PENGUIN REFERENCE BOOKS

THE PENGUIN DICTIONARY OF Musical Performers

Arthur Jacobs was born in Manchester in 1922 and educated at Manchester Grammar School and Merton College, Oxford. He became music critic of the *Daily Express* at the age of 25 and has since worked for many British and overseas newspapers and musical periodicals, as well as the BBC. He is a member of the editorial board of *Opera*, and for more than twenty years was a record-reviewer for the *Sunday Times*. In 1977 he was awarded a Leverhulme Research Fellowship to pursue his studies in Sullivan's life and music, chiefly from documentary archives in the United States. The result was his book *Arthur Sullivan: A Victorian Musician* (1984), which was acclaimed as a definitive biography.

He is (jointly with Stanley Sadie) the author of *The Pan Book of Opera* and has also edited *Choral Music* for Penguin, which was translated into Spanish and Japanese. He is well known as the author of *The Penguin Dictionary of Music*, which, in successive editions since 1958, is one of the longest-running reference books under a single compiler's name. A champion of opera in English, he has himself translated more than twenty operas from French, German, Italian and Russian. His translations of Rossini's *Cinderella* and *The Italian Woman in Algiers* have been in the repertoire of the English National Opera, and his translation of Berg's *Lulu* was used for the first complete staging of that work in the USA (Santa Fe, New Mexico, 1979). Among his more recent translations is Monteverdi's *The Coronation of Poppaea*.

Arthur Jacobs was a professor of musical history at the Royal Academy of Music from 1965 to 1979 and has lectured at various universities in the United States, Canada, Australia and Japan. From 1979 to 1984 he was head of the department of music at Huddersfield Polytechnic. Married with two sons, he enjoys swi[illegible] theatre-going and music.

THE PENGUIN DICTIONARY OF

Musical Performers

Arthur Jacobs

A biographical guide to significant interpreters of classical music – singers, solo instrumentalists, conductors, orchestras and string quartets – ranging from the seventeenth century to the present day

PENGUIN BOOKS

PENGUIN BOOKS

Published by the Penguin Group
Penguin Books Ltd, 27 Wrights Lane, London W8 5TZ, England
Penguin Books USA Inc.
375 Hudson Street, New York, New York 10014, USA
Penguin Books Australia Ltd, Ringwood, Victoria, Australia
Penguin Books Canada Ltd, 2801 John Street, Markham, Ontario, Canada L3R 1B4
Penguin Books (NZ) Ltd, 182–190 Wairau Road, Auckland 10, New Zealand

Penguin Books Ltd, Registered Offices: Harmondsworth, Middlesex, England

First published by Viking 1990
Published in Penguin Books 1991
10 9 8 7 6 5 4 3 2 1

Printed in England by Clays Ltd, St Ives plc

Contents

Introduction

Performers are in our day the most publicized members of the community of musicians. A Horowitz, a Menuhin, a Pavarotti magnetizes the public without regard to frontiers; so do the conductors – a Solti, Karajan or Bernstein. In the twentieth century recording has for the first time given a permanence to the performers' art, if not to their presence.

This book celebrates their achievements. The youngest were born after 1970, the earliest before 1600, but the spread is not even. Only gradually through history did the profession of performer distinguish itself, succeeding that of the general musician in whom the roles of performer, composer and teacher were combined. A decisive shift towards specialization occurs in the first half of the eighteenth century with the opera singers of Handel's day: the free market begins to operate. Singers both male and female, mainly but not exclusively Italian, travel to where the fees and honour are greatest, and composers write with the specialities of individual voices in mind.

The nineteenth century brought an explosion in the growth of performance as a public art, typified by the aura of legend that still attaches to such figures as Paganini and Jenny Lind. The twentieth century brought Caruso, McCormack, Kreisler and their successors into the home via the gramophone record: the performer became, in a new sense, a 'household name'.

Composers themselves continued to perform; many still do, happily accepting invitations to promote their works by conducting or playing them. But with such occasional (or 'secondary') performers this book is not concerned. Although Mozart and Beethoven launched most of their piano concertos in person, although Rossini as a matter of course supervised the first performance of his operas, they are not listed here; Paganini is, because his career was that of the travelling virtuoso and his work as a composer was part (but only part) of that. Also listed are a few musicians who, though ranking in history's eyes mainly as composers, pursued important concert or operatic careers going far beyond the promotion of their own works: Busoni, Mahler and Rakhmaninov, for instance.

The alphabetical list covers individual performers (executants and conductors), with entries also for the two most enduring forms of modern collective enterprise, the orchestra and the string quartet. The setting of a boundary for inclusion is the most difficult task confronting the compiler of such a work as this – an exercise in discrimination that cannot be based on completely objective criteria. Some talents occupy the public attention over many decades; others flash with a brief yet unmistakable importance, perhaps in launching new works or new techniques of playing, in either case altering permanently the music-lover's horizon. Recorded performances as well as achievements in the concert hall and opera house have been taken into consideration.

In particular, there must be an element of crystal-gazing in the selection of living artists according to what their long-term reputation promises to be. Among past artists an effort has been made to avoid those whose reputations seem to rest on little else but repetition from one music dictionary to the next and to rescue some who are in danger of slipping from print. Even the current twenty-volume edition of *The New Grove Dictionary of Music and Musicians* (1980) has no room for Ferenc Vecsey or Alexander

Barjansky, the respective dedicatees of Sibelius's Violin Concerto and Bloch's *Schelomo*. It has no entry for Peter Dawson, perhaps the last artist to unite the ballad singer's vast appeal with the tasteful insight of the serious interpreter; nor for Sir Henry Lytton, most celebrated of D'Oyly Carte Opera singers, or Harry Mortimer, conductor and organizer of unparalleled influence in the brass-band movement. Here they are.

Where possible, a performer's name is linked to the launch of something new – the importance of which, it is hoped, will be clear – and there is an index of more than 350 composers whose works are referred to in this connection.

In addition to the thousands of performers with full entries, the alphabetical list includes cross-references to some hundreds of musicians who are mentioned within these, usually as an orchestral conductor or quartet player, but occasionally as a less celebrated spouse or family member.

Not only *Grove* in its current and past editions but dozens of reference books (in ten languages) have been consulted for information, supplemented by periodicals and newspapers and, in the case of living artists, by biographies supplied at my personal request. Discrepancies in dates of birth (occasionally in dates of débuts also) arise in comparing different sources: the desire of performers to appear in print as younger than they are is hardly surprising. In such cases I have chosen the earliest believable quoted date. If any artist is thus misrepresented I tender an apology and, upon production of a birth certificate, promise to remedy the fault in any further printing.

Other corrections and updatings will, of course, be gratefully received and acted on.

Arthur Jacobs
June 1989

For this first paperback edition the opportunity has been taken to update information to mid-1990 and also (with thanks to David Cummings) to correct some errors from the original printing.

Arthur Jacobs
January 1991

Acknowledgements

I have found Alain Pâris's *Dictionnaire des interprètes* (Paris, revised edition, 1985) particularly informative on biographical dates and details of first performances difficult to trace in English-language sources. The latest edition of Nicolas Slonimsky's *Music Since 1900* (1972) and its 1986 *Supplement* have been almost as well thumbed as his seventh edition of *Baker's Biographical Dictionary of Musicians* (1984); I am also indebted to Mr Slonimsky and to David Cummings for privately supplying further biographical information.

The British Association of Concert Agents and individual agents, together with orchestras, opera houses and record companies both in Britain and abroad, have earned my gratitude in responding to requests for information about their artists. The resources of the Westminster Central Music Library and various other public and institutional libraries were constantly drawn on; I am particularly grateful to Christine Vann for zealous cross-checking. The BBC has been similarly helpful, particularly George Hall, its music information officer.

Specialized details came from the British Music Information Centre, the Centre de Documentation de la Musique Contemporaine (Paris), the Gaudeamus Foundation (Amsterdam) and the London representatives of a number of non-British governments. On guitarists, modern and historic, I have had the aid of Graham Wade, author of *Traditions of the Classical Guitar* (1980).

Helen Jeffrey of Penguin Books corrected and sharpened many points in the text, to its great advantage. Colleagues and friends stimulated some inquiries and answered others, and my wife, Betty, gave journalistic as well as wifely help.

Acknowledgements for the Thi[illegible]

[illegible]

How To Use This Book

Alphabetization

Gaps between words are ignored: Du Pré and Dupré both come after Duport. Capital-letter names like BBC Symphony Orchestra are listed as though BBC were a word. Names beginning with the prefix Mac, Mc, or M' are all listed as if spelt Mac.

Cross-references

A name in CAPITALS in the course of an entry indicates a cross-reference to another alphabetical entry.

Dates

Where only month and year are given for a date of birth or death, or only the year, this is the extent of ascertainable knowledge. Sometimes, where the exact date of birth is unknown, the date of baptism (bap.) is given; similarly, in default of precise dates, the expression '*fl.*' (flourished) is used as an approximation. A question-mark indicates an element of conjecture. The obsolete (pre-1918) Russian calendar has been adjusted into line with the modern calendar. Dates attached to premières refer, unless otherwise stated, to the actual performances and not to the date of a work's composition. The dates given for recordings and films are those of first release.

Transliteration

In general the standardized British system of transliteration of Russian and Bulgarian is followed. On the grounds of familiarity, however, an exception is made for Tch- instead of Ch- as in Tchaikovsky and for -oi rather than -oy in Bolshoi.

First Performances and Creations of Roles

The 'first performance' or 'première', without qualification, is the first public hearing anywhere of a particular composition. Qualifying phrases like 'first US performance' or 'first stage performance' are self-explanatory. 'First modern performance' means a twentieth-century revival after at least a century's lapse.

A stage performer is said to 'create' a role when he or she gives its 'first performance'; this conventional English-speaking usage is followed here. Readers should guard against sources that, misled by French usage, refer to the 'creation' of a role when only the first performance in a particular locality took place.

String Quartets

Members' names are always listed in the order first violin, second violin, viola and cello, and the instruments themselves are not routinely specified.

Names and Honours

Names are generally listed in the form professionally used, followed by an indication of any divergence from birth-name. 'Smith, Orlando [Henry]' indicates the performer omitted the middle name in professional use, 'Jones, [Mary] Amelia' that the middle name is used and the first name dropped. Where there has been an actual change or substitution of names, the word 'originally' is used (or 'née' for the change of a woman's name by marriage). Thus 'Brown (née Green), Sally (originally Sarah) [Phoebe]' shows that for professional purposes the performer has chosen to use her married name of Brown, to alter a legally bestowed forename and to omit her middle name.

Honours, which in Britain are widely regarded as representing genuine artistic recognition, are sparingly indicated here; a higher-ranking honour such as a knighthood overrides an earlier, lesser honour. Readers may find the following guide helpful.

The award most frequently granted to performing musicians (and others in like professions) is the OBE (Officer of the Order of the British Empire); fewer receive the higher-ranking CBE (Commander of the same order). A superior distinction attaches to the ranks of KBE and DBE (Knight Commander and Dame Commander of the order respectively), which carry the title 'Sir' or 'Dame'. Some foreign musicians have been awarded an honorary knighthood (Honorary KBE); it bestows no title.

None of these honours is hereditary. A baronetcy (also bearing the title 'Sir'), which is hereditary, is now rarely conferred in any field. Peerages of various ranks ('Lord' and 'Lady') were traditionally hereditary, but life peerages now also exist; no professional musician except Benjamin Britten has ever been made a peer.

All the foregoing honours may be conferred for a variety of services. The highest award made solely in recognition of intellectual distinction is the OM (Order of Merit), which is restricted to twenty-four people at any one time at the discretion of the Crown, irrespective of government advice. The title of CH (Companion of Honour), with numbers limited to sixty-five, is held in almost equal esteem. Among various other honours in the gift of the Crown, some, such as the CMG (Companion of the Order of St Michael and St George), have been given chiefly for services in the British Commonwealth overseas. Musical service rendered direct to the Court is customarily rewarded by an MVO or the higher CVO (Member and Commander of the Royal Victorian Order).

Locations of Performances

References to locations of performances normally give the name of city or town and, where relevant, the theatre, hall, festival, etc. Some special usages are as follows.

Unless otherwise indicated, 'Bayreuth' refers to the festival founded by Wagner in 1876 at Bayreuth (Germany) and now devoted to his operas, and 'Salzburg' (Austria) to that city's summer festival, which has been internationally important for both concerts and operas from the early 1920s.

The 'Bolshoi' is the principal opera and ballet theatre in Moscow, prominent both before and after the establishment of the Soviet regime in 1917. The name – meaning 'large' (corresponding to the British 'Grand Theatre') – is not unique to the institution, but nevertheless is internationally applied only to this theatre.

'Covent Garden' means the London theatre of that name, whether under present management as the home of the Royal Opera and Royal Ballet (formerly the Sadler's Wells Ballet) or under previous management.

'English National Opera' is the name acquired in 1974 by the former 'Sadler's Wells Opera'. Where an artist worked with the company only on one side of the change, the appropriate name alone is used.

'Glyndebourne' indicates the annual seasons of the Glyndebourne Festival Opera at Lewes, Sussex, and not, unless otherwise stated, the company's touring seasons.

'Metropolitan Opera' refers to the Metropolitan Opera House in New York, either leased to outside managements or, since 1908, under a continuous autonomous management.

'Paris Opera' indicates the city's principal state opera institution, founded under royal auspices in 1672, and from 1875 to 1989 housed in the building known as the Opéra. The 'Opéra-Comique' (always so accented and hyphenated) applies to the smaller Paris theatre that maintained an important and independent existence from 1807 to 1972.

The 'Proms' indicates the London promenade concert series begun in 1895 with Henry Wood as conductor and now run by the BBC as the Henry Wood Promenade Concerts.

'La Scala' is the usual abbreviation for the Teatro alla Scala in Milan. It opened in 1778 but has enjoyed primacy among Italian opera theatres only since about 1900. The 'Piccola Scala' opened in 1955, is a small theatre in the same building and under the same management.

Opera Titles

Titles of operas are in the original language if in English, French, German, Italian or Spanish, and in English translation if otherwise. Exceptionally, the short English title *The Ring* is used for Wagner's cycle *Der Ring des Nibelungen* (*The Nibelung's Ring*) comprising *Das Rheingold*, *Die Walküre*, *Siegfried* and *Götterdämmerung*.

Normally the composer's name is given with each opera title, but omitted for a select number of familiar operas very frequently referred to. In a few cases the title of such well-known works is given in an abbreviated form within square brackets. In the following alphabetical list of operas so treated, definite and indefinite articles are disregarded. English equivalents for foreign-language titles are provided in parentheses.

Aida – Verdi
Il barbiere di Siviglia [*Il barbiere*] (The Barber of Seville) – Rossini
The Bartered Bride [Czech: *Prodaná nevěsta*] – Smetana
La Bohème (Bohemian Life) – Puccini
Boris Godunov – Musorgsky
Butterfly, see Madama Butterfly
Carmen – Bizet
Cavalleria rusticana (The Rustic Code of Honour) – Mascagni
Così fan tutte [*Così*] (All Women Do So) – Mozart
Dido and Aeneas – Purcell
Don Carlos – Verdi
Don Giovanni – Mozart
Die Entführung aus dem Serail [*Die Entführung*] (The Abduction from the Seraglio) – Mozart
Falstaff – Verdi
Faust – Gounod
Fidelio – Beethoven
Figaro, see Le nozze di Figaro
Die Fledermaus (The Bat) – Johann Strauss (the younger)
Der fliegende Holländer (The Flying Dutchman) – Wagner
Götterdämmerung (Twilight of the Gods) – Wagner
Lohengrin – Wagner
Lucia di Lammermoor [*Lucia*] – Donizetti
Madama Butterfly [*Butterfly*] (Madam Butterfly) – Puccini
Die Meistersinger von Nürnberg [*Die Meistersinger*] (The Mastersingers of Nuremberg) – Wagner
The Mikado – Sullivan
Norma – Bellini
Le nozze di Figaro [*Figaro*] (The Marriage of Figaro) – Mozart
Otello (Othello) – Verdi
Pagliacci (Clowns) – Leoncavallo
Parsifal – Wagner
Porgy and Bess – Gershwin
Das Rheingold (The Rhinegold) – Wagner
Rigoletto – Verdi
The Ring (in full *The Nibelung's Ring*; Ger.: *Der Ring des Nibelungen*) – Wagner
Der Rosenkavalier (The Cavalier of the Rose) – Richard Strauss
Salome – Richard Strauss
Siegfried – Wagner
Tannhäuser – Wagner
Tosca – Puccini
La traviata (She Who Has Strayed) – Verdi
Tristan und Isolde [*Tristan*] (Tristan and Isolde) – Wagner
Il trovatore (The Troubadour) – Verdi
Die Walküre (The Valkyrie) – Wagner
Die Zauberflöte (The Magic Flute) – Mozart

A

Abbado, Claudio (b. 26 June 1933), Italian conductor. Prominent in opera and concert; made his Covent Garden and Metropolitan débuts 1968. Principal conductor, later music director, of La Scala, 1969–86; principal conductor, later music director, of the LONDON SYMPHONY ORCHESTRA, 1979–87; became music director of Vienna State Opera, 1986; appointed to BERLIN PHILHARMONIC ORCHESTRA, 1989. He also regularly conducts the CHICAGO SYMPHONY and other orchestras. Gave the première of Nono's *Il gran sole carico d'amore*, 1975, and the first performance since the composer's lifetime of Rossini's opera *Il viaggio a Reims* (Pesaro), 1984. His brother Marcello Abbado (b. 1926) is a composer and pianist.

Abbado, Marcello, *see* ABBADO, CLAUDIO.

Abel, Christian Ferdinand (b. Aug 1682; d. 3 Apr 1761), German violinist and bass viol player, also composer. Engaged at court at Köthen while Bach was music director there. Bach's three sonatas for bass viol and harpsichord may have been written for Abel to teach to the ruling prince.

Abendroth, Hermann (b. 19 Jan 1883; d. 29 May 1956), German conductor. Worked with the GÜRZENICH ORCHESTRA in Cologne, 1915–34, and was sufficiently 'acceptable' to succeed WALTER (dismissed, as a Jew, by the Nazis) as conductor of the GEWANDHAUS ORCHESTRA in Leipzig, 1934–45. He continued to work in Leipzig after 1945 under the communist East German regime.

Abramenkov, Andrey, *see* BORODIN QUARTET.

Abravanel, Maurice (b. 6 Jan 1903), Greek-born American conductor. Pupil in Berlin of Kurt Weill, whose work he conducted in Paris (first performance of *The Seven Deadly Sins*, 1933) and on Broadway. He held a famously long music directorship of the Utah Symphony Orchestra, 1947–79, and was the first to record the complete Mahler symphonies.

Abreu, Sergio (b. 5 June 1948) and **Eduardo** (b. 19 Sept 1949), Brazilian guitarists, brothers. Began their careers in 1963 and gave the first London performance of Castelnuovo-Tedesco's Concerto for two guitars, 1970.

Academy of Ancient Music, London concert-promoting society formed 1726. Title was adopted by an ensemble founded 1973; directed by HOGWOOD, it is dedicated to 'authentic' performance (on period instruments) of a mainly eighteenth-century repertory.

Academy of St Martin-in-the-Fields, London-based chamber orchestra founded 1959 by its conductor, MARRINER. Since 1974 it has often been directed from the violin by Iona Brown. Took its title from London church of that name where it gave concerts.

Accardo, Salvatore (b. 26 Sept 1941), Italian violinist. Made professional début in Naples aged thirteen. Particularly associated with Paganini: he was the first to record all six of Paganini's concertos, 1975. Dedicatee of Piston's Fantasia for violin and orchestra, 1973. Also conductor (of opera from 1987).

Achucarro, Joaquìn (b. 1 Nov 1936), Spanish

pianist. Made his début aged twelve, but decided on music as a career only after he had begun studying physics at university. Became well known on winning first prize at a Liverpool international competition, 1959. Recorded much of Falla's music, including the Concerto for keyboard (in both piano and harpsichord versions).

Ackerman, Otto (b. 18 Oct 1909; d. 9 Mar 1960), Romanian-born Swiss conductor. Noted for performances and recordings of Viennese operetta; he worked at the opera houses in Zurich, 1949–55, and Cologne, 1955–8.

Ackté (originally Achté), **Aino** (b. 23 Apr 1876; d. 8 Aug 1944), Finnish soprano. Made Paris début as Marguerite in *Faust*, 1897, and was the first to sing the title role of *Salome* in London, 1910. Director of Finnish National Opera, 1938–9.

Adam, Claus, *see* JUILLIARD QUARTET.

Adam, Theo (b. 1 Aug 1926), German bass-baritone. Member of the (East) Berlin State Opera from 1952. Famous as Wotan in *The Ring* (participated in both the BÖHM and JANOWSKI recordings), he appeared at the Bayreuth Festival from 1952 and at Covent Garden from 1967. Sang in the première of Berio's *Un re in ascolto*, 1984.

Adamberger, [Josef] **Valentin** (b. 6 July 1743; d. 22 Aug 1804), German tenor. Settled in Vienna and became a leading interpreter of Mozart's work. He sang in the first performances of Mozart's rescoring of Handel's *Messiah*, 1789, and *Die Entführung* (as Belmonte), 1782.

Adams, Suzanne (b. 28 Nov 1872; d. 5 Mar 1953), American soprano. Sang at the Metropolitan Opera and created the role of Hero in Stanford's *Much Ado About Nothing* in London, 1901. Married Leo STERN; after his death she taught singing in London, where she died.

Adler, Kurt Herbert (b. 2 Apr 1905; d. 9 Feb 1988), Austrian-born American conductor. Assistant to TOSCANINI at the Salzburg Festival, 1936, but was forced as a Jew to leave Austria, 1938. He notably raised the standards of the San Francisco Opera as artistic and then general director, 1953–82.

Adler, Larry (originally Lawrence) [Cecil] (b. 10 Feb 1914), American harmonica player. Made his instrument acceptable in 'serious' music; works written for him include Vaughan Williams's Romance for harmonica and orchestra, 1951. Also composer of film music. He settled in England after being victimized by the US anti-communist witch-hunt, 1949.

Adler, Peter Herman (b. 2 Dec 1899), Czech-born American conductor. Noted for televised US performances of opera. He conducted the première of Menotti's opera *Maria Golovin* in Brussels, 1958, and was music director of the Baltimore Symphony Orchestra, 1959–68.

Adni, Daniel (b. 6 Dec 1951), Israeli pianist. Made début aged twelve in Haifa and later studied with PERLEMUTER and ANDA. He performed in UK from 1970 and settled there; toured USA and Japan. Recorded Mendelssohn's complete *Songs Without Words*.

Aeolian Quartet, British string quartet. Founded as the Stratton Quartet (led by George Stratton), it took its newer name in 1944 when Max Salpeter became leader; other players were Colin Sauer, Watson Forbes and John Moore. Members in the 1970s were HURWITZ, Raymond Keenlyside, Margaret Major and Derek Simpson, who recorded the complete Haydn quartets in a new scholarly edition. It became inactive in 1981–2.

Agostini, Federico, *see* MUSICI, I.

Aguado, Dionisio (b. 8 Apr 1784; d. 29 Dec 1849), Spanish guitarist, also composer. Went to Paris, 1825, where his virtuosity attracted the interest of Paganini and Rossini.

Aguiari (also spelt Agujari), **Lucrezia** (known from her illegitimacy as 'La Bastardina') (b. 1743; d. 18 May 1783), Italian soprano. Sang in London, 1775–7. She had an unusually wide range and was praised by Mozart.

Ahlersmeyer, Matthieu (b. 29 June 1896; d. 23 July 1979), German baritone. Active chiefly in German theatres; he created the role of the Barber in Strauss's *Die schweigsame Frau* at Dresden, 1935, and was a member of the Hamburg State Opera, 1946–73.

Ahna, Heinrich de, *see* JOACHIM QUARTET.

Ahna, Pauline de (b. 4 Feb 1863; d. 13 May 1950), German soprano. Made her operatic début 1890. In 1894 she sang in the first performance of Strauss's *Guntram* and married the composer; he dedicated the Four Songs op. 27 to her, 1894.

Ahnsjö, Claes-Haakan (he uses the form Claes-H.) (b. 1 Aug 1942), Swedish tenor. Engaged at Munich Opera from 1973, and became widely famous in the roles of Mozart and others thereafter. Associated with DORÁTI in recordings of rare Haydn operas; also recorded Schubert opera arias and Swedish songs.

Ahronovitch, Yuri (b. 13 May 1932), Russian-born Israeli conductor. After holding important Russian posts, left USSR, 1972, and settled in Israel. Conductor of the GÜRZENICH ORCHESTRA in Cologne, 1975–86, and of STOCKHOLM PHILHARMONIC ORCHESTRA, from 1982. He conducted opera at Covent Garden, from 1974 (*Boris Godunov*), and performed there with the Royal Ballet (Prokofiev's *Romeo and Juliet*).

Ajemian, Anahid, *see* COMPOSERS QUARTET.

Ajmone-Marsan, Guido (b. 24 Mar 1947), Italian-born conductor, naturalized American 1962. After winning the Rupert Foundation Conducting Competition in London, 1973, became assistant to PREVIN with the LONDON SYMPHONY ORCHESTRA; later conducted in Chicago and London (Covent Garden, 1983). He was appointed music director of Essen Opera (West Germany), 1986.

Alain, Jehan (originally Jehan-Ariste) (b. 3 Feb 1911; d. 20 June 1940), French organist, also composer, brother of Marie-Claire ALAIN. Pupil of Dukas at the Paris Conservatory. Killed in action, 1940; Duruflé wrote an organ piece commemorating him.

Alain, Marie-Claire (b. 10 Aug 1926), French organist, sister of Jehan ALAIN. Pupil of Marcel DUPRÉ. Made début 1950, and won Geneva International Competition that year. Celebrated in classical and modern repertory, she specializes in performing her brother's music. Also internationally renowned as a teacher.

Alarie, Pierrette [Marguerite] (b. 9 Nov 1921), Canadian soprano. Active in US and European opera houses (Metropolitan, 1945, Paris, 1949). Married SIMONEAU, with whom she frequently performed and made recordings.

Alban Berg Quartet, Austrian string quartet founded 1971. Gives an annual series of concerts in Vienna and has won international distinction; it has recorded the complete Beethoven, Brahms, Berg and Webern quartets. Members, 1989: Günter Pichler, Gerhard Schulz, Thomas Kakuschka and Valentin Erben.

Albanese, Licia (b. 22 July 1913), Italian-born soprano, naturalized American 1945. A favourite of New York audiences, she remained with the Metropolitan Opera twenty-six years and gave 286 performances of 17 roles (including Violetta in *La traviata* 72 times).

Albani (originally Lajeunesse), [Marie-Louise Cécile] **Emma** (b. 1 Nov 1847; d. 3 Apr 1930), Canadian soprano. Took her name from Albany, New York, which had become her family's home. She was one of the leading performers in Victorian England. Made her début at Covent Garden 1872; sang in the first performances of Sullivan's cantata *The Golden Legend*, 1886, and Elgar's *The Apostles*, 1903. Created Dame, 1925.

Alberman, John, *see* ARDITTI QUARTET.

Alberni Quartet, London-based string quartet founded 1962. Its original members, from the Royal Academy of Music, were Dennis Simons, Howard Davis, John White and Gregory Baron. Members from 1975: Howard Davis, Peter Pople, Roger Best and David Smith. Internationally active, it was the first Western quartet to visit China, 1987; visiting artists in residence at the Royal Scottish Academy of Music, 1981–8.

Albert, Eugène [Francis Charles] **d'** (b. 10 Apr 1864; d. 3 Mar 1932), British pianist, later (as Eugen d'Albert) German. Made a brilliantly promising London début, 1881, and gave the first performance of Strauss's *Burleske* for piano and orchestra, 1890. He became equally celebrated as a composer and as head of the Berlin Music School, from 1907. The first of his six wives was CARREÑO.

Alboni, Marietta [Maria Anna Marzia] (b. 6 Mar 1823; d. 23 June 1894), Italian contralto. Exceptionally successful in opera in London, from 1847, and elsewhere, even rivalling LIND in the fees she commanded; toured USA, 1852. Very stout; in late years she performed seated.

Albrecht, Gerd (b. 19 July 1935), German conductor. Held conductorship of West Berlin Opera, 1972–4, then of the TONHALLE ORCHESTRA in Zurich, 1975–80. He conducted the première of Reimann's opera *Lear*, 1978 (also recorded).

Alcock, Walter [Galpin] (b. 29 Dec 1861; d. 11 Sept 1947), British organist. Pupil of Sullivan and Stainer. He was organist at the coronations of Edward VII, George V and George VI. Knighted, 1933. Also composed church music.

Alda (originally Davies), **Frances** [Jeanne] (b. 31 May 1883; d. 18 Sept 1952), New Zealand soprano, became American citizen 1939. Made her Metropolitan Opera début opposite CARUSO, 1908, and sang 266 performances of 23 roles there. She was married to (and later divorced from) the Metropolitan's director, Giulio Gatti-Casazza.

Aldulescu, Radu (b. 17 Sept 1922), Romanian cellist. Pupil of CASSADÓ. Having made his début in Bucharest, 1941, settled in Rome, then Paris; he has toured widely. Teaches at the Paris Conservatory and performs in a duo with Yonty SOLOMON.

Aler, John (b. 4 Oct 1949), American tenor. Specializes in Mozart roles. He has sung at Glyndebourne, from 1979, and the Vienna State Opera; made his Covent Garden début (as Ferrando in *Così*) 1986.

Alexander, Roberta (b. 3 Mar 1949), American soprano. Mimì in *La Bohème* was her début role at the Komische Oper, East Berlin, and at Covent Garden, 1984. Her Metropolitan Opera roles include Bess in *Porgy and Bess*.

Alexandrov, Yaroslav, *see* BORODIN QUARTET.

Alexanian, Diran (b. ?1881; d. 27 July 1954), Armenian cellist (born in Constantinople). As a student, played chamber music with Brahms and JOACHIM. He settled in Paris, where he collaborated on technical methods with CASALS; became a highly influential teacher in France and USA.

Alexeev (correct transliteration is Alexeyev), **Dmitry** (b. 10 Aug 1947), Russian pianist. Prizewinner at the Moscow Tchaikovsky Competition, 1974, and the Leeds Piano Competition, 1975. He began performing in the UK 1975 and the USA 1977 (début with GIULINI). Unusually, pursues concert and recording career both in the USSR and in the West; he accompanied HENDRICKS on a recording of spirituals.

Allan, Richard van, *see* VAN ALLAN.

Alldis, John (b. 10 Aug 1929), British choral director. Formed small London choir specializing in modern works; he was in charge of the London Symphony Chorus, then the London Philharmonic Choir, 1969–82, and has also held Continental posts. Conducted the first performance of Bedford's *Star Clusters, Nebulae, and Places in Devon*, 1972.

Allegranti, [Teresa] **Maddalena** (b. 1754; d. after 1801), Italian soprano. Famous for her operatic performances in Italian and German at Venice, London, 1781, and elsewhere. Mozart heard her in Dresden and praised her highly.

Allegri Quartet, London-based string quartet founded 1953. Its original members were Eli Goren, James Barton, Patrick Ireland and William Pleeth. Ireland remained as the one surviving member of a re-formed quartet, 1968, led by Hugh Maguire; Peter Carter took over as leader in 1977. Other members in 1989: David Roth, Roger Tapping and Bruno Schrecker. The quartet gave the first performance of Arnold's Quartet no. 2, 1976, written for them.

Allen, Thomas [Boaz] (b. 10 Sept 1944), British baritone. Performed at Covent Garden from 1972, Glyndebourne from 1973 and the Metropolitan Opera from 1981 (Papageno in *Die Zauberflöte*). He sang a leading role in the première of Musgrave's opera *The Voice of Ariadne* at Aldeburgh, 1974, and the title role in the first British stage production of Busoni's *Dr Faust* at English National Opera, 1986. CBE, 1989.

Aller, Eleanor, *see* HOLLYWOOD QUARTET and SLATKIN, LEONARD.

Allin, Norman (b. 19 Nov 1884; d. 27 Oct 1973), British bass. A leading British singer of the inter-war years; his operatic roles included King Marke (*Tristan*) and Mephistopheles (*Faust*). He made many song recordings from the 1920s, and was one of the original singers (designated by name in the score) of Vaughan Williams's *Serenade to Music*, 1938. CBE, 1958.

Alliot-Lugaz, Colette (b. 20 June 1947), French soprano. Performed in Mozart's and Rossini's operas, among others. She was a member of the Lyons Opera, 1976–83, and appeared at Glyndebourne, from 1981. Her recordings include French operetta and seventeenth-century music.

All-Union Radio and Television Symphony Orchestra, *see* MOSCOW RADIO SYMPHONY ORCHESTRA.

Almeida, Antonio [Jacques] **de** (b. 1 Jan 1928), French-born American conductor (father Portuguese, mother American). Conducted orchestra in Nice, 1968–78; he is a diligent researcher and editor, particularly of Offenbach's music. Made the first recording of Bizet's opera *Le Docteur Miracle*.

Altani, Ipolit [Karlovich] (b. 15 May 1846; d. 17 Jan 1919), Russian conductor. Chief conductor at the Bolshoi Theatre, 1882–1906, where he gave the first performance of Tchaikovsky's *Mazeppa*, 1884, and Rakhmaninov's *Aleko*, 1893.

Altmeyer, Jeannine (b. 2 May 1948), American soprano. Specializes in Wagner roles, which she has performed at Bayreuth, from 1979, and elsewhere. Sang Brünnhilde in the complete recording of *The Ring* under JANOWSKI, 1981–2.

Altschuler, Modest (b. 15 Feb 1873; d. 12 Sept 1963), Russian-born American conductor, previously cellist. He was an important promoter of Russian music through his New York series of concerts; gave the first performance of Skryabin's *Poem of Ecstasy*, 1904.

Alva, Luigi (originally Luis Ernesto Alva Talledo) (b. 10 Apr 1927), Peruvian tenor. Sang Paolino in Cimarosa's *Il matrimonio segreto* at the opening of the Piccola Scala in Milan, 1955. He was internationally admired as Almaviva in *Il barbiere*, which he recorded five times, and similar roles. First appeared at Covent Garden 1960 and at the Metropolitan Opera 1964.

Alwin, Karl, *see* SCHUMANN, ELISABETH.

Alwyn, Kenneth (originally Kenneth Alwyn Wetherell) (b. 28 July 1925), British conductor. Conducted BBC Northern Ireland Orchestra, then Royal Ballet, 1965–9. Also conducted musicals, and composed film music and television signature tunes.

Amadeus Quartet, British string quartet founded 1947. Made London début 1948. Its members were Norbert Brainin, Siegmund Nissel, Peter Schidlof and Martin Lovett; the first three were Austrian-Jewish refugees from the Nazis. The quartet is exceptional in that its membership never changed; it disbanded on Schidlof's death, 1987. The players won distinction for their performances of the classical repertory and of the works of Britten, whose Quartet no. 3 was written for them, 1975. Brainin was created CBE in 1960, the others in 1973.

Amadio, John [Bell] (b. 15 Nov 1884; d. 4 Apr 1964), Australian flautist, born in New Zealand. (Amadio was his stepfather's name.) Accompanied Luisa TETRAZZINI on European tour, 1920. Performed in Europe, USA and Australia with his second wife, AUSTRAL; they separated in the 1940s. He died at a rehearsal in Melbourne, aged seventy-nine.

Amar, Licco, *see* AMAR QUARTET.

Amar Quartet, German string quartet founded 1921. Its members were Licco Amar, Walter Caspar, Hindemith and Maurits Frank. Gave first performance of Hindemith's Quartet no. 2, 1922.

Ameling, Elly (originally Elisabeth) [Sara] (b. 8 Feb 1934), Dutch soprano. Pupil of BERNAC. Eminent performer of Bach and German lieder. She was the soloist in the première of Frank Martin's *La Mystère de la Nativité*, 1959. Made a few appearances in opera, including Ilia in

Mozart's *Idomeneo*. Her international distinction was marked by Dutch knighthood, 1971. She founded an annual prize at the international vocal competition at 's Hertogenbosch.

American Composers Orchestra, New York-based orchestra founded 1976. Made up of New York musicians, it gives about four concerts annually of new or revived American works. Principal conductor is Dennis Russell DAVIES.

Amici Quartet, London-based string quartet. Gave its first concert 1956; led by Lionel Bentley with various partners. Other members, 1988: Nicholas Dowding, Robert Hope Simpson and Bernard Richards.

Amicis, Anna Lucia De, *see* DE AMICIS.

Amoyal, Pierre [Alain] (b. 22 June 1949), French violinist. Studied with HEIFETZ in USA and made his name on US tour 1981; subsequently performed with SOLTI, BOULEZ, KARAJAN and others. Has recorded Prokofiev's two concertos and both his sonatas; also performs the Berg and Dutilleux concertos.

Amy, Gilbert [Claude Adolphe] (b. 29 Aug 1936), French conductor and composer. Successor to BOULEZ at the Domaine Musical concerts in Paris, 1967–74. Conducted French Radio's Nouvel Orchestre Philharmonique, 1976–81; became director of the Lyons Conservatory, 1984.

Ančerl, Karel (b. 11 Apr 1908; d. 3 July 1973), Czech conductor. Held various posts in Czechoslovakia (except when in Nazi concentration camps, 1939–45), and conducted the CZECH PHILHARMONIC ORCHESTRA, 1950–68. After communist coup, emigrated to Canada; conductor of the TORONTO SYMPHONY ORCHESTRA, 1969–73.

Anda, Géza (b. 19 Nov 1921; d. 14 June 1976), Hungarian-born pianist, naturalized Swiss 1955. Prominent performer of Mozart's and Bartók's concertos; published his own cadenzas to the former and recorded the complete set, conducting from the piano.

Anders, Peter (b. 1 July 1908; d. 10 Sept 1954), German tenor. Performed opera in Munich, Berlin and, after World War II, Hamburg. He was successful in Mozart operas, later in Wagner and Verdi (including *Otello*). He died after a car crash.

Anderson, George Frederick, *see* ANDERSON, LUCY.

Anderson, June (b. 30 Dec 1950), American soprano. Made her operatic début as Queen of the Night in *Die Zauberflöte* at the New York City Opera, 1978, and sang the same role in the film *Amadeus*. She performed the title role of Rossini's *Semiramide* in its first modern British revival (concert performance, Covent Garden, 1986).

Anderson (née Philpot), **Lucy** (b. 12 Dec 1797; d. 24 Dec 1878), British pianist. Teacher of Queen Victoria, and the first woman soloist in the Philharmonic Society's concerts, 1822. Married George Frederick Anderson (d. 1876), violinist and Master of the Queen's Music.

Anderson, Marian (b. 17 Feb 1902), American contralto. One of the first black solo artists to establish herself on the concert platform. Under Eleanor Roosevelt's patronage she gave famous concert before 75,000 people in Washington, 9 April 1939; appeared as Ulrica in Verdi's *Un ballo in maschera* at the Metropolitan Opera, 1955. Received many US honours; delegate to United Nations, 1957–8.

Andrade, Levine, *see* ARDITTI QUARTET.

André, Franz (b. 10 June 1893; d. 20 Jan 1975), Belgian conductor. Founding director of Belgium's radio orchestra, 1939–58. He gave the first performances of various modern works, including Milhaud's Symphony no. 7 (Venice), 1955. Also a composer.

André, Maurice (b. 24 May 1933), French trumpeter. Won Geneva International Competition, 1955. Well known as a performer of concertos (he has recorded at least thirty), and special arrangements; Boris Blacher, among others, has written a concerto for him. A high four-valved ('piccolo') trumpet that was designed for him has increased the brilliance of his performances.

Andreae, Volkmar (b. 5 July 1879; d. 18 June

1962), Swiss conductor. Held long conductorship of the TONHALLE ORCHESTRA in Zurich, 1906–49, and promoted much modern music. He conducted the first performance of Busoni's *Indian Fantasy* in Berlin, 1914. Also composer.

Angeles, Victoria de Los, *see* LOS ANGELES.

Anievas, Agustin (b. 11 June 1934), American pianist (father Spanish, mother Mexican). Made his New York début 1959, and lived for some years in Belgium. His recordings include all four concertos by Rakhmaninov.

Annibali, Domenico (b. *c.* 1705; d. 1779 or later), Italian male soprano (castrato). Engaged by Handel for his London operas, 1736–7, including *Giustino* and *Berenice*; he then went to Dresden and sang in many of Hasse's operas.

Anosov, Nikolay Pavlovich, *see* ROZHDESTVENSKY.

Ansermet, Ernest (b. 11 Nov 1883; d. 20 Feb 1969), Swiss conductor. Founding conductor, 1918–67, of the SUISSE ROMANDE orchestra. Distinguished also as ballet conductor and as guest with US orchestras, he took a leading part in performing new pieces by many composers, among them Stravinsky's *The Soldier's Tale*, 1918, and Britten's *The Rape of Lucretia* (Glyndebourne, 1946). He wrote a textbook on conducting and other works.

Appia, Edmond (b. 7 May 1894; d. 12 Feb 1961), Italian-Swiss violinist and conductor. Directed the radio orchestra in Geneva, from 1938, and was a guest conductor of more than fifty other orchestras. He also wrote on music.

Ara, Ugo, *see* FLONZALEY QUARTET.

Arad, Atar, *see* CLEVELAND QUARTET.

Aragall, Giacomo (originally Jaime) (b. 6 June 1939), Spanish tenor. Won a Verdi contest in Italy, 1963. He was engaged by La Scala and became highly successful as operatic tenor; first performed at Covent Garden, 1966 (in *Rigoletto*), and at the Metropolitan Opera, 1968.

Araiza, Francisco (b. 4 Oct 1950), Mexican tenor. After studying in Germany, became a member of Zurich Opera, 1977, and performed at Munich and Vienna. He won a high reputation in Mozart opera. Made his Covent Garden début 1983 (in Donizetti's *Don Pasquale*) and his Metropolitan début 1984 (in *Così*). Also active as song recitalist.

Arányi (originally Arányi de Hunyadvar), **Jelly [Eva] d'** (b. 30 May 1893; d. 30 Mar 1966), Hungarian-born British violinist. Great-niece of JOACHIM and pupil of HUBAY. Bartók's Violin Sonata no. 1, Ravel's *Tzigane* and Vaughan Williams's *Concerto accademico* were dedicated to her; she gave the first performances of the last two, 1924 and 1925. (*See also* BRAIN, AUBREY.) She was often partnered by HESS. Her elder sister, Adela (1886–1962), performed as a violinist under her married name, Fachiri.

Arban, [Joseph] Jean-Baptiste [Laurent] (b. 28 Feb 1825; d. 9 Apr 1889), French cornet player and conductor. His work as a teacher in Paris has led him to be regarded as the founder of modern trumpet and cornet technique. His is the well-known arrangement of the traditional tune 'The Carnival of Venice'.

Arbós, Enrique Fernández (b. 24 Dec 1863; d. 2 June 1939), Spanish violinist, conductor, composer and orchestrator. In Britain he performed and was professor at the Royal College of Music, 1894–1915. Conducted the Madrid Symphony Orchestra, 1904–36; gave the premières of Falla's *Nights in the Gardens of Spain*, 1916, and Prokofiev's Violin Concerto no. 2, 1935. He made orchestral arrangements of several pieces from Albéniz's *Iberia*.

Archambeau, Félicien d', *see* FLONZALEY QUARTET.

Archambeau, Iwan d', *see* FLONZALEY QUARTET.

Archilei, Vittoria (b. 1550; d. after 1620), Italian soprano, also lutenist and dancer. Became one of the most famous singers at the court of the Medici in Florence before 1600; her artistic skills are mentioned by the early opera composers Caccini and Peri.

Arditi, Luigi (b. 16 July 1822; d. 1 May 1903),

Italian conductor, also composer. Settled in London; in his long, prominent career in opera he conducted the first British performances of *Faust*, 1863, *Der fliegende Holländer* (in Italian), 1870, and Humperdinck's *Hänsel und Gretel*, 1894.

Arditti, Irvine, *see* ARDITTI QUARTET.

Arditti Quartet, London-based string quartet founded 1974. Original members were Irvine Arditti, Lennox Mackenzie, Levine Andrade and John Senter. In 1985 John Alberman and DE SARAM succeeded Mackenzie and Senter respectively. Devoted to modern music, its repertory includes 170 pieces written after 1970; gave the first performance, 1980, of Ferneyhough's Quartet no. 2, and has repeated it fifty times. The group has experimentally used electrically assisted (Raad) instruments. Made first visit to USA in 1988, when it gave the première of Cage's *Music for Four*.

Argenta (in full Argenta Maza), **Ataulfo** (b. 19 Nov 1913; d. 21 Jan 1958), Spanish conductor. Conducted the SPANISH NATIONAL ORCHESTRA, 1947–58, and was widely known as a guest conductor in Britain, from 1948, and elsewhere; he recorded many Spanish works. Died in a car accident.

Argerich, Martha (b. 5 June 1941), Argentinian pianist. International prizewinner at Bolzano and Geneva, 1957, but interrupted her career for further study before making London début, 1964, and winning the Warsaw Chopin Competition, 1965. She is distinguished in the romantic repertory. Also plays in a duo with KREMER. Her second marriage was to DUTOIT.

Arie, Raphael (b. 26 Aug 1920; d. 17 Mar 1988), Bulgarian-born Israeli bass. Initially studied violin, but came to prominence as bass in Italy (La Scala, from 1947) and elsewhere. He took part in the first performance of Stravinsky's *The Rake's Progress* (Venice), 1951.

Arkhipova, Irina [Konstantinovna] (b. 2 Dec 1925), Russian mezzo-soprano. Prominent at the Bolshoi Theatre, where she made her début as Carmen, 1956; took part in the first performance of Prokofiev's *The Story of a Real Man*, 1960. After appearing at La Scala, 1967, she became one of the best-known Soviet artists in the West. She sang Azucena in *Il trovatore* at Covent Garden, 1975.

Armstrong, Karan (b. 14 Dec 1941), American soprano of British and American parentage. Distinguished in such roles as Berg's Lulu (in the first Covent Garden performance, 1981) and Strauss's Salome. Performed in the première of Berio's *Un re in ascolto* (Salzburg Festival, 1984). Has also sung Butterfly, Tosca and Eva (*Die Meistersinger*). She is married to the stage director Götz Friedrich.

Armstrong, Richard (b. 7 Jan 1943), British conductor. Worked as music director of Welsh National Opera, 1973–86, with which he performed Berg's *Lulu*, Britten's *Billy Budd* and many works by Janáček as well as the older repertory. Won Janáček medal from the Czech government. Also conducted opera at Covent Garden, from 1982, Dresden and Philadelphia; at the Proms, 1989, conducted the first performance of Hoddinott's *Star Children*.

Armstrong, Sheila [Ann] (b. 13 Aug 1942), British soprano. Having won the Kathleen Ferrier prize, 1965, began to perform in opera (Glyndebourne from 1966 and Covent Garden from 1973) and concerts. She gave the première of McCabe's *Notturni ed alba* 1970, which is dedicated to her, and participated in the first recording of Elgar's *The Apostles*, 1973.

Arndt, Günther (b. 1 Apr 1907; d. 25 Dec 1976), German choral director and conductor. Directed the Berlin Motet Choir, 1950–60. He was prominent in twentieth-century music (first performance of Krenek's Six Motets, 1959) and also in operetta recordings.

Arnould (or Arnoult), [Madeleine] **Sophie** (b. 13 Feb 1740; d. 22 Oct 1802), French operatic soprano. A leading singer at the Paris Opera, 1757–78, she took principal roles in works by Rameau, Gluck and others.

Aronowitz, Cecil [Solomon] (b. 4 Mar 1916; d. 7 Sept 1978), British viola player (born in South Africa). Performed in London orchestras and chamber groups; founding member of the Melos Ensemble, 1950. He was head of string teaching at the Royal Northern College of Music and then at Snape Maltings School, 1977–8; collaborated with Britten.

Arrau, Claudio (b. 6 Feb 1903), Chilean pianist. Among the most eminent artists of his day. He was sent by the Chilean government to study in Berlin, and at seventeen was soloist with the BERLIN PHILHARMONIC ORCHESTRA. Won the Geneva International Competition, 1927. He developed an international career and settled in New York in 1941. Maintained a particular association with the Berlin Philharmonic and was awarded the high West German honour of the Verdienstkreuz, 1970, at the conclusion of the Beethoven bicentenary celebrations. Returned to Chile, 1984, after a seventeen-year absence. Frequently played the complete works of Bach, Mozart and Beethoven; he recorded both Brahms's concertos, and made three recordings of the cycle of Beethoven's, the third in his eighties.

Arroyo, Martina (b. 2 Feb 1936), American soprano of partly black, partly Hispanic descent. Made début at Carnegie Hall, New York, 1958 and the Metropolitan Opera 1959. Became famous as Aida (her début role at Covent Garden, 1968) and Tosca. Also sings modern music; gave the first performance of Stockhausen's *Momente*, 1962, and Barber's *Andromache's Farewell*, 1963.

Artôt, Désirée (b. 21 July 1835; d. 3 Apr 1907), Belgian soprano, previously mezzo-soprano. She was greatly praised by Berlioz and sang for Meyerbeer in his *Le Prophète* at Paris Opera, 1858. When she was in Russia, from 1868, Tchaikovsky proposed marriage to her. (*See also* WIENIAWSKI.)

Ascoli, Bernard d', *see* D'ASCOLI.

Ashkenazy, Vladimir [Davidovich] (b. 6 July 1937), Russian-born pianist, naturalized Icelandic 1972. A child prodigy, at the age of fifteen gave the first performance of Kabalevsky's Piano Concerto no. 3, 1953. He married an Icelandic fellow-student; left USSR for UK, 1963, moved to Iceland, 1968, and then to Switzerland. Shared first prize with OGDON in the Moscow Tchaikovsky Competition, 1962. He became distinguished in Russian composers as well as in the general repertory; recorded Chopin's complete works for solo piano. Has also played chamber music with PERLMAN and Lynn HARRELL. In the 1980s he has been prominent as a conductor. As music director of the ROYAL PHILHARMONIC ORCHESTRA from 1987 (*see* PREVIN), he returned with the orchestra to USSR in 1989.

Askenase, Stefan (b. 10 July 1896; d. 18 Oct 1985), Polish-born pianist, naturalized Belgian 1956. Trained in Vienna under Emil von SAUER. He was famous as a Chopin-player and a noted teacher at the Brussels Conservatory, 1954–6.

Atherton, David (b. 3 Jan 1944), British conductor. First music director of the LONDON SINFONIETTA, 1968–73. He became the youngest conductor to appear at Covent Garden and at the Proms, both 1968. Prominent in modern music, he conducted the première of Birtwistle's opera *Punch and Judy*, 1968, and Henze's *We Come to the River*, 1976; recorded the complete set of Schoenberg's works for chamber ensemble. Principal conductor of the ROYAL LIVERPOOL PHILHARMONIC ORCHESTRA, 1980–83. Music director of the San Diego Symphony Orchestra, California, 1980–87; of the Hong Kong Philharmonic Orchestra from 1989.

Atlantov, Vladimir [Andreyevich] (b. 19 Feb 1939), Russian tenor. Studied in Leningrad and Milan, and joined the Bolshoi Theatre company, 1967. He has sung widely in the West (New York, Paris and Vienna) in roles such as Cavaradossi (*Tosca*) and Otello (with which he made his début at Covent Garden, 1987, and which he has performed over 150 times). Also sings certain baritone roles. Married to MILASHKINA.

Atzmon (originally Groszberger), **Moshe** (b. 30 July 1931), Israeli conductor. Born in Budapest and emigrated to Israel, 1949. He studied at the Guildhall School of Music, London; held conducting posts in Sydney, 1969–72, and Hamburg, 1972–6.

Aubigny, Julie d', *see* MAUPIN.

Auer, Leopold (b. 7 June 1845; d. 15 July 1930), Hungarian violinist. Settled in St Petersburg

1868, and became leading soloist and teacher there; HEIFETZ was among his pupils. He at first rejected Tchaikovsky's Violin Concerto (*see also* BRODSKY), but afterwards played it. Moved to USA, 1918.

Augér, Arleen (b. 13 Sept 1939), American soprano. Member of Vienna State Opera, 1967–74. She possesses a high register that made her famous as Queen of the Night in *Die Zauberflöte*; her Metropolitan Opera début was as Marzelline in *Fidelio*, 1978. She has also recorded many of Bach's works under RILLING. Sang at Prince Andrew's wedding in Westminster Abbey, 1986.

Augusteo Orchestra, *see* SANTA CECILIA ORCHESTRA.

Austin, Frederic (b. 30 Mar 1872; d. 10 Apr 1952), British baritone. Sang in the performance in English of *The Ring* conducted in London by Hans RICHTER, 1908. He played the role of Peachum in his own version of *The Beggar's Opera*, 1920, which enjoyed a record long run.

Austral (originally Wilson), **Florence** (b. 26 Apr 1894; d. 16 May 1968), Australian soprano. Went to USA for advanced study, declined a Metropolitan Opera contract, but made her London concert début 1921; from 1922 she was prominent on the British opera stage in such roles as Brünnhilde and Aida. Made early recordings, from 1920, including Wagner opera. Married AMADIO.

Austrian Radio Symphony Orchestra, Vienna-based orchestra founded 1969. Conductors have included HORVAT, 1969–75, SEGERSTAM, 1975–82, and ZAGROSEK, from 1984.

Avdeyeva, Larissa [Ivanovna] (b. 21 June 1925), Russian mezzo-soprano. Member of the Bolshoi company in Moscow from 1952; she became noted in works by Tchaikovsky and other Russian composers. Sang in the first Bolshoi performance of Prokofiev's *War and Peace*, 1959, and has toured widely. She is married to SVETLANOV.

Avoglio, Christina Maria (dates unknown), Italian soprano. Esteemed by Handel; she sang in the first performance of his *Messiah* (Dublin), 1742, and *Samson*, 1743, and in many of his other works. Of any further career nothing is known.

Ax, Emanuel (b. 8 June 1949), Polish-born American pianist. Emigrated to New York with his family, 1961. He won the Rubinstein Competition in Tel Aviv, 1974; made New York début 1975 and performed in London at the Proms, 1983. Noted in Chopin and Schoenberg. He plays in a trio with KIM and MA.

Ayo, Felix (b. 1 July 1933), Spanish-born Italian violinist. Founding member and violinist-director of I MUSICI, 1952. He is also active as a soloist.

B

Babin, Victor (b. 31 Dec 1908; d. 1 Mar 1972), Russian-born American pianist. Studied with SCHNABEL in Berlin; emigrated to USA, 1937. He was also a composer and, from 1961 till his death, head of the Cleveland Institute of Music. Best known in a two-piano duo with his wife, VRONSKY.

Baccaloni, Salvatore (b. 14 Apr 1900; d. 31 Dec 1969). Italian bass. Sang at La Scala, 1926–40, where he began to specialize, at TOSCANINI's suggestion, in the comic roles of Italian opera. Also performed at Glyndebourne, 1936–9, and the Metropolitan Opera, 1940–62, and became one of the most celebrated of comic basses.

Bachauer, Gina (b. 21 May 1913; d. 22 Aug 1976), Greek-born British pianist of Greek and Austrian descent. Made her London début 1946 and her New York début 1950. She became a favourite of British audiences in the concerto repertory; her husband, Alec Sherman (b. 1907), conducted many of her performances.

Backhaus, Wilhelm (b. 26 Mar 1884; d. 5 July 1969), German-born pianist. Became Swiss citizen after World War II. Began touring at the age of sixteen; taught at the Royal Manchester College of Music, 1905–9. He made his US début 1912 and was still performing in his mid-eighties. Particularly celebrated in Beethoven. He made many recordings, including the Beethoven cello sonatas with Pierre FOURNIER.

Bacquier, Gabriel [Augustin-Raymond-Théodore-Louis] (b. 17 May 1924), French baritone. Sang with the Opéra-Comique, Paris, from 1956, and became internationally known in a variety of roles, including Scarpia (*Tosca*) and Boris Godunov. He made his début at Covent Garden 1962 and at the Metropolitan Opera 1964.

Badura-Skoda, Paul (b. 6 Oct 1927), Austrian pianist, also composer. (Skoda was his stepfather's name.) Famous as interpreter of Mozart and Schubert; he plays both modern and early instruments, and also performs with DEMUS. In 1970 gave the première of Frank Martin's Piano Concerto no. 2, dedicated to him. His wife, Eva, has been his partner in preparing scholarly music editions.

Bahr, Therese, *see* SCHNABEL.

Bahr-Mildenburg (originally von Bellschau-Mildenburg), **Anna** (b. 29 Nov 1872; d. 27 Jan 1947), Austrian soprano. Worked under MAHLER's conductorship at Hamburg and Vienna; sang Isolde and Elisabeth (*Tannhäuser*) at Covent Garden, 1906. In collaboration with her husband, the playwright Hermann Bahr, she wrote a book on Wagner.

Bailey, Lilian, *see* HENSCHEL, GEORGE.

Bailey, Norman [Stanley] (b. 23 Mar 1933), British baritone. Lived in South Africa and made opera début in Vienna, 1959. Appeared as Sachs in *Die Meistersinger* at Sadler's Wells, conducted by GOODALL, 1968. He continued to win fame in Wagner roles in English, but also sang them in German at New York City Opera, 1975, the Metropolitan, 1976, and elsewhere. CBE, 1977. His second wife is the soprano Kristine Ciesinski (b. 1952).

Baillie, Isobel (called Bella Baillie in early appearances) (b. 9 Mar 1895; d. 24 Sept 1983), British soprano. A leading exponent of oratorio for about thirty years from the mid-1920s, she is said to have sung Handel's *Messiah* more than 1,000 times. Taught in USA (Cornell University), 1961–2. Created Dame, 1978.

Bailly, Louis, *see* FLONZALEY QUARTET.

Baker, George (b. 10 Feb 1885; d. 8 Jan 1976), British baritone and, in youth, organist. Much associated with the operas of Gilbert and Sullivan, but was never a member of the D'Oyly Carte Company; he participated in SARGENT's recordings of these works when over seventy. He was also a competition adjudicator and BBC administrator, 1944–7. CBE, 1971. His wife was the soprano Olive Groves (1900–1974).

Baker, Janet [Abbott] (b. 21 Aug 1933), British mezzo-soprano. Celebrated in recital, in such larger works as Elgar's *The Dream of Gerontius* (recorded, 1964) and in a restricted range of operas. She famously sang many of Handel's operatic (originally castrato) heroes; made her Covent Garden début in Britten's *A Midsummer Night's Dream*, 1966, and also made her New York début that year. Created Kate in Britten's television opera *Owen Wingrave*, 1971, and gave the première of his solo cantata *Phaedra*, 1976. She retired from opera in 1982 after performing Gluck's *Orpheus* at Glyndebourne. Created Dame, 1976.

Balashov, Alexander, *see* SHOSTAKOVICH QUARTET.

Baldwin, Dalton (b. 19 Dec 1931), American pianist. Celebrated as accompanist to many famous singers, including AMELING, GEDDA, NORMAN and, particularly, SOUZAY. He regularly gives courses in both Europe and USA.

Ballista, Antonio (b. 30 Mar 1936), Italian pianist. Internationally prominent from the 1960s in modern works. Several have been dedicated to him, including Berio's *Erdenklavier* (Earth Keyboard), 1970. (*See also* CANINO.)

Balsam, Artur (b. 8 Feb 1906), Polish-born American pianist. Having studied in Berlin, made tour of USA with MENUHIN. Later, although occasionally a soloist (BBC's Mozart bicentenary programmes, 1956), he was principally known as an accompanist to such string players as Szymon GOLDBERG, MILSTEIN and ROSTROPOVICH.

Baltsa, Agnes (b. 19 Nov 1944), Greek mezzo-soprano. Established her operatic career at Frankfurt and West Berlin. She then became internationally known in a wide variety of roles, among them Carmen, Cherubino (*Figaro*) and Dido (Berlioz's *Les Troyens*). Has performed at Covent Garden, Vienna State Opera, from 1970, and the Metropolitan, from 1979.

Bamert, Matthias (b. 5 July 1942), Swiss conductor, also composer. Worked as assistant conductor to STOKOWSKI in New York, 1970–71, and then for Swiss radio. With the SCOTTISH NATIONAL ORCHESTRA, from 1985, he gave the premières of many works in its Musica Nova seasons, including Mark-Anthony Turnage's *Gross Intrusion*, 1987.

Banfalvy, Béla, *see* BARTÓK QUARTET.

Bantock, Granville (b. 7 Aug 1868; d. 16 Oct 1946), British conductor. Won prominence as composer and as head of the Birmingham School of Music, 1900–1934; earlier, his conducting of seaside concerts at New Brighton in Cheshire, 1897–1900, importantly promoted music by Elgar, Holbrooke and other British composers. He had previously conducted Stanford's opera *Shamus O'Brien*, 1896.

Bär, Olaf (b. 19 Dec 1957), German baritone. Emerged in the mid-1980s as one of the leading interpreters of German song. He made his operatic début 1981, and sang principally in Dresden; gave the first performance of Siegfried Matthus's *Die Weise von Liebe und Tod des Cornets Christoph Rilke*, 1985. Covent Garden début 1985.

Barabas, Sari (b. 14 Mar 1918), Hungarian soprano, formerly dancer. Made her singing début 1939 in Budapest. She performed in Munich, 1949–68, and also at Glyndebourne, 1953. Known in Mozart and in operetta.

Barbieri, Fedora (b. 4 June 1920), Italian mezzo-soprano. In Florence, 1942 and 1943, took part in revivals (rare at the time) of Monteverdi works. She became internationally known in such roles as Eboli (*Don Carlos*), with which she made her Metropolitan début, 1950. The visit of La Scala's company introduced her to Covent Garden, 1950.

Barbirolli, John (originally Giovanni Battista) (b. 2 Dec 1899; d. 29 July 1970), British conductor (father Italian, mother French). Conducted the SCOTTISH ORCHESTRA and then the NEW YORK PHILHARMONIC, 1937–42, as TOSCANINI's successor. His conductorship of the HALLÉ ORCHESTRA, from 1943 until his death, was decisive in consolidating its reputation and expanding its repertory to include, for example, Mahler's symphonies. He gave the first performances of Vaughan Williams's symphonies nos. 7 and 8, 1953 and 1956 (the latter was dedicated to him), and, in New York, of Britten's *Sinfonia da requiem*, 1941, and Grechaninov's Symphony no. 4, 1942. He was associated with other orchestras, among them the HOUSTON SYMPHONY ORCHESTRA, of which he was principal conductor, 1961–7; he also conducted the British National Opera Company, 1926–9, and occasionally at Covent Garden, 1928–33 and 1951–4. His second wife was ROTHWELL. Knighted, 1949, and made CH, 1969.

Barenboim, Daniel (b. 15 Nov 1942), Argentinian-born Israeli pianist and conductor. Followed both careers with distinction. He appeared as a child pianist in Buenos Aires, and moved with his family to Israel, 1952. In Salzburg he studied piano with Edwin FISCHER and conducting with MARKEVITCH. Made his piano début in London 1955 and New York 1956; from the mid-1960s he was equally prominent as a conductor, sometimes (for example in Mozart's concertos) from the keyboard. Conducted opera from 1973 (*Don Giovanni*, Edinburgh Festival); appeared at Bayreuth, 1981. He was soloist in the first performance of Goehr's Piano Concerto, 1972. Conductor of the ORCHESTRE DE PARIS, 1975–90; appointed artistic director of the new Bastille opera centre in Paris, but was dismissed, 1989, before its opening. Music director of the CHICAGO SYMPHONY ORCHESTRA from 1991. Married DU PRÉ.

Barere, Simon (b. 1 Sept 1896; d. 2 Apr 1951), Russian pianist. Settled in Berlin, later Stockholm, and made London début 1934; he toured internationally, and was highly regarded for his virtuoso technique. He died in Carnegie Hall, New York, after collapsing during his performance of Grieg's Piano Concerto.

Bar-Illan, David [Jacob] (b. 7 Feb 1930), Israeli pianist of Ukrainian-Jewish descent (born in Argentina). Settled in USA. He made his New York début 1960 and gave the first piano recital at the newly opened John F. Kennedy Center in Washington, 1971.

Barjansky, Alexander (b. 16 Dec 1883; d. 6 Jan 1961), Russian cellist. Left Russia before the 1917 Revolution, afterwards travelling on a Nansen (stateless) passport. Ernest Bloch's *Schelomo* (Solomon) for cello and orchestra, 1917, was dedicated to him (though KINDLER was the first to perform it); he gave the première of Delius's Cello Concerto, 1921. Edited various works for cello; died in Belgium.

Baron, Gregory, *see* ALBERNI QUARTET.

Baroni, Catarina, *see* BARONI, LEONORA.

Baroni, Leonora (b. Dec 1611; d. 6 Apr 1670), Italian singer and lutenist. Her singing won acclaim from connoisseurs in Naples (when she was sixteen), Genoa, Florence and Rome; appeared at domestic musical entertainments, sometimes with her mother (*see* BASILE) and sister, Catarina. She was attached to the French court, 1644–5.

Barrientos, Maria (b. 10 Mar 1883; d. 8 Aug 1946), Spanish soprano. Studied violin, piano and singing in Barcelona, then after further training in Italy appeared at Covent Garden, 1903, and, from 1916, at the Metropolitan Opera. She specialized in coloratura parts, among them the Queen of Shemakha in Rimsky-Korsakov's *The Golden Cockerel*. Performed mainly in concerts from 1920. Her recordings include sets of Falla's Spanish songs with the composer at the piano.

Barrios, [Pio] **Agustín** (b. 5 May 1885; d. 7 Aug 1944), Paraguayan guitarist. The first Latin American concert guitarist to establish himself in Europe, from 1934. He may be the first classical guitarist to have made a popular recording, 1910. Sometimes performed in Indian costume as 'Chief Nitsuga Mangoré'; he was was also a composer.

Barshai, Rudolf [Borisovich] (b. 28 Sept 1924), Russian-born viola player and conductor, naturalized British 1983. Had a distinguished career in USSR. He founded the MOSCOW CHAMBER ORCHESTRA, 1956, and conducted it until 1976; gave the first performance of Shostakovich's Symphony no. 14, 1969. Emigrated to Israel, 1976. He was conductor of the BOURNEMOUTH SYMPHONY ORCHESTRA, 1982–8, and music director of the Vancouver Symphony Orchestra, 1985–8.

Barstow, Josephine [Clare] (b. 27 Sept 1940), British soprano. Has developed a prominent operatic career: she created the role of Denise in Tippett's *The Knot Garden*, 1970, and the Young Woman in Henze's *We Come to the River*, 1976, and was the first in Britain to sing Jeanne, the hysterical heroine, in Penderecki's *The Devils of Loudun*, 1973. Made her New York début 1977. CBE, 1985.

Bartlett, Ethel (b. 6 June 1900; d. 17 Apr 1978), British pianist. Performed in piano duo with her husband, Rae Robertson (b. 29 Nov 1893; d. 4 Nov 1956), from 1928. They toured Europe and the Americas with conspicuous success; made many of their own arrangements and also commissioned new works. In Cincinnati they gave the first performance of Britten's *Scottish Ballad* for two pianos and orchestra, 1941.

Bartók Quartet, Hungarian string quartet founded 1957. Used the name of its leader, Péter Komlós, before obtaining the right to the present title from Bartók's widow, 1963. Other members, 1987: Béla Banfalvy, Géza Németh, and László Mező. The quartet won a UNESCO prize in 1981.

Bartoletti, Bruno (b. 10 June 1926), Italian conductor. Active at the Maggio Musicale, Florence, 1957–64, and at Rome Opera, 1965–73. He became principal conductor of Chicago Lyric Opera, 1964, and later its artistic director, 1985. Conducted the premières of Ginastera's opera *Don Rodrigo* (Buenos Aires), 1964, and Penderecki's *Paradise Lost* (Chicago), 1978.

Barton, James, *see* ALLEGRI QUARTET.

Barzin, Léon (b. 27 Nov 1900), Belgian-born American conductor. Taken to USA in infancy. He became a noted trainer of student orchestras and also a ballet conductor. As music director of New York City Ballet, 1948–58, and its predecessor, Ballet Society, he conducted the first stage performance of Stravinsky's *Agon*, 1957.

Bashmet, Yuri (b. 24 Jan 1953), Russian viola player. Studied in L'vov and Moscow, and won an international contest in Munich, 1976. Schnittke wrote for him a concerto, of which he gave the first performance in 1986. Has led his own ensemble, the Moscow Soloists, from 1986.

Basile, Andreana (b. *c.* 1580; d. *c.* 1640), Italian contralto. Sometimes accompanied herself on the harp or guitar. Her singing was prized in aristocratic circles in Naples (where she married a nobleman called Baroni), Mantua, Venice and Rome. Monteverdi declared her the finest singer he knew, and she was honoured by a book of poems. (*See also* BARONI, LEONORA.)

Bassi, Luigi (b. ? 5 Sept 1766; d. 13 Sept 1825), Italian baritone. Began his career in Italy, then went to Prague, where Mozart wrote for him the title role of *Don Giovanni*, 1787. He worked as both singer and stage director for an Italian company in Dresden from 1815 till his death.

Bastardina, La, *see* AGUIARI.

Bastianini, Ettore (b. 24 Sept 1922; d. 25 Jan 1967), Italian baritone, previously bass. In 1952 began singing such roles as Germont in Verdi's *La traviata* (Metropolitan Opera début, 1953) and Renato in his *Un ballo in maschera* (Covent Garden début, 1964). He was Prince Andrey in the first performance in the West of Prokofiev's *War and Peace* (Florence), 1953.

Bastin, Jules (b. 18 Aug 1933), Belgian bass. Made his début 1960 at the Monnaie (Brussels Opera). He has appeared mainly in Brussels and Paris (where he sang in the first complete production of Berg's *Lulu*, 1979); made Covent Garden début 1974, and US recital début (Washington) 1985. His many recordings include Berlioz's *Benvenuto Cellini* and *Béatrice et Bénédict*.

Bathori, Jane (originally Jeanne-Marie Berthier) (b. 14 June 1877; d. 21 Jan 1970), French mezzo-soprano. Made some early appearances in opera, but won particular fame in concerts, sometimes accompanying herself at the piano. She gave the first performances of several works by Ravel, including *Shéhérazade*, 1907, and sang much new music by Debussy, Satie and others. Poulenc wrote *Une chanson de porcelaine* for her eightieth birthday. She lived in Argentina during World War II, having frequently visited there.

Bâton, Charles, *see* BÂTON, HENRI.

Bâton, Henri (late seventeenth century), French player of the musette (bagpipes) and vielle (hurdy-gurdy). Helped to promote these rustic instruments to fashionable use: they were heard in Christmas concerts in Paris, 1731–3. His son, Charles Bâton (d. after 1754), followed a similar career and also wrote on music.

Battistini, Mattia (b. 27 Feb 1856; d. 7 Nov 1928), Italian baritone. Commanded international operatic reputation. From his débuts in Rome, 1878, and Covent Garden, 1883, sang a great range of parts, including those of Mozart and Wagner and (in his performances each season in Russia, 1893–1914) such Russian roles as Tchaikovsky's Onegin. He made important early recordings, 1903–24.

Battle, Kathleen (b. 13 Aug 1948), American soprano. Won an Olivier award for her Covent Garden début as Zerbinetta in Strauss's *Ariadne auf Naxos*, 1985. She made her Metropolitan début in a minor role in *Tannhäuser*, 1978; sang Nerina in the first Glyndebourne production of Haydn's *La fedeltà premiata*, 1979. Also a noted performer in recitals and orchestral concerts.

Baudo, Serge (b. 16 July 1927), French conductor. Music director of the ORCHESTRE DE PARIS, 1969–71, and Lyons Opera, 1971. Founded a Berlioz festival in Lyons, 1979. He conducted premières of many French works, including Messiaen's *Et exspecto resurrectionem mortuorum*, 1965, and *La Transfiguration*, 1969, and recorded all Martinů's symphonies. Also conducted at the Metropolitan Opera.

Bauer, Harold (b. 28 Apr 1873; d. 12 Mar 1951), British-born American pianist. Performed as a child violinist before turning to the piano. He was an admired trio partner of CASALS and THIBAUD. Ravel dedicated *Ondine* to him, and he gave the first performance of Debussy's *Children's Corner*, 1908. In New York he founded and directed the Beethoven Association, a concert series.

Baumann, Hermann [Rudolf Konrad] (b. 1 Aug 1934), German horn player. After orchestral experience, won an international radio competition, 1964, and concentrated on solo and chamber-music work. He had played early valveless horns with HARNONCOURT and others, as well as the modern horn. Has revived and made first recordings of works by Saverio Mercadante (two concertos) and others.

Baumgartner, Rudolf (b. 14 Sept 1917), Swiss violinist and conductor. Founded the Festival Strings Lucerne, with SCHNEIDERHAN, and, as its conductor, raised it to fame in concerts and on record. With this orchestra he gave many first performances, including those of Penderecki's Capriccio, 1965, and Ligeti's *Ramifications*, 1970. He was also director of the festival at Lucerne, 1968–80.

Bavarian Radio Symphony Orchestra, Munich-based orchestra founded 1949 under Eugen JOCHUM. Jochum remained as conductor until 1960; his successors have included Rafael KUBELÍK, 1961–79, and Colin DAVIS, from 1983.

BBC Northern (Symphony) Orchestra, *see* BBC PHILHARMONIC ORCHESTRA.

BBC Philharmonic Orchestra, Manchester-based orchestra founded 1934 as the BBC Northern Orchestra, conductor T. H. Morrison. It was later known as the BBC Northern Symphony Orchestra, of which Edward DOWNES became principal conductor in 1980. Took its present name 1982; Jan Pascal TORTELIER is to become principal conductor in 1992.

BBC Scottish Orchestra, *see* BBC SCOTTISH SYMPHONY ORCHESTRA.

BBC Scottish Symphony Orchestra, Glasgow-based orchestra founded 1935 as the BBC Scottish Orchestra, conductor Guy Warrack.

Took present title in 1967. Later conductors have included RICKENBACKER, 1978–80, and MAKSYMIUK, from 1983.

BBC Symphony Orchestra, London-based orchestra founded 1930. It is the main orchestra of the BBC. Principal conductors: BOULT, 1930–50, SARGENT, 1950–57, Rudolf SCHWARZ, 1957–63, DORÁTI, 1963–7, Colin DAVIS, 1967–71, BOULEZ, 1971–5, KEMPE, 1975–6, ROZHDESTVENSKY, 1978–81, PRITCHARD, 1982–9, and Andrew DAVIS, from 1989.

BBC Welsh Orchestra, *see* BBC WELSH SYMPHONY ORCHESTRA.

BBC Welsh Symphony Orchestra, Cardiff-based orchestra founded 1936 as the BBC Welsh Orchestra. It took its present title in 1974. OTAKA became conductor in 1987.

Bean, Hugh [Cecil] (b. 22 Sept 1929), British violinist. Pupil of SAMMONS and GERTLER. He was active as an orchestra leader (PHILHARMONIA ORCHESTRA, 1957–67) and member of the Music Group of London, a chamber ensemble, 1966–76. CBE, 1970.

Beard, John (b. *c.* 1717; d. 5 Feb 1791), British tenor. Trained at the Chapel Royal. He sang more of Handel's operatic and oratorio roles under the composer's direction than any other singer; these include the title roles in *Samson*, 1743, *Belshazzar*, 1745, and *Jephtha*, 1752. Received a doctorate from Oxford University, 1759, and was the manager of Covent Garden, 1761–7.

Becker, Hugo, *see* BECKER (JEAN), also FLESCH and HARRISON (BEATRICE).

Becker, Jean (b. 11 May 1833; d. 10 Oct 1884), German violinist. Known as the 'German Paganini'; performed in London, 1860. He settled in Florence, where he founded the important QUARTETTO FIORENTINO. His son Hugo Becker (1863–1941) was a noted cellist.

Bedford, Steuart [John Rudolf] (b. 31 July 1939), British conductor. Worked with Britten at the Aldeburgh Festival and elsewhere; conducted the première of Britten's *Death in Venice* in Aldeburgh, 1973, and made his Metropolitan début with the US première of the same opera, 1974. He was formerly married to the soprano Norma Burrowes (b. 1944), and is a brother of the composer David Bedford.

Beecham, Thomas (b. 29 Apr 1879; d. 8 Mar 1961), British conductor. Largely self-taught in music. Supported by family wealth, he gave London concerts with his own orchestra, 1905. Promoted and conducted opera at Covent Garden, 1910–13, including the first British performance of Strauss's *Elektra*, 1910. He founded the LONDON PHILHARMONIC ORCHESTRA, 1932, with which he worked in concerts and opera. Spent most of World War II in USA; on his return (the London Philharmonic having become independent) he founded the ROYAL PHILHARMONIC ORCHESTRA, 1946. Championed Sibelius and Delius, a close friend; gave the posthumous première of Delius's opera *Irmelin*, 1953. He was regarded as being one of the world's leading conductors. He had a flamboyant public manner and habitually conducted without a score. Knighted in 1916 and later that year inherited his father's baronetcy. (*See also* LABBETTE.)

Beethoven Quartet, Moscow-based string quartet active from 1923 to 1975. The leader, Dmitry Tsiganov, and cellist, Sergey Shirinsky, were members throughout that time: the other players from 1960 were Nikolay Zabaknikov and Fyodor Druinin. They gave first performances of most of Shostakovich's quartets (from no. 2, 1944, to no. 14, 1973), and, with the composer, of his Piano Quintet, 1940.

Begnis, Giuseppe De, *see* DE BEGNIS, GIUSEPPE.

Begnis, Giuseppina Ronzi De, *see* DE BEGNIS (GIUSEPPE) and RONZI.

Behrend, Siegfried (b. 19 Nov 1933), German guitarist. Made his début 1953 in Leipzig, and thereafter toured extensively. He became known for his mastery of difficult modern works, many of which, like Yun's *Gagok* (with voice and percussion, 1972), were written for him. His output of compositions, arrangements and editions of music exceeds 1,000, including about 200 film scores.

Behrens, Hildegard (b. 9 Feb 1937), German soprano. Made her débuts at Covent Garden (as Leonore in *Fidelio*) and the Metropolitan Opera in 1976. She came to fame when KARAJAN engaged her in the title role of *Salome* at the Salzburg Festival and for a recording, 1977. Much in demand as a Wagner specialist, she sang Brünnhilde in *The Ring* at Bayreuth, 1983.

Beinum, Eduard van, *see* VAN BEINUM.

Belkin, Boris (b. 26 Jan 1948), Russian-born Israeli violinist. Made his first appearance aged seven and later studied in Moscow; won a national violin contest. He emigrated to Israel, 1974. Played in USA and also in Paris under BERNSTEIN; toured Japan, 1979 and 1980; in London recorded both Prokofiev's violin concertos.

Bellezza, Vincenzo (b. 17 Feb 1888; d. 8 Feb 1964), Italian conductor. Made début at Covent Garden 1926, conducting Boito's *Mefistofele* (with SHALYAPIN in the title role); also took part in MELBA's farewell performance. He conducted the British première of Puccini's *Turandot*, 1927. Though mainly active in Italy, he again conducted opera in London in 1957–8.

Bellincioni, Gemma (b. 18 Aug 1864; d. 23 Apr 1950), Italian soprano. Helped to establish a new dramatic style when she created Santuzza in *Cavalleria rusticana*, 1890; she also created the title role in Giordano's *Fedora*, 1898. Under Strauss's baton sang Salome in the opera's first performance in Italy, 1906; she later gave more than 100 performances of the role. Her early recordings, 1903–5, have survived.

Bellison, Simeon (originally Semyon) (b. 4 Dec 1883; d. 4 May 1953), Russian-born American clarinettist. Emigrated to USA after 1917 Russian Revolution. He is said to have given more than 10,000 concerts; founded an ensemble of fifty clarinets and other instruments in New York, 1927. He was an authority on Jewish music.

Bellugi, Piero (b. 14 July 1924), Italian conductor. Held positions in USA till 1961 and in that year conducted the première of Milhaud's Symphony no. 10 in Portland, Oregon. He then returned to Italy, and later headed the Turin Radio–TV Symphony Orchestra, 1969–72. Conducted Handel's opera *Serse* at La Scala, 1962, but has been particularly active in modern works.

Belton, Ian, *see* BRODSKY QUARTET (2).

Běnačková, Gabriela (b. 25 Mar 1947), Czech soprano. Became known at the Prague National Theatre in such roles as Natasha in Prokofiev's *War and Peace*. From 1981 she has had a full international career on stage and in recordings, including Janáček's roles.

Bender, Paul (b. 28 July 1875; d. 25 Nov 1947), German bass. Engaged by Munich Opera in 1903 and gave his last performance there (Don Basilio in *Il barbiere*) seven days before his death; sang at the Metropolitan, 1922–7. A famous Wagner bass, he was also distinguished in recital, particularly in songs by Carl Loewe.

Bene, Adriana Ferrarese Del, *see* FERRARESE DEL BENE.

Benedetti, René, *see* PARRENIN QUARTET.

Benedetti Michelangeli (shortened to Michelangeli outside Italy), **Arturo** (b. 5 Jan 1920), Italian pianist. Also studied violin in childhood; winner of the Geneva International Competition, 1939. His post-war appearances (London, 1946, and New York, 1950) won him acclaim for his virtuoso display and intellectual rigour. Prone to illness, he severely restricted his concerts and often cancelled. Founding director of a piano school in his birthplace, Brescia, 1964–9.

Benoit, Henri, *see* CAPET QUARTET.

Bentley, Lionel, *see* AMICI QUARTET, BLECH QUARTET and LONDON STRING QUARTET (2).

Ben-Tovim, Atarah (b. 1 Oct 1940), British flautist, music director and educator. Performed as a flautist with major British orchestras, including the ROYAL LIVERPOOL PHILHARMONIC. From 1971 she organized, directed and introduced concerts with the expandable Atarah's Band: they were highly successful in presenting music to young children.

Benucci, Francesco (b. *c.* 1745; d. 5 Apr 1824),

Italian bass. From 1783 was principally in Vienna, where he was associated with Mozart. Sang the title role in the première of *Figaro*, 1786, Leporello in the first Vienna performance of *Don Giovanni*, 1788, and Guglielmo in the première of *Così*, 1790. He created the role of Count Robinson in Cimarosa's *Il matrimonio segreto*, 1792. Also sang opera in London, 1791–2.

Benyamini, Daniel, *see* TEL AVIV QUARTET.

Benzi, Roberto (b. 12 Dec 1937), French conductor. Gave concerts in Bayonne and Paris at the age of eleven, and appeared in two films. He established his adult career with *Carmen* at the Paris Opera, 1954, and has been a guest conductor with various European and US orchestras. Married to RHODES.

Berberian, Cathy (originally Catherine) (b. 4 July 1925; d. 6 Mar 1983), American mezzo-soprano. Studied and established herself in Italy. An extraordinary range of vocal utterance combined with stage personality made her a leading interpreter of modern, particularly Italian, music. She was married to Berio, 1950–66, and gave the premières of his *Circles*, 1960, and other works; Stravinsky revised for her his *Elegy for JFK* (originally for baritone). She was the first performer of the unaccompanied *Stripsody*, 1966, one of her own compositions.

Berbié, Jane (originally Jeanne Marie-Louise Bergougne) (b. 6 May 1934), French mezzo-soprano. Appeared at La Scala, 1958, and at Glyndebourne from 1967 (in the soprano role of Despina in *Così*, 1969 and 1971). A well-known interpreter of Rossini's coloratura mezzo-soprano parts, she sang Rosina in *Il barbiere* at Covent Garden, 1971.

Berganza (in full Berganza Vargas), **Teresa** (b. 16 Mar 1935), Spanish mezzo-soprano. One of the most celebrated singers of her generation, both in recital (usually accompanied by her husband, Felix Lavilla) and in opera. She made her British opera début 1958 at Glyndebourne (Cherubino in *Figaro*); sang at Covent Garden from 1960 (Rosina in *Il barbiere*) and at the Metropolitan from 1967 (Cherubino). Her repertory also includes Purcell's Dido.

Bergel, Erich (b. 1 June 1930), Romanian-born German conductor. Three years in gaol for subversion did not prevent his becoming conductor of the Cluj Philharmonic (Romania). He settled in West Germany, 1971, and thereafter toured widely. Made his first British appearance with the ROYAL PHILHARMONIC ORCHESTRA in 1973.

Berger, Erna (b. 19 Oct 1900; d. June 1990), German soprano. Became internationally famous in high coloratura roles such as the Queen of the Night (*Die Zauberflöte*). She was active at Berlin and Bayreuth from 1929 and made her Covent Garden début in 1934, but did not appear at the Metropolitan till 1949. After her opera career ended she continued as a recitalist till 1968 (aged sixty-seven).

Berger, Otto, *see* BOHEMIAN QUARTET.

Berghout, Phia (originally Sophia) [Rosa] (b. 14 Dec 1909), Dutch harpist. Made her début in 1926 and for twenty-five years played in the CONCERTGEBOUW ORCHESTRA OF AMSTERDAM. She not only encouraged the composition of new music for harp, but was director of the Eduard van Beinum Foundation, 1959–74, for which she organized international music courses.

Berglund, Joel [Ingemar] (b. 4 June 1903), Swedish bass-baritone. Well known as a Wagner singer (Bayreuth from 1942, Metropolitan as Sachs in *Die Meistersinger*, 1946). He was director of Royal Swedish Opera, 1949–52.

Berglund, Paavo [Allan Engelbert] (b. 14 Apr 1929), Finnish conductor. Notably increased the stature of the Finnish Radio Orchestra, with which he toured internationally. He made his British début 1965 with the BOURNEMOUTH SYMPHONY ORCHESTRA and was its principal conductor, 1972–9. In 1970 he gave (in Bournemouth and London) the first performances outside Finland of Sibelius's *Kullervo* symphony and also recorded it. Conducted the HELSINKI PHILHARMONIC ORCHESTRA, 1975–9.

Bergonzi, Carlo (b. 13 July 1924), Italian tenor, formerly baritone. Made his début as a tenor in 1951. He established himself as one of the most stylish of Verdi singers: Alvaro in *La forza del destino* was his London début role (Stoll Theatre,

1953), and he later recorded it with CALLAS and GOBBI. Made his Metropolitan début 1956 and celebrated twenty-five years there with a gala concert, 1981.

Berg Quartet, *see* ALBAN BERG QUARTET.

Beringer, Oscar (b. 14 July 1844; d. 21 Feb 1922), British pianist. Brought from Germany as a child by his father, a political refugee. He studied in Germany but based his professional life in London, where he ran an Academy for the Higher Development of Pianoforte Playing, 1873–97, and gave the first British performance of Brahms's Piano Concerto no. 2, 1882.

Bériot, Charles-Auguste de (b. 20 Feb 1802; d. 8 Apr 1870), Belgian violinist, also composer. Studied in Paris. He won notable success at his London début, 1826, and was internationally recognized as one of the finest players of the day. From 1829 he lived with the famous soprano MALIBRAN, and they were married in 1836; on her death later that year he withdrew from performance, though he resumed his career in 1838. Settled in Brussels, teaching at the Conservatory until he became blind in 1852.

Berlin Philharmonic Orchestra, German orchestra founded 1882. Principal conductors have included BÜLOW, 1887–92, NIKISCH, 1895–1922, FURTWÄNGLER, 1922–45 and 1948–54, CELIBIDACHE, 1945–52, and KARAJAN, 1955–89, succeeded by ABBADO. (*See also* BRANDIS QUARTET.)

Berlinsky, Valentin, *see* BORODIN QUARTET.

Berlin State Orchestra (or Berliner Staatskapelle), German orchestra now based in East Berlin. It is descended from a court ensemble of 1572. SUITNER was music director in the period 1964–71 and resumed the post in 1974.

Berman, Lazar [Naumovich] (b. 26 Feb 1930), Russian pianist. Studied in Moscow under GOLDENWEISER. He toured Western Europe (including London), 1958, but achieved prominence only in the 1970s (USA, 1976); among his recordings is Tchaikovsky's Piano Concerto no. 1 with KARAJAN.

Bernac [originally Bertin], **Pierre** (b. 12 Jan 1899; d. 17 Oct 1979), French baritone. In 1926 gave the first performance of Poulenc's song-set *Chansons gaillardes*, and his long subsequent career embraced much work with Poulenc as composer and pianist. He also sang German and English texts, and gave premières of songs by Lennox Berkeley, Hindemith and others.

Bernardi, Francesco, *see* SENESINO.

Bernstein, Leonard (originally Louis, but he legally changed it) (b. 25 Aug 1918; d. 14 Oct 1990), American pianist, conductor and composer. He combined these three roles in a way unparalleled in his generation. He worked as assistant to KOUSSEVITZKY, then assistant conductor of the NEW YORK PHILHARMONIC ORCHESTRA under RODZINSKI, making début 1943 (deputizing for WALTER); he was the first American-born musician to be regular conductor of that orchestra, 1958–69. Conducted at La Scala, 1953 (Cherubini's *Médée* with CALLAS) and at the Metropolitan, 1964, but was more closely associated with the Vienna State Opera, from 1966, the VIENNA PHILHARMONIC (with which he recorded all Beethoven's symphonies), the ISRAEL PHILHARMONIC and the LONDON SYMPHONY orchestras. He was a notable expositor of music on television.

Béroff, Michel (b. 9 May 1950), French pianist. Pupil of Yvonne LORIOD. He won the international Messiaen Competition, 1967, and performed at the Oxford Bach Festival, 1969, and afterwards with the BBC SYMPHONY ORCHESTRA. A specialist in Messiaen and other twentieth-century music, he has recorded all five Prokofiev piano concertos (as well as two Bach concertos).

Berry, Walter (b. 8 Apr 1929), Austrian bass-baritone. Made his début at the Vienna State Opera in Honegger's *Joan of Arc*, 1950. His Salzburg Festival appearances included the premières of operas by Egk, Liebermann and Einem (*Der Prozess*, 1953). Sang at the Metropolitan, 1966, and Covent Garden, 1976. He was married, 1957–70, to LUDWIG; they often performed together on stage and in recital.

Bertini, Gary (b. 1 May 1927), Russian-born Israeli conductor. Taken to Palestine as a boy.

After studying in Europe, he founded the Rinat Choir, later called the Israel Chamber Choir; toured widely. In 1965 conducted the ENGLISH CHAMBER ORCHESTRA and later gave many BBC concerts. He was music director of the DETROIT SYMPHONY ORCHESTRA, 1981–4; directed opera and concerts in Frankfurt from 1987. He conducted the first recording of Mahler's reconstruction of Weber's incomplete opera *Die drei Pintos*, 1976.

Best, Roger, *see* ALBERNI QUARTET.

Best, W[illiam] T[homas] (b. 11 Aug 1826; d. 10 May 1897), British organist. Civic organist at Liverpool, 1855–94. He was recognized internationally as a recital virtuoso. Opened the organs in the Royal Albert Hall, 1871, and Sydney Town Hall, 1892, and also played in Rome (in the presence of Liszt), 1882. He specialized in Bach and in organ arrangements of orchestral works.

Betti, Adolfo, *see* FLONZALEY QUARTET.

Bevignani, Enrico (b. 29 Sept 1841; d. 29 Aug 1903), Italian conductor, also composer. In London, where he was a favourite of PATTI, he conducted much opera, including the London premières of *Aida*, 1876, and *Pagliacci*, 1893. In Moscow, admired by Tchaikovsky, he conducted the first Bolshoi Theatre performance of *Yevgeny Onegin*, 1881.

Bezrodny, Igor, *see* MOSCOW CHAMBER ORCHESTRA.

Biggs, E[dward George] Power (b. 29 Mar 1906; d. 10 Mar 1977), British-born organist, naturalized American 1937. His activities as recitalist and broadcaster made him one of the best-known artists in USA. He studied surviving European baroque organs; commissioned and played new works, including Piston's Prelude and Allegro for organ and strings. He refused to perform on electronic organs.

Bigley, Roger, *see* LINDSAY QUARTET.

Bigot, Eugène (b. 28 Feb 1888; d. 17 July 1965), French conductor. Influential in Paris as the director of the Lamoureux Concerts, 1937–50, the chief conductor of Opéra-Comique, 1936–47, and chief conductor of the Paris Radio Orchestra, from 1947 until his death. He was also a composer.

Bigot (née Kiené), **Marie** (b. 3 March 1786; d. 16 Sept 1820), French (Alsatian) pianist. She was praised as a performer by Haydn and Beethoven, whose 'Appassionata' Sonata she is said to have played privately from manuscript. Her husband was librarian to Count RAZUMOVSKY, Beethoven's patron.

Bijlsma, Anner, *see* BYLSMA.

Billington (née Weichsell), **Elizabeth** (b. 27 Dec 1765; d. 25 Aug 1818), British soprano. A child prodigy (she was also a violinist and composer), she received some singing lessons from J. C. Bach. Sang opera with great success in London and was praised by Haydn. She went to Naples, where she became friends with Lady Emma Hamilton, and sang again in London from 1811. Died in retirement near Venice.

Biret, Idil (b. 21 Nov 1941), Turkish pianist. Studied in Paris. At the age of eleven she performed Mozart's Double Piano Concerto with KEMPFF; appeared with MENUHIN at the Istanbul Festival, 1973. She was a member of the jury at the Queen Elisabeth Competition, Brussels, 1978. Besides a wide classical repertory she plays music by Boucourechliev and other modern composers.

Birks, Ronald, *see* LINDSAY QUARTET.

Birmingham Symphony Orchestra, *see* CITY OF BIRMINGHAM SYMPHONY ORCHESTRA.

Bishop, Anna (originally Ann Riviere) (b. 9 Jan 1810; d. 18 Mar 1884), British soprano. Studied piano with MOSCHELES and singing with the composer Henry Bishop (1786–1855). She married Bishop, 1831, with whom she often appeared in concert, but left him for BOCHSA in 1839. They toured together, visiting St Petersburg and Naples, where she performed in twenty operas. In 1852 she sang in and directed the staging of the US première of Flotow's *Martha* in New York, and she also travelled to Australia. Gave her last concert at the age of seventy-three (New York).

Bishop-Kovacevich, Stephen (b. 17 Oct 1940), American pianist of Yugoslav descent. Known as Stephen Bishop until 1975. He made his boyhood début in San Francisco, 1951, and later moved to London and studied with HESS. Gave the first performances of concerto by Richard Rodney Bennett, 1969, and Tavener's *Palintropos*, 1979; he is well known in Beethoven, whose cello sonatas he recorded with DU PRÉ. Appointed to an international chair at the Royal Academy of Music, 1986. He is also a conductor.

Bispham, David [Scull] (b. 5 Jan 1857; d. 2 Oct 1921), American baritone. One of the few male Americans in his time to participate in international opera. He sang much in London (including Kurwenal in *Tristan*, Covent Garden, 1892), and appeared at the Metropolitan Opera, 1896–1903. Also a distinguished recitalist and an ardent proponent of singing in English.

Bitetti (originally Bitetti Ravina), **Ernesto** [Guillermo] (b. 20 July 1943), Argentinian guitarist. Became well known after his first tour abroad, 1965, and has often appeared as a soloist with orchestra. Rodrigo composed the *Sonata a la española* for him, 1969.

Bjoner, Ingrid (b. 8 Nov 1927), Norwegian soprano. Encouraged by FLAGSTAD. She made her career chiefly in Munich, where she sang the Empress when Strauss's *Die Frau ohne Schatten* reopened the National Theatre, 1963, and Isolde in the centenary performance of *Tristan*, 1965. She also appeared at Covent Garden, from 1967, and the Metropolitan, 1961–7.

Björling, Jussi (originally Johan) [Jonaton] (b. 5 Feb 1911; d. 6 Sept 1960), Swedish tenor. As a boy sang treble in a family quartet, which made recordings; trained in Stockholm and retained regular membership of Royal Swedish Opera till 1938. He became a major international star, especially in Italian opera; made Chicago début 1937 and Covent Garden début 1938 (in *Il trovatore*). Celebrated for his recordings, among them *La Bohème* with LOS ANGELES and BEECHAM, 1956. He died six months after suffering a heart attack while preparing for a Covent Garden performance. His son Rolf Björling (b. 1928) also become an operatic tenor; the Swedish baritone Sigurd Björling (1907–83) was not related to them.

Björling, Rolf, *see* BJÖRLING, JUSSI.

Björling, Sigurd, *see* BJÖRLING, JUSSI.

Blachut, Beno (b. 14 June 1913; d. 10 Jan 1985), Czech tenor. Member of Prague National Theatre from 1941. He made only occasional opera and concert appearances in the West (Edinburgh Festival with the Prague Company, 1970), but his recordings of Czech operas such as Smetana's *Dalibor*, 1952, and Janáček's *Jenůfa*, 1955, won him celebrity.

Black, Stanley (b. 14 June 1913), British conductor. Principal conductor of the BBC Northern Ireland Orchestra, 1968–9. He is best known as a guest conductor of various symphony orchestras in concerts of light music. Also composed more than 100 film scores.

Blades, James (b. 9 Sept 1901), British percussionist. More than anyone else in UK he established the importance of the role. Played with a circus and in silent-film orchestras, then in 1940 became principal percussionist of the LONDON SYMPHONY ORCHESTRA. He collaborated with Britten in creating the novel percussion parts of *The Prodigal Son* and other works. A skilled lecturer, he also wrote a standard textbook on percussion.

Blanc, Ernest (b. 1 Nov 1923), French baritone. Prominent at the Paris Opera from 1954. He sang at Bayreuth, 1958 and 1959, and at Glyndebourne (in Bellini's *I puritani* opposite SUTHERLAND, 1960), but gradually withdrew from an international career.

Bland, Charles (dates unknown), British tenor, son of Maria Theresa BLAND. His fame rests on his creation of the title role of *Oberon*, Weber's English opera, under the composer's direction, 1826.

Bland (née Romanzi), **Maria Theresa** (b. 1769; d. 15 Jan 1838), Italian-born British soprano, mother of Charles BLAND. In early appearances known as Romanzini. She was associated with the composers Dibdin and Storace, and was much admired at Drury Lane, where she sang for nearly forty years, 1786–1824. Suffered from mental illness in her later years.

Blech, Harry (b. 2 Mar 1910), British violinist and conductor. Led the BLECH QUARTET, 1934–50. He was founding conductor of the LONDON MOZART PLAYERS, 1949–84, the first British chamber orchestra to specialize in the Viennese classical period; it gained a devoted public. CBE, 1984.

Blech, Leo (b. 21 Apr 1871; d. 25 Aug 1958), German conductor, also composer of operas. Studied with Humperdinck. He led a distinguished career, chiefly in Berlin (at State Opera, 1926–37); banned thereafter as a Jew, he worked in Riga and then Stockholm. Returned to Berlin after the war, and was music director of the City Opera, 1949–53.

Blech Quartet, British string quartet founded 1934. Active until 1950, with wartime interruption. It was led throughout by Harry BLECH and there were three sets of other members: first David Martin, Frederick Riddle and Willem de Mont; secondly, Edward Silverman, Douglas Thompson and William Pleeth; and finally, Lionel Bentley, Keith Cummings and Douglas Cameron.

Blegen, Judith (b. 23 Apr 1941), American soprano. Studied violin and singing; appeared as both violinist and singer in the role of the schoolteacher heroine in *Help, Help, the Globolinks!*, 1969, which Menotti wrote for her. She sang at the Metropolitan Opera from 1970 and at Covent Garden, 1975, showing distinction in Mozart. Also performs with Kenneth COOPER and as a duettist with VON STADE.

Blomstedt, Herbert (b. 11 July 1927), American-born Swedish conductor. Having studied with BERNSTEIN in New York, held important conducting posts in Copenhagen (DANISH RADIO SYMPHONY ORCHESTRA, 1967–77), Stockholm and Dresden (DRESDEN STATE ORCHESTRA, 1975–85). He was then appointed music director of the SAN FRANCISCO SYMPHONY ORCHESTRA, 1985. Conscientiously refuses (as a Seventh-Day Adventist) to rehearse on Saturdays.

Bloomfield, Fannie, *see* ZEISLER.

Blumental, Felicja (b. 28 Dec 1915), Polish-born Brazilian pianist. Became resident in Brazil in World War II. Villa-Lobos wrote for her his Piano Concerto no. 5, of which she gave the première in London, 1955. Also plays harpsichord, and was the first to perform Penderecki's Partita for harpsichord and orchestra, 1972, dedicated to her.

Bochsa, Robert-Nicolas-Charles (b. 9 Aug 1789; d. 6 Jan 1856), French harpist and composer. Appointed harpist to Napoleon, then to the returning French king. He committed criminal forgery and, on being forced to leave France, took refuge in England. After becoming bankrupt, 1827, he was dismissed from the Royal Academy of Music, but retained his music directorship (assumed 1826) of the King's Theatre till 1830. He pursued a brilliant virtuoso career and also pursued Anna BISHOP, with whom he eloped, 1839. Their tours led to Sydney, where he died. His innovations in harp technique are historically important.

Bodanzky, Artur (b. 16 Dec 1877; d. 23 Nov 1939), Austrian-born American conductor. Having been assistant conductor to MAHLER in Vienna, he gave the first staged London performance of *Parsifal*, 1914. Became chief conductor of the German repertory at the Metropolitan, 1915, remaining almost continuously until his death. His Wagner performances were famous, but contained cuts now deemed unacceptable; he replaced the spoken dialogue in *Fidelio* (and other works) with his own recitatives.

Boettcher, Wolfgang, *see* BRANDIS QUARTET.

Bohemian Quartet, Prague-based string quartet founded 1892. Later known as the Czech Quartet. The original members were Karel Hoffmann, Josef Suk (1), NEDBAL and Otto Berger. Jiří Herold joined as viola player in 1902, and later cellists were WIHAN, 1897–1913 (who had been its mentor from the beginning), then Ladislav Zelenka. It disbanded in 1933.

Böhm, Karl (b. 28 Aug 1894; d. 14 Aug 1981), Austrian conductor. After gaining experience at Hamburg, worked as music director of Dresden State Opera, 1934–42; gave the first performances of Strauss's *Die schweigsame Frau*, 1935, and *Daphne*, 1938 (dedicated to him). He directed the Vienna State Opera in Nazi-ruled Austria, 1943–5, and again later, 1954–6, and appeared at Bayreuth from 1962. His Chicago concert appearance, 1956, and Metropolitan début, 1957, helped to build his world fame. He frequently conducted the VIENNA PHILHARMONIC ORCHESTRA and the LONDON SYMPHONY ORCHESTRA, of which he was appointed president in 1977. His country gave him the exclusive title 'Austrian General Music Director'.

Bohnke, Emil, *see* BUSCH QUARTET.

Bolet, Jorge (b. 15 Nov 1914; d. 16 Oct 1990), Cuban-American pianist. Born in Havana. He became a student at the Curtis Institute, Philadelphia, aged twelve (and, exactly fifty years from the day he auditioned, became head of its piano department). Later studied with GODOWSKY and Moriz ROSENTHAL. He is celebrated for his performances of Liszt and other grandiose romantics. His US military service in Japan led to his conducting the first performance there of *The Mikado*, 1946.

Bonci, Alessandro (b. 10 Feb 1870; d. 9 Aug 1940), Italian tenor. Sang internationally in opera (Covent Garden from 1900 and New York from 1907) and was one of the few Italians to make a name in the German lieder repertory. He continued to sing in Italy until 1935.

Bondini, Caterina (dates unknown), Italian soprano. Sang Susanna in the first Prague performances of *Figaro*, 1786, and (under Mozart's direction) Zerlina in the première of *Don Giovanni* (Prague), 1787. An anecdote tells that Mozart 'coached' her to scream by suddenly pinching her. Her husband, Pasquale Bondini, was the impresario of the Prague company.

Bonell, Carlos [Antonio] (b. 23 July 1949), British guitarist of Spanish descent. Cultivated unusual works, in distinguished company (such as BERGANZA and ZUKERMAN) or his own ensemble. He commissioned and gave the first performance of Stephen Oliver's Guitar Sonata, 1981. Also plays the *charango*, a small Bolivian guitar.

Boninsegna, Celestina (b. 26 Feb 1877; d. 14 Feb 1947), Italian soprano. Sang in opera at the age of fifteen and developed an international career; performed Verdi roles at Covent Garden from 1904. She is remembered for her successful early recordings.

Bonynge, Richard [Alan] (b. 29 Sept 1930), Australian conductor. As pianist and conductor he became coach and adviser to SUTHERLAND and helped to form her style. (They were married in 1954.) At her insistence he was engaged as her regular conductor for operatic performances and recordings. He made his Covent Garden début 1964 and was later music director of the Australian Opera, 1976–84. His performances revived unfamiliar music (ballet as well as opera) and encouraged vocal ornamentation in period styles. CBE, 1977; he was created Officer of the Order of Australia, 1983.

Borciani, Paulo, *see* QUARTETTO ITALIANO.

Bordoni, Faustina (b. 1700; d. 4 Nov 1781), Italian soprano. Travelled widely and came to London for three of Handel's opera seasons, 1726–8. Her professional and private rivalry with CUZZONI erupted in blows on stage in a performance of Bononcini's *Astianatte*, 1727. She was reckoned unsurpassed among contemporary singers. Married Hasse, 1730, who was court composer at Dresden, 1731–63, and sang much of his music at concerts and on stage; they eventually retired to Venice.

Borg, Kim (b. 7 Aug 1919), Finnish bass. Studied chemistry before taking up vocal career. He made his concert début in Helsinki, 1947, and afterwards became internationally known in opera: made début at Glyndebourne 1956 (as Don Giovanni) and at the Metropolitan 1959. He is one of the few non-Soviet singers to have sung as Boris Godunov at the Bolshoi Theatre. Also an accomplished recitalist and the composer of a trombone concerto and other works.

Borge, Victor [originally Borge Rosenbaum] (b. 3 Jan 1909), Danish pianist. Settled in USA, 1940. He became celebrated for his comic musical appearances; in New York his daily recitals ran for two and a half years from autumn 1953. Still performing at eighty.

Borgioli, Dino (b. 15 Feb 1891; d. 12 Sept 1960), Italian tenor. Partnered MELBA on her final Australian tour, 1924, and acquired a particular following in Britain. He sang at Covent

Garden from 1925 (opposite DAL MONTE and later SUPERVIA) and at Glyndebourne (in *Don Giovanni* and Donizetti's *Don Pasquale*), 1937–9. He taught much and was adviser to the New London Opera Company in its important London seasons, 1946–8.

Bori, Lucrezia (originally Lucrecia Borja y Gonzalez de Rianche) (b. 24 Dec 1887; d. 14 May 1960), Spanish soprano. Performed with CARUSO in Paris, 1910; she was Octavian in the Italian première of *Der Rosenkavalier*, Milan, 1911. Never appeared in Britain, but was a favourite artist at the Metropolitan, 1912–36, where she sang twenty-eight roles, from Mozart's Despina (*Così*) to Debussy's Mélisande. Her command of style, evident also on recordings, was much admired.

Borkh, Inge [originally Ingeborg Simon] (b. 26 May 1917), German soprano. Began her career in Switzerland, then won distinction in heavier operatic roles. She sang at Bayreuth from 1952 and made her débuts at the Metropolitan, 1954, and Covent Garden, 1959, as Salome. She had trained in drama as well as singing, and appeared in plays after leaving opera, 1977.

Borodin Quartet, Russian string quartet founded 1946 as the Moscow Philharmonic Quartet. Original players were Rostislav Dubinsky, Yaroslav Alexandrov, Dmitry Shebalin and Valentin Berlinsky. Members in 1988: Mikhail Kopelman, Andrey Abramenkov, Shebalin and Berlinsky. They recorded all Shostakovich's quartets.

Borsarello, Jacques, *see* LOEWENGUTH QUARTET.

Borwick, Leonard (b. 20 Feb 1868; d. 17 Sept 1925), British pianist. One of the few British solo instrumentalists of his day reckoned to be of leading international standard. He was a pupil of Clara SCHUMANN. Partnered JOACHIM in chamber music and GREENE in song. He also transcribed Debussy's *L'Après-midi d'un faune* and other orchestral works for piano.

Bos, Coenraad V[alẹntyn] (b. 7 Dec 1875; d. 5 Aug 1955), Dutch pianist. Became one of the most celebrated accompanists of his time: performed with CASALS and KREISLER and such singers as GERHARDT and SCHUMANN-HEINK. He settled in USA and taught at the Juilliard School, 1934–52. Died at Chappaqua, New York State.

Boschi, Giuseppe (b. *c.* 1675; d. after 1743), Italian bass. His voice would now be described as baritone. In London he created the role of Argante in Handel's *Rinaldo*, 1711; worked there again from 1720 to 1728, singing in other operas (including thirteen by Handel). His wife, the contralto Francesca Vanini (d. 1734), sang with him, but she apparently retired early.

Boskovsky, Alfred, *see* BOSKOVSKY, WILLI.

Boskovsky, Willi (b. 16 June 1909), Austrian violinist and conductor. Member of the VIENNA PHILHARMONIC ORCHESTRA from 1932 and later one of its leaders. As a conductor and specialist in music by the Strauss family, he upheld the dance-orchestra tradition of conducting with the violin bow. He conducted the Vienna Philharmonic's New Year's Day concert annually from 1954 to 1979. His brother Alfred Boskovsky (b. 1913) is a clarinettist.

Boston Pops Orchestra, American orchestra founded 1885. An offshoot of the BOSTON SYMPHONY ORCHESTRA, it gives a summer season of concerts made up mainly of lighter works. Its conductor for nearly half a century, 1930–79, was FIEDLER; he was followed by John WILLIAMS (2) from 1980.

Boston Symphony Orchestra, American orchestra founded 1881. Principal conductors (latterly styled music directors) have included HENSCHEL, 1881–4, NIKISCH, 1889–93, MUCK, 1906–8 and 1912–18, MONTEUX, 1919–24, KOUSSEVITZKY, 1924–49, MUNCH, 1949–62, LEINSDORF, 1962–9, STEINBERG, 1969–72, and OZAWA, from 1973.

Boué, Geori (originally Georgette) (b. 16 Oct 1918), French soprano. Prominent at the Paris Opera from 1942, in which year she sang the title role in Massenet's *Thaïs* at the centenary of the composer's birth. She also performed much operetta and played the title part in Sacha Guitry's film about the nineteenth-century soprano MALIBRAN, 1944. She often sang with her husband, the baritone Roger Bourdin (1900–1974).

Boukoff, Yuri (b. 1 May 1923), Bulgarian-born French pianist. Won a scholarship to France and underwent advanced training at the Paris Conservatory. He gained prizes at international competitions and pursued a world-wide career. In 1956 he was apparently the first European pianist to tour communist China.

Boulanger, Lili, *see* BOULANGER, NADIA.

Boulanger, Nadia (b. 16 Sept 1887; d. 22 Oct 1979), French pianist, organist, conductor, composer and teacher. Among her pupils of composition were US composers such as Copland, Roy Harris, Virgil Thomson (chiefly at the American Conservatory established 1921 at Fontainebleau). She was the first woman to conduct an entire symphony concert in London (4 November 1937) and the first to conduct the NEW YORK PHILHARMONIC (11 Feb 1939); she gave the première of Stravinsky's 'Dumbarton Oaks' Concerto (Washington, 1938) and remained in USA during World War II. Her sister Lili Boulanger (1893–1918), who died young, was also a composer.

Boulez, Pierre [Louis Joseph] (b. 26 Mar 1925), French conductor and composer. Unrivalled in combining both activities. Noted at first for his skill in conducting his own and other 'advanced' works (evolving a new hand-signalling technique), he proceeded to embrace a general repertory. Founder of the Domaine Musical concert series in Paris, 1954. At Donaueschingen, 1964, he was conductor of the first performance of Messiaen's *Couleurs de la cité céleste*. Conducted *Parsifal*, 1966–9, and *The Ring*, 1976–80, at Bayreuth. He was chief conductor of the BBC SYMPHONY ORCHESTRA, 1971–5, and music director of the NEW YORK PHILHARMONIC, 1971–7, with which he gave the première of Carter's Symphony of Three Orchestras, 1977. Founded the Institut de Recherche et de Coordination Acoustique/Musique (IRCAM) in Paris, 1974. At the Paris Opera he conducted the first complete version of Berg's *Lulu*, 1979.

Boult, Adrian [Cedric] (b. 8 Apr 1889; d. 22 Feb 1983), British conductor. Studied in London and Leipzig, where he observed the methods of NIKISCH, then in London conducted the first (private) performance of Holst's *The Planets*, 1918, and gained operatic and ballet experience. He was chief conductor of the BIRMINGHAM SYMPHONY ORCHESTRA, 1924–30, and of the BBC SYMPHONY ORCHESTRA, 1930–50. With the latter he attained particularly high standards in wide-ranging programmes: gave the first UK (concert) performance of Berg's *Wozzeck*, 1934, and the première of Vaughan Williams's *A Pastoral Symphony*, 1922, and Symphony no. 6, 1948. Conducted also in USA and European capitals. He directed the LONDON PHILHARMONIC ORCHESTRA, 1950–57, and worked again with the Birmingham Symphony, 1959–60. Knighted, 1937; CH, 1969.

Bour, Ernest (b. 20 Apr 1913), French conductor. Worked in concert and opera in France, Germany (SÜDWESTFUNK ORCHESTRA at Baden-Baden, 1964–79) and the Netherlands. An active promoter of new music, he gave the first performance of Bussotti's *Opus Cygne*, 1979.

Bourdin, Roger, *see* BOUÉ.

Bournemouth Municipal Orchestra, *see* BOURNEMOUTH SYMPHONY ORCHESTRA.

Bournemouth Sinfonietta, *see* BOURNEMOUTH SYMPHONY ORCHESTRA.

Bournemouth Symphony Orchestra, British orchestra founded 1893 as the Bournemouth Municipal Orchestra. Took present title in 1954. Its first conductor, GODFREY, remained till 1934; later conductors have included SCHWARZ, 1947–51, GROVES, 1951–61, SILVESTRI, 1961–9, BERGLUND, 1972–9, SEGAL, 1980–82, BARSHAI, 1982–8, and Andrew Litton, from 1988. An offshoot that plays a successful role as a chamber orchestra is the Bournemouth Sinfonietta, founded 1968; it has been conducted by DEL MAR, 1983–5, NORRINGTON, 1985–9, and then VÁSÁRY.

Bowman, James [Thomas] (b. 6 Nov 1941), British countertenor. The best-known such since Alfred DELLER, he worked much with Britten (who wrote for him the Voice of Apollo in *Death in Venice*, 1973), and has also sung many Handel opera and oratorio roles (some of which were intended for castrato); made Sadler's Wells Opera début in *Semele*, 1970.

Bowman, John (b. *c.* 1660; d. 23 Mar 1739),

British bass and actor. Said to have sung for Charles II at Nell Gwyn's lodgings when young. Later performed at court in Purcell's odes and took the role of Grimbald in the première of Purcell's *King Arthur*, 1690.

Boyko, Yefim, *see* TEL AVIV QUARTET.

Braham (originally Abraham), **John** (b. 20 Mar 1774; d. 17 Feb 1856), British tenor. Trained as a boy by LEONI (sometimes stated to have been his uncle); he went with STORACE to sing in Italy, where he was befriended by Nelson. Made his adult début at Covent Garden 1801. Weber wrote for him the hero's role, Sir Huon, in *Oberon* (London), 1826. He continued singing (latterly as baritone) until over seventy. Among his own compositions, the ballad 'The Death of Nelson' was extremely popular.

Brailowsky, Alexander (b. 16 Feb 1896; d. 25 Apr 1976), Russian pianist. Studied in Vienna with LESCHETIZKY and in Switzerland with BUSONI; made highly successful New York début 1924 and settled there. He specialized in Chopin and Liszt, and celebrated the 150th anniversary of Chopin's birth by performing his complete piano works in New York and Brussels, 1960.

Brain, Aubrey [Harold] (b. 12 July 1893; d. 20 Sept 1955), British horn player, father of Dennis BRAIN. Principal of BBC SYMPHONY ORCHESTRA, 1930–45. With d'ARÁNYI he gave the first performance of Ethel Smyth's Concerto for violin, horn and orchestra, 1927. Another son, Leonard Brain (1915–75), was an oboist.

Brain, Dennis (b. 17 May 1921; d. 1 Sept 1957), British horn player, son of Aubrey BRAIN. Principal horn of BEECHAM'S ROYAL PHILHARMONIC ORCHESTRA from 1946, later of the PHILHARMONIA. A distinguished soloist, he set new standards in horn technique. Britten wrote for him (and PEARS) his *Serenade* and the third canticle, *Still Falls the Rain* (first performances 1943 and 1955). He occasionally also performed as an organist. Killed in a car accident; Poulenc dedicated to his memory the *Elegy* for horn and piano, 1957. (*See also* HAAS, KARL.)

Brain, Leonard, *see* BRAIN, AUBREY.

Brainin, Norbert, *see* AMADEUS QUARTET.

Braithwaite, Nicholas [Paul Dallon] (b. 26 Aug 1939), British conductor, son of Warwick BRAITHWAITE. His work at Sadler's Wells Opera, 1970–74, included the first British performance of Penderecki's *The Devils of Loudun*, 1973. Music director of Glyndebourne Touring Opera, 1977–80. He has been principal conductor of the Manchester Camerata (chamber orchestra) since 1984, and in addition has been dean of the music faculty at the Victorian College of the Arts, Melbourne, since 1987.

Braithwaite, [Henry] Warwick (b. 9 Jan 1896; d. 18 Jan 1971), New Zealand conductor, father of Nicholas BRAITHWAITE. Active in British opera: he worked with Vic-Wells Opera (later Sadler's Wells), 1932–40, Welsh National Opera, 1956–60, and again with Sadler's Wells, 1960–68. Also conductor of the SCOTTISH ORCHESTRA, 1940–45.

Brambilla, Marietta, *see* BRAMBILLA, TERESA.

Brambilla, Teresa (b. 23 Oct 1818; d. 15 July 1895), Italian soprano. Made her début in Milan, 1831, and toured various countries, including Russia. In 1851 she created the role of Gilda in *Rigoletto*. Her sister, Marietta (1807–75), was a contralto, their father, Paolo Brambilla (1787–1838), a composer.

Branco, Pedro de Freitas, *see* FREITAS BRANCO.

Brandis, Thomas, *see* BRANDIS QUARTET.

Brandis Quartet, Berlin-based string quartet founded 1976. Its members – Thomas Brandis, Peter Brem, Wilfried Strehle and Wolfgang Boettcher – all performed with the BERLIN PHILHARMONIC ORCHESTRA.

Brandt, Marianne (originally Marie Bischoff) (b. 12 Sept 1842; d. 9 July 1921), Austrian mezzo-soprano. Made her operatic début 1867. She was the first to sing Brangaene in *Tristan und Isolde* in Berlin, London, 1882, and New York, 1886.

Brannigan, Owen (b. 10 Mar 1908; d. 9 May 1973), British bass. Prominent at Sadler's Wells Opera, 1943–8 and 1952–8; created the role of

Swallow in Britten's *Peter Grimes*, 1945. As a member of the English Opera Group he created other Britten roles, including Superintendent Budd in *Albert Herring*, 1947, and Noye in *Noye's Fludde*. Also popular light entertainer (often partnering LUSH) in traditional Northumbrian songs.

Branzell, Karin (b. 24 Sept 1891; d. 14 Dec 1974). Swedish mezzo-soprano. After working at the Berlin State Opera, sang for twenty-two seasons at the Metropolitan (first as Fricka in *Die Walküre*, 1924); also appeared at Covent Garden from 1935. In retirement she taught in New York and California.

Bream, Julian [Alexander] (b. 15 July 1933). British guitarist and lutenist. More than anyone else he established a British following for the guitar. Made his London début 1950, his US début 1958; has toured the world, made many broadcasts and films. He inspired and gave first performances of numerous works, including Britten's *Nocturnal*, 1964, and Brouwer's *Concerto elegiaco*, 1986. He regularly played guitar duets with John WILLIAMS (1) and, as lutenist, accompanied PEARS; from 1960 he has intermittently directed a consort of his own. CBE, 1985.

Brejaart, Jan, *see* GAUDEAMUS QUARTET.

Brem, Peter, *see* BRANDIS QUARTET.

Brema, Marie (originally Minny Fehrman) (b. 28 Feb 1856; d. 22 Mar 1925). British mezzo-soprano. Sang Lola in the British première of *Cavalleria rusticana*, 1891, and was the first British-born singer to appear at Bayreuth (as Ortrud in *Lohengrin* and Kundry in *Parsifal*, 1894). She was the soloist in the first performance of Elgar's *The Dream of Gerontius*, 1900, and later organized her own London seasons of opera in English.

Brendel, Alfred (b. 5 Jan 1931). Austrian pianist. His Vienna début at the age of seventeen included a sonata of his own. Pre-eminent in the Haydn-to-Schubert repertory, he performed the complete Beethoven sonatas in London, 1962, and New York, 1963; also plays Bartók and Schoenberg. Settled in London, 1974. He published a volume of essays on music, 1976. Honorary KBE, 1989.

Brent, Charlotte (b. *c.* 1735; d. 10 Apr 1802). British soprano. Pupil of Thomas Arne. She sang principal roles in his operas *Artaxerxes* and *Love in a Village*, both 1762, and won popularity: a published volume of over 400 songs was entitled *The Brent; or, English Syren*. She married the violinist and composer Thomas Pinto (1714–83).

Breuer, Menahem, *see* TEL AVIV QUARTET.

Bréval, Lucienne (originally Berthe Agnes Lisette Schilling) (b. 4 Nov 1869; d. 15 Aug 1935). Swiss-born French soprano. Sang at the Paris Opera, 1892–1919, and became distinguished in a wide range of works, including Wagner. She also appeared at Covent Garden, 1899, and Monte Carlo (title role in the première of Fauré's *Pénélope*, 1913).

Brewer, Bruce (b. 16 Oct 1941). American tenor. Settled in France. A specialist in the French and Italian baroque repertory, he sang at Aix-en-Provence in revival of Campra's opera *Le Carnaval de Venise*, 1975, and in London in Rameau's *La Princesse de Navarre*, 1979.

Briggs, Christopher Rawdon, *see* BRODSKY QUARTET (1).

Bright, Dora [Estella] (b. 16 Aug 1863; d. 16 Nov 1951). British pianist. Said to have been the first to devote a recital entirely to British music and the first woman composer commissioned by the Philharmonic Society (her Fantasia no. 2 for piano and orchestra; she was the soloist at its première, 1892). Also wrote about music.

Brilioth, Helge (b. 7 May 1931). Swedish tenor, formerly pianist, organist and baritone. Became internationally noted in Wagner's heroic tenor roles. He sang at Bayreuth from 1969 and from 1970 at Covent Garden (Siegmund) and the Metropolitan (Parsifal).

Brodsky, Adolph (b. 2 Apr 1851; d. 22 Jan 1929). Russian violinist. In Vienna in 1881 gave the first performance of Tchaikovsky's Concerto when AUER had rejected it. After leading Walter DAMROSCH'S NEW YORK SYMPHONY ORCHESTRA, 1891–4, he settled in Manchester, 1895. Worked briefly as leader of the

HALLÉ ORCHESTRA, then was principal of the Royal Manchester College of Music, 1896–1929; he also remained active as a soloist and quartet leader.

Brodsky Quartet (1), ensemble led by BRODSKY in Leipzig, 1870; other members were Jean BECKER, Ottokar Novácek and Julius KLENGEL. In the mid-1890s in Manchester he formed another group, with Christopher Rawdon Briggs, Simon Speelman and Carl Fuchs, to which Elgar's String Quartet was dedicated, 1918.

Brodsky Quartet (2), British string quartet. Named in honour of BRODSKY; it gave its first concert in 1973. Members: Michael Thomas, Ian Belton, Alexander Robertson (succeeded by Paul Cassidy, 1982) and Jacqueline Thomas.

Brosa, Antonio (b. 27 June 1894; d. 26 Mar 1979), Spanish violinist. Settled in London, and became well known as leader of the BROSA QUARTET. During World War II he lived in USA, where he was soloist in the première of Britten's Violin Concerto (New York), 1940, and led the PRO ARTE QUARTET, 1940–44. Returned to Europe, 1946; he gave the first performance of Gerhard's Violin Concerto, 1950.

Brosa Quartet, British string quartet led by BROSA, 1924–38. Other members were David Wise, Leonard Rubens and Anthony Pini.

Broschi, Carlo, *see* FARINELLI.

Brott, Boris (b. 14 Mar 1944), Canadian conductor. Assistant conductor of the TORONTO SYMPHONY ORCHESTRA, 1963–5, and conductor of the (British) NORTHERN SINFONIA, 1964–8. He has conducted the Hamilton Philharmonic Orchestra, Ontario, from 1969, and was also, 1972–7, chief conductor of the BBC WELSH ORCHESTRA. His father is the composer Alexander Brott.

Brouwenstijn, Gré (in full Gerarda Benthina van Swol-Brouwenstijn) (b. 26 Aug 1915), Dutch soprano. Joined the newly formed Netherlands Opera, 1948. Internationally noted, she sang at Covent Garden from 1951 (as Aida, Elisabeth in *Don Carlos* and other roles), and at Bayreuth, 1954–6. She was Leonore in Glyndebourne's first *Fidelio*, 1959. Retired in 1971.

Brouwer, Leo (b. 1 Mar 1939), Cuban guitarist, music administrator and composer. Studied composition in USA. He has toured internationally and recorded his own works for guitar. Exceptionally for a guitarist of stature, has composed mainly for other instruments, including prepared piano. (*See also* BREAM.)

Brown, Iona, *see* ACADEMY OF ST MARTIN-IN-THE-FIELDS.

Browning, John (b. 22 May 1933), American pianist. In 1956 made his New York début and won second prize (ASHKENAZY came first) in the Queen Elisabeth Competition, Brussels. He gave the première of Barber's Piano Concerto in 1962 and more than 400 performances of it in the ensuing twenty years. His international tours have included USSR and Japan; he has recorded Prokofiev's five piano concertos.

Brownlee, John [Donald Mackenzie] (b. 7 Jan 1900; d. 3 Jan 1969), Australian-born American baritone. Brought by MELBA to London, where he made his Covent Garden début in her farewell gala performance, 1926. He was prominent at the Paris Opera, 1926–33, and the Metropolitan, 1937–56. Became director of the Manhattan School of Music, 1956, and later its president, 1966.

Bruch, Max, *see* ROYAL LIVERPOOL PHILHARMONIC ORCHESTRA and SCOTTISH NATIONAL ORCHESTRA.

Bruck, Charles (b. 2 May 1911), Romanian-born French conductor. Held various orchestral posts, including conductorship of the French Radio Philharmonic Orchestra, 1965–70. He gave the first French performances of many works (by such composers as Janáček, Ligeti and Dallapiccola) and conducted the world première, in concert version, of Prokofiev's opera *The Fiery Angel* (Paris), 1954.

Brüggen, Frans (b. 30 Oct 1934), Dutch recorder player, flautist and conductor. In 1981 founded his own Orchestra of the Eighteenth Century to perform the classical repertory on authentic instruments. A virtuoso of the recorder, he is also an eminent exponent of the early transverse flute, and has played it on many recordings of (chiefly) eighteenth-century music; has often worked with BYLSMA and LEONHARDT. He commissioned and gave the première of Berio's *Gesti*, 1966, a piece that requires solo theatrical as well as musical performance.

Brunetti, Antonio (d. 25 Dec 1786), Italian violinist. Employed at Salzburg. Four works with orchestra were composed for him by the youthful Mozart, who, however, called him 'coarse, dirty . . . a disgrace to his employer, to himself and to the whole orchestra'.

Bruscantini, Sesto (b. 10 Dec 1919), Italian bass-baritone. Celebrated in comic roles. He appeared at La Scala from 1949 and sang with CALLAS in Rossini's *Il turco in Italia*, 1950. At Glyndebourne he was a favourite in Mozart (Alfonso in *Così*) and Rossini, 1951–6 and 1960. Continued performing into his sixties. He was married, 1953–7, to JURINAC.

Bruson, Renato (b. 13 Jan 1936), Italian baritone. First appeared at the Metropolitan Opera as Enrico in *Lucia di Lammermoor*, 1969, and made Covent Garden début 1976. In the 1980s he became one of the most admired Verdi singers (Posa in *Don Carlos*, and Iago in *Otello*).

Brymer, Jack (b. 27 Jan 1915), British clarinettist. In 1947 he was apppointed by BEECHAM to succeed KELL as first clarinet in the ROYAL PHILHARMONIC ORCHESTRA. Later played with other orchestras and became noted in concertos (made three recordings of Mozart's); he also directed wind ensembles and gave radio talks.

Bryn-Julson, Phyllis [Mae] (b. 5 Feb 1945), American soprano of Norwegian descent. After performing with the BOSTON SYMPHONY ORCHESTRA, 1966, became noted in twentieth-century works: she sang in the premières of Sessions's opera *Montezuma*, 1976, Maw's *La vita nuova* (London), 1979, and Del Tredici's *In Memory of a Summer Day*, 1980.

Buchbinder, Rudolf (b. 1 Dec 1946), Austrian pianist. His extensive recordings include the complete piano works of Haydn and, with STARKER, the complete cello sonatas of Beethoven. He appeared widely in Europe from the 1960s and performed with the NEW YORK PHILHARMONIC and other major US orchestras, 1983–4.

Buck, Peter, *see* MELOS QUARTET.

Buckman, Rosina (b. 1880; d. 30 Dec 1948), New Zealand soprano. Settled in Australia (where she performed with MELBA), then in Britain. At Covent Garden, from 1913, her roles included Aida and Isolde. She sang the heroine's part in the first performance of Ethel Smyth's opera *The Boatswain's Mate*, 1916. Her husband was the tenor Maurice D'Oisly (1888–1944).

Budapest Philharmonic Orchestra, Hungarian orchestra founded 1853. Its conductors have included the composer Ernst von Dohnányi, 1919–44, KLEMPERER, 1947–50, FERENCSIK, 1960–68, and András Kórodi, 1968–86.

Budapest Quartet, string quartet founded 1917. Originally made up of Hungarian musicians, but from early 1930s the players were Russian-Jewish. It was the quartet in residence at the Library of Congress in Washington, 1940–62, and then at the University of Buffalo, 1962–7, after which it disbanded. Its final members (from the 1930s) were Josef Roisman, Alexander SCHNEIDER, Boris Kroyt and Mischa Schneider. They were perhaps the most celebrated quartet players of their time. Bartók's Quartet no. 5, 1934, and Hindemith's no. 5, 1943, are dedicated to them.

Buesst, Aylmer (b. 28 Jan 1883; d. 25 Jan 1970), Australian conductor. Settled in London and became an operatic associate of BEECHAM; conducted the SCOTTISH ORCHESTRA, 1939–40. At Covent Garden on 6 Jan 1923 he conducted the British National Opera Company in Humperdinck's *Hänsel und Gretel*, apparently the first opera broadcast from a theatre in Europe.

Bülow, Hans [Guido] **von** (b. 8 Jan 1830; d. 12 Feb 1894), German pianist and conductor. As conductor to the court at Munich, he gave the first performances of *Tristan und Isolde*, 1865, and *Die Meistersinger*, 1868; championed Brahms also. He was the soloist in the première of Tchaikovsky's Piano Concerto no. 1 (after the composer had failed to secure a performance in Russia) in Boston, 1875. Conducted the BERLIN PHILHARMONIC ORCHESTRA, 1887–92. He married LISZT's illegitimate daughter, Cosima, who later became Wagner's mistress and then wife.

Bumbry, Grace [Ann Melzia] (b. 4 Jan 1937), American mezzo-soprano. Sang Venus in *Tannhäuser* at Bayreuth, 1961 (the first black singer to appear there). Eboli in *Don Carlos* was her début role (highly successful) at Covent Garden, 1963, and the Metropolitan, 1965. She later added soprano roles such as Tosca to her repertory.

Burchuladze, Paata (b. 12 Feb 1955), Soviet-Georgian bass. Trained partly in Italy. He won the Moscow Tchaikovsky Competition in 1982, made his British concert début 1983, Covent Garden début 1984 (as Ramfis in *Aida*) and Metropolitan début 1988. He sang Shostakovich's Suite on verses by Michelangelo at the Proms, 1986.

Burgos, Rafael Frühbeck de, *see* FRÜHBECK DE BURGOS.

Burnett, Richard [Leslie] (b. 23 June 1932), British pianist and harpsichordist. His aptitude in early pianos is backed by his own public collection (opened in 1977 at Finchcocks, Kent), where many such instruments are displayed in working order and concerts given.

Burrowes, Norma, *see* BEDFORD, STEUART.

Burrows, Stuart (b. 7 Feb 1933), British tenor. Celebrated as oratorio singer and in opera, particularly Mozart: he sang Tamino in *Die Zauberflöte* at Covent Garden, 1967, and Don Ottavio in *Don Giovanni* at the Metropolitan, 1971. Also presenter of his own television music show.

Burton, Philip, *see* GRILLER QUARTET.

Busch, Adolf [Georg Wilhelm] (b. 8 Aug 1891; d. 9 June 1952), German-born violinist, naturalized Swiss 1935, brother of Fritz BUSCH. Associated in youth with the composer Max Reger, at whose funeral he played, 1916. He won distinction as a soloist, quartet leader and teacher. Forbidden by the Nazis to perform with his Jewish son-in-law, Rudolf SERKIN, from 1933 he worked mainly in Switzerland, UK and USA. He was one of the founders of the Marlboro Festival at Vermont, 1950, which was of major importance in chamber music. Another brother, Hermann Busch (1897–1975), was a cellist.

Busch, Fritz (b. 13 Mar 1890; d. 14 Sept 1951), German-born conductor; became Argentinian citizen 1936, brother of Adolf BUSCH. His directorship of Dresden State Opera, 1922–33, was celebrated; conducted the first performances of Strauss's *Intermezzo*, 1924, and *Die aegyptische Helena*, 1933. Left Nazi Germany and conducted opera in Argentina. He was the first (and a highly influential) music director at Glyndebourne, 1934–9, and returned to conduct there in 1950–51. Also conductor of the STOCKHOLM PHILHARMONIC ORCHESTRA, 1937–40. At the Edinburgh Festival in 1951 he conducted the DANISH RADIO SYMPHONY ORCHESTRA.

Busch, Hermann, *see* BUSCH (ADOLF) and BUSCH QUARTET.

Busch Quartet, Austrian, later American, string quartet founded 1913 in Vienna as the Konzertverein Quartet. Ceased playing during World War I and re-formed in 1919 with the name the Busch Quartet and a membership of Adolf BUSCH, Karl Reitz, Emil Bohnke (succeeded by Karl Doktor, 1921) and Paul Grümmer. They emigrated to USA, 1940. The group again disbanded in 1945, but re-formed in 1946 and continued till Busch's death, 1952. Other final members were Bruno Straumann, Hugo Göttesmann and Hermann Busch.

Busoni, Ferruccio [Dante Michelangelo Benvenuto] (b. 1 Apr 1866; d. 27 July 1924), Italian composer and pianist (mother German). Internationally eminent as virtuoso performer, renowned in Liszt and his own famous transcriptions of Bach. He made his first US tour 1891, and from 1894 lived principally in Berlin; gave his last recital there in 1922. His piano pupils included Egon PETRI and the Australian composer Percy Grainger. He was also a conductor, and favoured modern works: first German performances of Sibelius's Symphony no. no. 2, 1905, and *Pohjola's Daughter*, 1908.

Bussani, Francesco (b. 1743; d. after 1807), Italian bass. Famous for his association with Mozart: he performed both as Bartolo and as

Antonio in the première of *Figaro*, 1786, and created the role of Don Alfonso in *Così*, 1790. He was also a stage manager and musical arranger.

Buths, Julius [Emil Martin] (b. 7 May 1851; d. 12 Mar 1920), German conductor and pianist. While he was director of the annual festivals at Düsseldorf, he translated Elgar's *The Dream of Gerontius* into German and conducted its first performance outside UK, 1901. In 1904 he was the soloist in the première of Delius's Piano Concerto.

Butler, Mark, *see* CHILINGIRIAN QUARTET.

Butt, Clara [Ellen] (b. 1 Feb 1872; d. 23 Jan 1936), British contralto. Her big-voiced ballad singing at concerts and on record made her a household word. While still a student she sang at the Albert Hall in Sullivan's *The Golden Legend*, 1902; Elgar wrote his *Sea Pictures* for her, 1908. Performed Gluck's Orpheus under BEECHAM at Covent Garden, 1920. A frequent concert partner was her husband, the baritone Kennerley Rumford (1870–1957). Created Dame, 1920 in recognition of her charity concerts in World War I.

Buxbaum, Friedrich, *see* ROSÉ QUARTET.

Bychkov, Semyon (b. 30 Nov 1952), Russian-born conductor, naturalized American 1983. Left USSR in 1975. He made successful guest appearances with major US and European orchestras and also conducted opera at the Aix-en-Provence Festival. Became music director of the Buffalo Philharmonic Orchestra, 1985, and of the ORCHESTRE DE PARIS, 1990.

Bylsma (also spelt Bijlsma), **Anner** (b. 17 Feb 1934), Dutch cellist. After orchestral work (leader of cellos in the CONCERTGEBOUW ORCHESTRA, 1962–8), concentrated on the revival of the baroque cello and its technique. He was the first to record on this instrument, 1976, and has made recordings of all Vivaldi's cello works. (*See also* BRÜGGEN and LEONHARDT.)

C

Caballé, Montserrat (b. 12 Apr 1933), Spanish soprano. Became celebrated not only in standard operatic roles (at Glyndebourne and the Metropolitan Opera from 1965 and Covent Garden from 1972) but in such rarities as Donizetti's *Lucrezia Borgia* (made first recording of it, 1966). Continued, despite her stoutness, to maintain success as opera and concert singer, and recorded with the pop star Freddie Mercury, 1988. She married, and often sang with, the tenor Bernabé Martí (b. 1934) and encouraged the career of CARRERAS.

Caffarelli, professional name adopted by Gaetano Majorano (b. 12 Apr 1710; d. 31 Jan 1783), Italian male soprano (castrato). Sang with Handel's company in London, 1738–9, creating the title roles in Handel's *Faramondo* and *Serse*. He was also a composer. Retired to Naples and bought a dukedom with the riches of his fame.

Caldwell, Sarah (b. 6 Mar 1924), American conductor. Specializes in opera; also often works as stage director for herself and other conductors. Founder and factotum of the Opera Group (later Company) of Boston, 1957, she prominently presented unusual works; conducted the first US stage performance of Prokofiev's *War and Peace*, 1974, and the US première of Tippett's *The Ice Break*, 1979. In 1973 she became the first woman to conduct at the Metropolitan Opera.

Callas (originally Kalogeropoulos), **Maria** [Anna Sophia Cecilia] (b. 3 Dec 1923; d. 16 Sept 1977), American soprano of Greek descent. Her Italian début, 1947, led to international acclaim; sang at La Scala from 1950, Covent Garden from 1952 and the Metropolitan from 1954. She was overweight, but slimmed drastically to become a compelling actress as well as singer in the title roles of *Norma* and Cherubini's *Médée* (she always sang the Italian version, as *Medea*). Also recorded mezzo-soprano roles, for example Carmen. Recordings and films helped to place her among the most celebrated of all twentieth-century performers. She was known for apparently temperamental cancellations and for a publicly exposed private life. Having married an Italian industrialist, 1949, she was billed as Maria Meneghini Callas; she separated from him, 1959, and became (temporarily) associated with the Greek shipowner Onassis. After 1968, her vocal powers weaker, she gave few opera performances but made an international concert tour with DI STEFANO, 1973–4. Died of a heart attack. (*See also* VOTTO.)

Calvé, Emma (originally Rosa-Noémie Calvet de Roquer) (b. 15 Aug 1858; d. 6 Jan 1942), French soprano. Celebrated in the French and Italian opera repertory, she partnered DE LUCIA in the première of Mascagni's *L'amico Fritz* in Rome, in 1891, and first sang at Covent Garden 1892. A famed role (really for mezzo-soprano) was Carmen: she sang in the thousandth performance of that opera at the Paris Opéra-Comique, 1904. Thereafter she appeared mainly in concerts.

Calvet, Joseph, *see* CALVET QUARTET.

Calvet Quartet, Paris-based string quartet formed 1919 with Joseph Calvet as leader. Other original members: Léon Pascal, Daniel Guilevitch and Paul Mass; finally, Jean Champeil, Maurice

Husson and Manuel Recasens. It disbanded in 1950.

Cambreling, Sylvain (b. 2 July 1948), French conductor. Worked in Lyons and Paris. In 1981 he became, jointly with PRITCHARD, music director of the Monnaie (Brussels Opera); helped to establish a new eminence for that company.

Camden, Archie (originally Archibald) [Leslie] (b. 9 Mar 1888; d. 16 Feb 1979), British bassoonist. Began his career in the HALLÉ ORCHESTRA before the first performance of Elgar's Symphony no. 1, 1908, and continued as a distinguished orchestral player, soloist and teacher for over sixty years. His recording of Mozart's Bassoon Concerto, 1927, was famous; Gordon Jacob wrote a concerto for him, 1947.

Cameron, [George] **Basil** (b. 1884; d. 26 June 1975), British conductor. Having assumed the German surname Hindenburg because of a supposed British prejudice in favour of foreigners, was driven back to his own name by the outbreak of war, 1914. Conducted in USA; in San Francisco gave the première of Bax's Symphony no. 4, 1938. From 1940 he was assistant conductor at the Proms. CBE, 1957.

Cameron, Douglas, *see* BLECH QUARTET and LONDON STRING QUARTET (2).

Campanini, Cleofonte (b. 1 Sept 1860; d. 19 Dec 1919), Italian conductor. In Milan he conducted the premières of Giordano's *Adriana Lecouvreur*, 1902, and Puccini's *Madama Butterfly*, 1904, and in New York the first US performances of *Otello*, 1902, and Debussy's *Pelléas et Mélisande*, 1908. Became principal conductor of Chicago Opera, 1910, and died in Chicago. His brother was the tenor Italo Campanini (1845–96), whose wife, Eva, was the sister of Luisa TETRAZZINI.

Campanini, Italo, *see* CAMPANINI, CLEOFONTE.

Campoli, Alfredo (b. 20 Oct 1906; d. 21 Mar 1991), Italian-born British violinist. Bliss's Concerto, 1955, is dedicated to him. Though highly esteemed as a soloist in the classical repertory (Proms début 1938), he achieved widest fame in the 1930s as leader of his own orchestra, which played light music, especially on radio.

Cangalovic, Miroslav (b. 18 Feb 1921), Yugoslav bass. During the period 1954–65 when performances by Russian operatic artists were generally unavailable in the West, the tours of the Belgrade Opera (including Edinburgh Festival, 1962) established him as a leading singer in such roles as Boris Godunov.

Caniglia, Maria (b. 5 May 1905; d. 16 Apr 1979), Italian soprano. Active at La Scala, 1930–51, and performed with that company at Covent Garden, 1950. She was admired in Verdi; sang opposite GIGLI on recordings of *Aida*, 1939, and other operas.

Canino, Bruno (b. 30 Dec 1935), Italian pianist, also composer and teacher at Milan Conservatory. Prominent in pioneering modern music, both as soloist and as duettist with BALLISTA; in New York they gave the first performance of Berio's Concerto for two pianos, 1963. He was also a pianist partner of BERBERIAN.

Cantelli, Guido (b. 27 Apr 1920; d. 24 Nov 1956), Italian conductor. His early-maturing gifts were encouraged by TOSCANINI. Conducted in New York, 1949, and at the Edinburgh Festival, 1950. Concerts and recordings with the PHILHARMONIA ORCHESTRA from 1951 helped establish him among the most gifted younger conductors. Conductor and stage director of *Così* at the Piccola Scala, Milan, 1956. He died in an air crash shortly after being chosen as music director of La Scala. A prize for young conductors commemorates him.

Cantelo, April [Rosemary] (b. 2 Apr 1928), British soprano. Married to Colin DAVIS, 1949–64, she was a well-known performer while his career was in bud. Notable in Purcell, she also sang with the Glyndebourne company (firstly at Edinburgh Festival, 1950), and created the roles of Helena in Britten's *A Midsummer Night's Dream*, 1960, and Beatrice in Williamson's *Our Man in Havana*, 1963.

Cape, Safford (b. 1 Feb 1906; d. 26 Mar 1973), American conductor and musicologist. In 1933 he established in Brussels the Pro Musica Antiqua group; explored medieval and Renaissance music with a pioneering devotion to historical interpretation. He retained authority in this field until he retired through ill health, 1967.

Capecchi, Renato (b. 6 Nov 1923), Italian baritone. His operatic versatility is said to have embraced 300 roles. Best known internationally in comic parts; made his Covent Garden début 1962 as Melitone in Verdi's *La forza del destino*. Soloist in the first performance of Wilfred Josephs's Jewish Requiem (Milan), 1965. He extended his career into his sixties, singing bass parts such as Bartolo in *Il barbiere*.

Capet, Lucien, *see* CAPET QUARTET.

Capet Quartet, Paris-based string quartet formed 1893 with Lucien Capet as leader. Other original members were Giron, Henri CASADESUS and Charles-Joseph Furet; Marcel CASADESUS was cellist from 1909 to 1914. The quartet was most famous (many recordings from 1925) with its final membership: Capet, Maurice Hewitt, Henri Benoit and Camille Delobelle. It disbanded in 1928.

Cappuccilli, Piero (b. 9 Nov 1929), Italian baritone. His début at La Scala, 1964, led to distinguished international career, especially in Verdi. His first appearances at both the Metropolitan Opera, 1960, and at Covent Garden, 1967, were in *La traviata*; KARAJAN engaged him as Posa *Don Carlos* at Salzburg, 1975, and for the recording.

Capuana, Franco (b. 29 Sept 1894; d. 10 Dec 1969), Italian conductor. Headed the San Carlo company (Naples), which brought opera back to post-war Covent Garden, 1946, and was music director of La Scala, 1949–52. He ranged notably outside the conventional Italian repertory, and gave the first Italian (concert) performance of Janáček's *Jenůfa* in Venice, 1941.

Caradori-Allan (née de Munck), **Maria** [Caterina Rosalbina] (b. 1800; d. 15 Oct 1865), Italian soprano. Settled in Britain. She made her début as Cherubino in *Figaro*, 1822. At a Manchester concert on 14 Sept 1836 she sang a duet with the dying MALIBRAN (who was never again heard). Near the end of her career she disappointed Mendelssohn with her performance in the première of his *Elijah* (Birmingham), 1846.

Carlos, Wendy (originally Walter) (b. 14 Nov 1939), American keyboard player. Worked with Robert Moog, inventor of the first commercially successful synthesizer, and (as Walter Carlos) made on that synthesizer the million-selling album *Switched-on Bach*, 1968; he also composed and synthesized the music for the film *A Clockwork Orange*, 1971. Underwent a physical operation to establish a sex change and in 1979 legally became Wendy.

Carlyss, Earl, *see* JUILLIARD QUARTET.

Carmirelli, Pina (originally Giuseppina) (b. 23 Jan 1914), Italian violinist. Known for her advocacy of Boccherini's chamber music, she founded the Boccherini Quintet, 1949, and the Carmirelli Quartet, 1954. In 1970 played the complete Beethoven violin sonatas with Rudolf SERKIN in New York. She was the violinist-director of I MUSICI, 1975–86.

Carreño, [Maria] Teresa (b. 22 Dec 1853; d. 12 June 1917), Venezuelan pianist. As a child studied in New York under GOTTSCHALK, then lived mainly in France and, from 1870, Britain. A powerful player in an era when women were rarely such, she was dubbed the Valkyrie of the piano. She toured widely (including Australia, 1910), composed much and was also on occasion an opera singer. Championed the music of her young ex-pupil Macdowell. She was married successively to SAURET, the baritone Giovanni Tagliapetra (1846–1921), d'ALBERT and Arturo Tagliapetra, a younger brother of her second husband. She died in New York, but her native country repossessed her ashes, 1938.

Carreras, José (b. 5 Dec 1946), Spanish tenor. Assisted in early career by his partner and compatriot CABALLÉ. His voice and handsome presence made him one of the most sought-after singers in roles such as Alfredo (*La traviata*) and Rodolfo (*La Bohème*); appeared from 1974 at Covent Garden and the Metropolitan Opera. He is also known for recordings of rarer operas, including Halévy's *La Juive*. In 1987 the onset of leukaemia interrupted his career, but he resumed the following year.

Carrodus (originally Carruthers), **John Tiplady** (b. 20 Jan 1836; d. 12 July 1895), British violinist. As principal violin at Covent Garden, played from 1869 until the night before his death. A chamber-music partner of GODDARD and PIATTI, and a noted teacher, he is credited with substantially raising British standards of string playing.

Carron (originally Cox), **Arthur** (b. 12 Dec 1900; d. 10 May 1967), British tenor. One of the few pre-1939 British singers to win leading operatic status. Sang Wagnerian and other roles at the Metropolitan Opera, 1936–46, and made final appearances (as Herod in *Salome*) at Covent Garden in 1952.

Carter, Peter, *see* ALLEGRI QUARTET.

Caruso, Enrico (b. 27 Feb 1873; d. 2 Aug 1921), Italian tenor. Acquired almost mythical standing as a paragon of operatic art, thanks partly to his successful early recordings, from 1901. He took part in the first performance of Giordano's *Fedora* at La Scala, 1898; appeared at Covent Garden from 1902, but was attached mainly to the Metropolitan Opera, 1903–20, where he sang 37 roles in 626 performances. Typifying his Italian and French repertory were Canio in *Pagliacci* and Don José in *Carmen*; he also performed in the première of Puccini's *La fanciulla del West* (Metropolitan), 1910. Died of pleurisy. A film of 1951, *The Great Caruso* (with LANZA), offered a fictionalized biography. (*See also* ALDA, DE LUCIA and PONSELLE.)

Carvalho (née Félix-Miolan), **Caroline** (originally Marie) (b. 31 Dec 1827; d. 10 July 1895), French soprano. Began performing as Marie Miolan but changed her name after marrying the French impresario Léon Carvalho in 1853. Celebrated in opera in Paris, where she created four Gounod heroines: Marguerite in *Faust*, 1859, Baucis in *Philémon et Baucis*, 1860, the title role in *Mireille*, 1864, and Juliet in *Roméo et Juliette*, 1867. Sang at Covent Garden between 1859 and 1872.

Casadesus, French family of musicians. Three brothers are known for publishing various pieces that they falsely ascribed to eighteenth-century composers: **Francis** (or François) [Louis] (b. 2 Dec 1870; d. 27 June 1954), violinist, conductor and composer; **Henri** [Gustave] (b. 30 Sept 1879; d. 31 May 1947), viol and viola d'amore player and composer; and **Marius** [Robert Max] (b. 24 Oct 1892; d. 13 Oct 1981), violinist, viol player and composer. Marius wrote the 'Adelaïde' Violin Concerto supposedly by Mozart. A fourth brother, **Marcel** [Louis Lucien] (b. 31 Oct 1882; d. 31 Oct 1914), was a cellist and, like Henri, played with the CAPET QUARTET. Another brother, Robert-Guillaume, was the father of Robert CASADESUS. Henri's grandson is the conductor Jean-Claude Casadesus (real surname Probst; b. 7 Dec 1935).

Casadesus, Gaby, *see* CASADESUS, ROBERT.

Casadesus, Jean, *see* CASADESUS, ROBERT.

Casadesus, Jean-Claude, *see* CASADESUS (family).

Casadesus, Robert (b. 7 Apr 1899; d. 19 Sept 1972), French pianist and composer. Pupil of DIÉMER. He was a friend of Ravel, whose complete piano works he recorded. Played under TOSCANINI in New York, 1935, and as duettist with FRANCESCATTI and with his wife, the pianist Gaby (originally Gabrielle) Casadesus (née L'Hôte; b. 1901). Their son, Jean Casadesus (1927–72), was also a pianist.

Casals, Pablo (also used the Catalan form, Pau) [Carlos Salvador Defilló] (b. 29 Dec 1876; d. 22 Oct 1973), Spanish cellist and conductor, also pianist and composer. Gave a solo cello recital in Barcelona at the age of fourteen; encouraged by the composer Albéniz, he studied in Madrid, then played in a Paris theatre orchestra. He was established as a concerto soloist by 1897 and enjoyed immense fame. Performed in London and Paris, 1899, and toured USA, 1901–2. As a solo recitalist he notably revived Bach's unaccompanied works; as a chamber musician he played in a trio with CORTOT and THIBAUD from 1905. In 1919 he was founding conductor of an orchestra in Barcelona. Articulately antifascist, he boycotted the regimes of Hitler and Mussolini and, after leaving Franco's Spain, settled in France and then Puerto Rico. His oratorio *El pessebre* (The Manger), 1960, was intended as a plea for peace. His pupils included SUGGIA, with whom he had a publicly acknowledged liaison, 1906–12; he married an American singer, Susan Metcalfe (and played her piano accompaniments); in 1957, aged eighty, he married a 28-year-old Puerto Rican cellist, Marta Montañez. (*See also* ALEXANIAN.)

Caspar, Walter, *see* AMAR QUARTET.

Cassadó, Gaspar [Moreu] (b. 30 Sept 1897; d. 24 Dec 1966), Spanish cellist. Pupil of CASALS. He attained international status as concerto player, duo partner of Arthur RUBINSTEIN and trio partner of MENUHIN and KENTNER. Composers who wrote for him included Dallapiccola (*Dialoghi* for cello and orchestra, 1960). His father was the organist and composer Joaquín Cassadó Valls (1867–1926).

Cassidy, Paul, *see* BRODSKY QUARTET (2).

Cassilly, Richard (b. 14 Dec 1927), American tenor. Appeared on Broadway in the first production of Menotti's *The Saint of Bleecker Street*, 1954, then developed a regular opera-house career: from 1968 at Covent Garden and from 1973 at the Metropolitan (Radamès in *Aida*).

Cassirer, Fritz (b. 29 Mar 1871; d. 26 Nov 1926), German conductor. Championed Delius; he conducted the première of the opera *Koanga* (at Elberfeld) and the first British performance of the choral work *Appalachia* (London). His hopes of a good career in London were disappointed.

Castelmary, Armand (originally Count Armand de Castan) (b. 16 Aug 1834; d. 10 Feb 1897), French bass. Sang the role of the Grand Inquisitor in the first performance of Verdi's French opera *Don Carlos*, 1867, and was also a famous interpreter of the title role of Boito's *Mefistofele*. He died on the stage of the Metropolitan in the middle of a performance of Flotow's *Martha*.

Catalani, Angelica (b. 10 May 1780; d. 12 June 1849), Italian soprano. Made her operatic début aged seventeen. She moved to London, where she attracted the extraordinary fee of £5,250 for two performances weekly over a seven-month season, 1808. In 1812 sang Susanna in the first London performance of *Figaro*. Subsequently in Paris she added theatre management to her singing, but from 1817 she was heard mainly in international concert tours.

Cavalieri, Lina (originally Natalina) (b. 25 Dec 1874; d. 8 Feb 1944), Italian soprano. Famed for her beauty; she sang at the *Folies Bergère* in Paris before embarking on an operatic career. First performed at the Metropolitan 1906 and at Covent Garden (as Tosca) 1908. Divorced from her first husband, she married an American millionaire, but she left him after a week, to public scandal; her third husband was the Italian tenor Lucien Muratore (1878–1954). She and her fourth husband were killed in an Allied air-raid on Florence. A posthumous film biography of her starred Gina Lollobrigida.

Cebotari (originally Cebutaru), **Maria** (b. 23 Feb 1910; d. 9 June 1949), Russian-born Austrian soprano. She created the role of Aminta in Strauss's *Die schweigsame Frau*, 1935, at Dresden; sang at Covent Garden with the Dresden company (as the Countess in *Figaro*), 1936, and with the Vienna State Opera (in the title role of *Salome*), 1947. She made several films, including one on the life of MALIBRAN.

Ceccato, Aldo (b. 18 Feb 1934), Italian conductor. Fulfilled various operatic engagements (Wexford Festival, 1968, and Covent Garden from 1970). He was conductor of the DETROIT SYMPHONY ORCHESTRA, 1973–7, and then the Hamburg Philharmonic, to 1983.

Cehanovsky, George (b. 14 Apr 1892; d. 25 Mar 1986), Russian-born American baritone. His forty-year service at the Metropolitan, 1926–66, perhaps a record, embraced 1,706 performances of 97 (mainly supporting) roles. He was married to RETHBERG.

Celibidache, Sergiu (b. 28 June 1912), Romanian conductor. Trained in Germany and, with FURTWÄNGLER under political suspicion, was suddenly thrust forward in 1945 as conductor of the BERLIN PHILHARMONIC ORCHESTRA, a post he held till 1952. Music director of the Swedish Radio Symphony Orchestra, 1964–71. He became music director of the Munich Philharmonic Orchestra, 1979, and took the orchestra to the USA in 1989. By his insistence on unusually long rehearsal he has deliberately curtailed his guest appearances, but his reputation is immense; he is also a composer.

Cellier, Alfred (b. 1 Dec 1844; d. 28 Dec 1891), British conductor, also composer (*see* DAVIES,

BEN), brother of François CELLIER. Held a leading position in British theatre music. Much associated with Sullivan, he conducted the first New York performance of *The Mikado*, 1885, and was music director for Sullivan's *Ivanhoe*, 1891.

Cellier, François (also known as Frank) (b. 1849; d. 5 Jan 1914), British conductor, brother of Alfred CELLIER. Succeeded his brother as music director for Richard D'Oyly Carte's promotions, 1878, and, as such, was Sullivan's intimate associate; he conducted at Sullivan's funeral in St Paul's, 1900. Also a composer.

Central Symphony Orchestra, *see* TOKYO PHILHARMONIC ORCHESTRA.

Cerquetti, Anita (b. 13 Apr 1931), Italian soprano. Had sung internationally in opera (Chicago, 1955–6) when she achieved new prominence in replacing the temperamental CALLAS as Norma (Rome, 1958). She retired through illness, 1961.

Chailly, Riccardo (b. 20 Feb 1953), Italian conductor. At the age of nineteen was appointed assistant conductor at La Scala, and began his substantial career with *Madama Butterfly* in Chicago, 1975. Additionally to operatic conducting, in 1982 he became music director of the (West) Berlin Radio Symphony Orchestra and was prominent in London and elsewhere; he succeeded HAITINK at the CONCERTGEBOUW ORCHESTRA, Amsterdam, 1988. His father is the composer Luciano Chailly.

Chalabala, Zdeněk (b. 18 Apr 1899; d. 4 Mar 1962), Czech conductor. Worked successively at various Czech opera houses (chief conductor at the Prague National Theatre, 1953–61); also regular guest conductor at the Bolshoi from 1956. Noted exponent of Czech orchestral music.

Chaliapin, Fyodor, *see* SHALYAPIN.

Challender, Stuart, *see* SYDNEY SYMPHONY ORCHESTRA.

Champeil, Jean, *see* CALVET QUARTET.

Chapman, Frank, *see* SWARTHOUT.

Charpentier, Marcel, *see* PARRENIN QUARTET.

Cherkassky, Shura (diminutive of Alexander) (b. 7 Oct 1911), Russian-born American pianist. Taken to USA in boyhood; he gave his first recital in Baltimore aged eleven and became a pupil of Josef HOFMANN. His international fame dates from a European tour in 1946, and is sustained (despite his diminutive stature) by performances of great force and impetus. Returned as a visiting artist to USSR; celebrated his seventy-fifth birthday with concerts in London, New York and elsewhere.

Chevillard, Camille (b. 14 Oct 1859; d. 30 May 1923), French conductor, also composer. In 1899 he succeeded his father-in-law, LAMOUREUX, at the orchestral concert series conducted by him, and became one of the most prominent Paris musicians. He gave the first performances of Debussy's *La Mer*, 1905, and Ravel's *La Valse*, 1920, and from 1914 was music director of the Paris Opera.

Chiara, Maria [Rita] (b. 24 Dec 1939), Italian soprano. Made her début as Desdemona in *Otello* in Venice, 1965, and has since performed widely in major opera houses, including the Metropolitan. Sang Liù in Puccini's *Turandot* in Covent Garden début, 1973.

Chicago Symphony Orchestra, American orchestra founded 1891. Theodore THOMAS was conductor till his death, 1905; a long period, 1905–42, under STOCK followed. The conductorships of REINER, 1953–63, and SOLTI, from 1969, enhanced its prestige through concerts and recordings; made its first European tour in 1971. BARENBOIM is to become music director in 1991.

Chilingirian, Levon, *see* CHILINGIRIAN QUARTET.

Chilingirian Quartet, London-based string quartet founded 1971 by Levon Chilingirian. Other original members were Mark Butler, Simon Rowland-Jones and Philip de Groote; later viola players were ERDELYI, from 1979, and Louise Williams, from 1986. It was attached successively to the universities of Liverpool and Sussex and from 1986 to the Royal College of Music.

Chiostri, Luigi, *see* QUARTETTO FIORENTINO.

Chorzempa, Daniel [Walter] (b. 7 Dec 1944), American organist of Polish and Alsatian parentage. Having made his first major appearances as pianist, became known in a wide-ranging organ repertory, which he performed from memory and with distinction (especially Liszt). He is also a conductor, and a composer of electronic and other works.

Christie, William (b. 19 Dec 1944), American harpsichordist and conductor. Settled in Paris, where he founded Les Arts Florissants, an ensemble devoted to baroque music, 1979. His notable operatic revivals include the Paris stage production, 1987 (and recording), of Lully's opera *Atys* and (on record, 1988) the first performance for about 250 years of Hasse's *Cleofide*.

Christoff, Boris (b. 18 May 1914), Bulgarian bass-baritone. Was funded by his king in 1941 to study in Italy and developed career there; he sang Pimen in *Boris Godunov* in Rome, 1946. Became world-famous as Boris Godunov himself, first at Covent Garden, 1949, and twice recorded the role. (In 1974 he returned to Covent Garden to sing a 25th-anniversary performance.) Invited by the Metropolitan Opera, 1950, but was politically barred because he was from a communist country; later sang in San Francisco and Chicago (1956–63), but never at the Metropolitan. Often called SHALYAPIN's successor, he was acclaimed for his acting as well as singing; famous also as King Philip in *Don Carlos* and in recital.

Chung, Kyung-Wha (b. 26 Mar 1948), Korean violinist, sister of Myung-Whun CHUNG. First musician of her country to win first-class international success. A child prodigy, she studied in New York under GALAMIAN and was joint Leventritt prizewinner with ZUKERMAN, 1967; she made her New York concerto début 1968 and her London début 1970. Her wide repertory embraces Walton's and Stravinsky's concertos as well as those more familiar. She often performs with her pianist brother, MYUNG-WHUN CHUNG, and cellist sister, Myung-Wha Chung (b. 1944).

Chung, Myung-Wha, *see* CHUNG, KYUNG-WHA.

Chung, Myung-Whun (b. 22 Jan 1953), Korean pianist and conductor, brother of Kyung-Wha CHUNG. Has often partnered his (older) sisters in a trio and was second prizewinner at the Moscow Tchaikovsky Competition, 1974. With encouragement from GIULINI at San Francisco, he began building a career as a conductor; made his Metropolitan Opera début 1986. In 1989, following the dismissal of BARENBOIM, he was made music director of the Bastille Opera project in Paris.

Cibber (née Arne), **Susanna** [Maria] (b. Feb 1714; d. 30 Jan 1766), British mezzo-soprano. Under Handel's guidance, earned admiration in the first performance of *Messiah* (Dublin), 1742, and its first London performance, 1743, and the première of *Samson*, 1743. She also acted in Shakespeare's and other plays. Retained her professional name, Mrs Cibber, even after eloping with her lover, John Sloper. She was a sister of the composer Thomas Arne.

Ciccolini, Aldo (b. 15 Aug 1925), Italian pianist. Made his début 1942 in his native Naples and in 1949 won the Long–Thibaud prize in Paris. He settled in Paris and proved a champion of French music: his recordings include all five of Saint-Saëns's piano concertos. In 1971 he became a professor at the Paris Conservatory.

Ciesinski, Kristine, *see* BAILEY.

Cigna, Gina (b. 6 Mar 1900), French soprano of Italian parentage. Used the surname of her husband, the tenor Maurice Sens, in her first appearance at La Scala, 1927. Then, as Cigna, she made a strong career: sang at Covent Garden (first as Marguerite in Berlioz's *La Damnation de Faust*) from 1933 and the Metropolitan from 1937. Injuries from a road accident obliged her to concentrate on teaching from 1947.

Cillario, Carlo Felice (b. 7 Feb 1915), Argentinian-born Italian conductor, formerly violinist. He studied in Italy and in Odessa; made his operatic début there in 1942 and his symphonic début in Bucharest, 1943. He became internationally well known, particularly in Italian opera. First appeared at the Metropolitan

1961 (in Verdi's *La forza del destino*) and at Glyndebourne 1966.

Cincinnati Symphony Orchestra, American orchestra founded 1895. Conductors have included STOKOWSKI, 1909–12, YSAŸE, 1918–22, REINER, 1922–31, Eugene GOOSSENS, 1931–46, SCHIPPERS, 1970–77, SUSSKIND, 1978–80, GIELEN, 1980–86, and LÓPEZ-COBOS, from 1986.

City of Birmingham Orchestra, *see* CITY OF BIRMINGHAM SYMPHONY ORCHESTRA.

City of Birmingham Symphony Orchestra, British orchestra founded 1920 as City of Birmingham Orchestra. Took present title 1948. Its conductors have included BOULT, 1924–30 and 1959–60, HEWARD, 1930–43, PANUFNIK, 1957–9, FRÉMAUX, 1969–78, and RATTLE, from 1980.

Civil, Alan (b. 13 June 1929; d. 19 Mar 1989), British horn player. Held leading positions with the ROYAL PHILHARMONIC, the PHILHARMONIA and, from 1966, the BBC SYMPHONY ORCHESTRA. He made an international career as a soloist in Mozart's concertos, among others. Sometimes played early valveless horns as well as the standard instrument. He was also a composer and occasional conductor.

Clark, Edward (b. 19 May 1888; d. 29 Apr 1962), British conductor. Pupil of Schoenberg in Berlin. An enthusiast for modern music, he conducted for Dyagilev's London ballet seasons, 1924–6, and was highly influential, while a BBC employee, 1927–36, in shaping radio music policy. He was married to the composer Elisabeth Lutyens.

Clark, James, *see* ENDELLION QUARTET.

Clemencic, René (b. 27 Feb 1928), Austrian recorder player and conductor, also composer. Working in Vienna, he has been prominent in the revival of early woodwind instruments; founded the Musica Antiqua ensemble, 1958. With a new group, which from 1969 was named the Clemencic Consort, he performed in concert, staged a number of little-known baroque operas and recorded prolifically.

Clemens, Clara, *see* GABRILOWITSCH.

Clement, Franz (b. 17 Nov 1780; d. 3 Nov 1842), Austrian violinist and composer. A travelling child prodigy, he gave concerts in London, 1790. Established himself in Vienna and was violinist-conductor at the Theater an der Wien, 1802–11, where in 1806 he played the Violin Concerto that Beethoven wrote for him (and, at the same concert, a set of his own variations with the violin held upside-down).

Cleva, Fausto (b. 17 May 1902; d. 6 Aug 1971), Italian-born conductor, naturalized American 1931. Joined the Metropolitan Opera as assistant chorus master in 1921; after holding other posts, returned as conductor, 1950, and gave 677 performances there. Best known in the Italian repertory. He died in Athens, having collapsed while conducting.

Cleveland Orchestra, American orchestra founded 1918. Principal conductors have included RODZINSKI, 1933–43, SZELL, 1946–70, MAAZEL, 1972–82, and Christoph von DOHNÁNYI, from 1984.

Cleveland Quartet, American string quartet founded 1969. All the original members – Donald Weilerstein, Peter Salaff, Martha Strongin-Katz and Paul Katz – then taught at the Cleveland Institute of Music. From 1976 it has been based at Rochester, New York State. Atar Arad joined as viola player in 1981 and was succeeded by James Dunham in 1987; William Preuil became first violinist in 1989.

Cliburn, Van (originally Harvey Lavan) (b. 12 July 1934), American pianist. Became a national hero on being the first American to win the Moscow Tchaikovsky Competition, 1958. He made a practice of beginning recitals with the US national anthem. Established a piano competition in Texas, 1962, named after him. His solo career faded surprisingly during the 1960s, and his venture into conducting in 1964 was not pursued. He made a return as concert pianist in 1989.

Clive (née Raftor), **Kitty** (originally Catherine) (b. 1711; d. 6 Dec 1785), British soprano. Sang in the first performance of Arne's *Alfred*, 1740, the masque that includes 'Rule, Britannia'. She was successful in ballad operas and also in acting Shakespeare. In 1733 she married George Clive, who was of noble family (but soon parted from him). She was a friend of such literary figures as Fielding, Johnson and Goldsmith.

Cluytens, André (b. 26 Mar 1905; d. 3 June 1967), Belgian-born conductor; became French citizen 1932. Held leading operatic and orchestral posts in Paris, then was chief conductor of the Belgian National Orchestra from 1960 until his death. Apart from French music, Wagner was a speciality; he was the first French conductor at Bayreuth, 1950.

Coates, Albert (b. 23 Apr 1882; d. 11 Dec 1953), British conductor, also composer (mother Russian). Invited in 1911 to conduct *Siegfried* in St Petersburg, he became principal conductor of the Maryinsky Theatre (opera and ballet) and, on his return to the West, a champion of Russian music, particularly Skryabin's. He conducted the first performance of Vaughan Williams's *A London Symphony* (revised version), 1920, and Gershwin's *A Cuban Overture* (under its original title, *Rhumba*) in New York, 1932, and also much opera. He settled in South Africa, 1946, and died there.

Coates, Edith [Mary] (b. 31 May 1908; d. 7 Jan 1983), British mezzo-soprano. Made her opera début at the Old Vic, London (in what was to become Sadler's Wells Opera). She sang in the first British performance of Rimsky-Korsakov's *The Snow Maiden*, 1933, and created the role of Auntie in Britten's *Peter Grimes*, 1945; appeared at Covent Garden, 1947–67. She was belatedly created OBE, 1977.

Coates, John (b. 29 June 1865; d. 16 Aug 1941), British tenor, previously baritone. Famous in oratorio (first performances of Elgar's *The Apostles*, 1903, and *The Kingdom*, 1904) and recital. He also sang in opera (Covent Garden from 1901); his roles included Tristan.

Cohen, Harriet (b. 2 Dec 1895; d. 13 Nov 1967), British pianist. Gave her first recital aged thirteen. She was prominent on the British musical scene; gave the first performance of Vaughan Williams's Concerto, 1933. Bax, with whom she had a lasting personal liaison, wrote various works for her, including a Concertante for left hand (and orchestra), 1950, when she had injured her right hand. CBE, 1937.

Cohen, Isidore, *see* JUILLIARD QUARTET.

Cohen, John, *see* PARRENIN QUARTET.

Cohen, Raymond, *see* COHEN, ROBERT.

Cohen, Robert (b. 15 June 1959), British cellist. Made London solo début 1971, US début 1979. His recordings include standard concertos and, with his parents, the violinist Raymond Cohen (b. 1919) and the pianist Anthya Rael (b. 1933), the complete Dvořák trios. Gave the first performance of Michael Berkeley's Concerto for cello and small orchestra, 1983.

Collegium Aureum, German ensemble founded 1964, mainly for studio recording. The players pursued an 'authentic' style using period instruments, and were pioneers in applying this approach to the classical period. They fell out of prominence after about ten years' work. Franzjosef Maier was the group's first violinist and director; it did not have a conductor.

Collier, Marie (b. 16 Apr 1926; d. 7 Dec 1971), Australian soprano. Her sudden death (in a fall from a window) cut off a strong career. At Covent Garden she sang the title role in Shostakovich's *Katerina Izmailova*, 1963, at Sadler's Wells the chief role in Janáček's *The Makropoulos Affair*, 1964, both first British performances.

Collingwood, Lawrance (b. 14 Mar 1887; d. 19 Dec 1982), British conductor. Studied in St Petersburg. In 1920 he joined the music staff of what was to become Sadler's Wells Opera; appointed chief conductor, 1931, and gave the first British performances of *Boris Godunov* in its original version, 1935, and of Rimsky-Korsakov's *The Snow Maiden*, 1933. Also influential conductor for recordings for HMV, 1922–71.

Collins, Anthony [Vincent Benedictus] (b. 3 Sept 1893; d. 11 Dec 1963), British conductor, previously viola player. Made London conducting début 1938. He spent the war in Hollywood, mainly as film composer and conductor, then returned to UK and made valued recordings of Sibelius symphonies; in his last years he again lived in California.

Collot, Serge, *see* PARRENIN QUARTET.

Colonne, Edouard (originally Judas Colonna) (b. 23 July 1838; d. 28 Mar 1910), French conductor and violinist. Founded the COLONNE ORCHESTRA in Paris, 1873. He was a champion of Berlioz, with over 100 performances of *La Damnation de Faust*, and of Bizet, with over 500 performances of the *L'Arlésienne* suites. At the Paris Opera conducted the French première of *Die Walküre*, 1893.

Colonne Orchestra (Orchestre Colonne), Paris-based orchestra founded 1873 by Edouard COLONNE. He conducted it till 1909, but only on his death a year later did the concerts take the name Concerts Colonne and only in 1979 was the orchestra itself so named. Other principal conductors have included PIERNÉ, 1910–34, and PARAY, 1934–40 and 1944–56.

Comissiona, Sergiu (b. 16 June 1928), Romanian conductor. Emigrated to Israel; he worked there, 1955–66, then in Sweden with the Gothenburg Symphony Orchestra, 1966–72. Music director of the Baltimore Symphony Orchestra, 1976–84, and conductor of the HOUSTON SYMPHONY ORCHESTRA, 1980–87. In 1987 he became music director of the New York City Opera, but he resigned the following year. Appointed conductor of the HELSINKI PHILHARMONIC ORCHESTRA, 1990.

Composers Quartet, American string quartet founded 1966 at the instigation of the composer Gunther Schuller and based mainly in New York. Specializes in modern works. Its violinists from the start were Matthew Raimondi and Anahid Ajemian; Jane Dane (replacing Jean Dupouy, 1974) and Mark Shuman (replacing Michael Rudiakov, 1977) later played viola and cello respectively. The quartet has performed the first three Carter quartets in a single programme many times (first 1975).

Concentus Musicus Wien, Austrian ensemble founded 1953 in Vienna by HARNONCOURT. Four years later it gave its first concerts as an orchestra performing baroque music on period instruments. Recorded hundreds of works (including all Bach's cantatas as well as the Brandenburg Concertos) to great acclaim.

Concertgebouw Orchestra of Amsterdam, Dutch orchestra founded 1888 with KES as conductor. Took title from its hall ('Concert Building'). Its later principal conductors have included MENGELBERG, 1895–1945, VAN BEINUM, 1945–59, HAITINK, 1961–88 (including periods jointly with JOCHUM, 1961–4, and KONDRASHIN, 1979–81), and CHAILLY, from 1988. Awarded the prefix 'Royal' in 1988.

Conlon, James (b. 18 Mar 1950), American conductor. Active in opera at the Metropolitan and Covent Garden (*Don Carlos*, 1979) and as symphonic conductor with major US and other orchestras. Conductor of the Rotterdam Philharmonic, 1983, and of Cologne Opera, from 1989.

Connell, Elizabeth (b. 22 Oct 1946), South African mezzo-soprano, later soprano. Based in UK. She sang with English National Opera, 1975–80, and at Bayreuth (Ortrud in *Lohengrin*), 1980, then (as soprano) at Covent Garden from 1985. Made Metropolitan début (Vitellia in Mozart's *La clemenza di Tito*), 1985.

Conrad, Doda (b. 19 Feb 1905), French bass, son of Marya FREUND. Born in Germany, he went with his mother to Paris; his first recital there was in 1932. Spent World War II in USA. He was a noted interpreter of songs by French and other composers, and gave the first performance of two songs by Musgrave (on Ezra Pound texts), 1951.

Cooper, Emil (b. 20 Dec 1877; d. 16 Nov 1960), Russian conductor. Active in opera; gave the first performance of Rimsky-Korsakov's *The Golden Cockerel*, 1909. Conducted Dyagilev's Russian opera troupe (with SHALYAPIN) in London, 1908–9. After 1922 worked mainly in Chicago, New York, 1944–50 (first US performance of Britten's *Peter Grimes*, 1947), and finally Montreal.

Cooper, Kenneth (b. 31 May 1941), American harpsichordist, also director of baroque music ensembles and musicologist. Held various US college appointments. On record has partnered MA in Bach and BLEGEN in cantatas by Handel and Domenico Scarlatti.

Coppola, Piero (b. 11 Oct 1888; d. 13 Mar

1971), Italian conductor and composer. Settled in Paris and became artistic director of French HMV. He conducted many recordings in Paris and, in London, Prokofiev's Piano Concerto no. 3 with the composer as soloist (issued 1933).

Corboz, Michel [-Jules] (b. 14 Feb 1934), Swiss conductor. Best known for choral work in Lausanne (with his own ensemble) and Lisbon (Gulbenkian Foundation Choir). Recorded rare French and Italian Renaissance and baroque music, as well as Monteverdi, Bach and others.

Corelli, Franco [Dario] (b. 8 Apr 1921), Italian tenor. His appearances at La Scala from 1954 led to international fame. Covent Garden début in *Tosca*, 1957; he made his Metropolitan début in *Il trovatore*, 1961, and sang there every year till 1974 in many Italian and a few French roles.

Corena, Fernando (b. 22 Dec 1916; d. 26 Nov 1984), Swiss bass. Studied in Geneva and Milan. He had a long career at the Metropolitan, 1954–78, where he performed the Sacristan in *Tosca* ninety-two times; recorded the role five times. He sang with Glyndebourne Opera in 1955 (title role of *Falstaff* at the Edinburgh Festival), and at Covent Garden from 1960.

Cortez, Viorica (b. 26 Dec 1935), Romanian mezzo-soprano. Made operatic début in Toulouse, 1965, and sang Carmen as her début role at Covent Garden, 1968, and the Metropolitan Opera, 1971. Her other roles have included Kundry in *Parsifal*.

Cortot, Alfred [Denis] (b. 26 Sept 1877; d. 15 June 1962), French pianist and conductor, also noted teacher. His passionate and wide-ranging involvement in music won him his compatriots' universal esteem until his collaboration with the Nazi occupation (1940–44). Pupil of one of Chopin's pupils, Emile Decombes. He developed a devotion to Wagner and went as a young man to Bayreuth and assisted Hans RICHTER; in 1902 he conducted an unsuccessful Wagner opera season in Paris. His solo career proceeded with distinction, and his trio with THIBAUD and CASALS, 1905–44, was the most celebrated and long-lasting of its kind. He continued to be known as a conductor. After World War II he prudently went to live in Switzerland (where he died), but he had been reacclaimed in Paris, 1949, for a recital marking the centenary of Chopin's death.

Cossotto, Fiorenza (b. 22 Apr 1935), Italian contralto. Sang small roles in Italy before her Covent Garden début as Neris in Cherubini's *Médée* (with CALLAS), 1959; she later recorded this role. Her first Metropolitan appearance was as Amneris in *Aida*, 1978. Prominent also in Vienna and Paris.

Cossutta, Carlo (b. 8 May 1932), Italian tenor. Brought up in Argentina, where he began his operatic career. Made Covent Garden début 1964 as the Duke in *Rigoletto*, Metropolitan début in *Norma*, 1973; famous in the title role of *Otello*. He sang in the first recording of Falla's *La vida breve* with LOS ANGELES, 1966.

Costa, Michael [Andrew Agnus] (originally Michele Andrea Agniello Costa) (b. 4 Feb 1808; d. 29 Apr 1884), Italian-born British conductor, also composer. Trained in Italy; came to London in 1829 and acquired unrivalled authority as operatic, orchestral and choral conductor. In 1847 he was appointed conductor of the newly established Royal Italian Opera at Covent Garden; remained there till 1868 and gave such works as *Rigoletto*, 1853, their first British performances. He was the first 'permanent' conductor at the Philharmonic Society, 1846–54, and conductor of the Sacred Harmonic Society (choir), 1848–82; was prominent at provincial choral festivals. Knighted in 1869.

Cotrubas, Ileana (b. 9 June 1939), Romanian soprano. Performed with Frankfurt Opera, then sang Debussy's Mélisande at Glyndebourne, 1969, where she returned to take the title role in the first modern revival of Cavalli's *Calisto*, 1970. Also sang at Covent Garden (début 1971 as Tatyana in Tchaikovsky's *Yevgeny Onegin*, in English) and the Metropolitan, from 1977. Retired from opera, 1989.

Couraud, Marcel (b. 20 Oct 1912), French conductor. Has specialized in choral music. Directed his own choir till 1954 and was appointed French radio's choral supervisor, 1967. With a small expert vocal group, Les Solistes des Chœurs, he performed much modern music; gave the première (and more than 130 later performances) of Xenakis's *Nuits*, 1968. He has also taught at US universities.

Coward, Henry (b. 26 Nov 1849; d. 19 June 1944), British conductor. Virtually self-educated in music, became a famous choir trainer in Sheffield. He took Yorkshire-based choirs on tour in Germany and Canada and on a six-month round-the-world trip, 1911. Also competition adjudicator, lecturer and composer. Knighted, 1926.

Cox, Jean (b. 16 Jan 1922), American tenor. Notable in Wagner. Spent his career mainly in Vienna (Volksoper, 1958–73) and Germany. He sang major roles at Bayreuth (including Lohengrin, Parsifal and Siegfried), 1966–75.

Crabbé, Armand [Charles] (b. 23 Apr 1883; d. 24 July 1947), Belgian baritone. Used the name Charles Morin when taking minor roles. He sang at Covent Garden, 1906–14, and reappeared there in 1937 in the title role of Puccini's *Gianni Schicchi*. Created the title role in Giordano's *Il re* at La Scala, 1929.

Craft, Robert (b. 20 Oct 1923), American conductor and writer on music. From 1948 he was Stravinsky's secretary, assistant conductor (they shared concerts of Stravinsky's music) and literary collaborator. A champion of the Second Viennese School, he conducted the first US performance of Berg's *Lulu* (incomplete version), 1963, and apparently influenced Stravinsky's own late embracing of Webern's principles. He conducted the first performances of Stravinsky's *In memoriam Dylan Thomas*, 1954, and *Requiem Canticles*, 1966.

Craig, Charles [James] (b. 3 Dec 1920), British tenor. Became a Covent Garden chorister and was encouraged by BEECHAM. He went on to sing principal roles with Carl Rosa Opera, Sadler's Wells Opera (later English National) and Covent Garden, 1952. With English National, 1983, recorded the title role of *Otello* in English.

Crass, Franz (b. 9 Feb 1928), German bass-baritone. Noted in Wagner (Bayreuth Festival from 1959) and as Rocco in *Fidelio* (two recordings). He also had a large concert repertory and was KLEMPERER's choice for recordings of Beethoven's *Missa solemnis*, 1960, and Mozart's Requiem, 1964.

Crespin, Régine (b. 23 Mar 1927), French soprano. At only twenty-four sang Elsa (*Lohengrin*) at the Paris Opera. Her Bayreuth appearance as Kundry (*Parsifal*), 1958, launched her high-level international career. Notable in French and German opera, for example as Dido in Berlioz's *Les Troyens* and as the Marschallin (in *Der Rosenkavalier*), her début role at Covent Garden, 1960 (she also recorded it, 1969).

Crickboom, Mathieu (b. 2 Mar 1871; d. 30 Oct 1947), Belgian violinist. A favoured student of YSAŸE and a noted chamber-music player; played second violin in Ysaÿe's Paris quartet, 1894–6. He was the dedicatee of Chausson's String Quartet. Taught at the Brussels Conservatory, 1919–44.

Croiza (originally Conelly), **Claire** (b. 14 Sept 1882; d. 27 Mar 1946), French mezzo-soprano. Distinguished in opera and in French solo song: she was the first to perform Honegger's *Six Poems of Cocteau*, 1924, and was also associated with Fauré and Poulenc. Her wide repertory at the Monnaie (Brussels Opera), from 1906, included Carmen, Delilah and Clytemnestra (*Elektra*). Sang at the Paris Opera from 1908 where she gave various first performances, among them Honegger's cantata *Judith*, 1925; had an enthusiastic London following.

Cropper, Peter, *see* LINDSAY QUARTET.

Crosdill, John (b. 1775; d. Oct 1825), British cellist. Prominent in London orchestras and provincial festivals. Having taught the cello to George IV when he was a prince, re-emerged from retirement to play at his coronation, 1821.

Cross, Joan (b. 7 Sept 1900), British soprano. Her historic role in British operatic life included the première of Britten's *Peter Grimes* (as Ellen), 1945. As a member of Sadler's Wells Opera, 1931–46, she had performed the heroine's role in the first British performance of Rimsky-Korsakov's *The Snow Maiden*, 1933. Sang many later Britten parts, including the title role of *Gloriana*, 1953. She was also an opera stage director and in 1948 founder with Anne Wood of what became the National School of Opera.

Crossley, Paul [Christopher Richard] (b. 17 May 1944), British pianist, also noted TV presenter. Pupil in Paris of Yvonne LORIOD and winner of the Messiaen Competition at Royan, 1967. Exponent of Messiaen and Tippett, whose Sonata no. 3, 1973, is dedicated to him; gave the first performance of Maw's *Personae*, 1973.

Cuenod, Hugues (b. 26 June 1902), Swiss tenor. Had extraordinarily long career. He performed in Paris from 1928 and was in the London première of Coward's *Bitter Sweet*, 1929; in the 1930s he gave recitals with HASKIL and made pioneer recordings of early music with BOULANGER. Taught and performed in Switzerland, 1940–46. He participated (as Sellem) in the première of Stravinsky's *The Rake's Progress*, 1951, and appeared in that and other roles at Glyndebourne from 1954; gave an 86th-birthday recital in London.

Culliford, Ingrid, *see* MARTINEZ.

Cummings, Keith, *see* BLECH QUARTET and LONDON STRING QUARTET (2).

Curtin (née Smith), **Phyllis** (b. 3 Dec 1922), American soprano. Uses surname of her first husband. She created the leading roles in Carlisle Floyd's *Susannah*, 1955, and *Wuthering Heights*, 1958; also sang at the Metropolitan (début as Fiordiligi in *Così fan tutte*, 1961), and Glyndebourne. After becoming dean of arts at Boston University, she continued to perform and in 1987 gave the first performance (in classical Greek) of Antoniou's *Paravasis*, specially composed for her.

Curzon, Clifford [Michael] (b. 18 May 1907; d. 1 Sept 1982), British pianist. Made début aged sixteen under WOOD in Bach's three-clavier concerto. He took lessons with SCHNABEL and studied in Paris with the harpsichordist LANDOWSKA and the musicologist BOULANGER. Distinguished in a mainly classical repertory, he gave the first performances of Rawsthorne's Concerto no. 2, 1951, and Lennox Berkeley's Sonata, 1946. Married the harpsichordist Lucille Wallace (1898–1977); knighted, 1977. He died in Lucerne a few days after collapsing at rehearsal.

Cutting, Thomas (dates unknown), British lutenist. In service to the courts of England and then Denmark, 1608. He was back in London in 1613. He may have been a relation of Francis Cutting, a composer for the lute, about whose career nothing is known.

Cuzzoni, Francesca (b. *c.* 1698; d. 1770), Italian soprano. Prominent in Handel's London opera seasons, 1723–7; at the rehearsal for her début (in *Ottone*) Handel overcame her rebelliousness by threatening to pitch her out of a window. Her jealous rivalry with BORDONI was famous. She was the first to sing many Handel heroines, including Cleopatra in *Giulio Cesare*, 1724. Also sang in Vienna and Florence, and again in London, 1734–6, under a management competing with Handel's.

Cvejic (also spelt Tzveych), **Biserka** (b. 5 Nov 1923), Yugoslav contralto. Brought up in Belgium. In Belgrade after World War II she had a career in lighter music before undertaking operatic study and making her formal début there in 1954. Appeared at Vienna State Opera, 1959, the Metropolitan, 1961 (Amneris in *Aida*), and Covent Garden, 1962 (also as Amneris).

Czech Philharmonic Orchestra, Prague-based orchestra. Arose from the Prague National Theatre and became independent in 1901. Its conductors have included TALICH, 1919–41, Rafael KUBELÍK, 1942–8, ANČERL, 1950–68, and NEUMANN, from 1968–90; Jiří Bělohlávek succeeded him.

Czech Quartet, *see* BOHEMIAN QUARTET.

Czerny, Carl (b. 21 Feb 1791; d. 15 July 1857), Austrian piano teacher, composer, pianist and writer on music. Historically important as the link between Beethoven (his teacher) and Liszt (his pupil). Liszt dedicated to him the *Transcendental Studies*, 1851. He was able to play all Beethoven's piano music by heart. Composed over 1,000 works in various forms, though only the piano studies remain in present-day usage.

Czerny-Stefańska, Halina (b. 30 Dec 1922), Polish pianist. Her teachers included CORTOT (in Paris). She was equal first prizewinner with DAVIDOVICH in the Warsaw International Chopin Competition, 1949; made London début 1949. Her daughter Elżbieta Stefańska-Łukowicz (b. 1943) is a harpsichordist.

Czerwenka, Oskar (b. 5 July 1924), Austrian bass. Member of the Vienna State Opera from 1951; he became celebrated in comic roles such as Ochs in *Der Rosenkavalier* (Glyndebourne, 1959, and Metropolitan Opera, 1961). Recorded the title role of Cornelius's *Der Barbier von Bagdad*, 1958.

Cziffra, György (or Georges) (b. 5 Nov 1921), Hungarian-born pianist, naturalized French 1968. Said to have performed publicly aged five (in a circus); studied with Ernst von Dohnányi. He toured internationally to 1941. Resumed study and career after the war and won the (Hungarian) Liszt Prize, 1955. He left Hungary in the political upheaval of 1956, settled in Paris and became celebrated in powerful virtuoso performances, for example of Liszt. He made many recordings, some with his son György (Georges) Cziffra (1942–81) as conductor.

D

D'Albert, Eugène, *see* ALBERT.

Dalberto, Michel (b. 2 June 1955), French pianist. Pupil of PERLEMUTER. Having won the Salzburg Mozart Competition, 1975, and the Leeds Piano Competition, 1978, made his formal Paris début with orchestra in 1980. He has toured internationally; his records include Fauré songs with NORMAN.

Dalley, John, *see* GUARNERI QUARTET.

Dal Monte, Toti (originally Antonietta Meneghelli) (b. 27 June 1893; d. 26 Jan 1975), Italian soprano. TOSCANINI, for whom she had sung in Beethoven's Symphony no. 9, took her to La Scala for the 1921–2 opera season. She then became celebrated at the Paris Opera, Covent Garden (1925, including the title role of *Lucia di Lammermoor*; *see also* BORGIOLI) and in USA (but never appeared at the Metropolitan). Her notable recordings include a *Madama Butterfly* with GIGLI, 1939.

Dam, José van, *see* VAN DAM.

Damrosch, Leopold (b. 22 Oct 1832; d. 15 Feb 1885), German-born American conductor, father of Walter DAMROSCH. Gave the US premières of Brahms's Symphony no. 1, 1877, and many other orchestral works, and conducted New York's first music festival, 1881. In 1884–5 he organized a season of German opera at the Metropolitan (including the first performance there of *Die Walküre*) and conducted every performance up to 9 Feb 1885; stricken with pneumonia, he died a week later. His son immediately took over.

Damrosch, Walter [Johannes] (b. 30 Jan 1862; d. 22 Dec 1950), German-born American conductor, son of Leopold DAMROSCH. In 1885 succeeded his father in the German repertory at the Metropolitan Opera, and in 1886 conducted the first US (concert) performance of *Parsifal*. His own Damrosch Opera Company was active in New York and elsewhere, 1894–9. He conducted the NEW YORK SYMPHONY ORCHESTRA, 1885–94 and 1902–28, and gave the premières of Gershwin's Piano Concerto, 1925, and *An American in Paris*, 1928.

Danco, Suzanne (b. 22 Jan 1911), Belgian soprano. Active in Italy from 1940; she performed as Ellen Orford in Britten's *Peter Grimes* at La Scala, 1947. Later she was highly successful at Glyndebourne, where she sang Fiordiligi in a televised *Così*, 1951 (Britain's first opera on television that was not produced by the BBC itself).

Dane, Jane, *see* COMPOSERS QUARTET.

Danise, Giuseppe, *see* SAYÃO.

Danish Radio Symphony Orchestra (also known as Danish State Radio Orchestra and Danish National Orchestra), Copenhagen-based orchestra founded 1925. Its principal conductors (sometimes overlapping) have included TUXEN, 1936–57, WÖLDIKE, 1950–67, Thomas Jensen, 1957–63, BLOMSTEDT, 1967–77, and SEGERSTAM, from 1988.

Dankworth, John [Philip William] (b. 20 Sept 1927), British saxophonist and conductor. Prominent from the 1950s in jazz as soloist and leader of his own band, with LAINE (whom he later married) as vocalist. Brought his jazz work to the classical platform; he collaborated with the composer Mátyás Seiber in *Improvisations for Jazz Band and Orchestra*, 1959. In 1969 he instituted at Wavendon a festival organization covering both classical and popular styles. He is also a composer of jazz and other pieces, and film music. CBE, 1974.

Dannreuther, Edward (originally Eduard) [Georg] (b. 4 Nov 1844; d. 12 Feb 1905), British pianist of German descent (born in Strasbourg). Prominent in London musical life (also as writer). He gave the first British performances of concertos by Grieg, 1874, Liszt (no. 2), 1874, and Tchaikovsky (no. 1), 1876. A friend of Wagner, he helped promote the London Wagner Festival of 1877 when Wagner stayed in his house.

Danon, Oscar (b. 7 Feb 1913), Yugoslav conductor. Became music director of the Belgrade Opera and Belgrade Philharmonic Orchestra, 1945, and later concentrated on opera conducting. He brought his company to UK, 1962, and established an authority particularly in Russian opera. Also conducted at the Vienna State Opera and elsewhere.

D'Arányi, Jelly, *see* ARÁNYI.

D'Archambeau, Félicien, *see* FLONZALEY QUARTET.

D'Archambeau, Iwan, *see* FLONZALEY QUARTET.

Darclée (originally Haricly), **Hariclea** (b. 10 June 1860; d. 10 Jan 1939), Romanian soprano. Famous as the first Tosca, 1900. She studied in Paris with FAURE, and made her début there 1888. Toured widely, and created the title roles of Catalani's *La Wally*, 1892, and Mascagni's *Iris*, 1898.

Darke, Harold [Edwin] (b. 29 Oct 1888; d. 28 Nov 1976), British organist. For fifty years, 1916–66, gave weekly recitals at a London church; he performed at the Royal Festival Hall to celebrate his seventy-fifth, eightieth and eighty-fifth birthdays. He was also conductor of a choral group (St Michael's Singers), 1919–66, and a composer. CBE, 1966.

Darré, Jeanne-Marie (b. 30 July 1905), French pianist. Made her Paris recital début 1920 and was thereafter prominent in French musical life. She became a professor at the Paris Conservatory, 1958, and later taught master-classes in USA.

Dart, [Robert] **Thurston** (b. 3 Sept 1921; d. 6 Mar 1971), British harpsichordist and scholar, also clavichord player and organist. Professor at Cambridge, 1962, founder of music faculty at London University, 1964, and editor of works by Byrd, Bach and others. As continuo player he worked with the Boyd Neel Orchestra (*see* NEEL), then took over its direction with the name Philomusica of London, 1955–9. He directed many recordings (often with the ACADEMY OF ST MARTIN-IN-THE-FIELDS) of Bach and eighteenth-century English music.

D'Ascoli, Bernard (b. 18 Nov 1958), French pianist. Became blind at the age of three and at eleven began to read music from braille. He won the Maria Canals Competition in Barcelona, 1978, and third prize at Leeds, 1981. He has toured widely; made his first US appearance in 1985 and played Schumann's Concerto at the Proms in 1986.

D'Aubigny, Julie, *see* MAUPIN.

David, Ferdinand (b. 19 June 1810; d. 18 July 1873), German violinist and conductor. Friend of Mendelssohn and soloist in the first performance of Mendelssohn's Violin Concerto, 1845. He visited Britain in 1839 and 1841. Principal violin teacher at the newly founded Leipzig Conservatory; his students included JOACHIM and WILHELMJ.

Davidovich, Bella (b. 16 July 1928), Russian pianist, mother of Dmitry SITKOVETSKY. Won equal first prize (with CZERNY-STEFAŃSKA) at the Warsaw International Chopin Competition, 1949. After her son had left USSR, she did likewise and emigrated to USA, 1978. Made New York recital début 1979.

Davies, Ben (originally Benjamin) [Grey] (b. 6

Jan 1858; d. 28 Mar 1943), British tenor. A great favourite of British audiences from the mid-1880s. He sang the lead in Alfred Cellier's long-running operetta *Dorothy*, 1887, and the title role in the première of Sullivan's opera *Ivanhoe*, 1891. He was still performing in 1926.

Davies, Cecilia (b. *c.* 1750; d. 3 July 1836), British soprano. Performed in London, Paris, Vienna and Milan (where she sang the title role in Sacchini's opera *Armida*, 1772). She was often partnered in concert by her sister Marianne (1744–*c.* 1818), who played flute, harpsichord and glass harmonica.

Davies, Dennis Russell (b. 16 Apr 1944), American conductor. Co-founder of the AMERICAN COMPOSERS ORCHESTRA in New York; his premières include Glass's Violin Concerto, 1987. He conducted *Der fliegende Holländer* at Bayreuth, 1978, and was music director of the Württemberg Opera, Stuttgart, 1980–87 (first performance of Glass's *Akhnaten*, 1984), then city music director at Bonn.

Davies, Fanny (b. 27 June 1861; d. 1 Sept 1934), British pianist. Studied with Clara SCHUMANN at Frankfurt; she performed in London with JOACHIM and PIATTI and championed Brahms's works. In 1907 she toured Germany with ELWES. Elgar's Concert Allegro (for solo piano), 1901, is dedicated to her.

Davies, Ioan, *see* FITZWILLIAM QUARTET.

Davies, Marianne, *see* DAVIES, CECILIA.

Davies, [Albert] **Meredith** (b. 30 July 1922), British conductor, formerly organist. Music director of the English Opera Group (Britten's organization), 1963–5, and shared with the composer the conducting of the first performance of Britten's *War Requiem*, 1962. Conductor of the Vancouver Symphony Orchestra, 1964–71, then the Royal Choral Society, 1972–85 (première of Burgon's *Magnificat and Nunc dimittis*, 1979); principal of Trinity College of Music, London, 1979–89. CBE, 1982.

Davies, Ryland (b. 9 Feb 1943), British tenor. Well known in Mozart opera. He first appeared at Glyndebourne 1968 and in 1969 sang Ferrando in *Così*, with his then wife, HOWELLS, as Dorabella. Performed at Covent Garden from 1970 and at the Metropolitan Opera from 1975.

Davies, Tudor (b. 12 Nov 1892; d. 2 Apr 1958), British tenor. As a member of the British National Opera Company, from 1922, sang in *La Bohème* opposite MELBA and created the title role in Vaughan Williams's *Hugh the Drover*, 1924. He later sang with other companies (and recorded) till 1946.

Davis, Andrew [Frank] (b. 2 Feb 1944), British conductor, formerly organist. Having studied conducting with FERRARA in Rome, became associate conductor of the BBC SCOTTISH ORCHESTRA, then the PHILHARMONIA, and conducted at Glyndebourne (Strauss's *Capriccio*, 1973) and Covent Garden. Music director of the TORONTO SYMPHONY ORCHESTRA, 1975–89 (toured with it internationally), then of the BBC SYMPHONY ORCHESTRA and Glyndebourne Opera, from 1989. At the Proms gave the first European performance of Tippett's *The Mask of Time*, 1984. CBE, 1988.

Davis, Colin [Rex] (b. 25 Sept 1927), British conductor, formerly clarinettist. Acquired London experience directing his own Kalmar Chamber Orchestra and Chelsea Opera Group before winning instant acclaim in replacing the indisposed KLEMPERER at a concert performance of *Don Giovanni*, 1959. He was conductor, later music director, of Sadler's Wells Opera, 1959–65, then worked with the BBC SYMPHONY ORCHESTRA, 1967–71, and at Covent Garden, 1971–86. He has been a regular guest conductor of the BOSTON SYMPHONY ORCHESTRA and in 1983 became music director of the BAVARIAN RADIO SYMPHONY ORCHESTRA, Munich. A notable exponent of Berlioz and Tippett, he gave the first performance of Tippett's Symphony no. 3, 1972, and his operas *The Knot Garden*, 1970, and *The Ice Break*, 1977; also conducted the première of Henze's *Tristan*, 1974. Knighted, 1980. He was appointed to an international chair at the Royal Academy of Music, 1988. His first wife was CANTELO.

Davis, Howard, *see* ALBERNI QUARTET.

Davis, Ivan (b. 4 Feb 1932), American pianist.

His big virtuoso style was noted in New York recital début, 1959. He won the international Liszt Prize, 1960, and made his London début 1966. Performed in a sixtieth-anniversary re-creation of Gershwin's *Rhapsody in Blue* in its original form (New York), 1984, and also recorded it.

Dawson, Peter [Smith] (b. 31 Jan 1882; d. 26 Sept 1961), Australian bass-baritone. Studied in London with SANTLEY and toured with ALBANI. He made his first recordings in 1904 and sold 13 million records of about 3,500 titles. He remained popular (mainly in the ballad repertory, though he had sung in opera at Covent Garden) till the 1940s, and died in Sydney. Also composed many songs, some under the pseudonym J. P. McCall.

De Ahna, Heinrich, *see* JOACHIM QUARTET.

De Ahna, Pauline, *see* AHNA.

De Almeida, Antonio, *see* ALMEIDA.

De Amicis, Anna Lucia (b. *c.* 1733; d. 1816), Italian soprano. Esteemed by the young Mozart; she sang in the first performance of his opera *Lucio Silla*, 1772. Sang also in London (first performance of J. C. Bach's *Orione*, 1763) and Naples, and was celebrated for both her high range and dramatic intensity.

Dean, Stafford, *see* HOWELLS.

Dearnley, Christopher [Hugh] (b. 11 Feb 1930), British organist. Widened the liturgical repertory at St Paul's Cathedral on becoming its organist, 1968; on occasion he has performed Viennese classical masses with orchestra. He has also edited church music.

De Begnis, Giuseppe (b. 1793; d. Aug 1849), Italian bass. Engaged by Rossini to create the role of Dandini in *La Cenerentola*, 1817; he was reckoned among the leading comic basses of his time. Sang in London, 1821–7 (with his wife, RONZI), and directed opera seasons in Bath and Dublin. He died in New York.

De Begnis, Giuseppina Ronzi, *see* DE BEGNIS (GIUSEPPE) and RONZI.

De Bériot, Charles-Auguste, *see* BÉRIOT.

De Burgos, Rafael Frühbeck, *see* FRÜHBECK DE BURGOS.

Decker, Franz-Paul (b. 23 June 1923), German conductor. Conducted the opening concert of the Brussels International Exhibition, 1958. He was music director of the Rotterdam Philharmonic, 1962–8, and the MONTREAL SYMPHONY, 1967–75 (with which he later gave the first performance of Prévost's *Il fait nuit lente*, 1981), then artistic director of the Calgary Symphony Orchestra.

De Fabritiis, Oliviero (b. 13 June 1902; d. 12 Aug 1982), Italian conductor. Active at Rome Opera, 1934–61, and elsewhere; he was the first to conduct Verdi's *Simon Boccanegra* at Covent Garden, 1965. His celebrated recordings include *Tosca*, 1938, and *Madama Butterfly*, 1939, both with GIGLI.

Defauw, Désiré (b. 5 Sept 1885; d. 25 July 1960), Belgian conductor, previously violinist and quartet leader. Directed the Brussels Conservatory concerts, 1926–40, and established the Belgian National Orchestra, 1937. He was conductor of what is now the MONTREAL SYMPHONY ORCHESTRA, 1940–48, and of the CHICAGO SYMPHONY ORCHESTRA, 1943–7, which he left under criticism.

De Freitas Branco, Pedro, *see* FREITAS BRANCO.

De Froment, Louis, *see* FROMENT.

DeGaetani, Jan (b. 10 July 1933; d. 15 Sept 1989), American soprano. Eminent in modern music with advanced vocal techniques (first performance of Crumb's *Ancient Voices of Children*, 1970), she had a varied further repertory including Stephen Foster songs. With the SCOTTISH NATIONAL ORCHESTRA, gave the première of Peter Maxwell Davies's *Stone Litany*, 1973. (*See also* GHIGLIA.)

De Gogorza, Emilio, *see* EAMES.

De Greef, Arthur (b. 10 Oct 1862; d. 29 Aug 1940), Belgian pianist. After study in Brussels, took advanced lessons from LISZT and

Saint-Saëns. He toured internationally and played a wide repertory; Grieg considered him an ideal exponent of his Piano Concerto, a work he widely popularized. He composed two piano concertos and other works.

De Groote, Philip, *see* CHILINGIRIAN QUARTET.

De Hidalgo, Elvira, *see* HIDALGO.

Delacôte, Jacques (b. 16 Aug 1942), French conductor, formerly flautist. Studied conducting with SWAROWSKY in Vienna, won the Mitropoulos Conducting Competition in New York, 1972, and conducted at the Vienna State Opera from 1972. In London he replaced ABBADO in Mahler's Symphony no. 3, 1973, and made his Proms début 1986.

De la Martinez, Odaline, *see* MARTINEZ.

De Lancie, John [Sherwood] (b. 26 July 1921), American oboist. In 1954 became first oboe of the PHILADELPHIA ORCHESTRA and in 1977 the director of that city's Curtis Institute. Jean Françaix wrote for him *The Flower Clock* (*L'Horloge de Flore*) and Benjamin Lees his Concerto.

De la Pau, Maria, *see* TORTELIER, PAUL.

Del Bene, Adriana Ferrarese, *see* FERRARESE DEL BENE.

Della Casa, Lisa (b. 2 Feb 1919), Swiss soprano. A member of Zurich Opera, then, 1947, of Vienna State Opera. Noted in Mozart (Glyndebourne début 1951 as the Countess in *Figaro*) and Strauss. She first sang Strauss's Arabella (her most celebrated role) at Munich in 1951, later with the Munich company at Covent Garden. She created three roles in Einem's *Der Prozess*, 1953.

Deller, Alfred (b. 31 May 1912; d. 16 July 1979), British countertenor. More than anyone else was responsible for the revival of this type of voice (previously the preserve of the English cathedral tradition). He performed Purcell and English lute songs with high virtuosity. Britten wrote several works for him: he was the original Oberon in Britten's *A Midsummer Night's Dream*, 1960. In 1950 he founded, as a vocal ensemble (with accompaniment), the Deller Consort, which he often conducted in concert and in recordings of Purcell, Handel and others. On his death the direction passed to his son Mark Deller (b. 1938). OBE, 1970.

Deller, Mark, *see* DELLER, ALFRED.

Del Mar, Norman [René] (b. 31 July 1919), British conductor, formerly horn player. He was BEECHAM's assistant with the ROYAL PHILHARMONIC ORCHESTRA, 1947–8, then music director of the English Opera Group, till 1956; conducted the first performance of Britten's *Let's Make an Opera!*, 1949. As conductor of the BBC SCOTTISH ORCHESTRA, 1960–65, he gave the premières of Lutyens's *Quincunx*, 1960, and Maw's *Scenes and Arias*, 1962. Champion of Strauss and author of a book on him. Also a noted teacher of conducting. CBE, 1975.

Del Monaco, Mario (b. 27 July 1915; d. 16 Oct 1982), Italian tenor. Gave up formal study and trained himself on past recordings. He won prominence with Verona Arena performances and the visit of the San Carlo company (Naples) to Covent Garden, 1946; made Metropolitan Opera début 1950. Enormously popular (also on records) as Radamès in *Aida*, Don José in *Carmen* and Canio in *Pagliacci*. He sang Otello 427 times (by his own reckoning) and was buried in his Otello costume.

Delobelle, Camille, *see* CAPET QUARTET.

De los Angeles, Victoria, *see* LOS ANGELES.

De Luca, Giuseppe (b. 25 Dec 1876; d. 26 Aug 1950), Italian baritone. Possessed one of the most polished and secure operatic voices of his time. He created the role of Sharpless in *Madama Butterfly* (Milan), 1904, and at seventy could still sing that part. At the Metropolitan Opera, from 1915, he sang fifty-two roles and created the title part of Puccini's *Gianni Schicchi*, 1918.

De Lucia, Fernando (b. 11 Oct 1860; d. 21 Feb 1925), Italian tenor. After début in Naples, sang (with CALVÉ) in the first performance of Mascagni's *L'amico Fritz*, 1891; in London he was the first Canio in *Pagliacci*, 1893, and Cavaradossi in *Tosca*, 1900. Retired from the stage in 1917 but sang at CARUSO's funeral, 1921.

Demessieux, Jeanne (b. 14 Feb 1921; d. 11 Nov 1968), French organist. A child prodigy, she held a Paris church appointment from her schooldays. Developed as a pre-eminent representative of the powerful French organ tradition through her performing, teaching (in France and Belgium) and composing.

De Mont, Willem, *see* BLECH QUARTET.

De Murska, Ilma, *see* DI MURSKA.

Demus, Jörg [Wolfgang] (b. 2 Dec 1928), Austrian pianist. Celebrated exponent of both modern and older types of piano. He made his Vienna début at fourteen, then became a pupil of GIESEKING and KEMPFF; he also studied composition and conducting. Toured widely as soloist and has performed as duettist with BADURA-SKODA and accompanist to FISCHER-DIESKAU and other singers.

Dénes, Vera, *see* TÁTRAI QUARTET.

Denzler, Robert (b. 19 Mar 1892; d. 25 Aug 1972), Swiss conductor. After conducting in Berlin, he was director of Zurich Opera, 1934–47. Because of the hostility of Nazi Germany to modern art, the honour fell to Zurich and to him of giving the first performances of Berg's opera *Lulu* (the incomplete two-act version), 1937, and Hindemith's opera *Mathis der Maler*, 1938.

De Pachmann, Vladimir, *see* PACHMANN.

De Peyer, Gervase [Alan] (b. 11 Apr 1926), British clarinettist. Studied in London (with THURSTON) and Paris. He was a founding member of the Melos Ensemble, 1950, and played first clarinet with the LONDON SYMPHONY ORCHESTRA, 1955–71. Also a soloist well known in concertos and chamber music, and occasionally a conductor. Gave the first performance of Musgrave's Clarinet Concerto, 1969.

De Reszke, Edouard (originally Eduard) (b. 22 Dec 1853; d. 25 May 1917), Polish bass, brother of Jean DE RESZKE. Made his operatic début under Verdi's baton in *Aida* (as the King) at its first Paris performance. With his brother he was a leading member of the Paris Opera thereafter; sang Mephistopheles at the 500th performance of *Faust*, 1887. He performed in London from 1880 and New York from 1891; retired in 1903. Failed to establish himself as a teacher, and died in poverty in Poland.

De Reszke, Jean (originally Jan) [Miecysław] (b. 14 Jan 1850; d. 3 Apr 1925), Polish tenor, previously baritone, brother of Edouard DE RESZKE. Sang John the Baptist in the Paris première of Massenet's *Hérodiade*, 1884; some later performances featured not only the brothers but their sister Joséphine, a soprano (1855–91). He was prominent in London opera seasons, 1887–1900, latterly in Wagner, and sang as Lohengrin in a command performance for Queen Victoria at Windsor, 1899.

De Reszke, Joséphine, *see* DE RESZKE, JEAN.

Dermota, Anton (b. 4 June 1910; d. 29 June 1989), Austrian tenor (born in what is now Yugoslavia). Studied organ and composition, then in 1936 made his Vienna and Salzburg vocal débuts in small roles. He became one of the leading singers of the Vienna State Opera; appeared with that company on its London visit, 1947, and sang Florestan in *Fidelio* at the reopening of its Vienna theatre, 1955.

Dern, Edouard, *see* YSAŸE QUARTET.

Dernesch, Helga (b. 3 Feb 1939), Austrian soprano. Prominent in Wagner: sang Sieglinde in *Die Walküre* at Covent Garden, 1970, and Isolde (opposite VICKERS) in KARAJAN's recording of *Tristan*, 1972. She now takes mezzo-soprano roles; created Goneril in Reimann's *Lear*, 1978, and made Metropolitan début 1985 as Marfa in Musorgsky's *Khovanshchina*. Married to KRENN.

Dervaux, Pierre (b. 3 Jan 1917), French conductor, formerly pianist and percussionist. Conducted at the Paris Opera, 1956–70, then the Quebec Symphony Orchestra, 1968–71; later music director at Nice, 1979–82. He made many orchestral and operatic recordings, chiefly of French music, and has been a noted teacher of conducting at Montreal and Nice.

De Sabata, Victor (b. 10 Apr 1892; d. 11 Dec 1967), Italian conductor. Made his name first as a composer; then, having become conductor at the Monte Carlo Opera, gave there the first performance of Ravel's *L'Enfant et les sortilèges*, 1925. Principally based at La Scala, 1929–53 (led its company on the 1950 London visit), he also gave notable symphonic performances elsewhere, including London, 1947. His recording of *Tosca* with CALLAS, DI STEFANO and GOBBI, 1950, is particularly celebrated.

De Saram, Rohan (b. 9 Mar 1939), British cellist of Sri Lankan parentage. Studied in Florence with CASSADÓ, and made his New York début 1960; from 1972 has been resident in London. Aside from the classical repertory he is noted in modern works, both as a soloist (first performance of Crosse's Cello Concerto, 1979), and as a member of the ARDITTI QUARTET.

De Sarasate, Pablo, *see* SARASATE.

Desmond, Astra (b. 10 Apr 1893; d. 16 Aug 1973), British contralto. Had an unusual speciality in Nordic songs: she sang Grieg in Norwegian, introduced Kilpinen's songs to Britain and wrote musicological studies of Grieg's and other songs. Took the title role in the first performance of Boughton's *Alkestis*, 1922, and was noted in Elgar's choral works.

Desormière, Roger (b. 13 Sept 1898; d. 25 Oct 1963), French conductor, equally prominent as composer. Conducted at the Paris Opéra-Comique from 1936, later also at the Paris Opera; during the Opéra-Comique's visit to Covent Garden, 1949, he conducted Debussy's *Pelléas et Mélisande*, of which he had made a celebrated recording, 1942. Until falling victim to paralysis in 1952, he remained in the forefront of French music: gave the first performances of Milhaud's *Salade*, 1924, Messiaen's *Trois petites liturgies de la présence divine*, 1945, and Boulez's *Le Soleil des eaux*, 1950.

De Souza, Ralph, *see* ENDELLION QUARTET.

Destinn, Emmy (originally Ema Kittlová) (b. 26 Feb 1878; d. 28 Jan 1930), Czech soprano. Adopted the name of her teacher, M. Loewe-Destinn. She was internationally distinguished in opera, with more than eighty roles. At the Metropolitan sang the heroine's part in the first performance of Puccini's *La fanciulla del West* (opposite CARUSO), 1910; she was Covent Garden's first Butterfly, 1905, and Berlin's first Salome, 1906. Czech patriotism led her to use the Czech form of her surname, Destinnová, after 1918.

Detroit Symphony Orchestra, American orchestra founded 1914. Its principal conductors have included GABRILOWITSCH, 1918–36, PARAY, 1951–63, EHRLING, 1963–73, CECCATO, 1973–7, DORÁTI, 1977–81, BERTINI, 1981–4, and HERBIG, from 1984.

Deutekom, Cristina (originally Stientje Engel) (b. 28 Aug 1932), Dutch soprano. Her outstanding coloratura ability made her a famous Queen of the Night in *Die Zauberflöte* (Metropolitan, 1967, Covent Garden, 1968, and recording, 1969). She later moved towards dramatic roles, for example Donna Anna in *Don Giovanni*.

Devienne, François (b. 31 Jan 1759; d. 5 Sept 1803), French flautist. Professor of flute at the foundation of the Paris Conservatory, 1795; his published 'method', 1794, is a prime source for the technique of the one-keyed classical flute. He was prominent in Paris concerts (also as bassoonist) from the 1780s, and composed successful operas as well as much instrumental music.

De Visée, Robert, *see* VISÉE.

De Vito, Gioconda (b. 26 July 1907), Italian violinist. Won an international prize at Vienna, 1932, and after World War II developed a career of major celebrity; she made London début 1948 and settled there. With FURTWÄNGLER conducting, recorded the Mendelssohn and Brahms concertos, 1952; the only modern concerto she played was Pizzetti's, 1945, dedicated to her. In 1961 she retired, a withdrawal in mid-career perhaps unparalleled among leading instrumentalists of this century.

Devos, Louis (b. 15 June 1926), Belgian tenor and conductor. Has specialized in singing modern music. He gave the first performance of Frank Martin's *Le Mystère de la nativité* under ANSERMET, 1958, took the role of Aaron in Schoenberg's *Moses und Aron* at the Vienna State Opera, 1973 (and on records), and was the soloist in the première of Penderecki's *Utrenja* (Cologne), 1972. He directs the Musica Polyphonica choir, which is distinguished in recordings of baroque music.

Devrient, Eduard [Philipp] (b. 11 Aug 1801; d. 4 Oct 1877), German baritone, also librettist and theatre historian. Was principally responsible for the first revival of Bach's *St Matthew Passion* (Berlin), 1829; his friend Mendelssohn was the conductor and he sang as Jesus. In 1833 he performed the title role of Marschner's *Hans Heiling*, to which he had written the libretto.

De Waart, Edo [in full Eduard] (b. 1 June 1941), Dutch conductor, formerly oboist. Won the Mitropoulos Conducting Competition in New York, 1964, and became assistant to BERNSTEIN. Made British début 1969. He was music director of the Rotterdam Philharmonic Orchestra, 1973–9, and of the SAN FRANCISCO SYMPHONY ORCHESTRA, 1977–85. Championed John Adams's music and conducted the first recording of his opera, *Nixon in China*, 1988. He appeared at Bayreuth, 1979. Became music director of the Netherlands Opera, 1985.

Dewaele, Jean-Claude, *see* PARRENIN QUARTET.

Diaz, Alirio (b. 12 Nov 1923), Venezuelan guitarist. Pupil of SEGOVIA at his courses in Siena; he later became his assistant and then successor, 1965. Eminent as soloist and editor. He played in USA under STOKOWSKI, 1968.

Diaz, Justino (b. 29 Jan 1940), Puerto Rican bass. Created the role of Antony in Barber's *Antony and Cleopatra* at the Metropolitan, 1966 (made début there 1963). He has also performed at Covent Garden (Escamillo in *Carmen*, 1976) and Salzburg, and on recordings of Handel oratorios, among other works.

Dichter, Cipa, *see* DICHTER, MISCHA.

Dichter, Mischa (b. 27 Sept 1945), American pianist of Polish descent (born in Shanghai). His parents settled in Los Angeles when he was two. Won second prize in the Moscow Tchaikovsky Competition, 1966, and made his London début 1977. He appears in two-piano programmes with his Brazilian-born wife, Cipa (b. 1944).

Dickie, Murray (b. 3 Apr 1924), British tenor. His career culminated in long attachment to Vienna State Opera, from 1951, mainly in character parts. He previously sang at Covent Garden (first performance of Bliss's *The Olympians*, 1949) and Glyndebourne.

Dickinson, Meriel (b. 8 Apr 1940), British mezzo-soprano. Prominent in modern music, especially with her brother, the composer and pianist Peter Dickinson. She was the soloist in the first performance of Crosse's *Memories of Morning: Night*, 1972, and made her New York début in Berio's *Laborintus* with the composer, 1986. Noted also in Handel opera.

Didur, Adam (b. 24 Dec 1874; d. 7 Jan 1946), Polish bass. Prominent at the Metropolitan Opera, 1908–33; sang the title role of *Boris Godunov* there in its first US performance, 1913. In 1933 he returned to Poland, where he taught after the war.

Diémer, Louis (b. 14 Feb 1843; d. 21 Dec 1919), French pianist. A pioneer from 1889 in the modern revival of the harpsichord. He toured when young as SARASATE's accompanist, and later became a leading Paris performer and teacher; CORTOT was among his pupils. Gave the first performance of Franck's Symphonic Variations, 1886, which is dedicated to him, as is Saint-Saëns's Piano Concerto no. 5.

Di Murska (also known as De Murska), **Ilma** (b. 4 Jan 1836; d. 14 Jan 1889), Croatian soprano. After Continental appearances, won prominence in London opera from 1865. She sang Senta there in the first British performance of *Der fliegende Holländer*, 1870. Later performed in USA and Australia, but her voice then deteriorated. She settled finally in Munich, where she poisoned herself.

Dinkin, Alvin, *see* HOLLYWOOD QUARTET.

Di Stefano, Giuseppe (b. 24 July 1921), Italian tenor. Celebrated for his operatic performances with CALLAS (for example at La Scala, where he sang from 1947) and for partnering her on her farewell concert tour, 1973–4. Highly esteemed in a limited repertory of Italian and a few French roles, he sang at the Metropolitan Opera from 1948; his British début was at the Edinburgh Festival, 1957.

Dixon, [Charles] **Dean** (b. 10 Jan 1915; d. 3 Nov 1976), American conductor. Became the first black musician to direct the NEW YORK PHILHARMONIC, 1941, and PHILADELPHIA ORCHESTRA, 1943. Sensing obstruction in an American career, he worked in Göteborg, Frankfurt (conducting radio orchestra, 1961–74) and Sydney; made his British début 1963. He reappeared with the Philadelphia Orchestra in 1975. Died in Switzerland.

Dmitriev, Alexander, *see* LENINGRAD SYMPHONY ORCHESTRA.

Dobbs, Mattiwilda (b. 11 July 1925), American soprano. Made her European début at the Holland Festival, 1952. One of the earliest black singers to win first-class status in opera, she sang very high coloratura parts such as the Queen of Shemakha in Rimsky-Korsakov's *The Golden Cockerel* (Covent Garden, 1954). Also performed at Glyndebourne from 1954 and the Metropolitan from 1956.

Dobrowen (originally Barabeichik), **Issay** [Alexandrovich] (b. 27 Feb 1891; d. 9 Dec 1953), Russian-born Norwegian conductor. His orphaned mother adopted the surname of a relative. He left Russia after the 1917 Revolution and worked in Dresden, Berlin and USA; conductor of the SAN FRANCISCO SYMPHONY ORCHESTRA, 1929–34. Then he returned to Europe, where he specialized after World War II in conducting (and occasionally stage-directing) Russian opera. Conducted CHRISTOFF's celebrated first recording of *Boris Godunov*, 1952.

Dohnányi, Christoph von (b. 8 Sept 1929), German conductor. Studied conducting with BERNSTEIN in USA. He was director of Hamburg State Opera, 1977–84, then became music director of the CLEVELAND ORCHESTRA. Conducted the first performances of Henze's operas *Der junge Lord* (Berlin), 1965, and *The Bassarids* (Salzburg), 1966. Has worked as an operatic stage director. Grandson of Hungarian composer Ernst von Dohnányi; SILJA is his wife.

Dohnányi, Ernst von, *see* BUDAPEST PHILHARMONIC ORCHESTRA.

D'Oisly, Maurice, *see* BUCKMAN.

Dokshitser, Timofey (b. 13 Dec 1921), Russian trumpeter. Long-serving member of the Bolshoi Theatre orchestra in Moscow, 1945–83, and noted soloist. He has recorded concertos specially written for him by Soviet composers, among them Vaynberg, 1967, as well as his own transcriptions of Kreisler violin pieces.

Doktor, Karl, *see* BUSCH QUARTET and DOKTOR, PAUL.

Doktor, Paul (b. 28 Mar 1919; d. 21 June 1989), Austrian-born viola player, naturalized American 1952. Worked in Switzerland during World War II, then settled in USA, where he performed, as soloist and chamber musician, and also taught. The Viola Concerto of Walter Piston was written for him, 1957. His father, Karl Doktor (1885–1949), played viola in the BUSCH QUARTET.

Dolby (also known as Sainton-Dolby), **Charlotte** [Helen] (b. 17 May 1821; d. 18 Feb 1885), British contralto. Appeared in London at Philharmonic Society concerts from 1841. Mendelssohn took her to perform in Leipzig, 1845, and dedicated to her the English edition of his Six Songs op. 57, 1843. She sang also in France and the Netherlands. Married SAINTON in 1860 and thereafter used the name Sainton-Dolby. Composed cantatas and songs.

Dolmetsch, [Eugène] **Arnold** (b. 24 Feb 1858; d. 28 Feb 1940), British (French-born) violinist and music scholar, father of Carl DOLMETSCH. A pioneer in revival of old instruments; began in the late 1880s to restore lutes, viols, clavichords and harpsichords. He then produced his own models of harpsichords, working with piano-making firms in Boston, 1905–11, and Paris, 1911–14. Later founded his own firm (and in 1925 a festival) in Haslemere (UK); its Dolmetsch recorders played a major role in school music. His third wife, Mabel (1874–1963), their children and some grandchildren continued his concerns.

Dolmetsch, Carl [Frederick] (b. 23 Aug 1911), British recorder player (and occasionally violinist), son of Arnold DOLMETSCH. Maintained the family manufacture of instruments at Haslemere and developed its festival. As a performer he toured internationally (usually with Joseph Saxby as harpsichord accompanist); his repertory included not only baroque music but new works written for him by Rubbra (Sonatina, 1964), Maw and others. CBE, 1954.

Dolmetsch, Mabel, *see* DOLMETSCH, ARNOLD.

Domgraf-Fassbaender, Willi (b. 19 Feb 1897; d. 13 Feb 1978), German baritone, father of Brigitte FASSBAENDER. Active at Berlin State Opera, 1928–45. In 1934 he sang (as Mozart's Figaro) at the opening night of the first season at Glyndebourne and remained a favourite there. Later he was chief stage director at Nuremberg Opera, 1953–62.

Domingo, Plácido (b. 21 Jan 1941), Spanish tenor. Educated in Mexico, where he studied piano and conducting as well as voice. Made his opera début in Mexico and USA, 1961; he first appeared in London 1969 (concert) and at Covent Garden 1971. He rose to highest international celebrity. With the Metropolitan Opera ('away' début 1966, 'house' début 1968) he has sung more than thirty roles. Though his chief fame is in the Italian repertory, he sang the title role of *Lohengrin* on Solti's recording, 1987. Menotti's opera *Goya*, 1986, was written for him. He was Alfredo in Zeffirelli's film of *La traviata*, 1982, and Don José in Rosi's film of *Carmen*, 1983. Has occasionally conducted concerts and opera (including Verdi's *Attila* at Barcelona, 1973).

Dominguez, Oralia (b. 15 Oct 1927), Mexican contralto. Sang opera in Mexico before coming to Europe. She performed from 1953 at La Scala, and in 1955 at Covent Garden (première of Tippett's *The Midsummer Marriage*) and Glyndebourne. Later based herself in Germany.

Donath (née Erwen), **Helen** (b. 10 July 1940), American soprano. From 1967 sang principally opera in Munich and Vienna; Covent Garden début 1982 (as Anne in Stravinsky's *The Rake's Progress*). With a large and distinguished repertory from Monteverdi to Britten, and with festival appearances including Salzburg (with KARAJAN) and Bayreuth, she has been curiously absent from the Metropolitan.

Donohoe, Peter (b. 18 June 1953), British pianist. His teachers included Yvonne LORIOD in Paris. Made his Proms début in London in 1979. Joint silver medallist at the Moscow Tchaikovsky Competition, 1982, he has returned with success to Russia and has appeared widely elsewhere (Japan, 1985). His repertory extends to Messiaen and to Muldowney's Piano Concerto (gave its first performance, 1983).

Doráti, Antal (b. 9 Apr 1906; d. 13 Nov 1988), Hungarian-born conductor, naturalized American 1947. Toured the world as ballet conductor with the company that succeeded Dyagilev's, 1933–41. He made his US concert début 1937, and was music director of the (new) American Ballet Theatre, 1937–41; conducted the première of Schuman's ballet score *Undertow*, 1945; made British concert début 1946. He was music director of the MINNEAPOLIS SYMPHONY ORCHESTRA (making it famous through records), 1949–60, and conductor of the BBC SYMPHONY ORCHESTRA, 1963–7, then STOCKHOLM PHILHARMONIC, 1966–74, the NATIONAL SYMPHONY (Washington), 1970–76, and the DETROIT SYMPHONY, 1977–81. A champion of Hungarian music, he conducted the posthumous première of Bartók's Viola Concerto (with PRIMROSE), 1949. Recorded all Haydn's symphonies. He conducted 'Concerts for Peace' in London, Berlin and Moscow a few weeks before his death.

Doret, Gustave (b. 20 Sept 1866; d. 19 Apr 1943), Swiss conductor. Active in Paris, he conducted the first performance of Debussy's *L'Après-midi d'un faune*, 1894. He also appeared as guest conductor in Amsterdam, London and elsewhere, and was equally prominent as a composer.

Dorus-Gras (née Van Steenkiste), Julie [-Aimée-Josephe] (b. 7 Sept 1805; d. 6 Feb 1896), Belgian soprano. Sang in the famous performance of Auber's *La Muette de Portici* in Brussels on 25 Aug 1829 that sparked off the Belgian revolution against the Dutch. At the Paris Opera, from 1831, she created the roles of Marguerite in Meyerbeer's *Les Huguenots*, 1836, and Teresa in Berlioz's *Benvenuto Cellini*, 1838.

Douglas, Barry (b. 23 Apr 1960), British pianist (born in Northern Ireland). Won the Moscow

Tchaikovsky Competition, 1986 (the first *outright* British winner; *see* DONOHOE and OGDON). In boyhood he also played clarinet and cello. Made his Proms début 1985 and returned to perform in USSR in 1987; New York recital début 1988. He has recorded chamber music with the TOKYO QUARTET and appeared (as himself) in Schlesinger's film *Madame Sousatzka*, 1989.

Dowding, Nicholas, *see* AMICI QUARTET.

Downes, Edward [Thomas] (b. 17 June 1924), British conductor. Attached to Covent Garden, 1952–69, and afterwards returned as guest; he conducted there the first British performance of Shostakovich's *Katerina Izmailova* (in his own translation), 1963, and the première of Peter Maxwell Davies's *Taverner*, 1972. Music director of Australian Opera, 1972–6; he conducted his own translation of Prokofiev's *War and Peace* as the first operatic performance in Sydney Opera House, 1973. Also well known as orchestral conductor, he gave the première of Birtwistle's *Chorales for Orchestra*, 1967. Became conductor of the BBC NORTHERN SYMPHONY (now BBC PHILHARMONIC) ORCHESTRA, 1980.

Downes, Ralph [William] (b. 16 Aug 1904), British organist and organ designer. His most famous construction is the organ in the Royal Festival Hall, London, 1951, with its then new capabilities in baroque organ tone. He was a well-known recitalist from the 1930s. Continued to supervise the maintenance of the Festival Hall organ into his eighties and gave his farewell performance on it in 1987.

Dragonetti, Domenico [Carlo Maria] (b. 10 Apr 1763; d. 16 Apr 1846), Italian double-bass player. Resident from 1794 in London, where his unique virtuosity put him among the highest-paid musicians. He often performed in a duo with his cellist friend LINDLEY. Visited Haydn in Vienna, 1798, and in 1808 he played there a cello sonata of Beethoven's on the double-bass with the enthusiastic composer at the piano. His technique is said to have inspired Beethoven's extraordinary demands on the double-basses in the Symphony no. 5.

Draper, Charles (b. 23 Oct 1869; d. 21 Oct 1952), British clarinettist. One of the earliest clarinet soloists to record prominently: made celebrated recordings of the Brahms and Mozart clarinet quintets with members of the LÉNER QUARTET, 1928–9. He gave the first performance of Stanford's Clarinet Concerto, 1904, with the composer conducting. The clarinettist Haydn Draper (1889–1934) was his nephew.

Draper, Haydn, *see* DRAPER, CHARLES.

Dresden State Orchestra (or Dresdner Staatskapelle), German orchestra. Performs in both concerts and opera; its descent may be traced to the Saxon imperial chapel, 1548. Principal conductors have included REINER, 1914–21, Fritz BUSCH, 1922–33, BÖHM, 1934–42, KEMPE, 1949–52, SANDERLING, 1964–7, BLOMSTEDT, 1975–85, and VONK, since 1985; Sinopoli to succeed in 1992.

Dreyfus, Huguette (b. 30 Nov 1928), French harpsichordist, also pianist. Won an international harpsichord competition at Geneva, 1958, and made world-wide appearances from the 1960s. She has recorded all Rameau's harpsichord works and teaches extensively.

Druinin, Fyodor, *see* BEETHOVEN QUARTET.

Dubinsky, Rostislav, *see* BORODIN QUARTET.

Dufallo, Richard (b. 30 Jan 1933), American conductor, formerly clarinettist. He was one of the four conductors of Stockhausen's *Carré* at its first performances in London and Paris, 1972, and conducted the première of Peter Maxwell Davies's opera *The Lighthouse* (Edinburgh), 1980. He has also conducted the CHICAGO SYMPHONY ORCHESTRA, 1970, the PHILADELPHIA ORCHESTRA, 1984, and the New York City Opera.

Dugazon (née Lefèbvre), **Louise-Rosalie** (b. 18 June 1755; d. 22 Sept 1821), French soprano (born in Berlin). Began her career as a dancer, then created over sixty roles at the Paris Opéra-Comique in now forgotten works such as Dalayrac's *Nina*, 1786. Her celebrity caused her name (her husband's, used even after her divorce in 1794) to be linked to role-types, as in a 'jeune Dugazon'.

Dumay, Augustin (b. 17 Jan 1949), French

violinist. Pupil of GRUMIAUX. He made his Paris début 1963 and played in Berlin under KARAJAN in 1979. Recorded the complete chamber music of Fauré, 1975.

Dunham, James, *see* CLEVELAND QUARTET.

Duparc, Elisabeth (known as 'La Francesina', 'The Frenchwoman') (d. ?1788), French soprano. Conspicuous among the mainly Italian singers engaged to sing Handel's and other Italian operas in London. She appeared in Handel's *Serse*, 1738, and also in some first performances of his English oratorios, including *Israel in Egypt*, 1739, and *Semele* (title role), 1744.

Duport, Jean-Pierre (b. 27 Nov 1741; d. 31 Dec 1818), French cellist. His outstanding talent was noted from his Paris début in 1761. After performing in Britain and Spain, he became a court musician to FREDERICK THE GREAT of Prussia. On a visit to that court in 1789 Mozart wrote variations on a minuet of Duport's, and Beethoven, visiting in 1796, performed as pianist with him.

Dupouy, Jean, *see* COMPOSERS QUARTET.

Dupré, Desmond [John] (b. 19 Dec 1916; d. 16 Aug 1974), British guitarist, lutenist, cellist and viol player. Having taught himself lute and viol, he was a leading expositor of those instruments at a time when they were little cultivated. Accompanied Alfred DELLER on the lute from 1951, and recorded as viol player with DART.

Du Pré, Jacqueline (b. 26 Jan 1945; d. 19 Oct 1987), British cellist. Pupil of William Pleeth in London (also had some lessons with Paul TORTELIER, CASALS and ROSTROPOVICH). She achieved a rare conquest of her audiences in Elgar's and other concertos, and as a sonata partner of BARENBOIM, whom she married in 1967. Gave the first performance of Goehr's Romanza for cello and orchestra, 1968, dedicated to her. In 1972 her performing career was halted by multiple sclerosis, though she continued to teach. (*See also* BISHOP-KOVACEVICH.)

Dupré, Marcel (b. 3 May 1886; d. 30 May 1971), French organist. His teachers in Paris included WIDOR, to whom he became assistant at St Sulpice Church; succeeded him in 1934. Ten recitals covering Bach's complete organ works (Paris, 1920) were followed by many overseas appearances, particularly in Britain and USA, winning him an unsurpassed authority. His organ improvisations were famous and were the sources of some of his compositions. Director of the Paris Conservatory, 1954–6.

Duprez, Gilbert [Louis] (b. 6 Dec 1806; d. 23 Sept 1896), French tenor, also composer. At the Paris Opera sang the title role in the first performance of Berlioz's *Benvenuto Cellini*, 1838; his other premières there included Donizetti's *La Favorite*, 1840. He was famous for his full-voiced high C (which Rossini compared to the sound emitted by a capon when its throat is cut).

Duruflé, Maurice (b. 11 Jan 1902; d. 16 June 1986), French organist, also composer. Holder of a Paris church post, he gave the first public performance of Poulenc's Concerto, 1941. His compositions include a well-known requiem (*see* WILLCOCKS) and fewer organ works than might be expected, among them the Prelude and Fugue on the Name of Alain (*see* ALAIN, JEHAN).

Dushkin, Samuel (b. 13 Dec 1891; d. 24 June 1976), Polish-born American violinist. Taken to USA as a child; pupil of AUER in New York. His friend Stravinsky wrote for him the Violin Concerto and Duo Concertant for violin and piano. He gave the first performances of these in Berlin, 1931 and 1932, with the composer as conductor and pianist respectively.

Dutoit, Charles [Edouard] (b. 7 Oct 1936), Swiss conductor, formerly orchestral viola player. Chief conductor of the Zurich Radio Orchestra, 1964–6, and music director of the Berne Symphony Orchestra, 1966–78; he was also a guest conductor of ballet (working with Massine and Nureyev) at the Vienna State Opera. Became music director of the MONTREAL SYMPHONY ORCHESTRA, 1977, and made it internationally known in recordings (particularly of Ravel and Stravinsky) and on concert tours. He conducted *Faust* at Covent Garden, 1985. The second of his three wives was ARGERICH.

Dutt, Hank, *see* KRONOS QUARTET.

Duval, Denise (b. 23 Oct 1921), French soprano. Her operatic career became prominent with the première of *Les Mamelles de Tirésias* (Poulenc, with libretto by Cocteau), 1947, in which she took principal role; repeated it in New York, 1953. Poulenc later set Cocteau's spoken monologue *La Voix humaine* as a solo opera, of which she gave the first performance in 1959. She retired from the stage in the mid-1960s, and thereafter taught.

Dvořáková, Ludmila (b. 11 July 1923), Czech soprano. Began her career in Bratislava and sang at the (East) Berlin State Opera from 1960. From the mid-1960s she was widely celebrated in heavy Wagnerian roles. Performed at Bayreuth from 1965 and sang Brünnhilde in *The Ring* at Covent Garden, 1967; also appeared as Leonore in *Fidelio* at the Metropolitan, 1966.

Dvorský, Petr (in some appearances Peter) (b. 25 Sept 1951), Czech tenor. Won first prize at the Geneva Competition, 1975, and became well known in Czech opera in the West, for example in a recording of Janáček's *Jenůfa* (with SÖDERSTRÖM, conducted by MACKERRAS), 1983. He made his début at Covent Garden in 1979.

Dyck, Ernest van, *see* VAN DYCK.

E

Eames, Emma (b. 13 Aug 1865; d. 13 June 1952), American soprano (born in Shanghai). Studied in Paris (where Gounod coached her as Marguerite in *Faust* and Juliet in *Roméo et Juliette*). She made her début at the Paris Opera 1889 and at Covent Garden 1891. Her chief fame was at the Metropolitan, 1899–1909, in the Gounod roles and as Tosca. Led a well-exposed private life; she took as her second husband the American baritone Emilio de Gogorza (1874–1949), but left him.

Easton, Florence (b. 25 Oct 1882; d. 13 Aug 1955), British soprano. Famous for the wide variety of her roles and her quickness in learning them. At the Metropolitan (regularly 1917–29) she created Lauretta in the first performance of Puccini's *Gianni Schicchi*, 1918, and also sang Brünnhilde in *The Ring*; she was Puccini's Turandot at Covent Garden, 1927, and Tosca at Sadler's Wells Opera, 1934. Sang in recital till 1943. She died in New York.

Eda-Pierre, Christiane (b. 24 Mar 1932), French soprano (born in Martinique). Began singing at the Paris Opera and Opéra-Comique in 1960. She has toured widely: guest (as Gilda in *Rigoletto*) at the Bolshoi Theatre, Metropolitan Opera and Wexford Festival, 1976. She had a leading role (the Angel) in the première of Messiaen's opera *St François d'Assise* in Paris, 1983.

Eddy, Nelson (b. 29 June 1901; d. 6 Mar 1967), American baritone. He was a major film star, from 1933, in musicals such as Herbert's *Naughty Marietta*, 1935 (his first opposite MACDONALD), and Friml's *Rose-Marie*, 1936. He previously sang with the Philadelphia Opera, taking the role of the Drum-major in the first US performance of Berg's *Wozzeck*, 1931.

Eden and Tamir, Israeli piano duo: Bracha Eden (b. 15 July 1928) and Alexander Tamir (b. 2 Apr 1931). Made their début in Israel 1954, New York 1955 and London 1957. They have widely explored the two-piano and one-piano duet repertory, and gave the first public performance of Stravinsky's piano-duet version of *The Rite of Spring*, 1968.

Edwards, Siân (b. 27 May 1959), British conductor. Studied in Leningrad. At short notice she took on the conducting of Weill's *Mahagonny* for Scottish Opera's new production, 1986. After appearing at Glyndebourne, she became the first woman ever to conduct at Covent Garden (Tippett's *The Knot Garden*, 1988). Conducted the first performances of Turnage's opera *Greek* at Munich and Edinburgh, 1988.

Eggard, Julius, *see* ROSÉ QUARTET.

Eggerth, Marta, *see* KIEPURA.

Egmond, Max van, *see* VAN EGMOND.

Egorov, Yuri, *see* YEGOROV.

Ehrling, Sixten (b. 3 Apr 1918), Swedish conductor. Conducted Royal Swedish Opera, 1953–60, and the DETROIT SYMPHONY ORCHESTRA, 1963–73, then became director of conducting studies at the Juilliard School. He is known particularly in interpreting Scandinavian music, and conducted Blomdahl's 'space opera' *Aniara* at its Stockholm première, 1959, and at Covent Garden, 1960.

Eisenberg, Maurice (b. 24 Feb 1900; d. 13 Dec 1972), German-born American cellist. Taken to USA as a child. He became a pupil of CASALS in Spain, then performed and taught in Paris, where he gave the first performance of Glazunov's Concerto-ballata (with the composer conducting), 1933. Later re-established in USA; he died while giving a lesson at the Juilliard School.

Elder, Mark [Philip] (b. 2 June 1947), British conductor. Worked at Glyndebourne and in Australia, then joined English National Opera, 1975, of which he became music director in 1979. He conducted there the first performance of Blake's *Toussaint*, 1977, and the British première of Shostakovich's *Lady Macbeth of Mtsensk*, 1987. Also appeared at Bayreuth, 1981. He conducted the Last Night of the Proms, 1987, and in the same season the first performance of Maw's *Odyssey*. Appointed CBE, 1989.

Elias, Rosalind (b. 13 Mar 1929), American mezzo-soprano. From 1954 has sung over forty-five roles with the Metropolitan Opera; she created Erika in Barber's *Vanessa*, 1958. Also sang with Scottish Opera (title role in Rossini's *La Cenerentola*, 1970) and at Glyndebourne.

Elman, Mischa (originally Mikhail) [Saulovich] (b. 20 Jan 1891; d. 5 Apr 1967), Russian-born violinist, naturalized American 1923. A pupil of AUER in St Petersburg, where he made his début 1904; in 1905 he gave in London the first UK performance of Glazunov's Concerto. Recognized thenceforth internationally as one of the greatest virtuosos of the time, he played more than fifteen concertos in a New York series, 1936–7, and gave the première of Martinů's Concerto no. 2 in Boston, 1943 (written for him). Sales of his records exceeded two million.

Elmo, Cloe (b. 9 Apr 1910; d. 24 May 1962), Italian mezzo-soprano. A leading performer at La Scala, 1936–45. In New York she was chosen by TOSCANINI to sing Mistress Quickly in his recording of *Falstaff*, 1950. She settled in Ankara and taught at the conservatory there from 1954 until her death.

Elwes, Gervase [Cary] (b. 15 Nov 1866; d. 12 Jan 1921), British tenor. In early career was a diplomat. After singing as an amateur, he won professional acclaim from 1904. Performed Elgar's *The Dream of Gerontius* about 150 times, and gave the first performance of Vaughan Williams's *On Wenlock Edge*, 1909. One of the first British singers to appear in his own recitals unassisted by other soloists. On his second US tour he was killed in a railway accident.

Endellion Quartet, London-based string quartet founded 1979. Called after the Cornish village of St Endellion. It won a New York young artists' competition, 1981, and has toured widely. Became quartet in residence to South-east Arts, 1986, in which year it recorded all Britten's works for string quartet. Original members: Andrew Watkinson, Louise Williams, Garfield Jackson and David Waterman; later second violinists were James Clark, 1984–6, then Ralph de Souza.

Endo, Akira, *see* LOUISVILLE ORCHESTRA.

Enescu, George (also known by French form, Georges Enesco) (b. 19 Aug 1881; d. 4 May 1955), Romanian violinist, equally famous as composer (also conductor and pianist). Trained in Paris, he based himself both there and in Romania. Toured internationally and made US début 1923. He was a chamber-music partner of CORTOT and others, and the most influential teacher of MENUHIN. Died in Paris. His native village is now called by his name.

Engen, Keith (or Kieth, the phonetic spelling he adopted for German use) (b. 5 Apr 1925), American bass. Active chiefly in Munich, where he took part in the première of Hindemith's opera *Die Harmonie der Welt*, 1957. Sang at Bayreuth in 1958 (King Henry in *Lohengrin*) and later.

English Chamber Orchestra, London-based orchestra founded 1948 by GOLDSBROUGH under his own name. Took present title 1960. It worked under Benjamin Britten at the Aldeburgh Festival and with other conductors, but had no regular conductor until TATE, from 1985.

English Concert, London-based chamber orchestra founded 1973 by PINNOCK, who usually directs from the harpsichord. It specializes in baroque music in a historical style with period instruments. The ensemble's name is also used when only a small number of performers appear.

Entremont, Philippe (b. 6 June 1934), French pianist and conductor. Won the Long–Thibaud Competition for piano in 1953, and gave the US première of Jolivet's Concerto in New York in the same year. He recorded all Ravel's solo piano music and all Saint-Saëns's concertos. Active as conductor from 1967; he was music director of the New Orleans Symphony Orchestra, 1981–4, and of Denver Symphony Orchestra, 1986–9.

Eötvös, Peter (b. 2 Jan 1944), Hungarian conductor, composer and performer on electronic instruments. Closely associated with both BOULEZ and Stockhausen, he became music director of the Ensemble Intercontemporain (Boulez's Paris foundation), 1979, and conducted Stockhausen's opera *Donnerstag*, both at its first performance (La Scala), 1981, and at Covent Garden, 1985. He also gave, with the BBC SYMPHONY ORCHESTRA, the first British performance of Stockhausen's *Spiel*, 1987.

Equiluz, Kurt (b. 13 June 1929), Austrian tenor. Sang in the Vienna Boys' Choir, won a Mozart competition in Vienna, 1949, then became a chorister of the Vienna State Opera. He took solo roles there from 1957, but became best known as a Bach singer (Evangelist in the Passions) with such specialist conductors as RILLING and HARNONCOURT.

Erb, Karl (b. 13 July 1877; d. 13 July 1958), German tenor. Completely self-taught as singer, he reached thirty before making his début. Sang with distinction (in over sixty-five roles) at the Munich Opera, 1913–25, and created the title role in Pfitzner's *Palestrina*, 1917. He and his wife, IVOGÜN, appeared together in *Die Entführung* at Covent Garden, 1927. He is fictionally immortalized as the tenor Erbe in Thomas Mann's novel *Dr Faustus* alongside the non-fictional KLEMPERER.

Erben, Valentin, *see* ALBAN BERG QUARTET.

Erdelyi, Csaba (b. 15 May 1946), Hungarian viola player. Emigrated to UK then, 1987, to USA. He was principal viola of the PHILHARMONIA ORCHESTRA and later, 1979–86, a member of the CHILINGIRIAN QUARTET. Also a noted soloist and partner of MENUHIN. He recorded Hoddinott's Concerto and also Strauss's songs with NORMAN.

Erede, Alberto (b. 8 Nov 1908), Italian conductor. Pupil of WEINGARTNER and Fritz BUSCH. He conducted *The Ring* at Turin, 1935, and was a member, along with Busch, of Glyndebourne's music staff, 1934–9. Conducted over 500 performances for the New London Opera Company, 1946–8, worked at the Metropolitan, 1950–55, was music director of the Deutsche Oper am Rhein, 1958–62, and conducted *Lohengrin* at Bayreuth, 1968. His appearance with English National Opera aged seventy-eight (conducting Rossini's *Mosè*), 1986, is without parallel in British opera annals.

Erlih, Devy (b. 5 Nov 1928), French violinist. Won the Long–Thibaud Competition, 1955, and went on to an international career, playing much French music. He married a daughter of the French composer Jolivet, and gave the first performance of Jolivet's unaccompanied *Suite rhapsodique*, 1967.

Ermler, Mark (b. 5 May 1932), Russian conductor. A member of the staff of the Bolshoi Theatre, 1957–87. He conducted the first public performance of Prokofiev's *The Story of a Real Man*, 1960, which had been banned under Stalin. Made his British début conducting the Bolshoi Ballet on its 1974 visit. He became principal guest conductor to the Royal Ballet, 1985, and conducted *Carmen* at Covent Garden in 1986.

Ernst, Heinrich [Wilhelm] (b. 6 May 1814; d. 8 Oct 1865), Austrian violinist. Emulated PAGANINI (with whom he performed at least once). He travelled widely and won the highest renown; Mendelssohn and Berlioz both admired him. Made his London début 1843 and settled there in 1855; he led a string quartet with JOACHIM, WIENIAWSKI and PIATTI, 1859. His own compositions are still prized by violinists.

Ershov, Ivan, *see* YERSHOV.

Eschenbach (originally Ringman), **Christoph** (b. 20 Feb 1940), German pianist and conductor. Won the Haskil Competition in Lucerne, 1965.

He made his British début 1966, his US début 1969; gave the première of Henze's Piano Concerto no. 2, 1968. From the 1970s he increasingly appeared as conductor (sometimes directing from the keyboard); worked at Covent Garden, 1984, and was principal conductor of the TONHALLE ORCHESTRA, Zurich, 1982–6. Appointed music director of the HOUSTON SYMPHONY ORCHESTRA, 1988.

Esipova, Anna, *see* YESIPOVA.

Eskdale, George [Salisbury] (b. 21 June 1897; d. 20 June 1960), British trumpeter. Principal trumpet of the LONDON SYMPHONY ORCHESTRA from 1932 until his death. His mid-1930s recording of Haydn's Trumpet Concerto (second and third movements) helped to bring about its modern popularity; he recorded the complete work in 1954.

Esswood, Paul [Lawrence Vincent] (b. 2 June 1942), British countertenor. Member of the choir at Westminster Abbey till 1971; he became known as a soloist with a broadcast of Handel's *Messiah* under MACKERRAS, 1965 (and afterwards recorded it). Made his operatic début in California in Cavalli's *Erismena*, 1968, and participated in the première of Penderecki's opera *Paradise Lost* (Chicago), 1978.

Estes, Simon (b. 2 Mar 1938), American bass-baritone. Won the Moscow Tchaikovsky Competition in the first year it was devoted to singing, 1966. He made his opera début in West Berlin, 1975, and was the first male black singer to appear at Bayreuth (as the Flying Dutchman, 1978). Sang a minor part in the first performance of Schuller's *The Visitation* (Hamburg), 1966, and took over a main role in its British (television) première.

Eto, Toshiya (b. 9 Nov 1927), Japanese violinist. Studied with SUZUKI in Japan (before Suzuki went over to group teaching), and with ZIMBALIST at the Curtis Institute, Philadelphia, where he later taught, 1953–61. He made his London début in 1968.

Evans, Anne (b. 20 Aug 1939), British soprano. Studied in London and Geneva, where she made her operatic début. Sang regularly with Sadler's Wells Opera from 1968 (including much Mozart), and in Marseilles and San Francisco. In 1986, in the Welsh National Opera production, she became the second British singer (after HUNTER) to undertake the complete Brünnhilde in *The Ring*; also performed as Kundry in *Parsifal* at English National Opera.

Evans, Geraint [Llewellyn] (b. 16 Feb 1922), British baritone. One of the most distinctive British opera singers, he made his Covent Garden début as the Nightwatchman in *Die Meistersinger*, 1948, and celebrated his twenty-fifth anniversary there in the title role of Donizetti's *Don Pasquale*. He was the first Mr Flint in Britten's *Billy Budd*, 1951. Performed also at the Salzburg Festival and the Metropolitan, from 1964. He occasionally worked as stage director for British and US opera companies. Knighted, 1969.

Evans, Nancy (b. 19 Mar 1915), British mezzo-soprano. Took the role of Nancy (specially written for her) in Britten's *Albert Herring*, 1947; she gave the first performances of Britten's *A Charm of Lullabies*, 1948, and, with orchestra, of Williamson's *Six English Lyrics*, 1969, dedicated to her. She was married first to the impresario Walter Legge (*see also* SCHWARZKOPF) and then to Eric Crozier, the librettist of *Albert Herring* and other Britten works. OBE, 1991.

Evera, Emily van, *see* PARROTT.

Ewing, Maria [Louise] (b. 27 Mar 1950), American mezzo-soprano, later soprano. Studied with STEBER and TOUREL and made her Metropolitan début 1976 as Cherubino (*Figaro*). In 1978 she made her first appearance at Glyndebourne as Dorabella (*Così*) under the stage direction of Peter Hall; they were married in 1982 and divorced in 1990. Sang Salome at Covent Garden, 1988.

F

Fábián, Márta (b. 27 Apr 1946), Hungarian cimbalom player. Has exploited her instrument's capabilities in folk, classical and modernist contexts, and elicited new works from Hungarian composers, including Szokolay and Kurtág. She is noted in such pieces as Boulez's *Éclat* (with its important cimbalom part), composed in 1965.

Fabritiis, Oliviero De, *see* DE FABRITIIS.

Faccio, Franco (b. 8 Mar 1840; d. 21 July 1891), Italian conductor. Worked at La Scala, 1871–90, where in 1873 he conducted the first Italian performance of a Wagner opera (*Lohengrin*). Famous for his Verdi performances, he conducted the première of *Otello*, 1887. Also a composer.

Fachiri, Adela, *see* ARÁNYI.

Faerber, Jörg (b. 18 June 1929), German conductor. Founded the Württemberg Chamber Orchestra in 1961 and has remained its conductor. Won note with a large recorded output of eighteenth-century music (including such unfamiliar composers as Michael Haydn, Krommer and Boismortier). He has also conducted British orchestras and the European Community Chamber Orchestra.

Fagan, Gideon (b. 3 Nov 1904; d. 21 Mar 1980), South African conductor, also composer. Worked in Manchester as conductor of the BBC NORTHERN ORCHESTRA, 1939–42. He later returned to South Africa and was music director of its broadcasting system, 1963–6.

Falcon, [Marie] **Cornélie** (b. 28 Jan 1814; d. 25 Feb 1897), French soprano. Had a short but brilliant career at the Paris Opera, 1832–8. She created the roles of Rachel in Halévy's *La Juive*, 1835, and Valentine in Meyerbeer's *Les Huguenots*, 1836; she won such success that the term 'falcon' was attached to that type of dramatic soprano voice.

Farberman, Harold (b. 2 Nov 1929), American conductor, also composer, formerly percussionist. Played percussion with the BOSTON SYMPHONY ORCHESTRA, 1952–63. He worked with various European and US orchestras and ensembles; he was the first conductor to record all four Ives symphonies. Conducted the Oakland Symphony Orchestra, California, 1971–9, and was later a guest conductor with BOURNEMOUTH SINFONIETTA.

Farinelli, professional name used by Carlo Broschi (b. 24 Jan 1705; d. 15 July 1782), Italian male soprano (castrato). Perhaps the most famous castrato of all; he was also a composer and (as amateur) a poet, harpsichordist and viola d'amore player. Sang in opera in Naples, Rome, Vienna and London, 1734–7, then served the Spanish court in Madrid, 1737–59, not only singing but also managing opera seasons. He retired to Bologna, where Gluck and Mozart were among his visitors.

Farley, Carole [Ann] (b. 29 Nov 1946), American soprano. Particularly known in the title role of Berg's *Lulu* (Metropolitan Opera, 1977, and elsewhere), of which she gave more than eighty performances in German, English and French. Made a film version of Poulenc's one-woman opera *La Voix humaine*; her unusual solo repertory includes Prokofiev's songs. She is married to the conductor SEREBRIER.

Farnadi, Edith (b. 25 Sept 1921; d. 12 Dec 1973). Hungarian-born Austrian pianist. A child prodigy, at the age of twelve both played and conducted Beethoven's Piano Concerto no. 1. She studied in Budapest and became a noted concerto soloist (under ANSERMET, BÖHM and others) and a recital partner of HUBERMAN. Taught in Budapest and later in Graz, where she died.

Farncombe, Charles [Frederick] (b. 29 July 1919). British conductor. A specialist in Handel operas, he has conducted twenty-eight on stage, possibly more than anyone since Handel himself. He was music director of the Drottningholm Court Theatre (a unique eighteenth-century theatre near Stockholm), 1970–79. CBE, 1977.

Farrar, Geraldine (b. 28 Feb 1882; d. 11 Mar 1967). American soprano. Her celebrated career at the Metropolitan Opera, 1906–22, included the title role in the first performance of Puccini's *Suor Angelica*, 1918; also sang as Butterfly at the opera's first US performance (with CARUSO), 1907. She appeared in silent films, 1915–19, and made vocal adaptations (with her own lyrics) of instrumental pieces by Rakhmaninov and others. Won an unusual following of young women (known as 'Gerryflappers').

Farrell, Eileen (b. 13 Feb 1920). American soprano. Had a considerable concert career (she sang and recorded Beethoven's Symphony no. 9 under TOSCANINI, 1959) before embarking on opera. She did not appear at the Metropolitan until 1960 (title role of Gluck's *Alceste*). Sang Wagner in notable concert performances but never on stage; she also performed jazz and blues.

Farulli, Piero, *see* QUARTETTO ITALIANO.

Fasano, Renato (b. 21 Aug 1902; d. 3 Aug 1979). Italian conductor, also composer, editor of baroque music and conservatory director. Founded an ensemble called the Collegium Musicum Italicum, 1948, which generated the Virtuosi di Roma, 1952; with this second group he significantly popularized the music of Vivaldi (and his Italian contemporaries) in small-scaled orchestral performances. His recordings include eighteenth-century operatic and choral works.

Fassbaender, Brigitte (b. 3 July 1939). German mezzo-soprano, daughter of Willi DOMGRAF-FASSBAENDER. At the Bavarian State Opera, Munich, from 1961, her roles ranged from Hänsel in Humperdinck's *Hänsel und Gretel* to Eboli in *Don Carlos*; in 1970 she was awarded the Bavarian title of Kammersängerin. Octavian in *Der Rosenkavalier* was her début role at Covent Garden, 1971, and the Metropolitan, 1974. She is also an accomplished recitalist.

Faure, Jean-Baptiste (b. 15 Jan 1830; d. 9 Nov 1914). French baritone. Began his operatic career in 1852 and still showed good tone on recordings made when he was nearly seventy. Based in Paris; he sang Posa in the première of *Don Carlos*, 1867, and the title role of Ambroise Thomas's *Hamlet*, 1868. His London opera début was in 1860; appeared as Mephistopheles in the first Covent Garden performance of *Faust*, 1863.

Favart (née Duronceray), **Marie-Justine-Benoîte** (b. 15 June 1727; d. 21 Apr 1772). French soprano. Married to the impresario and librettist Charles-Simon Favart. The career of both was hampered by the unwelcome attentions paid her by a powerful marshal, after whose death, 1750, she became a star performer at her husband's Paris theatre, the Comédie-Italienne, in such new operas as Pergolesi's *La serva padrona*. Offenbach's operetta *Madame Favart*, 1878, is based on her life.

Fedoseyev, Vladimir [Ivanovich] (b. 5 Aug 1932). Russian conductor. Appointed music director of the MOSCOW RADIO SYMPHONY ORCHESTRA, 1974, with which he has toured. He has also been a guest conductor of orchestras in Britain and elsewhere. His recordings include *Boris Godunov* and Glazunov symphonies.

Fejér, András, *see* TAKÁCS QUARTET.

Feltsman, Vladimir (b. 8 Jan 1952). Russian pianist. Pupil of Flier in Moscow, winner of the Long–Thibaud Competition in Paris, 1971; his repertory includes Messiaen and Schoenberg. His career was restricted by Soviet officialdom after he applied as a Jew to emigrate, 1979.

Eventually granted his exit permit, he made his New York début (and played for the US President) in 1987.

Fenby, Eric [William] (b. 22 Apr 1906), British pianist, conductor and composer. Long known as the amanuensis of the blind Delius and as his biographer, after his seventieth birthday he came to be in demand as a Delius interpreter, for example as the pianist partner of HOLMES. Conducted recording of *A Song of the High Hills* (for chorus and orchestra), 1984. OBE, 1962.

Fennell, Frederick (b. 2 July 1914), American conductor. As college professor (Eastman School of Music, Rochester), specialized in wind-band music, with notable recordings from the 1950s. He was resident conductor at the University of Miami, 1965–80; from 1972 made 'historical' recordings (using nineteenth-century wind instruments) for the Library of Congress in Washington.

Ferber, Albert (b. 29 Mar 1911; d. 11 Jan 1987), Swiss pianist. Made his début in Lucerne in 1920, then studied with GIESEKING and LONG; settled in Britain shortly before World War II. He recorded the complete piano works of Debussy and performed in forty-one countries.

Ferencsik, János (b. 18 Jan 1907; d. 12 June 1984), Hungarian conductor. Twice won his country's highest award, the Kossuth Prize. He was chief conductor of the HUNGARIAN STATE SYMPHONY ORCHESTRA from 1952 until his death, also of Hungarian State Opera, 1957–74, and the BUDAPEST SYMPHONY ORCHESTRA, 1960–68. As concert conductor, noted in Hungarian works, he first visited Britain 1957 and USA 1962; in Sydney he conducted the first performance of Sculthorpe's *Rain*, 1970.

Fernandez (originally Wiggins), **Wilhelmenia** (b. 5 Jan 1949), American soprano. Sang on Broadway as Bess (*Porgy and Bess*), 1977, then on US and European opera stages (Paris from 1979, as Musetta and then Mimì in *La Bohème*). She won wider celebrity as the star of Beineix's film *Diva*, 1981; sang Aida for Opera North, 1986.

Ferrara, Franco (b. 4 July 1911; d. 6 Sep 1985), Italian conductor. Made his début at Florence in 1938; his nervous problems led to withdrawal from public performance. He made a few records, but is chiefly noted as a teacher in Italy and elsewhere. Among his students were DE WAART, Andrew DAVIS and CHAILLY.

Ferrarese Del Bene (originally Gabrielli), **Adriana** (b. *c.* 1755; d. after 1799), Italian soprano. As an orphan in Venice she was called Ferrarese, i.e. from Ferrara; Del Bene was the name of her (presumed) husband. She was famous for her association with Mozart: he wrote two new songs for her in a Vienna performance of *Figaro*, 1789, and she was the first Fiordiligi in *Così*, 1790. Also performed in London, 1785, and Warsaw.

Ferras, Christian (b. 17 June 1933; d. 15 Sept 1982), French violinist. A child prodigy, he won first prize at an international competition at Scheveningen, 1948, and later took lessons from ENESCU. He was among the most highly regarded players of the 1960s and recorded the Beethoven, Brahms and Sibelius concertos with KARAJAN. Several works were written specially for him, including Honegger's Sonata for unaccompanied violin, 1948.

Ferrier, Kathleen [Mary] (b. 22 Apr 1912; d. 8 Oct 1953), British contralto. Achieved, chiefly in recital and in such works as Elgar's *The Dream of Gerontius*, a rare emotional bond with her audiences. She worked closely with Britten and created the title role in *The Rape of Lucretia*, 1946, and the contralto part in the *Spring Symphony*, 1949; gave the first performance (on radio) of Bliss's scena *The Enchantress*, 1951. She performed and recorded Mahler's *Das Lied von der Erde* with WALTER, who also accompanied her at the piano. She was noted in Bach, lieder and English folksong arrangements. The cancer of which she died prevented her from completing her series of Covent Garden performances as Gluck's Orpheus, 1953.

Feuermann, Emanuel (b. 22 Nov 1902; d. 25 May 1942), Austrian-born cellist, naturalized American a few weeks before his death. Active in pre-Hitler Germany; with the composer (viola) and Szymon GOLDBERG he recorded Hindemith's String Trio no. 2. As a Jewish refugee, made first US appearance 1934. He developed an outstanding career that was cut off by his early death after an operation. Performed in a trio with HUBERMAN and SCHNABEL, and with HEIFETZ and Arthur RUBINSTEIN.

Février, Jacques (b. 26 July 1900; d. 2 Sept 1979), French pianist. A friend of Poulenc from childhood, he was the dedicatee of Poulenc's Concerto for two pianos and gave its first performance with the composer, 1922. In 1933 he played Ravel's Concerto for the left hand with the authority of the composer, who had been dissatisfied with the original performance by WITTGENSTEIN.

Ffrangcon-Davies (originally Davies), **David** [Thomas] (b. 11 Dec 1855; d. 13 Apr 1919), British baritone. Had been ordained in the Church but became a noted singer of Victorian ballads, and made his London stage début with Carl Rosa Opera as the Herald in *Lohengrin*, 1890. Performed in Germany, USA and Canada. His book on singing, 1905, contained a preface by Elgar.

Fiedler, Arthur (b. 17 Dec 1894; d. 10 July 1979), American conductor. Celebrated for his long-running and hugely successful direction of the BOSTON POPS ORCHESTRA from 1930 till his death. Previously he had been a violinist and viola player with the BOSTON SYMPHONY ORCHESTRA and had organized a smaller touring group, the Arthur Fiedler Sinfonietta, 1924.

Field-Hyde, Margaret (b. 4 May 1905), British soprano, also violinist. Founded the Golden Age Singers, a five-strong madrigal group, in 1950. She had previously sung at Glyndebourne, taken part in (then rare) Monteverdi performances and given the first performance of Lutyens's *O saisons, o châteaux!*, 1947.

Fifer, Julian, *see* ORPHEUS CHAMBER ORCHESTRA.

Figner (née Mei), [Zoraida] **Medea** (originally Amedea) (b. 4 Apr 1858; d. 8 July 1952), Italian-born Russian soprano. Married, 1889–1903, to Nikolay FIGNER. After performing in Italy and elsewhere, she sang in Russia from 1887. She was the first to sing the heroine's roles in Tchaikovsky's *The Queen of Spades*, 1890, and *Yolanta*, 1892. Admired in a large repertory, including Wagner roles, she made important early recordings. Her last years were spent in Paris.

Figner, Nikolay [Nikolayevich] (b. 21 Feb 1857; d. 13 Dec 1918), Russian tenor. Sang widely in Western Europe (Covent Garden from 1897) and South America as well as in Russia, where he was the first Herman in Tchaikovsky's *The Queen of Spades*, 1890. (*See also* FIGNER, MEDEA.)

Finnilä, Birgit (b. 20 Jan 1931), Swedish contralto. Completed her studies in London and made concert début there in 1966; she then appeared with leading US and European orchestras. Her operatic performances have been very selective and include, for example, Erda in *The Ring* (Salzburg and Paris).

Fiorentino, Quartetto, *see* QUARTETTO FIORENTINO.

Firkušný, Rudolf (b. 11 Feb 1912), Czech-born American pianist. Made début aged ten in Prague; first appearance in London 1933, New York 1938. He was still performing when he was seventy-five, having won great esteem without cultivating a star role. His world-wide recitals prominently featured Czech composers, especially Janáček (with whom he had studied composition); his premières included concertos by Menotti, 1945, Hanson, 1948, and Martinů (no. 3, 1949, and no. 4, 1956).

Fischer, Ádám (b. 9 Sept 1949), Hungarian conductor, brother of Iván FISCHER. Won the Cantelli Conducting Competition in Milan, 1973. He worked as an opera conductor of companies at Helsinki, Karlsruhe, 1977–9, and Kassel, from 1987 (première of Tal's opera *The Tower* in Berlin, 1987). Has also conducted Vienna State Opera and the BOSTON SYMPHONY ORCHESTRA.

Fischer, Annie (originally Anny) (b. 5 July 1914), Hungarian pianist. Her teachers in Budapest included Ernst von Dohnányi; she made her début aged eight. During World War II lived in Sweden, but she returned to Hungary and developed an international career (noted for Beethoven and Schubert). Continued playing into the 1980s. She was married to Aladár

Toth (1898–1968), musicologist and director of Budapest State Opera, 1946–56.

Fischer, Edwin (b. 6 Oct 1886; d. 24 Jan 1960), Swiss pianist. Settled in Berlin, but went back to Switzerland in World War II. Celebrated in the standard Bach-to-Brahms repertory, he was one of the first modern pianists to revive the Mozartian role of conducting from the piano. Noted also in chamber music (for example with KULENKAMPFF and SCHNEIDERHAN) and as a teacher and music editor.

Fischer, György (b. 12 Aug 1935), Hungarian conductor, also pianist. Worked at Vienna State Opera, then Cologne Opera, from 1973. Made British début with Welsh National Opera, 1973. He also performs as accompanist to singers. Formerly married to POPP.

Fischer, Iván (b. 20 Jan 1951), Hungarian conductor, brother of Ádám FISCHER. Conductor of NORTHERN SINFONIA, 1979–82; musical director of Kent Opera from 1984 and artistic director from 1989. He has also conducted the LONDON SYMPHONY ORCHESTRA and opera at Covent Garden. In 1982, jointly with KOCSIS, he founded the Budapest Festival Orchestra. Acquired joint Dutch nationality, 1982.

Fischer, Paul, *see* ROSÉ QUARTET.

Fischer-Dieskau, Dietrich (b. 28 May 1925), German baritone, also occasionally from mid-1970s conductor. Made London début in concert with BEECHAM, 1951. In Schubert and Wolf, in concert and in recordings (often with SCHWARZKOPF), he became the pre-eminent male song-recitalist of his generation, with a repertory exceeding 1,000 songs; continued to record into his sixties. He was one of the singers for whom Britten wrote his *War Requiem*, 1962, and Reimann wrote the title role of the opera *Lear* for him, 1978. Within a wide operatic repertory he was also celebrated as Wozzeck on stage and, 1964, on record. He has written about Schubert songs. His fourth wife is VARADY.

Fiser, Lee, *see* LASALLE QUARTET.

Fisher, Sylvia [Gwendoline Victoria] (b. 18 Apr 1910), Australian soprano. Her notable roles at Covent Garden, 1949–58, included Leonore in *Fidelio* and the Marschallin in *Der Rosenkavalier*. She created the role of Miss Wingrave in the original television version of Britten's *Owen Wingrave*, 1971.

Fistoulari, Anatole (b. 20 Aug 1907), Russian-born conductor, naturalized British 1948. A child prodigy, he claims to have conducted Tchaikovsky's Symphony no. 6 at the age of seven. Active in the 1930s with the French-based Ballets Russes, then in Britain with various orchestras, from 1940. His many recordings (from the 1940s onwards) include much ballet and concertos with KEMPFF, CURZON and MILSTEIN. He was married, 1942–56, to MAHLER's daughter Anna.

Fitelberg, Grzegorz (b. 8 Oct 1879; d. 10 Jan 1953), Polish conductor, also composer. Had a long and pioneering career. Born in Russian Latvia, he was a violinist in the WARSAW PHILHARMONIC ORCHESTRA and then its chief conductor, 1909–11. Conducted in Russia, 1914–21, and in Paris for Dyagilev; he gave the first performance of Stravinsky's *Mavra*, 1922. Again worked in Warsaw, and managed to escape in World War II; on his return he became conductor of the (new) POLISH RADIO SYMPHONY ORCHESTRA and gave the première of Lutosławski's Symphony no. 1, 1948. His son Jerzy Fitelberg was a composer.

Fitzenhagen, Wilhelm [Karl Friedrich] (b. 15 Sept 1848; d. 14 Feb 1890), German cellist. Appointed professor at the Moscow Conservatory, 1870. He became a friend of Tchaikovsky and gave the first performance of his Variations on a Rococo Theme, 1877. (Fitzenhagen made his own edition, now regarded as distorting Tchaikovsky's intentions.) He was also a composer. Died in Moscow.

Fitzwilliam Quartet, London-based string quartet founded 1975. Its members were Christopher Rowland (later Daniel Zisman), Jonathan Sparey, Alan George and Ioan Davies. It recorded all Shostakovich's quartets with the encouragement of the composer. Disbanded in 1986.

Fizdale, Robert, *see* GOLD AND FIZDALE.

Fjeldstad, Oivin (b. 2 May 1903), Norwegian conductor. Chief conductor of the Norwegian Radio Orchestra and later the Oslo Philharmonic

1962–9; also conducted the National Youth Orchestra of Great Britain, 1961–8. He made the first (nearly) complete recording, with FLAGSTAD, of *Götterdämmerung*, 1955.

Flagello, Ezio (b. 28 Jan 1931), American bass. Has sung (and recorded) many operatic roles, forty-eight of them at the Metropolitan. He created Enobarbus in Barber's *Antony and Cleopatra* at the opening of the Metropolitan's new home, 1966.

Flagstad, Kirsten [Malfrid] (b. 12 July 1895; d. 7 Dec 1962), Norwegian soprano. After an unpromising early career became the most famous Wagnerian soprano of her time, particularly with her appearances at the Metropolitan Opera, 1935–41 (Sieglinde, then Isolde, Brünnhilde and others), and Covent Garden, 1936 (as Isolde and Brünnhilde) and 1948–51. During part of World War II she lived in Norway, and was afterwards accused (with her husband) of collaboration with the Nazis, a charge she denied. Sang Dido in Bernard Miles's tiny-scaled London production of *Dido and Aeneas* (with TEYTE), 1951. She was director of the Norwegian Opera, 1958–60. Strauss assigned to her the first performance of his Four Last Songs (London), 1950.

Fleisher, Leon (b. 23 July 1928), American pianist. As a boy studied with SCHNABEL and in 1952 was the first American to win the Queen Elisabeth Competition (Brussels); he performed at the Salzburg Festival, 1958. His distinguished career was interrupted in 1956 when his right hand was disabled; he played left-hand works and became a conductor. (He again performed as a two-handed pianist for a short time in 1982.)

Flesch, Carl (b. 9 Oct 1873; d. 14 Nov 1944), Hungarian violinist. Settled as a performer in Berlin (became trio partner of SCHNABEL and Hugo BECKER), but was particularly celebrated as a teacher in Philadelphia, 1923–8, Berlin, London, 1934–9, and Lucerne (where he died). His students included SZERYNG, NEVEU and Szymon GOLDBERG. An international competition in London commemorates him.

Fleury, Louis (b. 24 May 1878; d. 11 June 1926), French flautist. Made recital appearances with such well-known singers as CALVÉ and MELBA. Debussy wrote for him the most famous of all unaccompanied flute pieces, *Syrinx*, 1913.

Flipse, Eduard (b. 26 Feb 1896; d. 11 Sept 1972), Dutch conductor. An enthusiast for Mahler; for a long period he was chief conductor of the Rotterdam Philharmonic Orchestra, 1930–65. Also pianist and composer.

Flonzaley Quartet, string quartet founded 1902 in New York. Named after the Swiss residence of its patron, E. J. De Coppet. Its members were Adolfo Betti, Alfred Pochon, Ugo Ara (later Louis Bailly and then Félicien d'Archambeau) and Iwan d'Archambeau (later N. Moldavan). Stravinsky's Concertino for string quartet, 1920, and Bloch's Quartet no. 1, 1922, were dedicated to the ensemble. It disbanded in London in 1928.

Foldes (originally Földes), **Andor** (b. 21 Dec 1913), Hungarian-born pianist, naturalized American 1948. Played a Mozart concerto at the age of eight; he became a piano pupil of Dohnányi and later studied Bartók's works with the composer. Made his US début 1940 and from 1960 sometimes played and conducted simultaneously. His book on piano technique was translated into nine languages.

Foley, Allan James, *see* FOLI.

Foli, Signor, Italianized form of name adopted by Allan James Foley (b. 7 Aug 1835; d. 20 Oct 1899), Irish bass. After studying in Italy, sang in Britain, Russia and elsewhere. He participated in the first British performances of *Der fliegende Holländer*, 1870, and Berlioz's *L'Enfance du Christ*, 1880.

Forbes, Watson, *see* AEOLIAN QUARTET.

Forqueray, Antoine (b. 1671 or 1672; d. 28 June 1745), French viol player. One of the great exponents of the bass viol, he was in service to Louis XIV of France from 1690; also published pieces for viol and for harpsichord. He ill-treated (from jealousy?) his son Jean-Baptiste Forqueray (1699–1782), who was a viol player and composer.

Forqueray, Jean-Baptiste, *see* FORQUERAY, ANTOINE.

Forrester, Maureen [Katherine Stewart] (b. 25 July 1930), Canadian contralto. Won prominence from her New York recital début, 1956, and a subsequent performance there of Mahler's 'Resurrection' Symphony under WALTER. Her operatic roles include Gluck's Orpheus (stage début, Toronto, 1961) and Erda in *The Ring* (Metropolitan, 1975).

Forsell, [Carl] **John** (originally Johan) (b. 6 Nov 1858; d. 30 May 1941), Swedish baritone. Directed Royal Swedish Opera, 1923–39. Himself a famous Don Giovanni, he was the teacher of BJÖRLING and SVANHOLM.

Forzanti, Lionello, *see* QUARTETTO ITALIANO.

Foster, Lawrence [Thomas] (b. 23 Oct 1941), American conductor. A regular guest conductor with the ROYAL PHILHARMONIC ORCHESTRA, 1969–74; he has been music director of the HOUSTON SYMPHONY ORCHESTRA, 1971–8, and the Lausanne Chamber Orchestra, from 1985. He gave the first performance of Birtwistle's orchestral work *The Triumph of Time*, 1972, and conducted Walton's *Troilus and Cressida* at Covent Garden, 1976.

Foster, Muriel (b. 22 Nov 1877; d. 23 Dec 1937), British contralto. Among the most prominent British concert artists of her day. She was much prized as the Angel in Elgar's *The Dream of Gerontius* from its second Düsseldorf performance, 1902; soloist in the première of Elgar's *The Music Makers*, 1912.

Fournet, Jean (b. 14 Apr 1913), French conductor, formerly flautist. Conductor of the Dutch Radio Orchestra at Hilversum, 1961–73, and of the Rotterdam Philharmonic, 1968–73; he was also continuously active in France. On 78 and LP he recorded an exceptionally large amount of French orchestral music (some of it little known) with such soloists as MENUHIN and Paul TORTELIER, and also Dutch works.

Fournier, Jean, *see* FOURNIER (PIERRE) and JANIGRO.

Fournier, Pierre (b. 24 June 1906; d. 8 Jan 1986), French cellist. Led a distinguished international career, despite suffering from poliomyelitis. He made his first US tour 1948. Among the works dedicated to him are Poulenc's Cello Sonata, 1948, and Frank Martin's Concerto (première 1967). He was a chamber-music partner of BACKHAUS, SCHNABEL and others. From 1970 he was resident in Switzerland. His brother Jean Fournier (b. 1911) is a violinist.

Fou Ts'ong (b. 10 Mar 1934), Chinese-born pianist, naturalized British 1965. A prizewinner at European competitions from 1953; he studied in Poland and then settled in London, 1958. (Married to MENUHIN's daughter Zamira, 1961–70.) In 1980 he began returning regularly to China to perform and teach; became honorary professor at Beijing Conservatory.

Fowke, Philip [Francis] (b. 28 June 1950), British pianist. Made London recital début 1974 and has played regularly at the Proms from 1979; he has performed in USA from 1982 and toured widely elsewhere. His recordings include the Bliss Piano Concerto as well as standard works.

Fox, Virgil [Keel] (b. 3 May 1912; d. 25 Oct 1980), American organist. His career grew from a New York church appointment, 1946–65, to nationwide concerts (with a light show) that attracted huge audiences. Shared in inauguration of the organ of the Philharmonic Hall, New York, 1962; he was the first American to play at Bach's church (St Thomas's) in Leipzig.

Frager, Malcolm (b. 15 Jan 1935), American pianist. After winning the Queen Elisabeth Competition (Brussels), 1960, developed an international career; he had particular success in USSR from 1963. He has performed 'original' versions of familiar works, including the Schumann Concerto, and occasionally plays early pianos. (*See also* MILANOVA.)

Francescatti, Zino (originally René-Charles) (b. 9 Aug 1902), French violinist. Shortly after his Paris début, performed in Britain with Ravel as pianist, 1926. He toured internationally in the 1930s; made US début 1939 and then lived largely in New York until he retired to France. Eminent concerto player; also partnered Robert

CASADESUS for recordings of Beethoven sonatas.

Francesina, La, *see* DUPARC.

Franchomme, Auguste [Joseph] (b. 10 Apr 1808; d. 21 Jan 1884). French cellist, also composer. Prominent among Paris musicians, he became a close friend of Chopin and was the dedicatee of Chopin's Cello Sonata; they played its last three movements at Chopin's final Paris concert, 1848. He also befriended Mendelssohn and was a chamber-music partner of HALLÉ (in Paris).

François, Samson (b. 18 May 1924; d. 22 Oct 1970). French pianist (born in Frankfurt). Studied in Paris with CORTOT and became well known after World War II in Chopin and Ravel. Played the solo part in the première of his own Piano Concerto, 1951. He was one of the first Western artists to perform in communist China, 1964.

Frank, Maurits, *see* AMAR QUARTET.

Frankl, Peter (b. 2 Oct 1935). Hungarian-born pianist, naturalized British 1967. After studying in Budapest (his teachers included Kodály), won the Long–Thibaud Competition in Paris, 1957, and (with PAUK, an associate since student days) a duo competition in Munich. His international career (British début 1962, US début 1965) has continued the duo with Pauk; KIRSHBAUM became their trio partner. Frankl has recorded all Debussy's piano music.

Franklin, David [Henry Cyril] (b. 17 May 1908; d. 22 Oct 1973). British bass. Began his operatic career at pre-war Glyndebourne and was among the most prominent British singers at Covent Garden, 1947–50 (his roles included Ochs in *Der Rosenkavalier*). Retired after a throat operation and became a successful lecturer and broadcaster.

Frederick the Great (Friedrich II) (b. 24 Jan 1712; d. 17 Aug 1786). King of Prussia, amateur flautist and composer. As his house musician, C. P. E. Bach provided him with flute sonatas and other works; the fruit of J. S. Bach's visit of 1747 was the chamber work *The Musical Offering*, based on a theme by the King.

Freeman, Paul (b. 2 Jan 1936). American conductor. One of the few black conductors to win recognized status in recording (for example with the LONDON PHILHARMONIC and the ROYAL PHILHARMONIC ORCHESTRA) and concerts. Resident conductor of DETROIT SYMPHONY ORCHESTRA, 1970–79, then music director of Victoria Symphony Orchestra (British Columbia). He has prominently performed and recorded black composers.

Freire (originally Pinto Freire), **Nelson** [José] (b. 18 Oct 1944). Brazilian pianist. Made début aged five and won international competition in Rio de Janeiro at thirteen; later studied in Vienna. He made first appearances in Britain 1968, in USA 1969, and became well known in the solo repertory and in a duo with ARGERICH.

Freitas Branco, Pedro de (b. 31 Oct 1896; d. 24 Mar 1963). Portuguese conductor. Active in opera and concerts in Lisbon from the mid-1920s; organized the Portuguese National Radio Orchestra, 1934. He was chosen by Ravel to conduct the première of his Piano Concerto in G, with the composer as soloist, at the Paris Ravel Festival, 1931. His brother was the composer Luís de Freitas Branco.

Frémaux, Louis (b. 13 Aug 1921). French conductor. Chief conductor of the National Opera Orchestra of Monte Carlo, 1956–65, then active in Lyons. His music directorship of the CITY OF BIRMINGHAM SYMPHONY ORCHESTRA, 1969–78, improved the orchestra's standing (with important recordings), but ended abruptly. He was music director of the SYDNEY SYMPHONY ORCHESTRA, 1979–82.

Fremstad, Olive (b. 14 Mar 1871; d. 21 Apr 1951). Swedish-born American soprano. Also sang mezzo-soprano roles such as Carmen. The child of an unmarried mother, she was adopted by a Scandinavian-American couple. Studied in Berlin. Her Covent Garden appearances, 1902–3, included the first British performance of Ethel Smyth's German opera *Der Wald*, 1902. She became a major star at the Metropolitan, 1903–14 (title role in the US première of *Salome*, 1907), but left after a disagreement with the management.

Freni (originally Fregni), **Mirella** (b. 27 Feb 1935), Italian soprano. Made her début in 1955; sang Nannetta in *Falstaff* as her first role at Covent Garden, 1961, and La Scala, 1962. Later, especially under KARAJAN at Salzburg, took heavier roles such as Aida. Recordings range from Handel to Tchaikovsky (Tatyana in *Yevgeny Onegin*; also at Covent Garden, 1988).

Freund, Marya (b. 12 Dec 1876; d. 21 May 1966), German-born French soprano (born in Breslau, now Wrocław), mother of Doda CONRAD. Also studied violin. She took part in the première of Schoenberg's *Gurrelieder* (Vienna), 1913, and later settled in France. A notable interpreter of new music by various composers, she was the first in Britain to perform Schoenberg's *Pierrot lunaire* (three performances in two days), 1923.

Frick, Gottlob (b. 28 July 1906), German bass. His dark cast of voice made him celebrated in Wagner. He was based in East Germany (Dresden and Berlin) till 1953. Became known at Bayreuth from 1951, Covent Garden from 1951 (*The Ring*), the Metropolitan, 1961, and elsewhere. Also successful in comic roles.

Fricsay, Ferenc (b. 9 Aug 1914; d. 20 Feb 1963), Hungarian conductor. Worked with the HUNGARIAN STATE SYMPHONY ORCHESTRA, 1945–8. In 1947, replacing the indisposed KLEMPERER, he gave the Salzburg première of Einem's opera, *Dantons Tod*. Decisively established the orchestra of Berlin Radio as its music director, 1948–54 (then called RIAS, Radio in the American Sector), and made important recordings with it. After a short conductorship of the HOUSTON SYMPHONY ORCHESTRA, 1954, he became opera director in Munich and then returned to his Berlin orchestra, 1959; he inaugurated the rebuilt West Berlin Opera House, 1961. Died in Switzerland.

Fried, Miriam (b. 9 Sept 1946), Romanian-born Israeli violinist. Her parents emigrated when she was two. Studied in Tel Aviv, later in USA with Josef Gingold and GALAMIAN. Won the Paganini Competition (Genoa), 1968, and the Queen Elisabeth (Brussels), 1971. Her British début with the Menuhin Festival Orchestra at Windsor Castle, 1971, helped to launch an international career.

Fried, Oskar (b. 10 Aug 1871; d. 5 July 1941). German-born conductor, previously horn player, became naturalized citizen of USSR 1940. Friend and champion of Mahler, he was himself a composer. Having held important choral and orchestral positions in Berlin, he left Nazi Germany, 1934, and went to USSR. Conducted opera in Tbilisi and then a radio orchestra in Moscow (where he died).

Friedheim, Arthur (b. 26 Oct 1859; d. 19 Oct 1932), Russian-born German pianist, also composer. Studied with Anton RUBINSTEIN but disagreed with his method and went to LISZT; became both his student and his secretary. He was later recognized as a pre-eminent interpreter of Liszt's music. Professor at Royal Manchester College of Music, 1895–1904; from 1915 he worked mainly in USA and Canada. Died in New York.

Friedman, Ignaz (in Polish form, Ignacy) (b. 14 Feb 1882; d. 26 Jan 1948), Polish pianist. After studying with LESCHETIZKY in Vienna, began an international virtuoso's career, 1904; he is said to have given 2,800 concerts. With HUBERMAN and CASALS played Beethoven trios in Vienna to celebrate Beethoven centenary, 1927. In 1940 settled in Sydney, where he died.

Frijsh, Povla (originally Paula Frisch) (b. 3 Aug 1881; d. 10 July 1960), Danish soprano. First studied piano. She made her vocal début in Paris and developed her career there and in USA (début 1915). She is said to have introduced spirituals to Paris recital audiences. Died in USA.

Froment, Louis de (b. 5 Dec 1921), French conductor. Toured with his own Paris-based chamber orchestra (with RAMPAL as soloist) and conducted at the Opéra-Comique. He was conductor of the Luxembourg Radio–Television Orchestra, 1958–80 (afterwards a regular guest). With that and other orchestras he made many recordings, including all Debussy's orchestral works.

Frugoni, Orazio (b. 28 Jan 1921), Swiss-born Italian pianist. Made the first recording of early piano concerto (in E flat, unnumbered, 1784) by Beethoven. He was active in USA, 1947–67, then taught in Florence.

Frühbeck de Burgos, Rafael (b. 15 Sept 1933), Spanish conductor of German descent. (His father's surname was Frühbeck.) After final studies in Germany, he worked in Spain (conductor of the SPANISH NATIONAL ORCHESTRA, 1962–78) and elsewhere, for example with the NEW PHILHARMONIA ORCHESTRA, from 1969. He was music director for the city of Düsseldorf, 1966–71, and of the MONTREAL SYMPHONY ORCHESTRA, 1975–7. Recorded many zarzuelas as well as symphonic works.

Fuchs, Carl, *see* BRODSKY QUARTET (1).

Fueri, Maurice, *see* LOEWENGUTH QUARTET.

Fugère, Lucien (b. 22 July 1848; d. 15 Jan 1935), French baritone. Began as a café entertainer; he became a Parisian favourite in opera (the Father in the first performance of Gustave Charpentier's *Louise*, 1900) and operetta. He celebrated his eightieth birthday by singing the role of the Duke in Messager's *La Basoche*, which he had created thirty-eight years before.

Furet, Charles-Joseph, *see* CAPET QUARTET.

Furmedge, Edyth, *see* GILLY.

Furtwängler, [Gustav Heinrich Ernst Martin] **Wilhelm** (b. 25 Jan 1886; d. 30 Nov 1954), German conductor. Even after his death he continued through recordings to be highly esteemed and influential. He was chief conductor of the BERLIN PHILHARMONIC ORCHESTRA, 1922–45 and 1948–54, and of the VIENNA PHILHARMONIC, 1927–30; guest conductor in London from 1924 (Wagner at Covent Garden from 1935) and New York from 1925. His first performances included Bartók's Piano Concerto no. 1, 1927, Schoenberg's Variations for orchestra, 1928, and Hindemith's *Mathis der Maler* symphony, 1934. In 1934, under Nazi rule, he resigned his Berlin posts, but soon afterwards resumed and developed his career. Accusations (false or exaggerated) of Nazi complicity delayed his post-war return to international acceptance (London, 1948; never in USA). He conducted the first performance of Strauss's Four Last Songs (with FLAGSTAD), 1950, and the concert that reopened the Bayreuth Festival in 1951.

G

Gabrieli Quartet, London-based string quartet founded 1966. Original members were Kenneth Sillito, Brendan O'Reilly, Ian Jewel and Keith Harvey; John Georgiadis took over as leader in 1987. The group has given first performances of several works, including Crosse's Quartet no. 1, 1980.

Gabrielli, Caterina (b. 12 Nov 1730; d. 16 Feb or 16 Apr 1796), Italian soprano. Assumed the surname of the prince for whom her father worked as a cook. She became well known in Italy and from 1755 sang in Vienna, where she took part in the first performances of Gluck operas, including *L'innocenza giustificata*, 1755. She was involved in various theatrical scandals.

Gabrilowitsch, Ossip [Osip Solomonovich Gabrilovich] (b. 7 Feb 1878; d. 14 Sept 1936), Russian-born American pianist and conductor. First played in USA 1900. In both Europe and USA he gave series of 'historical' concerts showing the development of the concerto. Conducted the DETROIT SYMPHONY ORCHESTRA from 1918 until his death, but he kept up his piano career and was also a composer. He married the contralto Clara Clemens (1874–1962), daughter of Mark Twain.

Gadski, Johanna [Emilia Agnes] (b. 15 June 1872; d. 22 Feb 1932), German soprano. Celebrated chiefly in USA. She worked with Walter DAMROSCH's opera company from 1895 and became a leading Wagner singer at the Metropolitan; also sang at Covent Garden (Aida and other roles), 1898–1901. On US involvement in World War I, 1917, she returned to Germany, but she reappeared in USA in 1929 and then organized her own opera seasons. Killed in a car accident.

Galamian, Ivan [Alexander] (b. 5 Feb 1903; d. 14 Apr 1981), Persian-born American violinist of Armenian parentage. Celebrated teacher in Philadelphia and New York: PERLMAN and ZUKERMAN were among his pupils. He has edited many violin works and written books on violin technique.

Galkovsky, Alexander, *see* SHOSTAKOVICH QUARTET.

Gall [originally Galle], **Yvonne** (b. 6 Mar 1885; d. 21 Aug 1972), French soprano. Prominent at the Paris Opera, for example as Marguerite in *Faust*; she took part in its 200th Parisian performance, 1934. She also sang opera at Chicago, 1918–21, and was the soloist in the première of Florent Schmitt's Psalm 47, 1906. In 1958 she married the composer Henri Büsser.

Galli, Filippo (b. 1783; d. 3 June 1853), Italian bass. His operatic roles at La Scala, 1812–29, exceeded sixty. Elsewhere he gave first performances of Mustapha in Rossini's *L'Italiana in Algeri*, 1813, Assur in Rossini's *Semiramide*, 1823, and Henry VIII in Donizetti's *Anna Bolena*, 1830. He died a pauper in Paris.

Galli-Curci, Amelita (b. 18 Nov 1882; d. 26 Nov 1963), Italian soprano. Curci was her married name, 1910–20. A sensational performance as Gilda in *Rigoletto* inaugurated her operatic success at Chicago, 1916–36, and the Metropolitan, 1921–30. Through recordings, for example of the 'Bell Song' from Delibes's *Lakmé*, she became the epitome of coloratura singing. Her only appearances in Britain, 1924–34, were in concert.

Galliera, Alceo (b. 3 May 1910), Italian conductor, also composer. Spent World War II in Switzerland and held orchestral posts in Melbourne, Genoa and Strasbourg. He is best known from his many successful records, including those of concerts with ARRAU, David OISTRAKH and Pierre FOURNIER, and *Il barbiere* with CALLAS and GOBBI, 1957.

Galli-Marié (née Marié de l'Isle), **Celestine** [Laurence] (b. Nov 1840; d. 22 Sept 1905), French mezzo-soprano. The creator of the title roles of Ambroise Thomas's *Mignon*, 1866, and Bizet's *Carmen*, 1875, she sang in London with a visiting French company, 1886. She was also distinguished in Offenbach's operettas.

Galway, James (b. 8 Dec 1939), Irish flautist. After six years in the BERLIN PHILHARMONIC under KARAJAN, began a successful solo career in 1975. He performed a classical and near-pop repertory, with many new works (including Rodrigo's *Concierto pastoral*, 1979, and Corigliano's *The Pied Piper*, 1982) and special arrangements. Gave the first British performance of Musgrave's *Orfeo II*, 1976. He plays an eighteen-carat gold flute; has become a top-selling recording artist. His career was interrupted, 1978–9, by a severe accident.

Gamba, Piero (b. 16 Sept 1936), Italian conductor. A child prodigy; conducted a Beethoven and Dvořák concert at Harringay Arena, London, aged eleven. After a temporary withdrawal he emerged as a mature artist; appeared in London and elsewhere from 1959 and recorded all the Beethoven piano concertos with KATCHEN as soloist. Music director of Winnipeg Symphony Orchestra, 1970–80.

Ganz, Rudolph (b. 24 Feb 1877; d. 2 Aug 1972), Swiss-born American pianist and conductor, also composer, previously cellist. Made début as a cellist at the age of twelve. Taught piano in Chicago from 1901, and made New York début as a pianist 1906. He was music director of the ST LOUIS SYMPHONY ORCHESTRA, 1921–7, and later conducted successful seasons of young people's concerts, 1938–49.

Ganz, Wilhelm (b. 6 Nov 1833; d. 12 Sept 1914). German pianist and conductor. Active in Britain; he accompanied LIND, 1856, and conducted a concert series in London, 1871–81, in which Berlioz's *Symphonie fantastique* had its first complete London performance. Also taught singing at the Guildhall School of Music.

Ganzarolli, Wladimiro (b. 9 Jan 1932), Italian bass-baritone. Performed at La Scala from 1959 and became internationally known in Rossini and Mozart. He first appeared at Covent Garden 1965 (title role in *Figaro*); his recordings include Meyerbeer's *Les Huguenots* with SUTHERLAND, 1962.

Garbuzova (uses the spelling Garbousova in the West), **Raya** (b. 10 Oct 1905), Russian-born American cellist. Emigrated 1925 and settled in USA 1927. She became well known in appearances with major European and US orchestras. Among the works written for her is Barber's Cello Concerto (she gave the first performance, 1946). Also active as a teacher and music editor.

García, Manuel [del Popolo Vicente Rodríguez] (1) (b. 21 Jan 1775; d. 9 June 1832), Spanish tenor, also composer, father of Manuel GARCÍA (2), Maria MALIBRAN and Pauline VIARDOT-GARCIA. Sang in Paris then went to Italy; Rossini wrote the role of Almaviva in *Il barbiere* for him, 1816, and he sang at its first performances in Paris, London and New York. His was the first Italian opera company to visit USA (also Mexico), 1825–8. After returning to Paris, he concentrated on composition (he wrote over forty operas) and teaching.

García, Manuel [Patricio Rodríguez] **(2)** (b. 17 Mar 1805; d. 1 July 1906), son of Manuel GARCÍA (1). Spanish baritone and singing teacher. Having sung in his father's company in USA and Mexico, retired from the stage, studied physiology and won world fame by inventing the laryngoscope, 1855. He taught singing in Paris and for a longer period in London, 1848–95, where he settled (and died). LIND and SANTLEY studied with him.

Garcin (originally Salomon), **Jules Auguste** (b. 11 July 1830; d. 10 Oct 1896), French conductor. Took the name of his maternal grandfather. In 1885 he was appointed principal conductor of the Paris Opera and the orchestra of the SOCIÉTÉ DES CONCERTS DU CONSERVATOIRE, with which he gave the first performance of Franck's Symphony, 1889, and promoted Brahms's work against Parisian opposition. He was also a composer.

Gardelli, Lamberto (b. 8 Nov 1915), Italian-born Swedish conductor. Conducted Royal Swedish Opera, 1946–55, the DANISH RADIO SYMPHONY ORCHESTRA, 1959–61, and the BAVARIAN RADIO SYMPHONY ORCHESTRA, from 1982. He is best known in Italian opera, for example *Otello* (Covent Garden, 1979). Made the first complete recording of Rossini's *Guillaume Tell*, 1973.

Garden, Mary (b. 20 Feb 1874; d. 3 Jan 1967), American soprano (born in Scotland). Taken to USA as a child. She was the first Mélisande in Debussy's *Pelléas et Mélisande* in Paris, 1902, and also sang in its first US performance (New York), 1908. She had made her Paris début in 1900, replacing (in mid-performance) the star of Gustave Charpentier's *Louise*. Debussy dedicated his *Ariettes oubliées* to her, 1903. She formed the Chicago Civic Opera and became its director for the season 1921–2. After her performing career ended, she taught and lectured. Retired to Scotland, 1947, and died there.

Gardiner, John Eliot (b. 20 Apr 1943), British conductor. A specialist in Monteverdi, he brought out his own edition of the Vespers and performed it at a Prom in 1968. BOULANGER, with whom he studied in Paris, bequeathed him valuable material. Gave the first concert performance (London, 1975) and first stage performance (Aix-en-Provence, 1982) of Rameau's rediscovered opera *Les Boréades*; director of Lyons Opera, 1983–8. The composer H. Balfour Gardiner was his great-uncle.

Gaubert, Philippe (b. 3 July 1879; d. 8 July 1941), French conductor, also composer. Conductor of the orchestra of the SOCIÉTÉ DES CONCERTS DU CONSERVATOIRE in Paris, 1919–38. As music director of Paris Opera, 1924–39, he conducted the première of Roussel's *Padmâvatî*, 1923. His concert performances of Monteverdi's *Orfeo*, 1934–5, are said to have constituted the opera's first modern revival.

Gaudeamus Quartet, Dutch string quartet founded 1954. Its original members were Jos Verkoeyen, Jan Brejaart, Jan van der Velde and Joep Voigtschmidt. In name and purpose (promoting modern music), it is associated with the Gaudeamus Foundation. Members in 1989: Jan Wittenberg, Paul Hendriks, Hans Neuberger and Béla Santo.

Gauk, Alexander [Vasilyevich] (b. 15 Aug 1893; d. 30 Mar 1963), Russian conductor, also composer. As chief conductor of the LENINGRAD PHILHARMONIC ORCHESTRA, 1930–33, gave the first performance of Shostakovich's Symphony no. 3, 1930. Later worked in Moscow, where he salvaged Rakhmaninov's Symphony no. 1 (suppressed by the composer after its unsuccessful première, 1897) from the orchestral parts and performed it, 1945.

Gaultier, Denis (b. *c.* 1600; d. Jan 1672), French lutenist, also composer. Unlike many other musicians, he held no court or similar appointment but worked for different patrons. His compositions for lute, esteemed in themselves, were influential also on harpsichord style. The lutenist and composer Ennemond Gaultier (1575–1651) was his cousin; scholars do not always find it possible to ascribe authorship between them.

Gaultier, Ennemond, *see* GAULTIER, DENIS.

Gavazzeni, Gianandrea (b. 25 July 1909), Italian conductor, also composer and writer on music. Made his British début at the 1957 Edinburgh Festival with the Piccola Scala company from Milan and was later director of La Scala itself, 1965–72. He has made many opera recordings, including rarities such as Mascagni's *Iris*, 1956.

Gavrilov, Andrey (b. 21 Sept 1955), Russian pianist. Won the Moscow Tchaikovsky Competition in 1974. He studied with Svyatoslav RICHTER (who rarely accepts pupils), and in the 1980–81 season they shared concert performances of Handel's suites. His repertory includes the Berg Concerto (for piano and thirteen wind instruments) and Ravel's Concerto for the left hand. He first performed in London in 1976; exceptionally, moves freely between USSR and the West.

Gay, Maria (b. 13 June 1879; d. 29 July 1943), Spanish contralto. Self-taught; PUGNO 'discovered' her while travelling in Spain. She made her operatic début as Carmen (Brussels), 1902, which was also her Metropolitan début role (with TOSCANINI conducting), 1908. Sang at Covent Garden in 1906. Gay was her first husband's surname; in 1913 she married the tenor ZENATELLO.

Gayarre, Julián (originally Gayarre Sebástian) (b. 9 Jan 1844; d. 2 Jan 1890), Spanish tenor. Sang at Covent Garden from 1877, including the first British performances of Massenet's *Le Roi de Lahore* and Glinka's *A Life for the Tsar*. At La Scala he was Enzo in the première of Ponchielli's *La gioconda*, 1875. He suddenly lost his voice in mid-performance of Bizet's *Les Pêcheurs de perles* in Madrid, 1889.

Gayer [originally Ashkenasi], **Catherine** (b. 11 Feb 1937), American soprano. Trained in Germany and won distinction in modern opera: she took part in the first performances of Nono's *Intolleranza 1960*, 1961, Reimann's *Melusine* (title role), 1971, and Robin Orr's *Hermiston*, 1975. Her other roles include the Queen of the Night in *Die Zauberflöte* (Covent Garden, 1962).

Gazzelloni, Severino (b. 5 Jan 1919), Italian flautist. Combined mastery of the baroque repertory with a special disposition for the new music of severest technical difficulty. Works written for him include Haubenstock-Ramati's *Interpolation* (a 'mobile' for unaccompanied flute), 1958, and Schurmann's Sonatina, 1968.

Gedda (originally Ustinov), **Nicolai** [Harry Gustaf] (b. 11 July 1925), Swedish tenor. His father was Russian; Gedda was his mother's surname. From the Royal Swedish Opera, 1952, he proceeded straight to an international career. At La Scala he was in the first performance of Orff's *Il trionfo di Afrodite*, 1953; made his début at Covent Garden as the Duke in *Rigoletto*, 1955. Multilingual and with an exceptionally high register, he showed equal ease in Russian, German and French opera (and operetta) and performed on over 100 recordings.

Geistinger, Marie (b. 20 July 1828; d. 28 Sept 1903), Austrian soprano. Celebrated in operetta in Vienna. Offenbach praised her in the title role of his *La Belle Hélène*. She created main roles in the first performances of several operettas by the younger Johann Strauss, including *Die Fledermaus* (as Rosalinde), 1874, while she was also joint manager of her theatre.

Gencer, Leyla (b. 10 Oct 1924), Turkish soprano. Made her début in Ankara as Tosca, 1952, and developed a career mainly in Italian dramatic roles. Sang at La Scala from 1956, and participated in the première there of Pizzetti's *Assassinio nella cattedrale*, 1958; Covent Garden from 1962. Her Glyndebourne roles, from 1962, included Donizetti's Anna Bolena.

Gendron, Maurice (b. 26 Dec 1920; d. 20 Aug 1990), French cellist. Well known as a teacher at the Yehudi Menuhin School (UK) and elsewhere. He first appeared in London in 1945 when he gave the first West European performance of Prokofiev's Cello Concerto no. 1. Trio partner of Yehudi and Hephzibah MENUHIN, and occasional conductor.

George, Alan, *see* FITZWILLIAM QUARTET.

Georges, Jacques, *see* LOEWENGUTH QUARTET.

Georgiadis, John, *see* GABRIELI QUARTET.

Georgian, Karine, *see* KRAINEV.

Gerhardt, Elena (b. 11 Nov 1883; d. 11 Jan 1961), German-born soprano, later mezzo-soprano, naturalized British after leaving Nazi Germany. She was highly esteemed in songs by Schubert and Wolf, and made important recordings. Sang no opera. Died in London.

Geringas, David (b. 29 July 1946), Soviet-Lithuanian cellist. Pupil of ROSTROPOVICH. In 1970 he won the Moscow Tchaikovsky Competition. Settled in West Germany, 1976, where he performed and taught. At the Salzburg Festival of 1983 he gave the first performance of Krenek's Cello Concerto no. 1.

Germani, Fernando (b. 5 Apr 1906), Italian organist. Studied composition with Respighi. He was known as a soloist from the early 1920s. In 1936 he first visited London and took up a two-year teaching post at the Curtis Institute, Philadelphia. Became the first in Italy to perform the complete organ works of Bach, 1945. He was principal organist at St Peter's, Rome, 1948–59.

Gerster, Etelka (b. 25 June 1855; d. 20 Aug 1920), Hungarian soprano. Recommended by Verdi, made her début as Gilda in *Rigoletto* at Venice, 1876; thereafter performed in London (Bellini's *La sonnambula*), 1877, New York, 1878, and elsewhere. She was considered a younger rival to PATTI, but did not win Patti's immortality.

Gertler, André (originally Endre) (b. 16 July 1907), Hungarian violinist. Settled in Belgium, 1928, and became noted as a soloist in modern music (and also as the leader of his own string quartet, 1931–51). In 1945 he gave the first European performance of Bartók's Sonata for solo violin: performed Berg's Concerto about 150 times.

Geszty, Sylvia (b. 28 Feb 1934), Hungarian soprano. Famous in coloratura roles such as the Queen of the Night in *Die Zauberflöte* (Covent Garden début, 1966) and Zerbinetta in Strauss's *Ariadne auf Naxos* (Glyndebourne, 1971). She sang in Moscow and at the Salzburg Festival. Became professor of singing at Stuttgart, 1975.

Gewandhaus Orchestra of Leipzig, German orchestra. Its foundation may be traced to a concert in 1781; named after its hall ('Cloth House'). Principal conductors have included Mendelssohn, 1835–47, NIKISCH, 1895–1922, FURTWÄNGLER, 1922–8, WALTER, 1929–33, ABENDROTH, 1934–45, and, under the post-war East German regime, KONWITSCHNY, 1949–62, NEUMANN, 1964–8, and MASUR, from 1970.

Geyer, Steffi (b. 28 Jan 1888; d. 11 Dec 1956), Hungarian violinist. Settled in Switzerland. Bartók, who was in love with her, wrote a concerto for her, 1907, which she never performed; since its première, 1958, it has been called no. 1. Othmar Schoeck, also enamoured of her, likewise wrote a concerto for her. She married the composer Walter Schulthess.

Ghiaurov, Nikolay, *see* GYAUROV.

Ghiglia, Oscar (b. 13 Aug 1938), Italian guitarist. Self-taught at first, later took formal study in Rome and with SEGOVIA. He won a French radio and television guitar contest in 1963; made his concert début in London and New York 1966, in Paris 1968. He has taught in USA. His recordings include songs by Peter Maxwell Davies, accompanying DEGAETANI.

Ghiuselev, Nikolay, *see* GYUZELEV.

Giannini, Dusolina (b. 19 Dec 1900; d. 29 June 1986), American soprano, daughter of Ferruccio GIANNINI. Created the role of Hester in *The Scarlet Letter*, 1938, an opera by her brother, Vittorio Giannini. Having already appeared in concert, she made her professional opera début in Hamburg, 1925, sang Aida at Covent Garden, 1928, and took various roles at the Metropolitan, 1936–41. She performed as Tosca in New York City Opera's opening performance, 1944.

Giannini, Ferruccio (b. 15 Nov 1868; d. 17 Sept 1948), Italian tenor, father of Dusolina GIANNINI. Made one of the earliest operatic recordings, 1896. He settled in Philadelphia and ran a small theatre where operas, plays and concerts were given. Died in Philadelphia.

Gibson, Alexander [Drummond] (b. 11 Feb 1926), British conductor. Worked at Sadler's Wells Opera (finally as music director, 1957–9), and then as music director of the SCOTTISH NATIONAL ORCHESTRA, 1959–1984. Conducted the première of Weir's *Ballad*, 1981. He was the founding music director of Scottish Opera, 1962–87. From 1967 he also conducted widely in USA; gave the first US performance of Monteverdi's opera *Il ritorno d'Ulisse*, 1974. His recordings include all Mozart's works for violin and orchestra (with SZERYNG). Knighted, 1977.

Giebel, Agnes (b. 10 Aug 1921), German soprano (born in the Netherlands). Grew up in Essen. She won distinction as a Bach performer, particularly on German radio and recordings from 1951, and developed a notable concert career without operatic appearances. Her repertory embraced Berg, Britten and Henze as well as Bach's *St Matthew Passion* (twice recorded) and Brahms's *German Requiem*.

Gielen, Michael [Andreas] (b. 20 July 1927),

Austrian conductor, also composer, formerly pianist. Performed Schoenberg's complete piano works in Buenos Aires, 1949. He was principal conductor at the Royal Swedish Opera, 1960–65; at Cologne he conducted the première of Bernd Alois Zimmermann's *Die Soldaten*, 1965. His skilled advocacy of modern music won little support during his conductorship of the CINCINNATI SYMPHONY ORCHESTRA, 1980–86. He then became conductor of the SÜDWESTFUNK ORCHESTRA at Baden-Baden.

Gieseking, Walter (b. 5 Nov 1895; d. 26 Oct 1956), German pianist (born in France). Recognized in his lifetime as one of the most eminent exponents of the classical German and Austrian repertory and also of Debussy and Ravel (recorded their complete piano music). He made his début in London 1923 and in New York 1926. Gave the first performance of concertos by Petrassi, 1939, and others. Having remained active in Germany during World War II, he later had to answer accusations of Nazi collaboration before resuming world career (New York reappearance in 1953).

Gigli, Beniamino (b. 20 Mar 1890; d. 30 Nov 1957), Italian tenor. Among the most celebrated performers of his time, particularly on records and in many recital tours, including those from 1947 to 1956 immediately before retirement. Previously he was prominent in opera, mainly Italian: Metropolitan début as Faust in Boito's *Mefistofele*, 1920, Covent Garden début 1930 in the title role of Giordano's *Andrea Chenier*. Made his last Covent Garden appearance 1946 in *La Bohème* opposite his daughter Rina Gigli (b. 1916).

Gigli, Rina, *see* GIGLI, BENIAMINO.

Gigout, Eugène (b. 23 Mar 1844; d. 9 Dec 1925), French organist. Appointed to Paris church (St Augustin), 1863, and remained over sixty years until he died. He was active as a concert soloist (toured Britain and elsewhere) and teacher; composed much for his instrument and was famous for his improvisations.

Gilbert, Kenneth (b. 16 Dec 1931), Canadian harpsichordist, also organist. Made London début 1968 and then became very active in France and Germany (teacher at Stuttgart and Strasbourg). Noted for combining scholarship and performance, he has edited the complete sonatas of Domenico Scarlatti; he also edited, and recorded, the complete harpsichord works of François Couperin.

Gilels, Elena, *see* GILELS, EMIL.

Gilels, Emil [Grigoryevich] (b. 19 Oct 1916; d. 14 Oct 1985), Russian pianist. Pupil of NEUHAUS and one of the chief representatives of Soviet music (twice awarded the Order of Lenin). In 1944 he gave the first public performance of Prokofiev's Sonata no. 8, the composer having previously played it to a restricted gathering. World War II interrupted his career, and his New York début was not made until 1956, his London début 1959. His daughter Elena (b. 1948) is also a pianist. (*See also* KOGAN.)

Gilly, Dinh (b. 19 July, 1877; d. 19 May 1940), Algerian-born French baritone. Prominent at the Paris Opera, 1902–8, and at the Metropolitan, 1909–14, where he sang Sonora in the first performance of Puccini's *La fanciulla del West*, 1910; at this opera's first British performance (Covent Garden, 1911) he took the principal baritone role, Rance. Made notable recordings, 1920–28, and with his wife, the contralto Edith Furmedge (1890–1956), directed a singing school in London.

Gilmore, Patrick Sarsfield (b. 25 Dec 1829; d. 24 Sept 1892), Irish-born American bandmaster and promoter. Successful military band concerts (sometimes with cannon addition) led to his 'National Peace Jubilee' in Boston, 1867, with six bands and an orchestra of 1,000, and to an even larger ten-day event in 1872, with an orchestra of up to 2,000 and GODDARD as pianist. He was also a composer; the song 'When Johnny Comes Marching Home' is ascribed to him.

Gimpel, Bronislav (b. 29 Jan 1911; d. 1 May 1979), Austrian-born American violinist, brother of Jakob GIMPEL. Emigrated to USA, 1937. Known as a soloist (for example in recordings of Bach's unaccompanied works) and in chamber music. He was leader of the (American) Warsaw Quartet, 1962–7, and of the New England Quartet, 1967–73. He died eight days before a projected joint recital with his brother.

Gimpel, Jakob (b. 16 Apr 1906; d. 12 Mar 1989), Austrian-born American pianist, brother of Bronislav GIMPEL. His Vienna début, 1923, led to a successful career in Germany, which was interrupted by the Nazis; went to Palestine and was associated with HUBERMAN. He settled in Los Angeles, 1938, where in addition to performing he wrote film scores and taught.

Girard, Narcisse (b. 27 Jan 1797; d. 16 Jan 1860), French conductor. Gave the première (which the composer called a massacre) of Berlioz's *Harold en Italie* (with URHAN), 1834. He was prominent in Paris as a conductor of both concerts (*see* SOCIÉTÉ DES CONCERTS DU CONSERVATOIRE) and opera. He died while conducting a performance of Meyerbeer's *Les Huguenots*.

Giron, *see* CAPET QUARTET.

Giuliani, Mauro [Giuseppe Sergio Pantaleo] (b. 27 July 1781; d. 8 May 1829), Italian guitarist, also composer and cellist. Settled in Vienna, 1806, where he led a distinguished career. He collaborated with Hummel and Moscheles in works for guitar and piano, and played cello in the première of Beethoven's Symphony no. 7, 1813. Returned to Italy, 1819. As well as the standard guitar he played the lyre-guitar, with its projecting 'wings'.

Giulini, Carlo Maria (b. 9 May 1914), Italian conductor. Made his concert début in Rome, 1944, and his opera début at Bergamo, 1950; proceeded to win highest reputation in both fields. As principal conductor at La Scala, 1953–6, he conducted the famous Visconti production of *La traviata* with CALLAS and DI STEFANO; made Covent Garden début 1958 with Visconti's production of *Don Carlos*. He worked with the CHICAGO SYMPHONY and the VIENNA SYMPHONY ORCHESTRA, and was music director of the LOS ANGELES PHILHARMONIC, 1978–84. His recordings include Bruckner, Mahler and both Brahms's piano concertos (with ARRAU).

Giuranna, Bruno (b. 6 Apr 1933), Italian viola player. Made his solo début under KARAJAN in 1954. He has participated in distinguished ensembles: founding member of I MUSICI, 1952–9, and the Italian String Trio, 1958, and he later joined the VÉGH QUARTET, 1978. Has taught courses in Italy and elsewhere.

Gladkowska, Konstancja (b. 10 June 1810; d. 20 Dec 1889), Polish soprano. She was a fellow-student of Chopin at the Warsaw Conservatory; he fell in love with her and declared that she inspired the slow movement of his Piano Concerto no. 2 and a waltz (op. 70 no. 3). Made her operatic début 1830, but no great success followed.

Glennie, Evelyn (b. 10 July 1965), British percussionist, also pianist. She is profoundly deaf but can sense music's vibrations. Gave London début recital as percussionist 1986; studied the marimba in Japan. Gave première of Richard Rodney Bennett's percussion concerto, 1990. In 1987 performed and recorded Bartók's Sonata for two pianos and percussion with SOLTI, PERAHIA and fellow-percussionist David Corkhill.

Globokar, Vinko (b. 7 July 1934), French-born Yugoslav trombonist, also composer. Trained principally in Paris and Berlin. His virtuosity combined with his many new sound effects and theatrical presentation led various composers to write for him, including Berio (*Sequenza V*, 1966) and Kagel (*Der Atem*, 1970). His advanced and sometimes eccentric instrumental techniques are exploited in some of his own compositions. He has also led ensembles and taught, mainly in Cologne.

Glossop, Peter (b. 6 July 1928), British baritone. Chorus-member and then soloist at Sadler's Wells Opera. He won an international competition in Sofia and made his début at Covent Garden in 1961; his many roles there included the title parts of Verdi's *Nabucco* and *Simon Boccanegra*. Also sang at the Salzburg Festival, from 1970 (Iago in KARAJAN's recorded and filmed *Otello*), and at the Metropolitan (début as Scarpia in *Tosca*, 1969).

Glover, Jane [Alison] (b. 13 May 1949), British conductor. Made her reputation firstly as a musicologist, specializing in Monteverdi and Cavalli, but then became known for her conducting. She conducted at the Glyndebourne Festival from 1981, at the Proms from 1985 and at English National Opera from 1989. Succeeded Harry BLECH as artistic director of the

LONDON MOZART PLAYERS, 1984. She is also a successful television presenter.

Gluck, Alma [originally Reba Fiersohn] (b. 11 May 1884; d. 27 Oct 1938), American soprano (born in Romania). Taken to USA as a child. She appeared with the Metropolitan Opera to 1913 (for example as Sophie in Massenet's *Werther*), but thereafter was a concert singer. Won praise from connoisseurs of vocal refinement as well as achieving huge American popularity. Her recording of 'Carry Me Back to Old Virginny', 1915, reputedly sold two million copies. Gluck was her first husband's surname; her second husband was ZIMBALIST.

Gobbi, Tito (b. 24 Oct 1913; d. 5 Mar 1984), Italian baritone, also from mid-1960s operatic stage director. Sang opera in Italy from 1935, emerging after the war as a major performer: Salzburg Festival (as Don Giovanni), 1948, and Covent Garden with visiting La Scala company, 1950. He was famous as Scarpia in *Tosca* (Metropolitan début, 1956; recorded with CALLAS, 1964) and as Iago in *Otello*. Sang in the first performance of Pizzetti's *Epithalamium* (with chorus and orchestra), 1939; he made more than twenty-five films, not all operatic. The title of Commendatore (Italian state honour) was conferred on him.

Goddard, Arabella (b. 12 Jan 1836; d. 6 Apr 1922), British pianist (born in France). As a child, studied in Paris with KALKBRENNER; at the age of eight she played before Queen Victoria and had six waltzes of her own published. She studied further with, and afterwards married, the music critic J. W. Davison. Often played at the Philharmonic Society concerts. She toured USA, India and Australia, 1873–6, and retired in 1882; died in France. (*See also* CARRODUS and GILMORE.)

Godfrey, Dan (originally Daniel) [Eyers] (b. 20 June 1868; d. 20 July 1939), British conductor. Conducted the (civilian) London Military Band, then worked in Johannesburg. In 1893 he organized for Bournemouth corporation a band that became the BOURNEMOUTH MUNICIPAL ORCHESTRA. As its conductor, till 1934, he gave programmes that helped to promote such British composers as Parry, Elgar and Ethel Smyth. He was also a pioneer in the early recording of orchestral music, from 1925. His father, Dan Godfrey (1831–1903), and son, also called Dan Godfrey (sometimes Dan Godfrey, junior; 1893–1935), were both conductors. The former was the first British Army bandmaster to receive a commission.

Godfrey, Isidore (b. 27 Sept 1900; d. 12 Sept 1977), British conductor. As music director of the D'Oyly Carte Opera Company, 1929–68, he conducted the popular works by Gilbert and Sullivan as well as *Cox and Box* (Burnand and Sullivan), and made many US and other tours. He recorded these pieces (most of them many times over) from 1933. OBE, 1965.

Godowsky, Leopold (b. 13 Feb 1870; d. 21 Nov 1938), Lithuanian-born pianist, naturalized American 1891. Trained in Berlin, he emigrated to USA, and thereafter travelled extensively. His career as an outstanding player ended with a stroke suffered while recording Chopin's nocturnes, 1930. He continued composing and arranging; some of his virtuoso transcriptions (such as the Strauss waltzes) remain standard.

Goehr, Walter (b. 28 May 1903; d. 4 Dec 1960), German conductor. Emigrated to Britain, 1933 (at first used the pseudonym George Walter). He was conductor of the influential Morley College concerts in London from 1943 until his death. Gave the first performances of Britten's *Serenade*, 1943, and Tippett's *A Child of Our Time*, 1944. His son is the composer Alexander Goehr.

Gogorza, Emilio de, *see* EAMES.

Golani, Rivka (b. 22 Mar 1946), Israeli-born viola player, naturalized Canadian 1983. Emigrated to Canada in 1974. She gave the premières of many works, including Colgrass's Chaconne, 1984, and made the first recordings, 1989, of Elgar's Cello Concerto in the arrangement by TERTIS and of Bax's Phantasy for viola and orchestra. Became resident in Britain in 1987; she is married to the conductor Thomas SANDERLING.

Gold and Fizdale, American-based two-piano duo: Arthur Gold (Canadian, b. 6 Feb 1917) and Robert Fizdale (American, b. 12 Apr 1920). Both studied at the Juilliard School. A concert of John Cage's works, 1944, launched a career in which they specialized in modern works. Composers who wrote for them include Poulenc, Milhaud and Berio (Concerto for two pianos and orchestra, first performance 1972).

Goldberg, Reiner (b. 17 Oct 1939), German tenor. Attached to Dresden State Opera and later to East Berlin Opera, 1977. He is distinguished in the Wagner repertory. Made Covent Garden début 1982 (in *Die Meistersinger*). He sang the title roles of *Parsifal* in H. J. Syberberg's film, 1983, and of Strauss's early opera *Guntram* in its first recording, 1985.

Goldberg, Szymon (b. 1 Jan 1909), Polish-born violinist, later conductor; became American citizen 1953. Led the BERLIN PHILHARMONIC ORCHESTRA, 1929–34, but was forced out (as a Jew) by Nazi pressure. Toured much with Lili KRAUS; spent two and a half years in Japanese captivity in World War II. He was founding conductor of the NETHERLANDS CHAMBER ORCHESTRA, 1955–79; also guest conductor of the BBC SYMPHONY and other orchestras.

Goldenweiser, Alexander [Borisovich] (b. 10 Mar 1875; d. 26 Nov 1961), Russian pianist. Belonged to Leo Tolstoy's entourage, and was associated too with Rakhmaninov and Skryabin. In 1906 he became professor at Moscow Conservatory, a post he held for fifty-five years until his death; spent two periods as director. He was also a composer.

Goldman, Edwin Franko (b. 1 Jan 1878; d. 21 Feb 1956), American bandmaster. Inaugurated famous outdoor band series in New York, 1918. (Earlier he had played cornet in the Metropolitan Opera orchestra.) As well as performing his own and other new, specially written works, he gave the US première of Berlioz's *Symphonie funèbre et triomphale*, 1947. His son Richard Franko Goldman (1910–80) took over the band and was also a composer, theorist and conservatory director.

Goldman, Richard Franko, *see* GOLDMAN, EDWIN FRANKO.

Goldovsky, Boris (b. 7 June 1908), Russian-born American pianist and conductor. Settled in USA, and became celebrated as an operatic conductor, stage director and supporter of opera in English. He was director of opera at various colleges; conducted the first US stage performances of Mozart's *Idomeneo*, 1947, and *La clemenza di Tito*, 1952.

Goldsbrough, Arnold [Wainwright] (b. 26 Oct 1892; d. 14 Dec 1964), British conductor. Founded the Goldsbrough Orchestra, 1948, which later became the ENGLISH CHAMBER ORCHESTRA. A pioneer in reviving eighteenth-century performing style, he was also a harpsichordist, organist, editor and, 1924–9, music director at Morley College, London.

Goldsbrough Orchestra, *see* ENGLISH CHAMBER ORCHESTRA and GOLDSBROUGH, ARNOLD.

Goldschmidt, Berthold (b. 18 Jan 1903), German-born conductor, also composer, naturalized British 1947. Emigrated to Britain, 1935. He conducted the Glyndebourne Opera company at the first Edinburgh Festival, 1947; gave the first performance of Deryck Cooke's partial completion of Mahler's Symphony no. 10, 1960. (*See also* MARTINEZ and RATTLE.)

Goldschmidt, Otto [Moritz David] (b. 21 Aug 1829; d. 24 Feb 1907), German pianist and conductor, also composer. Married the soprano LIND. After they settled in London, he founded the Bach Choir, 1875, and in the following year gave the first complete performance in Britain of Bach's Mass in B minor.

Golschmann, Vladimir (b. 16 Dec 1893; d. 1 Mar 1972), French-born conductor of Russian descent, naturalized American 1947. Conducted ballet in Paris (first performance of Milhaud's *Le Bœuf sur le toit*, 1920) and the SCOTTISH ORCHESTRA in Glasgow, 1928–30. He emigrated to USA, where he was conductor of the ST LOUIS SYMPHONY ORCHESTRA, 1931–58.

Goltz, Christel (b. 8 July 1912), German soprano. Created the title role in Liebermann's *Penelope*, 1954. She made her Covent Garden début as Salome, 1951, and sang there in the first British stage performance of Berg's *Wozzeck*, 1952. Her repertory included about 120 operas.

Gomez, Jill (b. 21 Sept 1942), British soprano (born in British Guiana). Cultivated a wide concert repertory. She made her stage début with Glyndebourne Touring Opera, 1968; created the roles of Flora in Tippett's *The Knot Garden*, 1970, and the Countess in Musgrave's *The Voice of Ariadne*, 1974.

Goodall, Reginald (b. 13 July 1901; d. 5 May 1990), British conductor. Celebrated in Wagner, particularly for his Sadler's Wells Opera (later English National) performances of *Die Meistersinger* in English, 1968, and a complete *Ring*, 1973 (later recorded). Earlier at Sadler's Wells he had launched Britten's *Peter Grimes* at the theatre's post-war reopening, 1945. Despite being on Covent Garden's staff he was allotted no performances there during SOLTI's music directorship, 1961–71; he resumed appearances with *Parsifal*, 1971. Knighted, 1986.

Goodman, Benny (originally Benjamin) [David] (b. 30 May 1909; d. 13 June 1986), American clarinettist. Famous in jazz (with his own band from 1934), then in classical works (recorded Mozart's Quintet with the BUDAPEST QUARTET, 1938). He commissioned and gave the premières of Bartók's *Contrasts* (with Bartók as pianist and SZIGETI as violinist), 1939, and of Copland's Concerto, 1950. Appeared in *The Benny Goodman Story*, a film biography, 1956.

Goossens, Eugène (b. 28 Jan 1867; d. 31 July 1958), British violinist and conductor, father of Eugene [Aynsley] GOOSSENS, Leon GOOSSENS and Sidonie GOOSSENS. Active chiefly in opera; he was principal conductor of the Carl Rosa Opera Company, 1899–1915. Another daughter, Marie (b. 1894), is a harpist (still teaching at 95). His Belgian-born British father, also called Eugène Goossens (1845–1906), was a conductor.

Goossens, [Aynsley] **Eugene** (b. 26 May 1893; d. 13 June 1962), British conductor, also composer, son of Eugène GOOSSENS. Much associated with BEECHAM. He conducted the première of Stanford's opera *The Critic*, 1916, and the first British concert performance of Stravinsky's *The Rite of Spring*, 1921. Later divided his work between Britain and USA (conductor of the CINCINNATI SYMPHONY ORCHESTRA, 1931–46). He went to Australia, 1947, as director of the New South Wales Conservatorium and conductor of the SYDNEY SYMPHONY ORCHESTRA; after being convicted of importing pornography, 1956, returned to Britain. Conducted his own opera *Don Juan de Mañara* at Covent Garden, 1937. Knighted, 1955.

Goossens, Leon [Jean] (b. 12 June 1897; d. 13 Feb 1988), British oboist, son of Eugène GOOSSENS. One of the most celebrated British musicians of his time; various British composers wrote expressly for him, including Vaughan Williams (Concerto, first performance 1944). He played in the Covent Garden orchestra and then the LONDON PHILHARMONIC, 1932–9. CBE, 1950. In 1962 his teeth and lips were severely damaged in a car accident, but he recovered his technique and resumed performances in 1966 (when he was nearing seventy).

Goossens, Marie, *see* GOOSSENS, EUGÈNE.

Goossens, Sidonie (b. 19 Oct 1899), British harpist, daughter of Eugène GOOSSENS. Married for a time to GREENBAUM. She was a member of the BBC SYMPHONY ORCHESTRA from its foundation, 1930, and remained for fifty years; the first solo harpist to broadcast in Britain, 1923, and the first to appear on television, 1936. In 1988 she returned to the Proms to take the solo harp part in Vaughan Williams's *Serenade to Music*, in the first performance of which she had played fifty years before.

Goren, Eli, *see* ALLEGRI QUARTET.

Gorr, Rita (originally Marguerite Geirnaert) (b. 18 Feb 1926), Belgian mezzo-soprano. Sang at Bayreuth, 1958, Covent Garden, 1959–71 (début as Amneris in *Aida*), and the Metropolitan Opera (début 1967 as Amneris). Performed the title role in the first recording of Roussel's *Padmâvatî*, 1969.

Goss, John (b. 27 Dec 1800; d. 10 May 1880), British organist, also composer. Appointed organist of St Paul's Cathedral, 1838, and retained the post (though latterly he was not active) till his death. He was a pupil of Mozart's pupil, the composer Thomas Attwood; among his own students (at the Royal Academy of Music) was Sullivan. Reginald GOSS-CUSTARD was his great-nephew.

Goss-Custard, Henry, *see* GOSS-CUSTARD, REGINALD.

Goss-Custard, Reginald (b. 29 Mar 1877; d. 13 June 1956), British organist. Held appointments in London churches, but was known chiefly as a recitalist and broadcaster; toured USA, 1916. He composed organ music. His brother Henry Goss-Custard (1871–1964) was also an organist; his great-uncle was John GOSS.

Gostling, John (b. *c.* 1650; d. 17 July 1733), British bass. A clergyman and member of the Chapel Royal, from 1679; he was a favourite soloist of Charles II. His powerful low notes are said to have inspired Purcell's anthem *They That Go down to the Sea in Ships*, 1685.

Göttesmann, Paul, *see* BUSCH QUARTET.

Gottschalk, Louis Moreau (b. 8 May 1829; d. 18 Dec 1869), American pianist, also conductor and composer. Studied piano with HALLÉ in Paris and became celebrated there at the age of nineteen both as a performer and for his Creole pieces, which were forerunners of ragtime. He won the praise of Chopin and Berlioz; returned to USA 1852 (where he is said to have given eighty-five recitals and travelled fifteen thousand miles by rail in four and a half months). Having become involved in an amorous scandal, he left USA suddenly in 1865. He fainted while playing his composition *Morte!!* in Brazil, and died there. (*See also* HOFFMAN, RICHARD.)

Gould, Glenn [Herbert] (b. 25 Sept 1932; d. 4 Oct 1982), Canadian pianist. His early performances (Washington, 1955, and London, 1958) won him renown that grew to notoriety because of his eccentricities, such as using very low seating. Specialized in Bach (two celebrated recordings of the 'Goldberg' Variations) and Schoenberg (all of whose piano works he recorded). In 1964 he gave up concert performances in favour of recordings (on which some obtrusive vocalizing may be heard). Also composer and writer and maker of radio programmes, not only on music. His fame approaches cult status.

Gow, Nathaniel (b. 28 May 1763; d. 19 Jan 1831), British violinist, also trumpeter and cellist. Became leader of a famous Edinburgh dance-band, which played his own and other Scottish music; it performed before royalty in London. He was the composer of the famous ballad 'Caller Herring'. Other members of his family were also musicians, including his father, Neil (or Niel) Gow (1727–1807).

Gow, Neil, *see* GOW, NATHANIEL.

Gracis, Ettore (b. 24 Sept 1915), Italian conductor. Active in pioneer revivals of Italian eighteenth-century music, for example Piccinni's opera *La molinara*, 1960. He conducted at the Maggio Musicale, Florence, and, 1959–71, at the Teatro la Fenice, Venice.

Graf, Hans, *see* MOZARTEUM ORCHESTRA.

Graffman, Gary (b. 14 Oct 1928), American pianist. Took lessons with HOROWITZ and Rudolf SERKIN after making his début with the PHILADELPHIA ORCHESTRA, 1947. Appeared in London from 1956 and became known as a soloist and chamber musician. He was forced to retire in 1979 when his right hand became incapacitated by carpal tunnel syndrome.

Grandjany, Marcel [Georges Lucien] (b. 3 Sept 1891; d. 24 Feb 1975), French-born harpist, previously organist, naturalized American 1945. Made his London début 1922; he composed various works, including songs, and was a distinguished teacher in New York (where he was resident from 1936) and Montreal.

Grappelli (originally Grappelly), **Stephane** (b. 26 Jan 1908), French violinist. After his classical training he turned to jazz and organized the famous Parisian Quintette du Hot Club with the guitarist Django Reinhardt, 1934. His performances with MENUHIN and their recordings, from 1973, drew the attention of classical listeners. Continued playing after he was eighty.

Gray, Linda Esther (b. 29 May 1948), British soprano. Pupil of TURNER. She became noted as Wagner's Isolde in the Welsh National Opera performances conducted by GOODALL, 1979 (later recorded). Has sung at Glyndebourne from 1973 (roles include Electra in Mozart's *Idomeneo*) and at Covent Garden; made US début as Sieglinde in *Die Walküre*, 1981.

Greef, Arthur de, *see* DE GREEF.

Greenbaum, Hyam (b. 12 May 1901; d. 13 May 1942), British violinist and conductor. Music director to the theatre impresario C. B. Cochran, then conductor of the BBC Television Orchestra, 1936–9 (the first musician to hold such a post). Helped orchestrate Walton's film scores. He was married to Sidonie GOOSSENS; his sister Kyla (originally Betty) Greenbaum (b. 1922), a pianist, was active particularly in modern music.

Greenbaum, Kyla, *see* GREENBAUM, HYAM.

Greenberg, Noah (b. 9 Apr 1919; d. 9 Jan 1966), American conductor. Founded the New York Pro Musica Antiqua (later shortened to New York Pro Musica), 1952, a pioneer group that brought medieval works with appropriate instrumentation to wide public notice; made European tour with *The Play of Daniel*, 1960. He was equally successful in promoting Renaissance music.

Greene, Harry Plunket (b. 24 June 1865; d. 19 Aug 1936), Irish baritone. Made his London début 1888 and became a favourite artist in oratorio and recital; noted in German song (*see also* BORWICK). He took part in the opening concerts of the Wigmore Hall, London, 1901. Wrote several books, including *Interpretation in Song*, 1912. He married a daughter of the composer Hubert Parry.

Gregor-Smith, Bernard, *see* LINDSAY QUARTET.

Greindl, Josef (b. 23 Dec 1912), German bass. Began his operatic career 1936. Appeared from 1943 at Bayreuth and developed a noted postwar career: performed at Vienna State Opera, 1956–69, and Covent Garden from 1963 (replacing WIENER as Sachs in *Die Meistersinger*). Sang Moses in the first German staging of Schoenberg's *Moses und Aron*, 1959. He is also a teacher and stage director.

Grey, Madeleine (b. 11 June 1896), French soprano. Much associated with leading French composers. She was the first to sing Ravel's *Deux mélodies hébraïques*, 1920, and the complete *Chansons madécasses*, 1926, as well as Canteloube's *Songs of the Auvergne*, 1926 (also first to record it). Toured with Ravel as pianist, 1928.

Griller, Sidney [Aaron] (b. 10 Jan 1911), British violinist. Formed the GRILLER QUARTET, 1928, and in recognition of its achievement was awarded the CBE, 1951. He taught at the Royal Academy of Music, in California, 1949, and elsewhere.

Griller Quartet, London-based string quartet founded 1928 by Sidney GRILLER, its leader. Other members were Jack O'Brien, Philip Burton and Colin Hampton. The personnel remained unchanged until the quartet disbanded in 1961. Among the works dedicated to it was Bliss's Quartet no. 2. (*See also* THURSTON.)

Grimaldi, Nicolo, *see* NICOLINI.

Grinke, Frederick (b. 8 Aug 1911; d. 16 Mar 1987), Canadian-born British violinist. Noted as orchestra leader, chamber musician, teacher at the Royal Academy of Music from 1944, and soloist in various British works that were written for him, including Vaughan Williams's Sonata (first performance, BBC, 1954). Such composers as Arthur Benjamin, Lennox Berkeley, Ireland and Rubbra partnered him in their violin-and-piano works.

Grisi, Giuditta (b. 28 July 1805; d. 1 May 1840), Italian mezzo-soprano, sister of Giulia GRISI. The first to sing the role of Romeo in Bellini's *I Capuleti e i Montecchi*, 1830. She performed in Vienna, Paris and London as well as in Italian cities.

Grisi, Giulia (b. 22 May 1811; d. 29 Nov 1869), Italian soprano, sister of Giuditta GRISI. Sang Juliet to her sister's Romeo in Bellini's *I Capuleti e i Montecchi*, 1830. From her Paris début in 1832 she was one of the most celebrated opera singers there and in London. She was the first Norina in Donizetti's *Don Pasquale* (Paris, 1843) and sang the title role in the first London performance of Donizetti's *Lucrezia Borgia* opposite the Italian tenor MARIO. He became her lifelong companion (she was already married and could not be divorced); they sang together in St Petersburg, 1849, and New York, 1854. Her roles also embraced Mozart and Meyerbeer.

Grist, Reri (b. 29 Feb 1932), American soprano. Moved from Broadway shows to opera, and sang Blonde in *Die Entführung* at Santa Fe, 1959. One of the few black singers to achieve success on the international opera circuit in the 1960s, she had a speciality in light coloratura roles: sang at Covent Garden (Rimsky-Korsakov's *The Golden Cockerel*, 1962), the Metropolitan (from 1966), and the Salzburg Festival. Took part in the first US performance of Nono's *Sul ponte di Hiroshima*, 1971.

Groote, Philip de, *see* CHILINGIRIAN QUARTET.

Grossi, Giovanni Francesco (known as 'Siface' from one of his operatic characters) (b. 12 Feb 1653; d. 29 May 1697), Italian male soprano (castrato). Sang in London, 1687, where he made much impression with the rarity and accomplishment of his voice: Purcell's harpsichord piece *Sefauchi's Farewell*, 1687, was composed in his honour. He was murdered by hired assassins after an imprudent love affair.

Groves, Charles [Barnard] (b. 10 Mar 1915), British conductor. Conducted the BOURNEMOUTH MUNICIPAL ORCHESTRA, 1951–61, Welsh National Opera, 1961–3, and the the ROYAL LIVERPOOL PHILHARMONIC ORCHESTRA, 1963–77 (first British conductor to present complete cycle of Mahler symphonies with his own orchestra). He gave the première of Harvey's *Persephone Dream*, 1973. His music directorship of English National Opera, 1978–9, ended unexpectedly. Recordings include large-scaled Delius works. Knighted, 1973.

Groves, Olive, *see* BAKER, GEORGE.

Gruberová, Edita (b. 23 Dec 1946), Czech soprano. Joined the Vienna State Opera, 1970, and developed an international career, with speciality in coloratura parts. The Queen of the Night in *Die Zauberflöte* was her début role at Glyndebourne, 1973, and the Metropolitan Opera, 1977. She sang Constanze in SOLTI's recording of *Die Entführung*, 1987, and the title role of *Lucia di Lammermoor* at Covent Garden, 1988.

Gruenberg, Erich, *see* LONDON STRING QUARTET (2).

Grumiaux, Arthur (b. 21 Mar 1921; d. 16 Oct 1986), Belgian violinist. Began his career in 1939, but did not play publicly under the German occupation. From 1945 (London début) he won celebrity as a soloist with a broad repertory, including the Berg and Walton concertos, and in chamber music (partner of HASKIL in Mozart and Beethoven sonatas). Created a Belgian baron, 1973.

Grümmer, Elisabeth (b. 31 Mar 1911; d. 6 Nov 1986), German soprano. First worked as an actress but was encouraged by KARAJAN to study singing. She made her operatic début in 1940. Sang Eva in *Die Meistersinger* at Covent Garden under BEECHAM, 1951, and the same role at Salzburg, 1953. Known also in Mozart and Strauss roles, and as a concert singer.

Grümmer, Paul, *see* BUSCH QUARTET.

Grützmacher, Friedrich [Wilhelm Ludwig] (b. 1 Mar 1832; d. 23 Feb 1903), German cellist and composer. Served the King of Saxony at Dresden from 1860. He made an edition of Boccherini's Cello Concerto in B flat that was long standard but is now recognized as an unscholarly concoction.

Guadagni, Gaetano (b. *c.* 1725; d. Nov 1792), Italian male alto (castrato), later male soprano. Worked in the London season of 1748–9 with Handel (who revised solos in *Messiah* and *Samson* for him). In Vienna he was the original Orpheus in Gluck's opera of that title, 1762. Returned later to London; also performed in Italian cities and in Potsdam for FREDERICK THE GREAT.

Guadagno, Anton (b. 2 May 1925), Italian-born American conductor. Became assistant conductor at the Metropolitan, then was music director of Philadelphia Lyric Opera, 1966–72; also appeared at the Vienna Volksoper. Conducted various operatic recital records with CABALLÉ, CORELLI and others.

Gualda, Sylvio (b. 12 Apr 1939), French percussionist. As well as performing in Paris orchestras he has been active as a soloist in new works; among those written for him are *Heptade* for trumpet and six percussion by Jolivet, 1972, and *Psappha* and *Aïs* by Xenakis, 1977 and 1981.

Guarneri Quartet, American string quartet founded 1964. Members: Arnold Steinhardt, John Dalley, Michael Tree and David Soyer. It recorded all Beethoven's quartets and, with Arthur RUBINSTEIN, Schumann's piano quintet.

Gueden, Hilde (b. 15 Sept 1917; d. 17 Sept 1988), Austrian soprano. Made her début in 1939 and, as a member of the visiting Vienna State Opera, first appeared at Covent Garden 1947; Metropolitan Opera début 1951 (as Gilda in *Rigoletto*). Sang the heroine's role (Anne Trulove) in the first US performance of Stravinsky's *The Rake's Progress*, 1953. She was also a successful performer in operetta.

Guest, Douglas [Albert] (b. 9 May 1916), British organist. Director of music at Westminster Abbey, 1963–81. At the abbey's 900th anniversary celebrations, 1966, his innovations included a liturgical performance of Beethoven's *Missa solemnis*. CVO, 1975.

Guest, George [Howell] (b. 9 Feb 1924), British organist and conductor. As director of music at St John's College, Cambridge, from 1951, made many recordings from Palestrina to Britten; took the choir to USA and Canada. He was also a noted recitalist. President of the Royal College of Organists, 1978–80. OBE, 1988.

Gui, Vittorio (b. 14 Sept 1885; d. 17 Oct 1975), Italian conductor, also composer. Active in Florence, where he formed the orchestra that was the foundation for the city's festival, 1933. He was the first Italian conductor at the Salzburg Festival, 1933, and a leading champion of Brahms in Italy. Conducted at Covent Garden in 1938 and (with CALLAS in *Norma*) 1952. He initiated the modern revival of Rossini's *Le Comte Ory* with his Florence performance of 1952; it was also among the operas he conducted at Glyndebourne, 1952–64, and one of his many recordings. Gave his last concert (in Florence) two weeks before his death at the age of ninety.

Guilbert, Yvette (b. 20 Jan 1865; d. 2 Feb 1944), French singer and *diseuse*. In topical and traditional songs she became a star of Paris entertainments in the 1890s; visited Britain, from 1893, and USA. Her interpretative art is said to have been praised by Verdi and Gounod. After an illness she reappeared in 1901 with a wider repertory.

Guilevitch, Daniel, *see* CALVET QUARTET.

Guilmant, [Félix] **Alexandre** (b. 12 Mar 1837; d. 29 Mar 1911), French organist, also composer. Held Paris church post, 1871–1901, and was a celebrated recitalist; performed in Britain, USA, from 1893, and Russia. He was cofounder of the Schola Cantorum, a music academy in Paris, 1894; taught organ there and at the Paris Conservatory.

Gulbenkian Orchestra, Lisbon-based chamber orchestra founded 1962. It is supported by the Gulbenkian Foundation. Principal conductors have included TABACHNIK, 1973-5, and SCIMONE, from 1979.

Gulbranson (originally Norgren), **Ellen** (b. 4 Mar 1863; d. 2 Jan 1947), Swedish soprano. Prominent in Wagner: she sang Brünnhilde in *The Ring* at Bayreuth from 1896 and later at Covent Garden.

Gulda, Friedrich (b. 16 May 1930), Austrian pianist. After winning the Geneva International Competition, 1946, pursued a virtuoso career (New York début 1950), with a specialization in the Bach-to-Beethoven repertory. From around 1960 he showed an intense interest in jazz and improvisation. Composed for jazz ensemble, and occasionally played flute and saxophone; he also gave some piano recitals that mixed classical and jazz styles. His recordings include Bach's complete *Well-tempered Clavier*, 1986.

Guller, Youra (originally Georgette) (b. 16 May 1895; d. 11 Jan 1981), French pianist. A child prodigy; toured as a performer before entering the Paris Conservatory, from which she graduated with highest honours at the age of twelve. In mid-career she withdrew through ill health, but she resumed 1959. Made New York début 1971, and recorded Bach, Chopin and others in the later 1970s.

Gulli, Franco (b. 1 Sept 1926), Italian violinist. Member of the Virtuosi di Roma (*see* FASANO) and active in chamber music. As a soloist he has played over fifty concertos; he gave the first modern performance of

Paganini's Concerto no. 5, 1959 (later recorded), and the première of Gian Francesco Malipiero's Concerto no. 2, 1963, which is dedicated to him. Teaches in USA.

Gürzenich Orchestra, Cologne-based orchestra. Developed from an earlier foundation, it took its name in 1857 from its hall. Its principal conductors have included HILLER, 1850–84, ABENDROTH, 1915–34, WAND, 1946–75, AHRONOVITCH, 1975–86, and then JANOWSKI.

Guschlbauer, Theodor (b. 14 Apr 1939), Austrian conductor. Active in opera: at Vienna Volksoper, 1964–6, Lyons Opera, 1969–75, and the (French) Rhine Opera, from 1983. He has also worked as an orchestral conductor at Strasbourg, from 1983, and has recorded rarely heard German and Austrian orchestral works by such composers as Monn and Dittersdorf.

Gutheil-Schoder, Marie (b. 16 Feb 1874; d. 4 Oct 1935), German soprano. Engaged by MAHLER in 1900 for the Vienna Court Opera (later State Opera), where she was exceptionally successful. She also worked as an operatic stage director and was the soloist in the first performance of Schoenberg's one-person opera *Erwartung*, 1924.

Gutman, Natalia (b. 14 Nov 1942), Russian cellist. Made her début aged nine and in 1962 was runner-up in the Moscow Tchaikovsky Competition. Also a composer. With her husband, the violinist Oleg Kagan (1940–90), gave the première of Schnittke's Double Concerto, 1982.

Guy, Barry [John] (b. 22 Apr 1947), British double-bass player. Active in both jazz and classical field. Founder, 1971, and artistic director of the London Jazz Composers' Orchestra. He is also a composer (not only for his instrument), drawing on jazz and non-jazz elements.

Guzikow, Michal Józef (b. 2 Sept 1806; d. 21 Oct 1837), Polish-Jewish xylophone player. Began as a street musician. Toured Vienna and Paris from 1835. His virtuoso skill in playing transcriptions (of, for example, Paganini's violin pieces) enraptured Mendelssohn and others and introduced the instrument to the classical field.

Gyaurov, Nikolay (b. 13 Sept 1929), Bulgarian bass. Trained in Moscow. He has been prominent on Western stages from 1957 (at first was also a member of the Sofia Opera). Made his Covent Garden début 1962 (as the Father Guardian in Verdi's *La forza del destino*). He is recognized as one of the finest basses in the SHALYAPIN mould; well known in the title role of *Boris Godunov* (recording under KARAJAN, 1970).

Gyuzelev, Nikolay (b. 17 Aug 1936), Bulgarian bass. First graduated as a painter, then won a vocal competition in Sofia and made his operatic début there in 1960. He toured internationally with Bulgarian National Opera; appeared at the Metropolitan Opera, 1965, and other major houses. Noted equally in Verdi and in Russian roles (Boris Godunov at Covent Garden, 1984).

H

Haas, Karl [Wilhelm Jakob] (b. 27 Dec 1900; d. 7 July 1970), German-born British player of the viola d'amore and other instruments. Came to Britain in 1939 as a Jewish refugee from Nazi Germany. He was founding director of the London Baroque Ensemble, 1943–66; the use of 'baroque' in the title is one of the first British standardizations of the term in the musical sense. Dennis BRAIN was among its members.

Haas, Monique (b. 20 Oct 1906; d. 6 June 1987), French pianist. Recorded all the solo piano music of Debussy and Ravel and was a duo partner of ENESCU and Pierre FOURNIER. Among the works dedicated to her is Milhaud's Sonata no. 2, 1950. She married the composer Marcel Mihalovici.

Habeneck, François-Antoine (b. 22 Jan 1781; d. 8 Feb 1849), French conductor, previously violinist. Introduced Beethoven's symphonies to France and gave the first performances of Berlioz's *Symphonie fantastique*, 1830, and, at the Paris Opera, Rossini's *Guillaume Tell*, 1829, Meyerbeer's *Les Huguenots*, 1836, and Berlioz's *Benvenuto Cellini*, 1838. Berlioz wrote scathingly of him, but his performances were esteemed by Wagner and other authorities. He was also a composer.

Hacker, Alan [Ray] (b. 30 Sept 1938), British clarinettist. A victim of poliomyelitis, he plays from a wheelchair. He is much associated with modern music; took part in the first performance of Birtwistle's *Ring a Dumb Carillon*, 1965 (also recorded), and David Blake's Clarinet Quintet, 1981. He pioneered the reconstruction of the original solo parts of Mozart's Clarinet Concerto and Quintet and performed them on a specially built instrument with a lower extension, as used by STADLER. Teacher at York University, 1976–86, and also conductor (Opera North, 1989). OBE, 1989. (*See also* PRUSLIN.)

Hadley, Henry, *see* SAN FRANCISCO SYMPHONY ORCHESTRA.

Haebler, Ingrid (b. 20 June 1926), Austrian pianist. Well known for her recordings of all Mozart's piano concertos and sonatas. She studied with MAGALOFF and LONG, and won competitions at Geneva, 1952, and Munich, 1954. She was a duo partner of SZERYNG.

Haefliger, Ernst (b. 6 July 1919), Swiss tenor. Known in opera (Glyndebourne, 1956), and as the Evangelist in Bach's Passions. He sang in the first performances of Orff's *Antigonae* (Salzburg), 1949, and of several works by his compatriot Frank Martin, including the oratorio *Golgotha*, 1949.

Haendel, Ida (b. 15 Dec 1923), Polish-born violinist, naturalized British 1940. Pupil of FLESCH and ENESCU. She made her London concerto début 1937; emigrated to Canada, 1952. Sustained a high reputation, almost exclusively in the repertory of popular concertos, and also gave the (broadcast) première of Dallapiccola's *Tartininia seconda* (for violin and orchestra), 1957. CBE, 1991.

Hagegård, Erland, *see* HAGEGÅRD, HÅKAN.

Hagegård, Håkan (b. 25 Nov 1945), Swedish

baritone. Studied with GOBBI. In Bergman's film of *Die Zauberflöte*, 1974, he sang Papageno, which had been his début role at Royal Swedish Opera, 1968. He performed at Glyndebourne from 1973 (Count in Strauss's *Capriccio*) and the Metropolitan Opera from 1978 (title role in Donizetti's *Don Pasquale*). The baritone Erland Hagegård (b. 1944) is his cousin.

Hagen-Groll, Walter (b. 15 Apr 1927), German choral director. Active at Salzburg Festival, Vienna State Opera and elsewhere; chorus master of the (New) Philharmonia Chorus in London, 1971–5. He was the regular choral director on KARAJAN's opera recordings from 1969.

Hager, Leopold (b. 6 Oct 1935), Austrian conductor. Chief conductor of the MOZARTEUM ORCHESTRA, 1969–81; with it he toured Japan and elsewhere and made recordings, including several rarely heard early Mozart operas. He also conducted at the Salzburg Festival and at the Metropolitan, 1976.

Hague Philharmonic Orchestra, The, *see* RESIDENTIE ORCHESTRA OF THE HAGUE.

Haitink, Bernard [Johan Herman] (b. 4 Mar 1929), Dutch conductor. Chief conductor of the CONCERTGEBOUW ORCHESTRA OF AMSTERDAM, 1961–88 (at first jointly with JOCHUM), and of the LONDON PHILHARMONIC, 1967–79. He made US début 1957, British début 1961. Conducted at Glyndebourne from 1972 and became its music director in 1977; worked as music director designate at Covent Garden from 1987, and took post as music director in September 1988. He gave the first performance of Malcolm Arnold's *Philharmonic Concerto*, 1976, and Maw's *The World in the Evening*, 1988. Honorary KBE, 1977.

Halíř, Karel (also known by Germanized form, Carl) (b. 1 Feb 1859; d. 21 Dec 1909), Bohemian violinist. Pupil of JOACHIM and second violinist in Joachim's quartet, 1897, then founded his own quartet. He was an enthusiastic early performer of Tchaikovsky's Violin Concerto; gave the first performance, 1905, of Sibelius's Concerto in its revised and now standard form. Taught in Berlin, where he died.

Hall, Marie [Mary Paulina] (b. 8 Apr 1884; d. 11 Nov 1956), British violinist. Pupil of WILHELMJ in London and ŠEVČÍK in Prague. Made London concert début 1903, New York début 1905. She was considered one of the finest players of her time. Gave the first performance of Vaughan Williams's *The Lark Ascending*, 1921, dedicated to her.

Hall, Michael, *see* NORTHERN SINFONIA.

Hallé, Charles (originally Carl Halle) (b. 11 Apr 1819; d. 25 Oct 1895), German-born British pianist and conductor. Moved to Paris, 1836, where he performed with FRANCHOMME and became acquainted with Liszt, Chopin, Berlioz and Wagner. He then settled in Manchester, and in 1858 inaugurated the orchestral series from which the HALLÉ ORCHESTRA and the Hallé Concerts developed. He also conducted the LIVERPOOL PHILHARMONIC ORCHESTRA, 1883–95. In London he was active as a pianist (he was apparently the first to play all Beethoven's sonatas in a series of recitals) and conductor. Became principal of the Royal Manchester College of Music on its inception, 1893. He was an enthusiast for Gluck (first performance in English of *Iphigénie en Tauride*, as a concert work, 1860) and Berlioz. His second wife was the violinist NERUDA.

Hallé Orchestra, Manchester-based orchestra founded 1858 by Charles HALLÉ. Later conductors have included Hans RICHTER, 1899–1911, HARTY, 1920–33, BARBIROLLI, 1943–70, LOUGHRAN, 1971–83, and SKROWACZEWSKI, 1984–91.

Halleux, Laurent, *see* PRO ARTE QUARTET.

Hamari, Julia (b. 21 Nov 1942), Hungarian mezzo-soprano. Made her concert début in Vienna, 1966. She has recorded much in the German song repertory. Her work in opera has been mainly on records; sang Olga in SOLTI's recording of Tchaikovsky's *Yevgeny Onegin*, 1974.

Hambourg, Boris, *see* HAMBOURG, MARK.

Hambourg, Jan, *see* HAMBOURG, MARK.

Hambourg, Mark (b. 31 May 1879; d. 26 Aug

1960). Russian-born pianist; became British citizen 1896. Pupil of LESCHETIZKY; made London début 1889 and US début 1898. He gave the first London performance of Busoni's Concerto, 1910. Very popular as a soloist, he also formed a trio with his brothers, Jan (violinist, 1882–1947) and Boris (cellist, 1884–1954).

Hammond, Joan [Hood] (b. 24 May 1912), New Zealand soprano. Studied and made début in Sydney; after her London concert début, 1938, she appeared in opera in London, New York, Moscow and Leningrad (Tatyana in Tchaikovsky's *Yevgeny Onegin* in Russian). Sang the title role in the first British professional performance of Dvořák's *Rusalka*, 1959. She was a popular concert and recording artist in the era of 78s; made a million-selling record of 'O My Beloved Father' from Puccini's *Gianni Schicchi*. Retired in 1965; created Dame, 1974. She returned to UK to teach master-classes, 1988.

Hammond-Stroud, Derek (b. 10 Jan 1929), British baritone. His London recital début was in 1954, but he built his chief career from 1961 at Sadler's Wells Opera (later English National). Notable in comic roles, for example Bunthorne in Sullivan's *Patience*, but also as Beckmesser in *Die Meistersinger* and Alberich in *The Ring* (also recorded).

Hampton, Colin, *see* GRILLER QUARTET.

Handl, Max, *see* ROSÉ QUARTET.

Handley, Vernon (b. 11 Nov 1930), British conductor. From 1962 he developed the Guildford Symphony Orchestra to a fully professional basis; also taught at the Royal College of Music. Conductor of the ULSTER ORCHESTRA, 1985–9. He is a champion of lesser-known British music, of which he has recorded much; began the first complete recording of Moeran's orchestral works in 1988. That year he also conducted the première of Barry's *Chevaux-de-frise* at the Proms and appeared as a guest conductor in Japan.

Hannikainen, Pekka, *see* HANNIKAINEN, TAUNO.

Hannikainen, Tauno [Heikki] (b. 16 Feb 1896; d. 12 Oct 1968), Finnish conductor, also cellist. Pupil of CASALS in Paris. He held conducting posts in USA, 1942–50, but was chiefly known for his work as conductor of the Helsinki Symphony Orchestra, 1950–63, and his speciality in Finnish music, which was displayed in his concerts with the LONDON SYMPHONY ORCHESTRA, 1952–3. His father, Pekka Hannikainen (1854–1924), was a conductor and his three brothers were also musicians.

Hanzl, Jiří, *see* VLACH QUARTET.

Harada, Koichiro, *see* TOKYO QUARTET.

Harada, Sadao, *see* TOKYO QUARTET.

Hardenberger, Håkan (b. 27 Oct 1961), Swedish trumpeter and cornetist. Made his British début at a brass-band festival playing Elgar Howarth's Trumpet Concerto, 1984, and rapidly achieved international impact. He gave the first performances of Crosse's *Array* for trumpet and strings (Proms, 1986) and of Birtwistle's *Endless Parade* for trumpet and orchestra, 1987, both written for him.

Harle, John (b. 27 Sept 1956), British alto and soprano saxophonist. Active as a soloist, also leading his own Myrrha Saxophone Quartet, 1976–81. Founded the Berliner Band in London, 1982, which concentrated on pre-Nazi German music. He gave the first performances of Muldowney's Concerto, 1984, and Richard Rodney Bennett's Sonata for (soprano) saxophone, 1988.

Harnoncourt, Nikolaus (b. 6 Dec 1929), German cellist, bass viol player and conductor. One of the pioneers in the orchestral revival of 'authentic' instruments, particularly with his group the CONCENTUS MUSICUS WIEN from 1953. With LEONHARDT he embarked on the recording of all Bach's cantatas. In his performances and recordings he has concentrated on the Bach period, but also embraced operas by Monteverdi and Mozart. From the 1980s he has conducted standard orchestras, including the VIENNA PHILHARMONIC and the CONCERTGEBOUW, in the eighteenth-century repertory.

Harnoy, Ofra (b. 31 Jan 1965), Israeli cellist. Resident in Canada from 1972. In 1982 she was the youngest performer ever to receive the New York Concert Artists' Guild award. She made the first recording of a newly discovered Offenbach concerto and gave the first US performance of Bliss's Cello Concerto, both 1983.

Harper, Heather [Mary] (b. 8 May 1930), British soprano (born in Northern Ireland). Worked at Glyndebourne (at first as understudy) from 1955, performed in the first British staging of Schoenberg's one-person drama *Erwartung*, 1960, and made her Covent Garden début 1962 in Britten's *A Midsummer Night's Dream*. She sang in the first performances of Britten's *War Requiem*, 1962, and Tippett's Symphony no. 3, 1972. Michael Berkeley composed his *Songs of Awakening Love* for her, 1986. CBE, 1965.

Harrell, Lynn (b. 30 Jan 1944), American cellist. Pupil of Leonard ROSE. Made his New York début 1960; he was principal cellist (and the youngest player) with the CLEVELAND ORCHESTRA, 1965–71. Went on to lead an international career; London début 1975 (with ASHKENAZY). He made the first recording of Herbert's Cello Concerto no. 2, 1988. Has held an international chair at the Royal Academy of Music since 1986. His father was the baritone Mack Harrell (1909–60).

Harrell, Mack, *see* HARRELL, LYNN.

Harrington, David, *see* KRONOS QUARTET.

Harrison, Beatrice (b. 9 Dec 1892; d. 10 Mar 1965), British cellist, sister of May HARRISON. A child prodigy; studied with Hugo BECKER in Berlin, where she also performed in a duo with d'ALBERT. Made adult London début 1911, and often collaborated with her sister. She gave the first British performances of Delius's Cello Concerto, 1923, and Kodály's Sonata for solo cello, 1924. The combination of her cello and the sound of the nightingales in her Surrey garden was heard in a famous broadcast, 1924, and issued on record, 1925.

Harrison, George, *see* SHANKAR.

Harrison, May (b. Mar 1891; d. 8 June 1959), British violinist (born in India), sister of Beatrice HARRISON. Studied in London and with AUER in St Petersburg, and then pursued a distinguished career. She and Beatrice gave the first performance of Delius's Double Concerto (dedicated to them), 1920; partnered by Arnold Bax she gave the première of Delius's Sonata no. 3, which he also dedicated to her.

Harrison, Sidney (b. 4 May 1903; d. 8 Jan 1986), British pianist. Chiefly known as teacher and popularizer: he was the first in Britain to give piano lessons on television, 1950. Taught latterly at the Royal Academy of Music; author and composer of educational and other works.

Harrison, William, *see* PYNE.

Harshaw, Margaret (b. 12 May 1909), American mezzo-soprano and from about 1950 soprano. Sang at the Metropolitan Opera from 1942. She specialized in Wagner roles, including Brünnhilde (which she also performed at Covent Garden from 1953). Appeared at Glyndebourne, 1954, but not on the general European circuit. College teacher from 1962.

Hartman, Imre, *see* LÉNER QUARTET.

Harty, [Herbert] **Hamilton** (b. 4 Dec 1879; d. 19 Feb 1941), British conductor, also pianist and composer (born in Northern Ireland). As conductor of the HALLÉ ORCHESTRA, 1920–33, he raised it to very high standards; gave the British premières of Mahler's Symphony no. 9, 1930, and Shostakovich's Symphony no. 1, 1932, and (as pianist with the composer conducting) the first public performance of Lambert's *The Rio Grande*, 1929. He left the Hallé in acrimonious circumstances, and thereafter was based in London. Conducted the first performances of Walton's Symphony no. 1, in both its unfinished and its completed forms, 1934 and 1935. Married to NICHOLLS. Knighted, 1925. His arrangements of movements from Handel's *Water Music* and *Fireworks Music* were universally performed.

Harvey, Keith, *see* GABRIELI QUARTET.

Harwood, Elizabeth [Jean] (b. 27 May 1938; d. 21 June, 1990), British soprano. Sang at Glyndebourne from 1960 and Sadler's Wells Opera (later English National) from 1961; made her

Metropolitan début 1975 (Fiordiligi in *Così*). She alternated principal roles with SUTHERLAND on an Australian tour, 1965; sang the title role in KARAJAN's recording of Lehár's *Die lustige Witwe*.

Haskil, Clara (b. 7 Jan 1895; d. 7 Dec 1960), Romanian-born pianist, naturalized Swiss 1949. Studied both piano and violin in Paris with distinction. Liability to illness restricted her career. Although she performed from 1920, not till after 1945 did she gain major recognition; especially noted in Mozart and Schubert, and also played Bartók and Hindemith. She was a regular duo partner of GRUMIAUX and worked with CASALS. Died in Brussels.

Hasson, Maurice (b. 6 July 1934), French violinist. Studied with SZERYNG. He made his Paris début 1950, London début 1973 and US début 1978. From 1960 to 1973 he was based in Venezuela, but he later settled in London. His recordings include Bach and Vivaldi two-violin concertos with Szeryng.

Haugland, Aage (b. 1 Feb 1944), Danish bass-baritone of Norwegian parentage. After making his début with Norwegian Opera, joined Danish Royal Opera, 1973 (roles include Boris Godunov). He developed a Wagner speciality, and appeared at Covent Garden as Hunding in *Die Walküre*, 1975; sang at the Metropolitan Opera from 1979 and at Bayreuth from 1983.

Hauk, Minnie (originally Amalia Mignon Hauck) (b. 16 Nov 1851; d. 6 Feb 1929), American soprano. Made her début at fourteen. She was the first in USA to sing Juliet in Gounod's *Roméo et Juliette*, 1867, Carmen, 1878, and the title role of Massenet's *Manon*, 1885. Successful also in Berlin and London; sang Carmen over 500 times, in French, English, German and Italian.

Hausmann, Robert (b. 13 Aug 1852; d. 18 Jan 1909), German cellist. Introduced by JOACHIM to PIATTI, with whom he studied in London and Italy. Gave the first performances of Brahms's Cello Sonata no. 2 (dedicated to him), 1886, and (with Joachim) his Double Concerto, 1887. He was the cellist in Joachim's quartet, 1879–1907.

Hayashi, Yasuko (b. 10 July 1943), Japanese soprano. Studied in Milan. She is celebrated as Madam Butterfly (La Scala, 1972, Covent Garden, 1975, and Chicago, 1978); has also sung principal roles in *Don Giovanni* and *La traviata*.

Hayes, Roland (b. 3 June 1887; d. 1 Jan 1977), American tenor. One of the first black singers to become established in the concert hall; made US formal début 1917. He later studied with HENSCHEL in London. He was admired in German and other songs as well as spirituals, of which he published his own editions. Continued performing into his mid-sixties.

Heger, Robert (b. 19 Aug 1886; d. 14 Jan 1978), German conductor. Had a long operatic career in Germany and Austria from 1909. He conducted a famous pre-LP recording of *Der Rosenkavalier* with Lotte LEHMANN and Elisabeth SCHUMANN, 1933; gave the first British performance, with the visiting Bavarian State Opera, of Strauss's *Capriccio*, 1953.

Heifetz, Benar, *see* KOLISCH QUARTET.

Heifetz, Jascha (originally Yosif) (b. 2 Feb 1901; d. 10 Dec 1987), Russian-born violinist, naturalized American 1925. Child prodigy; studied at St Petersburg Conservatory with AUER. He went to Berlin, where his concerts, from 1912, launched him on a world career. Emigrated to USA, 1917, and made London début 1920. He revisited Russia in 1934. Ceased solo appearances about 1971 (when he was the subject of a French film). Considered technically the finest of modern violinists; he played much chamber music (for example with PIATIGORSKY and FEUERMANN), transcribed over 200 pieces as solo works and gave first performances of concertos by Walton, 1939, Gruenberg, 1944, and others.

Heiller, Anton (b. 15 Sept 1923; d. 25 Mar 1979), Austrian organist, also composer. Won an international competition in Haarlem, 1952; received various Austrian state awards and from 1971 was professor at the Vienna Academy. In his earlier years he was also active as a harpsichordist and conductor.

Heinze, Bernard [Thomas] (b. 1 July 1894; d. 9

June 1982), Australian conductor. Worked with the Australian Broadcasting Commission from 1929 and conducted the MELBOURNE SYMPHONY ORCHESTRA, 1932–49; director of the New South Wales Conservatorium, 1956–66. He powerfully influenced Australian musical life. Conducted the first performance of Sculthorpe's *Sun Music III*, 1967. Knighted, 1949; created Companion of the Order of Australia, 1976.

Helffer, Claude (b. 18 June 1922), French pianist. Pupil of Robert CASADESUS. Distinguished in twentieth-century music, he recorded all Schoenberg's solo piano works and all three Boulez sonatas, and gave the first performances of Amy's *Epigramme*, 1965, Xenakis's *Erikhthon*, 1974, and Boucourechliev's Concerto, 1975. Toured widely and made US début 1966.

Hellmesberger, Ferdinand, *see* HELLMESBERGER, JOSEPH.

Hellmesberger, Georg, *see* HELLMESBERGER, JOSEPH.

Hellmesberger, Joseph (b. 3 Nov 1828; d. 24 Oct 1893), Austrian violinist, also conductor. Gave orchestral and choral concerts in Vienna, and taught such well-known violinists as AUER and BRODSKY. From 1849 to 1891 he led a string quartet, which was Vienna's most famous; Brahms gave his first Vienna concert with it (as pianist and composer), 1862. His father, Georg (1800–1873), and sons, Joseph (1855–1919) and Ferdinand (1863–1940), were also conductors in Vienna.

Helsinki Philharmonic Orchestra, Finnish orchestra. It has grown from an orchestra founded 1882 by KAJANUS and conducted by him up to 1933. Later conductors have included Paavo BERGLUND, 1975–9 (from 1978 with Ulf Söderblöm), KAMU, 1981–90, and COMISSIONA, from 1990.

Heltay, László [István] (b. 5 Jan 1930), Hungarian-born conductor, naturalized British 1962. Settled in Britain, 1956. He founded the Kodály Choir at Merton College, Oxford, 1957, and conducted an *Ode* dedicated by Kodály to the college, 1964. In 1970 he formed the Brighton Festival Chorus, with which he gave the first performance of Havergal Brian's Psalm 23 (composed 1901). Conductor, Royal Choral Society, since 1985.

Hempel, Frieda (b. 26 June 1885; d. 7 Oct 1955), German soprano. Made operatic début 1905 and won fame in Mozart, for example as the Queen of the Night in BEECHAM's London performances of *Die Zauberflöte*, 1910. Sang the Marschallin in the first Berlin and first New York performances of *Der Rosenkavalier*, 1911 and 1913. She lived mainly in USA from 1912; in 1955, knowing she was incurably ill, returned to Germany.

Hemsley, Thomas [Jeffery] (b. 12 Apr 1927), British baritone. Sang Aeneas opposite FLAGSTAD's Dido in London, 1951, then performed in opera in Germany (Bayreuth, 1968–70) and Switzerland. In Britain he created the roles of Mangus in Tippett's *The Knot Garden*, 1970, and Caesar in Hamilton's *The Catiline Conspiracy*, 1974. He is well known also in concert and occasionally works as an opera stage director.

Henderson, Roy [Galbraith] (b. 4 July 1899), British baritone. Made his London début 1925 and sang as Mozart's Figaro at the opening of Glyndebourne, 1934; he was a soloist in the first performance of Delius's *Idyll*, 1933, and Vaughan Williams's *Dona nobis pacem*, 1936. Also choral director and teacher (notably of FERRIER). CBE, 1970.

Hendricks, Barbara (b. 20 Nov 1948), American soprano. Pupil of TOUREL. After appearing with San Francisco Opera, she sang at Glyndebourne, 1974 (in the title role of Cavalli's *La Calisto*). Became resident in Paris in 1977. Following the acceptance of black singers in the complete range of roles, she performed Juliet (Gounod's *Roméo et Juliette*) at the Paris Opera, 1982, Sophie (*Der Rosenkavalier*) at the Metropolitan, 1986, and Mimì in a film of *La Bohème*, 1988. As a concert singer she gave the first performance of Del Tredici's *Final Alice* (with SOLTI conducting), 1976. (*See also* ALEXEEV.)

Hendriks, Paul, *see* GAUDEAMUS QUARTET.

Henri, Louie, *see* LYTTON.

Henschel, [Isador] **George** (originally Georg) (b. 18 Feb 1850; d. 10 Sept 1934), German-born baritone and conductor, also pianist and composer, naturalized British 1890. Sang in Bach's *St Matthew Passion* under Brahms's conductorship, 1875, and made London début 1877; in USA he was conductor of the newly founded BOSTON SYMPHONY ORCHESTRA, 1881–4. After settling in Britain, he conducted a London orchestral concert series, 1886–97, and was conductor of the SCOTTISH ORCHESTRA, 1893–5. He continued as a singer (performing at London's Schubert centenary celebrations, 1928, aged seventy-eight), and made recordings with his own piano accompaniments. In Boston at the age of eighty-one he conducted a near-repetition of his first programme there. Knighted, 1914. His first wife, Lilian Bailey (1870–1901), was a singer, and she often performed with him; their daughter Helen Henschel (d. 1973) was both a singer and a pianist.

Henschel, Helen, *see* HENSCHEL, GEORGE.

Herbeck, Johann [Franz von] (b. 25 Dec 1831; d. 28 Oct 1877), Austrian conductor, also composer. As conductor of an important Viennese orchestral concert series, 1859–70 and 1870–75, he gave the first performance of Schubert's 'Unfinished' Symphony (thirty-five years after the composer's death), 1865. He also conducted opera.

Herbig, Günther (b. 30 Nov 1931), German conductor of Austrian parentage (born in Czechoslovakia). Held appointments in East Germany (Dresden Philharmonic, 1972–7, and Berlin Symphony Orchestra, 1977–84), and was also a guest conductor with the BBC PHILHARMONIC, 1981–3. He became music director of the DETROIT SYMPHONY ORCHESTRA, 1984, and of the TORONTO SYMPHONY ORCHESTRA, 1990.

Herincx, Raimund [Fridrik] (b. 23 Aug 1927), British bass-baritone of Belgian parentage. Sang with Welsh National and Sadler's Wells Opera (later English National), including major Wagner and Stravinsky roles. At Covent Garden he took part in the first performance of Tippett's *The Knot Garden*, 1970, and Peter Maxwell Davies's *Taverner*, 1972.

Hermstedt, [Johann] **Simon** (b. 29 Dec 1778; d. 10 Aug 1846), German clarinettist, also conductor. Served a German ducal court. Highly esteemed, he performed throughout Germany as a soloist, often accompanied by Spohr (whose Clarinet Concerto no. 1, 1809, was written for him) and sometimes by Weber, who wrote for him two works that are now lost.

Herold, Jiří, *see* BOHEMIAN QUARTET.

Hersee, Rose (b. 1845; d. 26 Nov 1924), British soprano. Performed in Britain and USA, then joined the new Carl Rosa Opera. She was Susanna in *Figaro* at the company's London opening, 1875, and sang Carmen every night for three weeks when the company gave the opera its first production in Australia, 1879. Her father was the critic and librettist Henry Hersee.

Hertz, Alfred (b. 15 July 1872; d. 17 Apr 1942), German-born American conductor. At the Metropolitan Opera he conducted the US premières of *Salome*, 1907, and *Der Rosenkavalier*, 1913; his performance of *Parsifal* there in 1903 was the first to defy the Wagner family's ban on staging this work outside Bayreuth. During his conductorship of the SAN FRANCISCO SYMPHONY ORCHESTRA, 1915–30, it became one of the first US orchestras to employ women (other than as harpists). In 1922 he started giving concerts at the Hollywood Bowl.

Herz, Henri (originally Heinrich) (b. 6 Jan 1803; d. 5 Jan 1888), Austrian pianist. Studied in Paris and settled there; won enormous success as a teacher and virtuoso. He visited London, 1834, and toured USA, Mexico and the West Indies, 1845–51. Later established a piano factory in Paris. Also prolific composer for piano.

Hess, Myra (b. 25 Feb 1890; d. 25 Nov 1965), British pianist. Celebrated for organizing London's wartime National Gallery concerts, 1939–46. She was a cherished soloist in Britain (début under BEECHAM 1907) and USA (from 1922), and also played in a duo with SCHARRER, her cousin (both were pupils of MATTHAY). Gave the first performance of Bridge's Sonata, 1925. She made Bach's 'Jesu, Joy of Man's Desiring' (from Cantata 147) famous in her piano transcription, published 1926. Created Dame, 1941.

Heward, Leslie [Hays] (b. 8 Dec 1897; d. 3 May 1943), British conductor, also composer. Conducted the Cape Town Orchestra, 1924–7, and was also music director of South African radio. He succeeded BOULT as conductor of the CITY OF BIRMINGHAM ORCHESTRA, 1930, and held the post until his early death.

Hewitt, Maurice, *see* CAPET QUARTET.

Hickox, Richard [Sidney] (b. 5 Mar 1948), British conductor. Has directed the London Symphony Chorus, from 1976, and conducted it in Moscow, 1983; music director of the NORTHERN SINFONIA, 1982–90. He conducted Gluck's *Armida* and other rare operas for the Spitalfields Festival (London). In 1985 he conducted opera at Covent Garden and gave the first performance of Burgon's *Revelations* for chorus and orchestra.

Hidalgo, Elvira de (b. 27 Dec 1888; d. 22 Jan 1980), Spanish soprano. Had a distinguished career, especially in coloratura roles, from 1908. She made her début at the Metropolitan 1910 (Rosina in *Il barbiere*); her sole Covent Garden appearance was as Gilda in *Rigoletto*, 1924. Taught from 1936 in Athens, where she was the only teacher of CALLAS, and later in Ankara.

Hill, Martyn (b. 14 Sept 1944), British tenor. In 1986 he made the first recording of Carter's *In Sleep, In Thunder* and sang and played the piano as Mozart in Rimsky-Korsakov's *Mozart and Salieri* (concert performance). His opera roles include Quint in Britten's *The Turn of the Screw*.

Hill, Ureli Corelli (b. *c.* 1802; d. 2 Sept 1875), American violinist and conductor. Conducted the first US performance with orchestra of Handel's *Messiah*, 1831, and later studied with Spohr in Germany. A founder-member of the Philharmonic Society in New York, 1842, he conducted the US premières of Beethoven's symphonies nos. 5 and 7, 1841 and 1843. After business difficulties he committed suicide.

Hillebrecht, Hildegard (b. 26 Nov 1927), German soprano. Active in opera at Zurich and Düsseldorf/Duisburg, and from 1961 at Munich with the Bavarian State Opera. She is well known in Wagner and Strauss; sang the Empress at the first Covent Garden performance of Strauss's *Die Frau ohne Schatten*, 1967.

Hiller, Ferdinand [von] (b. 24 Oct 1811; d. 11 May 1885), German conductor and composer. Conducted in Paris, London and St Petersburg. He was chiefly influential as city music director in Cologne, 1850–84, where he directed the newly expanded conservatory and conducted the city orchestra (known from 1857 as the GÜRZENICH ORCHESTRA).

Hillis, Margaret (b. 1 Oct 1921), American conductor. An outstanding choral director: trained choruses for the CHICAGO SYMPHONY ORCHESTRA (under REINER), 1957, and the SAN FRANCISCO SYMPHONY ORCHESTRA, 1982. Deputizing for SOLTI, she conducted Mahler's Symphony no. 8 in New York, 1977.

Hillyer, Raphael, *see* JUILLIARD QUARTET.

Hilpert, Friedrich, *see* QUARTETTO FIORENTINO.

Hindemith, Paul, *see* AMAR QUARTET.

Hines (originally Heinz), **Jerome** [Albert Link] (b. 8 Nov 1921), American bass. Made Metropolitan Opera début 1946; went on to perform over forty roles there, including Don Giovanni, Wotan and Boris Godunov, 1954, which he later sang at the Bolshoi Theatre, 1962. He was also a composer.

Hislop, Joseph (b. 5 Apr 1884; d. 6 May 1977), British tenor. Studied in Stockholm and made operatic début there; sang at Covent Garden, 1920–28 (as Faust, with SHALYAPIN, 1928), and in USA. As a teacher in Stockholm, 1936–48, his pupils included Jussi BJÖRLING and Birgit NILSSON. He later taught in London.

Hobson, Ian (b. 7 Aug 1952), British pianist. Studied in Cambridge, London and Yale, and became a teacher at the University of Illinois, 1975. In 1981 he won the Leeds Piano Competition. Recorded Hummel sonatas; he has also worked as a conductor, sometimes from the piano.

Hodgson, Alfreda [Rose] (b. 7 June 1940),

British contralto. Made concert début 1961 and became noted in major Mahler performances; sang in the Israeli première of Handel's *Messiah*, 1974. She has toured widely and performed with English National Opera, from 1974, and at Covent Garden, from 1983.

Hoengen, Elisabeth, *see* HÖNGEN.

Höffgen, Marga (b. 26 Apr 1921), German contralto. Made concert début in Berlin, 1952, and won international note in Bach and Handel. On the opera stage she sang, almost exclusively, as Erda in *The Ring* (Covent Garden, 1959, and Bayreuth, from 1960).

Hoffman, Grace (b. 14 Jan 1925), American mezzo-soprano. Sang at Florence and Zurich, then La Scala, 1953, and the Metropolitan, 1958. She was well known as Eboli in *Don Carlos* (Covent Garden début 1961) and Brangaene in *Tristan*.

Hoffman, Richard (b. 24 May 1831; d. 17 Aug 1909), British pianist, also composer. Settled in USA, but retained British nationality. He travelled and performed with LIND on her American tour, 1850–52; often appeared in a piano duo with GOTTSCHALK. His New York concert of 1897 marked the fiftieth anniversary of his début there.

Hoffmann, Bruno (b. 15 Sept 1913), German glass harmonica player. Constructed a four-octave modern form of the instrument and performed on it in London from 1938 and in USA from 1964.

Hoffmann, Karel, *see* BOHEMIAN QUARTET.

Hoffnung, Gerard (b. 22 Mar 1925; d. 28 Sept 1959), German-born British artist, humorist and amateur tuba player. A childhood refugee from the Nazis; worked in London as a cartoonist, famously satirizing conductors and others. In 1956 he organized the first Hoffnung Music Festival, which included (dis)arrangements of classics and such specially composed spoofs as Malcolm Arnold's *A Grand, Grand Overture* for three vacuum-cleaners, floor-polisher, rifles and orchestra, 1956.

Hofmann, Josef [Casimir] (originally Józef Kazimierz) (b. 20 Jan 1876; d. 16 Feb 1957), Polish-born pianist; became American citizen 1926. Made a sensational New York début aged eleven. He was the sole pupil of Anton RUBINSTEIN in Germany, and toured Russia frequently from 1896; Rakhmaninov dedicated his Piano Concerto no. 3 to him, 1909. Built an unsurpassed American-based career as a performer and teacher, and was director of the Curtis Institute in Philadelphia, 1926–38. He composed music under the name Michel Dvorsky.

Hofmann, Peter (b. 12 Aug 1944), German tenor. Made his operatic début 1972. He became celebrated as Siegmund in *The Ring* (at Bayreuth and Covent Garden, 1976) and other Wagner roles, including Parsifal (recorded under KARAJAN, 1981).

Hogwood, Christopher (b. 10 Sept 1941), British harpsichordist and conductor. Founding director of the ACADEMY OF ANCIENT MUSIC, 1973, a small orchestra of period instruments devoted mainly to eighteenth-century music; with it he recorded all Mozart's symphonies. Was previously associated with MUNROW. He has also conducted the BOSTON SYMPHONY and other major orchestras in the standard repertory. He became artistic director of the Handel and Haydn Society of Boston, the oldest US concert-giving body, 1986, and music director of the St Paul Chamber Orchestra in Minneapolis, 1988; conducted Mozart operas in Paris, 1987.

Holl, Robert (originally Robertus) [Theodore Johannes Maria] (b. 10 Mar 1947), Dutch bass. Studied with HOTTER in Munich and became a member of the Bavarian State Opera, though he later devoted himself entirely to concert work. Recorded Schubert's *Winterreise* (rare for bass) and Musorgsky songs, and appeared at the Vienna and Salzburg festivals. He is also a composer.

Holliger, Heinz (b. 21 May 1939), Swiss oboist, also composer. Studied composition with BOULEZ. From the mid-1960s he was conspicuous in the avant-garde repertory and developed new effects, such as sounding notes simultaneously. Works that have been written for him, or jointly for him and his wife, the harpist Ursula Holliger (née Hänggi; b. 1937), include double concertos by Henze, 1966, and Lutosławski, 1980, and Carter's Oboe Concerto, of which he gave the first performance in 1988. (*See also* NICOLET.)

Holliger, Ursula, *see* HOLLIGER, HEINZ.

Hollins, Alfred (b. 11 Sept 1865; d. 17 May 1942), British pianist and organist. Blind from birth, but he studied with BÜLOW in Germany and developed a career as a soloist and church organist. Toured USA, from 1886, and Australia several times. He was also a composer.

Hollreiser, Heinrich (b. 24 June 1913), German conductor. After being on the staff of Vienna State Opera, he was principal conductor of Berlin State Opera, 1961–4. At Hamburg he conducted the first German performance of Britten's *Peter Grimes*, 1947; also conducted at Bayreuth and internationally.

Hollweg, Werner (b. 13 Sept 1936), German tenor. Sang with minor opera companies before appearing as Belmonte in *Die Entführung* at the Maggio Musicale, Florence, 1969; performed many times in Mozart operas at Salzburg. His recordings include rare Loewe songs. Sang in Beethoven's Symphony no. 9 under KARAJAN in Osaka, 1970.

Hollywood Quartet, American string quartet founded 1948. Its original members, who were all Hollywood film studio musicians, were Felix SLATKIN, Paul Shure, Paul Robyn and Eleanor Aller; Alvin Dinkin joined as viola player in 1954. It disbanded in 1961.

Holm, Renate (b. 10 Aug 1931), German soprano. Pupil of IVOGÜN. She was noted as an operetta singer, then in 1960s sang with the Vienna State Opera and won success in coloratura roles, including Blonde in *Die Entführung* at Salzburg, 1961.

Holm, Richard (b. 3 Aug 1912; d. 20 July 1988), German tenor. Active with Bavarian State Opera, Munich, with which he sang in the first British performance of Strauss's *Capriccio*, 1953. He also performed with the Covent Garden company and at Glyndebourne, 1950.

Holmes, Ralph (b. 1 Apr 1937; d. 4 Sept 1984), British violinist. Made London début 1951, US début (under BARBIROLLI) 1966. He cultivated an unusually wide concerto repertory, and gave the first performance of Richard Rodney Bennett's Concerto, 1976, among others; sometimes directed from the violin. He recorded the Delius sonatas with FENBY. His distinguished career was cut short by early death.

Holst, Henry (b. 25 July 1899), Danish violinist. Gained wide experience as a performer and teacher: taught at the Royal Manchester College of Music, 1931–45, then in London and Copenhagen, 1963, and also in Japan. In 1941 he gave the first European performance (after US première by HEIFETZ) of Walton's Violin Concerto.

Holst, Imogen [Clare] (b. 12 Apr 1907; d. 9 Mar 1984), British conductor. Founding conductor of the Purcell Singers, 1953–67. From 1952 she was music assistant to Britten; his ballet *The Prince of the Pagodas*, 1957, is dedicated jointly to her and Ninette de Valois. She was the daughter (and biographer) of the composer Gustav Holst. CBE, 1975.

Homer (née Beatty), **Louise** (b. 30 Apr 1871; d. 6 May 1947), American contralto. Sang at the Metropolitan Opera, 1900–1929, and performed in Converse's *The Pipe of Desire*, 1905, the first American opera to be given there. She was a notable Orpheus in TOSCANINI's revival of Gluck's opera, 1909. Married to the composer Sidney Homer; Samuel Barber was her nephew.

Honegger-Moyse, Blanche, *see* MOYSE.

Höngen, Elisabeth (b. 7 Dec 1906), German mezzo-soprano. Joined Vienna State Opera, 1943, and made first Covent Garden appearance with that company in 1947; she sang at the Metropolitan Opera only in 1952. Known as Verdi's Lady Macbeth and Clytemnestra in *Elektra* (twice recorded). She taught in Vienna from 1957.

Hopf, Hans (b. 2 Aug 1916), German tenor. Sang with Bavarian State Opera in Munich from 1949 and at Covent Garden from 1951. He specialized in Wagner roles (made New York début in *Die Meistersinger*, 1952) and such other heavy parts as Verdi's Otello.

Hopkins, John [Raymond] (b. 19 July 1927), British conductor. After holding UK posts, worked with the New Zealand National Orchestra, 1956–63 (also conducting opera). He was director of music to the Australian Broadcasting Commission in Sydney, 1963–73, then a college dean in Melbourne. Conducted and made first recordings of Australian works, including Sculthorpe's *Sun Music I*, 1965. OBE, 1970.

Horák, Josef (b. 24 Mar 1931), Czech bass clarinettist. Began to make a solo career on his instrument in 1955. With SPAARNAY he is jointly responsible for its modern emergence, creating a new repertory and range of sounds. In 1959 Hindemith arranged his Bassoon Sonata for him.

Horenstein, Jascha (b. 6 May 1887; d. 2 Apr 1973), Russian-born American conductor (mother Austrian). Moved to Vienna 1911, and conducted there and in Berlin. Forced as a Jew to leave Nazi Germany, he eventually went to USA, 1940. After 1945 he earned a high reputation in Bruckner, Mahler and Berg; gave the first (concert) performance in Paris of Berg's *Wozzeck*, 1950. Mahler's symphonies and Robert Simpson's Symphony no. 3 are among his celebrated late recordings, 1969–71. Also conducted *Fidelio*, 1961, and *Parsifal* at Covent Garden.

Horne, Marilyn [Bernice] (b. 16 Jan 1934), American mezzo-soprano. After making US opera début 1954, worked much in Europe (Covent Garden début as Marie in Berg's *Wozzeck*, 1965). She developed a remarkable coloratura facility that was evident when she partnered SUTHERLAND (for example in *Norma* at her Metropolitan début, 1970). Stravinsky's reworking of two Hugo Wolf songs, 1968, is dedicated to her. Married, 1960–76, to Henry LEWIS, and later to ZACCARIA.

Horowitz, Vladimir (b. 1 Oct 1903; d. 5 Nov 1989), Russian-born pianist, naturalized American 1942. Began career in Russia (*see* MILSTEIN); made London and New York débuts 1928. In 1933 he performed in the NEW YORK PHILHARMONIC ORCHESTRA's Beethoven cycle under TOSCANINI (whose daughter he married). Reclusive behaviour and long absences from the platform only heightened his immense reputation, particularly in Liszt and other romantic composers. Gave the first performance (in Cuba) of Barber's Sonata, 1949. He returned to USSR for a performance that was televised world-wide, 1986. In 1988 it was announced that his true date of birth was 1903 and not, as had been generally stated, 1904.

Horszowski, Mieczysław (b. 23 June 1892), Polish-born pianist, naturalized American 1948. In an extraordinarily long career he played a Beethoven concerto at the age of ten in Warsaw and a Mozart concerto at ninety in New York. His chief reputation was made in the 1950s, when his partners included CASALS. Recorded all the Beethoven sonatas, and continued recording into his nineties.

Horvat, Milan (b. 28 July 1919), Yugoslav conductor. Graduated in law as well as music. He was active in Zagreb, and also in Dublin (RADIO TELEFÍS EIREANN SYMPHONY ORCHESTRA, 1953–8) and Vienna (AUSTRIAN RADIO SYMPHONY ORCHESTRA, 1969–75). His recordings include works by Boydell and other Irish composers.

Hotter, Hans (b. 19 Jan 1909), German bass-baritone, formerly organist. Made operatic début 1929. Settled in Munich, where he sang in the first performances of Strauss's *Friedenstag*, 1938, and *Capriccio*, 1942. Became a Wagner favourite at Covent Garden, from 1948, especially as Sachs in *Die Meistersinger* and Wotan in *The Ring* (of which he was stage director, 1961–4). Similarly esteemed at Bayreuth, from 1952, and the Metropolitan, 1950–54. In 1989, aged eighty, he took a minor role in a London performance of Schoenberg's *Gurrelieder*.

Hotteterre, Jacques (b. 29 Sept 1674; d. 16 July 1762), French flautist, also bassoonist, composer and instrument maker. He was the most famous of a large family of musicians; active at French court. His renowned book on flute playing, 1707, was the first in any language.

Houston Symphony Orchestra, American orchestra founded 1913. Its principal conductors have included STOKOWSKI, 1955–61, BARBIROLLI, 1961–7, PREVIN, 1967–9, COM-

ISSIONA, 1980–87, and ESCHENBACH, from 1988.

Hout, Lucien van, *see* YSAŸE QUARTET.

Howard (originally Swadling), **Ann** [Pauline] (b. 22 July 1936), British mezzo-soprano. With Sadler's Wells Opera (later English National), sang Carmen, among other roles, and was in the first British performances of Richard Rodney Bennett's *The Mines of Sulphur*, 1965, and Ligeti's *Le Grand Macabre*, 1982. She has also performed at Covent Garden and with US companies. She sang the role of Caliban in John Eaton's *The Tempest* at Santa Fe, 1989.

Howarth, Elgar (b. 4 Nov 1935), British trumpeter and conductor, also composer. He arranged music for the Philip Jones Brass Ensemble, with which he performed. Conducting the LONDON SINFONIETTA, since 1973, he has specialized in twentieth-century music. In the field of opera he conducted the premières of Ligeti's *Le Grand Macabre* (Stockholm), 1978, and Osborne's *The Electrification of the Soviet Union*, 1987. Also conductor of the Grimethorpe Colliery Band, 1972–6; and with it gave the first performances of Birtwistle's *Grimethorpe Aria*, 1973, and Gruber's *Demilitarized Zones* (Zagreb), 1979.

Howell, Gwynne [Richard] (b. 13 June 1938), British bass. Made opera début 1968 (after earlier town-planning career) with Sadler's Wells Opera (later English National); his roles at Covent Garden in major international casts have included Pimen in *Boris Godunov*, Capulet in Bellini's *I Capuleti e i Montecchi* (also recorded, 1986). He sang the title role of *Boris* with Canadian Opera, 1986.

Howells, Anne [Elizabeth] (b. 12 Jan 1941), British mezzo-soprano. Performed with Welsh National Opera, then at Covent Garden from 1967 – début as Flora in *La traviata*, Ophelia in the first UK performance of Searle's *Hamlet*, 1969. She sang the heroine (Cathleen) in the first performance of Maw's *The Rising of the Moon* at Glyndebourne, 1970; made Metropolitan début 1975. She was married, 1966–81, to Ryland DAVIES, then to the bass Stafford Dean (b. 1937).

Hubay, Jenő (b. 15 Sept 1858; d. 12 Mar 1937), Hungarian violinist, also composer. A child prodigy, he became a pupil of JOACHIM in Berlin; after Paris début, 1878, studied with VIEUXTEMPS. He taught in Brussels, then from 1886 at the Budapest Conservatory, of which he was later director, 1919–34; his pupils there included SZIGETI and TELMÁNYI. His father, Károly Hubay (or Karl Huber; 1828–85), was a violinist and conductor.

Hubay, Károly, *see* HUBAY, JENŐ.

Huberman, Bronislav (b. 19 Dec 1882; d. 15 June 1947), Polish violinist. Studied with an assistant of JOACHIM. He gave concerts from the age of eleven; made London début 1894; and appeared with PATTI in her final Vienna concert, 1895. In 1896 he played Brahms's Concerto to the composer's approval in Vienna and made his US début. Continued an illustrious career (*see also* FEUERMANN). He organized, largely from Jewish refugee musicians, the PALESTINE SYMPHONY ORCHESTRA, 1936. Died in Switzerland.

Hughes, Arwel, *see* HUGHES, OWAIN ARWEL.

Hughes, Owain Arwel (b. 21 Mar 1942), British conductor. Researched the original ending that Alfano wrote for Puccini's unfinished *Turandot*, and in 1983 conducted its first (concert) performance. He was principal conductor of the Huddersfield Choral Society, 1984–6, and frequent conductor of the HALLÉ ORCHESTRA, with which he gave the première of Arnold's *Welsh Dances*, 1989. His father, Arwel Hughes (1909–88), was a composer and conductor.

Hungarian Quartet, string quartet founded 1935 in Budapest. It transferred to the Netherlands, 1937, and then to California, 1950. Disbanded in 1970. VÉGH was originally first violinist, with Péter Szeransky, Dénes Koromzay and Vilmos Palotai. When SZÉKELY became leader, 1935, Végh moved to second violin (later succeeded by Alexander Moskovsky, 1940–59, then Michael Kuttner, 1959–70); Palotai was replaced by Gabriel Magyar in 1956.

Hungarian State Symphony Orchestra, Budapest-based orchestra. Developed from an orchestra founded 1923 and took present title 1952. Principal conductors have included FRICSAY, 1945–8, and FERENCSIK, 1952–84.

Hunt, Arabella (b. *c.* 1645; d. 26 Dec 1705), British soprano and lutenist. Active at the courts of Queen Mary and Queen Anne (to whom, as a princess, she gave singing lessons). Purcell is said to have written some of his songs for her, but she did not appear in public theatrical performance.

Hunter, Rita [Nellie] (b. 15 Aug 1933), British soprano. Sang with Sadler's Wells Opera (later English National) from 1960. Her excessive weight did not prevent her from having exceptional success as Brünnhilde in *The Ring* from 1970 (also recorded, in English); she sang Brünnhilde, Aida and other roles at the Metropolitan from 1972. CBE, 1980. Settled in Australia.

Hurford, Peter [John] (b. 22 Nov 1930), British organist. Graduated in law and music; pupil of MARCHAL. He gave organ recitals at the Royal Festival Hall, London, from 1957. Music director at St Albans Abbey, 1958–78, where he founded an organ festival. He made many recordings and international tours. Also a composer and editor. OBE, 1984.

Hurst, George (b. 20 May 1926), British conductor of Romanian and Russian descent. Studied at the Royal Conservatory, Toronto, and with MONTEUX; made London début 1953. He was conductor of the BBC NORTHERN SYMPHONY ORCHESTRA, 1958–68, and was later associated with the BOURNEMOUTH SYMPHONY ORCHESTRA.

Hurwitz, Emanuel [Henry] (b. 7 May 1919), British violinist. Pupil of HUBERMAN. Noted in chamber music and as a teacher, he was leader of the Melos Ensemble, 1956–72, and of the AEOLIAN QUARTET, 1970–82. Also occasional conductor. CBE, 1978.

Hüsch, Gerhard [Heinrich Wilhelm Fritz] (b. 2 Feb 1901; d. 21 Nov 1984), German baritone. Made celebrated pre-1939 recordings of Schubert, Schumann and the Finnish song composer Kilpinen. He also sang in opera (Bayreuth from 1930 and Covent Garden, 1930 and 1938). Noted teacher in Munich and London.

Husson, Maurice, *see* CALVET QUARTET.

Hutcheson, Ernest (b. 20 July 1871; d. 9 Feb 1951), Australian pianist. Studied in Leipzig, then settled in USA as teacher and performer. In 1915 and 1919 he played concertos by Tchaikovsky, Liszt and Macdowell in a single evening. Member of staff of the Juilliard School from its inception, 1924, and president, 1937–45.

Hyde, Walter (b. 6 Feb 1875; d. 11 Nov 1951), British tenor. Performed in light opera, then at Covent Garden, 1908–24 (including Siegmund in the first performance of *The Ring* in English). He sang the hero's role in the first British production of Delius's *A Village Romeo and Juliet*, 1910. Prominent also in concert.

Hyde-Smith, Christopher, *see* ROBLES.

I

Ikeda, Kikuei, *see* TOKYO QUARTET.

Imai, Nobuko (b. 18 Mar 1943), Japanese viola player. Studied in Tokyo and USA; resident in the Netherlands. She participated in the first performance of Tippett's Triple Concerto, 1980 (also recorded), and performed Walton's Viola Concerto as part of the composer's eightieth-birthday celebrations, 1982. Made New York recital début 1987. She became artistic adviser for the new Casals Hall in Tokyo, 1988.

Inbal, Eliahu (b. 16 Feb 1936), British and Israeli conductor (born in Jerusalem). Holds both nationalities. He won the Cantelli Conducting Competition in Milan, 1963, and made London début 1965. Became music director of the Frankfurt Radio Symphony Orchestra, 1974; he has also conducted opera (Glyndebourne, 1981). Recordings include all Schumann's orchestral works, all Mahler's symphonies and (with ARRAU) Chopin's complete works for piano and orchestra.

Inghelbrecht, Désiré-Emile (b. 17 Sept 1880; d. 14 Feb 1965), French conductor, also composer (mother English). Friend and champion of Debussy. In Paris he conducted the première of Cocteau's spectacle *Les Mariés de la tour Eiffel*, 1921, with music by Honegger, Milhaud, Auric, Poulenc and Tailleferre. Founding conductor of French National Radio Orchestra, 1934–45, and conductor at Paris Opera, 1945–50.

Ireland, Patrick, *see* ALLEGRI QUARTET.

Ireland, Robin, *see* LINDSAY QUARTET.

Irish Radio–Television Orchestra, *see* RADIO TELEFÍS EIREANN SYMPHONY ORCHESTRA.

Irving, [Kelville] **Ernest** (b. 6 Nov 1878; d. 24 Oct 1953), British conductor. As music director for Ealing Film Studios, from 1935 until his death, commissioned and conducted some celebrated film scores, including Vaughan Williams's for *Scott of the Antarctic*, 1948. He was also a composer, especially of film music.

Irving, Robert [Augustine] (b. 28 Aug 1913), British conductor. Noted as music director of Sadler's Wells (later Royal) Ballet, 1949–58, and Balanchine's New York City Ballet, from 1958. He conducted many ballet premières, some with specially commissioned music, for example Auric's *Tricolore* in New York, 1978. At the Stravinsky Festival (New York), 1972, he conducted seven different programmes of Stravinsky's music in eight days.

Isaac, Adèle (b. 8 Jan 1854; d. 22 Oct 1915), French soprano. Pupil of DUPREZ. Her career was mainly at the Paris Opéra-Comique and, later, Paris Opera: at the former she took all three principal soprano roles in the first performance of Offenbach's *Les Contes d'Hoffmann*, 1881. Retired from the stage in 1894.

Isaacs, Edward [Maurice] (b. 14 July 1881; d. 31 July 1953), British pianist. As director of a midday concert series in Manchester, from 1923, he introduced many young performers who later became famous, including KENTNER and LYMPANY. He was blind from 1928, but still occasionally performed piano concertos, for example at the Proms in 1928 and 1929.

Isomura, Kazuhide, *see* TOKYO QUARTET.

Israel Philharmonic Orchestra, Tel Aviv-based orchestra founded by HUBERMAN 1936 as the Palestine Symphony Orchestra. Its first concert was conducted by TOSCANINI. Took present name in 1948. Music directors have included MARTINON, 1958–69, and MEHTA, from 1977 (who had been music adviser from 1969).

Istomin, Eugene (b. 26 Nov 1925), American pianist of Russian parentage. After studying with Rudolf SERKIN and HORSZOWSKI in Philadelphia, made New York concerto début 1943. Noted in trio with Isaac STERN and Leonard ROSE. He commissioned and gave the first performance of Roger Sessions's Piano Concerto, 1956. Married CASALS's widow, the cellist Marta Casals (née Montañez), 1975.

Italiano, Quartetto, *see* QUARTETTO ITALIANO.

Iturbi, Amparo, *see* ITURBI, JOSÉ.

Iturbi, José (b. 28 Nov 1895; d. 28 June 1980), Spanish pianist and from 1936 conductor. Played in USA from 1928 and settled there; made considerable international career. His fingers represented Chopin's in the film *A Song to Remember*, 1945, and he appeared in several other films. In some performances and recordings of concertos (even Liszt's) he both conducted and played. Performed in a piano duo with his sister Amparo Iturbi (1898–1969).

Ivanov, Konstantin [Konstantinovich] (b. 21 May 1907), Russian conductor. Chief conductor of the USSR STATE SYMPHONY ORCHESTRA, 1946–65, with which he toured Western Europe and USA in the 1960s. He made recordings with important Soviet soloists, among them GILELS and NIKOLAYEVA. Also a composer.

Iványi, József, *see* TÁTRAI QUARTET.

Ivogün, Maria (originally Ilse Kempner) (b. 18 Nov 1891; d. 2 Oct 1987), Hungarian-born German soprano. Her adopted surname was fabricated from that of her mother, Ida von Günther. Engaged by WALTER in 1913 for the Munich Opera, with which she remained till 1925; she then went to Berlin City Opera. Retired from the stage in 1934 and later taught (her students included SCHWARZKOPF). She was famous in high coloratura parts such as Zerbinetta in Strauss's *Ariadne auf Naxos*. Married to ERB, then, from 1933, to her accompanist, Michael Raucheisen (1889–1984).

Iwaki, Hiroyuki (b. 6 Sept 1932), Japanese conductor. Studied with KARAJAN, and was based in Hamburg, 1966–9. Became chief conductor of the MELBOURNE SYMPHONY ORCHESTRA in 1974. He was active also as a conductor of Japanese orchestras, particularly the NHK SYMPHONY ORCHESTRA, of which he has been principal conductor from 1969. Conducted the first performance of works by Takemitsu (*Arc Part II*, 1966, and *A Way a Lone II*, 1982), Mayuzumi and other Japanese composers.

J

Jachmann-Wagner, Johanna, *see* WAGNER, JOHANNA.

Jackson, Francis [Alan] (b. 20 Oct 1917), British organist. Worked at York Minster, 1946–82. He is a noted recitalist; also composer, conductor and consultant on organ design. OBE, 1978.

Jackson, Garfield, *see* ENDELLION QUARTET.

Jackson, Isaiah (b. 22 Jan 1945), American conductor. Made his London début with the Dance Theatre of Harlem, 1981. In 1986–90 he was principal conductor (later music director) of the Royal Ballet, the first black musician to occupy such a prominent post in UK. Gave the first performance of Burgon's ballet score *Prometheus*, 1988; made Proms début 1987. He has conducted the CLEVELAND ORCHESTRA and other major US orchestras.

Jacob, Benjamin (b. 15 May 1778; d. 24 Aug 1829), British organist, also harpsichordist and conductor. Studied harmony with the composer Samuel Arnold. One of the best London organists of his time, he was (with the composers Samuel Wesley and William Crotch) a pioneer in promoting Bach's keyboard music in Britain.

Jacob, Joseph, *see* YSAŸE QUARTET.

Jacobi, Georg (later known by French form, Georges) (b. 13 Feb 1840; d. 13 Sept 1906), German violinist and conductor, also composer. Settled in Paris, where he conducted many Offenbach operettas. Moved to London, 1871; conducted the first British performance of *Die Fledermaus*, 1876, and the première of Sullivan's ballet *Victoria and Merrie England*, 1897.

Jacobs, Paul (b. 22 June 1930; d. 25 Sept 1983), American pianist, also harpsichordist. He was prominent in twentieth-century music: gave the first complete cycle of Schoenberg's piano music in Paris, 1956; he recorded Schoenberg and Elliott Carter among others, and was the dedicatee of Richard Rodney Bennett's *Cycle 2*. Also orchestral pianist to the NEW YORK PHILHARMONIC. He died of AIDS.

Jacobs, René (b. 30 Oct 1946), Belgian countertenor. After studying with DEVOS, developed a prominent career in baroque music in ensembles directed by HARNONCOURT and others. He was noted in Handel opera, and sang in MALGOIRE's recording of *Tamerlano*, 1985. His work as a conductor includes the first recording of Cavalli's opera *Giasone*, 1989.

Jadlowker, Hermann (b. 17 July 1877; d. 13 May 1953), Latvian tenor. The original Bacchus in Strauss's *Ariadne auf Naxos* at Stuttgart, 1912. He had previously sung in Berlin and at the Metropolitan Opera, 1910–12. Returned in 1929 to his birthplace, Riga, and became a synagogue cantor; he emigrated to Palestine, 1938.

Jalas (originally Blomstedt), **Jussi** (b. 23 June 1908), Finnish conductor. Son-in-law of Sibelius and a famous interpreter of his music: in 1957 he revived Sibelius's *Kullervo* symphony, which was originally given in 1892 but had been suppressed by the composer. Conducted opera and symphony concerts in Helsinki from 1945.

Janáček Quartet, Prague-based string quartet. Gave its first public performance 1947. The original members were Jiří Trávníček, Miroslav Matyáš, Jiří Kratochvil and Karel Krafka. Members in 1988: Bohumil Smejkal, Adolf Sýkora, Kratochvil and Břetislav Vybiral.

Janigro, Antonio (b. 21 Jan 1918; d. 1 May 1989), Italian cellist and conductor. Pupil of ALEXANIAN and CASALS. Forced to remain in Yugoslavia during World War II, he settled in Zagreb as a performer and teacher; founding conductor of a chamber ensemble, the Solisti di Zagreb, 1954–67. Made US début 1956 and performed in a trio with Jean FOURNIER and BADURA-SKODA. He was conductor of various orchestras, including the Angelicum in Milan, 1965–7.

Janis (originally Yanks, shortened from Yankelevitch), **Byron** (b. 24 Mar 1928), American pianist. Pupil of Josef and Rosina LHÉVINNE and later of HOROWITZ. He played in USSR, 1960 and 1962; his career was then interrupted by illness, but he resumed in 1972. In 1967 in France he discovered Chopin's own manuscripts (previously unlocated) of two waltzes.

Janotha, [Maria Cecylia] **Natalie** (b. 8 June 1856; d. 9 June 1932), Polish pianist. Pupil of Clara SCHUMANN; became court pianist in Berlin. A pet dog and prayer-book were conspicuous at her recitals. She specialized in Chopin; published an early fugue of his for the first time, 1898, and later recorded it, 1905. She was long resident in Britain, but was deported as an enemy alien, 1916; thereafter settled in The Hague, where she died.

Janowitz, Gundula (b. 2 Aug 1937), German soprano. Sang from 1960 at the Vienna State Opera (encouraged by KARAJAN) and Bayreuth. She became well known in Mozart opera (Ilia in *Idomeneo* at Glyndebourne, 1964, and the Countess in *Figaro* at the reopening of the Paris Opera, 1973) and as a recitalist.

Janowski, Marek (b. 18 Feb 1939), German conductor (born in Poland). Taken to Germany as a child. With the Cologne Opera he gave the first British performance of Henze's *Der junge Lord*, 1969. Worked as city music director in Dortmund, 1975–80, completed a recording of *The Ring*, in 1984, and was music director of the ROYAL LIVERPOOL PHILHARMONIC ORCHESTRA, 1983–6; appointed music director of the GÜRZENICH ORCHESTRA, 1986.

Jansons, Mariss (b. 14 Jan 1943), Soviet-Latvian conductor, son of Arvid YANSONS. Prefers the original Latvian spelling of his name to the English phonetic transliteration of Russian script. He studied in Leningrad and took courses in Austria with SWAROWSKY and KARAJAN. Became assistant to MRAVINSKY with the LENINGRAD PHILHARMONIC, then chief conductor of the Oslo Philharmonic, 1979. He made many British appearances, notably with the BBC WELSH SYMPHONY ORCHESTRA.

Janssen, Herbert (b. 22 Sept 1895; d. 3 June 1965), German-born American baritone. Made début with Berlin State Opera, 1922. He sang at Covent Garden, 1926–39, and Bayreuth, 1930–37; much admired in Wagner. After leaving Nazi Germany, he was prominent at the Metropolitan Opera, 1939–52, and was also distinguished in recital.

Janssen, Werner (b. 1 June 1899), American conductor, also composer. His conducting of Sibelius's music in Helsinki, 1934, won the composer's approval. Occasionally conducted the NEW YORK PHILHARMONIC ORCHESTRA. With his own Janssen Symphony Orchestra in Los Angeles, 1940–52, he gave many first performances, among them *Genesis* (for narrator and orchestra), 1945, by seven composers, including Schoenberg and Stravinsky.

Janzer, Georges, *see* VÉGH QUARTET.

Järvi, Neeme (b. 7 June 1937), Soviet-Estonian conductor. Held opera post in Tallinn from 1963, and won a conducting competition in Rome, 1971. He emigrated to USA, 1980, having previously conducted at the Metropolitan Opera, 1979. Became music director of the Göteborg Symphony Orchestra in Sweden, 1982, and of the SCOTTISH NATIONAL ORCHESTRA, 1984, which he left suddenly in 1988. At the Proms, 1989, gave the first British performance of Pärt's Symphony no. 3, dedicated to him. His extensive recorded repertory includes all Prokofiev's symphonies and works by the Estonian-Swedish composer Eduard Tubin.

Jeanrenaud, Joan, *see* KRONOS QUARTET.

Jensen, Thomas, *see* DANISH RADIO SYMPHONY ORCHESTRA.

Jerger, Alfred (b. 9 June 1889; d. 18 Nov 1976), Austrian baritone. Long-standing member of Vienna State Opera, 1921–53; at Dresden he was the first Mandryka in Strauss's *Arabella*, 1933 (and at Covent Garden, 1934). He was also a stage director, libretto reviser and, in his youth, a conductor. When nearly eighty he sang a small role (the Notary) in SOLTI's recording of *Der Rosenkavalier*, 1969.

Jeritza (originally Jedlitzka), **Maria** (b. 6 Oct 1887; d. 10 July 1982), Czech soprano. Her beauty assisted the operatic fame she won chiefly in Vienna and New York. Sang several Strauss roles and created Ariadne in his *Ariadne auf Naxos*, 1912, and the Empress in *Die Frau ohne Schatten*, 1919. She was also well known in Puccini and in Korngold's *Die tote Stadt* (first US performance 1921, her Metropolitan Opera début).

Jerusalem, Siegfried (b. 17 April 1940), German tenor, formerly orchestral bassoonist. Made vocal début 1977 and quickly became prominent in Wagner; he sang as Lohengrin in Hamburg, 1976, and performed at Bayreuth from 1977. His recordings include the title role in Offenbach's *Les Contes d'Hoffmann*, 1979.

Jewel, Ian, *see* GABRIELI QUARTET.

Joachim, Joseph (b. 28 June 1831; d. 15 Aug 1907), Hungarian violinist, also conductor and composer. One of the chief masters of the violin as a soloist and quartet leader. He was a child prodigy; studied in Leipzig under Mendelssohn's guidance, and at the age of twelve performed in London, where he returned almost annually in his maturer years. In 1868 he gave the première of Bruch's Violin Concerto no. 1 in its revised form. A friend and champion of Brahms, he gave the first performance of his Violin Concerto, 1879, and Double Concerto, 1887 (with HAUSMANN), and conducted the UK première of his Symphony no. 1, 1877. Married the mezzo-soprano Amalie Weiss (1839–99), but they were divorced in 1882; lived (and taught) in Berlin from 1868 and died there. (*See also* BORWICK [ERNST] and JOACHIM QUARTET.)

Joachim Quartet, Berlin-based string quartet founded 1869 by JOACHIM. He was always leader, but the other members often changed. His original colleagues were Ernst Schiever, Heinrich de Ahna and Wilhelm Müller. In London Joachim performed regularly with Louis Ries, Ludwig Straus and PIATTI, but this group was not called the Joachim Quartet (which as such did not appear in London till 1900).

Jobin, Raoul (b. 8 Apr 1906; d. 20 Jan 1974), Canadian tenor. Sang opera in Paris, then at the Metropolitan, 1940–50, where he was prominent in French works; created Luca in Menotti's *The Island God*, 1942. He returned to Paris Opera after the war in a wide general repertory; retired in 1957 and taught in Montreal.

Jochum, Eugen (b. 1 Nov 1902; d. 26 Mar 1987), German conductor. Active in both opera and concerts in Hamburg, 1934–49. In 1949 in Munich he formed the BAVARIAN RADIO SYMPHONY ORCHESTRA, which he conducted till 1960; performed at the Edinburgh Festival, 1957. He was also conductor of the CONCERTGEBOUW ORCHESTRA OF AMSTERDAM with HAITINK, 1961–4, and conductor laureate of the LONDON SYMPHONY ORCHESTRA, 1975–8. His many recordings include two sets of the nine Bruckner symphonies. His elder brother Otto Jochum (1898–1969) was a choirmaster and composer.

Jochum, Otto, *see* JOCHUM, EUGEN.

Johannesen, Grant (b. 30 July 1921), American pianist. Pupil of Robert CASADESUS and Egon PETRI. He toured Europe with the NEW YORK PHILHARMONIC ORCHESTRA under MITROPOULOS, 1956–7, and made extensive further tours. Duo partner (and husband, 1963–73) of NELSOVA. He became director, 1974, and later president of the Cleveland Institute of Music.

Johns, [Paul] Emile (b. *c.* 1798; d. 10 Aug 1860), Polish-born American pianist, also composer. Active in New Orleans from 1920. He was the only American to receive a dedication from Chopin (Mazurkas op. 7, 1832), whom he came to know while visiting Paris; died in Paris on a later visit.

Johnson, Anthony Rolfe, *see* ROLFE JOHNSON.

Johnson, Edward (b. 22 Aug 1878; d. 20 Apr 1959), Canadian tenor. Sang in Italy as a young man under the name Eduardo di Giovanni, and went on to perform with Chicago Opera and the Metropolitan, 1922–35. He then worked as the Metropolitan's general manager, 1935–50.

Johnson, Emma (b. 20 May 1966), British clarinettist. Won BBC TV Young Musician of the Year Award, 1984, which led to her début in London and Vienna, 1985. She was immediately engaged to record both standard works and rarities, including Crusell's Concerto no. 2 and Bottesini's Duo for clarinet and double bass with orchestra, 1986 (first recording).

Johnson, Graham [Rhodes] (b. 10 July 1950), British pianist (born in Rhodesia). Founded the Songmakers' Almanac, a varying group of vocal soloists, 1976, and began a unique London concert series of thematic programmes, for which he is pianist and commentator. As an accompanist he worked with LOS ANGELES, PEARS, SCHWARZKOPF and others.

Johnston, James (b. 13 Aug 1903), British tenor. Born in Northern Ireland, began his career there and in Dublin. He was prominent in London opera between 1945 and 1960. Sang in the first British performance of Verdi's *Simon Boccanegra* (Sadler's Wells Opera), 1948, made his Covent Garden début in the première of Bliss's *The Olympians*, 1949, and appeared at Glyndebourne in 1952.

Jones, Aled (b. 29 Dec 1970), British treble. Soloist on recording under HOGWOOD of Handel's *Athaliah*; he sang in Bernstein's *Chichester Psalms* conducted by the composer in London, May 1986. His retirement was announced in 1987. He has also worked as a stage actor and television presenter.

Jones, Geraint [Iwan] (b. 16 May 1917), British organist, harpsichordist and conductor, also impresario. Active as a harpsichordist from 1940. He played Bach's complete organ works in London, 1945–6, and in 1951 conducted *Dido and Aeneas* in Bernard Miles's garden-staging with FLAGSTAD as Dido (also in London).

Jones, Gwyneth (b. 7 Nov 1936), British soprano. Made early appearances as a mezzo-soprano. Sang with Welsh National Opera from 1963 and at Covent Garden from 1964, where her roles included Leonora in *Il trovatore* and Sieglinde in *Die Walküre*; the latter was her début role at the Metropolitan, 1972. Performed at Bayreuth from 1966. Created Dame, 1986.

Jones, Parry (b. 14 Feb 1891; d. 26 Dec 1963), British tenor. Sang in USA, survived the German sinking of the *Lusitania*, 1915, and then joined the Carl Rosa Opera Company. He was soloist in the British première of Kodály's *Psalmus hungaricus*, 1927; at Covent Garden, 1949–53, sang in the first British stage performance of Berg's *Wozzeck*, 1952.

Jones, Philip (b. 12 Mar 1928), British trumpeter and conductor. Played with major London orchestras to 1971. He was founding director of the Philip Jones Brass Ensemble, 1951–87, the first of its kind to have a long and brilliant international success; its many commissions included Richard Rodney Bennett's *Commedia IV*, 1974, and McCabe's *Desert II*, 1981. CBE, 1986.

Jones (originally Joyner), **[Matilda] Sissieretta** (b. 5 Jan 1868; d. 24 June 1933), American soprano. Being black, she was considered but deemed unacceptable for such roles as Aida at the Metropolitan Opera. Known as 'the Black Patti' (*see* PATTI); she led a concert group called the Black Patti's Troubadours, 1893–1910.

Jordá, Enrique (b. 24 Mar 1911), Spanish conductor. Went to Paris as a medical student, but then turned to music; studied organ with Marcel DUPRÉ. After conducting the SPANISH NATIONAL ORCHESTRA, 1940–45, he went to Cape Town. As conductor of the SAN FRANCISCO SYMPHONY ORCHESTRA, 1954–63, he gave the first performances of Milhaud's symphonies nos. 8 and 12, 1958 and 1962. Worked in Antwerp to 1976.

Jordan, Armin, *see* SUISSE ROMANDE, ORCHESTRE DE LA.

Joseffy, Rafael (b. 3 July 1852; d. 25 June 1915), Hungarian-born American pianist. After making Berlin début, won success in USA from 1879 and settled in New York; toured much with Theodore THOMAS and his orchestra. He was an influential teacher and a champion of Brahms's piano works.

Jourdan-Morhange, Hélène (b. 30 Jan 1888; d. 15 May 1961), French violinist. Much associated with Ravel; his Violin Sonata, 1927, is dedicated to her, and she gave the first performance of his *Berceuse sur le nom de Gabriel Fauré*, 1922. Her career was cut short by rheumatism.

Journet, Marcel (b. 25 July 1867; d. 5 Sept 1933), French bass. Sang Wagner, Verdi and, reputedly, sixty-five French operas; he also took some baritone roles. Performed at Covent Garden, the Metropolitan, 1900–1908, and Paris Opera, from 1908 (*Lohengrin*). At La Scala under TOSCANINI he created the role of Simon Magus in Boito's (posthumous) *Nerone*, 1924. Recorded from 1905.

Joy, Geneviève (b. 4 Oct 1919), French pianist. Prominent in Paris as an interpreter of twentieth-century works. In 1970 the twenty-fifth year of her duo with the pianist Jacqueline Robin (b. 1917) was marked by new works from ten composers, including Milhaud, Jolivet and Ohana as well as her husband, Henri Dutilleux.

Joyce, Eileen [Alannah] (b. 21 Nov 1912; d. 25 Mar 1991), Australian pianist. Studied in Leipzig and then settled in London, where she became highly popular (for example at the Proms from 1942); she changed her dresses in mid-concert to match the colours to the music. Gave the first British performances of Shostakovich's Piano Concerto no. 1, 1936, and no. 2, 1958. She played on several film soundtracks, notably excerpts from Rakhmaninov's Concerto no. 2 in David Lean's *Brief Encounter*, 1945. Also harpsichordist. CMG, 1981.

Judenkünig, Hans (b. *c.* 1450; d. Mar 1526), German lutenist. Active in Vienna. He wrote two famous instruction books containing his own compositions and arrangements, *c.* 1519 and 1523.

Juilliard Quartet, New York-based American string quartet founded 1946 in association with the Juilliard School of Music. Robert Mann has remained leader; the other original members were Robert Koff (succeeded by Isidore Cohen, Earl Carlyss and Joel Smirnoff), Raphael Hillyer (succeeded by Samuel Rhodes) and Arthur Winograd (succeeded by Claus Adam, then Joel Krosnick). It was appointed resident quartet at the Library of Congress, Washington, 1962.

Jullien, Louis [alleged, with no evidence produced, to have had thirty-four additional baptismal names: Georges Maurice Adolphe Roch Albert Abel Antonio Alexandre Noé Jean Lucien Daniel Eugène Joseph-le-Brun Joseph-Barême Thomas Thomas Thomas-Thomas Pierre Cerbon Pierre-Maurel Barthélemi Artus Alphonse Bertrand Emanuel Dieudonné Josué Vincent Luc Michel Jules-de-la-Plane Jules-Bazin Julio-César] (b. 23 Apr 1812; d. 14 Mar 1860), French conductor and promoter. Known especially for his promenade concerts at cheap prices, at which he pioneered the technique and showmanship of baton conducting. He was active in Paris and regularly from 1840 in London; also composer. Confined in his last weeks to a lunatic asylum.

Jung, Manfred (b. 9 July 1940), German tenor. Unusually, was chorus-member at Bayreuth, 1970–73, where he was to win fame as a soloist from 1976 (for example in the title role of *Parsifal* and Siegfried in *Götterdämmerung*, which was also televised). Made Metropolitan début 1981.

Jungwirth, Manfred (b. 4 June 1919), Austrian bass. Made operatic début while a German army conscript in Bucharest, 1942, and won Geneva International Competition, 1948. He made his UK début 1965 at Glyndebourne as Ochs in *Der Rosenkavalier*, his most celebrated role; sang at Vienna State Opera from 1967.

Jürgens, Jürgen (b. 5 Oct 1925), German conductor, also editor of baroque music. Prominent as director of the Hamburg Monteverdi Choir from 1955. In concert and recording he revived a rare opera, Gagliano's *Dafne* of 1608; he has also recorded modern Italian music.

Jurinac, Sena (abbreviation of Srebrenka) (b. 24 Oct 1921), Yugoslav soprano (mother Austrian). Sang with Vienna State Opera from its post-war reopening in 1945 (and visited Covent

Garden with the company, 1947). She was among the most celebrated Mozart singers: made Glyndebourne company début (at the Edinburgh Festival) as Fiordiligi in *Così*, 1950. Well known also in Strauss (the Composer in *Ariadne*). She first appeared in the USA 1959, at San Fransisco Opera. Married, 1953–7, to BRUSCANTINI.

K

Kabaivanska, Raina [Yakimova] (b. 15 Dec 1934), Bulgarian soprano. Studied in Italy, where she made her operatic début, 1959, under the name Raina Kabai. Built an international career, prominently in Verdi and Puccini. She sang Desdemona in *Otello* at Covent Garden, 1962, and took the title role on the first recording of Donizetti's *Fausta*, 1981.

Kabos, Ilona (b. 7 Dec 1893; d. 28 May 1973), Hungarian-born British pianist. Became a noted teacher in London and, annually from 1965, at the Juilliard School; OGDON and KALICHSTEIN were among her pupils. With KENTNER (to whom she was married, 1931–45), she gave the first performance of Bartók's Concerto for two pianos, 1942.

Kagan, Oleg, *see* GUTMAN.

Kajanus, Robert (b. 2 Dec 1856; d. 6 July 1933), Finnish conductor. Prominent in making Sibelius's music known; he gave the first performance, 1915, of the Symphony no. 5 and made the first recordings (with the LONDON SYMPHONY ORCHESTRA) of nos. 1 and 2. He was resident orchestral conductor at Helsinki from 1882 until 1932. Composed orchestral and other music.

Kakuschka, Thomas, *see* ALBAN BERG QUARTET.

Kalichstein, Joseph (b. 15 Jan 1946), Israeli pianist. In New York he was a pupil of KABOS and STEUERMANN, and gained the Leventritt Prize, 1969. He has performed with major European, US and Japanese orchestras and recorded both Mendelssohn concertos (with PREVIN). He plays in a trio with the violinist LAREDO and the cellist Sharon Robinson.

Kalisch, Paul, *see* LEHMANN, LILLI.

Kalkbrenner, Frédéric (originally Friedrich Wilhelm Michael) (b. between 2 and 8 Nov 1785; d. 10 June 1849), German-born French pianist, also composer. Born while his parents were on a coach journey. He was a prizewinning student at the Paris Conservatory, and acquired fame in Europe as a pianist and pedagogue: Chopin dedicated to him his Piano Concerto no. 1. He lived in London, 1814–23, then in Paris, where he was a partner in the Pleyel piano business.

Kalter (originally Aufrichtig), **Sabine** (b. 28 Mar 1889; d. 1 Sept 1957), Austrian mezzo-soprano. Had a prominent operatic career in Hamburg until she was forced out as a Jew by the Nazi race laws. Sang at Covent Garden, 1935–9, for example as Fricka in *The Ring* and Brangaene in *Tristan und Isolde*. Died in London.

Kamnitzer, Peter, *see* LASALLE QUARTET.

Kamu, Okko [Tapani] (b. 7 Mar 1946), Finnish conductor, also composer, formerly violinist. Won the international KARAJAN Conducting Competition in 1969, when he was already a conductor at the Finnish National Opera. Made his London début with the NEW PHILHARMONIA ORCHESTRA, 1970; chief conductor of the HELSINKI PHILHARMONIC ORCHESTRA, 1981–90. Conducted the première of Sallinen's Symphony no. 3, 1975, which was dedicated to him, and also the first British performance of Sallinen's Symphony no. 5, 1987.

Kanawa, Kiri Te, *see* TE KANAWA.

Kapell, William (b. 20 Sept 1922; d. 29 Oct 1953), American pianist. Died in an air crash, having won exceptional praise in USA and elsewhere. (He never played in UK.) He had notably championed Khachaturian's Piano Concerto; Copland's Fantasy for piano, 1957, was dedicated to his memory.

Kappel, Gertrude (b. 1 Sept 1884; d. 3 Apr 1971), German soprano. Celebrated in Wagner (Brünnhilde and Isolde). In her long career, 1906–37, appeared at Covent Garden, 1912–14 and 1924–6, and the Metropolitan, 1928–36 (including the title role in the first performance of Strauss's *Elektra*, 1932).

Kapuscinski, Richard, *see* LASALLE QUARTET.

Karajan, Herbert (originally Heribert) **von** (b. 5 Apr 1908; d. 16 July 1989), Austrian conductor, also stage and film director for some of his own opera performances. His success as a conductor was unsurpassed. Music director of the Berlin State Opera, 1938–45; despite former Nazi Party membership from 1935, he made his London début with the PHILHARMONIA ORCHESTRA in 1947. Worked as artistic director at La Scala, 1948–68 (conducted the première of Orff's *Trionfi di Afrodite*, 1953), and also Vienna State Opera, 1957–64; made Metropolitan Opera début 1967. As 'conductor for life' of the BERLIN PHILHARMONIC ORCHESTRA, from 1955 (he resigned three months before his death) he made a prodigious number of recordings, among them all Beethoven's symphonies (four times), Wagner (including the complete *Ring* cycle), Verdi operas, Mahler and Webern. A foundation in his name promotes a biennial competition for young conductors.

Karas, Anton (b. 7 July 1906; d. 9 Jan 1985), Austrian zither player and café musician. Worked in Vienna. He played on the soundtrack for Carol Reed's film *The Third Man*, 1949; it included the 'Harry Lime Theme' which became hugely popular and is said to have sold four million records.

Karr, Gary [Michael] (b. 20 Nov 1941), American double-bass player. Made his New York début as a solo recitalist in 1962 and was soloist on the NEW YORK PHILHARMONIC's European tour, 1964. Today's most celebrated exponent of his instrument, he commissioned and premièred the concertos of Henze, 1967, and Schuller, 1968.

Kars, Jean-Rodolphe (b. 15 Mar 1947), Austrian pianist (born in Calcutta). Uses the French form of his forenames. He studied at the Paris Conservatory and was also a private pupil of KATCHEN. Made his London début 1967 and won the Messiaen Competition at Royan the following year.

Katchen, Julius (b. 15 Aug 1926; d. 29 Apr 1969), American pianist. A child prodigy (made début with the PHILADELPHIA ORCHESTRA at eleven), he studied philosophy in Paris and became resident there. He made the first LP record issued by a British company (Brahms's Piano Sonata in F minor), 1950. A fine career was cut short by early death. Played in a trio with Josef SUK (2) and STARKER and occasionally conducted.

Katims, Milton (b. 24 June 1909), American viola player and conductor. Played first viola in TOSCANINI's New York-based NATIONAL BROADCASTING COMPANY SYMPHONY ORCHESTRA, then was music director of the Seattle Symphony Orchestra, 1954–76. He later became director of a music college in Houston.

Katin, Peter [Roy] (b. 14 Nov 1930), British-born Canadian pianist. His paternal grandparents were Russian. In his boyhood he was a Westminster Abbey chorister. Well known as an interpreter of Chopin, Rakhmaninov, and others. He held a professorship at the University of Western Ontario, 1978–84. Recorded Walton's Sinfonia concertante with the composer conducting.

Katz, Mindru (b. 3 June 1925; d. 30 Jan 1978), Romanian-born pianist, naturalized Israeli 1959. Made his London concerto début 1958 (under BOULT). He played all the Beethoven concertos under Josef KRIPS at the Israel Festival, 1964. Died while giving a recital in Istanbul.

Katz, Paul, *see* CLEVELAND QUARTET.

Kaufman, Louis (b. 10 May 1905), American

violinist. Toured Europe from 1950. He performed many modern and unusual works; gave the première of Wirén's Concerto in Stockholm, 1953, and the first London performance of Piston's, 1956.

Keene, Christopher (b. 21 Dec 1946), American conductor. Prominent in opera. After working with Menotti at the Spoleto Festival in Italy, he conducted at New York City Opera, from 1970; became its director in 1988. At Santa Fe he conducted the first performance of Villa-Lobos's opera *Yerma*, 1971.

Keenlyside, Raymond, *see* AEOLIAN QUARTET.

Kegel, Herbert (b. 29 July 1920), German conductor. One of the most prominent conductors in East Germany; he became chief conductor of the Dresden Philharmonic, 1977. His repertory includes a wide range of modern composers, among them Penderecki and Britten (whose *War Requiem* he conducted in Leipzig, 1966).

Keilberth, Joseph (b. 19 Apr 1908; d. 20 July 1968), German conductor. A noted interpreter of Wagner and Strauss, he conducted at the Bayreuth Wagner Festival from 1952, and in that year appeared with the Hamburg State Opera at the Edinburgh Festival. He was artistic director of the Bavarian State Opera, Munich, from 1959; died there after collapsing in a performance of *Tristan*.

Kelemen, Zoltán (b. 12 Mar 1926; d. 9 May 1979), Hungarian bass. Noted in Wagner: sang Alberich in *The Ring* at Bayreuth, 1964, later at Covent Garden, 1970, the Metropolitan Opera, and in KARAJAN's complete recording. He took part in the first performance of Bernd Alois Zimmermann's *Die Soldaten*, 1965.

Kell, Reginald [Clifford] (b. 8 June 1906; d. 5 Aug 1981), British clarinettist. A principal player for BEECHAM (LONDON PHILHARMONIC ORCHESTRA, 1932–6), and a noted soloist and leader of his own wind ensemble. Between 1948 and 1971 he lived mainly in USA, and he died on a return visit there.

Kellogg, Clara [Louise] (b. 9 July 1842; d. 13 May 1916), American soprano and operatic impresario. Sang Marguerite in the first New York performance of *Faust*, 1863, and made her London début in that role, 1867. In collaboration with LUCCA she organized an opera company in USA, 1872, then managed her own company, 1873–9.

Kelly, Michael (b. 25 Dec 1762; d. 9 Oct 1826), Irish tenor. After appearances in Italy, went to Vienna, where he became a friend of Mozart. Created the roles of Basilio and Curzio in the première of *Figaro*, 1786. Later, in London, he was an operatic tenor, composer and stage manager at the King's Theatre, and also an unsuccessful publisher; became bankrupt in 1811.

Kemble, Adelaide (b. 1814; d. 4 Aug 1879), English soprano. In 1839 she went to Italy, took lessons with PASTA and made successful appearances in such works as *Norma*. Also won acclaim in London, but married in 1843 and left the profession; she later became known as a novelist. Her father was the actor Charles Kemble.

Kemp, Barbara (b. 12 Dec 1881; d. 17 Apr 1959), German soprano, also stage director. Noted in Wagner, she was a member of the Berlin Court Opera (later State Opera) from 1913 to 1931. She married its director, the composer Max von Schillings, and took the title role in the first Berlin and New York performances of his opera *Mona Lisa*, 1915 and 1923.

Kempe, Rudolf (b. 14 June 1910; d. 12 May 1976), German conductor. Worked in Dresden and then Munich (as director of Bavarian State Opera, 1952–4), and also as a guest conductor at the Vienna State Opera. After conducting the Munich company on its Covent Garden visit, 1953, he was engaged by Covent Garden itself for *The Ring* and other operas. He was BEECHAM's associate and then in 1961 succeeded him as chief conductor (later artistic director) of the ROYAL PHILHARMONIC ORCHESTRA. Conducted the TONHALLE ORCHESTRA, 1965–72, and the BBC SYMPHONY ORCHESTRA, 1975–6. He recorded all Strauss's orchestral works.

Kempen, Paul van (b. 16 May 1893; d. 8 Dec 1955), Dutch conductor. Made his career chiefly in Dresden and elsewhere in Germany. For political reasons he was at first unwelcome in the Netherlands after the war, but he conducted a radio orchestra there in the period 1949–53.

Kempff, Wilhelm (b. 25 Nov 1895), German pianist, also composer. Began his distinguished career in 1916; he appeared as a soloist with the BERLIN PHILHARMONIC ORCHESTRA first in 1918 and as late as 1979. Although he toured internationally, gave no recital in London until 1951 or in New York until 1964. His recordings include all Beethoven's and Schubert's piano sonatas.

Kennedy, Daisy, *see* MOISEIWITSCH.

Kennedy, David, *see* KENNEDY-FRASER.

Kennedy, Nigel (b. 28 Dec 1956), British violinist. Studied at the Yehudi Menuhin School, initially as a pianist, and the Juilliard School. He regularly appears as a jazz as well as classical violinist; made London concert début 1977. His recording of Vivaldi's *The Four Seasons* achieved unprecedented sales, exceeding 600,000.

Kennedy-Fraser, Marjory (b. 17 Oct 1857; d. 22 Nov 1930), British contralto. Collected, edited and performed folksongs of the Hebrides, from 1905. Her father, David Kennedy (1825–86), was also a singer and song collector. She took the title role in Bantock's opera *The Seal Woman*, 1924, for which she wrote the libretto. She was also a pianist and composer.

Kentner, Louis (originally Lajos) [Philip] (b. 19 July 1905; d. 21 Sept 1987), Hungarian-born pianist; became British citizen 1946. Settled in Britain, 1935; married, 1931–45, to KABOS. He was an influential performer of Liszt and Bartók (first European performance of Bartók's Piano Concerto no. 3, London, 1946), and also championed British composers. Walton's Violin Sonata, 1949, was written for him and MENUHIN (who had become his brother-in-law by his second marriage, 1946). The two were renowned partners in recital and also appeared in a trio with CASSADÓ. CBE, 1978.

Kern, Adele (b. 25 Nov 1901; d. 6 May 1980), German operatic soprano. Famous in Mozart soubrette roles in Munich and Vienna and, 1927–35, at the Salzburg Festival. She also sang at Covent Garden, 1931 and 1933.

Kern, Patricia (b. 4 July 1927), British mezzo-soprano. Prominent at Sadler's Wells Opera (later English National); sang the title role in Rossini's *La Cenerentola* and Cherubino in *Figaro*. She performed with Scottish Opera (Britten's Lucretia), Covent Garden, from 1967, and New York City Opera as well as other companies in USA and Canada; also at Glyndebourne, 1984.

Kersey, Eda (b. 15 May 1904; d. 13 July 1944), British violinist. Esteemed both as a soloist and as a chamber musician. She gave the première of Bax's Violin Concerto and the first British performance of Barber's, both 1943.

Kertész, István (b. 28 Aug 1929; d. 16 Apr 1973), Hungarian-born German conductor. Equally committed to opera and concert, he was principal conductor of the LONDON SYMPHONY ORCHESTRA, 1965–8, while retaining his music directorship of Cologne Opera, from 1964; also made guest appearances at Covent Garden from 1966. His many recordings include the first complete version of Mozart's *La clemenza di Tito*, 1967. He drowned while swimming in Israel.

Kes, Willem (b. 16 Feb 1856; d. 21 Feb 1934), Dutch conductor, previously violinist. The first conductor of the CONCERTGEBOUW ORCHESTRA OF AMSTERDAM, 1888–95, he established it in the first rank. He then worked in Glasgow (conductor of the SCOTTISH ORCHESTRA, 1895–8), Moscow and Koblenz.

Keys, Ivor [Christopher Banfield] (b. 8 Mar 1919), British pianist, organist and conductor. Known particularly for the opera performances he directed as professor at the University of Birmingham, 1968–86, including Keiser's *Masaniello* (first modern performance), 1973, and Handel's *Giulio Cesare*, 1977. He is also a composer. CBE, 1976.

Khaikin, Boris [Emanuilovich] (b. 26 Oct 1904; d. 10 May 1978), Russian conductor. Noted in opera; in Leningrad he conducted the premières of Prokofiev's *The Duenna*, 1946, and *The Story of a Real Man*, 1948 (private performance, after which the opera was politically banned till 1960). Worked at the Bolshoi Theatre from 1954. He conducted the LENINGRAD PHILHARMONIC on an Italian tour, 1966.

Khokhlov, Pavel [Akinfievich] (b. 2 Aug 1854; d. 20 Sept 1919), Russian baritone. Active mainly at the Bolshoi Theatre, where he sang the title role in the first public performance of Tchaikovsky's *Yevgeny Onegin*, 1881, and repeated the role more than 130 times. He performed in other Russian operas as well as in Mozart, Meyerbeer and Wagner.

Khuner, Felix, *see* KOLISCH QUARTET.

Kibkalo, Yevgeny (b. 12 Feb 1932), Russian baritone. After joining the Bolshoi company, underwent additional training in Milan. He sang in the first Bolshoi performances of Prokofiev's *War and Peace* (as Andrey), 1959, and took the principal role in Prokofiev's *The Story of a Real Man* when it was freed from its political ban, 1960. His other roles have included Demetrius in Britten's *A Midsummer Night's Dream*.

Kiepura, Jan (b. 16 May 1902; d. 15 Aug 1966), Polish tenor. Had an international operatic career (Vienna State Opera, 1926, and the Metropolitan, 1938), but his popularity broadened enormously when he appeared in Hollywood musical films, for example *My Song Goes Round the World*, 1934. Married Marta Eggerth (b. 1912) and performed with her in a three-year Broadway run of Lehár's *The Merry Widow*, from 1956, and in other shows.

Kim, Young-Uck (b. 1 Sept 1947), Korean violinist. Sent to USA at the age of eleven. He became a pupil of GALAMIAN and performed with the PHILADELPHIA ORCHESTRA under ORMANDY when he was fifteen. Also appears in a trio with AX and MA.

Kimm, Fiona [Mary] (b. 24 May 1952), British mezzo-soprano. Active in opera. She has performed many young male parts, among them Fyodor in *Boris Godunov* (during her first Covent Garden season, 1983); Edward Cowie's solo theatre piece, *Kate Kelly's Roadshow*, 1982, was written for her; she sang in the first performances (Munich and Edinburgh) of Turnage's opera *Greek*, 1988.

Kincszes, Veronika (b. 8 Sept 1948), Hungarian soprano. Joined the Hungarian State Opera, 1973, and has become known for her performances and recordings of Hungarian operas and choral works. She made her US début in Chicago, 1981; sang the title role in Puccini's *Suor Angelica* at Montreal, 1986.

Kindler, Hans (b. 8 Jan 1892; d. 30 Aug 1949), Dutch-born American cellist and conductor. First cellist of the PHILADELPHIA ORCHESTRA, 1914–20, and soloist in the first performance of Bloch's *Schelomo*, 1917 (though its dedicatee was BARJANSKY). He conducted the première of Stravinsky's *Apollon musagète* in Washington, 1928, and was conductor of the newly founded NATIONAL SYMPHONY ORCHESTRA there, 1931–48.

King, James (b. 26 Dec 1925), American tenor. After starting as a baritone, made his début as a tenor in San Francisco, 1961, and became one of the world's leading performers of heavier roles, such as Wagner's Siegmund and Parsifal. He sang at the Bayreuth Wagner Festival from 1965 and at Covent Garden from 1966; participated in both SOLTI's and BÖHM's complete recordings of *The Ring*.

King, Thea (b. 22 May 1925), British clarinettist. Well known for championing the twentieth-century British repertory (Stanford, Finzi and Frankel) and for revivals of earlier music; she made recordings of Crusell's three clarinet concertos (dating from 1811 to 1828). In 1985 she recorded Mozart's Concerto and Clarinet Quintet using an instrument with an authentic extended compass. Married to THURSTON.

Kipnis, Alexander (b. 13 Feb 1891; d. 14 May 1978), Russian-born bass; became American citizen 1931. Father of Igor KIPNIS. Had a distinguished opera and recital career in Germany and Austria. After being forced out (as a Jew) by the Nazi race laws, he settled in USA, where he had been a visiting performer since 1923. Noted in Wagner; he sang at Covent Garden from 1927 and at Glyndebourne (as Sarastro in *Die Zauberflöte*) in 1936.

Kipnis, Igor (b. 27 Sept 1930), American harpsichordist, son of Alexander KIPNIS. Made his New York recital début 1961; he has toured and taught widely, and recorded also on clavichord and piano. His repertory includes modern harpsichord works, for example George

Rochberg's *Nach Bach* (After Bach), in addition to baroque pieces.

Kirchgässner, Marianne [Antonia] (b. 5 June 1769; d. 9 Dec 1808), German glass harmonica player. Blind from the age of four. She toured to Salzburg, Munich, London, 1794, and elsewhere. Mozart, having heard her in Vienna, wrote for her two solo pieces and one with flute, oboe, viola and cello. The peculiar vibrations of her instrument were dubiously blamed for her early death.

Kirkby, Emma (b. 26 Feb 1949), British soprano. Made London début 1974. She cultivated an unusual restraint of vibrato, and quickly won fame as an interpreter of familiar and unfamiliar baroque music. Performed much with PARROTT (to whom she was married, 1971–83) and ROOLEY; has occasionally appeared on stage.

Kirkby-Lunn, Louise (b. 8 Nov 1873; d. 17 Feb 1930), British mezzo-soprano. At twenty-two she was selected by Stanford to sing in the first performance of his opera *Shamus O'Brien*; went on to lead a distinguished career at Covent Garden, 1901–22, and the Metropolitan, 1902–8. She sang Kundry in the first US performance in English of *Parsifal* (Boston), 1904, and performed in Elgar's *Sea Pictures* when MAHLER conducted it in New York, 1910.

Kirkpatrick, John (b. 18 Mar 1905), American pianist. In 1939 gave (from memory) the first performance of Ives's extremely complex *Concord Sonata* (published 1919). He became a professor at Yale and curator of the Ives collection there.

Kirkpatrick, Ralph (b. 10 June 1911; d. 13 Apr 1984), American harpsichordist and pianist (*see* ROSEN, CHARLES). He is chiefly famous for the original research leading to his biography of Domenico Scarlatti, 1953, and for establishing a numerical catalogue of that composer's work. Taught at Yale, 1940–78.

Kirshbaum, Ralph (b. 4 Mar 1946), American cellist. Has been resident in London from 1971. He recorded Elgar's and Walton's concertos; formed a successful trio with PAUK (violin) and FRANKL (piano).

Kirstein, Jack, *see* LASALLE QUARTET.

Kirsten, Dorothy (b. 6 July 1917), American soprano. In 1975 celebrated thirty years with the Metropolitan Opera, where she sang such roles as Puccini's Butterfly and Mimì (*La Bohème*). Performed at the Bolshoi and other Soviet theatres, 1962. She appeared in *The Great Caruso*, 1951, and other films.

Klee, Bernhard (b. 19 Apr 1936), German conductor. Has held operatic and orchestral posts at Düsseldorf from 1977. He has been guest conductor with the BERLIN PHILHARMONIC, from 1968, and various British orchestras, especially the BBC PHILHARMONIC, from 1985. Piano accompanist to MATHIS, his wife. His recordings include Zemlinsky's *Lyrische Symphonie* and the first recording of Mozart's unfinished opera *Zaide*, 1973.

Kleiber, Carlos (b. 3 July 1930), German-born conductor; became Austrian citizen 1980. Son of Erich KLEIBER. When young, emigrated with his parents to Argentina; uses Spanish forename. Acclaimed in opera, he conducted at Covent Garden from 1974 and at the Bayreuth Wagner Festival, 1974–6. His work as an orchestral conductor has included guest performances with the CHICAGO SYMPHONY ORCHESTRA, 1979.

Kleiber, Erich (b. 5 Aug 1890; d. 27 Jan 1956), Austrian-born conductor; became Argentinian citizen 1938. Father of Carlos KLEIBER. As music director of Berlin State Opera, conducted the première of Berg's *Wozzeck*, 1925; later, hostile to the Nazi regime, he left Germany for Argentina. He was reappointed to his Berlin position (now in East Germany), 1954, but again resigned in protest at political pressure. At Covent Garden, 1950–53, he gave Berg's *Wozzeck* its first British stage production, 1952, and was much admired for his *Rosenkavalier*. Noted too as a concert conductor (appeared with the LONDON SYMPHONY ORCHESTRA, 1935). He was also a composer.

Klein, Peter (b. 25 Jan 1907), German-born Austrian tenor. Celebrated as Mime in *The Ring* (Covent Garden from 1947) and other character parts. He was a member of Vienna State Opera from 1942, and sang various roles at the Metropolitan Opera, 1949–51.

Klemperer, Otto (b. 14 May 1885; d. 6 July 1973). German-born conductor, also composer; became Israeli citizen 1970. Having assisted MAHLER in preparing the première of his Symphony no. 8 in Munich, 1910, he developed an outstanding career as a conductor, particularly at the Berlin State Opera, 1927–33, and its branch the Kroll Opera. Conducted the first Berlin performances of Stravinsky's *Oedipus rex*, Hindemith's *Cardillac* and Schoenberg's *Erwartung*, among other works. As a Jew he was forced out of Germany by the Nazi race laws, 1933, and emigrated to USA; he was conductor of the LOS ANGELES PHILHARMONIC ORCHESTRA, 1933–9, with which he gave the première of Toch's *Pinocchio: A Merry Overture*, and of the BUDAPEST PHILHARMONIC ORCHESTRA, 1947–50. From 1959, despite partial paralysis, he was prominent in London as principal conductor of the PHILHARMONIA ORCHESTRA. At Covent Garden he both conducted and directed the productions of *Fidelio*, 1961, and other operas.

Klengel, August Alexander (b. 29 June 1783; d. 22 Nov 1852), German pianist. Admired by Moscheles and Chopin; active in the revival of Bach's works. He was also an organist and composer.

Klengel, Julius (b. 24 Sept 1859; d. 27 Oct 1933), German cellist. Noted as an orchestral musician and quartet player (*see* BRODSKY QUARTET 1); taught in Leipzig, where his pupils included FEUERMANN, SUGGIA and PIATIGORSKY. Also composer of four cello concertos and other works.

Kletzki, Paul (original Polish spelling Pavel Klecki) (b. 21 Mar 1900; d. 5 Mar 1973), Polish-born conductor; took Swiss nationality 1947. Before World War II held a conducting post in Kharkov, USSR; made his British début with the PHILHARMONIA ORCHESTRA in 1947. He was principal conductor of the LIVERPOOL PHILHARMONIC, 1954–5, and of the SUISSE ROMANDE orchestra, 1967–9. Also composer.

Klien, Walter (b. 27 Nov 1928), Austrian pianist. Eminent in the classical repertory, he was the first to record the complete solo piano works of Brahms; also recorded all Schubert's piano sonatas. He has toured widely and accompanied such singers as PATZAK and PREY.

Klimov, Valery Alexandrovich (b. 16 Oct 1931). Russian violinist. Pupil of David OISTRAKH; won the Moscow Tchaikovsky Competition, 1958. He made his British début with the BBC SYMPHONY ORCHESTRA in 1967.

Klindworth, Karl (b. 25 Sept 1830; d. 27 July 1916), German pianist. A pupil of LISZT and friend of Wagner; he made the voice-and-piano scores of *The Ring*. Much in demand as a teacher, he lived in London, 1854–68, then taught till 1881 at the newly founded Moscow Conservatory. Also conductor.

Klobucar, Berislav (b. 28 Aug 1924), Yugoslav conductor. Active at the Vienna State Opera from 1953. He conducted at the Bayreuth Wagner Festival, 1968, and was appointed concert and opera conductor at Nice, 1982.

Klosé, Hyacinthe Eléonore (b. 11 Oct 1808; d. 29 Aug 1880), French clarinettist. A distinguished teacher at the Paris Conservatory, 1839–68. He was influential in improving the mechanism of the clarinet, and wrote tutors for it and the newly invented saxophone.

Klose, Margarete (b. 6 Aug 1902; d. 14 Dec 1968), German operatic mezzo-soprano. Active chiefly in Berlin, but was also esteemed elsewhere; she sang Ortrud in *Lohengrin* under BEECHAM at Covent Garden, 1935.

Knappertsbusch, Hans (b. 12 Mar 1888; d. 25 Oct 1965), German conductor. Established his reputation in long tenures at the Bavarian State Opera, Munich, 1922–36, and the Vienna State Opera, 1936–50; noted also for his concerts and recordings with the VIENNA PHILHARMONIC ORCHESTRA. He travelled little, but conducted at Covent Garden (*Salome*), 1937, and the Bayreuth Wagner Festival, 1951–7.

Kneisel, Franz (b. 26 Jan 1865; d. 26 Mar 1926), Hungarian-born American violinist of German parentage. Performed as soloist and led his own string quartet, 1885–1917, which gave the first performance of Dvořák's 'American' Quartet (op. 96), 1894. He was also leader (concertmaster) of the BOSTON SYMPHONY ORCHESTRA, 1885–1903.

Knight, Gillian [Rosemary] (b. 1 Nov 1934),

British contralto. Active in opera; sang at Covent Garden from 1970 (first performance of Peter Maxwell Davies's *Taverner*, 1972). She had a distinguished long career with the D'Oyly Carte Opera Company, from 1958, in its performances (and recordings) of Gilbert and Sullivan.

Kniplová, Naděžda (b. 18 Apr 1932), Czech soprano. A member of Prague National Opera, she also made guest appearances at Hamburg and other major Western opera centres. Her reputation in strongly dramatic parts (such as Tosca and Emilia Marty in Janáček's *The Makropoulos Affair*) has been sustained by her recordings.

Knüpfer, Paul (b. 21 June 1865; d. 4 Nov 1920), German bass. Member of the Berlin Court Opera (later State Opera) from 1888 until his death. At Covent Garden, 1904–14, he sang Gurnemanz in the first British staging of *Parsifal* and Ochs in the British première of *Der Rosenkavalier*.

Knushevitsky, Svyatoslav [Nikolayevich] (b. 6 Jan 1908; d. 19 Feb 1963), Russian cellist. Gave the first performance of Khachaturian's Cello Concerto, 1946. In 1940 he formed a trio with David OISTRAKH (violin) and OBORIN (piano), which became well known for concerts and recordings; with it he made his British début in 1958.

Knyvett, Charles (b. 22 Feb 1752; d. 19 Jan 1822), British countertenor. A prominent singer in the Handel commemoration festival of 1784; he was also a concert promoter. His sons Charles (1773–1852) and William (1779–1856) were both musicians.

Kochański, Paul (originally Pawel) (b. 14 Sept 1887; d. 12 Jan 1934), Polish violinist. Collaborated with Szymanowski in performances and arrangements of his music and wrote cadenzas for both his concertos. He taught in Russia and, having emigrated to USA in 1921, at the Juilliard School, from 1924.

Kocsis, Zoltán (b. 30 May 1952), Hungarian pianist, also organist. Won a national competition at the age of eighteen, toured USA and made his British début the following year. He recorded Bach's keyboard concertos and his own transcriptions from Wagner operas. He is also a conductor and composer. (*See also* FISCHER, IVÁN.)

Kodousek, Joseph, *see* VLACH QUARTET.

Koeckert, Rudolf (b. 27 June 1913), German violinist (born in what is now part of Czechoslovakia). Active as an orchestral leader, but particularly known for leading the KOECKERT QUARTET.

Koeckert, Rudolf Joachim, *see* KOECKERT QUARTET.

Koeckert Quartet, German (but originally Prague-based) string quartet founded 1939. First known as the Prague German Quartet or the Sudeten German Quartet, it was later based in Munich and in 1947 took the name of its leader, Rudolf KOECKERT. Other members from 1975 were his son, Rudolf Joachim Koeckert, Franz Schessl and Josef Merz.

Koff, Robert, *see* JUILLIARD QUARTET.

Kogan, Leonid [Borisovich] (b. 14 Nov 1924; d. 17 Dec 1982), Russian violinist. Won the Queen Elisabeth Competition in Brussels 1951, and thereafter achieved a distinguished international career; first appeared in Britain 1955 and in USA 1958. He was the first Soviet violinist to perform (and record) Berg's Concerto; Khachaturian's Concerto-rhapsody for violin and orchestra, 1962, is dedicated to him. He, his wife, Elizaveta (sister of GILELS), and their son Pavel gave the first performance of Mannino's Concerto for three violins, 1965, which was dedicated to them.

Kohler, Irene (b. 7 Apr 1912), British pianist. Studied in London and with STEUERMANN in Vienna. She was active in London from her twenties (first appearance at a Prom in 1934); gave the European première of Eugene Goossens's *Fantasy Concerto*, 1943. She taught and performed in Japan, 1979 and 1981.

Kohout, Antonín, *see* SMETANA QUARTET.

Kolisch, Rudolf (b. 20 July 1896; d. 1 Aug 1978), Austrian-born American violinist. As a result of a childhood injury he had to hold the instrument in his right hand and bow with the left. Studied violin with ŠEVČÍK and composition with Schoenberg. He was known chiefly as the leader of the KOLISCH and PRO ARTE quartets.

Kolisch Quartet, Vienna-based string quartet founded 1922 by KOLISCH, its leader. For most of its existence the other members were Felix Khuner, Jenö Lehner and Benar Heifetz. Unusually, they played the standard repertory from memory and championed difficult modern works: gave the first performances of Schoenberg's quartets nos. 3 and 4, Berg's *Lyric Suite* and Bartók's Quartet no. 5. Disbanded in 1939.

Kollo (originally Kollodziewski), **René** (b. 20 Nov 1937), German tenor. Had an early career as a singer in light entertainment before suddenly coming to fame in Wagner: sang at Bayreuth, 1969, and the Paris Opera (title role in *Parsifal*), 1974, and made Metropolitan début as Lohengrin, 1976. Also continued to sing operetta. His recordings include the first of Korngold's *Die tote Stadt*, 1976.

Komlós, Péter, *see* BARTÓK QUARTET.

Komlóssy, Erzsébet (b. 9 July 1933), Hungarian mezzo-soprano. A member of the Hungarian National Opera, she is well known from that company's recordings. Also sang under CASALS in Athens in his oratorio *El pessebre* (The Manger), 1966, and as Azucena in *Il trovatore* at Covent Garden, 1970.

Kondrashin, Kirill [Petrovich] (b. 6 Mar 1914; d. 7 Mar 1981), Russian conductor. After working at the Bolshoi Theatre, 1943–56, concentrated on the concert repertory. As conductor of the Moscow Philharmonic, 1960–75, he gave the first performance of Shostakovich's Symphony no. 4, 1962 (twenty-six years after it was written) and the new, politically controversial Symphony no. 13. In 1979 he became music director of the CONCERTGEBOUW ORCHESTRA in Amsterdam, where he died of a heart attack shortly after conducting a concert.

Konetzni (originally Konerczny), **Anny** (b. 12 Feb 1902; d. 6 Sept 1968), Austrian soprano, previously contralto, sister of Hilde KONETZNI. Became well known in Wagnerian roles in the inter-war years, and returned to sing Brünnhilde in *Die Walküre* at Covent Garden in 1951.

Konetzni (originally Konerczny), **Hilde** (b. 21 Mar 1905; d. 20 Apr 1980), Austrian soprano, sister of Anny KONETZNI. Highly successful in opera; appeared in various Mozart, Strauss and Wagner roles at Covent Garden, 1938–9. She returned there with the visiting Vienna State Opera as Leonore in *Fidelio*, 1947.

Kontarsky, Alfons (b. 9 Oct 1932), German pianist, brother of Aloys KONTARSKY. Famous for two-piano duo with his elder brother, he has also performed and recorded other chamber music.

Kontarsky, Aloys (b. 14 May 1931), German pianist, brother of Alfons KONTARSKY. With his brother in a two-piano duo from 1955 he gave many first performances of modern works, including Bernd Alois Zimmermann's *Dialogues* for two pianos and orchestra, 1960, and Stockhausen's *Mantra*, 1970. He has also performed and recorded as a soloist.

Konwitschny, Franz (b. 14 Aug 1901; d. 28 July 1962), German conductor (born in what is now Czechoslovakia). Appointed conductor of the GEWANDHAUS ORCHESTRA in Leipzig in 1949, he held that position for the rest of his life, and later combined it with posts in Dresden and East Berlin. He conducted *The Ring* at Covent Garden, 1959. Died on tour in Yugoslavia.

Kónya, Sándor (b. 23 Sept 1923), Hungarian-born German tenor. Became a member of the (West) Berlin City Opera, 1955. He sang at the Bayreuth Wagner Festival as Lohengrin, 1958, the role in which he made his Covent Garden début, 1963.

Konzertverein Quartet, *see* BUSCH QUARTET.

Koopman, Ton (b. 2 Oct 1944), Dutch harpsichordist and organist. Has recorded all the Bach keyboard concertos and a wide variety of other baroque and pre-baroque music. He formed the Amsterdam Baroque Orchestra in 1977.

Kopelman, Mikhail, *see* BORODIN QUARTET.

Korchagin, Alexander, *see* SHOSTAKOVICH QUARTET.

Korchinska, Maria (b. 16 Feb 1895; d. 17 Apr 1979), Russian-born British harpist. Settled in Britain in 1926. Active in performing new works, she took part in the première of Britten's

A Ceremony of Carols, 1942. With BERGHOUT she organized an annual international congress for harpists.

Kord, Kazimierz (b. 18 Nov 1930), Polish conductor. Artistic director of the WARSAW PHILHARMONIC ORCHESTRA from 1977, and was also conductor of the SÜDWESTFUNK ORCHESTRA at Baden-Baden, 1980–86. He has worked as a guest conductor in Britain, USA (Metropolitan Opera, 1972), and elsewhere.

Korjus, Miliza (b. 18 Aug 1907; d. 21 Aug 1980), Polish-born American soprano. Sang in opera in Berlin and Vienna, but achieved widest fame in stage and film musicals such as *The Great Waltz* (fanciful film biography of the younger Johann Strauss), 1938. Lived in USA from 1936 and died there.

Kórodi, András, *see* BUDAPEST PHILHARMONIC ORCHESTRA.

Koromzay, Dénes, *see* HUNGARIAN QUARTET.

Koshetz, Nina, form of name preferred for Western use by Nina Ivanovna Koshitz (b. 30 Dec 1894; d. 14 May 1965), Russian-born American soprano. Toured in Russia with RAKHMANINOV as pianist. She made a reputation in USA from the 1920s for performing (and recording) Russian songs; shared a New York recital with Prokofiev as composer and pianist, 1930.

Košler, Zdeněk (b. 3 Mar 1928), Czech conductor. Won a conducting competition in New York, 1963, and assisted BERNSTEIN there in 1963–4. After working in East Berlin, he was conductor of the Prague Symphony Orchestra, 1971–80, and chief conductor of the Prague National Theatre (opera), 1980–85, to which he returned as artistic director, 1990. Also guest conductor in Britain, 1975, and elsewhere.

Kostecký, Lubomir, *see* SMETANA QUARTET.

Kostelanetz, André (b. 22 Dec 1901; d. 13 Jan 1980), Russian-born American conductor. Settled in USA, 1922. He became known mainly for his own light orchestral arrangements, but was also a guest conductor of the NEW YORK PHILHARMONIC and other orchestras. Commissioned and gave the first performance of Copland's *Lincoln Portrait* (Cincinnati), 1942, and conducted the New York Philharmonic in the première of Walton's *Capriccio burlesco*, 1968, dedicated to him. Married, 1938–59, to PONS.

Köth, Erika (b. 15 Sept 1927; d. 21 Feb 1989), German soprano. Had major European career, principally in Munich and Vienna, but also Milan, Moscow and London (with the visiting Munich company from 1953). Her unusually high coloratura voice was well suited to such roles as Zerbinetta in Strauss's *Ariadne auf Naxos* and Donizetti's Lucia.

Koussevitzky, Serge (Sergey Alexandrovich Kusevitsky) (b. 26 July 1874; d. 4 June 1951), Russian-born American conductor, previously double-bass player. Leader of the double-basses at the Bolshoi Theatre; he established himself as a remarkable soloist, performing some of his own adaptations and compositions. Having married into a wealthy family, he launched himself as conductor of his own orchestra, 1909, and purchased a publishing house; he contracted Skryabin, Stravinsky, Rakhmaninov and others, and remained a champion of Skryabin's music, giving the première of *Prometheus* in Moscow, 1911. Continued conducting in Russia after the 1917 Revolution, but left in 1920; in Paris he conducted the first performance of Ravel's arrangement of Musorgsky's *Pictures at an Exhibition*, 1922. Settled in USA and was conductor of the BOSTON SYMPHONY ORCHESTRA, 1924–49; he achieved unsurpassed orchestral standards and commissioned music from Stravinsky (*Symphony of Psalms*, 1931) and Copland (*Short Symphony*, 1932), among others. Later the Koussevitzky Foundation, commemorating his wife, funded the creation of Britten's *Peter Grimes*, Bartók's Concerto for Orchestra and other works. He founded the Tanglewood (formerly Berkshire) Festival, 1955. (*See also* BERNSTEIN.)

Kovács, Dénes (b. 18 Apr 1930), Hungarian violinist. Won the Carl Flesch Prize in London, 1955. He has toured widely and recorded both Bartók's violin concertos. Director of the Liszt Academy of Music in Budapest, 1971–80.

Kovařovic, Karel (b. 9 Dec 1862; d. 6 Dec 1920), Czech conductor, also composer. As opera director at the Prague National Theatre, from 1900, gave the first performance of Dvořák's *Rusalka*, 1901, and championed other Czech works. He prepared his own revision and reorchestration of Janáček's *Jenůfa*.

Kraemer, Nicholas, *see* NEW IRISH CHAMBER ORCHESTRA.

Krafka, Karel, *see* JANÁČEK QUARTET.

Kraft, Anton (b. 30 Dec 1749; d. 28 Aug 1820), Bohemian cellist, also composer. A leading player in Haydn's princely orchestra at Eszterháza from 1778 and later a touring virtuoso. Haydn's well-known Concerto in D, 1781 (once thought to be one of Kraft's own compositions), was written for him, as was the cello part in Beethoven's Triple Concerto. He played in the latter's première, 1808, and was in the orchestra for the first performance of Beethoven's Symphony no. 7, 1813.

Krainev, Vladimir (b. 1 Apr 1944), Russian pianist. Pupil of NEUHAUS; shared first prize in the Moscow Tchaikovsky Competition with LILL, 1970. He has played in a duo with his wife, the cellist Karine Georgian (b. 1944).

Krasner, Louis (b. 21 June 1903), Russian-born violinist. Taken to USA at the age of five. He commissioned Berg's Violin Concerto, and gave the first performance of it, 1936, and of Schoenberg's, 1940; also made the first recordings of both.

Kratochvil, Jiří, *see* JANÁČEK QUARTET.

Kraus, Alfredo (b. 24 Sept 1927), Spanish tenor of Austrian descent. Sang opposite SUTHERLAND in *Lucia di Lammermoor* at Covent Garden, 1959. He has performed at the Metropolitan from 1962 and achieved international distinction in Mozart, Verdi (Duke in *Rigoletto*) and Massenet (title role of *Werther*); recorded many of these stage roles.

Kraus, Ernst (b. 8 June 1863; d. 6 Sept 1941), German tenor, father of Richard KRAUS. Prominent at Bayreuth, 1899–1909. At Covent Garden he sang Herod in the first British performance of *Salome*, 1910.

Kraus, Lili (b. 4 Mar 1903; d. 6 Nov 1986), Hungarian pianist; later took New Zealand and then American nationality. Became well known in the 1930s as a soloist and in a duo with Szymon GOLDBERG. On tour in 1942 she was interned by the Japanese for three years, but afterwards resumed a vigorous concert career. She played twenty-five Mozart concertos in one season in New York, 1966–7. University teacher in Texas, 1967–83.

Kraus, Otakar (b. 10 Dec 1909; d. 28 July 1980), Czech-born British baritone. Settled in London, 1940, and achieved a distinctive career in opera (Covent Garden from 1951) and as a singing teacher. He created the roles of Tarquinius in Britten's *The Rape of Lucretia* with the English Opera Group, 1946, and Nick Shadow in Stravinsky's *The Rake's Progress* in Venice, 1951.

Kraus, Richard (b. 16 Nov 1902; d. 11 Apr 1978), German conductor, son of Ernst KRAUS. Active at various German opera houses. He notably revived Busoni's seldom heard *Doktor Faust with* FISCHER-DIESKAU at Berlin in 1955.

Krause, Tom (b. 5 July 1934), Finnish baritone. Has achieved success in many languages. He sang at Glyndebourne in Strauss's *Capriccio*, 1963, and at Hamburg in the first performance of Krenek's opera *Der goldene Bock*, 1964. Collaborated with SÖDERSTRÖM in a complete recording of Sibelius's songs, and has also recorded leading roles in operas by Gluck, Mozart and others.

Krauss, Clemens (b. 31 Mar 1893; d. 16 May 1954), Austrian conductor. Had a long association with the VIENNA PHILHARMONIC ORCHESTRA (and was conducting it on tour when he died suddenly in Mexico), but won his chief fame as an opera director in Vienna, 1929–35, Berlin, 1935–6, and Munich, 1937–42. A close friend of Strauss, he was the first conductor of *Arabella* (Dresden, 1933) and *Capriccio* (Munich, 1942), in which he collaborated on the libretto. Appeared at Covent Garden both before and after World War II. He was married to URSULEAC, whom he accompanied at the piano in recital. His recordings include Beethoven piano concertos with BACKHAUS and Brahms's Alto Rhapsody with FERRIER, 1947.

Kreisler, Fritz (b. 2 Feb 1875; d. 29 Jan 1962), Austrian-born violinist, also composer; became French citizen, 1938, and then American, 1943. His long career spanned the upheavals of two world wars. Won little note in his first US appearances assisting Moriz ROSENTHAL, 1889. His major success began with his performances with the BERLIN PHILHARMONIC ORCHESTRA, 1899, and his international fame was much aided by recordings. He first played in London 1902 and in 1910 gave the première of Elgar's Concerto, which was written for him. Performed publicly till 1947. His very large repertory included highly successful pieces of his own (such as *Caprice viennois*); he also published pieces attributed to various eighteenth-century composers, afterwards admitting the hoax. His cadenzas to the Beethoven and Brahms concertos were adopted by many other violinists.

Kremer, Gidon (b. 27 Feb 1947), Soviet violinist of a Latvian family. Pupil of David OISTRAKH; won the Moscow Tchaikovsky Competition, 1970. As well as the classical concertos (including Beethoven's with modern-style cadenzas by Schnittke), he plays and has recorded a great variety of modern music; gave the first performance of Gubaidulina's *Offertorium*, 1984. In a recording of the Bach Double Concerto he performed (by superimposition of tracks) both solo parts. He has been resident mainly in the West from the mid-1970s, and founded the Lockenhaus Festival in Austria, 1981; performed at a Leningrad festival in 1988 (*See also* MAISKY.)

Krenn, Werner (b. 21 Sept 1942), Austrian tenor, formerly orchestral bassoonist. Equally active in concert and opera, notably in Mozart. He sang Titus in the first international recording of *La clemenza di Tito*, 1967, and became a member of Vienna State Opera in 1972. Married to DERNESCH.

Krenz, Jan (b. 14 July 1926), Polish conductor. Became known when he was appointed conductor of the POLISH RADIO SYMPHONY ORCHESTRA (at Katowice), 1953, which he took on successful international tours (Cheltenham Festival, 1967), presenting Polish and other works. He was director of the Warsaw Opera, 1968–73, and made many recordings of Polish and other music; held an orchestral post in Bonn, 1979–83. He is also a composer.

Kreutzer, Rodolphe (b. 16 Nov 1766; d. 6 Jan 1831), French violinist and composer of German descent. Chiefly famous because Beethoven admired his playing and dedicated to him (without explicit permission) the Violin Sonata op. 47, published 1805. There is no evidence that Kreutzer ever played the work in public.

Krips, Henry (originally Heinrich) (b. 10 Feb 1912; d. 25 Jan 1987), Austrian-born conductor; became Australian 1944. Brother of Josef KRIPS. Emigrated to Australia, 1938, and conducted the Australian Broadcasting Corporation's orchestras in Perth and Adelaide. He was a guest with Sadler's Wells Opera in London, 1967, where he later settled and specialized in lighter Viennese music. Also composer.

Krips, Josef (b. 8 Apr 1902; d. 13 Oct 1974), Austrian conductor, brother of Henry KRIPS. On staff of Vienna State Opera, 1933–8. He took a leading part in Vienna's resumption of operatic and concert life after 1945 and also conducted at the first post-war Salzburg Festival, 1946. He was conductor of the LONDON SYMPHONY ORCHESTRA, 1950–54 (making many successful recordings, especially of the Austro-German classics) and later of the SAN FRANCISCO SYMPHONY ORCHESTRA, 1963–70. Continued to work as opera conductor: appeared at Covent Garden with Vienna State Opera, 1947, and with Covent Garden's own company from 1963 and also at the Metropolitan from 1966.

Kroll, William (b. 30 Jan 1901; d. 10 Mar 1980), American violinist. Studied in Berlin, and led a distinguished career in chamber music: he was leader of the Coolidge Quartet 1936–1944, and others. He gave, with the composer's wife, the first performance, 1941, of Harris's Violin Sonata no. 1. Also composer.

Krombholc, Jaroslav (b. 30 Jan 1918; d. 16 July 1983), Czech conductor. Long active in opera at the Prague National Theatre and other houses; conducted at Covent Garden, 1959, and at Sadler's Wells Opera, 1961 (*The Bartered Bride*) and later. He was a celebrated exponent of Czech music with orchestras in London and elsewhere.

His opera recordings include the first of Martinů's *Julietta*, 1964.

Kronos Quartet, San Francisco-based string quartet founded 1973 by its first violinist, David Harrington. Other members, from 1978: John Sherba, Hank Dutt and Joan Jeanrenaud. The group almost exclusively plays twentieth-century music; it gave the first performance of Reich's *Different Trains* (with tape) in London, 1988.

Krosnick, Joel, *see* JUILLIARD QUARTET.

Kroyt, Boris, *see* BUDAPEST QUARTET.

Krumpholtz, Jean-Baptiste (originally Jan Křtitel) (b. 3 May 1742; d. 19 Feb 1790), Czech harpist, also composer, brother of Wenzel KRUMPHOLTZ. An innovator in harp design. He studied composition with Haydn, 1773, then settled in Paris. Married a young pupil, Anne-Marie Steckler, and when she left him for a lover (apparently the celebrated composer Dussek), drowned himself in the Seine; she became well known in London as a harpist.

Krumpholtz, Wenzel (originally Václav) (b. *c.* 1750; d. 2 May 1817), Czech violinist and mandolinist, brother of Jean-Baptiste KRUMPHOLTZ. Beethoven wrote for him a sonata for mandolin and piano and composed a vocal trio in his memory.

Kubelík, Jan (b. 5 July 1880; d. 5 Dec 1940), Czech-born Hungarian violinist, also composer, father of Rafael KUBELÍK. Pupil of ŠEVČIK. His early concerts in Europe and USA (London début 1900) won a sensational success and initiated a career that continued till the 1939–40 season when he played nearly fifty works in ten Prague concerts. His recordings, mostly of short pieces, include Mozart's 'L'amerò, sarò costante' as MELBA's accompanist. On his marriage to a Hungarian in 1903 he took Hungarian nationality.

Kubelík, Rafael [Jeronym] (b. 29 June 1914), Czech-born conductor, also composer; became Swiss citizen 1967. Son of Jan KUBELÍK. Toured Britain with the CZECH PHILHARMONIC ORCHESTRA, 1938, and was its principal conductor, 1942–8. He left Czechoslovakia in 1948 after communist coup there; conducted the CHICAGO SYMPHONY ORCHESTRA, 1950–53, and gave the première of Harris's Symphony no. 7, 1952. As music director of Covent Garden, 1955–8, he gave the first London performances of Janáček's *Jenůfa* and Berlioz's *Les Troyens* (both in English). He had a short-lived, controversial appointment as music director of the Metropolitan Opera, 1971–4, but a long-term, fruitful tenure at the BAVARIAN RADIO SYMPHONY ORCHESTRA in Munich, 1961–79. On his recorded set of the nine Beethoven symphonies he conducted nine different orchestras, including the CLEVELAND and the VIENNA PHILHARMONIC. He married the Australian soprano Elsie Morison (b. 1929).

Kubiak, Teresa (b. 26 Dec 1937), Polish soprano. Appeared as Lisa in Tchaikovsky's *The Queen of Spades* at Glyndebourne, 1970, and the Metropolitan, 1973. Later she recorded, under BERNSTEIN, one of the two vocal parts in Shostakovich's Symphony no. 14.

Kuhlmann, Kathleen (b. 7 Dec 1950), American mezzo-soprano. Sang in opera in USA, then at La Scala (Meg Page in *Falstaff*, 1980), Glyndebourne (title role in Rossini's *La Cenerentola*, 1983) and Covent Garden. She was Penelope in the first performance of the Henze–Monteverdi *Il ritorno d'Ulisse* at Salzburg, 1985.

Kuhn, Gustav (b. 25 Aug 1947), Austrian conductor. Conducted opera at Glyndebourne and Salzburg, 1980, and in Chicago, 1981. He was an orchestral music director in Bonn, 1983–6.

Kuijken, Barthold, *see* KUIJKEN, SIGISWALD.

Kuijken, Sigiswald (b. 16 Feb 1944), Belgian violinist, viol player and conductor. Founded a baroque orchestra called La PETITE BANDE, 1972; in London he has conducted the ORCHESTRA OF THE AGE OF ENLIGHTENMENT. Among his collaborators in 'authentic' performances have been LEONHARDT and his brothers, Wieland Kuijken (b. 1938), viol player and cellist, and Barthold Kuijken (b. 1949), flautist and recorder player.

Kuijken, Wieland, *see* KUIJKEN, SIGISWALD.

Kulenkampff, Georg (b. 23 Jan 1898; d. 4 Oct

1948), German violinist. Noted teacher in Berlin and Lausanne, and author of a posthumously published memoir. He died of spinal paralysis, having won distinction in his shortened career; recorded Beethoven sonatas with the young SOLTI as pianist, 1947.

Kullak, Theodor (b. 12 Sept 1818; d. 1 Mar 1882), German pianist, also composer. Pupil of CZERNY. In 1846 he became court pianist to the King of Prussia in Berlin, where he later founded his own academy; it eventually had about 100 teachers.

Kullman, Charles (b. 13 Jan 1903; d. 8 Feb 1983), American tenor of German parentage. Family surname was originally Kullmann. Having appeared at the Berlin State Opera, Covent Garden and elsewhere, he made his Metropolitan Opera début (as Faust) 1935. Went on to sing thirty-three roles there and acquired a noted personal following; he retired in 1960.

Kunz, Erich (b. 20 May 1909), Austrian baritone. Sang in the Glyndebourne chorus, 1934, and returned in 1948 as a soloist (Guglielmo in *Così*). He was well known in other Mozart roles and as Beckmesser in *Die Meistersinger*.

Kunzel, Erich (b. 21 Mar 1935), American conductor. Resident conductor (previously associate) of the CINCINNATI SYMPHONY ORCHESTRA, 1969–74. He conducted the orchestra on recordings of works by Duke Ellington and Dave Brubeck with the composers as pianists.

Kupper, Annelies (b. 21 July 1906; d. 7 Dec 1987), German soprano. Worked as a music teacher before embarking on a major opera career. She sang at the Bavarian State Opera, Munich, 1946–66, and created the title role in Strauss's *Die Liebe der Danae* at Salzburg, 1952. She also performed the role in London, 1953, where she had previously appeared as Chrysothemis in Strauss's *Elektra*.

Kurtz, Efrem (b. 7 Nov 1900), Russian-born conductor; took American nationality 1944. Active in Germany from 1921 and in 1927 toured UK and South America with the dancer Anna Pavlova. Well known as a ballet conductor, he was also music director of the HOUSTON SYMPHONY ORCHESTRA, 1948–54, and, jointly with PRITCHARD, the LIVERPOOL PHILHARMONIC ORCHESTRA, 1955–7. He revisited Russia in 1966, conducting Leningrad and Moscow orchestras. Married to Elaine Shaffer, 1925–73.

Kurz, Selma (b. 15 Nov 1874; d. 10 May 1933), Austrian soprano. Engaged for the Vienna Court Opera (later State Opera) under MAHLER's directorship in 1899 and remained until 1929. Her coloratura voice and remarkable trill made her famous in such roles as Gilda (*Rigoletto*). MELBA's jealousy of her has been cited as a reason for her infrequent London appearances (Covent Garden, 1904–5, 1907 and 1924).

Kusche, Benno (b. 30 Jan 1916), German bass-baritone. Made début in Koblenz 1938. He sang at Covent Garden as La Roche in the first British performance of Strauss's *Capriccio*, 1953; first performed at the Metropolitan Opera 1971.

Kuttner, Michael, *see* HUNGARIAN QUARTET.

Kuznetsova, Maria [Nikolayevna] (b. 1880; d. 26 Apr 1966), Russian soprano. Distinguished member of the Maryinsky Theatre (now the Kirov) in St Petersburg. She later created the leading role of Fevronia in Rimsky-Korsakov's *The Legend of the Invisible City of Kitezh*, 1907. Also a dancer, she appeared in the first performance of Strauss's *Josephslegende*, Paris, 1914; from the 1920s was based in Paris and toured widely (including Japan, 1936).

Kvapil, Radoslav (b. 15 Mar 1934), Czech pianist. A specialist in his country's music, he has recorded all Janáček's piano works and (for the first time ever) all Dvořák's, completed 1979. In 1978 he gave what may have been the first performance of a concerto by Beethoven's contemporary Antonín Rejcha.

Kynaston, Nicolas (b. 10 Dec 1941), British organist. Pupil of GERMANI and DOWNES. He was organist at Westminster Cathedral, 1960–71, and a noted soloist at the Royal Festival Hall, London, from 1966. He has toured USA, Japan, Korea and elsewhere.

L

Labbette, Dora (b. 4 Mar 1898; d. 3 Sept 1984), British soprano. Had prominent career in recital and oratorio from 1917; her recordings include Delius songs with BEECHAM as accompanist. She came late to opera (at Covent Garden, 1935), for which she used the name Lisa Perli (from her birthplace, Purley).

Labèque, Katia (b. 3 Mar 1950) and **Marielle** (b. 6 Mar 1952), French pianists, sisters. Perform as a duo on both one and two pianos. They recorded Messiaen's *Visions de l'Amen* under the composer's guidance when still in their teens. Gave the European première of Berio's Concerto, 1973 (and played it at their US début, 1978), and the first performance of Gershwin's own two-piano arrangement of *An American in Paris*, 1984 (also recorded).

Labinsky, Andrey [Markovich] (b. 1871; d. 8 Aug 1941), Russian tenor. As a soloist at the Maryinsky Theatre, St Petersburg, 1897–1911, created the role of Vsevolod in Rimsky-Korsakov's opera *The Legend of the Invisible City of Kitezh*, 1907. He later sang at the Bolshoi, 1912–24.

Lablache, Luigi (b. 6 Dec 1794; d. 23 Jan 1858), Italian bass of French and Irish descent. Maintained highest international reputation over a long period. At La Scala his first role was Dandini in Rossini's *La Cenerentola*, 1817, and he made his London début in Cimarosa's *Il matrimonio segreto*, 1830; sang the title role in the first performance of Donizetti's *Don Pasquale*, 1834. His greatest success was achieved in the première of Bellini's *I puritani* in Paris, 1835. Continued to sing opera in London into his sixties.

Lagoya, Alexandre, *see* PRESTI.

Laidlaw, Anna Robena (b. 30 Apr 1819; d. 29 May 1901), British pianist. Visited Germany while young and met Schumann, whose *Phantasiestücke* were published in 1838 with a dedication to her. She was successful in London and Leipzig, but retired on her marriage, 1855.

Laine, Cleo (originally Clementina Dinah Campbell) (b. 28 Oct 1927), British singer. Noted in jazz (especially with DANKWORTH, her husband) and in works written specially for her, such as Richard Rodney Bennett's *Soliloquy* for voice and instruments, 1966. She has also performed (and recorded, 1974) Schoenberg's *Pierrot lunaire* in English.

Lambert, [Leonard] Constant (b. 23 Aug 1905; d. 21 Aug 1951), British conductor and composer. Music director of Vic-Wells Ballet (later Sadler's Wells), 1931–47; he conducted Purcell's *The Fairy Queen* in the production that reopened Covent Garden after the war, 1946. The dedicatee of Walton's *Façade*, he took part as reciter in an early performance, 1926. (*See also* HARTY.)

Lamond, Frederic [Archibald] (b. 28 Jan 1868; d. 21 Feb 1948), British pianist. Studied in Germany, where he had some lessons from BÜLOW and LISZT. He made his début in Berlin 1885 and in London 1886 (with Liszt in the audience). Lived mainly in Germany until shortly before World War II. He was also a composer.

Lamoureux, Charles (b. 28 Sept 1834; d. 21 Dec

1899). French conductor, also violinist. After introducing Handel oratorios to Paris audiences in the 1870s, founded his own orchestral concert series, 1881. He conducted the première of Chabrier's *España*, 1883. Powerfully fostered French taste for Wagner: performed extracts in concert, then the first French productions of *Lohengrin*, 1887, and *Tristan*, 1899. He took his orchestra to London in a joint arrangement with WOOD, 1899. His successor was his son-in-law, CHEVILLARD.

Lanchbery, John (b. 15 May 1923). British conductor. Noted in conducting ballet (principal conductor of Royal Ballet at Covent Garden, 1960–72) and arranging some of the most successful ballet scores (such as *La Fille mal gardée*, after Hérold). He also composed film scores and recorded the complete Tchaikovsky ballets. OBE, 1990.

Lancie, John de, *see* DE LANCIE.

Landowska, Wanda [Alexandra] (b. 5 July 1877; d. 16 Aug 1959). Polish-born harpsichordist; became French by marriage. Prominent from 1912 in reviving the harpsichord. She commissioned and gave the first performances of the concertos by Falla, 1926, and Poulenc, 1929, and was the first to record Bach's *Well-tempered Clavier* complete. Spent her later years in USA (where she died); she gave her final recital in New York at seventy-five.

Langdon, Michael (b. 12 Nov 1920). British bass. Prominent at Covent Garden from 1950, where he sang in the first performance of Britten's *Billy Budd*, 1951; noted as Ochs in *Der Rosenkavalier*. He was director of the National Opera Studio, 1978–86. CBE, 1973.

Langlais, Jean (b. 15 Feb 1907). French organist, also composer. Pupil of MARCHAL, Marcel DUPRÉ and (for composition) Dukas. An international recitalist, he made his first US appearance 1952. He was church organist at St Clotilde, Paris, from 1945, and taught music at a college for the blind, 1930–68. Gave his final professional recital aged eighty at the Royal Festival Hall in London, 1988.

Langlois, Philippe, *see* LOEWENGUTH QUARTET.

Langridge, Philip [Gordon] (b. 16 Dec 1939). British tenor, formerly violinist. Sang at the Proms from 1970 and Glyndebourne from 1974 (Don Ottavio in *Don Giovanni*, 1977). He made a recording as Aaron in Schoenberg's *Moses und Aron* under SOLTI, and created the title role in Birtwistle's *The Mask of Orpheus*, 1986. Married to MURRAY.

Lanza, Mario [originally Alfredo Arnold Cocozza) (b. 31 Jan 1921; d. 7 Oct 1959). American tenor of Italian descent. Famous from appearances in musicals and films, especially the title role in *The Great Caruso*, 1951 (*see* CARUSO). He lived in Rome from 1956 and died there from cardiac arrest.

Laredo, Jaime (b. 7 June 1941). Bolivian-born American violinist. Resident in USA from childhood; pupil of GALAMIAN. In 1959 he won the Queen Elisabeth Competition, Brussels, and gave the first performance of Milhaud's *Concert royal*. Recorded Bach's complete works for violin and keyboard with GOULD. The Bolivian government issued postage stamps in his honour. (*See also* KALICHSTEIN.)

Larrocha (in full Larrocha y de la Calle), **Alicia de** (b. 23 May 1923). Spanish pianist. Specializing in Spanish music, made London début 1953 and US début (San Francisco) 1955, and played in a duo with CASSADÓ. She became head of a piano academy in Barcelona, 1959. Her reputation flowered in the 1980s with recordings of Mozart concertos under SOLTI.

LaSalle Quartet, New York-based string quartet founded 1949. Its original members were Walter Levin, Henry Meyer, Peter Kamnitzer and Richard Kapuscinski (succeeded by Jack Kirstein, 1965, and Lee Fiser, 1975). Its first performances included Penderecki's Quartet no. 1, 1962. Disbanded 1988.

Laskine, Lily (b. 31 Aug 1893; d. 4 Jan 1988). French harpist. Active in Paris from 1949; she was prominent as a soloist and international teacher. Jolivet wrote for her his Harp Concerto, 1952, and Roussel his only work for solo harp, the Impromptu, of which she gave the first performance, 1919.

Latham-Koenig, Jan (b. 15 Dec 1953). British

conductor of French, Polish and Danish descent. Founded the Koenig Ensemble, 1976. He conducted English National Opera (*Tosca*), 1987, but has worked mainly outside UK, for example in Italy at the Montepulciano Festival, 1981–6. Made US début 1985.

Laubenthal (originally Neumann), **Horst** [Rüdiger] (b. 8 Mar 1938), German tenor, adopted son (and sole pupil) of Rudolf LAUBENTHAL. Won note as a recitalist and Bach singer, and from 1967 he has also sung opera in Berlin and elsewhere. He took a principal role on the first recording of Korngold's *Violanta*, 1980.

Laubenthal, Rudolf (b. 18 Mar 1886; d. 2 Oct 1971), German tenor, father by adoption of Horst LAUBENTHAL. Won high international repute in Wagner (Covent Garden as Siegfried and other roles, 1926–30). At the Metropolitan Opera he sang Stewa in the first US production of Janáček's *Jenůfa*, 1924.

Lauri-Volpi, Giacomo (b. 11 Dec 1892; d. 17 Mar 1979), Italian tenor. His roles at the Metropolitan Opera, from 1923, included Calaf in the US première of Puccini's *Turandot*, 1926. Sang Arnold in the centenary performance of Rossini's *Guillaume Tell* at La Scala, 1929; he also made important recordings. Performed at a gala in Barcelona aged seventy-nine.

Lavilla, Felix, *see* BERGANZA.

Lawrence, Marjorie (b. 17 Feb 1907; d. 13 Jan 1979), Australian soprano. Sang at the Metropolitan from 1934: she was notably athletic, riding her horse into the scenic flames when performing Brünnhilde in *Götterdämmerung*. Stricken with poliomyelitis in 1941, she continued to sing opera in New York and Paris till 1946 with restricted movement; performed Wagner's Venus (in *Tannhäuser*) and Isolde from a couch. Her autobiography *Interrupted Melody* was filmed, 1955.

Lazarus, Henry (b. 1 Jan 1815; d. 6 Mar 1895), British clarinettist, also basset-horn player. Had long career in London as soloist and as orchestral musician with Royal Italian Opera, 1838–83. He was also a celebrated chamber-music player and teacher.

Lear (née Shulman), **Evelyn** (b. 8 Jan 1926), American soprano. Her career developed mainly in Europe; made début in Berlin 1958. A specialist in twentieth-century roles, she sang in the first performances of Egk's *Die Verlobung in San Domingo*, 1963, and Levy's *Mourning Becomes Electra* (her Metropolitan début), 1967. In Berg's *Lulu* she performed the title role (also recorded) and later the mezzo-soprano role of Geschwitz. Her second marriage, 1955, was to STEWART.

Ledger, Philip [Stevens] (b. 12 Dec 1937), British conductor and keyboard player. Became Britain's youngest cathedral organist (Chelmsford, 1961). While he was director of music at the University of East Anglia, 1965–73, he collaborated with Britten and others at the Aldeburgh Festival. Appointed principal of the Royal Scottish Academy of Music and Drama, 1982.

Leginska (originally Liggins), **Ethel** (b. 13 Apr 1886; d. 26 Feb 1970), British pianist, also conductor and composer. Made New York recital début 1913 and settled in USA (married, 1906–17, to the composer Emerson Whythorne). She was the first woman to conduct at the Hollywood Bowl, 1925; conducted her own opera, *Gale*, in Chicago, 1935.

Legros, Joseph (b. 7 Sept 1739; d. 20 Dec 1793), French tenor, also composer and concert director. Sang in Rameau operas, then became Gluck's leading tenor in Paris. He was the first tenor to sing Orpheus, 1774, and played principal roles in *Iphigénie en Aulide* and *Iphigénie en Tauride*, 1774 and 1779.

Lehel, György (b. 10 Feb 1926; d. 26 Sept 1989), Hungarian conductor. Chief conductor of the Budapest Radio–Television Symphony Orchestra from 1962. He brought it to the Cheltenham Festival, 1968, and gave the first performance of Crosse's Chamber Concerto. Champion of new Hungarian music. He appeared as a guest conductor in New Zealand, 1988–9.

Lehmann, Lilli (b. 24 Nov 1848; d. 7 May 1929), German soprano. A singer of immense reputation, she performed 170 roles. Made début in Prague in 1865, had minor roles at the opening season of Bayreuth, 1876, and sang Brünnhilde in *The Ring* there, 1896. At the Metropolitan, from 1885, she was Isolde in the first US performance of *Tristan*, 1886 (opposite NIEMANN). Performed at and helped to organize Salzburg festivals, and taught at the Salzburg Mozarteum from 1926. Her recital repertory included about 600 songs; sang in public when over seventy. She also edited songs for publication. Married the tenor Paul Kalisch (1855–1964), who sometimes sang Tristan with her.

Lehmann, Lotte (b. 27 Feb 1888; d. 26 Aug 1976), German-born soprano, naturalized American 1945. Pre-eminent in her long operatic career to 1945, after which she continued as a recitalist and distinguished teacher. Made operatic début in Hamburg, 1909, then sang at Vienna State Opera, 1914–38, and created major Strauss roles: the Composer in *Ariadne auf Naxos* (second version), 1916, and the Dyer's Wife in *Die Frau ohne Schatten*, 1919. She was also the first to sing Puccini's Turandot in Vienna, 1926. Performed at Covent Garden, 1924–38, and at the Metropolitan Opera, from 1934. On the Nazi annexation of Austria, 1938, emigrated to USA.

Lehner, Jenö, *see* KOLISCH QUARTET.

Leibowitz, René (b. 17 Feb 1913; d. 29 Aug 1972), Polish-born French conductor. Taken to France in boyhood. He was an influential theorist and teacher (his composition students included Boulez), also composer. Conducted the first recording of Webern's Symphony, *c.* 1951, and of Satie's *Socrate*, 1952, and recorded many standard orchestral works.

Leider, Frida (b. 18 Apr 1888; d. 4 June 1975), German soprano. Distinguished in Wagner, she was a member of Berlin State Opera, 1923–40, and sang at Bayreuth, 1928–38, and Covent Garden, 1924–38 (where her first roles were Isolde and Brünnhilde). Performed the title role in a rare revival of Gluck's *Armide*, 1928. She also sang at the Metropolitan, and elsewhere.

Leinsdorf (originally Landauer), **Erich** (b. 4 Feb 1912), Austrian-born conductor, naturalized American 1942. Worked at the Metropolitan Opera from 1937 and was briefly conductor of the CLEVELAND ORCHESTRA, 1943. He made his chief impact as music director of the BOSTON SYMPHONY ORCHESTRA, 1962–9, and on records, which included opera (first recording of Korngold's *Die tote Stadt*, 1976).

Leitner, Ferdinand (b. 4 Mar 1912), German conductor. As music director of Stuttgart Opera, 1950–69, conducted the first performances of Orff's *Oedipus der Tyrann*, 1959, and *Prometheus*, 1968 (also recorded); he made the first recording, 1969, of Busoni's opera *Doktor Faust*. Conductor of the RESIDENTIE ORCHESTRA OF THE HAGUE, 1976–80.

Lemeshev, Sergey [Yakovlevich] (b. 10 July 1902; d. 26 June 1977), Russian tenor. Sang with the Bolshoi Opera, 1931–56, and was admired in such parts as Lensky (Tchaikovsky's *Yevgeny Onegin*) and the Duke of Mantua (*Rigoletto*).

Lemmens, Jaak Nikolaas, *see* LEMMENS-SHERRINGTON.

Lemmens-Sherrington (née Sherrington), **Helen** (b. 4 Oct 1834; d. 9 May 1906), British soprano. Married the Belgian organist and composer Jaak Nikolaas Lemmens (1823–81) in 1857. She was educated at the Brussels Conservatory. Made London début 1856 and was in great demand at choral festivals; she sang at the first performance of Sullivan's cantata *Kenilworth*, 1864.

Lemnitz, Tiana [Luise] (b. 26 Oct 1897), German soprano. Had a long and distinguished career at Berlin State Opera, 1934–57. She declined invitations to USA but sang at Covent Garden from 1936 (début as Eva in *Die Meistersinger*). Noted in Mozart, and also in the title role of Janáček's *Jenůfa*.

Léner, Jenö, *see* LÉNER QUARTET.

Léner Quartet, Austro-Hungarian quartet founded 1918 and based originally in Budapest. Its members throughout were Jenö Léner, Josef Smilovits, Sandor Roth and Imre Hartman. Achieved the highest European and US celebrity; its recordings included Mozart's Oboe Quartet with Leon GOOSSENS and Clarinet Quintet with Charles DRAPER. Disbanded 1948.

Leningrad Philharmonic Orchestra, Russian orchestra founded 1921. KOUSSEVITZKY had conducted an antecedent orchestra, 1917–20. Its conductors have included Emil COOPER, 1921–3, MALKO, 1926–9, GAUK, 1930–33, STIEDRY, 1934–7, MRAVINSKY, 1938–88, and Kurt SANDERLING (co-conductor), 1941–60. TEMIRKANOV's appointment was announced in 1988.

Leningrad Symphony Orchestra, Russian orchestra. Evolved from a radio orchestra, founded 1931. Its conductors have included YANSONS, to 1968, and TEMIRKANOV, 1968–76, then Alexander Dmitriev.

Lenya (also spelt Lenja), **Lotte** (originally Karoline Wilhelmine Blamauer) (b. 18 Oct 1898; d. 27 Nov 1981), Austrian-born actress and singer. She was celebrated for creating leading roles in stage works by Kurt Weill (whom she married in 1926), notably *Die Dreigroschenoper* (Berlin, 1928; later recorded and filmed) and *Die sieben Todsünden* (Paris, 1933). Refugees from the Nazis, she and Weill settled in USA, where she performed in his English-language shows, including *Lost in the Stars*, 1949.

Leonhardt, Gustav (b. 30 May 1928), Dutch harpsichordist, organist and scholar. A leader in the 'authentic' performance of baroque composers, particularly noted in Frescobaldi, Froberger and other lesser-known figures. Made his début as a harpsichordist in Vienna, 1950; he is a church organist in Amsterdam, and also plays early music with BRÜGGEN, BYLSMA and others. In 1967 he acted the part of Bach (and performed on organ and harpsichord) in Jean-Marie Staub's film biography.

Leoni, Michael (d. 1797), British tenor. Jewish, he worked as a London synagogue cantor, and then in the theatre (first performance of Sheridan's *The Duenna*, with music by both the Linleys, 1775). He is said to have been BRAHAM's uncle. Gave up his London career to become a cantor in Kingston, Jamaica, where he died.

Leonova, Darya Mikhailovna (b. 21 Mar 1829; d. 6 Feb 1896), Russian contralto. Made her début in the young male role of Vanya in Glinka's *A Life for the Tsar*, 1852, coached by the composer. She created important Russian opera roles, including the Hostess in *Boris Godunov*, 1874; toured USA, Western Europe and (with Musorgsky as her pianist) within Russia.

Leppard, Raymond [John] (b. 11 Aug 1927), British harpsichordist, conductor and music editor. Conducted the bicentenary revival of Handel's *Samson* at Covent Garden, 1959. His performance of his own edition of Monteverdi's *L'incoronazione di Poppea* at Glyndebourne, 1962, initiated a wave of interest in Monteverdi (and later Cavalli). After his conductorship of the BBC NORTHERN SYMPHONY ORCHESTRA, 1973–80, worked largely in USA, where he conducted (and made the first recording of) Virgil Thomson's opera *The Mother of Us All*, 1976. CBE, 1983.

Leschetizky, Theodor (original Polish spelling Teodor Leszeticki) (b. 22 June 1830; d. 14 Nov 1915), Polish pianist and teacher (born in what was then the Austrian-ruled part of Poland). Studied in Vienna with CZERNY; in St Petersburg he was a friend of Anton RUBINSTEIN. Returned to Vienna, 1878, where he became one of the most influential of all piano teachers (his students included PADEREWSKI and SCHNABEL). The second of his four marriages, 1880–92, was to his student Anna YESIPOVA with whom he gave duet recitals. He was also a composer.

Leslie, Henry [David] (b. 18 June 1822; d. 4 Feb 1896), British conductor, also composer. Took charge of an amateur choir, 1855, which became celebrated under his name, especially in unaccompanied works. It was dissolved in 1880, but he later conducted a re-formed choir, 1885–7.

Leutgeb, Ignaz (b. *c.* 1745; d. 27 Feb 1811), Austrian horn player, also composer. A friend of Mozart, who wrote three horn concertos (K417, 1783, K447 and K495) for him in Vienna; some of Mozart's other works may likewise have been intended for him.

Leveridge, Richard (b. 1670 or 1671; d. 22 Mar 1758), British bass, also composer. Greatly popular, he sang on the London stage for more than fifty years from 1695, when he was in the first performance of Purcell's *The Indian Queen*. Performed for a single season with Handel: premières of *Il pastor fido*, 1712, and *Teseo*, 1713.

Levi, Hermann (b. 7 Nov 1839; d. 13 May 1900), German conductor. Worked mainly in Munich; won distinction as Wagner conductor at Bayreuth (despite Wagner's baiting of him as a Jew) and conducted the first performance of *Parsifal*, 1882. He was a friend of Clara SCHUMANN and also a noted Brahms interpreter and opera translator.

Levin, Walter, *see* LASALLE QUARTET.

Levine, James [Lawrence] (b. 23 June 1943), American conductor, also pianist. Worked at the Metropolitan Opera from 1971; he became principal conductor there, 1973, and then music director (a post created for him), 1975. Made his British opera début 1970, conducting the Welsh National Opera (at Llandudno), and his British concert début 1973; conducted at Bayreuth from 1982. He has often directed concertos from the keyboard.

Lewenthal, Raymond (b. 29 Aug 1926), American pianist. Studied in Paris with CORTOT, and made his US début 1948. He has devoted recitals and records to the works of the eccentric nineteenth-century French composer Alkan and other neglected figures.

Lewis, Anthony *see* MEDICI QUARTET.

Lewis, Anthony [Carey] (b. 2 Mar 1915; d. 5 June 1983), British scholar and conductor. Active in conducting early revivals (and recordings) of stage and other works by Monteverdi, Handel and Rameau; he made the first complete recordings of Purcell's *King Arthur*, 1950, and *The Fairy Queen*, 1957. Principal of the Royal Academy of Music, 1968–82. Knighted, 1972.

Lewis, Henry (b. 16 Oct 1932), American conductor. Worked with various US orchestras and founded the Los Angeles Chamber Orchestra; he also made recordings with European orchestras. Became the first black musician to conduct at the Metropolitan Opera, 1972. He was married, 1960–76, to HORNE.

Lewis, Richard (b. 10 May 1914), British tenor. From 1947 worked notably at Glyndebourne (Mozart and many other roles, including Nero in *L'incoronazione di Poppea*), and also at Covent Garden, where he performed in the premières of Walton's *Troilus and Cressida* (as Troilus), 1954, and Tippett's *King Priam* (as Achilles), 1962. He had a varied concert repertory; sang in the first performance of Stravinsky's *Canticum sacrum* at Venice, 1956. CBE, 1963.

Lhévinne, Josef (originally Iosif Arkadyevich Levin) (b. 13 Dec 1874; d. 2 Dec 1944), Russian pianist. Regarded as an outstanding teacher. He made his concerto début in Moscow at fifteen; with his wife, Rosina LHÉVINNE, lived mainly in Berlin, 1907–19, but they were interned during World War I; settled in USA, 1919, they were soon afterwards naturalized. Joined staff of the newly founded Juilliard School in 1922.

Lhévinne (née Bessi), **Rosina** (b. 28 Mar 1880; d. 9 Nov 1976), Russian pianist. Married Josef LHÉVINNE in 1899, and made her own career, appearing in Vienna, 1910. In USA she matched her husband's reputation as a teacher and continued to be active into her seventies; her pupils included CLIBURN.

Liberace, Walter (originally Władziu) [Valentino] (b. 16 May 1919; d. 4 Feb 1987), American pianist of Italian and Polish parentage. Acquired notoriety and a fortune in the 1950s as a glamorized entertainer playing his own arrangements of Chopin and others. In 1980 he was sued for 'palimony' by his homosexual ex-partner. Died after developing AIDS.

Licette, Miriam (b. 9 Sept 1882; d. 11 Aug 1969), British soprano. Made her début in Rome as Butterfly, 1911, and became well known in Mozart and other roles in London. She joined BEECHAM's opera company in 1915 and sang in his English-language recording of *Faust*, 1932.

Ligendza, Catarina (originally Katarina Beyron) (b. 18 Oct 1937), Swedish soprano. Studied with GREINDL in Vienna and became prominent in Wagner opera. She had major roles at Bayreuth from 1971, including Brünnhilde (in *The Ring*) and Isolde, and sang Senta in *Der fliegende Holländer* at Covent Garden, 1972.

Lill, John [Richard] (b. 17 Mar 1944), British pianist. Made London début 1963 and won (jointly with KRAINEV) the Moscow Tchaikovsky Competition in 1970. He returned to USSR the next year in concerts with the LONDON SYMPHONY ORCHESTRA. A specialist in Beethoven, in 1984 he played all Beethoven's piano sonatas, all five concertos and the solo in the 'Choral Fantasy' (in California) within thirty days. OBE, 1978.

Lincke, Joseph (b. 8 June 1783; d. 26 March 1837), German cellist. In Vienna he became a member of SCHUPPANZIGH's string quartet and played, with the composer, Beethoven's two cello sonatas, 1815, which were written for him. He was himself a composer.

Lind, Jenny (originally Johanna Maria) (b. 6 Oct 1820; d. 2 Nov 1887), Swedish soprano. Became a legend as the 'Swedish nightingale'. She delighted Chopin and Mendelssohn: sang under Verdi's direction in London in the first performance of his *I masnadieri*, 1847. Famous in Bellini and Donizetti roles, she acquired even wider celebrity in concert after giving up opera at twenty-nine; in 1850–51 she gave ninety-three concerts on a US tour promoted by Barnum. Married Otto GOLDSCHMIDT, 1852, and lived thereafter in London; in 1883 (past sixty) she became a vigorous teacher of singing at the Royal College of Music.

Lindley, Robert (b. 4 Mar 1776; d. 13 June 1855), British cellist. The leading London exponent of his instrument, he was also famous for his extraordinary partnership (for fifty-two years from 1794) with the double-bass player DRAGONETTI; they played at Philharmonic concerts, operatic performances and elsewhere. He was professor at the newly opened Royal Academy of Music from 1822.

Lindsay Quartet, London-based string quartet founded 1966. Its members were Peter Cropper, Ronald Birks, Roger Bigley (replaced by Robin Ireland, 1985) and Bernard Gregor-Smith. Gave the first performance of Tippett's Quartet no. 4, 1979.

Linley, Elizabeth Ann (b. 5 Sept 1754; d. 28 June 1792), British soprano. Eloped with and later married, 1773, the playwright Sheridan, after which she withdrew from a prominent career in London concerts and stage performances. She was the daughter and pupil of the elder Thomas Linley (composer).

Lipatti, Dinu (diminutive of Constantin) (b. 19 Mar 1917; d. 2 Dec 1950), Romanian pianist, also composer. Awarded only second prize at competition in Vienna, 1934, causing the resignation of CORTOT from the jury. In 1943 he escaped from Romania and settled in Switzerland; made London concerto début 1947. Illness restricted his career, but his recordings (the first in piano duet with BOULANGER, 1937) aroused an extraordinary following, which continued after his early death.

Lipiński, Karol Józef (b. 30 Oct 1790; d. 16 Dec 1861), Polish violinist, also conductor and composer. Performed in Italy with PAGANINI, 1818, and was seriously considered his rival. Toured elsewhere, then settled in Dresden, 1839, where he formed his own string quartet and taught JOACHIM and WIENIAWSKI, among others.

Lipp, Wilma (b. 26 April 1925), Austrian soprano. Member of the Vienna State Opera from 1945. She was celebrated as the Queen of the Night in *Die Zauberflöte*, which was her début role at La Scala, and which she recorded four times. Also sang at Covent Garden, 1951, Glyndebourne, San Francisco and elsewhere.

List, Eugene (b. 6 July 1918; d. 28 Feb 1985), American pianist. On army service in 1945 played at Potsdam before Churchill, Truman and Stalin. Subsequently held US college appointments. He made a recording of Hanson's Piano Concerto, 1983.

Liszt, Ferenc (Germanized as Franz) (b. 22 Oct 1811; d. 31 July 1886), Hungarian pianist and composer. Occupies a prime place in the development of piano technique as well as being famous as a composer. He exhibited a wide repertory, including (a rarity in his day) Bach fugues; his long fingers gave him a keyboard stretch of a 10th. He was the pioneer of the solo piano recital (as distinct from a recital shared with others). Also held full-time conducting post at Weimar, 1848–58, where he gave the first performances of *Lohengrin*, 1850, and Cornelius's opera *Der Barbier von Bagdad*, 1858.

Litton, Andrew, *see* BOURNEMOUTH SYMPHONY ORCHESTRA.

Litvinne, Félia, French form of name adopted by Felya [Vasilyevna] Litvinova (née Françoise-Jeanne Schütz) (b. 1861; d. 12 Oct 1936), Russian soprano. Taken to France as a child. After studying in Paris, she sang in New York, Brussels (as Brünnhilde in the first French-language performance of *Die Walküre*, 1887), Moscow and, from 1890, St Petersburg; also at Covent Garden (début 1899 as Isolde). Made early recordings, from 1902, and became famous teacher in Paris.

Liverpool Philharmonic Orchestra, *see* ROYAL LIVERPOOL PHILHARMONIC ORCHESTRA.

Lloyd, Edward (b. 7 Mar 1845; d. 31 Mar 1927), British tenor. Celebrated in oratorios; he sang in the first performances of Gounod's *Redemption*, 1882, and Elgar's *The Dream of Gerontius*, 1900. Toured USA, 1890 and 1892. He gave no stage performances.

Lloyd, Robert [Andrew] (b. 2 Mar 1940), British bass. Turned to singing after beginning a career as an academic historian. He sang at Covent Garden from 1972 and in 1983 became the first British singer to portray Boris Godunov there; Metropolitan début 1988. Also made many concert appearances and recordings; star of BBC film *Six-foot Cinderella*, 1988. CBE, 1991.

Lloyd-Jones, David [Mathias] (b. 19 Nov 1934), British conductor. Active with Sadler's Wells Opera (later English National) (first British performance of Prokofiev's *War and Peace*, 1972) and as artistic director of Opera North from its inception, 1978, till 1990. With it he conducted the première of Josephs's *Rebecca*, 1983. He is also a music editor, notably of *Boris Godunov*, 1975, which he has conducted and translated.

Lloyd Webber, Julian (b. 14 Apr 1951), British cellist. Lloyd is actually a forename but is used as surname. His teachers included Pierre FOURNIER. He has given first performances of many works, some specially written for him, including a concerto by Rodrigo, 1982, and a reconstruction of Sullivan's Cello Concerto (edited by MACKERRAS with David Mackie), 1986. He was the first to record Bridge's *Oration* (cello and orchestra), 1976. His brother is the composer Andrew Lloyd Webber; their father, W(illiam) S(outhcombe) Lloyd Webber (1914–82), was an organist and composer.

Lockey, Charles (b. 23 Mar 1820; d. 3 Dec 1901), British tenor. Church musician in London; he sang under Mendelssohn's direction in the first performance of his *Elijah* (Birmingham), 1846. A disorder of the larynx compelled him to retire in 1859.

Lockhart, James (b. 16 Oct 1930), British conductor, also pianist. At Aldeburgh he gave the first performance of Walton's opera *The Bear*, 1967. He was music director of Welsh National Opera, 1968–85, and held opera posts also at Kassel and Koblenz. As a pianist he was known particularly as a recital partner of Margaret PRICE. Became head of the Opera School at the Royal College of Music, 1986.

Loder, Kate [Fanny] (b. 21 Aug 1825; d. 30 Aug 1904), British pianist. Played Mendelssohn's Concerto in G minor in the composer's presence in London in 1844 and in that year became a professor at the Royal Academy of Music. Brahms's *German Requiem* was first heard in Britain at her house, 1871, with a two-piano accompaniment by her and the composer Cipriani Potter. She was a niece of the composer Edward Loder.

Loewenguth, Alfred, *see* LOEWENGUTH QUARTET.

Loewenguth, Roger, *see* LOEWENGUTH QUARTET.

Loewenguth Quartet, Paris-based string quartet founded 1929. Alfred Loewenguth was leader throughout, originally with Maurice Fueri, Jacques Georges and Jacques Neilz, and finally with Philippe Langlois, Jacques Borsarello and Roger Loewenguth. The quartet was noted especially in the French repertory. It disbanded in 1983.

Loh, Anton, *see* ROSÉ QUARTET.

Lombard, Alain (b. 4 Oct 1940), French conductor. Opera conductor at Lyons, 1961–5; made US début 1963. As music director of the Strasbourg Philharmonic Orchestra, 1972–83, he made many recordings, including the two Ravel concertos with QUEFFÉLEC.

London (originally Burnstein), **George** (b. 5 May 1919; d. 24 Mar 1985), Canadian-born American bass-baritone. Active in opera from 1941. He made his Vienna State Opera début 1949 as Amonasro in *Aida*, the role in which he also made his first and last appearances, 1951 and 1960, at the Metropolitan. In 1960 he became the first American to sing Boris Godunov at the Bolshoi. Suffered partial paralysis in 1967 and thereafter took artistic administration posts in Washington, 1968–77.

London Mozart Players, British chamber orchestra founded 1949 by Harry BLECH. Specializes in Haydn and Mozart. GLOVER succeeded Blech in 1984.

London Philharmonic Orchestra, British orchestra founded 1932 by BEECHAM. It was used by him for opera seasons as well as in regular concerts and recordings. When Beecham left wartime Britain, the orchestra changed to self-governing management and engaged its own conductors, including VAN BEINUM, 1949–51, BOULT, 1950–57, STEINBERG, 1958–60, PRITCHARD, 1962–6, HAITINK, 1967–79, SOLTI, 1979–83, TENNSTEDT, 1983–7, and from 1990 Franz Welser-Möst.

London Sinfonietta, British chamber orchestra founded 1968. Performs mainly modern music; it is often made up of only twelve to twenty-four players, with high specialization of individual parts. Principal conductors have included ATHERTON, HOWARTH and RATTLE.

London String Quartet (1), British string quartet founded 1908 as the New String Quartet. It changed title in 1911. C. Warwick-Evans was cellist throughout; other original members were SAMMONS, Charles W. Petre, and H. Waldo Warner, and other final members were John Pennington, Petre (after wartime interruption) and PRIMROSE. In 1916 it gave the première of Delius's Quartet no. 3 (original version in three movements). Ceased performing 1934. (*See also* TUBB.)

London String Quartet (2), British string quartet active from 1958 to 1961. The original members, Erich Gruenberg, Lionel Bentley, Keith Cummings and Douglas Cameron, had previously performed as the New London Quartet, 1950–56. John Tunnell or Carl Pini sometimes played second violin.

London Symphony Orchestra, British orchestra founded 1904 as a self-governing organization. It was conducted by Hans RICHTER, 1904–11; the permanent conductors were Josef KRIPS, 1950–54, MONTEUX, 1961–4, KERTÉSZ, 1965–8, PREVIN, 1968–79, ABBADO, 1979–87, and Michael Tilson THOMAS, from 1988.

Long, Marguerite [Marie-Charlotte] (b. 13 Nov 1874; d. 13 Feb 1966), French pianist. Exercised great influence as a soloist and teacher; championed Debussy and Ravel (first performance of *Le Tombeau de Couperin*, 1919, and the Piano Concerto in G, 1932). She opened an academy in Paris in association with THIBAUD, 1941, and in 1943 they founded the competition that still bears their names.

López-Cobos, Jesus (b. 25 Feb 1940), Spanish conductor. Artistic director of the SPANISH NATIONAL ORCHESTRA, 1984–8, and music director of West Berlin Opera, 1981–90; he became music director of the CINCINNATI SYMPHONY ORCHESTRA in 1986, and has been appointed additionally to the Lausanne Chamber Orchestra from 1990. Guest conductor in London and other centres, including opera at Covent Garden, 1975, and in Paris.

Lorengar, Pilar [originally Pilar Lorenza García] (b. 16 Jan 1921), Spanish soprano. Noted in Mozart: she was Pamina in *Die Zauberflöte* at Glyndebourne, 1957, and Donna Anna in *Don Giovanni* at Covent Garden, 1963. Sang at the Metropolitan from 1966, and in the first German performances of Falla's *La Atlántida*, 1962.

Lorenz, Max (b. 17 May 1901; d. 11 Jan 1975), German tenor. Noted in Wagner: made his début 1927 and was a leading attraction at Bayreuth, 1933–44 and 1952. He also sang at the Metropolitan, from 1931, and Covent Garden, from 1934. Created the main role in Einem's *Der Prozess* at Salzburg, 1953.

Loriod, Jeanne, *see* LORIOD, YVONNE.

Loriod, Yvonne (b. 20 Jan 1924), French pianist. Second wife of Messiaen; she was the first performer of all his works with a piano part as well as Boulez's Sonata no. 2, 1950, and other pieces; she also plays all Mozart's concertos. Her sister Jeanne (b. 1928) is an exponent of the Ondes Martenot (see MARTENOT).

Los Angeles, Victoria de (originally Victoria Gómez Cima) (b. 1 Nov 1923), Spanish soprano. Has won equal distinction in recital (over 1,000 songs, including many Spanish) and opera. Having made her début in 1944, she sang at Salzburg and Covent Garden from 1950 (in such roles as Butterfly and Mimì in *La Bohème*), and the Metropolitan Opera from 1951 (*Faust*). Was seen little on stage after 1961. She made many recordings (*see* BJÖRLING, JUSSI), among them the first of Falla's opera *La vida breve*, 1966.

Los Angeles Philharmonic Orchestra, American orchestra founded 1919. Its principal conductors have included RODZINSKI, 1929–33, KLEMPERER, 1933–9, MEHTA, 1962–78, GIULINI, 1978–84, and PREVIN, 1986–9; SALONEN is appointed from 1992.

Lott, Felicity [Ann] (b. 8 May 1947), British soprano. Sang with English National Opera from 1975 and notably at Glyndebourne from 1977, including the title role of Strauss's *Arabella*, 1985. She also performed with the CHICAGO SYMPHONY ORCHESTRA, 1984, and at Prince Andrew's wedding in Westminster Abbey, 1986. CBE, 1990.

Lough, Ernest (b. 17 Nov 1911), British treble. His recording in 1926 of Mendelssohn's 'Oh for the Wings of a Dove' (with THALBEN-BALL) was internationally famous, and his 'Hear ye, Israel', 1927, from Mendelssohn's *Elijah* attained its millionth sale in 1962. He continued as an adult church chorister but did not turn professional.

Loughran, James (b. 30 June 1931), British conductor. Succeeded BARBIROLLI as principal conductor of the HALLÉ ORCHESTRA, 1971–83, and made many appearances elsewhere; New York début 1972. He has occasionally conducted opera, including the first performance of Malcolm Williamson's *Our Man in Havana*, 1963.

Louisville Orchestra, American orchestra founded 1866. Under the conductorship of WHITNEY, 1937–67, and MESTER, 1967–79, it commissioned and recorded many new works by American and other composers. In 1980 Akira Endo became conductor, and he was succeeded by Lawrence Leighton Smith in 1983.

Lovett, Martin, *see* AMADEUS QUARTET.

Löwe, Ferdinand (b. 19 Feb 1865; d. 6 Jan 1925), Austrian conductor. Active in Vienna. A champion of Bruckner, under whom he had studied, he gave the (posthumous) first performance of Bruckner's Symphony no. 9, 1903. The editions that he and others made of the Bruckner symphonies are now regarded as false to the composer's intentions.

Lubin, Germaine [Léontine Angélique] (b. 1 Feb 1890; d. 27 Oct 1979), French soprano. Won conspicuous Parisian operatic success in a wide repertory ranging from Rameau to the first performance of d'Indy's *La Légende de St Christophe*, 1920; she was noted in Wagner roles (such as Isolde) both in French and in German (Bayreuth from 1938). Sang under Nazi auspices during the wartime occupation of Paris and was afterwards penalized; she emerged to give a final recital, 1950, and to teach.

Lubin, Steven (b. 22 Feb 1942), American pianist. Made New York début 1972. As soloist and leader of his own chamber ensemble he is celebrated for his performances of Mozart, Beethoven and others on 'period' pianos, or rather their reproductions; his recordings include all Beethoven's piano concertos. Also writer on music.

Luca, Giuseppe De, *see* DE LUCA.

Lucas, Brenda, *see* OGDON.

Lucca, Pauline (b. 25 April 1841; d. 28 Feb 1908), Austrian soprano. Sang opera in Prague, Vienna, Berlin, New York and elsewhere. Favoured by Meyerbeer, she took the role of Selika in his *L'Africaine* at its first British and first German performances (London and Berlin), 1865; also sang Elisabeth in the British première of *Don Carlos*, 1868.

Lucia, Fernando De, *see* DE LUCIA.

Ludwig, Christa (b. 16 Mar 1924), German mezzo-soprano. Celebrated in concert (for example Brahms and Mahler) and opera. She was married, 1957–70, to BERRY, with whom she often sang. At Vienna State Opera, from 1955, she created the central role in Einem's

Der Besuch der alten Dame, 1971; sang at the Metropolitan, from 1959, Bayreuth, from 1966, and Covent Garden (début as Amneris in *Aida*, 1968).

Lukomska, Halina (b. 29 May 1929), Polish soprano. Won 's Hertogenbosch competition, 1956, then studied in Italy under DAL MONTE and became well known in modern works. She recorded Lutosławski songs and also Boulez's *Pli selon pli* under the composer's direction, 1970.

Lupu, Radu (b. 30 Nov 1945), Romanian pianist. Trained at the Moscow Conservatory (pupil of NEUHAUS) and won the Leeds Piano Competition, 1969; made London début 1969 and New York début 1972. He has toured widely, including China; gave the first performance of André Tchaikowsky's Piano Concerto, 1975. He has made many recordings, among them the complete Mozart violin sonatas with Szymon GOLDBERG. Resident in UK.

Lush, Ernest (b. 23 Jan 1908; d. 12 May 1988), British pianist. Joined the BBC as staff accompanist, 1928, and became a household name to radio listeners, especially in partnership with BRANNIGAN; left the BBC in 1966. In concert and recordings he partnered Pierre FOURNIER, RICCI, HAMMOND and others.

Luxon, Benjamin (b. 24 Mar 1937), British baritone. His broad repertory includes folksongs (with banjoist partner) as well as opera and formal concert pieces. Much associated with Britten, he created the title role in *Owen Wingrave* (televised), 1971; he also sang a double role in the first performance of Peter Maxwell Davies's opera *Taverner*, 1972. He has recorded Victorian ballads with TEAR and PREVIN (piano). Made his Metropolitan Opera début in the title role of Tchaikovsky's *Yevgeny Onegin*, 1980. CBE, 1986.

Lympany, Moura (originally Mary Johnstone) (b. 18 Aug 1916), British pianist. Her mother's surname was Limpenny. She studied with MATTHAY; made her début 1929 and was still performing sixty years later. Noted in the Russian repertory, she gave in London the first performance outside USSR of Khachaturian's Piano Concerto, 1940, and was the first in the West to record all twenty-four Rakhmaninov preludes. CBE, 1979.

Lysy, Alberto (b. 11 Feb 1935), Ukrainian-born Argentinian violinist and conductor. Made his New York début 1961 and founded his own chamber orchestra in Buenos Aires in 1966. In Gstaad he has been much associated with MENUHIN as a teacher, and also directs his own ensemble, the Camerata Lysy (founded 1977).

Lytton, Henry (originally Henry Alfred Jones) (b. 3 Jan 1865; d. 15 Aug 1936), British baritone. Famous for his long career with D'Oyly Carte Opera Company, 1884–1934, which brought him a knighthood, 1930. He was known mainly in Gilbert and Sullivan comic roles, but also sang in the first performance of Edward German's *Merrie England*, 1902. His wife was the soprano Louie Henri (originally Webber; 1865–1947).

M

M', names beginning with this are listed as if spelt MAC.

Ma, Yo-Yo (b. 7 Oct 1955), Chinese cellist (born in Paris). Made first public appearance aged five; after moving with his parents to New York, he played on television under BERNSTEIN, 1963. Studied with Leonard ROSE. He has attained high international status as a soloist; performs in a trio with AX and KIM. (*See also* COOPER, KENNETH.)

Maag, Peter (b. 10 May 1919), Swiss conductor. Held orchestral and operatic posts in Düsseldorf and Bonn, 1954–9, then retired to a Buddhist monastery for two and a half years. He resumed conducting at Vienna, in Italy and, from 1984, at Berne. US début 1959; made many recordings.

Maas, Robert, *see* PRO ARTE QUARTET.

Maazel [Varencove], **Lorin** (b. 6 Mar 1930), American conductor (born in Paris). Child-prodigy conductor (with NEW YORK PHILHARMONIC, 1942), also violinist. In 1960 he became the youngest and the first American conductor at Bayreuth. He was music director of the CLEVELAND ORCHESTRA, 1972–82, and then of Vienna State Opera 1982–4; music director of PITTSBURGH SYMPHONY ORCHESTRA since 1986. Conducted the first performances of Dallapiccola's opera *Ulisse*, 1968, and Berio's *Un re in ascolto*, 1984. In London he conducted all Beethoven's symphonies in a single day for charity, 1988. His second wife, 1969–83, was the pianist Israela Margalit.

Mácal, Zdeněk, *see* SYDNEY SYMPHONY ORCHESTRA.

McCarthy, John (b. 20 Nov 1919), British conductor and chorus master, also church music director. Organized a pool of singers from which he drew choruses for many famous conductors' recordings (chiefly as the Ambrosian Singers or the Ambrosian Opera Chorus); it attained a dominant position in London recordings from the 1950s. Chorus master to the LONDON SYMPHONY ORCHESTRA, 1961–6. OBE, 1990.

McCormack, John (b. 14 June 1884; d. 16 Sept 1945), Irish-born tenor, naturalized American 1917. One of the world's most popular artists through records and ballad concerts. In his early career he also sang in opera (Covent Garden from 1907 and with US companies from 1909); in 1911 he created Lieutenant Merrill in Victor Herbert's opera *Natoma*. Made a papal count, 1928.

McCracken, James [Eugene] (b. 16 Dec 1926; d. 30 Apr 1988), American tenor. Sang small roles at the Metropolitan Opera from 1953, then developed a major career in Europe, especially as Otello (Covent Garden, 1964). He was married to the soprano Sandra Warfield (b. 1929).

MacDonald, Jeanette (b. 18 June 1907; d. 14 Jan 1965), American soprano. Her career was chiefly in musicals (New York from 1922) and musical films (including *The Merry Widow*, 1934, with Maurice Chevalier, and many with EDDY). She also sang in opera at Montreal (Juliet in Gounod's *Roméo et Juliette*) and Chicago, 1940.

M'Guckin (sometimes spelt McGuckin), **Barton** (28 July 1852; d. 17 Apr 1913), Irish tenor. Sang in London from 1875, especially in opera; his leading roles included Phoebus in Arthur Goring Thomas's *Esmeralda* (first performance 1883), and Des Grieux in the first British performance of Massenet's *Manon*, 1885, opposite ROZE. He toured in USA, 1887–8.

McIntyre, Donald [Conroy] (b. 22 Oct 1934), New Zealand bass-baritone. Studied in London and then sang at Sadler's Wells Opera (later English National). At Covent Garden he created the role of Heyst in Richard Rodney Bennett's *Victory*, and he sang Prospero in the first British performance of Berio's *Un re in ascolto*, 1989. Noted in Wagner, especially at Bayreuth from 1967; he was Wotan in its centenary performance of *The Ring*, 1976, which was televised. OBE, 1977.

Macintyre, Margaret (b. ?1865; d. Apr 1943), British soprano (born in India). Prominent in London opera and concert; she created Rebecca in Sullivan's *Ivanhoe*, 1891. Also sang at La Scala as Sieglinde in the first performance there of *Siegfried*, 1899, and in Moscow.

McKellar, Kenneth (b. 23 June 1927), British tenor. Sang in concert and opera (Carl Rosa Opera Company from 1953); he was a soloist on BOULT's first recording of Handel's *Messiah*, 1954. Won his widest reputation in lighter music, especially with a Scottish flavour.

Mackenzie, Lennox, *see* ARDITTI QUARTET.

Mackerras, [Alan] **Charles** [MacLaurin] (b. 17 Nov 1925), Australian conductor (born in New York). Came to London, 1946, then studied with TALICH in Prague. He worked prominently at Sadler's Wells Opera (later English National): as principal conductor, 1970–80, he gave the first British performances of Janáček's *Katya Kabanova*, 1951, and *The Makropoulos Affair*, 1964. Also conducted Janáček notably in Paris and Vienna (with recordings). He was equally prominent in reviving Handel opera in his own editions; recorded *Messiah* three times; arranged a popular ballet score (after Gilbert and Sullivan's operettas), *Pineapple Poll*, 1951. He was conductor of the SYDNEY SYMPHONY ORCHESTRA, 1982–5, and became music director of Welsh National Opera in 1986. Knighted, 1979. (*See also* LLOYD WEBBER and ORCHESTRA OF THE AGE OF ENLIGHTENMENT.)

McKie, William [Neil] (b. 22 May 1901; d. 1 Dec 1984), Australian organist. Worked in Melbourne, then at Westminster Abbey, 1941–63, where he directed the music at the coronation of Elizabeth II, 1953. Knighted, 1953.

MacKinlay, Jean Sterling, *see* STERLING.

Macmillan, Ernest (b. 18 Aug 1893; d. 6 May 1973), Canadian conductor, also organist and composer. Held a long and influential conductorship of the TORONTO SYMPHONY ORCHESTRA, 1931–56. He was the first Canadian to be knighted, 1935, for services to music.

MacNeil, Cornell (b. 24 Sept 1922), American baritone. Sang in the first performance of Menotti's *The Consul*, 1950, and in 1959 performed at the Metropolitan and La Scala. He took the role of Germont in Zeffirelli's film of *La traviata*, 1982.

Madeira (née Browning), **Jean** (b. 14 Nov 1918; d. 10 July 1972), American contralto, previously pianist. Sang at the Metropolitan Opera from 1948 and Bayreuth from 1956; noted as Carmen. She created the role of Circe in Dallapiccola's *Ulisse* (Berlin, 1968).

Maderna, Bruno (b. 21 Apr 1920; d. 13 Nov 1973), Italian-born conductor and composer, became West German citizen 1963. As well as being ranked among the foremost modernist composers, he was prominent as a conductor of new works by others; his premières include Nono's *Intolleranza 1960* in Venice, 1961, and Druckman's *Windows* in Chicago, 1972.

Magaloff, Nikita (b. 8 Feb 1912), Russian-born pianist, naturalized Swiss 1956. Left Russia as a boy, 1918, and settled in Paris, where he took lessons with Prokofiev. In 1939 he moved to Switzerland, and in 1947 toured USA. Well known as a Chopin interpreter and as a teacher. He recorded with SZIGETI, whose daughter he married.

Maguire, Hugh, *see* ALLEGRI QUARTET.

Magyar, Gabriel, *see* HUNGARIAN QUARTET.

Mahler, Gustav (b. 7 July 1860; d. 18 May 1911), Austrian composer and conductor. His conductorship of the Vienna Court Opera, 1897–1907 was historic in establishing high standards. As conductor of the VIENNA PHILHARMONIC, 1898–1901, he gave the first performance of Bruckner's Symphony no. 6, 1899. In New York he conducted at the Metropolitan Opera from 1908 (first US performance of *The Bartered Bride*, 1909) and with the NEW YORK PHILHARMONIC ORCHESTRA gave the first complete cycle in the USA of Bruckner symphonies.

Maier, Franzjosef, *see* COLLEGIUM AUREUM.

Mainardi, Enrico (b. 19 May 1897; d. 10 Apr 1976), Italian cellist, also composer. In 1933 he recorded Strauss's *Don Quixote* with the composer conducting; gave the first performances of concertos by Pizzetti, 1934, and Gian Francesco Malipiero, 1939. Trio partner of Edwin FISCHER and KULENKAMPFF, and well-known teacher in Rome and elsewhere. (*See also* ZECCHI.)

Maisky, Mischa (b. 10 Jan 1948), Soviet-Lithuanian cellist. Pupil of ROSTROPOVICH in Moscow; emigrated to Israel, 1973, and later studied with PIATIGORSKY in California. Made London début 1976. He has performed in a duo with ARGERICH and recorded the Brahms Double Concerto with KREMER.

Major, Margaret, *see* AEOLIAN QUARTET.

Majorano, Gaetano, *see* CAFFARELLI.

Makarov, Nikolay [Petrovich] (b. 16 Feb 1810; d. 17 Dec 1890), Russian guitarist and composer for his instrument. Performed internationally and in 1856 organized an international competition in Brussels for guitar compositions.

Maksymiuk, Jerzy (b. 9 Apr 1936), Polish conductor, also composer. Conducted concerts and opera in Warsaw and founded the Polish Chamber Orchestra, 1972, which he took on successful tours to Britain, 1977, and elsewhere. He was also conductor of the POLISH RADIO SYMPHONY ORCHESTRA and, from 1983, the BBC SCOTTISH SYMPHONY ORCHESTRA.

Malcolm, George [John] (b. 28 Feb. 1917), British harpsichordist, pianist and conductor. While master of the music at Westminster Cathedral, 1947–59, he conducted the first performance of Britten's *Missa brevis*, 1959, written for his choir. Eminent as harpsichordist, he also plays Bach on the piano.

Małcużyński, Witold (b. 10 Aug 1914; d. 17 July 1977), Polish-born Argentinian pianist. Studied with PADEREWSKI in Switzerland and made a reputation chiefly in Chopin. In 1946 he recorded for the BBC on the piano Chopin played in London in 1848.

Malgoire, Jean-Claude (b. 25 Nov 1940), French conductor. Worked as orchestral oboist till 1974; in 1967 he founded a small baroque orchestra, La Grande Écurie et la Chambre du Roy, which became internationally prominent in recording. Conducted baroque opera in London, Aix-en-Provence (tercentenary revival of Lully's *Psyché*, 1987) and elsewhere.

Malibran (née García), **Maria** [Felicia] (b. 24 Mar 1808; d. 23 Sept 1836), French mezzo-soprano, daughter of Manuel GARCÍA (1). Married a French merchant named Malibran and later, 1836, the violinist BÉRIOT. She was famous for combining vocal and dramatic excitement. Made her opera débuts in London and New York 1825 and in Paris 1828; she sang Rossini heroines (for example the title role of *La Cenerentola*), and, among soprano roles, Leonore in the first English-language production of *Fidelio* in London, 1835. (*See also* BOUÉ, CARADORI-ALLAN and CEBOTARI.)

Malko, Nikolay [Andreyevich] (b. 4 May 1883; d. 23 June 1961), Russian-born conductor, naturalized American 1946. Gave the first performance of Myaskovsky's Symphony no. 5 in Moscow, 1920, and of Shostakovich's no. 1 in Leningrad, 1926. He worked outside USSR from 1928; conducted in London, 1933, and was in USA during World War II. He conducted the Yorkshire Symphony Orchestra, 1954–6, and the SYDNEY SYMPHONY ORCHESTRA, from 1956. Died in Sydney.

Mancinelli, Luigi (b. 6 Feb 1848; d. 2 Feb 1921), Italian conductor, also composer. Took the baton at a performance of *Aida*, 1874, when the scheduled conductor was drunk, and went on to develop an important career in Italian opera. Conducted in London from 1887 and in New York from 1893; he was conductor of the first US performance of *Tosca*, 1901.

Mandini, Maria (dates unknown), Italian soprano. Active from 1783 in Vienna, where Mozart wrote for her the role of Marcellina in *Figaro*, 1786. Her husband was Stefano Mandini (*c.* 1750–*c.* 1810), an Italian baritone active in Vienna; there he created the role of Count Almaviva in *Figaro*, 1786, and sang in the first performance of Cimarosa's *Il matrimonio segreto*, 1792. His brother Paolo Mandini (1757–1842) was a tenor.

Mandini, Paolo, *see* MANDINI, MARIA.

Mandini, Stefano, *see* MANDINI, MARIA.

Mann, Robert, *see* JUILLIARD QUARTET.

Manners, Charles, *see* MOODY.

Manning, Jane [Marian] (b. 20 Sept 1938), British soprano. Made her London début 1964 in songs by Dallapiccola, Webern and Messiaen, and has kept a speciality in modern works. She commissioned and gave the first performance of Birtwistle's *Nenia on the Death of Orpheus*, 1970; took eight roles in Weir's ten-minute *King Harald's Saga*, 1979. Appeared with own ensemble, Jane's Minstrels, in 1988. Married to the critic and composer Anthony Payne. OBE, 1990.

Manns, August [Friedrich] (b. 12 Mar 1825; d. 1 Mar 1907), German-born conductor, naturalized British 1894. A leading figure in London music, particularly at the Crystal Palace concerts, 1855–1901. There he introduced Schubert's Symphony no. 9, 1856, and many other works to Britain, and gave the first performances of many British works, including the young Sullivan's music to *The Tempest*, 1862, and Ethel Smyth's *Serenade*, 1890. Knighted, 1903.

Mantovani, Annunzio Paolo (b. 15 Nov 1905; d. 29 Mar 1980), Italian-born British conductor, previously violinist. Known by surname only. He made his London solo début at sixteen, broadcast from 1927 and was music director for Noël Coward, 1945. Later won fame for the special sound of his orchestral strings.

Mar, Norman Del, *see* DEL MAR.

Mara (née Schmeling), **Gertrud Elisabeth,** (b. 23 Feb 1749; d. 20 Jan 1833), German soprano. Sang in Vienna (where Mozart was not impressed with her) and other cities before making her London début 1784. She performed opera with distinction (sometimes in English), and later taught in Moscow. Died in the Baltic port of Reval (now Tallinn).

Marais, Marin (b. 31 May 1656; d. 15 Aug 1728), French bass viol player, also composer. Studied composition with Lully and performed in his operas. He served as a French court musician, 1676–1725, and was an internationally acknowledged virtuoso. Several of his nineteen children became musicians.

Marchal, André (b. 6 Feb 1894; d. 27 Aug 1980), French organist. Blind from birth, he held two Paris church appointments, 1915–45 and 1945–63. A celebrated recitalist, he toured widely (including Australia, 1953), and shared in the inauguration of the Royal Festival Hall organ in London, 1954. Recorded the complete organ works of Bach, François Couperin and Franck.

Marchesi, Blanche, *see* MARCHESI, SALVATORE.

Marchesi (née Graumann), **Mathilde** (b. 24 Mar 1821; d. 17 Nov 1913), German mezzo-soprano. Famous in concert and particularly as a teacher in Vienna and Paris; her students included GARDEN and MELBA. On the death of her husband, Salvatore MARCHESI, she settled in London, where she died.

Marchesi, Salvatore (b. 15 Jan 1822; d. 20 Feb 1908), Italian baritone. Held the noble titles of Cavaliere and Marchese. He was celebrated in opera in Berlin and London, where he sang Mephistopheles in the first English-language performance of *Faust*, 1864. Translated French and German operas into Italian. He was married to Mathilde MARCHESI, from 1852; their

French-born daughter Blanche Marchesi (1863–1940) performed as a soprano and taught singing in London.

Marchisio, Barbara (b. 6 Dec 1833; d. 19 Apr 1919), Italian contralto, and **Carlotta** (b. 8 Dec 1835; d. 28 June 1872), Italian soprano, sisters. Sang in opera together in Italy, where they were admired by Rossini, and in London and Paris. They took part in the first performance of Rossini's *Petite messe solennelle*, 1864.

Marcolini, Marietta (b. *c.* 1780), Italian contralto. Famous in Rossini's coloratura roles. She created created the heroine's parts in his operas *La pietra del paragone*, 1812, and *L'Italiana in Algeri*, 1813.

Marcoux, Vanni (original forenames Jean Emile Diogène) (b. 12 June 1877; d. 21 Oct 1962), Italian-born bass-baritone of French parentage. His début, 1894, inaugurated a distinguished French career: he was the first Frenchman to play Boris Godunov, 1922, and Ochs in *Der Rosenkavalier*, 1926. Sang at Covent Garden from 1905. He worked as an opera administrator in Bordeaux, 1948–51. Some sources mistakenly refer to him as Vanni-Marcoux.

Margalit, Israela, *see* MAAZEL.

Mario, Giovanni [Matteo] (b. 17 Oct 1810; d. 11 Dec 1883), Italian tenor. Of noble birth, with the title Cavaliere di Candia. He sang in Paris, then made London début in Donizetti's *Lucrezia Borgia*, 1839; playing the title role was Giulia GRISI, who became his lifelong companion and often sang with him. He took part in the British première of *Rigoletto*, 1853, and in the first French performance of Verdi's *Un ballo in maschera*, 1861; also sang in New York.

Markevitch, Igor (b. 27 July 1912; d. 7 Mar 1983), Russian-born conductor, also composer, naturalized Italian 1947 and naturalized French 1982. Having studied in Paris with CORTOT and BOULANGER (and later with SCHERCHEN), he worked as a conductor in Stockholm, Paris (the Lamoureux concerts, 1957–61), Montreal, 1958–61, Rome (SANTA CECILIA ORCHESTRA, 1973–5) and elsewhere. Also taught conducting at various centres, including Moscow. Partial deafness restricted his later career.

Marriner, Neville (b. 15 Apr 1924), British violinist and conductor. Founded chamber orchestra named ACADEMY OF ST MARTIN-IN-THE-FIELDS, 1959, and remained at its head while music director of the Los Angeles Chamber Orchestra, 1969–79, and the MINNESOTA SYMPHONY ORCHESTRA, 1979–86. With the Academy he recorded a huge repertory, mainly baroque, but also including Mozart, Bartók, and others. Knighted, 1985.

Marsalis, Branford, *see* MARSALIS, WYNTON.

Marsalis, Wynton (b. 18 Oct 1961), American trumpeter. Active in both jazz and the symphonic repertory. He performed as soloist with an orchestra at the age of sixteen. Made highly successful recordings of Haydn's and other concertos from 1983; by multi-tracking, he has sometimes recorded as many as eight trumpet parts simultaneously. Made European débuts 1985. In jazz he often performs with his brother Branford Marsalis (b. 1960), a tenor saxophonist.

Marshall, Lois [Catherine] (b. 29 Jan 1925), Canadian soprano, made London début with BEECHAM in 1956. Despite being partly paralysed by poliomyelitis, she has sung in opera (for example as Queen of the Night in *Die Zauberflöte*). Gave the first performance of Morawetz's *From the Diary of Anne Frank*, 1970. She made nine visits to USSR; retired in 1982 after some late appearances as a mezzo-soprano.

Marshall, Margaret (b. 4 Jan 1949), British soprano. Won a Munich competition, 1974, and gave her first London recital 1975. Her opera début as Eurydice (Gluck's *Orpheus*) in Florence, 1978, was followed by Mozart roles at Glyndebourne, La Scala, 1982, and elsewhere. She has sung extensively in concert, with US début 1980.

Marsick, Martin [Pierre Joseph] (b. 9 Mar 1848; d. 21 Oct 1924), Belgian violinist. An organist in his boyhood, he studied with JOACHIM, settled in Paris and became eminent there as soloist, quartet leader and teacher; his pupils included FLESCH and THIBAUD. Saint-Saëns dedicated to him his Violin Sonata no. 1, 1885.

Martenot, Maurice (b. 14 Oct 1898; d. 10 Oct

1980), French musician. Studied cello and composition, but became celebrated as the inventor and player of one of the first practical electronic instruments, 1928, now known as the Ondes (waves) Martenot. (*See also* LORIOD, YVONNE.)

Martí, Bernabé, *see* CABALLÉ.

Martin, David, *see* BLECH QUARTET.

Martin, Maud, *see* TORTELIER, PAUL.

Martinelli, Giovanni (b. 22 Oct 1885; d. 2 Feb 1969), Italian tenor. Became undisputed leader of his operatic field after the death of CARUSO, 1921. He sang at Covent Garden from 1912 (début as Cavaradossi in *Tosca*), but most regularly at the Metropolitan, 1913–45 (thirty-six roles, including Fernando in the first performance of Granados's *Goyescas*, 1916). At the age of eighty-one in Seattle he performed as the Emperor in Puccini's *Turandot*, 1967.

Martinez, Odaline de la (originally Odaline de la Caridad Martinez) (b. 31 Oct 1949), Cuban-American conductor and composer. Studied at the Royal Academy of Music from 1972 and settled in London. In 1976, jointly with the flautist Ingrid Culliford, she founded Lontano, a chamber ensemble devoted to modern music, and in 1984 she became the first woman to conduct a complete programme at the Proms. In London she conducted the first (concert) performance of Goldschmidt's opera *Beatrice Cenci*, 1988 (composed 1950).

Martinon, Jean (b. 10 Jan 1910; d. 1 Mar 1976), French conductor, also composer. After World War II (when he was a prisoner of war) took leading posts in Bordeaux and Paris and regularly conducted the LONDON PHILHARMONIC ORCHESTRA, 1947–9. He was conductor of the ISRAEL PHILHARMONIC ORCHESTRA, 1958–69, and the CHICAGO SYMPHONY ORCHESTRA, 1963–8, from which he resigned amid conservative hostility; his adventurous programmes included the first performance of Stravinsky's Variations (in memory of Aldous Huxley), 1965, when he carried out the composer's suggestion to perform the work twice over.

Marton, Eva (b. 18 June 1943), Hungarian soprano. Made opera début 1968 in Budapest, then sang prominently with Frankfurt Opera, 1972–7, and at the Metropolitan from 1976 (début as Eva in *Die Meistersinger*); she performed Puccini's Turandot there and, 1987, at Covent Garden. Took the title role on the first recording of Korngold's *Violanta*, 1980.

Mascheroni, Edoardo (b. 4 Sept 1852; d. 4 Mar 1941), Italian conductor, also composer. Conducted the first production in Italy of *Fidelio*, 1886. Verdi supported his appointment as chief conductor at La Scala, 1891–4, where he gave the première of *Falstaff*, 1893.

Masi, Enrico, *see* QUARTETTO FIORENTINO.

Mass, Paul, *see* CALVET QUARTET.

Massary, Fritzi (originally Friederike Massaryk) (b. 21 Mar 1882; d. 3 Jan 1969), Austrian soprano. Noted in operetta, principally in Berlin and Vienna; being Jewish, she fled the Nazis and went to London, 1933, then settled in California. Created six Oscar Straus roles, including Vera in *Der letzte Walzer*, 1920, and starred in Coward's *Operette*, 1938.

Masson, Diego (b. 21 June 1935), Spanish-born French conductor. Worked with BOULEZ as a percussionist before turning to conducting. He conducted the première of Stockhausen's *Stop*, 1969 (dedicated to him), and the first French performance of Boulez's '*. . . explosante-fixe . . .*'. He also conducts a general repertory and gave the first performance of Harper's *Hedda Gabler* with Scottish Opera, 1985. He is the son of the painter André Masson.

Masterson, [Margaret] Valerie (b. 3 June 1937), British soprano. Sang Gilbert and Sullivan roles in the D'Oyly Carte Opera Company (also recorded), 1966–70, and then joined Sadler's Wells Opera (later English National), 1971, where she became noted in Handel. Also performed at Covent Garden (première of Henze's *We Come to the River*, 1976), Paris, Aix-en-Provence and elsewhere.

Masur, Kurt (b. 18 July 1927), German conductor. Held orchestral and operatic posts in East German cities (Dresden, Berlin, Leipzig) and in 1970 became conductor of the GEWANDHAUS ORCHESTRA in Leipzig. Appointed to NEW YORK PHILHARMONIC from 1992.

Masurok, Yuri [Antonovich] (b. 18 July 1931), Polish-born Russian baritone. Member of Bolshoi Opera, from 1963, with which he sang Tchaikovsky's Onegin and other roles. Made Covent Garden début 1975 in Verdi's *Un ballo in maschera*; he became well known at other Western opera theatres and also on record.

Mata, Eduardo (b. 5 Sept 1942), Mexican conductor, also composer. After holding posts in Mexico, became music director of the Dallas Symphony Orchestra, 1977; he toured Mexico with the NEW PHILHARMONIA ORCHESTRA, 1976. Recorded works by Falla and Latin American composers.

Matačić, Lovro von (b. 14 Feb 1899; d. 4 Jan 1985), Yugoslav conductor. Conductor of the Dresden State Orchestra, 1956–8, and succeeded SOLTI at Frankfurt Opera, 1961–6. He made many recordings; that of Lehár's *Die lustige Witwe*, 1963, is celebrated.

Materna, Amalie (b. 10 July 1844; d. 18 Jan 1918), Austrian soprano. Long associated with Vienna Court Opera; sang Amneris in the first Austrian performance of *Aida*, 1874, and the title role in the première of Goldmark's *Die Königin von Saba*, 1875. Famous in Wagner, she performed as Brünnhilde in the first (Bayreuth) performance of the complete *Ring*, 1876.

Mathieson, Muir (b. 24 Jan 1911; d. 2 Aug 1975), British conductor. Celebrated as music director for films. He induced Bliss to write the music for *Things to Come*, 1935, and the 69-year-old Vaughan Williams for *Forty-ninth Parallel*, 1941. Later he commissioned the 19-year-old Richard Rodney Bennett for *Interpol*, 1956. OBE, 1957.

Mathis, Edith (b. 11 Feb 1938), Swiss soprano. Had distinguished career in opera: Salzburg from 1960, Glyndebourne, 1965 (Sophie in *Der Rosenkavalier*), and the Metropolitan from 1970 (début as Pamina in *Die Zauberflöte*). She sang in the first recording of Haydn's opera *Il mondo della luna*, 1977. Married to KLEE.

Matteis, Nicola (d. 1707 or later), Italian violinist and composer. Settled in London soon after 1670; esteemed by the diarist Evelyn, he is thought to have associated with Purcell. His son, also called Nicola (or Nicholas) Matteis (of uncertain dates), was likewise a violinist and composer.

Matthay, Tobias [Augustus] (b. 19 Feb 1858; d. 15 Dec 1945), British pianist. Gave his first London recital 1884 and in 1900 founded his own piano school. His special method of teaching was very influential in Britain; his students included Harriet COHEN, HESS and LYMPANY.

Matthews, David, *see* MEDICI QUARTET.

Matthews, Denis [James] (b. 27 Feb 1919; d. 24 Dec 1988), British pianist, also writer on music. Well known in Mozart and Beethoven. In 1956 he gave the first performance of Rubbra's Piano Concerto (and also recorded it). Professor at Newcastle University, 1972–84; CBE, 1975. He committed suicide.

Matyáš, Miroslav, *see* JANÁČEK QUARTET.

Matzenauer, Margarete (b. 1 June 1881; d. 19 May 1963), Hungarian contralto. Her opera début in 1901 was followed by valuable early recordings. At the Metropolitan Opera, 1911–30 (début as Amneris in *Aida*), she sang the Kostelnička (Sextoness) in Janáček's *Jenůfa* at its first US performance, 1924. Also took soprano roles.

Mauceri, John [Francis Peter] (b. 12 Sept 1945), American conductor. Active in both USA and Europe; he conducted the first European performance of Bernstein's *Mass* in Vienna, 1973, and the première of Menotti's opera *Tamu-Tamu* at Spoleto, 1974. Made Metropolitan Opera début 1976 and became music director of Scottish Opera in 1987.

Maupin, married name and sole stage name of Julie (or Emilie) d'Aubigny (b. *c.* 1670; d. 1707), French soprano. Sang at the Paris Opera from 1690 in operas by Lully and others. Campra wrote for her the heroine's role in *Tancrède*, 1702, and Couperin on occasion accompanied her at the harpsichord. A tempestuous character, she fought duels in men's clothing and had both male and female lovers.

Maurel, Victor (b. 17 June 1848; d. 22 Oct 1923), French baritone. Made his Paris Opera début 1868 and became one of the most celebrated artists of the day. He sang Wagner at Covent Garden from 1873 and took the title role in the first performance of Verdi's revised version of *Simon Boccanegra*, 1881. Verdi then gave him the creation of Iago (*Otello*), 1887, and Falstaff, 1893.

May, Florence (b. 6 Feb 1845; d. 29 June 1923), British pianist. Studied in Germany with Clara SCHUMANN. After becoming an admirer and acquaintance of Brahms, she vigorously promoted his music in her subsequent London performances and in a biography, 1905.

Mayer, Sebastian, *see* WEBER, JOSEPHA.

Mayr, Richard (b. 18 Nov 1877; d. 1 Dec 1935), Austrian bass-baritone. Member of Vienna State Opera from 1902; celebrated as Baron Ochs in *Der Rosenkavalier* (from its first production in Vienna, 1911). He sang in the first performance of Mahler's Symphony no. 8, 1910, and of Strauss's *Die Frau ohne Schatten*, 1919; also performed at Bayreuth, Covent Garden and the Metropolitan.

Mazurok, *see* MASUROK.

Mc, names beginning thus are listed as if spelt MAC.

Medici Quartet, London-based string quartet formed 1974. Members: Paul Robertson, David Matthews, Paul Silverthorne (later Ivo-Jan van der Werff) and Anthony Lewis (1).

Mehta, Mehli, *see* MEHTA, ZUBIN.

Mehta, Zubin (b. 29 Apr 1936), Indian conductor. The sole Indian to make a major reputation in Western classical music. His father, Mehli Mehta (b. 1908), was a violinist and conductor in Bombay. Studied in Vienna and USA. He conducted the MONTREAL SYMPHONY ORCHESTRA, 1961–7, which he took to USSR, 1962; made his Metropolitan Opera début 1965, (*Aida*). Much associated with the ISRAEL PHILHARMONIC ORCHESTRA, he became its music director 1977. He was also music director of the LOS ANGELES PHILHARMONIC, 1962–78, and the NEW YORK PHILHARMONIC, 1978–91. Conducted the first performances of Barber's *Essay no. 3*, 1978, and of Penderecki's *Kosmogonia* (for chorus and orchestra), 1970, and Symphony no. 2 (in Lucerne), 1980, dedicated to him.

Melachrino, George [Miltiades] (b. 1 May 1909; d. 18 June 1965), British conductor of Greek descent. Formed the Melachrino Strings, 1945, an orchestra devoted to light music. Its distinctive, lush sound was highly popular on records and radio.

Melba, Nellie (originally Helen Porter Mitchell) (b. 19 May 1861; d. 23 Feb 1931), Australian soprano. Took her professional surname from her birthplace, Melbourne; her married name was Armstrong. She studied in Paris, made opera début (as Gilda in *Rigoletto*) in Brussels, 1887, and became one of the most celebrated singers of her day. (Peach Melba and Melba Toast are named after her.) Sang at Covent Garden, 1888–1914 (and a few later performances to 1926), and at the Metropolitan from 1893. Her coloratura skills illuminated such roles as Donizetti's Lucia and Delibes's Lakmé. Recorded from 1904, including the duet from *La Bohème* with CARUSO. Created Dame, 1918. Made final tour to Australia with BORGIOLI, 1924; retired and died there. She was subject of a film biography, 1953.

Melbourne Symphony Orchestra, Australian orchestra originating before 1900 and called the Victorian Symphony Orchestra, 1950–65. Its conductors have included HEINZE, 1932–49, SUSSKIND, 1953–5, WÖSS, 1956–60, TZIPINE, 1961–5, VAN OTTERLOO, 1967–71, Fritz Rieger, 1971–2, and IWAKI, from 1974.

Melcher, Wilhelm, *see* MELOS QUARTET.

Melchior, Lauritz (originally Lebrecht Hommel) (b. 20 Mar 1890; d. 18 Mar 1973), Danish-born tenor, previously baritone; became American citizen 1947. Sang in concert in London, 1919, and acquired international fame from his Covent Garden début as Siegmund, 1924.

Thereafter he specialized in Wagner (Bayreuth from 1924, Metropolitan, 1926–50); performed as Tristan over 200 times.

Melkus, Eduard (b. 1 Sept 1928), Austrian violinist. Noted for his stylish performances of the baroque repertory, both as soloist (usually on an authentic baroque violin) and as director of the Capella Academica, which he founded in Vienna in 1965. His records include Bach's Double Violin Concerto with himself playing both parts.

Melnikov, Ivan [Alexandrovich] (b. 4 Mar 1832; d. 8 July 1906), Russian baritone. Sang with the Maryinsky (now Kirov) Opera in St Petersburg, 1867–92, also working as a stage director in the last years. There he created the title role of *Boris Godunov*, 1874.

Melos Quartet, Stuttgart-based string quartet founded 1965. Made its début in 1966; members are Wilhelm Melcher, Gerhard Ernst Voss, Hermann Voss and Peter Buck. The name Melos, apart from its Greek signification (melody), echoes the names Melcher and Voss.

Mendelssohn, Felix, *see* GEWANDHAUS ORCHESTRA OF LEIPZIG.

Mengelberg, Willem (b. 28 Mar 1871; d. 21 Mar 1951), Dutch conductor. Unique in his fifty-year conductorship, 1895–1945, of the CONCERTGEBOUW ORCHESTRA. Championing Mahler, he conducted all nine symphonies in Amsterdam, 1920. Strauss dedicated to him *Ein Heldenleben*, 1898, and Rakhmaninov *The Bells*, 1913; he gave the first performance of Kodály's *Háry János* suite, 1927. Also appeared at the Royal Philharmonic Society concerts in London, 1911–14. In 1921 he went to New York to conduct the New York Symphony Orchestra; at his suggestion it merged with the NEW YORK PHILHARMONIC, 1928, which he conducted on regular visits till 1930. His support for the Nazi occupying power in World War II barred him from later Dutch appearances; he died in Switzerland.

Menter, Sophie (b. 29 July 1848; d. 23 Feb 1918), German pianist. Had lessons from LISZT; she was married, 1872–86, to POPPER, and taught in St Petersburg, 1883–7. She was also a composer: Tchaikovsky orchestrated her *Hungarian Gypsy Airs* for piano and orchestra, and she played it under his direction at Odessa, 1893.

Menuhin, Hephzibah, *see* MENUHIN, YEHUDI.

Menuhin, Jeremy, *see* MENUHIN, YEHUDI.

Menuhin, Yaltah, *see* MENUHIN, YEHUDI.

Menuhin, Yehudi (b. 22 Apr 1916), American-born violinist of Russian parentage; took Swiss nationality 1970 and British nationality 1985. Studied in San Francisco under PERSINGER and in Paris under ENESCU; a child prodigy of unsurpassed gifts, he made a famous recording of Elgar's Violin Concerto with the composer conducting, 1932. In maturity his world celebrity continued. Bartók's Sonata for solo violin, 1944, was one of various works written for him, and in 1952 he revived Mendelssohn's early Concerto in D minor. Strongly motivated by humanitarian causes: he gave more than 500 wartime concerts for the Red Cross, played to survivors of the Nazi concentration camps at Belsen, 1945, and controversially defended FURTWÄNGLER from charges of Nazi taint; he made a notable East–West *rapprochement* with Nehru in India and shared concerts with SHANKAR, and was president of the International Music Council of UNESCO, 1969–75. Also active as conductor and formerly as festival director at Bath (1958–69) and Windsor. He was soloist in the first performances of the concertos by Lennox Berkeley, 1961, and Panufnik, 1972. Often played with KENTNER (at one time his brother-in-law): Walton's Violin Sonata, 1949, was written for them. He gave many recitals with his pianist sister, Hephzibah (1920–81) and in a trio with Kentner and CASSADÓ. His sister Yaltah (b. 1922) was also a pianist, as is his son Jeremy (b. 1951). His honorary KBE of 1965 became a formal knighthood in 1985; he was also awarded the much rarer distinction of OM, 1987.

Merrick, Frank (b. 30 Apr 1886; d. 19 Feb 1981), British pianist. In his long career he championed, as performer and editor, the music of John Field. Gave London recitals to mark his seventy-fifth and eightieth birthdays. He was also a composer; wrote songs (some in Esperanto) and was prizewinner in a competition to complete Schubert's 'Unfinished' Symphony, 1928.

Merrill, Robert (b. 4 June 1917), American baritone. His career was almost entirely at the Metropolitan Opera, 1945–75, and almost entirely in the Italian repertory. Germont in *La traviata* was his début role there and at Covent Garden, 1967.

Merz, Josef, *see* KOECKERT QUARTET.

Mesplé, Mady (originally Madeleine) (b. 7 Mar 1931), French soprano. Noted for her high range. Delibes's Lakmé was her début role, 1953, and she sang it at the 500th performance of that work at the Opéra-Comique, 1960. She took part in the première of Menotti's *The Last Savage* in Paris, 1963, and sang under BOULEZ in Schoenberg's *Die Jakobsleiter*.

Messager, André, *see* SOCIÉTÉ DES CONCERTS DU CONSERVATOIRE, ORCHESTRE DE LA.

Mester, Jorge (b. 10 Apr 1935), American conductor of Hungarian parentage (born in Mexico). As conductor of the LOUISVILLE ORCHESTRA, 1967–79, which had a policy of commissioning and recording new works, he conducted many first recordings, including Blacher's *Orchestra Ornament*, 1968, and Penderecki's *De natura sonoris II*, 1972.

Metcalfe, Susan, *see* CASALS.

Meyer, Henry, *see* LASALLE QUARTET.

Meyer, Kerstin [Margareta] (b. 3 Apr 1928), Swedish mezzo-soprano. Often partnered SÖDERSTRÖM in concert and performed a wide operatic repertory. In Hamburg she sang in the premières of Schuller's *The Visitation*, 1966, and Goehr's *Arden muss sterben*, 1967. Made many appearances at Glyndebourne, beginning with the first English-language performance of Henze's *Elegy for Young Lovers*, 1961; also at Bayreuth and the Metropolitan. Translated Einem's *Der Besuch der alten Dame* into Swedish for a Stockholm production and sang the title role.

Mező, László, *see* BARTÓK QUARTET.

Michelangeli, a shortened surname commonly used outside Italy for Arturo BENEDETTI MICHELANGELI.

Michelucci, Roberto, *see* MUSICI, I.

Milán, Luis (b. *c.* 1500; d. after 1561), Spanish vihuelist. Worked at the ducal court of Valencia and wrote a book about courtly life. The volume he published in 1536 is the earliest collection of music for vihuela (and therefore, in modern terms, for guitar).

Milanov (originally Kunc), **Zinka** (b. 17 May 1906; d. 30 May 1989), Yugoslav soprano. Engaged by TOSCANINI to sing Verdi's Requiem at Salzburg, 1937, and was prominent at the Metropolitan Opera, 1937–66, principally in Verdi and Puccini. She sang Tosca and Leonora (*Il trovatore*) at Covent Garden, 1956–7.

Milanova, Stoika (b. 5 Aug 1945), Bulgarian violinist. Pupil of David OISTRAKH in Moscow; won the Carl Flesch Competition in London, 1970. She has toured widely (Japan and Australia, 1976) and played in a duo with FRAGER and also LUPU.

Milashkina, Tamara [Andreyevna] (b. 13 Sept 1934), Russian soprano. Sang as soloist with Bolshoi Opera from 1958; she was the first Soviet singer to appear at La Scala, 1962. Known in Russian opera: filmed as Fevronya in Rimsky-Korsakov's *The Legend of the Invisible City of Kitezh*, 1966. Married to ATLANTOV.

Milder-Hauptmann (née Milder), [Pauline] **Anna** (b. 13 Dec 1785; d. 29 May 1838), Austrian soprano (born in Constantinople). Daughter of a Viennese courier. Beethoven wrote for her the heroine's role in *Fidelio*, 1805, and Schubert 'Der Hirt auf dem Felsen' and another song. In Berlin she participated in Mendelssohn's historic revival of Bach's *St Matthew Passion*, 1829.

Millo, Aprile (b. 14 Apr 1958), American soprano of Italian descent. Elvira in Verdi's *Ernani* was her début role at La Scala, 1982, and the Metropolitan, 1984. She was later engaged at the Vienna State Opera and elsewhere.

Milnes, Sherrill [Eustace] (b. 10 Jan 1935), American baritone. His appearances with New

York City Opera, from 1964 (first US performance of Prokofiev's *The Fiery Angel*, 1965), led to international success and over thirty complete opera recordings, especially of Italian works. He sang at Covent Garden from 1971 (Renato in Verdi's *Un ballo in maschera*). Has also occasionally conducted.

Milstein, Nathan [Mironovich] (b. 31 Dec 1904), Russian-born violinist, naturalized American 1942. In his youth played Glazunov's Concerto under the composer, 1920. He formed a duo with HOROWITZ, with whom he left USSR. Made US début 1929 under STOKOWSKI in Philadelphia, and maintained his place among foremost violinists; he composed his own cadenza for Beethoven's Concerto.

Minneapolis Symphony Orchestra, *see* MINNESOTA ORCHESTRA.

Minnesota Orchestra, American orchestra founded 1903 as Minneapolis Symphony Orchestra. Changed its name in 1968. Its principal conductors have included ORMANDY, 1931–6, MITROPOULOS, 1937–49, DORÁTI, 1949–60, SKROWACZEWSKI, 1960–79, and MARRINER, 1979–86.

Minton, Yvonne [Fay] (b. 4 Dec 1938), Australian mezzo-soprano. Developed her career in Britain. She sang in the first performance of Maw's opera *One Man Show*, 1964, then in a varied repertory at Covent Garden, including Marfa in Musorgsky's *Khovanshchina* and Thea in the première of Tippett's *The Knot Garden*, 1970. Retired from opera 1983 but continued to give concerts. CBE, 1980.

Mintz, Shlomo (b. 30 Oct 1957), Russian-born Israeli violinist. Went as a child to Israel and, encouraged from the age of nine by Isaac STERN, moved to New York at seventeen to study at the Juilliard School. He gave his first New York recital 1973 and appeared at Salzburg 1980. Recorded compositions and transcriptions by Kreisler, 1981, also major concertos and Paganini's caprices. He gave the first performance of Neikrug's Concerto, 1984. Became adviser to the Israel Chamber Orchestra in 1989.

Miolan, Marie, *see* CARVALHO.

Mitchinson, John [Leslie] (b. 31 Mar 1932), British tenor. Noted in Elgar's *The Dream of Gerontius* and in Mahler (Symphony no. 8 in BERNSTEIN'S recording). With Welsh National Opera he sang as Tristan and in the first British production of Martinů's *The Greek Passion*, 1981 (both also recorded).

Mitropoulos, Dimitri (b. 1 Mar 1896; d. 2 Nov 1960), Greek-born conductor, also pianist and composer; became American citizen 1946. Studied in Brussels and Berlin, and made US début 1936. He was music director of the MINNEAPOLIS SYMPHONY ORCHESTRA, 1937–49, and then the NEW YORK PHILHARMONIC, 1949–57. His many premières included Hindemith's Symphony in E flat, 1941, Copland's *Statements*, 1942, and Krenek's Piano Concerto no. 3 (as pianist and conductor, from memory), 1946. Gave the first US (concert) performances of Busoni's opera *Arlecchino* and Schoenberg's *Erwartung*, both 1951. He also conducted at the Metropolitan Opera, including the première of Barber's *Vanessa*, 1958. Died in Milan while rehearsing Mahler's Symphony no. 3. An international conducting competition commemorates him. (*See also* STEBER.)

Młynarski, Emil (b. 18 July 1870; d. 5 Apr 1935), Polish conductor, also pianist, violinist and composer. Studied piano with Anton RUBINSTEIN and violin with AUER. As conductor of Warsaw Opera, from 1897, he was the first to organize regular orchestral concerts in Warsaw. Conducted the first performance of Szymanowski's opera *King Roger*, 1926; also promoted Polish music abroad. He was conductor of the Scottish Symphony Orchestra, 1910–15, and taught in Philadelphia, 1929–31. His daughter married Arthur RUBINSTEIN.

Mödl, Martha (b. 22 Mar 1912), German soprano. Began her career as mezzo-soprano: made Covent Garden début as Carmen, 1949, before becoming prominent in Wagner: sang at Bayreuth from 1951 and the Metropolitan from 1957 (début as Brünnhilde in *Siegfried*). She was in the first performance of Reimann's *Gespenstersonate* in Berlin, 1984 as a mezzo-soprano, and she sang the Countess in Tchaikovsky's *The Queen of Spades* at Nice, 1989.

Moffo, Anna (b. 27 June 1932), American soprano of Italian parentage. Made early appearance as Butterfly on Italian television (1956). International success followed in many lighter-voiced roles: Nannetta in Verdi's *Falstaff* at Salzburg and Gilda in *Rigoletto* at the Metropolitan (and seventeen other roles there from 1959). She made her Covent Garden début as Gilda, 1964.

Moiseiwitsch (German spelling of Russian Moiseivich), **Benno** (b. 22 Feb 1890; d. 9 Apr 1963), Russian-born pianist; took British nationality 1937. Pupil of LESCHETIZKY in Vienna. He made his British début 1908, US début 1919, and toured widely. His performances of Rakhmaninov won the composer's admiration; he also championed, as few did, the music of a very different Russian composer, Metner. Married, 1914–24, to the Australian violinist Daisy Kennedy (1893–1981).

Moldavan, N., *see* FLONZALEY QUARTET.

Molinari, Bernardino (b. 11 Apr 1880; d. 25 Dec 1952), Italian conductor. As artistic director of the AUGUSTEO ORCHESTRA, 1912–43, championed Italian composers. He also conducted in New York, 1928, Latin America and elsewhere. Gave the first performance of Respighi's *Pines of Rome*, 1924, and of Barber's Symphony no. 1 (Rome), 1936.

Molinari-Pradelli, Francesco (b. 4 July 1911), Italian conductor, also pianist. Active chiefly in opera, he first conducted at La Scala 1946, at Verona Arena 1950, Covent Garden 1955 (*Tosca*, with TEBALDI) and the Metropolitan Opera 1966. Made many operatic recordings.

Molique, [Wilhelm] Bernard (b. 7 Oct 1802; d. 10 May 1869), German violinist, also composer. Visited London in 1840 and later; 1849–66; worked there as a soloist, chamber musician and teacher. His technical dexterity was praised by Berlioz, Mendelssohn and Schumann.

Moll, Kurt (b. 11 Apr 1938), German bass. Member of Hamburg Opera from 1970 and became known internationally in Wagner (Bayreuth from 1974). He made his Covent Garden début as Caspar in Weber's *Der Freischütz*, 1977. His many recordings include the principal role of Schubert's *Die Zwillingsbrüder* on its first recording, 1975.

Monaco, Mario del, *see* DEL MONACO.

Mont, Willem de, *see* BLECH QUARTET.

Montañez, Marta, *see* CASALS and ISTOMIN.

Monte, Toti dal, *see* DAL MONTE.

Monteux, Claude, *see* MONTEUX, PIERRE.

Monteux, Pierre (b. 4 Apr 1875; d. 1 July 1964), French conductor, previously violinist. Led historic career. While conducting for Dyagilev's ballet in Paris, 1911–14, he gave the first performances of Stravinsky's *Petrushka*, 1911, *The Rite of Spring*, 1913, and *The Nightingale*, 1914, and Ravel's *Daphnis et Chloé* and Debussy's *Jeux*, both 1912. He was conductor of the BOSTON SYMPHONY ORCHESTRA, 1919–24, founding conductor of the Paris Symphony Orchestra, 1929–35, and then conducted the SAN FRANCISCO SYMPHONY ORCHESTRA, 1935–52. At eighty-six he was appointed (on a twenty-five year contract) principal conductor of the LONDON SYMPHONY ORCHESTRA, 1961. His many orchestral premières included Prokofiev's Symphony no. 3 (Paris), 1929, and Sessions's Symphony no. 2 (San Francisco), 1947; he was the dedicatee of Pijper's Symphony no. 3, 1926. His son Claude Monteux (b. 1920) is a flautist and conductor.

Montgomery, Kenneth (b. 28 Oct 1943), British conductor (born in Northern Ireland). Studied with BOULT and (in Siena) with CELIBIDACHE. He appeared at Glyndebourne, 1967, and was later music director of Glyndebourne Touring Opera, 1975–6. Conducted the BOURNEMOUTH SINFONIETTA and the Netherlands Radio Orchestra.

Montreal Symphony Orchestra, Canadian orchestra. Began as the orchestra of the Concerts Symphoniques and took present title 1953. Its principal conductors have included Wilfrid Pelletier, 1936–40, DEFAUW, 1941–8, MARKEVITCH, 1958–61, MEHTA, 1961–7, and DUTOIT, from 1977.

Moody (also known as Moody-Manners), **Fanny** (b. 23 Nov 1866; d. 21 July 1945), British soprano and operatic manager. Having made her début in 1887, sang Tatyana in the first

British performance of Tchaikovsky's *Yevgeny Onegin*, 1892. She ran an opera company in conjunction with her husband, the bass Charles Manners (1857–1935).

Moór, Emanuel (b. 19 Feb 1863; d. 20 Oct 1931), Hungarian pianist, also composer. Toured as accompanist to Lilli LEHMANN, among others. In later years he was concerned mainly with a double-keyboard piano, which he invented in 1921.

Moore, Gerald (b. 30 July 1899; d. 13 Mar 1987), British pianist. More than anyone else heightened the status of the profession of 'the unashamed accompanist' (title of his book, 1943). In recital and on hundreds of recordings, 1921–67, he partnered the leading singers of the day, from John COATES and MCCORMACK to LOS ANGELES, Janet BAKER and FISCHER-DIESKAU, and such instrumentalists as CASALS. Lectured widely on song interpretation. CBE, 1954.

Moore, Grace (b. 5 Dec 1898; d. 26 Jan 1947), American soprano. Won chief fame in musicals and films, notably *One Night of Love* (title of its theme song), 1934. From 1928 she sang at the Opéra-Comique and the Metropolitan. The composer Gustave Charpentier coached her for the title role in his *Louise*, an opera she also filmed (directed by Abel Gance), 1939, and recorded, 1943. She died in an air crash; a film of her life, 1953, starred Kathryn Grayson. (*See also* TIBBETT.)

Moore, John, *see* AEOLIAN QUARTET.

Moreschi, Alessandro (b. 11 Nov 1858; d. 21 Apr 1922), Italian male soprano (castrato). The last of the castrati, he sang at the Sistine Chapel, 1883–1913. His recordings, 1902 and 1904, give a quavering hint of how this type of voice sounded.

Morin, Charles, *see* CRABBÉ.

Morison, Elsie, *see* KUBELÍK, RAFAEL.

Morrison, T. H., *see* BBC PHILHARMONIC ORCHESTRA.

Mortimer, Harry (b. 10 Apr 1902), British cornetist, trumpeter and conductor. His career, from 1924, as solo cornetist, conductor, adjudicator and BBC supervisor of brass and military bands, 1942–6, was of unparalleled influence in its field. Played trumpet with the HALLÉ ORCHESTRA, 1927–30, and 1931–5, and gave the first performance of Geoffrey Bush's Trumpet Sonata, 1946. CBE, 1984.

Moscheles, Ignaz (b. 23 May 1794; d. 10 May 1870), German pianist, conductor and composer. Met Beethoven in Vienna and prepared the piano score of his *Fidelio*. He first appeared in London 1821 and later settled there; conducted the first British performance of Beethoven's *Missa solemnis*, 1832. He was a friend of Mendelssohn (with whom he often performed) and Chopin. Gave 'historical' recitals (harpsichord and piano), a rarity at the time. In 1846 he moved to Leipzig as principal professor at the newly founded conservatory. Taught the young Sullivan, who boarded with him.

Moscow Chamber Orchestra, Russian orchestra founded 1956 by BARSHAI. Its later directors have been Igor Bezrodny, 1976–83, then TRETYAKOV under whom it became the USSR State Chamber Orchestra.

Moscow Philharmonic Quartet, *see* BORODIN QUARTET.

Moscow Radio Symphony Orchestra (properly All-Union Radio and Television Symphony Orchestra), Soviet orchestra founded 1930–31. Its principal conductors have included GAUK, 1953–61, ROZHDESTVENSKY, 1961–74, and then FEDOSEYEV.

Moskovsky, Alexander, *see* HUNGARIAN QUARTET.

Motlík, Jaroslav, *see* VLACH QUARTET.

Mottl, Felix [Josef] (b. 24 Aug 1856; d. 2 July 1911), Austrian conductor. Assisted Hans RICHTER in the preparation of the first performance of *The Ring* at Bayreuth, 1876. At Karlsruhe, 1881–1903, he was conductor of a famous and pioneering concert and operatic series. He was the first to mount a performance of Berlioz's *Les Troyens* in all its five acts on a single evening, 1890. Conducted at Covent Garden (including *The Ring*, 1898) and in New York. He died in Munich after collapsing in mid-performance of *Tristan*.

Moučka, Viktor, *see* VLACH QUARTET.

Moyse, Marcel [Joseph] (b. 17 May 1889; d. 1 Nov 1984), French flautist. Perhaps the most famous twentieth-century flautist, he was active in Paris from 1913. Gave the first performances of Ibert's Concerto, 1934 (dedicated to him), and, with his daughter-in-law, Blanche Honegger-Moyse, Martinů's Concerto for flute and violin, 1936.

Mozarteum Orchestra, Salzburg-based chamber orchestra founded 1922. Won note under its founding conductor, PAUMGARTNER, 1922–38 and 1945–69; later conductors have included HAGER, 1969–81, WEIKERT, 1981–4, and Hans Graf, from 1984. On occasion it has expanded to symphonic size.

Mravinsky, Yevgeny [Alexandrovich] (b. 4 June 1903, d. 20 Jan 1988), Russian conductor. Conducted at Leningrad's opera and ballet theatre (now Kirov), 1932–8, and then began a long and distinguished conductorship of the LENINGRAD PHILHARMONIC ORCHESTRA. He gave the first performances of Shostakovich's symphonies nos. 5 (1937), 6 (1939), 8 (1943, dedicated to him), 9 (1945) and 10 (1953), and of other Soviet works.

Muck, Carl (or Karl) (b. 22 Oct 1895; d. 3 Mar 1940), German conductor, previously pianist. Distinguished as opera conductor in Berlin, 1892–1912, with over 100 different operas. He also conducted there the first performance of Busoni's Piano Concerto, 1902, with the composer as soloist, and championed Bruckner's symphonies. His conductorship of the BOSTON SYMPHONY ORCHESTRA, 1906–8 and again from 1912, was broken by US entry into World War I; he was arrested and interned, 1918. Conductor of the Hamburg Philharmonic, 1922–3; also conducted at Bayreuth from 1901 and made historic Wagner recordings there, 1927.

Mudarra, Alonso (b. *c.* 1510; d. 1 Apr 1580), Spanish vihuelist and guitarist. Cathedral musician in Seville from 1546 to his death. Works for his instrument are prominent in the three volumes of his compositions published in 1546; their dedication to a royal councillor indicates Mudarra's status.

Mühlen, Raimund von zur, *see* ZUR MÜHLEN.

Mühlfeld, Richard [Bernhard Herrmann] (b. 28 Feb 1856; d. 1 June 1907), German clarinettist. Famous for his association with Brahms, who wrote for him the Clarinet Quintet (of which he gave the first performance, 1891), the two clarinet sonatas and other works. He was also a conductor and, 1890, music director of the ducal theatre of Saxe-Meiningen.

Mule, Marcel (b. 24 June 1901), French saxophonist. Credited with major share in establishing a classical status for the instrument. He formed a saxophone quartet, 1928, and persuaded various composers to write for him, including Glazunov (Saxophone Quartet, 1932) and Ibert (Concertino, 1935). Also taught at the Paris Conservatory.

Müller, Iwan (b. 3 Dec 1786; d. 4 Feb 1854), German clarinettist. Achieved a lasting technical improvement in the instrument, 1809, and also claimed the invention of the alto clarinet, meant to succeed the basset-horn. He worked in London, 1815–20 and later; his clarinet tutor, 1825, is dedicated to George IV.

Müller, Wilhelm, *see* JOACHIM QUARTET.

Mullings, Frank (b. 10 May 1881; d. 19 May 1953), British tenor. Notable in opera as Otello (first at Manchester, 1916). He sang at Covent Garden, from 1919, where he was Apollo in the first performance of Boughton's *Alkestis*, 1924. Latterly performed mainly in concert.

Mullova, Viktoria (b. 27 Nov 1959), Russian-born Austrian violinist. Won Moscow Tchaikovsky Competition, 1982. She escaped to Sweden, 1983, and was granted Austrian nationality. Made London début 1984. Her recordings include Vivaldi concertos with ABBADO and Sibelius's with OZAWA.

Munch (originally Münch), **Charles** (b. 26 Sept 1891; d. 6 Nov 1968), French conductor, also violinist. He was over forty when he won prominence in Paris, from 1932. Gave the première of Messiaen's *L'Ascension*, 1935, and the first public performance of Poulenc's Organ Concerto, 1941; conducted the orchestra of the SOCIÉTÉ DES CONCERTS DU CONSERVATOIRE, 1938–46. He succeeded KOUSSEVITZKY as conductor of the BOSTON SYMPHONY ORCHESTRA, 1949–62, with which he gave many new works, including Piston's Symphony no. 6, 1955, and Barber's *Prayers of Kierkegaard*, 1965. In 1967 he founded the ORCHESTRE DE PARIS, and was touring USA with it when he died.

Münchinger, Karl (b. 29 May 1915; d. 24 Sep 1990), German conductor. Founding director of the STUTTGART CHAMBER ORCHESTRA, from 1945. With it he recorded much Bach (including the Brandenburg Concertos three times) and toured widely (USSR, 1959).

Munrow, David (b. 12 Aug 1942; d. 15 May 1976), British player of recorder, crumhorn and many other early woodwind instruments. In concert and on television, as soloist and founder-director of the Early Music Consort, 1967, he did more than anyone else to popularize Renaissance consorts. Peter Maxwell Davies wrote for the group as a stage band in his opera *Taverner*, 1972. Munrow also played modern works for the recorder (first performance of Lutyens's *The Tears of Night*, 1972) and arranged period music for film. Committed suicide.

Muratore, Lucien, *see* CAVALIERI.

Murray, Ann (b. 27 Aug 1949), British mezzo-soprano. Made opera début 1974 with Scottish Opera, then sang with English National Opera (notably in the title role of Handel's *Xerxes*, 1985), at Covent Garden, from 1976 (début as Cherubino in *Le nozze di Figaro*), and at Aix-en-Provence Festival. In concert she has often performed with the Songmakers' Almanac (*see* JOHNSON, GRAHAM). Married to LANGRIDGE.

Murska, Ilma di, *see* DI MURSKA.

Musici, I, Rome-based ensemble founded 1952. Originally made up of eleven strings and one harpsichord. The members played without a conductor and at first concentrated on Vivaldi and other composers of the Italian baroque. Their violinist-directors have been AYO, 1952–67, Roberto Michelucci, 1967–72, and ACCARDO, 1972–6. CARMIRELLI, having shared with Accardo from 1975, continued until Federico Agostini took over in 1986.

Muti, Riccardo (b. 28 July 1941), Italian conductor. Became principal opera conductor at Florence, 1970. He succeeded KLEMPERER as conductor of the NEW PHILHARMONIA ORCHESTRA, 1973–82, ORMANDY at the PHILADELPHIA ORCHESTRA, 1980–92, and ABBADO at La Scala, 1986. Made many orchestral and opera recordings, including the first recording of Cherubini's Requiem in D minor for male voices and orchestra, 1985.

Mutter, Anne-Sophie (b. 29 June 1963), German violinist. Conspicuously favoured by KARAJAN, with whom she recorded major concertos from the age of fifteen. Made London début 1977, Washington 1980. In 1986 she gave the first performance of Lutosławski's *Chain 2* (violin and orchestra) and was appointed (aged only twenty-three) to an international chair at the Royal Academy of Music.

Muzio, Claudia (originally Claudina) (b. 7 Feb 1889; d. 24 May 1936), Italian soprano. Made her opera début 1910 and became celebrated in Italy, New York and Buenos Aires as well as on records; sang at only one Covent Garden season, 1914. At the Metropolitan she created the role of Giorgetta in Puccini's *Il tabarro*, 1918, and was the first to sing Tatyana (Tchaikovsky's *Yevgeny Onegin*) there, 1920.

N

Nägeli, Philip, *see* VÉGH QUARTET.

Nakura, Yoshiko, *see* TOKYO QUARTET.

Nápravník, Eduard (b. 24 Aug 1839; d. 23 Nov 1916), Czech conductor. Went to Russia in 1861, where he became highly influential as chief conductor of the imperial theatres, from 1869 till his death. He gave the first performances of Dargomizhsky's *The Stone Guest*, 1872, *Boris Godunov*, 1874, five Tchaikovsky operas, including *The Queen of Spades*, 1890, and Borodin's Symphony no. 2, 1877.

Nash, Heddle (b. 14 June 1896; d. 14 Aug 1961), British tenor. Studied in Milan. He sang in Mozart roles at Glyndebourne, 1934–8, and at Covent Garden, and was also an admired concert singer in Elgar's *The Dream of Gerontius* (recorded, 1945). His last operatic role was in the first staging of Benjamin's *A Tale of Two Cities*, 1957. His son John Heddle Nash (b. 1928) is a baritone.

Nash, John Heddle, *see* NASH, HEDDLE.

National Broadcasting Company Symphony Orchestra, New York-based orchestra founded 1937 to create an American post of prestige for TOSCANINI. On his retirement, 1954, and the withdrawal of support by the broadcasting company, the musicians established the Symphony of the Air as a co-operative, with BARZIN as music director. It did not last.

National Orchestra of France, *see* ORCHESTRE NATIONAL DE FRANCE.

National Orchestra of Spain, *see* SPANISH NATIONAL ORCHESTRA.

National Philharmonic Orchestra of Warsaw, *see* WARSAW PHILHARMONIC ORCHESTRA.

National Symphony Orchestra, Washington-based orchestra founded 1931. Its principal conductors have included DORÁTI, 1970–76, and ROSTROPOVICH, from 1977.

Navarra, André [Nicolas] (b. 13 Oct 1911; d. 31 July 1988), French cellist. Made his Paris concerto début 1931 and first appeared in Britain 1950 (Elgar's Concerto at Cheltenham Festival); gave the first performance of Jolivet's Concerto, 1962. He was also a well-known teacher.

NBC Symphony Orchestra, *see* NATIONAL BROADCASTING COMPANY SYMPHONY ORCHESTRA.

Neaman, Yfrah (b. 13 Feb 1923), Lebanese-born violinist of Jewish-Palestinian parentage, naturalized British 1948. Studied in Paris and settled in London. He was an influential teacher at the Guildhall School and artistic director of the Carl Flesch Competition. Gave the first British performances of the violin concertos of Piston, 1952, and Gerhard, 1955. OBE, 1983.

Neary, Martin [Gerard James] (b. 28 Mar 1940), British organist. Also conducts widely (for example with the BOURNEMOUTH SYMPHONY ORCHESTRA). Conducted first performance of Tavener's *Ultimos Ritos*, 1974. Organist and Master of Music at Winchester Cathedral 1972–87, and at Westminster Abbey from 1988.

Neate, Charles (b. 28 Mar 1784; d. 30 Mar

1877), British pianist and cellist. Became a close friend of Beethoven in Vienna in 1815. As a founding member of the Philharmonic Society of London, he arranged for it to purchase some of Beethoven's works.

Nedbal, Oskar (b. 26 Mar 1874; d. 24 Dec 1930), Czech viola player and conductor, also composer. Friend of Dvořák, and member of the BOHEMIAN QUARTET. He was conductor of the CZECH PHILHARMONIC ORCHESTRA, 1896–1906, and later conducted both opera and concerts in Vienna.

Neel, [Louis] Boyd (b. 19 July 1905; d. 30 Sept 1981), British conductor. In 1933 founded his own string orchestra, which became the most famous British chamber orchestra of its time (*see also* DART). It gave the first performance of Britten's Variations on a theme of Frank Bridge, 1937. He was dean of the Royal Conservatory of Music, Toronto, 1953–70. CBE, 1953.

Neidlinger, Gustav (b. 21 Mar 1910), German bass-baritone. Celebrated in Wagner; sang at Bayreuth from 1952 and Covent Garden from 1963. He took part in three different recordings of *Das Rheingold* and *Götterdämmerung*. Made Metropolitan Opera début 1972.

Neilz, Jacques, *see* LOEWENGUTH QUARTET.

Nelsova, Zara (originally Sara Nelson) (b. 23 Dec 1918), Canadian-born cellist; took American nationality 1953. Made London début 1932. She introduced several new works, including Bloch's three suites for unaccompanied cello, 1956, dedicated to her. She was married to JOHANNESEN.

Németh, Géza, *see* BARTÓK QUARTET.

Nemeth, Maria (b. 13 Mar 1897; d. 28 Dec 1967), Hungarian soprano. Settled in Vienna (and died there), and was prominent at Vienna State Opera, 1924–42. She was celebrated in strongly dramatic roles (Puccini's Turandot was her sole part at Covent Garden, 1931), and also sang the Queen of the Night in *Die Zauberflöte*.

Nendick, Josephine [Anne] (b. 2 Feb 1931), British soprano. Conspicuous in new music, she has made festival appearances at Aldeburgh, 1957 (her début), Darmstadt, 1958 (with BOULEZ), Warsaw and elsewhere. Also sang in Berlioz's *Les Troyens* at the Proms, 1967. She has held various teaching appointments.

Neruda (also known as Norman-Neruda), **Wilma** [Maria Francisca] (b. 21 Mar 1839; d. 15 Apr 1911), Czech violinist. Married the Swedish composer Ludvik Norman; they were divorced in 1869 and in 1888 she married HALLÉ, with whom she toured Australia and elsewhere. She was considered the leading woman violinist of her time.

Nesterenko, Yevgeny [Yevgenyevich] (b. 8 Jan 1938), Russian bass. Joined the Bolshoi company, 1971, and has frequently visited the West, from 1973. Made his début at the Metropolitan 1975 (as Boris Godunov) and at Covent Garden 1978 (Don Basilio in *Il barbiere*). Well known also in concert repertory, including Verdi's Requiem and Shostakovich's Symphony no. 14.

Netherlands Chamber Orchestra, Amsterdam-based orchestra founded 1955. It was prominent under its founding director, Szymon GOLDBERG, 1955–79; he was succeeded by Antoni ROS-MARBÁ.

Neuberger, Hans, *see* GAUDEAMUS QUARTET.

Neuhaus, Heinrich (also known by Russian form, Genrikh) (b. 12 Apr 1888; d. 10 Oct 1964), Russian pianist. Studied with Godowsky in Vienna. As a professor in Moscow, from 1922, he was one of the most influential of all piano teachers; his pupils included GILELS and Svyatoslav RICHTER. The Polish composer Szymanowski was his cousin.

Neumann, Václav (b. 29 Oct 1920), Czech viola player and conductor. Founding member of the SMETANA QUARTET. He conducted opera and concerts at Berlin, Leipzig and Stuttgart, and was then appointed conductor of the CZECH PHILHARMONIC ORCHESTRA, 1968–90. Made the first recording of Janáček's *The Excursions of Mr Brouček*, 1962.

Nevada (originally Wixom), **Emma** (b. 7 Feb 1859; d. 20 June 1940), American soprano. Took professional name from her birthplace near

Nevada City, California. She was prominent in London opera, 1882–1922, and particularly famous in coloratura roles; in the New York seasons of 1884 to 1889 she alternated with PATTI. Her daughter Mignon Nevada (1886–1971) was also an operatic soprano.

Nevada, Mignon, *see* NEVADA, EMMA.

Neveu, Ginette (b. 11 Aug 1919; d. 28 Oct 1949), French violinist. Performed as a soloist with a Paris orchestra at the age of seven. She won the Wieniawski Competition, 1935 (when David OISTRAKH was second), and became recognized as an outstanding artist. Made US début 1937 and British début 1945. She was killed in an air crash.

New Irish Chamber Orchestra, Dublin-based orchestra founded 1970. André Prieur was conductor to 1979, and Nicholas Kraemer became artistic director in 1985.

New London Quartet, *see* LONDON STRING QUARTET (2).

New Philharmonia Orchestra, *see* PHILHARMONIA ORCHESTRA.

New String Quartet, *see* LONDON STRING QUARTET (1).

Newton, Ivor (b. 15 Dec 1892; d. 21 Apr 1981), British pianist. One of the most celebrated accompanists of his time; his career lasted for more than sixty years. He worked in Britain and internationally with MELBA, SHALYAPIN, FLAGSTAD, MENUHIN, CALLAS and many others.

New York Philharmonic Orchestra, American orchestra founded 1842. In 1928 it merged with the New York Symphony Orchestra (and for some years thereafter used the title Philharmonic Symphony Orchestra of New York). Its principal conductors have included MAHLER, 1909–11, MENGELBERG, 1923–9, TOSCANINI, 1928–36, BARBIROLLI, 1937–42, RODZINSKI, 1943–7, WALTER, 1947–9, STOKOWSKI with MITROPOULOS, 1949–51, Mitropoulos solely, 1951–7, BERNSTEIN, 1958–69, BOULEZ, 1971–7, MEHTA, 1978–91; MASUR appointed from 1992.

New York Symphony Orchestra, *see* NEW YORK PHILHARMONIC ORCHESTRA.

Ney, Elly (b. 27 Sept 1882; d. 31 Mar 1968), German pianist. Pupil of LESCHETIZKY and Emil von SAUER; made début 1905. She was celebrated in Beethoven: recorded the Sonata op. 111 in 1936 and (when she was seventy-six) 1958.

Nezhdanova, Antonina [Vasilyevna] (b. 17 July 1873; d. 26 June 1950), Russian soprano. She had a long, distinguished career at the Bolshoi, 1920–36, where she often sang opposite SOBINOV; her roles included Rimsky-Korsakov's Snow Maiden. Later in Paris sang Gilda (*Rigoletto*) opposite CARUSO, 1913. She was also an accomplished recitalist.

NHK Symphony Orchestra, Tokyo-based orchestra founded 1926, serving the national broadcasting system, it used various names before adopting its present one, 1951. Principal conductors have included WÖSS, 1951–4, SCHÜCHTER, 1958–61, and IWAKI, from 1969.

Nicholls, Agnes (b. 14 July 1877; d. 21 Sept 1959), British soprano. Married to HARTY. She sang in the first performance of Elgar's *The Kingdom*, 1906, and as Brünnhilde in *The Ring* (in English) at Covent Garden, 1908.

Nicholson, Sydney [Hugo] (b. 9 Feb 1875; d. 30 May 1947), British organist. Founder of the School of English Church Music, 1927, which later became the influential Royal School of Church Music (royal charter, 1945). Knighted, 1947.

Nicolet, Aurèle (b. 22 Jan 1926), Swiss flautist. Played principal flute in the BERLIN PHILHARMONIC ORCHESTRA to 1959. As a soloist he has toured widely, and works have been written for him by Takemitsu (*Voice* for solo flute, 1971) and others. His recordings include Ligeti's Double Concerto with Heinz HOLLIGER, 1976.

Nicolini, professional name used by Nicolo Grimaldi (bap. 5 Apr 1673; d. 1 Jan 1732). Italian male alto (castrato). Active in Italy from about 1695. He came to London in 1708 and sang the title role in *Rinaldo* (Handel's first opera for London), 1711. Never retired: engaged to sing in Pergolesi's *Salustia* in Naples, 1731, he became ill and died before its première, 1732.

Nicolini (originally Nicolas), **Ernest** (b. 23 Feb 1834; d. 19 Jan 1898), French tenor. Sang in Paris, Milan and London; he partnered PATTI on stage and married her in 1886. He was the first in London to sing Radamès (*Aida*), 1876, and Lohengrin, 1879.

Niemann, Albert (b. 15 Jan 1831; d. 13 Jan 1917), German tenor. Chosen by Wagner as Siegmund in the first Bayreuth performance of *Die Walküre*, 1876. He was the first to sing this role in Britain, 1882, and also the first to sing Tristan in USA, 1886 (New York, opposite Lilli LEHMANN).

Nikisch, Arthur (b. 12 Oct 1855; d. 23 Jan 1922), Hungarian conductor. Eminent in interpretation and technical discipline. He was conductor of both the GEWANDHAUS ORCHESTRA in Leipzig and the BERLIN PHILHARMONIC ORCHESTRA from 1895 to the end of his life. Conducted concerts in Boston from 1889 and in London from 1895, and took the LONDON SYMPHONY ORCHESTRA to USA, 1912; in Paris he gave the first performance of Skryabin's *Divine Poem*, 1905. Occasionally conducted opera.

Nikolayeva, Tatyana [Petrovna] (b. 4 May 1924), Russian pianist, also composer. Pupil of GOLDENWEISER; won prize for her Bach performance at the Leipzig Competition, 1950. Her wide repertory of concertos includes Stravinsky's. Teacher at Moscow Conservatory and judge at international competitions.

Nilsson (née Svennsson), [Märta] **Birgit** (b. 17 May 1918), Swedish soprano. Pre-eminent in such Wagner roles as Brünnhilde (*The Ring*), Isolde (*Tristan*) and Senta (*Der fliegende Holländer*), and also as Strauss's Elektra and Puccini's Turandot. She sang at Covent Garden from 1957 and the Metropolitan from 1959. Retired from public performance in 1986.

Nilsson, Christine (originally Kristina) (b. 20 Aug 1843; d. 22 Nov 1921), Swedish soprano. Won highest operatic fame. She made her début in Paris, 1864, and became particularly well known in London and New York, where she sang in *Faust* at the opening of the new Metropolitan Opera House, 1883. Took part in the first performance in London of Balfe's opera *The Talisman*, 1874; she gave a farewell concert there in 1891.

Nimsgern, Siegmund (b. 14 Jan 1940), German bass-baritone. Has performed in both concert and opera: he first sang at Covent Garden 1973 (Amfortas in *Parsifal*) and the Metropolitan 1978. Made his London début in a concert performance of Berlioz's *La Damnation de Faust*, 1973.

Nissel, Siegmund, *see* AMADEUS QUARTET.

Nixon, Marni (originally Margaret) (b. 22 Feb 1930), American soprano. Her unusual recital and recorded repertory includes Ives songs. On film soundtracks she has dubbed the singing of many celebrities, among them Audrey Hepburn in *My Fair Lady*, 1964.

Noble, Dennis [William] (b. 25 Sept 1899; d. 14 Mar 1966), British baritone. Among the most famous inter-war singers of oratorio; he was the soloist in the first performance of Walton's *Belshazzar's Feast*, 1931. Also sang in opera at Covent Garden, with leading roles in premières of Goossens's *Judith*, 1929, and *Don Juan de Mañara*, 1937.

Nordica (originally Norton), **Lillian** (b. 12 May 1857; d. 10 May 1914), American soprano. Celebrated in opera; sang at La Scala (Elvira in *Don Giovanni*), 1879, Paris Opera, the Metropolitan and in London (Covent Garden and Drury Lane), 1887–1902. She was a famous Isolde (*Tristan*) and was also noted in oratorio.

Norena, Eidé (originally Kaja Hanson Eidé) (b. 26 Apr 1884; d. 19 Nov 1968), Norwegian soprano. Sang in Stockholm, then at La Scala under TOSCANINI; performed at Covent Garden and also at Paris Opera, 1925–37. She was admired in a variety of roles, including all three heroines in Offenbach's *Les Contes d'Hoffmann*.

Norman, Jessye (b. 15 Sept 1945), American soprano. Sang Aida at La Scala and Cassandra in Berlioz's *Les Troyens* at Covent Garden, 1972, and developed a highly successful operatic and concert career. Cassandra was also her début role at the Metropolitan, 1983. In a rare demonstration of black solidarity she closed the world-televised Nelson Mandela campaign concert, 1988. (*See also* DALBERTO.)

Norman-Neruda, Wilma, *see* NERUDA.

Norrington, Roger [Arthur Carver] (b. 16 Mar 1934), British conductor, formerly tenor. Founded the Heinrich Schütz Choir in 1962. He was much associated with Monteverdi, whose operas he gave as principal conductor (later director) of Kent Opera, 1966–84; conducted the first stage performance in Britain of Rameau's *Les Boréades*, 1985. With his London Classical Players, from 1978, he was a pioneer in reviving orchestral works by Beethoven and Berlioz with 'authentic' instruments and strict observance of original tempos; took this orchestra to USA in 1988. He was conductor of the BOURNEMOUTH SINFONIETTA, 1985–9. Music directtor, orchestra of St Luke's (New York), 1990. CBE, 1990.

Northern Sinfonia, Newcastle-based orchestra founded 1958. First conducted by Michael Hall; later conductors have included Rudolf SCHWARZ, 1964–73, HICKOX, 1982–90, and Heinrich SCHIFF, from 1990. In recent years it has used the title Northern Sinfonia of England.

Nourrit, Adolphe (b. 3 Mar 1802; d. 8 Mar 1839), French tenor, much esteemed. He created many major operatic roles in Paris, including those in Rossini's *Moïse* and *Guillaume Tell*, 1827 and 1829, Auber's *La Muette de Portici*, 1828, and Halévy's *La Juive*, 1835. Sang also in Italy. Subject to depression, he threw himself from a hotel window in Naples and was killed.

Novácek, Ottokar, *see* BRODSKY QUARTET (1).

Novaës, Guiomar (b. 28 Feb 1895; d. 7 Mar 1979), Brazilian pianist. A child prodigy, she was subsidized by her government to enter the Paris Conservatory, where she studied with PHILIPP. Made débuts in Paris 1911, London 1912 and New York 1915; she frequently toured USA. Specialized in romantic composers and modern Latin Americans, including her husband, Octavio Pinto.

Novák, Jiří, *see* SMETANA QUARTET.

Novello, Clara [Anastasia] (b. 10 June 1818; d. 12 Mar 1908), British soprano. Sang in the first British (private) performance of Beethoven's *Missa solemnis*, 1832, and in the Italian première of Rossini's *Stabat mater* (under the composer), 1841. She gave up her career on her marriage, but later resumed and became a favourite soloist in choral festivals. Her father was the publisher and organist Vincent Novello (1781–1861).

Novello, Ivor, *see* NOVELLO-DAVIES.

Novello, Vincent, *see* NOVELLO, CLARA.

Novello-Davies (originally Davies), **Clara** (b. 7 Apr 1861; d. 1 Mar 1943), British singer and choral conductor. Helped herself to the additional name Novello, presumably for the glamour given to it by Clara NOVELLO. Her son was the actor, singer and composer Ivor Novello (1893–1951).

Novotná, Jarmila (b. 23 Sept 1907), Czech soprano. Well known at Vienna State Opera, 1933–8 (title role in the first performance of Lehár's *Giuditta*, 1934). She then sang at the Metropolitan Opera, 1940–56 (début as Mimì in *La Bohème*). Retired to Vienna.

Nuovo Quartetto Italiano, *see* QUARTETTO ITALIANO.

Nyiregyházi, Erwin (b. 19 Jan 1903; d. 13 Apr 1987), Hungarian-born American pianist. A child prodigy, he played as a soloist with the BERLIN PHILHARMONIC ORCHESTRA aged twelve; studied with LAMOND. He made a highly impressive US début 1920, and settled in USA. Personal problems interrupted his career (he married ten times), and he seldom performed in public from the mid-1930s. A semi-private come-back in San Francisco, 1974, led to a new, successful recording, 1977. Also composer.

O

Oberlin, Russell [Keys] (b. 11 Oct 1928), American countertenor. An early associate of GREENBERG in the New York Pro Musica, from 1952, devoted to early music. He sang in the first Covent Garden performance of Britten's *A Midsummer Night's Dream*, 1961. From the mid-1960s he was active as lecturer.

Oborin, Lev [Nikolayevich] (b. 11 Sept 1907; d. 5 Jan 1974), Russian pianist. Gave the first performance of Khachaturian's Piano Concerto, 1937. He had a long and distinguished role in Soviet concert life and played in a trio with David OISTRAKH and KNUSHEVITSKY. Taught ASHKENAZY.

Obraztsova, Elena [Vasilyevna] (b. 7 July 1937), Russian mezzo-soprano. As a student, sang Marina in *Boris Godunov* at the Bolshoi Theatre, and afterwards joined that company. She won the Moscow International Tchaikovsky Competition, 1970. Made her Metropolitan début as Amneris in *Aida*, 1976, and her Covent Garden début in the same role, 1985. She has also sung Oberon in Britten's *A Midsummer Night's Dream* (originally for countertenor).

O'Brien, Jack, *see* GRILLER QUARTET.

Ochman, Wiesław (b. 6 Feb 1937), Polish tenor. His roles have included Lensky in Tchaikovsky's *Yevgeny Onegin* at Glyndebourne, 1968, and Mozart's Idomeneo at Salzburg, 1972. He appeared at Chicago (Alfredo in *La traviata*, 1972) before making his Metropolitan début, 1975.

Ochs, Siegfried (b. 19 Apr 1858; d. 5 Feb 1929), German choral conductor, also composer. Best known for writing and falsely attributing to Handel a song called 'Dank sei dir, Herr' (Thanks be to thee, O Lord). He conducted the first work by Schütz to be recorded (*Saul, Saul, was verfolgst du mich*), 1928.

Odnoposoff, Adolfo, *see* ODNOPOSOFF, RICARDO.

Odnoposoff, Ricardo (b. 24 Feb 1914), Austrian-born Argentinian violinist. Made his début in Argentina aged five. He studied in Berlin with FLESCH, won an international competition in Brussels, 1937, and developed an international career. Later taught in Vienna and Berlin. His brother Adolfo Odnoposoff (b. 1917) is a cellist.

Ogdon, John [Andrew Howard] (b. 27 Jan 1937; d. 1 Aug 1989), British pianist. In 1962 he was joint winner (with ASHKENAZY) of the Moscow Tchaikovsky Competition. Had made London début 1958 with Busoni's Piano Concerto, a piece typical of his unusual repertory: gave the premières of Rawsthorne's *Ballad* (for solo piano), 1967, and Williamson's Piano Concerto no. 3, 1964 (dedicated to him), and the first London performance of Sorabji's *Opus Clavicembalisticum*, 1988 (of three and a half hours' duration). Also duo-pianist with his wife, Brenda Lucas (b. 1935). The mental disorder that restricted his career from the mid-1970s was described in a film biography, *Virtuoso*, 1989; he died of bronchial pneumonia.

Ohlsson, Garrick (b. 3 Apr 1948), American pianist. In 1970 became the first American to win the Chopin International Competition in Warsaw. He performed Busoni's rarely heard Piano Concerto in New York, 1989; among his recordings are Skryabin's Concerto and all Weber's four sonatas. His keyboard stretch (a 13th in the left hand and a 12th in the right) is exceptional.

Oisly, Maurice d', *see* BUCKMAN.

Oistrakh, David [Fyodorovich] (b. 30 Sept 1908; d. 24 Oct 1974), Russian violinist, latterly also conductor, father of Igor OISTRAKH. The first Soviet string player to establish an unsurpassed reputation in the West. He won an international competition in Brussels in 1937, but did not make his formal London début till 1954; at his New York début, 1955, he gave the first US performance of Shostakovich's Concerto no. 1 (written for him, as was Khachaturian's). His repertory included over thirty concertos. He was a trio partner of OBORIN and KNUSHEVITSKY, and memorably played two-violin works with MENUHIN and also with his son. Gave his final concert (conducting in Amsterdam) two days before his death there.

Oistrakh, Igor [Davidovich] (b. 27 Apr 1931), Russian violinist, also viola player and from 1968 conductor, son of David OISTRAKH. He won an international contest in Poznań (Poland), 1952, and made his first UK appearance 1953. His piano partner is his wife, Natalya Zertsalova (b. 1930).

Olczewska, Maria, *see* OLSZEWSKA.

Olenina-d'Alheim, Marya [Alexeyevna] (b. 19 Sept 1869; d. 27 Aug 1970), Russian soprano. Married Pierre d'Alheim, the French translator of *Boris Godunov*, and together they organized concerts in Moscow and Paris. She herself was a distinguished performer of (and writer on) Musorgsky. Settled in Paris, but later returned to USSR, 1959, and died there, aged 100.

Olivero, Magda (originally Maria Maddalena) (b. 25 Mar 1912), Italian soprano. Developed her career solely in Italy; she retired in 1941, but re-emerged with remarkable success in 1951. Appeared in London, 1952, Paris and elsewhere in leading Verdi and other roles. At the age of sixty-three she made her Metropolitan début as Tosca, 1975. She retired once again in 1982.

Olszewska, Maria (originally Marie Berchtenbreitner) (b. 12 Aug 1892; d. 17 May 1969), German mezzo-soprano. Created the role of Brigitte in Korngold's *Die tote Stadt* at Hamburg, 1920. She sang with Vienna State Opera between 1921 and 1930 and made Covent Garden début 1924, Metropolitan début 1933; her notable roles included Brangaene in *Tristan*. (Her adopted surname Olszewska is usually misspelt as Olczewska in British references.)

Ondříček, František (also known by Germanized form, Franz) (b. 29 Apr 1857; d. 12 Apr 1922), Czech violinist. Gave the first performance of Dvořák's Concerto, 1883. He toured widely before settling in Vienna, 1907, as a soloist and quartet leader; was also a composer. His father was the violinist and conductor Jan Ondříček (1832–1900), five of whose other children were also professional violinists.

Ondříček, Jan, *see* ONDŘÍČEK, FRANTIŠEK.

Onegin (née Hoffmann), **Sigrid** [Elisabeth Elfriede Emilie] (b. 1 June 1889; d. 16 June 1943), Swedish-born Russian contralto (father German, mother French). Her first husband was a Russian who adopted the surname Onegin. She sang at Stuttgart Opera from 1912, later at Munich, Covent Garden, 1927, Berlin and Bayreuth, 1933. Famous as Gluck's Orpheus and Wagner's Erda, but also took parts for a higher range, such as Verdi's Lady Macbeth.

Onnou, Alphonse, *see* PRO ARTE QUARTET.

Orchestra of . . ., *see*, in general, next word of title, or place-name.

Orchestra of the Age of Enlightenment, London-based orchestra. Began giving concerts in 1986, using eighteenth-century instruments for music of that period. Unlike other such London groups, it is self-governing and has no permanent conductor. Its conductors have included Sigiswald KUIJKEN and (for what may have been the first 'authentic' performance of Schubert's Symphony no. 9, a work the composer never heard) MACKERRAS.

Orchestra of the Conservatory Concerts Society, *see* SOCIÉTÉ DES CONCERTS DU CONSERVATOIRE, ORCHESTRE DE LA.

Orchestre de Paris, French orchestra founded 1967 by MUNCH to replace the orchestra of the SOCIÉTÉ DES CONCERTS DU CONSERVATOIRE. Its principal conductors have been BAUDO, 1969–71 (with KARAJAN as music adviser), SOLTI, 1972–5, BARENBOIM, 1975–90, and then BYCHKOV.

Orchestre National de France, Paris-based orchestra founded 1934. It has worked with many conductors, none of them permanent, including MUNCH, CLUYTENS, CELIBIDACHE and MAAZEL.

O'Reilly, Brendan, *see* GABRIELI QUARTET.

Ormai, Gábor, *see* TAKÁCS QUARTET.

Ormandy, Eugene (originally Jenö Blau) (b. 18 Nov 1899; d. 22 Mar 1985), Hungarian-born conductor, previously violinist, naturalized American 1927. Went to USA, 1921. He was music director of the MINNEAPOLIS SYMPHONY ORCHESTRA, 1931–6, and then for a famously long period, 1936–80, conducted the PHILADELPHIA ORCHESTRA as STOKOWSKI's associate and, 1938, successor; became conductor laureate, 1980. He made many foreign tours with the orchestra. Conducted his large repertory from memory; his numerous first performances included Rakhmaninov's *Symphonic Dances*, 1941, Barber's *Medea*, 1947, Bartók's Piano Concerto no. 3, 1946 (with SÁNDOR as soloist), and Virgil Thomson's Suite no. 1 from *Louisiana Story*, 1948, and *A Joyful Fugue*, 1962. Among his foreign awards was an honorary KBE, 1976.

Orpheus Chamber Orchestra, New York-based orchestra founded 1972 by the cellist Julian Fifer (who became executive director). It works without a conductor and is self-governing; it has recorded Mozart and Stravinsky.

Ortiz, Cristina (b. 17 Apr 1950), Brazilian-born pianist, naturalized British 1977. In 1969 became the youngest competitor (and first woman) to win the Van Cliburn Competition in Texas. Studied in USA with Rudolf SERKIN, and made New York recital début 1971. She then settled in London, but also toured widely (Salzburg Festival début 1983). Her recordings include both Shostakovich concertos.

Östman, Arnold (b. 24 Dec 1939), Swedish conductor. Prominent in orchestral performance of eighteenth-century music on period instruments. He became music director of the Drottningholm Court Theatre in Sweden, 1980. Made his London début with Cologne Opera, 1983, and conducted at Covent Garden, 1984.

Otaka, Tadaaki (b. 8 Nov 1947), Japanese conductor. Underwent advanced training in Vienna. He became principal conductor of the TOKYO PHILHARMONIC ORCHESTRA, 1974, and of the BBC WELSH SYMPHONY ORCHESTRA, 1987.

Otten, Joseph, *see* ST LOUIS SYMPHONY ORCHESTRA.

Otterloo, Willem van, *see* VAN OTTERLOO.

Otto, Lisa (b. 14 Nov 1919), German soprano. Made her début 1941 and became well known in Mozart opera. At Salzburg, 1953–4, she sang Despina in *Così* and Blonde in *Die Entführung* (the latter also at Glyndebourne, 1956).

Oubradous, Fernand (b. 15 Feb 1903), French bassoonist and conductor. In Paris in 1927 he founded an oboe, clarinet and bassoon trio, for which original works were written by Ibert (Five Pieces, 1935) and others. He formed his own chamber orchestra in Paris, 1940, and later conducted and taught in Lille, Nice and Salzburg.

Oudin, Eugène [Espérance] (b. 24 Feb 1858; d. 4 Nov 1894), American baritone, also opera translator (originally a lawyer). Made New York début 1886. He came to London, where he created the part of the villain (The Templar) in Sullivan's *Ivanhoe*, 1891, and sang the title role of Tchaikovsky's *Yevgeny Onegin* at its first British production, 1892.

Oundjian, Peter Haig, *see* TOKYO QUARTET.

Ousset, Cécile (b. 23 Jan 1936), French pianist. Won several competitions, including the Queen

Elisabeth in Brussels, 1956. She made her British début at the Edinburgh Festival, 1980, and has toured widely; recorded all Beethoven's sets of piano variations.

Ozawa, Seiji (b. 1 Sept 1935), Japanese conductor (born in China). Won French conducting competition, 1959, and studied in USA. Became BERNSTEIN's assistant on the NEW YORK PHILHARMONIC ORCHESTRA's Japan tour, 1961. He was music director of the TORONTO SYMPHONY ORCHESTRA, 1965–9, the SAN FRANCISCO SYMPHONY ORCHESTRA, 1970–76, and the BOSTON SYMPHONY ORCHESTRA (at first overlapping), from 1973, which he took to China, 1979, Europe and Japan. Also performed as a guest conductor with other orchestras (London début 1965 with the LONDON SYMPHONY ORCHESTRA). He conducted the first performances of Takemitsu's *Autumn* (Tokyo), 1973, Ligeti's *San Francisco Polyphony*, 1975, Peter Maxwell Davies's Symphony no. 2, 1981, Panufnik's *Sinfonia votiva*, 1982, and Messiaen's opera *St François d'Assise* (Paris), 1983.

Ozim, Igor (b. 3 May 1931), Yugoslav violinist. His teachers included ROSTAL in London, where he won the Carl Flesch Competition, 1951. In 1957 he gave the first performance of Milko Kelemen's Concerto, one of several Yugoslav works written for him. Taught at Ljubljana, then Cologne, 1963.

P

Pachmann (or de Pachmann), **Vladimir** (b. 27 July 1848; d. 6 Jan 1933), Russian pianist. Specializing in Chopin, achieved sensational success, particularly from US tour, 1891. He became notorious for such eccentricities as addressing the audience. Married, 1884–95, to his Australian pupil Marguerite Oakey, who edited some Chopin works showing his fingerings. Died in Rome.

Paderewski, Ignacy [Jan] (b. 18 Nov 1860; d. 29 June 1941), Polish pianist, also composer. As one of his country's most celebrated citizens, he was briefly prime minister of the newly established Polish republic, 1919, and in 1940 joined the Polish government in exile in France. After studying with LESCHETIZKY, he made London début 1890 and New York début 1891. Toured extensively, with an arduous schedule (more in recital than with orchestra), and became a concert favourite, especially in Beethoven and Chopin (and his own Minuet in G). He died in New York.

Paganini, Niccolò (b. 27 Oct 1782; d. 27 May 1840), Italian violinist, also viola player and composer. His career (mostly as a performer of his own works) set new levels of virtuosity and showmanship; for example he would snip three violin strings successively and continue to perform on the fourth. Made London début 1831; in Paris he commissioned (but did not play) Berlioz's *Harold en Italie*, 1834. Settled in Parma, where in 1835–6 he directed the ducal concerts. Illness plagued his last years; he died in Nice. The 'theme of Paganini' used by Brahms, Rakhmaninov and others is from no. 24 of his (unaccompanied) caprices, published 1820.

Pagliughi, Lina (b. 27 May 1907; d. 2 Oct 1980), American-born Italian soprano. Studied in Milan; she sang opera at La Scala from 1930 and at Covent Garden from 1938; retired in 1957 and taught in Milan. She was one of the most famous of coloratura singers in such roles as Gilda (*Rigoletto*) and Lucia.

Palestine Symphony Orchestra, *see* ISRAEL PHILHARMONIC ORCHESTRA.

Palm, Siegfried (b. 25 Apr 1927), German cellist and opera administrator. His exceptional solo technique was exploited by such composers as Penderecki, of whose *Capriccio per Siegfried Palm* (for solo cello) he gave the first performance, 1968; also gave the première of Yun's *Glissées*, 1970. He was prominent in chamber music; administrator of West Berlin Opera, 1976–81.

Palmer, Felicity [Joan] (b. 6 Apr 1944), British soprano, also mezzo-soprano. Studied in London and Munich. From 1970 she sang a wide concert repertory, including Boulez. Made opera début in Houston, 1970, and performed Dido with Kent Opera, 1971. Her varied later repertory includes Brangaene in *Tristan* and Katisha in English National Opera's *Mikado*, 1986.

Palotai, Vilmos, *see* HUNGARIAN QUARTET.

Pampanini, Rosetta (b. 2 Sept 1896; d. 2 Aug 1973), Italian soprano. Distinguished in Puccini: sang Butterfly at La Scala under TOSCANINI, 1925. She continued to appear there till 1927; also performed Verdi and Puccini at Covent Garden, from 1928, and elsewhere.

Panerai, Rolando (b. 17 Oct 1924), Italian baritone. Distinguished as Figaro in Rossini's *Il barbiere* (Covent Garden début, 1960). He made his Italian début 1947, and sang in the first stage performance of Prokofiev's *The Fiery Angel* (Venice), 1955; performed at Salzburg from 1957. His many recordings include the title role in Paisiello's *Il barbiere di Siviglia*.

Panufnik, Andrzej (b. 24 Sept 1914), Polish-born conductor and composer (mother British), naturalized British 1961. Conducted in Cracow and Warsaw, and as guest in Berlin and London. He moved to Britain in 1954; after conducting the CITY OF BIRMINGHAM SYMPHONY ORCHESTRA, 1957–9, he concentrated on composition. Knighted, 1991.

Panzéra, Charles [Auguste Louis] (b. 16 Feb 1896; d. 6 June 1976), Swiss baritone. Settled in France. Although he sang at the Paris Opéra-Comique from 1919, his chief distinction was in concert; at twenty-six he gave the first performance of Fauré's last song cycle, *L'Horizon chimérique*, 1922, dedicated to him. He championed much other French music, was a prolific recording artist and wrote on interpretation.

Paradis, Maria Theresia von (b. 15 May 1759; d. 1 Feb 1824), Austrian pianist, also composer. Became blind at the age of five. She toured to Paris, London, 1784, and Berlin. Salieri, with whom she had studied, dedicated an organ concerto to her and Mozart a piano concerto (presumed to be K456 in B flat, 1784). Her own works include concertos and operas.

Paray, Paul (b. 24 May 1886; d. 10 Oct 1979), French conductor, also composer. After directing concerts in Monte Carlo, conducted a major Paris series (COLONNE ORCHESTRA), 1934–40 and from after the liberation, 1944–56. He was also conductor of the DETROIT SYMPHONY ORCHESTRA, 1951–63. His many first performances included Ravel's (orchestrated) *Don Quichotte à Dulcinée*, 1934 (with SINGHER). When he was ninety-one he conducted a concert in Nice honouring Chagall's ninetieth birthday.

Parepa-Rosa (originally Parepa de Boyescu), **Euphrosyne** (b. 7 May 1836; d. 21 Jan 1874), British soprano (father Romanian). Made London opera début 1855. While on tour in USA, 1867, she married ROSA; became the leading soprano in the opera company he founded. She encouraged the young W. S. Gilbert. Sang in Germany and again in USA, but recurring illness led to early death.

Parikian, Manoug (b. 15 Sept 1920; d. 24 Dec 1987), Turkish-born British violinist of Armenian descent. Distinguished as orchestral leader (PHILHARMONIA ORCHESTRA, 1949–57) and in chamber music (duo partner of MALCOLM and others), he was also well known as soloist. Gave the first performances of Goehr's Concerto (dedicated to him), 1962, and of both Crosse's concertos, 1966 and 1970.

Paris Orchestra, *see* ORCHESTRE DE PARIS.

Parish-Alvars, Elias (b. 28 Feb 1808; d. 25 Jan 1849), British harpist. Based mainly in Vienna from 1834. An innovator in harp technique, he aroused the enthusiasm of Berlioz, Liszt and Mendelssohn. His own works, including two concertos, are still reckoned extremely difficult.

Parkening, Christopher (b. 14 Dec 1947), American guitarist. A favoured pupil of SEGOVIA from childhood; he also studied cello. Won popularity in USA (and became head of the University of California's newly founded guitar department); he withdrew from performance in 1979, but later resumed international touring, 1982. Gave the première of Castelnuovo-Tedesco's Guitar Concerto no. 2, 1966, dedicated to him.

Parker, Jon Kimura (b. 25 Dec 1959), Canadian pianist of partly Japanese descent. While a student at the Juilliard School, played with its orchestra on European tour, 1983. In 1984 he won the Leeds Piano Competition and made London and New York solo débuts. The following year he was featured in a Canadian television documentary, *Local Boy Makes Great*, and appeared with the TORONTO SYMPHONY ORCHESTRA in a Toronto gala for Elizabeth II.

Parratt, Walter (b. 10 Feb 1841; d. 27 Mar 1924), British organist, also composer. The leading organist in Britain, he was appointed to St George's, Windsor, 1882. Knighted, 1892, and became Master of the Queen's Music, 1893 (a post that he held into the reigns of Edward VII and George V). His compositions include church music. Professor at Oxford, 1908–18.

Parrenin, Jacques, *see* PARRENIN QUARTET.

Parrenin Quartet, French string quartet founded 1944. Original members were Jacques Parrenin (who has remained as leader throughout), Marcel Charpentier, Serge Collot and Pierre Penasson; John Cohen, Jean-Claude Dewaele and René Benedetti joined in 1980.

Parrott, Andrew [Haden] (b. 10 Mar 1947), British conductor. Noted in both baroque and modern music: founder-director of the Taverner Choir, 1973. Made Proms début 1977, conducting Monteverdi's Vespers. He sang with the Electric Phoenix group, and was musical assistant to Tippett; conducted the first performance of Weir's *A Night at the Chinese Opera*, 1987. His first wife, 1971–83, was KIRKBY, and in 1986 he married the soprano Emily van Evera (b. 1955).

Parry, John (b. *c.* 1710; d. 7 Oct 1782), British harpist. He was blind; served a Welsh music-loving baronet. In London his playing impressed Handel and won the patronage of the future George III; he was editor of apparently the first published collection of Welsh folksongs, 1742. He should not be confused with the John Parry (1776–1851) who was a clarinettist and conductor.

Parsons, Geoffrey [Penwill] (b. 15 June 1929), Australian pianist. Came to Britain, 1950, as accompanist to DAWSON, and concentrated on accompanying as a career: worked with HÜSCH, 1955, and studied with WÜHRER in Munich, 1956. Performing with singers such as SCHWARZKOPF, 1961, and Janet BAKER and various leading instrumentalists, he became recognized as a leader in his field. OBE, 1977.

Partridge, Ian (b. 12 June 1938), British tenor. Noted in Bach's Passions (as the Evangelist) and other baroque works, and also in recital repertory (recordings of Schubert, Warlock and Britten). He sang as the bard Iopas in Covent Garden's performance of Berlioz's *Les Troyens*, 1969. His sister Jennifer Partridge (b. 1942) is his pianist partner.

Partridge, Jennifer, *see* PARTRIDGE, IAN.

Pascal, Léon, *see* CALVET QUARTET.

Pasdeloup, Jules [Etienne] (b. 15 Sept 1819; d. 13 Aug 1887), French conductor. His first performances included Saint-Saëns's Symphony no. 2, 1859, dedicated to him. He was greatly influential in Paris musical life, especially in the earlier years of his Popular Concerts of Classical Music (in a hall seating nearly 5,000), which he conducted from 1861 to 1884.

Pasero, Tancredi (b. 11 Jan 1893; d. 17 Feb 1983), Italian bass. Sang from 1918 at La Scala and was still performing there in 1952; noted in Verdi (for example as King Philip in *Don Carlos*). Appeared at the Metropolitan from 1929 and Covent Garden from 1931.

Pasta (née Negri), **Giuditta** [Maria Costanza] (b. 28 Oct 1797; d. 1 Apr 1865), Italian soprano. Acclaimed as one of the greatest operatic artists of her day for her great range and dramatic power. Made début 1815, London 1817; in 1831 she created the title roles of Donizetti's *Anna Bolena* and Bellini's *La sonnambula* and *Norma*. Sang again in London, also St Petersburg and elsewhere.

Patanè, Franco, *see* PATANÈ, GIUSEPPE.

Patanè, Giuseppe (b. 1 Jan 1932; d. 29 May 1989), Italian conductor. Active chiefly in opera (at West Berlin Opera, 1962–8), and was also co-conductor of the American Symphony Orchestra in New York, 1982–4. Conducted at Covent Garden from 1973. He died in mid-performance of Rossini's *Il barbiere*. His father, Franco Patanè (1908–68), was also a conductor.

Patey (née Whytock), **Janet Monach** (known as 'Madame Patey') (b. 1 May 1842; d. 28 Feb 1894), British contralto. Of great repute in oratorio and ballad concerts. She sang in the first performances of Sullivan's *The Martyr of Antioch*, 1880, and *The Golden Legend*, 1886. Her husband was the bass John George Patey (1835–1901).

Patey, John George, *see* PATEY, JANET MONACH.

Paton, Mary Anne (b. Oct 1802; d. 21 July 1864), British soprano. Born in Edinburgh. She first sang in London while still a child. Having appeared in the first British performance of Weber's *Der Freischütz*, 1824, created the heroine's role in his *Oberon* (London), 1826. Toured USA.

Patti, Adelina (originally Adela) [Juana Maria] (b. 10 Feb 1843; d. 27 Sept 1919), Spanish-born Italian soprano. Won enormous international reputation in her long career: she made her opera début at sixteen in New York, 1859, and in 1911 emerged from retirement to make famous, if faltering, recordings. London début 1861, Paris 1862, both in Bellini's *La sonnambula*; she sang the title role in the first London performance of *Aida*, 1876. Also famous in ballads, for example 'Home, Sweet Home'. Gave her official London farewell concert in 1906. The second of her three husbands (from 1886 till his death) was the tenor Ernest NICOLINI. She died at her castle home in Wales.

Patzak, Julius (b. 9 Apr 1898; d. 26 Jan 1974), Austrian tenor. Self-taught, he sang with Bavarian State Opera in Munich, 1928–45, and later with Vienna State Opera. Recorded the role of Florestan in *Fidelio* three times. He was also admired as a song recitalist.

Pau, Maria de la, *see* TORTELIER, PAUL.

Pauer, Ernst (b. 21 Dec 1826; d. 9 May 1905), Austrian pianist. Worked much in London. He gave an unusual series of chronological (harpsichord and piano) recitals from 1861. Taught at the Royal Academy of Music and then the Royal College of Music. He was also a music editor, arranger and composer.

Pauk, György (b. 26 Oct 1936), Hungarian-born violinist, naturalized British 1967. After winning the Munich Sonata Competition, 1957 (with FRANKL, who continued as his regular partner), settled in London; made first Festival Hall appearance 1961. His wide international touring has included return visits to Hungary. Gave the first British performance of Penderecki's Violin Concerto, 1979, and (with IMAI and KIRSHBAUM) the première of Tippett's Triple Concerto, 1980.

Paul, Tibor (b. 29 Mar 1909; d. 11 Nov 1973), Hungarian-born conductor, naturalized Australian 1955. Active in Budapest till 1944. Thereafter he worked mainly with radio orchestras in Australia, except for a period in Dublin with the RADIO TELEFÍS EIREANN SYMPHONY ORCHESTRA, 1960–67. Died in Sydney.

Pauly, Rosa (b. 15 Mar 1894; d. 14 Dec 1975), Hungarian soprano. Sang opera at major German and Austrian theatres to 1935 (when the Nazi regime penalized her as a Jew). She was noted in the title role of Strauss's *Elektra* at Salzburg and Covent Garden, 1938, under BEECHAM. Emigrated to Palestine, where she taught and died.

Paumgartner, Bernhard (b. 14 Nov 1887; d. 27 July 1971), Austrian conductor, also musicologist and opera translator. Active principally in Salzburg; he was director of the Mozarteum (college), 1917–38 and 1945–59 (KARAJAN was among his students of conducting), and founded the MOZARTEUM ORCHESTRA, 1922. As conductor and organizer, he was involved in the Salzburg Festival from its inception in 1920.

Pavarotti, Luciano (b. 12 Oct 1935), Italian tenor. Became one of the major box-office stars of opera (also made many concert appearances). He won an Italian singing competition, 1961; first performed outside Italy in 1963 (in *Lucia di Lammermoor* at Amsterdam), and also sang as a substitute for DI STEFANO at Covent Garden that year. Worked much with SUTHERLAND (including Australian tour). He sang at the Metropolitan from 1968 (in *La Bohème*). Apart from Mozart's *Idomeneo* (Glyndebourne, 1964, Salzburg and recording), his repertory clings to the stock Italian line of Bellini, Donizetti, Verdi and Puccini. Appeared in the film *Yes, Giorgio*, 1982.

Pears, Peter [Neville Luard] (b. 22 June 1910; d. 3 Apr 1986), British tenor. His mature career and private life were intimately associated with Britten. His first recital with Britten as pianist, 1937, included the première of Britten's cycle *On This Island*; sang the title role of Britten's *Peter Grimes*, 1945, and was equally prominent in all his later operas. He also performed

Dowland, Bach and Schubert with distinction, and created Pandarus in Walton's *Troilus and Cressida*, at Covent Garden, 1954. He was a founder-director of the Aldeburgh Festival, 1948. Knighted, 1977. (*See also* BRAIN [DENNIS] and BREAM.)

Peerce, Jan (originally Jacob Pincus Perelmuth) (b. 3 June 1904; d. 15 Dec 1984), American tenor. Sang in Beethoven's Symphony no. 9 under TOSCANINI in New York, 1938. From 1941 to 1968 he was one of the most constant and popular American-born stars of the Metropolitan Opera (in such works as *La traviata* and *Tosca*). Also appeared as guest artist with the Bolshoi, 1956, and in films; made Broadway début as Tevye in *Fiddler on the Roof*, 1971.

Peeters, Flor (b. 4 July 1903; d. 4 July 1986), Belgian organist and composer, also music editor. Toured widely as a recitalist. From 1923 he held cathedral post at Mechelen; taught in Belgium and the Netherlands, and was director of the Antwerp Conservatory, 1952–68. Created a Belgian baron, 1971.

Pegreffi, Elisa, *see* QUARTETTO ITALIANO.

Pekinel, Güher and **Süher** (both b. 29 Mar 1953), Turkish piano duo (female identical twins). Made début with orchestra in Turkey when they were nine; studied in USA with Rudolf SERKIN and others. They first performed at the Salzburg Festival 1984. Recordings include Stravinsky and Bernstein.

Pelletier, Wilfrid, *see* MONTREAL SYMPHONY ORCHESTRA.

Penasson, Pierre, *see* PARRENIN QUARTET.

Pennington, John, *see* LONDON STRING QUARTET (1).

Perahia, Murray (b. 19 Apr 1947), American pianist. The first American to win the Leeds Piano Competition, 1972. He played at the Aldeburgh Festival, 1973, and became one of its directors; settled in London. Recorded all the Mozart piano concertos conducting from the keyboard. He is noted also in duos (for example with CURZON and LUPU) and other chamber music. (Among so many Jewish musicians he is one of the very few to be of the Sephardic branch.)

Perlemuter, Vlado (b. 26 May 1904), Polish pianist (born in Kaunas, now in Lithuania). Resident in France. He studied in Paris with CORTOT; after learning all Ravel's piano works, he played them to the composer. Noted teacher. Gave London recital aged 86.

Perli, Lisa, *see* LABBETTE.

Perlman, Itzhak (b. 31 Aug 1945), Israeli violinist. Achieved eminence despite losing the use of his legs through poliomyelitis when aged four. He appeared on television in USA, 1958, then studied with GALAMIAN in New York (where he later settled). He made his US professional début 1963, London 1968; chamber music partner of ASHKENAZY and Lynn HARRELL. Recordings include Berg and Stravinsky concertos as well as Joplin's rags; he also sang the tiny role of the jailer in *Tosca* on LEVINE's recording, 1980.

Persiani (née Tacchinardi), **Fanny** (b. 4 Oct 1812; d. 3 May 1867), Italian soprano. Donizetti wrote the title role of *Lucia di Lammermoor* for her brilliant, high-ranging voice. She gave its first performance (Naples), 1835, and was later active in London, Paris and elsewhere. Married the composer Giuseppe Persiani.

Persimfans, conductorless orchestra active in Moscow, 1922–32. (The name is a Russian abbreviation for First Symphonic Ensemble.) It failed not because its artistic results were poor but because too many rehearsals were required to reach collective agreement and satisfactory realization.

Persinger, Louis (b. 11 Feb 1887; d. 31 Dec 1966), American violinist, also pianist and conductor. Studied in Leipzig. He was noted as a teacher in San Francisco, from 1916, and then in New York; his pupils included the boy MENUHIN, whom he accompanied at his New York début, 1926. On his seventy-fifth birthday he gave a recital divided between violin and piano.

Pertile, Aureliano (b. 9 Nov 1885; d. 11 Jan 1952), Italian tenor. His long career at La Scala, 1916–46, embraced the title roles in two operas about Nero, Boito's and Mascagni's *Nerone*, 1924 and 1935. He sang also at Covent Garden, 1927–31 (in such works as *Aida* and *Il trovatore*), and elsewhere.

Pešek, Libor (b. 22 June 1933), Czech conductor. Became conductor in residence of the CZECH PHILHARMONIC, 1982, and made his London début 1985 with the PHILHARMONIA ORCHESTRA. In 1987 he was appointed principal conductor of the ROYAL LIVERPOOL PHILHARMONIC ORCHESTRA. His recordings include Berg's Chamber Concerto and Martinů's opera *The Greek Passion*.

Petite Bande, La, ensemble founded 1972 and directed by Sigiswald KUIJKEN. Another prominent member is LEONHARDT. It performs baroque music on period instruments.

Petre, Charles W., *see* LONDON STRING QUARTET (1).

Petri, David, *see* PETRI, MICHALA.

Petri, Egon (b. 23 Mar 1881; d. 27 May 1962), German-born pianist, previously violinist (father Dutch), naturalized American 1938. Became pupil and assistant to BUSONI and a distinguished interpreter of his music. He taught at the Royal Manchester College of Music, 1905–11. Made New York début 1932 and settled in USA.

Petri, Hanne, *see* PETRI, MICHALA.

Petri, Michala (b. 7 July 1958), Danish recorder player. Made recital début at nine and studied in Germany. She began extensive international touring and recording in the mid-1970s, playing modern as well as baroque works. Performs with her mother, Hanne Petri (b. 1929), a pianist and harpsichordist, and her brother David (b. 1962), a cellist.

Petrov (originally Krause), **Ivan** [Ivanovich] (b. 29 Feb 1920), Russian bass. As a soloist with the Bolshoi Theatre, from 1943, he has performed as Boris Godunov and Borodin's Prince Igor. Sang the title role in the first recording of Rakhmaninov's *Aleko*, 1957.

Petrov, Nikolay [Arnoldovich] (b. 14 Apr 1943), Russian pianist. Studied with GOLDENWEISER; he won second prize at the Van Cliburn Competition in Texas, 1962, and later served on its jury. Made London début 1965. He gave the first performance of Khachaturian's Concerto-rhapsody for piano and orchestra, 1968.

Petrov, Osip [Afanasyevich] (b. 15 Nov 1806; d. 12 Mar 1878), Russian bass. Sang in many historic Russian premières, including Glinka's *A Life for the Tsar* (as Susanin), 1836, and *Ruslan and Ludmila* (as Ruslan), 1842. In 1876 Tchaikovsky wrote a choral hymn to honour the celebrations of his fifty years on the stage.

Peyer, Gervase de, *see* DE PEYER, GERVASE.

Philadelphia Orchestra, American orchestra founded 1900. It won fame under STOKOWSKI, 1912–38; later music directors have been ORMANDY, 1938–80 (previously Stokowski's associate, 1936–8), MUTI, 1980–92 and SAWALLISCH from 1993.

Philharmonia Hungarica, orchestra founded 1957. It assembled musicians who had left Hungary for Vienna after the political repressions of 1956, and settled at Marl in northern Germany in 1959. Principal conductors, not always Hungarian, have included SEGAL, 1979–85, and after him Gilbert VARGA. It also worked with DORÁTI on recordings of the complete Haydn symphonies.

Philharmonia Orchestra, London-based orchestra founded 1945 by Walter Legge. It was formed mainly to make recordings, but assumed a major concert role. Principal conductors have been KARAJAN, 1950–59, KLEMPERER, 1959–73, MUTI, 1973–82, and SINOPOLI, from 1984. In 1964 Legge attempted to disband the orchestra for commercial reasons, but the players established a self-governing management and Klemperer stayed with them. They took the name New Philharmonia Orchestra, but returned to the original in 1977.

Philipp, Isidore (b. 2 Sept 1863; d. 23 Feb 1958), Hungarian-born French pianist. Taken to Paris aged three; studied under Saint-Saëns and others. He became one of the most celebrated of teachers: from 1903 he was professor at the Paris Conservatory, and his pupils included

SCHWEITZER. Lived in New York, 1941–55, where he performed Franck's Sonata for violin and piano when he was ninety-one.

Pianka, Uri, *see* TEL AVIV QUARTET.

Piatigorsky, Gregor (originally Grigory) [Pavlovich] (b. 17 Apr 1903; d. 6 Aug 1976), Russian-born cellist; became American citizen 1942. Worked in Berlin, partnering SCHNABEL and FLESCH in chamber music. Made his début in USA 1929, and later performed there in a trio with HEIFETZ and Arthur RUBINSTEIN. As one of the leading soloists of his day (also famous as teacher), he gave the first performances of concertos by Hindemith, 1941, and Walton, 1957, among others, and composed and transcribed for his instrument.

Piatti, Alfredo [Carlo] (b. 8 Jan 1822; d. 18 July 1901), Italian cellist, also composer. Encouraged by Liszt, made Paris début 1844; Mendelssohn wrote at least part of a concerto for him. He settled in London, where he became highly successful as soloist, quartet player with JOACHIM and teacher. Gave the first performance of Sullivan's Cello Concerto, 1866. Died in Italy. (*See also* CARRODUS.)

Piccaver (originally Peckover), **Alfred** (b. 25 Feb 1884; d. 23 Sept 1958), British tenor. Had a long and distinguished career at Vienna Court Opera (later State), 1910–37. He sang in the first Austrian performance of Puccini's *La fanciulla del West*, 1913. Also performed at Covent Garden and later taught in London, but in 1955 returned to Vienna, where he died.

Pichler, Günter, *see* ALBAN BERG QUARTET.

Pierné, [Henri Constant] **Gabriel** (b. 16 Aug 1863; d. 17 July 1937), French conductor, also composer. Conducted the COLONNE ORCHESTRA in Paris, 1910–34; he gave the premières of Stravinsky's *Firebird*, 1910, and Saint-Saëns's *Carnival of the Animals* (never performed in the composer's lifetime), 1922.

Pilarczyk, Helga [Käthe] (b. 12 Mar 1925), German soprano. First studied piano. At Hamburg State Opera, 1953–67, she won fame in modern roles, such as the Woman in Schoenberg's *Erwartung* (also recorded) and Berg's Lulu. Sang in the first performance of Henze's *König Hirsch* at Berlin, 1956, and as Salome at Covent Garden, 1959.

Pini, Anthony, *see* BROSA QUARTET.

Pini, Carl, *see* LONDON STRING QUARTET (2).

Pini-Corsi, Antonio (b. June 1858; d. 22 Apr 1918), Italian baritone. After début 1878, specialized at first in comic roles, then sang Ford in the première of *Falstaff*, 1893 (also in the first British performance, 1894). He performed at the Metropolitan from 1899 and last appeared in Italy in 1917.

Pinnock, Trevor [David] (b. 16 Dec 1946), British harpsichordist and conductor. Made London début as harpsichordist 1968. In 1972 he founded the ENGLISH CONCERT, which won an important place in performance on baroque instruments. As a soloist he recorded the complete keyboard works of Rameau. On visits to USA he has held university posts and conducted Handel opera as well as founding the Classical Band.

Pinto, Thomas, *see* BRENT.

Pinza, Ezio (originally Fortunio) (b. 18 May 1892; d. 9 May 1957), Italian bass. Sang in the première of Boito's *Nerone*, 1924. Achieved chief operatic fame in twenty-two consecutive seasons, from 1926, at the Metropolitan, particularly in Verdi and Mozart. He also performed at Covent Garden, from 1930, Salzburg and elsewhere. In 1949 he won a new audience when he appeared in the first production of Rodgers and Hammerstein's *South Pacific*. (*See also* RETHBERG.)

Pishchugin, Sergey, *see* SHOSTAKOVICH QUARTET.

Pitt, Percy (b. 4 Jan 1870; d. 23 Nov 1932), British conductor, also composer. Conductor and adviser at Covent Garden, collaborating with BEECHAM; on the collapse of Beecham's financial enterprise, 1922, he became artistic director of the British National Opera Company, and remained till 1924. As the first music director of the BBC, 1924–30, he established its musical standards.

Pittsburgh Symphony Orchestra, American orchestra founded 1895. Its principal conductors have included REINER, 1938–48, STEINBERG, 1952–76, PREVIN, 1976–86, and MAAZEL, from 1986.

Pitz, Wilhelm (b. 25 Aug 1897; d. 21 Nov 1973), German conductor, previously violinist. Trained the chorus of the newly restarted Bayreuth Festival, 1951–73. He was the first chorus master of the Philharmonia Chorus, 1957–71, and as such collaborated in concerts with GIULINI, KLEMPERER and others. OBE, 1969.

Plaidy, Louis (b. 28 Nov 1810; d. 3 Mar 1874), German pianist, previously violinist. He was engaged by Mendelssohn as piano teacher at the Leipzig Conservatory, 1843–65, where Grieg and Sullivan were among his students.

Plançon, Pol [-Henri] (b. 12 June 1851; d. 11 Aug 1914), French bass. Active at the Paris Opera (first performances of Massenet's *Le Cid*, 1885, and Saint-Saëns's *Ascanio*, 1890) and from 1891 in London (première of Stanford's *Much Ado About Nothing*, 1901). He was notable for his successful and stylish early recordings, from 1902.

Plasson, Michel (b. 2 Oct 1933), French conductor. Won an international competition at Besançon, 1962, then studied with STOKOWSKI and others in USA. Conductor of opera at Toulouse, 1968–82 (latterly as general administrator); also worked at Covent Garden, from 1979, and the Metropolitan. In Paris he conducted the première of Landowski's opera *Montségur*, 1985. His many recordings include all Honegger's symphonies.

Pleeth, William, *see* ALLEGRI QUARTET, BLECH QUARTET and DU PRÉ.

Pleyel, Camille, *see* PLEYEL, MARIE DENISE.

Pleyel (née Moke), **Marie Denise** (b. 4 Sept 1811; d. 30 Mar 1875), French pianist. Briefly engaged to Berlioz, 1830, but in 1831 married Camille Pleyel (1788–1855), the composer, pianist and piano manufacturer. She obtained legal separation from him in 1835 and settled in Belgium. Admired by many composers, she was the dedicatee of Chopin's Nocturnes op. 9, 1833, and Liszt's *Reminiscences of Norma*, 1841.

Plowright, Rosalind [Anne] (b. 21 May 1949), British soprano. Won competition in Sofia, 1979. She sang in the Glyndebourne chorus, and as soloist with English National Opera, 1975; made US début 1982. She sang at Covent Garden 1983 as Donna Anna (*Don Giovanni*), and later roles have included Aida (opposite PAVAROTTI) and Strauss's Ariadne. As a concert singer she has worked with MEHTA and SINOPOLI.

Ployer, Barbara (*fl.* 1770–90), Austrian amateur pianist. Pupil of Mozart, who in 1784 wrote for her in Vienna the concertos K449 in E flat and K453 in G.

Pludermacher, Georges (b. 26 July 1944), French pianist. Won an international competition in Zurich, 1979, and became noted in modern music, for example Xenakis (created his *Synaphai*, with orchestra, 1971) and Boucourechliev. He plays in a piano duo with Yvonne LORIOD.

Pochon, Alfred, *see* FLONZALEY QUARTET.

Pogorelich, Ivo (b. 20 Oct 1958), Yugoslav pianist. Trained in Moscow (and married his teacher, Aliza Kezeradze, 1980). He won a Montreal competition in 1980. At the Warsaw International Chopin Competition that year his failure to win recognition provoked a scandal, and ARGERICH resigned from the jury. When invited to record Tchaikovsky's Piano Concerto no. 1 with KARAJAN, 1983, he refused to accommodate the conductor's wishes and the recording was cancelled. He later recorded it with ABBADO; he has also recorded Bach and Chopin. Tours widely; lives in London.

Polacco, Giorgio (b. 12 Apr 1873; d. 30 Apr 1960), Italian conductor. Studied in St Petersburg, Venice and Milan. He conducted TETRAZZINI's US début in San Francisco, 1905, and worked at the Metropolitan Opera from 1912. Invited by GARDEN, became principal conductor of the newly formed Chicago Civic Opera, 1922; he retired through ill health, 1930.

Polish Radio Symphony Orchestra, Katowice-based orchestra re-formed 1945 under ROWICKI's conductorship after wartime collapse.

Subsequent principal conductors have included MAKSYMIUK, 1976–7, Stanisław Wislocki, 1977–81, and Anton Wit, from 1983.

Pollini, Maurizio (b. 5 Jan 1942), Italian pianist. Won Warsaw Chopin Competition, 1960 (as youngest contestant), then studied with BENEDETTI MICHELANGELI. He toured and recorded with great success, specializing in both Chopin and Schoenberg; made US début 1968. Also conductor of orchestras and opera, from 1982.

Pommier, Jean-Bernard (b. 17 Aug 1944), French pianist and conductor. His piano teachers included ISTOMIN. Played under KARAJAN at Salzburg, 1971, and Berlin, and in 1973–4 conducted the NEW YORK PHILHARMONIC. He has performed as conducting soloist with the ENGLISH CHAMBER ORCHESTRA, 1980, the NORTHERN SINFONIA and others.

Pons, Lily (originally Alice Joséphine) (b. 12 Apr 1898; d. 13 Feb 1976), French soprano. First studied piano. She won her chief fame at the Metropolitan, from her sensational début in 1931 (as Lucia) to 1959; also sang at Covent Garden, 1935, on recordings and in films, with exceptional coloratura range. Settled in USA and was married, 1938–59, to KOSTELANETZ, with whom she performed in concert as late as 1972.

Ponselle (originally Ponzillo), **Rosa** (b. 22 Jan 1897; d. 25 May 1981), American mezzo-soprano. In an unprecedented début, 1918, sang opposite CARUSO in the first operatic performance of her life, which was also the first production at the Metropolitan of Verdi's *La forza del destino*. She subsequently sang twenty-one other roles there, to 1937, and also appeared at Covent Garden (début as Norma, 1929). In retirement she became a noted teacher.

Pople, Peter, *see* ALBERNI QUARTET.

Popp, Lucia (b.12 Nov 1939), Czech-born Austrian soprano. Has appeared with Vienna State Opera from 1963; made début at Covent Garden 1966 (Oscar in Verdi's *Un ballo in maschera*) and at the Metropolitan 1967. Her later international roles have included Sophie in *Der Rosenkavalier* and then the Marschallin in the same opera. She is also celebrated in the concert repertory, and has given recitals accompanied by her (former) husband, György FISCHER. She is currently married to the tenor Peter Seiffert (b. 1954).

Popper, David (b. 9 Dec 1843; d. 7 Aug 1913), Czech cellist, also composer. Worked in Vienna, then from 1896 till his death taught at the Budapest Conservatory. He was married to MENTER.

Postnikova, Viktoria [Valentinovna] (b. 12 Jan 1944), Russian pianist. Pupil of Yakov Flyer in Moscow; she shared second prize in the Leeds Piano Competition of 1966. Her highly successful London début (Proms, 1967) began a distinguished international career. In 1969 she married ROZHDESTVENSKY, with whom she occasionally performs in a piano duo.

Pougnet, Jean (b. 20 July 1907; d. 14 July 1968), British violinist of Anglo-French parentage (born in Mauritius). Known as soloist in lighter, salon music as well as in concertos. He was leader of the LONDON PHILHARMONIC ORCHESTRA, 1942–5, among others.

Pouishnoff, Lev (b. 11 Oct 1891; d. 28 May 1959). Russian-born pianist, naturalized British 1935. Settled in Britain, where he made his début 1921. A popular recitalist and active exponent of Rakhmaninov's music, he gave the British première of the Piano Concerto no. 4, 1930. In 1938 he became the first classical pianist to give a performance televised from London.

Poulet, Gaston (b. 10 Apr 1892; d. 14 Apr 1974), French violinist and conductor. Worked as orchestral leader in Paris under MONTEUX, then as a soloist; gave the first performance of Debussy's Violin Sonata, 1917, with the composer at the piano. He conducted his own Paris concert series from 1929, and continued to hold posts in Nazi-occupied Paris when others, such as PARAY, would not. His son Gérard Poulet (b. 1938) is a violinist.

Poulet, Gérard, *see* POULET, GASTON.

Poulton, [Edith Eleanor] **Diana** [Chloe] (b. 18 Apr 1903), British lutenist. Pupil of Arnold DOLMETSCH. She was one of the first twentieth-century professional lutenists and the first professor of lute at the Royal College of Music, from 1971. Also recitalist, adviser on theatrical productions, teacher and author of a book on Dowland.

Powell, Maud (b. 22 Aug 1868; d. 8 Jan 1920), American violinist. The first American woman violinist to achieve a concert career. She studied in Leipzig, Paris and with JOACHIM in Berlin; made London début 1883. Gave the first performances in USA of concertos by Tchaikovsky, 1889, Dvořák, 1894, and Sibelius, 1906. She was also a quartet leader, 1894–8, with male partners. As a touring soloist with Sousa's band she played before Edward VII at Windsor in 1903.

Prague German Quartet, *see* KOECKERT QUARTET.

Prausnitz, Frederik (originally Frederick) [William] (b. 26 Aug 1920), German-born American conductor. He adopted the spelling 'Frederik' from a misprint. A specialist in modern works, he has appeared as guest conductor with the BBC SYMPHONY (giving the first British performance of Varèse's *Ecuatorial*, 1966), and other orchestras.

Pré, Jacqueline du, *see* DU PRÉ.

Presti, Ida (b. 31 May 1924; d. 24 Apr 1967), French guitarist. Her early death cut off a brilliant career. She was known as a soloist and in a celebrated guitar duo with her husband, Alexandre Lagoya (b. 1929). Poulenc's *Sarabande*, 1960, was written for her, and Castelnuovo-Tedesco's *Well-tempered Guitars* (twenty-four preludes and fugues), 1962, for the duo.

Preston, Simon [John] (b. 4 Aug 1938), British organist and conductor, also harpsichordist. Organist and lecturer at Christ Church, Oxford, 1970–81; conducted the first performance of Walton's *Jubilate Deo*, 1972. He became organist of Westminster Abbey, 1981, and in 1987 left to concentrate on recital career. Toured widely.

Prêtre, Georges (b. 14 Aug 1924), French conductor. Active in French cities; conducted the first performance of Poulenc's *La Voix humaine*, 1959. He recorded opera with CALLAS, and toured USA with the ROYAL PHILHARMONIC ORCHESTRA, 1963. Also appeared at Covent Garden, 1961, and the Metropolitan Opera, 1964. He became music director of Paris Opera in 1970, but resigned the following year.

Preuil, William, *see* CLEVELAND QUARTET.

Previn, André (originally Andreas Ludwig Priwin) (b. 6 Apr 1929), German-born pianist and conductor, also composer and notable television presenter, of Russian-Jewish descent, naturalized American 1943. Taken to USA in boyhood. He became a successful Hollywood film composer and jazz pianist. From 1962 worked as regular symphonic conductor: with HOUSTON SYMPHONY ORCHESTRA, 1967–9, LONDON SYMPHONY ORCHESTRA, 1968–79 (recorded all the Vaughan Williams symphonies), PITTSBURGH SYMPHONY ORCHESTRA, 1976–86, and LOS ANGELES PHILHARMONIC ORCHESTRA, from 1986 (he left in 1989 after a disagreement). He became music director of the ROYAL PHILHARMONIC ORCHESTRA, 1985, but later confined himself to its principal conductorship while ASHKENAZY took the (organizing) directorship.

Previtali, Fernando (b. 16 Feb 1907; d. 1 Aug 1985), Italian conductor. Worked with Rome Radio Orchestra, 1936–43 and 1945–53, and at La Scala and other Italian theatres; conducted other orchestras, including the CLEVELAND, 1955. He gave the first performance of Dallapiccola's opera *Volo di notte*, 1940. Also composer.

Prévost, Germain, *see* PRO ARTE QUARTET.

Prey, Hermann (b. 11 July 1929), German baritone. Notable career in both opera and recital. He sang Wolfram in *Tannhäuser* at the Metropolitan, 1960, and Bayreuth, 1965; made Covent Garden début as Figaro in *Il barbiere*, 1973. In 1976 he founded an annual Schubert festival at Hohenems. His many recordings include operatic roles and Schubert and Brahms songs.

Přibyl, Vilém (b. 10 Apr 1925; d. 21 July 1990), Czech tenor. Sang as amateur before joining a Czech provincial opera company. He won note in the title role of Smetana's *Dalibor* during Prague National Theatre's visit to the Edinburgh

Festival, 1964. Afterwards performed at Covent Garden (Florestan in *Fidelio*, 1967), Salzburg and elsewhere.

Price, Leontyne (originally Mary Violet) (b. 10 Feb 1927), American soprano. Her Tosca on US television (a black singer in the role of an Italian singer), 1955, was considered a landmark. Gave the first performance of Barber's *Prayers of Kierkegaard*, 1954, and later was Cleopatra in the première of his *Antony and Cleopatra*, 1966. She was noted as Aida at Vienna State Opera, 1958, Covent Garden and La Scala. Received the Presidential Medal of Freedom, the highest US civil award. Married, 1952–72, to WARFIELD.

Price, Margaret [Berenice] (b. 13 Apr 1941), British soprano. Well known in Mozart; made début as Cherubino (*Le nozze di Figaro*) at Welsh National Opera, 1962, then at Covent Garden. She has also sung Desdemona in *Otello* (Paris Opera and the Metropolitan) and other Verdi roles. Noted recitalist, often accompanied by LOCKHART. CBE, 1982.

Prieur, André, *see* NEW IRISH CHAMBER ORCHESTRA.

Primrose, William (b. 23 Aug 1903; d. 1 May 1982), British viola player. Studied violin with YSAŸE, who directed him to the viola; played with the LONDON STRING QUARTET (1). Living from 1939 in USA, he was noted as soloist, partner of HEIFETZ and PIATIGORSKY and teacher. He commissioned Bartók's Viola Concerto and gave its first performance, 1949. CBE, 1953.

Pringsheim, Klaus (b. 24 July 1883; d. 7 Dec 1972), German conductor, also composer. A disciple of Mahler, conducted a complete cycle of Mahler symphonies in Berlin, 1923–4. He taught in Japan, 1931–7 and again later, and exercised a marked influence on Japanese composers.

Printemps, Yvonne (b. 25 July 1894; d. 18 Jan 1977), French soprano. Famous in French operetta and in lighter music. Poulenc wrote some songs for her, and Hahn his operetta *Mozart* (1925), based on a play by her husband, Sacha Guitry. Noël Coward's musical play *Conversation Piece*, 1934, was also written for her.

Pritchard, John [Michael] (b. 5 Feb 1921; d. 5 Dec 1989), British conductor. Associated from 1949 with Glyndebourne, first as répétiteur and finally, 1969–78, music director. He conducted at Covent Garden from 1952 (including the first performances of Tippett's *The Midsummer Marriage*, 1955, and *King Priam*, 1962). Music director of the ROYAL LIVERPOOL PHILHARMONIC, 1957–63 (at first jointly with KURTZ), the LONDON PHILHARMONIC and, 1982–9, the BBC SYMPHONY ORCHESTRA. He was also joint music director (with CAMBRELING) at the Monnaie (Brussels Opera), 1981–9, and in 1986 was appointed music director of San Francisco Opera. Knighted, 1983.

Pro Arte Quartet, Brussels-based string quartet. Made its début 1913. With the original membership of Alphonse Onnou, Laurent Halleux, Germain Prévost and Robert Maas it won the highest distinction and many works were written for it, including Bartók's Quartet no. 4, 1928. After transferring to USA, 1940, it was led by BROSA, 1940–44, and KOLISCH, 1944–7. The title then became attached to the quartet of the University of Wisconsin and ceased to carry its former prestige.

Procter, [Mary] **Norma** (b. 15 Feb 1928), British contralto. Among the best known of her generation in oratorio (for example Mendelssohn's *Elijah* and Elgar's *The Dream of Gerontius*). She also sang with Britten's English Opera Group and at Covent Garden (Gluck's *Orpheus*, 1961).

Prohaska, Jaro (originally Jaroslav) (b. 24 Jan 1891; d. 28 Sept 1965), Austrian bass-baritone. Member of the Vienna Boys' Choir as a child. He was noted in Wagner roles at Berlin State Opera, 1931–52, and Bayreuth, 1933–44. Later worked as college teacher.

Pruslin, Stephen [Lawrence] (b. 16 Apr 1940), American pianist. Settled in Britain and made London début 1970. A specialist in modern music, he commissioned Peter Maxwell Davies's Piano Sonata, 1981, gave the first performance of Birtwistle's *Linoi* (with HACKER), 1968, and wrote the libretto of Birtwistle's opera *Punch and Judy*, 1968.

Pugno, [Stéphane] **Raoul** (b. 23 June 1852; d. 3

Jan 1914), French pianist, also organist and composer. Became well known as soloist and in duo with YSAŸE; Saint-Saëns dedicated to him a celebrated toccata, 1899. He made famous early recordings, 1903, and toured widely; died in Moscow.

Pujol (originally Pujol Vilarrubí), **Emilio** (b. 7 Apr 1886; d. 15 Nov 1980), Spanish guitarist, teacher, writer on music and composer. Toured internationally (London, 1912) and gave the first performance of Falla's *Homage to Debussy*, 1922. He was also prominent from 1936 in reviving the vihuela and publishing its sixteenth-century music.

Punto, Giovanni (Italianized form of original name, Jan Václav Stich) (b. 28 Sept 1746; d. 16 Feb 1803), Bohemian horn player. Active in Paris, where he met Mozart, and elsewhere. He was one of the four wind players (*see also* RAMM) for whom Mozart intended a sinfonia concertante, 1778; Beethoven wrote a sonata for him and partnered him in its first performance, 1800. He was also a violinist and composer.

Putnam, Ashley (b. 10 Aug 1952), American soprano. In 1978 sang the title role in the first US performance of Musgrave's *Mary Queen of Scots* (also recorded) and made her European début as Musetta in *La Bohème* at Glyndebourne. She performed at Covent Garden as Janáček's Jenůfa, 1986.

Puyana, Rafael (b. 14 Oct 1931), Colombian harpsichordist. Studied in USA (with LANDOWSKA, among others). He made his US début 1957, London 1966, and has lived in Paris as his country's representative at UNESCO. Plays modern as well as baroque works; he gave the first performance of Montsalvatge's *Concierto del albaycin*, 1978, dedicated to him.

Pyne, Louisa [Fanny] (b. 27 Aug 1832; d. 20 Mar 1904), British soprano and operatic manager. Performed in childhood and went on to appear in opera in London and New York. She sang leading roles with the Pyne–Harrison Company, 1859–64, which she had formed with the tenor William Harrison (1813–68), including that in the first performance of Benedict's *The Lily of Killarney*, 1862.

Q

Quartetto Fiorentino, Italian string quartet founded 1865 by Jean BECKER. His colleagues were Enrico Masi, Luigi Chiostri and Friedrich Hilpert (succeeded by Louis Spitzer-Hegyesi, 1875). The quartet played an important role in setting high standards as an ensemble rather than focusing on a famous leader. Disbanded in 1880.

Quartetto Italiano, Italian string quartet founded 1945 as the Nuovo Quartetto Italiano. Changed its name in 1951. Members were Paulo Borciani, Elisa Pegreffi, Piero Farulli (succeeded by Lionello Forzanti, 1979) and Franco Rossi. Exceptionally, they played from memory. Ceased activity in 1986.

Queffélec, **Anne** (b. 17 Jan 1948), French pianist. Studied with BRENDEL, DEMUS and BADURA-SKODA; won first prize at an international competition in Munich, 1968. She is known chiefly in Scarlatti, Mozart and the French repertory. Her father, Henri, and brother, Yann, are both well-known writers.

Queler (née Rabin), **Eve** (b. 1 Jan 1936), American conductor. Noted for New York concert performances of opera, among them Puccini's *Edgar*, of which she gave US première, 1977. Her performance of Massenet's *Le Cid*, 1976, was recorded, making her apparently the first woman conductor of a commercially recorded opera. She became the first woman guest conductor of the PHILADELPHIA ORCHESTRA in 1976.

R

Raaff, Anton (bap. 6 May 1714; d. 28 May 1797). German tenor. Sang the title role in the first performance of Mozart's *Idomeneo* in Munich, 1781. He was already celebrated in opera in Vienna, Naples and Florence.

Rachmaninov (also spelt Rachmaninoff), **Sergey**, *see* RAKHMANINOV.

Radio Telefís Eireann Symphony Orchestra, Dublin-based orchestra originating from a small studio ensemble of 1925. Principal conductors have included Albert ROSEN, 1968–81, and Bryden THOMSON, 1984–6.

Rael, Anthya, *see* COHEN, ROBERT.

Raimondi, Matthew, *see* COMPOSERS QUARTET.

Raimondi, Ruggero (b. 3 Oct 1941), Italian bass. Famous in Mozart and Verdi operas: his Don Giovanni was seen at Glyndebourne, 1969, and in Joseph Losey's film, 1979. Also sang at the Metropolitan Opera, from 1970 (including Silva in Verdi's *Ernani*), and appeared as Escamillo in Francesco Rosi's film of *Carmen*, 1984.

Raisa, Rosa (originally Rose Burchstein) (b. 23 May 1893; d. 28 Sept 1963), Polish-born American soprano. Studied in Naples. She created the title role of Puccini's *Turandot* at La Scala, 1926. Sang at Covent Garden, 1914 and 1926, and became particularly celebrated with Chicago Opera, 1913–36, where she performed thirty-four roles. She was famous as Norma and Tosca.

Rakhlin, Natan, *see* USSR STATE SYMPHONY ORCHESTRA.

Rakhmaninov, Sergey [Vasilyevich] (various spellings used, in USA mostly Serge Rachmaninoff) (b. 1 Apr 1873; d. 28 Mar 1943), Russian pianist, conductor and composer. Studied with his cousin ZILOTI. He conducted opera in Moscow from the 1897–8 season and appeared as both pianist and conductor in London, 1899. Made his first US tour 1909 and, after taking up residence there in 1921, continued touring as highly popular pianist. His last concert tour took place two months before his death. A finger-span of up to a 12th contributed to his power. He was soloist in the first performances of his piano concertos nos. 2, 3 and 4 (1901, 1909 and 1927).

Ralf, Torsten (b. 2 Jan 1901; d. 27 Apr 1954), Swedish tenor. Noted in such Wagner roles as Lohengrin, in which he made his débuts at Covent Garden, 1935 (as a replacement arriving with three and a half hours to spare), and the Metropolitan, 1945. He created the role of Apollo in Strauss's *Daphne* at Dresden, 1938.

Ramey, Samuel (b. 28 May 1940), American bass. Made his début with New York City Opera 1973. Noted as Mozart's Figaro (his first role at Glyndebourne, 1976, and Covent Garden, 1982), he has developed a speciality in rare 'coloratura bass' roles, as in Rossini's *Semiramide* (Aix-en-Provence, 1980).

Ramin, Günther (b. 15 Oct 1898; d. 27 Feb 1956), German organist and conductor, also composer. In 1940 become cantor of St

Thomas's Church, Leipzig (the twelfth in succession to Bach there); he took the choir on various tours (including USSR, 1953). Also directed the Berlin Philharmonic Choir, 1935–43.

Ramm, Friedrich (b. 1744; d. 1808), German oboist. Played in the orchestra at Mannheim, where he became friendly with Mozart, 1777, and gave repeated performances of Mozart's Oboe Concerto in C. He was also one of the players for whom Mozart intended a sinfonia concertante for flute, oboe, horn (*see* PUNTO) and bassoon.

Rampal, Jean-Pierre (b. 7 Jan 1922), French flautist. Celebrated in Bach and other baroque composers (he has recorded the complete Bach sonatas with PINNOCK). Known also in modern music, he was soloist in the first performances of Jolivet's Flute Concerto, 1950, and of Hovhaness's Symphony no. 36 for flute and orchestra (Washington), 1979. Among the French works dedicated to him is Poulenc's Sonata, 1956.

Ranalow, Frederick [Baring] (b. 7 Nov 1873; d. 8 Dec 1953), Irish baritone. Sang in Beecham's opera company before playing the principal role of Macheath in the famous revival of *The Beggar's Opera* in Frederic AUSTIN'S musical arrangement, 1920. He went on to perform the part more than 1,400 times.

Randegger, Alberto (b. 13 Apr 1832; d. 18 Dec 1911), Italian conductor, also composer. Settled in London, 1854, where he directed much opera and conducted the first two seasons of symphony concerts at the Queen's Hall (opened 1895). He was an influential singing teacher.

Rankl, Karl (b. 1 Oct 1898; d. 6 Sept 1968), Austrian-born British conductor, also composer. Worked under KLEMPERER in Berlin, 1928–31, and came to Britain as a Jewish refugee from the Nazis. His music directorship of the newly constituted Covent Garden Opera, 1946–51, met some sustained criticism. He then conducted the SCOTTISH NATIONAL ORCHESTRA (1952–7).

Rascher, Sigurd (b. 15 May 1907), German saxophonist. Influential from the mid-1930s in establishing the saxophone as a solo concert instrument. Works written for and first performed by him include Glazunov's Concerto (Nyköping, Sweden, 1934) and Ibert's Concertino de camera, 1935.

Raskin, Judith (b. 21 June 1928; d. 21 Dec 1984), American soprano. Sang in the premières of Douglas Moore's *The Ballad of Baby Doe*, 1956 (title role), and Menotti's *The Labyrinth*, 1963, and in the London recording (conducted by the composer) of Stravinsky's *The Rake's Progress*, 1964. She also performed at the Metropolitan and, 1963, Glyndebourne.

Rasoumovsky, Andrey Kyrilovich, *see* RAZUMOVSKY.

Rattle, Simon (b. 19 Jan 1955), British conductor. In 1976 made his London professional début (with the NEW PHILHARMONIA ORCHESTRA) and became the youngest conductor to appear at the Proms (with the LONDON SINFONIETTA, with which his association has continued). In Liverpool he conducted the first performance of H.K. Gruber's *Frankenstein!!*, 1978. His work at Glyndebourne, from 1977, has included a notable *Porgy and Bess*, 1986. As principal conductor of the CITY OF BIRMINGHAM SYMPHONY ORCHESTRA, from 1980, he has presented adventurous programmes and enhanced its status; took it to Berlin, 1987, where he revived Goldschmidt's Ciaconna sinfonica of 1936 in the presence of its 84-year-old *émigré* composer. Appeared with major US orchestras from 1979 and at English National Opera (Janáček's *Katya Kabanova*), 1985. CBE, 1987. His wife is the soprano Elise Ross (b. 1947).

Raucheisen, Michael, *see* IVOGÜN.

Rautawaara, Aulikki (b. 2 May 1906), Finnish soprano. A favourite Mozart singer of early seasons at Glyndebourne, 1934–8. She also performed at the Salzburg Festival and in films, and later established herself in Helsinki as a teacher. The composer Einojuhani Rautavaara is her cousin.

Rauzzini, Venanzio (bap. 19 Dec 1746; d. 8 Apr 1810), Italian male soprano (castrato). The young Mozart wrote *Exsultate, jubilate* (with its famous Alleluia) for him in Milan. He himself was a composer of standing and also, from 1777, a concert promoter in Bath, where Haydn visited him, 1794, and where he died.

Rawnsley, John (b. 14 Dec 1949), British baritone. Sang at Glyndebourne from 1981. With English National Opera (début 1982 as Amonasro in *Aida*) he performed the title role in Jonathan Miller's production of *Rigoletto*, 1983, which went to USA, 1984, and was recorded and televised. Also appeared at Covent Garden, Brussels and Geneva.

Razumovsky, Andrey Kyrilovich (b. 2 Nov 1752; d. 23 Sept 1836), Russian amateur violinist. He was a count, later a prince. As Russian ambassador in Vienna from 1792, he became a friend and patron of Beethoven (whose three string quartets op. 59 are dedicated to him). The string quartet he established in 1808 was placed at Beethoven's service; its members included SCHUPPANZIGH and LINCKE.

Read, Ernest (b. 22 Feb 1870; d. 9 Oct 1965), British conductor and educationist. Founded youth orchestras in London from 1926 and a series of London orchestral concerts for children from 1944, in both areas pioneering the field. He also wrote music textbooks.

Recasens, Manuel, *see* CALVET QUARTET.

Reed, William H[enry] (b. 29 July 1876; d. 2 July 1942), British violinist. Closely associated with Elgar, he gave the first performance of his Violin Sonata, 1919, and wrote two books on him. Joined the LONDON SYMPHONY ORCHESTRA on its founding, 1904, and was its leader for an exceptional length of time, 1912–35.

Reeves, Sims (originally John) (b. ? 26 Sept 1818; d. 25 Oct 1900), British tenor. Studied in Paris and Milan, where he appeared in opera, but won greatest fame as a concert singer. He sang in the premières of choral works by Sullivan, including *The Prodigal Son*, 1869, and in the first British performance of Berlioz's *La Damnation de Faust*, conducted by the composer, 1848.

Rehfuss, Heinz [Julius] (b. 25 May 1917; d. 27 June 1988), German-born Swiss (later American) baritone. Performed a wide concert and opera repertory. He sang in the first recording (under the composer) of Stravinsky's *Oedipus rex* (as Creon), 1954, and in the première of Nono's opera *Intolleranza 1960*, 1961. Taught in many European, US and Canadian centres.

Reich, Günter (b. 22 Nov 1921; d. 15 Jan 1989), German baritone. In his youth emigrated to Palestine, but returned to Germany for education and career; member of Stuttgart Opera from 1968. Well known in twentieth-century works, he twice recorded the role of Moses in Schoenberg's opera *Moses und Aron*. Sang in the première of Penderecki's *Die schwarze Maske*, 1986.

Reilly, Tommy (originally Thomas) [Rundle] (b. 21 Aug 1919), Canadian harmonica player. Settled in Britain, 1935. From the 1950s he performed classical works, both original and arrangements made for him. Gave the first performance of Farnon's Prelude and Dance for harmonica and orchestra (Oslo), 1966. Also composer.

Reiner, Fritz (in Hungarian form, Frigyes) (b. 19 Dec 1888; d. 15 Nov 1963), Hungarian-born conductor, naturalized American 1928. Conducted the DRESDEN STATE ORCHESTRA, 1914–21, among others, then emigrated to USA. He was chief conductor of the CINCINNATI SYMPHONY ORCHESTRA, 1922–31, and the CHICAGO SYMPHONY ORCHESTRA, from 1953 until his death. Conducted the first performances of various American works, including Schuman's *Circus Overture*, 1944, and Copland's Clarinet Concerto (with GOODMAN), 1950, and of Stravinsky's *The Rake's Progress* (at the Metropolitan), 1953.

Reinhardt, Django, *see* GRAPPELLI.

Reinhold, Henry Theodore (d. 14 May 1751), German-born British bass. His origins are not known. After settling in London, he often worked with Handel, for example in the first performances of *Israel in Egypt*, 1739, and *Samson*, 1743. Also took part in theatrical productions of works by Arne and others.

Reitz, Karl, *see* BUSCH QUARTET.

Reizen, Mark, *see* REYZEN.

Remedios, Alberto (b. 27 Feb 1935), British tenor. Prominent at Sadler's Wells Opera (later English National) from 1957, in such roles as Siegmund and Siegfried in *The Ring*, 1973 (also recorded). He sang opera in Australia, USA (Metropolitan, 1976), and elsewhere. His brother Ramon Remedios (b. 1940) is also an operatic tenor.

Remedios, Ramon, *see* REMEDIOS, ALBERTO.

Reményi, Ede (originally Eduard Hoffmann) (b. 17 Jan 1828; d. 15 May 1898), Hungarian violinist, also composer. Toured with Brahms as pianist, 1852, and influenced Brahms's Hungarian Dances. He also played in London, 1877, USA, China and elsewhere. Died while performing at a concert in San Francisco.

Remoortel, Edouard van, *see* VAN REMOORTEL.

Rényi, Albert, *see* TÁTRAI QUARTET.

Residentie Orchestra of The Hague (sometimes known as The Hague Philharmonic Orchestra), Dutch orchestra founded 1904. Its principal conductors have included VAN OTTERLOO, 1949–73, and VONK, from 1980.

Resnik, Regina (b. 30 Aug 1922), American mezzo-soprano. Began her career as soprano in such roles as Leonora in *Il trovatore* at the Metropolitan, and Sieglinde in *The Ring* at Bayreuth, 1953. As mezzo-soprano, sang Fricka (*The Ring*) there in 1961. She was the Baroness in the première of Barber's *Vanessa*, 1958, and Claire in the first US performance of Einem's *Der Besuch der alten Dame*, 1972. Also stage director.

Reszke, Edouard de, *see* DE RESZKE, EDOUARD.

Reszke, Jean de, *see* DE RESZKE, JEAN.

Reszke, Joséphine de, *see* DE RESZKE, JEAN.

Rethberg, Elisabeth (originally Lisbeth Sättler) (b. 22 Sept 1894; d. 6 June 1976), German-born American soprano. Sang opera in Dresden, then at the Metropolitan, 1922–42 (thirty roles including fifty-one performances as Aida); toured widely with PINZA. She returned to Dresden to create the title role in Strauss's *Die aegyptische Helena*, 1928. Her second husband, from 1957, was CEHANOVSKY.

Revoil, Fanely (b. 25 Sept 1910), French soprano. Celebrated in operetta in Paris, for example in the title roles of Messager's *Véronique* and Hahn's *Ciboulette*. She took part in the first performance of Roussel's opera *Le Testament de Tante Caroline*, 1936.

Reyzen, Mark [Osipovich] (b. 3 July 1895). Russian bass. Had major operatic career first in Leningrad then, 1930–54, at the Bolshoi: he returned there (as Gremin in Tchaikovsky's *Yevgeny Onegin*) for a ninetieth-birthday performance in 1985. Sang in Britain (concerts only), at the Paris Opera and elsewhere; he made recordings of various classic Russian roles (including Musorgsky's Boris Godunov, 1948).

Rhené-Bâton (originally René Bâton) (b. 5 Sept 1879; d. 23 Sept 1940), French conductor. Worked with the Dyagilev ballet in London and the Netherlands. In Paris he gave important first performances, including Debussy's *Printemps*, 1913, and Ravel's *L'alborada del gracioso*, 1919; Roussel dedicated to him his Symphony no. 2, 1922.

Rhodes, Jane [Marie Andrée] (b. 13 Mar 1929), French soprano. Active at the Paris Opera and Opéra-Comique, where her roles ranged from Carmen to Tosca, she sang Salome at the Metropolitan Opera, 1962. She was Renata on the first recording of Prokofiev's *The Fiery Angel*, 1957. In 1966 she married BENZI (who had conducted her Carmen).

Rhodes, Samuel, *see* JUILLIARD QUARTET.

Ricci, Ruggiero (b. 24 July 1918), American violinist. His distinguished career began with a recital in San Francisco at the age of ten, with his teacher, PERSINGER, at the piano. Toured extensively from 1957. He has played about sixty concertos and was the first to perform those by Ginastera, 1963, and Einem, 1970. A specialist in Paganini, he gave the first US performance of the newly found Concerto in E minor, 1977.

Ricciarelli, Katia (b. 16 Jan 1946), Italian soprano. Made her début in 1969; first appeared at Covent Garden, 1974, and the Metropolitan, 1975, as Mimì in *La Bohème*. Much in demand, especially in Italian lyrical roles, she was Desdemona in Zeffirelli's film of *Otello*, 1986. Her many recordings include the first of Cherubini's *Anacréon*, 1971.

Richards, Bernard, *see* AMICI QUARTET.

Richter, Hans (b. 4 Apr 1843; d. 5 Dec 1916), Austro-Hungarian conductor. Gave *The Ring* its first complete performance (Bayreuth), 1876. In Vienna he conducted the premières of Tchaikovsky's Violin Concerto, 1881, and Brahms's Symphony no. 3 (1883). Became a leading orchestral conductor in London, from 1877, and Manchester with the HALLÉ ORCHESTRA, 1899–1911. Encouraged Elgar and conducted the first performances of the 'Enigma' Variations, 1899, and the Symphony no. 1, 1908, dedicated to him. He instigated and was conductor of the first English-language performances of *The Ring* at Covent Garden, 1908–9. Died in Bayreuth.

Richter, Karl (b. 15 Oct 1926; d. 15 Feb 1981), German organist and conductor. Worked as church organist in Leipzig, then settled in Munich, 1951, and won world-wide reputation as founder and conductor of the Munich Bach Orchestra and Choir. He took them to USSR for performances of the *St John Passion* and the Mass in B minor, 1968. Made many recordings, especially of Bach.

Richter, Svyatoslav [Teofilovich] (b. 20 Mar 1915), Russian pianist. Studied with NEUHAUS. He has combined an unsurpassed authority with a disposition to cancel his concerts. Gave the first public performances of Prokofiev's piano sonatas nos. 6, 7 and 9 (1940, 1943 and 1951), and made a rare appearance as conductor for the première of Prokofiev's Cello Concerto no. 2, 1952 (with ROSTROPOVICH). He has played in the West from 1960, and was much associated with Britten at the Aldeburgh Festival.

Richter-Haaser, Hans (b. 6 Jan 1912; d. 16 Dec 1980), German pianist, also conductor and composer. Made his youthful début at a Schubert commemoration, 1928. After World War II, when he was taken prisoner by the French, he built a wider career and became internationally known in Beethoven. Made first New York appearance in 1959.

Rickenbacher, Karl Anton (b. 20 May 1940), Swiss conductor. Has worked with various orchestras in Germany, Britain and elsewhere. He was principal conductor of the BBC SCOTTISH SYMPHONY ORCHESTRA, 1978–80.

Ridderbusch, Karl (b. 29 May 1932), German bass. Noted in Wagner. He sang at Bayreuth and the Metropolitan from 1967, and at Covent Garden (three roles in *The Ring*) from 1971. Performed on many operatic recordings, including the first of Pfitzner's *Palestrina*, 1973.

Riddle, Frederick, *see* BLECH QUARTET.

Riegel, Kenneth (b. 29 Apr 1938), American tenor. Noted in character parts such as the title role in Zemlinsky's *Der Zwerg* (The Dwarf), which he performed entirely on his knees (Covent Garden, first London performance, 1985). He made his Metropolitan Opera début 1973; sang Don Ottavio in Joseph Losey's film of *Don Giovanni* and Alwa in the first complete staging of Berg's *Lulu* in Paris, 1979 (also recorded).

Rieger, Fritz, *see* MELBOURNE SYMPHONY ORCHESTRA.

Ries, Ferdinand (bap. 28 Nov 1784; d. 13 Jan 1838), German pianist, also composer. Son of Beethoven's teacher Franz Anton Ries (1755–1846). In Vienna he became Beethoven's friend and an early performer of his music. Worked in London, 1813–24, where he was considered a leading pianist.

Ries, Franz Anton, *see* RIES, FERDINAND.

Ries, Louis, *see* JOACHIM QUARTET.

Rifkin, Joshua (b. 22 Apr 1944), American pianist, conductor and musicologist. Became widely known in the 1970s for reviving the ragtime music of Scott Joplin in a classical recital context (and on record). As a Bach scholar and conductor he promoted the idea that the Mass in B minor required only soloists, not a chorus (recording, 1983).

Rignold, Hugo [Henry] (b. 15 May 1905; d. 30 May 1976), British conductor. Began career as a dance-band violinist. He conducted Sadler's Wells Ballet (later named Royal Ballet) and the CITY OF BIRMINGHAM SYMPHONY ORCHESTRA, 1960–68. Worked also in South Africa.

Rilling, Helmuth (b. 29 May 1933), German organist and conductor. In 1954, while still a student in Stuttgart, founded the choir with which he first became celebrated. Of high repute as a Bach conductor. Gave first performance (and recording, 1969) of the Mass for Rossini written by Verdi and twelve other composers.

Rippon, Michael [George] (b. 10 Dec 1938), British bass-baritone. Notable in such declamatory concert works as Henze's *El Cimarrón* and Walton's *Belshazzar's Feast*. His first performances include Birtwistle's *Epilogue*, 1972, and Peter Maxwell Davies's *Le Jongleur de Notre Dame*, 1978. He also sang in Mozart and other opera at Glyndebourne, from 1970, and Covent Garden.

Roberton, Hugh [Stevenson] (b. 23 Feb 1874; d. 7 Oct 1952), British conductor, also composer and arranger. Founder and conductor throughout its existence, 1906–51, of the celebrated (amateur) Glasgow Orpheus Choir. He travelled with it to London and elsewhere.

Roberts, Bernard (b. 23 July 1933), British pianist. Made London début 1957. Without major exposure to international audiences he has built a distinct personal following, especially in Beethoven, whose thirty-two piano sonatas he has twice recorded. Also professor at the Royal College of Music.

Robertson, Alexander, *see* BRODSKY QUARTET (2).

Robertson, James (b. 17 June 1912), British conductor. As music director of Sadler's Wells Opera, 1946–54, gave the first British performance of Wolf-Ferrari's *I quatro rusteghi* (as 'The School for Fathers'), 1946. He conducted a remarkable repertory with the (amateur) John Lewis Partnership Society in London. Conductor of the New Zealand National Orchestra, 1954–7.

Robertson, Paul, *see* MEDICI QUARTET.

Robertson, Rae, *see* BARTLETT.

Robeson, Paul (b. 9 Apr 1898; d. 23 Jan 1976), American bass. His world popularity was unequalled in his day by any other black performer. Gave first concert 1925. He was particularly famous in spirituals and in the song 'Ol' Man River' from Kern's *Show Boat*, in which he played in London, 1928, and in the 1936 film version (but not in the original New York production). Acted the title role in Shakespeare's *Othello*, firstly in London, 1930. His espousal of Soviet communism restricted his later US career, but he returned to Carnegie Hall, New York, in 1958.

Robin, Jacqueline, *see* JOY.

Robin, Mado (b. 29 Dec 1918; d. 10 Dec 1960), French soprano. Her extremely high voice extended to the C above so-called top C. She sang at the Paris Opera from 1945, at San Francisco (for example as Gilda in *Rigoletto*), 1954, and in USSR, 1959.

Robinson, Anastasia (b. *c.* 1692; d. Apr 1755), British soprano, later contralto. Handel wrote for her the solo soprano part in his *Ode for Queen Anne's Birthday*, 1714, the contralto role of Cornelia in *Giulio Cesare*, 1724, and other parts. She was a person of culture and a friend of Pope; secretly married the elderly Earl of Peterborough, 1724.

Robinson, Ann Turner (d. 5 Jan 1741), British soprano. Identified with the 'Mrs Robinson' who sang in several original Handel performances, including the opera *Radamisto*, 1720, and his first London oratorio, *Esther*, 1732.

Robinson, Eric, *see* ROBINSON, STANFORD.

Robinson, [Peter] **Forbes** (b. 21 May 1926; d. 13 May 1987), British bass. His career with Covent Garden, from 1954, embraced the title role in the première of Tippett's *King Priam* (Coventry), 1962, and the role of Moses in the first British production of Schoenberg's *Moses und Aron*, 1965.

Robinson, Miss (forename and dates unknown),

British mezzo-soprano. Sang in Handel's last London oratorio season, 1744–5. It is not always easy to distinguish between the performances of this singer, Anastasia ROBINSON and Ann Turner ROBINSON, all of whom were associated with Handel.

Robinson, Sharon, *see* KALICHSTEIN.

Robinson, Stanford (b. 5 July 1904; d. 25 Oct 1984), British conductor. Much associated with opera and light music at the BBC. He conducted the first British (stage) performance of Alessandro Scarlatti's opera *Il trionfo dell'onore*, 1951, and also the UK première of Schoenberg's *Friede auf Erden* (BBC, 1931). His brother Eric Robinson (1908–74) was also a conductor.

Robles, Marisa (b. 4 May 1937), Spanish harpist. Resident in Britain from 1959; noted as recitalist and television performer. In chamber-music performances she was frequently partnered by her (then) husband, the flautist Christopher Hyde-Smith (b. 1935).

Robyn, Paul, *see* HOLLYWOOD QUARTET.

Rodzinski, Arthur (b. 1 Jan 1892; d. 27 Nov 1958), Polish-born conductor; took American nationality 1933. Conductor of the CLEVELAND ORCHESTRA, 1933–43, which he made first-class; with it he gave the first US (concert) performance of Shostakovich's *Lady Macbeth of Mtsensk*, 1935. Later he had short, stormy conductorships of the NEW YORK PHILHARMONIC, 1943–7, and the CHICAGO SYMPHONY ORCHESTRA, 1947–8. In New York he conducted the première of Hindemith's *Symphonic Metamorphoses of Themes of Weber*, 1944.

Rogé, Pascal (b. 6 Apr 1951), French pianist. Studied at the Paris Conservatory and privately with KATCHEN. He made his orchestral début at the age of eleven, 1962, and London recital début in 1969. Won the Long–Thibaud Competition, 1971. His recordings include all the concertos of Saint-Saëns and Ravel.

Rogers, Nigel [David] (b. 21 Mar 1935), British tenor. Studied under HÜSCH in Munich and began his career there. He won distinction in baroque performances: twice recorded the title role of Monteverdi's *Orfeo* (1974, 1985). Also sang in the London première of Goehr's opera *Arden muss sterben*, 1974. His group Chiaroscuro gave the first modern revival of Handel's cantata *Il trionfo del tempo e del disinganno*, 1987. He has taught courses in Europe, USA and Australia.

Rogg, Lionel (b. 21 Apr 1936), Swiss organist. Performer of highest repute, concentrating on the organ after an equally distinguished start as pianist. In 1961 in Geneva he played Bach's complete works for organ, which he later recorded three times; his other recordings include all Buxtehude's organ works. Also harpsichordist (with modern as well as baroque repertory), composer and international teacher.

Rögner, Heinz, *see* YOMIURI NIPPON SYMPHONY ORCHESTRA.

Roisman, Josef, *see* BUDAPEST QUARTET.

Rolfe Johnson, Anthony (b. 5 Nov 1940), British tenor. Widely known in Handel oratorio (title role on recording of *Jephtha*, 1985) and in opera. He sang at Glyndebourne, from 1974, Covent Garden, 1985, and Hamburg State Opera (title role in Mozart's *La clemenza di Tito*), 1986. Took part in the first recordings (under DORÁTI) of rare Haydn operas. Occasionally, from 1988, he has been jointly singer and director of Bach performances.

Romanzini, *see* BLAND, MARIA THERESA.

Ronald, Landon (originally Landon Ronald Russell) (b. 7 June 1873; d. 14 Aug 1938), British conductor, son of Henry RUSSELL. As musical adviser to the Gramophone Company (HMV) from 1900, he attracted artists to the new medium and himself conducted Grieg's Piano Concerto (abridged) with BACKHAUS as early as 1911; his 1925 recording of Tchaikovsky's Symphony no. 4 was the first electrical recording to be released commercially in Britain. Previously toured as MELBA's piano accompanist, 1894. He was also a composer (his works include the song 'Down in the Forest') and principal of the Guildhall School of Music, 1910–35. Knighted, 1922.

Ronzi (or Ronzi De Begnis), **Giuseppina** (b. 11 Jan 1800; d. 7 June 1853), French-born Italian soprano. Created the title role in Donizetti's *Maria Stuarda* in Naples, 1834. Her first appearance in London was in Rossini's *Il turco in Italia*, 1821, with her husband, DE BEGNIS (from whom she later separated). She returned to London, 1843, and sang Norma in English.

Rooley, Anthony (b. 10 June 1944), British lutenist. A key figure in the early-music revival in Britain, in 1969 he became joint organizer with TYLER of the Consort of Musicke (sole director from 1972); KIRKBY emerged as its leading singer. Directed many 'authentic' performances (sometimes staged) of late-Renaissance and early-baroque works, including the first modern professional production, 1983, of *Cupid and Death* (first performed 1653) by Locke and Christopher Gibbons.

Rooy, Anton van, *see* VAN ROOY.

Rosa (originally Rose), **Carl** [Augustus Nikolaus] (b. 22 Mar 1842; d. 30 Apr 1889), German violinist and conductor. Settled in London. With his wife, PAREPA-ROSA, he organized an American touring company. In London, after her early death, he formed the Carl Rosa Opera Company, whose leading singers included SANTLEY. He staged first performances in English of *Der fliegende Holländer*, 1876, *Aida*, 1880, and other works, and launched new British operas by such composers as Goring Thomas and Stanford (*The Canterbury Pilgrims*, 1884).

Rosbaud, Hans (b. 22 July 1895; d. 29 Dec 1962), Austrian conductor. Gave many important premières, from Bartók's Piano Concerto no. 2. (with the composer as soloist), 1933, to Ligeti's *Atmospheres*, 1961; also conducted the first radio performance, 1954, and the first stage performance (Zurich), 1957, of Schoenberg's *Moses und Aron*. He was conductor of the Frankfurt Radio Orchestra, 1928–37, the SÜDWESTFUNK ORCHESTRA at Baden-Baden, from 1948 till his death, and the TONHALLE ORCHESTRA, from 1950 till his death.

Rosé, Arnold [Josef] (b. 24 Oct 1863; d. 25 Aug 1946), Romanian-born Austrian violinist. His fifty-seven-year period, 1881–1938, as one of the joint leaders of the VIENNA PHILHARMONIC ORCHESTRA is unparalleled. In 1882 he founded the ROSÉ QUARTET, which became prominent in new music; continued as leader until 1938 when, being Jewish, he had to flee the Nazi occupation of Austria. Settled in Britain, where he died. He was married to MAHLER's sister Justine.

Rose, Bernard [William George] (b. 9 May 1916), British organist and conductor. Became organist of Magdalen College, Oxford, 1957 (Emeritus Fellow, 1981), and made its choir famous. He was president of the Royal College of Organists, 1974–6, and has edited music by Tomkins and others. His son Gregory Rose (b. 1948), a conductor, founded the ensemble Singcircle.

Rosé, Eduard, *see* ROSÉ QUARTET.

Rose, Gregory, *see* ROSE, BERNARD.

Rose, Leonard [Joseph] (b. 27 July 1918; d. 16 Nov 1984), American cellist. Made New York début 1944. After gaining orchestral experience, he developed a career as soloist (and also as trio partner of Isaac STERN and ISTOMIN); British début at the Edinburgh Festival, 1951. He gave the première of William Schuman's *A Song of Orpheus* (cello and orchestra), 1962.

Rosé Quartet, Vienna-based string quartet founded 1882 by Arnold ROSÉ. He remained its leader through various changes until his forced emigration, 1938. The other original members were Julius Eggard, Anton Loh and Eduard Rosé; his colleagues in 1938 were Paul Fischer, Max Handl and Friedrich Buxbaum. The group gave the first performances of Schoenberg's quartets nos. 1 and 2, 1907 and 1908, and Webern's Five Movements, 1910.

Rosen, Albert (b. 14 Feb 1925), Austrian-born conductor; became Czech citizen 1949. He was in Palestine during World War II, then worked in Prague. Conducted the RADIO TELEFÍS EIREANN SYMPHONY ORCHESTRA in Dublin, 1968–81; noted for rare operas at the Wexford Festival (for example Humperdinck's *Königskinder*, 1986). In London he gave the first British stage performance of Rimsky-Korsakov's *Christmas Eve*, 1988.

Rosen, Charles (b. 5 May 1927), American pianist, also musicologist. Entered the Juilliard

School at the age of seven and later studied with Moriz ROSENTHAL and his wife; in 1951 made New York solo début. He is a noted exponent of Beethoven and Schoenberg; gave the première with Ralph KIRKPATRICK of Carter's Concerto for piano and harpsichord, 1961. His writings include the influential book *The Classical Style*, 1971.

Rosenthal, Manuel (originally Emmanuel) (b. 18 June 1904), French conductor, also composer. Music director of the ORCHESTRE NATIONAL DE FRANCE, 1944–7, which he had joined in 1934 as fourth percussionist. He was appointed director of the Seattle Symphony Orchestra, 1949, but was dismissed for marital irregularity, 1951; he later returned to Seattle, however, to conduct *The Ring*, 1986. Made a celebrated ballet arrangement, *Gaîté parisienne* (after Offenbach), 1938.

Rosenthal, Moriz (b. 17 Dec 1862; d. 3 Sept 1946), Polish pianist. Pupil of Karol Mikuli (who had studied with Chopin) as a child, and later of LISZT, 1876–8. Despite his diminutive stature he was a powerful virtuoso, admired by Brahms. In 1888–9 he toured USA (accompanied for a time by KREISLER) and in 1895 performed in London. Resident in USA from 1938.

Rosing, Vladimir (b. 23 Jan 1890; d. 24 Nov 1963), Russian-born American tenor. Made concert début with HEIFETZ, 1910, and sang opera at St Petersburg from 1912. He was Herman in the first London performance of Tchaikovsky's *The Queen of Spades*, 1915. In USA he ran his own touring company, 1923–9, and worked for others as singer and stage director.

Ros-Marbá, Antoni (b. 2 Apr 1937), Spanish conductor. Chief conductor of the SPANISH NATIONAL ORCHESTRA, 1978–81, in 1979 he succeeded Szymon GOLDBERG as conductor of the NETHERLANDS CHAMBER ORCHESTRA. He has recorded Spanish and other music.

Ross, Elise, *see* RATTLE.

Rossi, Franco, *see* QUARTETTO ITALIANO.

Rossi, Mario (b. 29 Mar 1902), Italian conductor. Noted principally as conductor of the Turin Radio Orchestra, 1946–69, with which he conspicuously promoted new works. Conducted opera at Florence and La Scala, and also on recordings.

Rossi-Lemeni, Nicola (b. 6 Nov 1920; d. 12 Mar 1991), Turkish-born Italian bass (father Italian, mother Russian). Studied law and had undergone no regular vocal training before making successful opera début at Venice, 1946. Advised by SERAFIN (whose daughter was his first wife; his second was ZEANI), he became noted in Russian opera. Sang Boris Godunov at Covent Garden, 1951, and San Francisco, 1952; sang the role of Becket in the first performance of Pizzetti's *Assassinio nella cattedrale*, Milan, 1958.

Rostal, Max (b. 7 Aug 1905), Austrian-born British violinist. Lived in London, 1934–58, where he performed and taught; mentor of the newly formed AMADEUS QUARTET. He was a notable exponent of Bartók, and gave the first performance of concertos by Alan Bush, 1948, and others. CBE, 1977. Later settled in Switzerland.

Rostropovich, Mstislav [Leopoldovich] (b. 27 Mar 1927), Russian cellist, also pianist and conductor. His status and repertory are distinguished; he was soloist in the premières of Prokofiev's Cello Concerto no. 2 (under Svyatoslav RICHTER), 1952, Shostakovich's two cello concertos, 1959 and 1966, Britten's Cello Symphony, 1964, Bliss's Concerto, 1970, and many other works written for him. Has recorded Dvořák's Concerto seven times. In 1970 he fell foul of Soviet officialdom after supporting the author Solzhenitsyn; he and his wife, VISHNEVSKAYA, left USSR, 1974, and in 1978 were stripped of their citizenship. Made London conducting début 1974; became music director of the NATIONAL SYMPHONY ORCHESTRA (Washington), 1977, with which he returned to USSR in 1990. Also performs as piano accompanist to his wife.

Roswaenge (originally Rosenving-Hansen), **Helge** (b. 29 Aug 1897; d. 19 June 1972), Danish tenor. Particularly famous in opera at Berlin, 1930–44, and the Vienna State Opera, 1936–58. He sang Tamino in *Die Zauberflöte* on recordings under TOSCANINI, 1937, and BEECHAM, 1938.

Roth, David, *see* ALLEGRI QUARTET.

Roth, Sandor, *see* LÉNER QUARTET.

Rothenberger, Anneliese (b. 19 June 1924), German soprano. Well known in such youthful operatic roles as Sophie in *Der Rosenkavalier* (Glyndebourne, 1959–60, and in film, 1960), and also in operetta. She became a member of Vienna State Opera, 1958, made her Metropolitan Opera début in 1960 and created the title role in Sutermeister's opera *Madame Bovary* in Zurich, 1967.

Rothmüller, [Aaron] **Marko** (b. 31 Dec 1908), Yugoslav baritone, also composer. As a Jew his early career in Germany was interrupted. For a time he sang regularly in Zurich, where he took part in the première of Hindemith's opera *Mathis der Maler*, 1938. His post-war British successes included the title role of Berg's *Wozzeck* in its first British stage performance (Covent Garden), 1952, and seasons at Glyndebourne, 1949–55. Among his compositions are a symphony and string quartet; he has also written a book on Jewish music.

Rothwell, Evelyn (b. 24 Jan 1911), British oboist. Pupil of Leon GOOSSENS. She gave the first performance of Mozart's rediscovered Oboe Concerto (K314) in Salzburg, 1934. Many British works have been dedicated to her, including Rubbra's Oboe Sonata, 1958. Married BARBIROLLI, 1939. OBE, 1984.

Rowicki, Witold (b. 26 Feb 1914; d. 1 Oct 1989), Russian-born Polish conductor, also composer. Given charge of rebuilding the POLISH RADIO SYMPHONY ORCHESTRA at Katowice, 1945–50, after its wartime collapse, and similarly the WARSAW PHILHARMONIC, 1950–55 and 1958–77. He made his first appearance in Britain 1958, in USA 1961. Lutosławski's Concerto for Orchestra, 1954, is among the Polish works dedicated to him.

Rowland, Christopher, *see* FITZWILLIAM QUARTET.

Rowland-Jones, Simon, *see* CHILINGIRIAN QUARTET.

Royal Concertgebouw Orchestra of Amsterdam, *see* CONCERTGEBOUW ORCHESTRA OF AMSTERDAM.

Royal Liverpool Philharmonic Orchestra, British orchestra founded as the Liverpool Philharmonic Orchestra. The origins of its concert series may be traced back to the 1840s (*see* ZEUGHEER); acquired the title 'Royal' in 1957. Its conductors have included the composer Max Bruch, 1880–83, HALLÉ, 1883–95, SARGENT, 1942–8, PRITCHARD (at first jointly with KURTZ), 1955–63, GROVES, 1963–77, WELLER, 1977–80, ATHERTON, 1980–83, JANOWSKI, 1983–6, and PEŠEK, from 1987.

Royal Philharmonic Orchestra, London-based orchestra founded 1946 by BEECHAM after he had lost control of the LONDON PHILHARMONIC ORCHESTRA. At first it had a tenuous connection with the Royal Philharmonic Society, founded 1813. On Beecham's death KEMPE became principal conductor, 1961 (later made 'conductor for life'); he was succeeded by DORÁTI, 1975, then WELLER, 1980. PREVIN, named music director in 1985, abandoned the policy-making role (which was assumed by ASHKENAZY) in 1987, and was then titled principal conductor.

Roze, Marie (originally Hippolyte Ponsin) (b. 2 Mar 1846; d. 21 June 1926). French soprano. Sang opera in Paris and with various British companies; she was particularly admired as Carmen. Took the title role in the first British performance of Massenet's *Manon* (in English, Liverpool), 1885; also toured in USA.

Rozhdestvensky (originally Anosov), **Gennadi** [Nikolayevich] (b. 4 May 1931), Russian conductor. Took his mother's name to avoid trading on the reputation his father, Nikolay Anosov (1900–1962), enjoyed as conductor. He was a prominent symphonic and opera conductor in Moscow (first Soviet performance of Britten's *A Midsummer Night's Dream*, 1965), and became well known in the West after his London début, 1956. He was chief conductor of the STOCKHOLM PHILHARMONIC, 1974–7, and the BBC SYMPHONY ORCHESTRA, 1978–81; introduced Schnittke's Symphony no. 1 to Britain, 1986. He also performs in piano duet with his wife, POSTNIKOVA.

Rubens, Leonard, *see* BROSA QUARTET.

Rubini, Giovanni Battista (b. 7 Apr 1794; d. 3 Mar 1854), Italian tenor. Created the leading roles in Bellini's *La sonnambula*, 1831, and *I puritani*, 1835, and Donizetti's *Anna Bolena*, 1830. His close collaboration with Bellini is said to have been crucial to the composer's style. He sang in London from 1831 (his roles included Don Giovanni, a baritone part), toured with LISZT in Germany and became director of singing at the Russian court.

Rubinstein, Anton [Grigorievich] (b. 28 Nov 1829; d. 20 Nov 1894), Russian pianist, also composer, brother of Nikolay RUBINSTEIN. A child prodigy, performed in Paris at the age of ten, 1839; he later acquired a commanding reputation second only to LISZT's. By playing from memory, not usual at that time, he won additional distinction. On a triumphant US tour, 1872–3, he also gave duo recitals with WIENIAWSKI. He was director of the St Petersburg Conservatory, 1862–7 and 1887–91.

Rubinstein, Arthur (originally Artur) (b. 29 Jan 1887; d. 20 Dec 1982), Polish-born pianist; became American citizen 1946. He preferred the English spelling of his forename. Established himself (particularly from 1937) as one of the great musical celebrities. At the age of eight he played a Mozart concerto in Berlin under JOACHIM; made London début 1912 and gave charity recitals there with YSAŸE during World War I; duo partner of CASSADÓ. He was a noted interpreter of Spanish music (made his own famous arrangement of Falla's *Ritual Fire Dance*) as well as of Chopin. Stravinsky transcribed for him three dances from *Petrushka*, 1921. Also appeared in films and wrote a successful autobiography. He was acclaimed on his return to Poland, 1958, but in Jewish remembrance of Nazi atrocities refused to revisit Germany. Active as a recitalist until nearly ninety. He lived mostly in Paris; married a daughter of MŁYNARSKI, 1932. Made honorary KBE, 1977. (*See also* SZERYNG.)

Rubinstein, Nikolay [Grigorievich] (b. 14 June 1835; d. 23 Mar 1881), Russian pianist and conductor, brother of Anton RUBINSTEIN. His brilliant piano technique enabled him to undertake the first performance of Balakirev's *Islamey*, 1869, dedicated to him. He contemptuously declined to give the première of Tchaikovsky's Piano Concerto no. 1, but afterwards performed it with distinction. He conducted the first performances of Tchaikovsky's Variations on a Rococo Theme, 1877, and Symphony no. 4, 1878.

Rudel, Julius (b. 6 Mar 1921), Austrian-born conductor; took American nationality 1944. Conducted at the New York City Opera from 1944 and was later its director, 1957–79. In Washington he gave the first performance of Ginastera's opera *Bomarzo*, 1969. Appeared at Covent Garden in 1985.

Rudiakov, Michael, *see* COMPOSERS QUARTET.

Rudolf [Johann Joseph Rainer], Archduke of Austria (b. 8 Jan 1788; d. 24 July 1831), Austrian patron of music and amateur pianist and composer. Pupil of Beethoven. He was pianist in the first performance of Beethoven's Triple Concerto, 1808. The dedication to him of Beethoven's Piano Trio in B flat, op. 97, 1811, gave it the nickname the 'Archduke' Trio.

Rudolf, Max (b. 15 June 1902), German-born conductor, naturalized American 1946. Settled in USA and was active at the Metropolitan Opera in both conducting and management. He was music director of the CINCINNATI SYMPHONY ORCHESTRA, 1958–70. Wrote *The Grammar of Conducting*, 1950.

Ruffo, Titta (originally Ruffo Cafiero Titta) (b. 9 June 1877; d. 6 July 1953), Italian baritone. In his long career, 1898–1931, he is credited with effecting a change in taste towards a more robust type of baritone singing. Appeared in London only in 1903; sang much in USA (début in Philadelphia, 1912, as Rigoletto) and Argentina.

Rumford, Kennerley, *see* BUTT.

Russell, Henry (b. 24 Dec 1812; d. 8 Dec 1900), British singer, father of Landon RONALD. Performing music for all ranges of voice, became famous as singer–pianist; he was rare among soloists in his time in undertaking complete recitals without assistance from other performers.

Active in Boston and New York before returning to Britain in the mid-1840s. He wrote at least 250 songs, of which 'A Life on the Ocean Wave' was chosen as the march of the Royal Marines, 1899.

Růžičková, Zuzana (b. 14 Jan 1928), Czech harpsichordist. Won an international competition at Munich, 1956, and became widely known through recordings. She was co-founder of the Prague Chamber Soloists, with which she played from 1962 to 1967. Married to the composer Victor Kalabis.

Rybenský, Jaroslav, *see* SMETANA QUARTET.

Rysanek, Leonie (b. 12 Nov 1926), Austrian soprano. Her reputation was made as Sieglinde in the first post-war Bayreuth Festival, 1951. In 1952 she joined Bavarian State Opera in Munich and the following year appeared with it in London; made her Metropolitan Opera début as Lady Macbeth (replacing CALLAS at short notice), 1959. Her sister Lotte Rysanek (b. 1928) was also a soprano.

Rysanek, Lotte, *see* RYSANEK, LEONIE.

Rzewski, Frederic [Anthony] (b. 13 Apr 1938), American pianist. Devoted to new music, he took part in the first performances of Stockhausen's *Klavierstück X*, 1962, and *Plus–Minus*, 1964. Also composer; his music often expounds a socialist message.

S

Sabata, Victor De, *see* DE SABATA.

Sacher, Paul (b. 28 Apr 1906), Swiss conductor. Founded the Basle Chamber Orchestra, 1926, with which he gave many first performances, including those of Bartók's Music for Strings, Percussion and Celesta, 1937, and Strauss's *Metamorphosen*, 1946. Undertook a similarly adventurous series in Zurich from 1941. He also appeared as guest conductor in Britain, USA (1955 only) and elsewhere, and continued to be active into his eighties.

Sack, Erna [Dorothea] (b. 6 Feb 1898; d. 2 Mar 1972), German soprano, previously contralto. Developed a soprano voice of exceptional range, up to the C above so-called top C. Famous in concert and on record, she also had a noted career in opera, and was the first to sing Isotta in Strauss's *Die schweigsame Frau*, 1935.

Sádlo (originally Zátvrský), **Miloš** (b. 13 Apr 1912), Czech cellist. Adopted the surname of a teacher. He was the first outside USSR to play Khachaturian's Cello Concerto and gave the first modern performance of the rediscovered Haydn Concerto in C, 1962. Also active in various Czech chamber-music ensembles.

Safonov, Vasily [Ilyich] (b. 6 Feb 1852; d. 27 Feb 1918), Russian pianist and conductor. Director of the Moscow Conservatory, 1889–1905; his piano pupils included the composers Skryabin and Metner. Conducted in New York from 1904 and in London from 1906, and returned to Russia 1909. He was one of the first conductors to dispense with a baton.

St Cecilia Orchestra, *see* SANTA CECILIA ORCHESTRA.

St Louis Symphony Orchestra, American orchestra. Dates back to a differently named foundation of 1880 (and is therefore the second-oldest US orchestra after New York's). Its original conductor was Joseph Otten; later conductors have included GOLSCHMANN, 1931–58, SEMKOW, 1976–9, and Leonard SLATKIN, from 1979.

Sainton, Prosper [Philippe Catherine] (b. 5 June 1813; d. 17 Oct 1890), French violinist. Settled in Britain, 1845, and took major part in London musical life. He performed as orchestral leader at concerts and, 1847–71, Covent Garden opera, and was a member of string quartets. Also composer and conductor; he conducted the first performance of Sterndale Bennett's *Ode* at the opening of the 1862 International Exhibition. Married the contralto and composer DOLBY.

Sainton-Dolby, Charlotte, *see* DOLBY.

Salaff, Peter, *see* CLEVELAND QUARTET.

Salmond, Felix [Adrian Norman] (b. 19 Nov 1888; d. 19 Feb 1952), British cellist. His début in 1909 included the first performance of Bridge's *Phantasie Trio*, and he later gave the première of Elgar's Concerto, 1919, conducted by the composer. (Its failure was ascribed to inadequate rehearsal time.) In 1922 he settled in USA; he was an influential teacher at the Curtis Institute, Philadelphia, 1925–42. His father was the baritone Norman Salmond (1858–1914).

Salmond, Norman, *see* SALMOND, FELIX.

Salomon, Johann Peter (b. 20 Feb 1745; d. 28 Nov 1815), German violinist, also impresario and composer. Settled in London, 1781. As concert promoter he arranged Haydn's two London visits, 1790–91 and 1794–5; the symphonies Haydn wrote for London (nos. 93–104) are often called the 'Salomon' set. Salomon led the Philharmonic Society's orchestra at its first concert, 1813. Died (after a riding accident) in London.

Salonen, Esa-Pekka (b. 30 June 1958), Finnish conductor, also composer, formerly horn player. Studied in Italy. Acclaimed on his London conducting début in 1983 (when he replaced Michael Tilson THOMAS at a few days' notice), he proceeded to US début 1984. In 1985 he became principal conductor of the Swedish Radio Orchestra. Made the first recording of Lutosławski's Symphony no. 3, 1986. He is to be music director of the LOS ANGELES PHILHARMONIC ORCHESTRA from 1992.

Salpeter, Max, *see* AEOLIAN QUARTET.

Salzedo, Carlos (originally Léon Carlos Salzédo) (b. 6 Apr 1885; d. 17 Aug 1961), French-born harpist, also composer, of Spanish descent, naturalized American 1923. Preferred to use an authentically Spanish form of name. He moved to USA 1909, and became prominent in modern music. He was much associated with the composer Edgard Varèse, and in the first performance of Varèse's *Ionisation* (under SLONIMSKY) played the Chinese blocks. Gave the première of Dello Joio's Harp Concerto, 1947, and explored new harp sonorities in his own compositions.

Sammons, Albert [Edward] (b. 23 Feb 1886; d. 24 Aug 1957), British violinist. Became prominent orchestral leader after BEECHAM heard him playing in a London hotel orchestra. Also a noted soloist, he was the dedicatee of Delius's Concerto, 1919, and the first to record Elgar's Concerto in its complete form, 1929. As leader of the LONDON STRING QUARTET (1) he took part in the première of Elgar's Piano Quintet, 1919.

Samosud, Samuil [Abramovich] (b. 14 May 1884; d. 6 Nov 1964), Soviet conductor (born in Georgia). Active in Petrograd (later Leningrad), 1917–36, and then in Moscow. He was a prominent opera conductor in both cities: gave the première of Shostakovich's *The Nose* (Leningrad), 1930. His orchestral first performances included Prokofiev's Symphony no. 7, 1952.

Samuel, Harold (b. 23 May 1879; d. 15 Jan 1937), British pianist. Worked mainly as accompanist at first, then gave highly successful series of Bach recitals in London, 1921. Thereafter specialized as a soloist in Bach, making many US tours. Collaborated in published Bach editions and was also composer.

Sanderling, Kurt (b. 9 Sept 1912), German conductor. Left Germany under Nazi persecution, 1936, and went to Moscow, then Leningrad. He conducted the LENINGRAD PHILHARMONIC (under MRAVINSKY's direction), 1941–60, with noted success. Returned to Berlin, where he was principal conductor of the East Berlin Symphony Orchestra, 1960–77. He has also appeared as guest conductor in several cities (London, 1972), and recorded many Soviet works as well as Sibelius's symphonies. His son Thomas Sanderling (b. 1942) is likewise a conductor (*see also* GOLANI).

Sanderling, Thomas, *see* SANDERLING, KURT.

Sanderson, Sibyl (b. 7 Dec 1865; d. 15 May 1903), American soprano. Massenet wrote the title roles of his operas *Esclarmonde* and *Thaïs* for her voice and physical beauty. She won acclaim in Paris in their first performances, 1889 and 1894, but was less successful when singing opera in London and New York.

Sándor, György (b. 21 Sept 1912), Hungarian-born American pianist. Studied piano with Bartók and composition with Kodály in Budapest. Emigrated to USA, 1939. He was much associated with Bartók's music, and gave the (posthumous) première of the Piano Concerto no. 3, 1946. He recorded all Prokofiev's solo piano works.

San Francisco Symphony Orchestra, American orchestra founded 1911. Originally conducted by Henry Hadley; later principal conductors have included MONTEUX, 1935–52, JORDÁ, 1954–63, Josef KRIPS, 1963–70, OZAWA, 1970–76, DE WAART, 1977–85, and BLOMSTEDT, from 1985.

Sanromá, Jesús María (b. 7 Nov 1902; d. 12 Oct 1984), Puerto Rican pianist. Studied in Boston from the age of fourteen and later in Europe with CORTOT and SCHNABEL. In USA he became a noted soloist; gave the first performance of Hindemith's Piano Concerto, 1947. He was appointed chairman of university music department in Puerto Rico, 1951.

Santa Cecilia Orchestra, Rome-based orchestra founded 1907 as the Augusteo Orchestra. Principal conductors have included MOLINARI, 1912–43, PREVITALI, 1952–71, MARKEVITCH, 1973–5, SCHIPPERS, 1977, and SINOPOLI, 1983–7.

Santley, Charles (b. 28 Feb 1834; d. 22 Sept 1922), British baritone. One of the few Britons to star in international opera casts in mid-Victorian London. He sang in the first British performance of *Faust* (as Valentin), 1863 (the grateful composer later added an aria for him), and in the first London performance of Nicolai's *Die lustigen Weiber von Windsor*, 1864; also took the title role of *Der fliegende Holländer*, 1870 (the first London performance of any Wagner opera). In 1907 he eventually received the knighthood that Victorian usage had withheld from actors and singers.

Santo, Béla, *see* GAUDEAMUS QUARTET.

Sanzogno, Nino (b. 13 Apr 1911; d. 4 May 1983), Italian conductor, also composer. Prominent in Italian opera, he inaugurated the Piccola Scala at Milan, 1955, and brought its company to the 1957 Edinburgh Festival. At La Scala he conducted the first Italian performance of Walton's *Troilus and Cressida*, 1956, and the première of Poulenc's *Dialogues des carmélites*, 1957. Introduced British audiences to concert works by Dallapiccola and others.

Saram, Rohan de, *see* DE SARAM.

Sarasate (in full Sarasate y Navascuéz), **Pablo** [Martín Melitón] **de** (b. 10 Mar 1844; d. 20 Sept 1908), Spanish violinist. Performed publicly at eight, studied in Paris and was a European celebrity from the 1860s (*see* DIÉMER); composed virtuoso violin pieces such as the famous *Zigeunerweisen* (Gypsy Airs). He was the dedicatee of many works of which he gave the first performance, including Saint-Saëns's concertos nos. 1 and 3, 1867 and 1881, Lalo's *Symphonie espagnole*, 1875, Bruch's *Scottish Fantasy*, 1880, and Mackenzie's Violin Concerto, 1885. Also keen quartet player.

Sargent, [Harold] **Malcolm** [Watts] (b. 29 Apr 1895; d. 3 Oct 1967), British conductor, also pianist and, in youth, composer. Best known as chief conductor of the Proms, 1948–66; also conducted the Royal Choral Society, 1928–67, the LIVERPOOL PHILHARMONIC ORCHESTRA, 1942–8, and the BBC SYMPHONY ORCHESTRA, 1950–57. He was much associated with Gilbert and Sullivan (*see* BAKER, GEORGE). His premières included Walton's *Belshazzar's Feast*, 1931, and Vaughan Williams's Symphony no. 9, 1958, as well as the first (film) performance of Britten's *Young Person's Guide to the Orchestra*, 1946. He talked skilfully on radio and was a member of the wartime BBC 'Brains Trust'. Knighted, 1947.

Sass, Sylvia (b. 12 July 1951), Hungarian soprano. A member of the Budapest Opera from 1972, she developed an international career. Her appearance with Scottish Opera (Desdemona in *Otello*, 1975) preceded her Covent Garden début, 1976. Among her many recordings are Cherubini's *Médée* (title role) and Bartók's *Bluebeard's Castle*.

Sauer, Colin, *see* AEOLIAN QUARTET.

Sauer, Emil von (b. 8 Oct 1862; d. 27 Apr 1942), German pianist. Pupil of Nikolay RUBINSTEIN and, for a shorter period, of LISZT. His performing career was long, 1882–1936, and distinguished. He edited the complete piano works of Brahms, taught at a Vienna academy and recorded both Liszt's piano concertos at the age of seventy-seven. Composed two concertos for piano, among other works.

Sauret, Emile (b. 22 May 1852; d. 12 Feb 1920), French violinist. The record of his early study is uncertain; it may have been in Paris or Brussels. He made his London début 1862 and was among the leading players of the 1870s. From 1890 he was mainly in London (where he died), but he taught for a time in Chicago, 1903–6. Composed and transcribed music for violin.

Sawallisch, Wolfgang (b. 26 Aug 1923), German conductor, also pianist. Became the youngest conductor to appear at Bayreuth when he conducted *Tristan und Isolde* there in 1957; made his London orchestral début the same year. After working as music director of the SUISSE ROMANDE orchestra, 1970–80, he became music director, 1971, then general director of Bavarian State Opera in Munich. He is appointed music director of the PHILADELPHIA ORCHESTRA from 1993.

Saxby, Joseph, *see* DOLMETSCH, CARL.

Sayão, Bidú (originally Balduina de Oliveira Sayão) (b. 11 May 1902), Brazilian soprano. Began her operatic career in Rome. She sang in Milan, Paris and elsewhere, and won a particular following at the Metropolitan Opera, 1937–1952 (in such roles as Zerlina in *Don Giovanni*, Mimì in *La Bohème* and Massenet's Manon). Her husband was the baritone Giuseppe Danise (1883–1963).

Schack (various Czech spellings include Cziak), **Benedikt,** (b. 7 Feb 1758; d. 10 Dec 1826), Czech tenor. Settled in Vienna. His friend Mozart wrote for him the role of Tamino in *Die Zauberflöte*; it is thought that he played the (magic) flute as well as singing in the first production, 1791 (his wife, Elisabeth, was the Third Lady). He was also a composer, and Mozart wrote a set of variations for piano on one of his themes.

Schack, Elisabeth, *see* SCHACK, BENEDIKT.

Schalk, Franz (b. 27 May 1863; d. 2 Sept 1931), Austrian conductor. A pupil of Bruckner, he gave early performances of Bruckner's symphonies (in altered and now denigrated versions). He was director of the Vienna State Opera, 1918–29, at first jointly with Strauss, and gave the first performance of Strauss's *Die Frau ohne Schatten*, 1919. Conducted also at the Metropolitan Opera and Covent Garden. His brother Josef Schalk (1857–1911) was a pianist and fellow-promoter of Bruckner.

Schalk, Josef, *see* SCHALK, FRANZ.

Scharrer, Irene (b. 2 Feb 1888; d. 11 Jan 1971), British pianist. Made orchestral début at the Proms, 1905, and proceeded to win a high British reputation; she also appeared in USA from 1925. Gave her last performance 1958 (with HESS, her cousin). A celebrated recording, 1934, popularized a scherzo from a concerto by the otherwise forgotten composer Litolff.

Scherchen, Hermann (b. 21 June 1891; d. 12 June 1966), German conductor. A leader in promoting modern music, especially of the Schoenberg school. Apart from writing a handbook on conducting, he gave many first performances, among them Berg's Chamber Concerto, 1927, and Violin Concerto, 1936, Webern's Variations op. 30, 1943, and the first stage performance of Dallapiccola's opera *Il prigioniero*, 1950. Made many London visits, but did not appear in New York till 1964. He was active until a heart attack four days before his death. His daughter Tona Scherchen-Hsiao (b. 1938) is a composer.

Scherman, Thomas [Kielty] (b. 12 Feb 1917; d. 14 May 1979), American conductor. His Little Orchestra Society contributed much unfamiliar music to New York's concert life, 1947–75. He commissioned and in 1947 gave the first performance of David Diamond's suite *Romeo and Juliet*.

Schessl, Franz, *see* KOECKERT QUARTET.

Schidlof, Peter, *see* AMADEUS QUARTET.

Schiever, Ernst, *see* JOACHIM QUARTET.

Schiff, András (b. 21 Dec 1953), Hungarian pianist. Studied music in Budapest and further in UK with MALCOLM. He won prizes at the Moscow Tchaikovsky Competition, 1974, and the Leeds Piano Competition, 1975; made his London début 1976. He is noted for his Bach performances and recordings (despite the current orthodoxy that the modern piano falsifies Bach).

Schiff, Heinrich (b. 18 Nov 1951), Austrian cellist. Began learning piano, then, from nine, cello; he became a pupil of NAVARRA in Germany. First appeared in Vienna and

London 1973, in New York 1983. He gave the first London performance of Bernd Alois Zimmermann's Cello Concerto, 1984, and the première of Henze's *Seven Love-Songs*, 1986. Having occasionally conducted since the mid-1980s, he was appointed artistic director of the NORTHERN SINFONIA from 1990.

Schikaneder, Emanuel [Johann Joseph] (b. 1 Sept 1751; d. 21 Sept 1812), German baritone, also actor, composer, dramatist and impresario. For his company and to his libretto Mozart composed *Die Zauberflöte*, in which he sang Papageno (Vienna), 1791. He became mad in his last year and died in poverty.

Schiller, Madeline (b. *c.* 1842; d. 11 July 1911), British pianist. Studied in Leipzig and, after marrying a Boston merchant, settled in USA. On 12 Nov 1881 in New York she gave the first performance of Tchaikovsky's Piano Concerto no. 2, antedating the generally claimed Moscow première by six months.

Schindler, Anton [Felix] (b. 13 June 1795; d. 16 Jan 1864), Austrian violinist. Performed as theatre musician in Vienna and was Beethoven's secretary, apparently unpaid, from 1820 almost without pause until the composer's death, 1827. He later worked in Germany as a conductor. His biography of Beethoven is regarded as vital, despite its errors.

Schiøler, Annette, *see* TELMÁNYI.

Schiøtz, Aksel [Hauch] (b. 1 Sept 1906; d. 19 Apr 1975), Danish tenor. Shared with PEARS the role of Male Chorus in the first performances (at Glyndebourne) of Britten's *The Rape of Lucretia*, 1946. Made his New York début 1947. A brain tumour stopped his career in 1950, and he had to learn to speak and sing again; briefly reappeared as baritone and also taught. He received a Danish knighthood in 1947.

Schipa, Tito (originally Raffaele Attilio Amadeo) (b. 2 Jan 1888; d. 16 Dec 1965), Italian tenor. From his first appearances at La Scala, 1915–16, won distinction in the lighter operatic tenor repertory (the Duke in *Rigoletto* and the title role of Massenet's *Werther*); Puccini wrote for him the role of Ruggero in *La Rondine*, 1917. Long an operatic favourite in New York and Chicago, he appeared in London only in concert. His (pre-LP) recordings were famous.

Schippers, Thomas (b. 9 Mar 1930; d. 16 Dec 1977), American conductor. Conducted the first performances of Menotti's *The Consul*, 1950, and his (televised) *Amahl and the Night Visitors*, 1951. In 1955 he became the youngest ever to conduct the NEW YORK PHILHARMONIC ORCHESTRA and at the Metropolitan Opera, where he conducted the première of Barber's *Antony and Cleopatra*, 1966. Also appeared at La Scala and, 1963, Bayreuth. He was music director of the CINCINNATI SYMPHONY ORCHESTRA, 1970–77. Died of cancer.

Schlusnus, Heinrich (b. 6 Aug 1888; d. 18 June 1952), German baritone. Much esteemed in Verdi, with a long career at Berlin State Opera, 1917–45, he was also in demand (and made many recordings) as a song recitalist. Performed in USA from 1927, but apparently never in Britain.

Schmedes, Erik (b. 27 Aug 1866; d. 21 Mar 1931), Danish tenor, previously baritone. Prominent at the Vienna State Opera, 1896–1924, at first under MAHLER's conductorship. Esteemed in Wagner, he made important recordings from 1902. Sang in USA from 1908; seemingly never performed in Britain.

Schmidt, Joseph (b. 4 Mar 1904; d. 16 Nov 1942), Romanian tenor. Studied in Vienna. His diminutive stature (he was less than five feet tall) prevented operatic appearances, but he won admiration internationally and particularly in Germany through radio and recordings as well as concerts. A Jewish refugee from Nazi Germany, he died in a Swiss internment camp.

Schmidt-Isserstedt, Hans (b. 5 May 1900; d. 28 May 1973), German conductor. Active particularly in Hamburg, where he conducted the North German Radio Orchestra, 1945–71. Also conductor of the STOCKHOLM PHILHARMONIC ORCHESTRA, 1955–64, and guest conductor with more than 120 orchestras elsewhere; conducted *Figaro* at Glyndebourne, 1958. With the VIENNA PHILHARMONIC he recorded all Beethoven's symphonies and (with BACKHAUS) piano concertos.

Schnabel, Artur (b. 17 Apr 1882; d. 15 Aug 1951), Austrian-born pianist, naturalized American 1944. One of the most highly esteemed musicians of his time as performer and teacher. Pupil of LESCHETIZKY. He settled in Berlin, where he marked the Beethoven centenary in 1927 by performing a cycle of all thirty-two sonatas (also repeated the set elsewhere and was first to record it); famous for reviving the (then neglected) Schubert sonatas. Left Germany, 1933, as a Jew under Nazi threat, but returned to Europe after the war; died in Switzerland. He was also a composer and developed an advanced atonal idiom. Married to the soprano Therese Bahr (1876–1959); their son Karl Ulrich Schnabel (b. 1909) was a pianist. (*See also* FEUERMANN and FLESCH.)

Schnabel, Karl Ulrich, *see* SCHNABEL, ARTUR.

Schnéevoigt, Georg [Lennart] (b. 8 Nov 1872; d. 28 Nov 1947), Finnish conductor. After holding posts in Germany and Russia, founded an orchestra; it merged with another to form the Helsinki City Orchestra, of which he was joint conductor with KAJANUS, 1916–32, and then sole conductor till 1941. He later worked with the LOS ANGELES PHILHARMONIC ORCHESTRA, 1927–9, among others. Made important early recordings of Sibelius symphonies.

Schneider, [Abraham] **Alexander** (b. 21 Oct 1908), Russian-born American violinist. Worked in Germany and became second violinist of the BUDAPEST QUARTET. He settled in USA, 1939, and from 1952 led his own quartet. Much associated with CASALS, whom he persuaded out of retirement in 1950 to grace the Prades Festival. He also conducted (for example his own Brandenburg Players) and again played in the Budapest Quartet, 1955–64.

Schneider, Hortense [Catherine Jeanne] (b. 30 Apr 1833; d. 6 May 1920), French soprano. The most famous of the original stars of Offenbach operettas, she was the first to perform (in Paris) the title roles of *La Belle Hélène*, 1864, *La Grande-duchesse de Gérolstein*, 1867, and *La Périchole*, 1868 (also in London, 1868).

Schneider, Mischa, *see* BUDAPEST QUARTET.

Schneiderhan, Wolfgang [Eduard] (b. 28 May 1915), Austrian violinist. Leader of the VIENNA PHILHARMONIC, 1938–51, and of his own string quartet. With BAUMGARTNER, his former pupil, he formed the Festival Strings Lucerne, 1956. Later also conductor. He often performed with his wife, SEEFRIED.

Schnorr von Carolsfeld, Ludwig (b. 2 July 1836; d. 21 July 1865), German tenor. Settled in Dresden, and became noted in Wagner. He and his wife, Malvina (1825–1904), took the title roles of *Tristan und Isolde* in the opera's first performance, 1865, a few weeks before his early death. On his deathbed he is said to have broken into song and called on Wagner's name.

Schnorr von Carolsfeld, Malvina, *see* SCHNORR VON CAROLSFELD, LUDWIG.

Schöffler, Paul (b. 15 Sept 1897; d. 21 Nov 1977), German-born Austrian bass. Sustained a long career: performed at Vienna State Opera, 1937–65. Well known in Wagner, he also sang Danton in Einem's *Dantons Tod*, 1947, and Jupiter in the first performance of Strauss's *Die Liebe der Danae*, 1952. He died in Amersham, UK.

Schönzeler, Hans-Hubert (b. 22 June 1925), German-born conductor, also musicologist and composer, naturalized British 1947. Educated in Australia and Paris. He conducted a London ensemble, 1957–61, specializing in twentieth-century music; made the first recordings of Rubbra's Symphony no. 10, 1977, and Australian works. Author of a book on Bruckner, 1970.

Schorr, Friedrich (b. 2 Sept 1888; d. 14 Aug 1953), Hungarian-born American bass-baritone. Appeared at Graz as Wotan (*Die Walküre*), 1912, and came to be considered one of the world's major Wagner singers. He was prominent at Covent Garden, 1924–33, and the Metropolitan Opera, 1924–43 (leading role in the US première of Krenek's *Jonny spielt auf*, 1929). Later worked as college teacher and operatic stage director in New York.

Schranz, Károly, *see* TAKÁCS QUARTET.

Schrecker, Bruno, *see* ALLEGRI QUARTET.

Schreier, Peter (b. 29 July 1935), German tenor, and from 1970 conductor. Sang with East German opera companies (Dresden, Berlin), then won international fame in Mozart operas; performed at the Salzburg Festival and Vienna State Opera from 1967 and at the Metropolitan from 1967. As singer, he has recorded over thirty operas, from *Die Zauberflöte* (three times) to Dessau's *Einstein*, 1978. Also distinguished recitalist.

Schröder, Jaap (b. 31 Dec 1925), Dutch violinist. Prominent in the revival of eighteenth-century music on period instruments; he founded and led, 1975–81, the Quartetto Esterhazy, which was devoted to this. Recorded with HOGWOOD and others.

Schröder-Devrient (née Schröder), **Wilhelmine** (b. 6 Dec 1804; d. 26 Jan 1860), German soprano. Admired by Beethoven (who rehearsed her in Vienna for a production of *Fidelio*, 1822), Weber, Goethe and the young Wagner, she sang in the first London production of *Fidelio*, 1832. Known as the 'Queen of Tears' (she was observed actually to weep on stage), she was famous for her dramatic power. Her other roles included Desdemona in Rossini's *Otello*. Married for a short time to the actor Carl Devrient.

Schuch, Ernst von (b. 23 Nov 1846; d. 10 May 1914), Austrian conductor. Engaged as court conductor in Dresden, 1873, and remained in charge of opera there till the year of his death, raising the company to the highest level. He introduced Puccini's work to his audiences and conducted the first performance of Strauss's *Salome*, *Elektra* and *Der Rosenkavalier*, 1905, 1909 and 1911. Raised to Austrian nobility, 1897.

Schüchter, Wilhelm (b. 15 Dec 1911; d. 27 May 1974), German conductor. After holding posts in Germany, conducted the NHK SYMPHONY ORCHESTRA in Japan, 1958–61. He then returned to Germany and worked as concert and opera conductor in Dortmund until his death. Made European and Japanese recordings.

Schulz, Gerhard, *see* ALBAN BERG QUARTET.

Schumann (née Wieck), **Clara** [Josephine] (b. 13 Sept 1819; d. 20 May 1896), German pianist, also composer. In 1840 married (against her father's wishes) Schumann, whose songs she inspired. She survived him by forty years and became one of the best-known interpreters of his music; first soloist in his Piano Concerto, 1845. She was also a noted performer of Chopin and Brahms, a very close friend. First played in London 1856; she continued teaching after her retirement from the concert platform, 1891.

Schumann, Elisabeth (b. 13 June 1888; d. 23 Apr 1952), German-born soprano, naturalized American 1944. Made her début 1909 in Hamburg and became internationally known in opera, especially Mozart (Vienna State Opera, 1919–38, and Covent Garden, 1924–31). Strauss admired her (she was a famous Sophie in *Der Rosenkavalier*) and toured USA as her piano accompanist, 1921. Being Jewish, she left Austria on the Nazi annexation of 1938, settled in USA and taught there. The second of her three husbands was the conductor and pianist Karl Alwin (1891–1945), who often accompanied her.

Schumann-Heink (née Rössler), **Ernestine** (b. 15 June 1861; d. 17 Nov 1936), Austrian-born contralto; became American citizen 1908. Purchased her release from a Berlin opera contract in order to sing regularly in USA. She was a favourite at the Metropolitan, from 1899, and gave farewell performances there aged seventy, 1932. With a repertory of about 150 operatic parts, she was particularly noted in Wagner and took three roles in the first complete *Ring* at Covent Garden, 1892. She was the first Clytemnestra in Strauss's *Elektra*, 1909, and at the end of her New York career played Katisha in *The Mikado*, 1931.

Schuppanzigh, Ignaz (b. 20 Nov 1776; d. 2 Mar 1830), Austrian violinist and conductor. A friend of Beethoven (who called him a Falstaff, presumably because of his stoutness), he was first violinist in the first performances of most of Beethoven's string quartets, from before 1800, and was leader at the première of the Symphony no. 9, 1824. In 1824 Schubert dedicated to him his Octet and the Quartet in A minor.

Schuricht, Carl (b. 3 July 1880; d. 7 Jan 1967), German conductor, also composer. Pupil of Humperdinck and Reger. He lived in Switzerland from 1944 and died there. Played a prominent part in the post-war reopening of the Salzburg Festival, 1946, and conducted the VIENNA PHILHARMONIC ORCHESTRA on its first US tour, 1955. He made many recordings in the (pre-electric) 1920s.

Schwarz, Gerard (b. 19 July 1947), American trumpeter and conductor. Co-principal trumpeter of the NEW YORK PHILHARMONIC ORCHESTRA, 1973–7. A noted soloist, he commissioned and gave the first performance of Schuller's Trumpet Concerto, 1979. Became music director of the Los Angeles Chamber Orchestra, 1978, and of the Seattle Symphony Orchestra, 1983; in New York he conducted the première of Panufnik's *Arbor cosmica*, 1984.

Schwarz, Rudolf (b. 29 Apr 1905), Austrian-born conductor; became British citizen 1952. His early career in Germany was terminated by Nazi persecution; he was rescued from Belsen concentration camp by British forces, and returned to conducting. Worked with BOURNEMOUTH MUNICIPAL ORCHESTRA, 1947–51, CITY OF BIRMINGHAM SYMPHONY, 1951–7, BBC SYMPHONY, 1957–63, and NORTHERN SINFONIA, 1964–73 (of which he was appointed conductor laureate, 1982). At Birmingham he gave the first performance of Bliss's *Meditations on a Theme by John Blow*, 1955. CBE, 1973.

Schwarzkopf, [Olga Maria] **Elisabeth** [Friederike] (b. 9 Dec 1915), German soprano. After working in Berlin, 1938–42, joined Vienna State Opera, with which she made her first Covent Garden appearance, 1947. Later sang regularly with the Covent Garden company (including several roles in English), but did not appear at the Metropolitan till 1964. Under Stravinsky's conductorship she created the role of the heroine, Anne Trulove, in *The Rake's Progress* at Venice, 1951. Won international prominence in many fields, latterly in teaching; her performances of Mozart and Strauss were particularly admired, as was her singing of Wolf's songs. She married Walter Legge, founder of the PHILHARMONIA ORCHESTRA and record-company chief; she holds the Grosses Verdienstkreuz (high West German honour) and other awards.

Schweitzer, Albert (b. 14 Jan 1875; d. 4 Sept 1965), French (Alsatian) organist, music scholar, theologian and medical missionary. Organist of the Paris Bach Society, 1905–13. His chief musical fame comes from his 1905 book on Bach (originally in French, later published in a longer German edition, 1908). Awarded Nobel Peace Prize, 1952, and honorary OM, 1954.

Scimone, Claudio (b. 23 Dec 1934), Italian conductor. Founded the ensemble I Solisti Veneti in Padua, 1959, with which he has performed baroque and modern music. Also critic and, from 1974, director of the Padua Conservatory. He became conductor of the GULBENKIAN ORCHESTRA in Lisbon, 1979; conducted the first recording of Rossini's opera *Ermione*, 1988.

Sciutti, Graziella (b. 17 Apr 1927), Italian soprano, later also stage director. In her early career, from 1950, especially at the Aix-en-Provence Festival and the Piccola Scala in Milan, she came to specialize in lighter roles, such as Despina in *Così fan tutte* and Norina in Donizetti's *Don Pasquale*. Sang at Covent Garden from 1956 and at the Metropolitan Opera from 1961. She directed her own performance in Poulenc's one-woman opera *La Voix humaine* at Glyndebourne, 1977.

Scott, Charles Kennedy (b. 16 Nov 1876; d. 2 July 1965), British conductor. Studied organ in Brussels and in 1904 founded the Oriana Madrigal Society, an influential London choir; he conducted it till 1961, mainly performing Tudor and new British music. Also music editor and composer.

Scott, John [Gavin] (b. 18 June 1956), British organist. Youngest organ soloist ever to appear at the Proms, 1977 (playing Reubke's Sonata on Psalm 94): he played at Prince Charles's wedding, 1981. Won a Bach competition at Leipzig, 1984, and has toured USSR, Australia and elsewhere. Became Organist and Director of Music, St Paul's Cathedral, 1990.

Scotti, Antonio (b. 25 Jan 1866; d. 26 Feb 1936), Italian baritone. Notable in such roles as Falstaff and Scarpia (*Tosca*); he was the first to sing the latter in London, 1900, and New York, 1901. He enjoyed a long career, performing at the Metropolitan from 1899 to 1933. Ran his own (financially unsuccessful) US touring company, 1919–22.

Scottish National Orchestra, orchestra founded 1891 as the Scottish Orchestra. Renamed in 1950. Its principal conductors have included HENSCHEL, 1893–5, KES, 1895–8, the composer Max Bruch, 1898–1900, BARBIROLLI, 1933–6, SZELL, 1936–9, BUESST, 1939–40, Warwick BRAITHWAITE, 1940–45, SUSSKIND, 1946–52, RANKL, 1952–7, SWAROWSKY, 1957–9, GIBSON, 1959–84, JÄRVI, 1984–8, and Bryden THOMSON, 1988–91.

Scottish Orchestra, *see* SCOTTISH NATIONAL ORCHESTRA.

Scotto, Renata (b. 24 Feb 1933), Italian soprano. Made her Italian début 1954 and in 1957 successfully replaced CALLAS for a single performance of Bellini's *La sonnambula* at the Edinburgh Festival. She became noted in roles of pathos; sang the title role of *Madama Butterfly* in her first appearances at Covent Garden, 1962, and the Metropolitan, 1965. Has recorded over thirty operas, some of them more than once.

Seaman, Christopher (b. 7 Mar 1942), British conductor, formerly orchestral percussionist. Principal conductor of the BBC SCOTTISH SYMPHONY ORCHESTRA, 1971–7, and the Utrecht Symphony Orchestra, 1979–83. From 1978 he conducted many of the BBC's Robert Mayer concerts for young audiences. Gave the first performance of Panufnik's Symphony no. 6, 1978.

Seefried, Irmgard (b. 9 Oct 1919; d. 24 Nov 1988), German soprano of Austrian parentage. Became a member of the Vienna State Opera, 1943, with which she sang at Covent Garden, 1947; also appeared frequently at other major centres. She was esteemed in Mozart opera (Susanna in *Le nozze di Figaro*) and also as recitalist. With her husband, the violinist SCHNEIDERHAN, she gave the first performance of Henze's *Ariosi* at the Edinburgh Festival, 1964.

Segal, Uri (b. 7 Mar 1944), Israeli conductor. Studied in London and won the Mitropoulos Conducting Competition in New York, 1969. He was principal conductor of the German-based PHILHARMONICA HUNGARICA, 1979–85, and of the BOURNEMOUTH SYMPHONY ORCHESTRA, 1980–82. Has appeared as guest conductor with the CHICAGO SYMPHONY, the ISRAEL PHILHARMONIC and other orchestras.

Segerstam, Leif [Selim] (b. 2 Mar 1944), Finnish conductor, also composer, formerly pianist and violinist. Music director of Royal Swedish Opera, 1968–72, and Finnish National Opera, 1973–4, and principal conductor of the AUSTRIAN RADIO SYMPHONY ORCHESTRA, 1975–82. He was appointed to the DANISH RADIO SYMPHONY ORCHESTRA, 1988. Led his own quartet on recordings of four of his string quartets.

Segovia, Andrés (b. 21 Feb 1893; d. 2 June 1987), Spanish guitarist. A self-taught, pre-eminent performer, he is chiefly responsible for the guitar's twentieth-century standing as a classical solo and concerto instrument. Gave his first recital aged fifteen in Granada; his Paris début, 1924, and first US appearances, 1928, initiated a long international career. As well as extensively arranging music (particularly by Bach), he stimulated many modern composers to write for him, among them Roussel and Rodrigo (*Fantasia for a Gentleman*, of which Segovia gave the première, 1954).

Seidl, Anton (b. 7 May 1850; d. 28 Mar 1898), Hungarian conductor. Encouraged by Wagner, he became a major interpreter of Wagner's work, especially at the Metropolitan Opera, 1885–96 (340 performances). He gave the première of Dvořák's 'New World' Symphony (New York), 1893, and was one of the first to perform Bruckner symphonies in USA. Conducted at Covent Garden in 1897 (a year before his early death).

Seiffert, Peter, *see* POPP.

Sellick, Phyllis [Doreen] (b. 16 June 1911), British pianist. Celebrated in piano duet with her husband, Cyril SMITH; solo début 1933. She made the first recordings of Walton's Sinfonia concertante, 1946 (with the composer conducting), and Tippett's Sonata no. 1.

Sembrich, Marcella (originally Prakseda Marcellina Kochańska, with some variant spellings) (b. 15 Feb 1858; d. 11 Jan 1935), Polish-born American soprano. Made her débuts at Covent

Garden, 1880, and the Metropolitan, 1883, in the title role of *Lucia di Lammermoor*, a part well suited to her exceptional coloratura skills. At a concert at the Metropolitan in 1884 she also performed as pianist and violinist. Retired from opera in 1909, but continued to give recitals and taught in Philadelphia and New York.

Semkow, Jerzy (also known in the West by Germanized form, Georg) (b. 12 Oct 1928), Polish conductor. Trained in Leningrad under MRAVINSKY and conducted in Moscow before working as artistic director of Warsaw National Opera, 1959–62. Later he conducted at Covent Garden, 1970, was music director of the ST LOUIS SYMPHONY ORCHESTRA, 1976–9, and recorded the original version of *Boris Godunov*, 1976 (the first complete recording to be released in the West).

Sénéchal, Michel (b. 11 Feb 1927), French tenor. Sang the title role in a rare revival of Rameau's opera *Platée* at Aix-en-Provence Festival, 1956, and was later heard at Glyndebourne, 1966, and La Scala. In 1980, he became director of the school of the Paris Opera.

Senesino, professional name adopted (from his birthplace, Siena) by Francesco Bernardi (b. *c.* 1680; d. before 27 Jan 1759), Italian male mezzo-soprano (castrato). Engaged by Handel for his London seasons, 1720–28, he sang in thirty-two operas (thirteen by Handel). After another period with Handel, 1730–33, he moved to a rival management. Greatly esteemed for vocal skill, but caricatured as ugly and stout.

Sens, Maurice, *see* CIGNA.

Senter, John, *see* ARDITTI QUARTET.

Serafin, Tullio (b. 1 Sept 1878; d. 2 Feb 1968), Italian conductor. A young assistant to TOSCANINI, then principal conductor at La Scala, 1909–14 and 1917–18; at the Metropolitan Opera, 1924–34, he gave the first US performance of Puccini's *Turandot*, 1926. He helped guide the careers of such singers as CALLAS (with whom he made important opera recordings) and SUTHERLAND. Active into his eighties.

Serebrier, José (b. 3 Dec 1938), Uruguayan conductor, also composer. Studied in USA and became associate to STOKOWSKI. His repertory is eclectic; gave the first US performances of Wagner's early Overture in D, 1986, and of Massenet's opera *Chérubin*, 1987, as well as the première of Mennin's Symphony no. 9, 1987, and other works. He was the first to record Shostakovich's film music for *King Lear*, and his other recordings include Poulenc's *La Voix humaine* with his wife, FARLEY, as soloist. Also conducted extensively in Australia, from 1979, and Europe.

Serkin, Peter (b. 24 July 1947), American pianist, son of Rudolf SERKIN. Studied with his father, but acknowledges the greater influence of HORSZOWSKI. He has developed an unconventional, mainly modern repertory. In 1973 founded a group called Tashi (with clarinet, violin and cello), with which he remained till 1980. From that time he has performed and recorded Beethoven and Brahms as well as Schoenberg, Takemitsu (première of *Riverrun* for piano and orchestra, 1985) and others. Occasionally plays an early model of piano.

Serkin, Rudolf (b. 28 Mar 1903), Austrian-born pianist of Russian parentage, naturalized American 1939, father of Peter SERKIN. Settled in USA, 1933. He won eminence for his intense, intellectual, commanding style. Noted chamber-music player, especially at the Marlboro Festival in Vermont, and recital-partner of CARMIRELLI. Martinů's Sonata, of which he gave the première in 1957, is dedicated to him. He was head of the piano department of the Curtis Institute, Philadelphia, 1939–76, and its director, 1968–76. Holds high West German, French and other honours and was awarded (US) Presidential Medal of Freedom, 1963. He married a daughter of Adolf BUSCH.

Ševčík, Otakar (b. 22 Mar 1852; d. 18 Jan 1934), Czech violinist. After his early performing career, became internationally noted as a teacher in Russia, from 1875, Prague, London and various US centres. He was said to have had more than 5,000 students, among them Jan KUBELÍK and SCHNEIDERHAN.

Shacklock, Constance (b. 16 Apr 1913), British mezzo-soprano. Prominent in Covent Garden's new post-war company, 1946–56; her roles included Brangaene (*Tristan*) and Amneris (*Aida*). She also sang opera in Moscow (Amneris, 1957) and elsewhere, and from 1961 to 1966 was a star in the London production of Rodgers and Hammerstein's *The Sound of Music*. OBE, 1970.

Shaffer, Elaine, *see* KURTZ.

Shafran, Daniil (Westernized as Daniel) [Borisovich] (b. 13 Jan 1923), Russian cellist. Won an all-USSR competition for violinists and cellists, 1937, and was joint prizewinner with ROSTROPOVICH of a competition in Prague, 1950. He toured in Western Europe and, from 1960, USA.

Shalyapin, Fyodor [Ivanovich] (b. 13 Feb 1873; d. 12 Apr 1938), Russian bass. The most celebrated of all Russian singers, his recordings (about 200) reinforced his authority as singer and operatic actor. He was a member of the Bolshoi Theatre, 1899–1914, and sang internationally from 1901. Performed in Paris in Dyagilev's opera and ballet series, 1908–13, and then in London, 1913–14. He returned to Russia after the 1917 Revolution, but left permanently in 1921. To such famous Russian roles as Boris and Varlaam in *Boris Godunov* and Galitzky and Konchak in Borodin's *Prince Igor* he added Mephistopheles in *Faust*, among others. He was also a powerfully dramatic solo recitalist.

Shankar, Ravi (b. 7 Apr 1920), Indian sitarist, also composer. His virtuosity and communicative manner, shown in tours of Europe and USA, 1956–7, were mainly responsible for the acceptance of Indian music by Western concert audiences. His partners in performance have included MENUHIN and the Beatles singer George Harrison (b. 1943). Among his compositions are two concertos for sitar and orchestra, 1971 and 1976, and the music to the film *Gandhi*, 1983.

Shaw, Robert [Lawson] (b. 30 Apr 1916), American conductor. Conducted the first performance of Hindemith's *When Lilacs Last in the Dooryard Bloom'd* (requiem for President Roosevelt) in New York, 1946. In 1948 he founded the Robert Shaw Chorale, a professional group, which toured internationally with distinction. He was music director of the Atlanta Symphony Orchestra, 1967–88, and brought it to Europe in 1988.

Shebalin, Dmitry, *see* BORODIN QUARTET.

Sherba, John, *see* KRONOS QUARTET.

Sherman, Alec, *see* BACHAUER.

Shilling, Eric (b. 11 Oct 1920), British bass. From 1945 he sustained a much admired, long career with Sadler's Wells Opera (later English National), excelling in operetta in such roles as Frank in *Die Fledermaus* and the Lord Chancellor in Sullivan's *Iolanthe*; sang in the first British production of Reimann's *Lear*, 1989. He also sang in the première of Antony Hopkins's opera *Three's Company*, 1953.

Shirinsky, Sergey, *see* BEETHOVEN QUARTET.

Shirley, George [Irving] (b. 18 Apr 1932), American tenor. Appeared at the Metropolitan from 1961, at Glyndebourne from 1966 and at Covent Garden from 1967. He was one of the first male black singers to be engaged internationally on 'colour-blind' impartiality; his roles have included Tamino in *Die Zauberflöte* and David in *Die Meistersinger*.

Shirley-Quirk, John (b. 28 Aug 1931), British baritone. Celebrated chiefly in solo song and in such large-scale concert works as the Bach Passions, Elgar's *The Dream of Gerontius* and Walton's *Belshazzar's Feast*. He has worked with distinction in opera, especially Britten's: created the principal baritone roles in the three church parables, 1964–8, and *Death in Venice*, 1973. His operatic repertory also embraces Arkel in Debussy's *Pelléas et Mélisande* and Tchaikovsky's Onegin.

Shislov, Andrey, *see* SHOSTAKOVICH QUARTET.

Shore, John (b. *c.* 1662; d. 1752), British trumpeter, also lutenist and probably violinist. The original performer of difficult trumpet parts in many of Purcell's works, he served James II and William III. His father, Matthias (or Matthew) Shore (d. ?1700), was also a trumpeter, as was William Shore (d. 1707), probably an uncle.

Shore, Matthias, *see* SHORE, JOHN.

Shore, William, *see* SHORE, JOHN.

Shostakovich, Dmitry, *see* SHOSTAKOVICH, MAXIM.

Shostakovich, Maxim [Dmitryevich] (b. 10 May 1938), Russian-born pianist and conductor, naturalized American 1987. Soloist in the first performance, 1957, of the Piano Concerto no. 2 by his father, Dmitry Shostakovich. He conducted prominently in USSR (including the première of his father's Symphony no. 15, 1972), but when on tour in West Germany in 1981 announced that he would not return. Settled in USA, and conducted there and in Europe. His son, also named Dmitry (b. 1961), is a pianist.

Shostakovich Quartet, Moscow-based string quartet founded 1967. Members: Andrey Shislov, Alexander Balashov (replaced by Sergey Pishchugin, 1977), Alexander Galkovsky and Alexander Korchagin.

Shuard, Amy (b. 19 July 1924; d. 18 Apr 1975), British soprano. Gained first operatic experience in South Africa. As a member of Sadler's Wells Opera, 1949–55, she was Katya Kabanova in the first British performance of Janáček's opera. Sang at Covent Garden, from 1954, in such roles as Wagner's Brünnhilde and Puccini's Turandot and in the theatre's first production of Schoenberg's *Erwartung*, 1961.

Shuman, Mark, *see* COMPOSERS QUARTET.

Shumsky, Oscar (b. 23 Mar 1917), American violinist. At the age of eight played with the PHILADELPHIA ORCHESTRA under STOKOWSKI. After studying with ZIMBALIST, he became an orchestral violinist and soloist; also conducted at the Stratford Festival in Ontario, 1959–69. He won new prominence in his sixties: performed again in London, 1981, and in 1986 made a recording of Mozart's Sinfonia concertante (as viola player) with his violinist son, Eric.

Shure, Paul, *see* HOLLYWOOD QUARTET.

Siegel, Jeffrey (b. 18 Nov 1942), American pianist. His teachers included Rosina LHÉVINNE; he was a prizewinner at the Queen Elisabeth Competition in Brussels, 1968. In Budapest in 1984 he gave the first performance of Liszt's lately discovered Fantasy on Verdi's *Ernani* (of 1847); also played it at his first Carnegie Hall (New York) recital, 1985.

Siems, Margarethe (b. 30 Dec 1879; d. 13 Apr 1952), German soprano. Chosen by Strauss to create roles of very varied requirements: Chrysothemis in *Elektra*, 1909, the Marschallin in *Der Rosenkavalier*, 1911, and Zerbinetta in *Ariadne auf Naxos*, 1912. She sang at first mainly in Dresden, then internationally (Covent Garden début 1913). Active as teacher till 1940.

Siepi, Cesare (b. 10 Feb 1923), Italian bass. Prominent in opera, particularly at the Metropolitan for twenty-three seasons from 1950. He was famous as Mozart's Don Giovanni (his Covent Garden début role, 1962) and Figaro, and as Mephistopheles in *Faust*. Made four recordings of *Don Giovanni*.

Siface, *see* GROSSI.

Siki, Béla (b. 21 Feb 1923), Hungarian-born Swiss pianist. Studied in Budapest, then in Geneva with LIPATTI. He won the Geneva International Competition, 1947, and became well known as interpreter of Liszt and Bartók; has often adjudicated international competitions. He later settled in USA and became a piano professor in Seattle, 1965, and Cincinnati, 1980.

Silja, Anja (b. 17 Apr 1935), German soprano. Prominent at the Bayreuth Festival from 1960 (début as Senta in *Der fliegende Holländer*); she revealed a strong dramatic personality, which she later applied to recordings of Schoenberg's *Erwartung* and Berg's *Wozzeck* and *Lulu*. Also sang in London (at first with Frankfurt Opera, 1963), and the Metropolitan, from 1972. Married Christoph von DOHNÁNYI.

Silk, Dorothy [Ellen] (b. 4 May 1883; d. 30 July 1942), British soprano. Conspicuous from 1920 in concerts of Bach and other baroque composers. She sang in the first performance of Holst's opera *Sāvitri*, 1921.

Sillito, Kenneth, *see* GABRIELI QUARTET.

Sills, Beverly (originally Belle Miriam Silverman) (b. 25 May 1929), American soprano, also operatic manager. Her US stage début with Philadelphia Civic Opera, 1947, led to a world-wide career and especial fame in coloratura roles such as Elvira (Bellini's *I puritani*) and Lucia. She sang at Vienna State Opera from 1967 and at Covent Garden from 1970, but achieved greatest celebrity as an adored star with New York City Opera, which she had joined in 1955 and of which she was director, 1979–88.

Siloti, Alexander, *see* ZILOTI.

Silveri, Paolo (b. 28 Dec 1913), Italian baritone. Sang with the visiting Naples company at Covent Garden, 1946, then with Covent Garden's own group, to 1949 (for example in the title role of *Boris Godunov* in English). He had made his début (in Italy), however, as a bass, 1939; flirted with the tenor range (Otello) in 1959, but reverted to baritone shortly after. He taught singing in Rome from 1970.

Silverman, Edward, *see* BLECH QUARTET.

Silverstein, Joseph (b. 21 March 1932), American violinist and conductor. Worked for twenty-one years, 1962–83, as leader of the BOSTON SYMPHONY ORCHESTRA, and also became its assistant conductor, 1971. He was appointed music director of the Utah Symphony Orchestra in 1983.

Silverthorne, Paul, *see* MEDICI QUARTET.

Silvestri, Constantin (b. 13 May 1913; d. 23 Feb 1969), Romanian-born conductor, also composer, naturalized British 1967. Began his conducting career in Romania, but left in 1957 and made his London début that year. He was conductor of the BOURNEMOUTH SYMPHONY ORCHESTRA from 1961 until his death and also conducted at Covent Garden, 1963.

Simionato, Giulietta (b. 12 May 1910), Italian mezzo-soprano. Famous in coloratura parts (a rarity among mezzo-sopranos in her day) such as the title role in Rossini's *La Cenerentola*, which she twice recorded. She had a long career at La Scala, 1939–66, where she sang Valentine (soprano) in a rare revival of Meyerbeer's *Les Huguenots*, 1962 (also recorded). Appeared at the Metropolitan from 1949 and Covent Garden from 1953.

Simmons, Calvin (b. 27 Apr 1950; d. 21 Aug 1982), American conductor. One of the few black conductors to become known, he conducted *Figaro* at Glyndebourne, 1976, and was appointed conductor of the Oakland Symphony Orchestra in California, 1979. Early death (by drowning) cut off a promising career.

Simon, Abbey (b. 8 Jan 1920), American pianist. Toured widely following his New York recital début, 1940; teacher at the Juilliard School. He recorded the complete piano works of Ravel and all the Rakhmaninov concertos. Resident in Switzerland.

Simoneau, Léopold (b. 3 May 1918), Canadian tenor. Much esteemed in Mozart opera, he sang at Glyndebourne from 1951 (Idamante in the first British professional staging of *Idomeneo*) and the Metropolitan from 1963. Teacher in San Francisco, from 1971. He married ALARIE.

Simonov, Yuri [Ivanovich] (b. 4 Mar 1941), Russian conductor. Won an international conducting competition at Rome, 1968, and in 1970 became chief conductor of the Bolshoi Theatre. He has toured with Bolshoi Opera (New York, 1975) and Ballet, and appeared as guest conductor at Covent Garden, from 1982. Gave the first performance of Shchedrin's ballet *Anna Karenina*, 1972 (also recorded).

Simons, Dennis, *see* ALBERNI QUARTET.

Simpson, Derek, *see* AEOLIAN QUARTET.

Simpson, Robert Hope, *see* AMICI QUARTET.

Singher, Martial [Jean-Paul] (b. 14 Aug 1904; d. 9 Mar 1990), French baritone. Sang at the Paris Opera, 1930–41, but achieved particular fame in USA as performer (Metropolitan from 1943) and teacher in New York and Philadelphia. He was the first to sing Ravel's song cycle *Don Quichotte à Dulcinée*, 1934, which he also recorded.

Sinopoli, Giuseppe (b. 2 Nov 1946), Italian conductor, also composer. Graduated in medicine before studying conducting with

SWAROWSKY in Vienna, 1972. He was active in Italy in modern music, then in standard opera. Conductor of the SANTA CECILIA ORCHESTRA, 1983–7, and the PHILHARMONIA, from 1984; he made his Bayreuth début 1985. Appointed principal conductor of the DRESDEN STATE ORCHESTRA from 1992.

Sitkovetsky, Dmitry (b. 27 Sept 1954), Russian violinist, son of Bella DAVIDOVICH. Emigrated to USA, 1977, later followed by his mother. He studied in New York with GALAMIAN and in 1977 won the Kreisler Competition in Vienna; made his Proms début 1986. He has recorded the Mozart violin concertos as soloist–director. Performed again in USSR, 1989.

Sivori, [Ernesto] **Camillo** (b. 25 Oct 1815; d. 19 Feb 1894), Italian violinist. Studied briefly with PAGANINI and built a career of the first rank; his tours included a long visit to the Americas, 1846–50. He lived mainly in France from the 1850s. During the Paris uprising of 1870 came to London, where he took part in the inaugural concerts of the Royal Albert Hall. In Paris, 1876, led the first performance (to an invited audience) of Verdi's String Quartet at the composer's request. Also composed more than forty published works.

Škampa, Milan, *see* SMETANA QUARTET.

Skrowaczewski, Stanisław (b. 3 Oct 1923), Polish-born conductor, naturalized American 1966. Active as a pianist until wartime bomb injury; he later studied conducting in Paris with KLETZKI. Conducted Polish orchestras, made US début 1958 and was conductor of the MINNEAPOLIS SYMPHONY ORCHESTRA, 1960–79. From 1984 until 1991 he was principal conductor of the HALLÉ ORCHESTRA. Also composer and occasional opera conductor (Metropolitan début 1970).

Slatkin, Felix, *see* HOLLYWOOD QUARTET and SLATKIN, LEONARD.

Slatkin, Leonard (b. 1 Sept 1944), American conductor. Studied piano, violin and viola. He made his European début as guest conductor with the ROYAL PHILHARMONIC ORCHESTRA, 1974, and has conducted at Vienna State Opera, in USSR and elsewhere. Appointed music director of the ST LOUIS SYMPHONY ORCHESTRA, 1979. His parents, Felix Slatkin (1915–63), violinist and conductor, and Eleanor Aller (b. 1917), cellist, both played in the HOLLYWOOD QUARTET.

Slezak, Leo (b. 18 Aug 1873; d. 1 June 1946), Austrian tenor (born in Moravia). One of the most successful in his field. His début in 1895 was in Brno as Lohengrin, the role in which he made his much quoted wisecrack, 'When does the next swan go?'; it was also his début role at Covent Garden, 1900. Sang over forty parts with the Vienna State Opera (formerly Court Opera), 1901–26, appeared at the Metropolitan (début as Otello, 1909) and acted in films. His son was the American film star Walter Slezak.

Slobodskaya, Oda (b. 10 Dec 1888; d. 29 July 1970), Russian soprano. Began her career in Petrograd (now Leningrad), 1919, and sang in Paris in the first public performance of Stravinsky's opera *Marva*, 1922. Having made her home in London, she appeared at Covent Garden (British première of Delius's *Koanga*, 1935) and won special celebrity for her recitals, broadcasts and recordings of Russian song. She was active well into her seventies.

Slonimsky, Nicolas (originally Nikolay Leonidovich) (b. 27 Apr 1894), Russian-born pianist, conductor, composer and writer, naturalized American 1931. Best known as author of music reference books. He went to USA, 1923, and in 1927 formed the Chamber Orchestra of Boston. Conducted various first performances, including Ives's *Three Places in New England* (New York), 1931, and Varèse's *Ionisation* (with SALZEDO), 1933, and *Ecuatorial*, 1934.

Smallens, Alexander (b. 1 Jan 1889; d. 24 Nov 1972), Russian-born American conductor. Taken to USA as a child. In his early career he worked with Pavlova's ballet company and Chicago Opera, conducted the première of *Porgy and Bess* in Boston, 1935, and in 1956 took the opera on a European tour.

Smart, George [Thomas] (b. 10 May 1776; d. 23 Feb 1867), British organist, harpsichordist, violinist and conductor. Played violin in the orchestra for Haydn's concerts in London, 1794. A founder-member of the Philharmonic Society of

London, 1813, he conducted some of its early concerts, including the first performance of Beethoven's Symphony no. 9, 1826. Became organist of the Chapel Royal, 1822. On his tour of Europe, 1825, he visited Beethoven in Vienna; he was a friend of Weber (who died at Smart's London home) and a champion of his music. Also composer. Knighted (in Ireland), 1811. His brother Henry Smart (1778–1823) was a violinist and composer, and Henry's son Henry [Thomas] Smart (1813–79) was an organist and composer.

Smart, Henry, *see* SMART, GEORGE.

Smart, Henry [Thomas], *see* SMART, GEORGE.

Smejkal, Bohumil, *see* JANÁČEK QUARTET.

Smetáček, Václav (b. 30 Sept 1906; d. 18 Feb 1984), Czech conductor, previously oboist. Conducted from the 1930s and toured UK 1938. He was associated, 1942–72, with what became the Prague Symphony Orchestra, and also appeared as guest conductor with more than 100 orchestras, among them the Tokyo Symphony, 1961. His prolific recorded output includes Czech orchestral rarities.

Smetana Quartet, Czech quartet founded 1945. A successor to the former Czech Conservatory Quartet, its founding members were Jaroslav Rybenský, Lubomir Kostecký, NEUMANN and Antonín Kohout. Jiří Novák became first violin in 1946 and Milan Škampa viola in 1955, but there were no further changes until the quartet disbanded, 1989.

Smilovits, Josef, *see* LÉNER QUARTET.

Smirnoff, Joel, *see* JUILLIARD QUARTET.

Smirnov, Dmitry [Alexeyevich] (b. 19 Nov 1882; d. 27 Apr 1944), Russian tenor. A member of the Moscow Bolshoi Opera, 1904–10, then of the Imperial Opera in St Petersburg, he sang at the Metropolitan from 1910 (the Duke in *Rigoletto*). Settled in Paris after the 1917 Revolution but later returned to USSR on tour. He made important (pre-1930) recordings of excerpts from Russian operas.

Smith, Cyril [James] (b. 11 Aug 1909; d. 2 Aug 1974), British pianist. Well known in duo, from 1941, with his wife, SELLICK. In 1956 he lost the use of his left arm, but the duo continued, playing new works and special arrangements, such as that of Bliss's Concerto for two pianos, 1968 (also recorded). OBE, 1971.

Smith, David, *see* ALBERNI QUARTET.

Smith, Jennifer (b. 13 July 1945), British soprano. Born and educated in Portugal; pupil of BERNAC in Paris. She has become internationally prominent in eighteenth-century music (first recording of Rameau's opera *Les Boréades*, 1982). Also active in twentieth-century music, she participated in the première, 1976, and a recording of Geoffrey Burgon's Requiem.

Smith, Lawrence Leighton, *see* LOUISVILLE ORCHESTRA.

Smith, Ronald (b. 3 Jan 1922), British pianist, also composer. Made his Proms début 1942. He became an authority on the eccentric French composer and pianist Alkan, whose music he has extensively performed (some for the first time in Britain) and recorded. He should not be confused with Ronald [Aubrey] Smith (b. 1928), music educationist.

Snítil, Václav, *see* VLACH QUARTET.

Sobinov, Leonid [Vitalyevich] (b. 7 June 1872; d. 14 Oct 1934), Russian tenor. In 1897 first appeared at the Bolshoi Theatre, with which his career was principally associated; he was later director, 1917–18, and was honoured by a gala there in 1933. Famed in such roles as Lensky (Tchaikovsky's *Yevgeny Onegin*) and Des Grieux (Massenet's *Manon*). He also sang in the West (La Scala, from 1901) and made historic early recordings, to 1910.

Société des Concerts du Conservatoire, Orchestre de la, Paris-based orchestra. Active from 1828 to 1967, when it was replaced by the ORCHESTRE DE PARIS. Its principal conductors included HABENECK, 1828–49, GIRARD, 1849–60, GARCIN, 1885–92, the composer André Messager, 1908–18, GAUBERT, 1919–38, MUNCH, 1938–46, and CLUYTENS, 1949–67.

Söderblöm, Ulf, *see* HELSINKI PHILHARMONIC ORCHESTRA.

Söderström (in full Söderström-Olow), [Anna] **Elisabeth** (b. 7 May 1927), Swedish soprano. Sang at Royal Swedish Opera from 1950. Her unusually wide concert and opera repertory won her international distinction, particularly in Mozart and Strauss. She performed frequently at Glyndebourne from 1957 (Strauss's *Intermezzo* in English, 1974); also sang at the Metropolitan, 1959–64. Her other roles range from Nero in Monteverdi's *L'incoronazione di Poppea* to Janáček's Katya Kabanova.

Soldat, Marie (b. 25 Mar 1863; d. 30 Sept 1955), Austrian violinist. Formed her own all-women string quartet in Berlin, 1887, and another in Vienna, 1899. A pupil of JOACHIM, she was a noted performer of Brahms's Violin Concerto (at that time hardly touched by women players).

Solomon (originally Solomon Cutner) (b. 9 Aug 1902; d. 2 Feb 1988), British pianist. He was always known professionally by his first name only. At the age of eight played Tchaikovsky's Concerto no. 1 at the Queen's Hall, London. Prominent as concerto soloist, he gave the première of Bliss's Concerto (New York), 1939; performed in a trio with FRANCESCATTI and Pierre FOURNIER at the Edinburgh Festival, 1955. In 1956 he had a stroke, which barred further appearances, but his celebrity remained, mainly through his recordings of Beethoven. CBE, 1946.

Solomon, John (b. 2 Aug 1856; d. 1 Feb 1953), British trumpeter. A chief influence in the British orchestral development of the trumpet (which, in his youth, was still often replaced by the cornet). He was first trumpet under WOOD on the opening of the Proms, 1895, and a founder-member of the LONDON SYMPHONY ORCHESTRA, 1904. Played in public until he was eighty.

Solomon, Yonty (b. 6 May 1938), South African pianist. Moved to London, 1963, to become a pupil of HESS, and later studied with Charles ROSEN. He has toured widely. Works dedicated to him include Richard Rodney Bennett's Five Studies, 1964. Persuaded the reclusive composer Sorabji to allow him to give the first public performances, from 1977, of about twenty works, including Concerto for solo piano (just under two hours' duration).

Solti, Georg (originally György) (b. 21 Oct 1912), Hungarian-born conductor, also pianist, naturalized British 1972. Made conducting début 1938 in Budapest, but, facing restrictions as a Jew, went to Switzerland. Barred from advance as conductor, he concentrated on piano; won Geneva Piano Competition, 1942. After the war his conductorship of the Bavarian State Opera in Munich, 1946–52, established its new high status. He conducted orchestral concerts in London from 1949, was music director at Covent Garden, 1961–71 (first British performance of Schoenberg's *Moses und Aron*, 1965), and made the first stereo recording of *The Ring*, 1966. As music director of the CHICAGO SYMPHONY ORCHESTRA from 1969 (his appointment is to end in 1991), continued to give new works, including Tippett's Symphony no. 4, 1977 and Lutosławski's Symphony no. 3, 1983. In 1987 he recorded Bartók's Sonata for two pianos and percussion with PERAHIA (his first piano-duo recording) and GLENNIE. His honorary KBE, 1971, became a regular knightood on his British naturalization. (*See also* KULENKAMPFF.)

Sontag, Henriette (originally Gertrud Walburga) (b. 3 Jan 1806; d. 17 June 1854), German soprano. Her reputation was unsurpassed in her day. Weber, having heard her in Vienna, chose her for the title role in the first performance of *Euryanthe*, 1823. She sang in the première of Beethoven's Symphony no. 9 in Vienna in 1824, and performed in opera (Mozart, Rossini and Donizetti) in London from 1828. Broke off her career, 1830, after her marriage, but resumed in 1849. She went with an Italian opera company to Mexico, where she caught cholera and died.

Sor (or Sors), [Joseph] **Fernando** [Macari] (b. 14 Feb 1778; d. 10 July 1839), Spanish guitarist, also composer and author. Worked in Madrid, Paris and, 1815–23, London. He wrote an influential textbook for his instrument, 1830.

Sotin, Hans (b. 10 Sept 1939), German bass. In 1970 made his Glyndebourne début as Sarastro in *Die Zauberflöte* and sang in Beethoven's Symphony no. 9 under MEHTA at a United Nations celebration in New York. He is particularly well known in Wagner, and first performed at the Bayreuth Festival in 1972.

Soukup, Soběslav, *see* VLACH QUARTET.

Souliotis (also spelt Suliotis), **Elena** (b. 28 May 1943), Greek soprano. Her début in Naples, 1964, led to a prominent but brief career in opera and operatic recordings. She was said to have damaged her voice by undisciplined use. Sang as Verdi's Lady Macbeth and in other roles at Covent Garden, 1969–73.

South-west German Radio Orchestra, *see* SÜDWESTFUNK ORCHESTRA.

Souza, Ralph de, *see* ENDELLION QUARTET.

Souzay (originally Tisserand), **Gérard** [Marcel] (b. 8 Dec 1918), French baritone. Succeeded his teacher, BERNAC, as the leading interpreter of French song. In 1945 he gave his first Paris recital and appeared in London in a centenary commemoration of Fauré's birth. Chosen to take part in the first performance of Stravinsky's *Canticum sacrum*, 1956. He began to perform in opera in 1960: made his début in New York in the title role of Monteverdi's *Orfeo*.

Soyer, David, *see* GUARNERI QUARTET.

Soyer, Roger [Julien Jacques] (b. 1 Sept 1939), French bass. Prominent in opera at the Aix-en-Provence Festival, Paris Opera, from 1963, and elsewhere. He is a celebrated Don Giovanni (Metropolitan Opera, 1972, and, under BARENBOIM, at Edinburgh Festival, 1973, and in recording). His other recorded roles include Arkel in Debussy's *Pelléas et Mélisande*.

Spaarnay, Harry [Willem] (b. 14 Apr 1944), Dutch bass clarinettist, formerly jazz saxophonist. He is one of the very few musicians (*see also* HORÁK) to have made an extensive solo career playing bass clarinet. Has performed many new works written for him or for his ensemble, including Yun's *Monologue* for bass clarinet (Melbourne, 1983).

Spani, Hina (originally Higinia Tuñón) (b. 15 Feb 1896; d. 11 July 1969), Argentinian soprano. Sang in Italy, 1915–34, and toured widely. She was active principally in Buenos Aires as a member of its opera company, 1915–40, and director of the university music school, from 1952. Her repertory embraced more than seventy roles.

Spanish National Orchestra (Orquesta Nacional), Madrid-based orchestra. The present foundation of 1940 followed on from a previous concert series. Its conductors have included ARGENTA, 1947–58, FRÜHBECK DE BURGOS, 1962–78, ROS-MARBÁ, 1978–81, and LÓPEZ-COBOS, 1984–8.

Sparey, Jonathan, *see* FITZWILLIAM QUARTET.

Speelman, Simon, *see* BRODSKY QUARTET (1).

Sperry, Paul [John] (b. 14 Apr 1934), American tenor. Made London and New York débuts 1969. He has commissioned and given first performances of works by US and European composers, including Maderna's *Boswell's Journal*, 1972, Henze's *Voices*, 1974, and Rands's *Cantico del sole*, 1983. Teaches in New York.

Spitzer-Hegyesi, Louis, *see* QUARTETTO FIORENTINO.

Spivakovsky, Jascha, *see* SPIVAKOVSKY, TOSSY.

Spivakovsky, Tossy (b. 4 Feb 1907), Russian-born American violinist. Made his concert début aged ten in Berlin and based his career there (though also toured world-wide) until threatened by the Nazi regime as a Jew. He worked in Melbourne from 1933 and settled in USA, 1940. In 1943 gave the US première of Bartók's Violin Concerto no. 2 (the only performance heard by the composer himself). He wrote his own cadenzas to Beethoven's and other concertos. His brother Jascha Spivakovsky (b. 1896) was a pianist.

Stabile, Mariano (b. 12 May 1888; d. 11 Jan 1968), Italian baritone. In 1921 was chosen by TOSCANINI to sing the title role of *Falstaff* at La Scala; this led to international fame, particularly in Verdi. He sang Falstaff over 1,000 times, up to 1961. His repertory of at least fifty other parts included Mozart's Figaro (his first Glyndebourne role, 1936), Beckmesser in *Die Meistersinger* and Ambroise Thomas's Hamlet.

Stade, Frederica von, *see* VON STADE.

Stader (originally Molnár), **Maria** (b. 5 Nov 1911), Hungarian-born Swiss soprano (her adoptive parents were Swiss). Prominent in concerts at the Salzburg Festival, she also sang as Queen of the Night in *Die Zauberflöte* at Covent Garden, 1949–50. Taught singing in Switzerland and USA.

Stadler, Anton [Paul] (b. 28 June 1753; d. 15 June 1812), Austrian clarinettist. Mozart wrote for him the solo parts of his Clarinet Quintet and Clarinet Concerto (first performances 1784 and 1791); both works were designed for a clarinet with a lower-range extension, which Stadler invented (now named a basset clarinet). He also played the obbligato parts written for clarinet and basset-horn (a standard, lower-pitched instrument) in the première of Mozart's opera *La clemenza di Tito*, 1791. He and his brother Johann Stadler (1755–1804) were both clarinettists in the Austrian court orchestra.

Stadler, Johann, *see* STADLER, ANTON.

Starker, János (b. 5 July 1924), Hungarian-born cellist of Russian parentage, naturalized American 1954. Left Hungary for France and then settled in USA, 1948. After working as leading cellist in US orchestras, he became a professor at Indiana University, 1958, and also began to develop a noted (though never sensational) solo career. Made London recital début 1956 and gave the first performance of Miklós Rózsa's Concerto, 1969, dedicated to him. He played in a trio with KATCHEN and Josef SUK (2). (*See also* BUCHBINDER.)

Staudigl, Joseph (b. 14 Apr 1807; d. 28 Mar 1861), Austrian bass. Having established himself in opera in Vienna, he visited London with a German-language company and took part in the first performance in Britain of Meyerbeer's *Les Huguenots*, 1842. He followed this with opera in English, 1843, and, at the composer's choice and under his baton, sang the title role of Mendelssohn's *Elijah* at its première in Birmingham, 1846. He became insane in 1856. His son, also Joseph Staudigl (1850–1916), was a baritone.

Steber, Eleanor (b. 17 July 1916), American soprano. Sang twenty-eight major roles at the Metropolitan Opera, 1940–62, including Marie in Berg's *Wozzeck* and the title role of Barber's *Vanessa* in its first production, 1958. She gave the première of Krenek's *The Ballad of the Railroads* (with MITROPOULOS as pianist), 1950. Also performed with the Glyndebourne company at the Edinburgh Festival, 1947.

Stefano, Giuseppe di, *see* DI STEFANO.

Stefańska-Łukowicz, Elżbieta, *see* CZERNY-STEFAŃSKA.

Steibelt, Daniel (b. 22 Oct 1765; d. 2 Oct 1823), German pianist and conductor, also composer. Worked in Paris, London (married an Englishwoman) and other cities, including Vienna, where he was worsted in a piano contest with Beethoven. Became opera conductor in St Petersburg, and died there.

Stein, Horst (b. 2 May 1928), German conductor. Spent several periods with Hamburg Opera, finally as its music director, 1972–7. He was also associated with Bayreuth and Vienna State Opera, where he conducted the first performance of Einem's *Der Besuch der alten Dame*, 1971. Worked as music director of the SUISSE ROMANDE orchestra in Geneva, 1980–85.

Steinberg, [Hans] **William** (originally Wilhelm) (b. 1 Aug 1899; d. 16 May 1978), German-born conductor, naturalized American 1944. Active in Frankfurt (where he gave the first performance of Schoenberg's opera *Von heute auf morgen*, 1930) and Berlin. He left Nazi Germany as a Jewish refugee and in 1936 founded the PALESTINE SYMPHONY ORCHESTRA with HUBERMAN; Steinberg became its first regular conductor. Later he worked as music director of the PITTSBURGH SYMPHONY ORCHESTRA, 1952–76, and (concurrently) the LONDON PHILHARMONIC, 1958–60, and the BOSTON SYMPHONY, 1969–72.

Steinhardt, Arnold, *see* GUARNERI QUARTET.

Steinitz, [Charles] **Paul** [Joseph] (b. 25 Aug 1909; d. 22 Apr 1988), British organist and conductor. As founding conductor of the London (originally South London) Bach Society, 1947, and organist at St Bartholomew-the-Great, 1949–61, he gave there in 1952 the first British performance of Bach's *St Matthew Passion* to be sung in German; it became an annual event. He also conducted the première of Rubbra's *Song of the Soul*, 1953, and the first British performance of Dallapiccola's *Canti di prigionia*, 1963.

Stephens, Catherine (b. 18 Sept 1794; d. 22 Feb 1882), British soprano and actress. Played Ophelia in *Hamlet* opposite John Philip Kemble, 1817, and sang Susanna in the first performances in English of *Le nozze di Figaro*, 1819. Weber, in London in 1826, wrote for her his last composition, an English song 'From Chindara's Warbling Fount'. She retired in 1835.

Sterling, Antoinette (b. 23 Jan 1850; d. 9 Jan 1904), American contralto. Settled in London and made her London début at a Covent Garden promenade concert in 1873. With a range descending to low E flat, she was an admired concert artist, adept in the lighter, ballad repertory: gave the first performance of Sullivan's 'The Lost Chord', 1877. She was the mother of Jean Sterling MacKinlay (1882–1958), singer and actress, and [Malcolm] Sterling MacKinlay (1876–1952), singing teacher and writer.

Stern, Isaac (b. 21 July 1920), Russian-born American violinist. Taken as infant to USA; pupil of PERSINGER. He first played with an orchestra 1936, made New York début 1937 and European début 1947 (in Munich). Rose to highest rank as soloist and in 1960 formed a notable trio with ISTOMIN and Leonard ROSE. He led a successful campaign to save Carnegie Hall, New York, from demolition, 1960. Gave the first performances of concertos by Schuman, 1947, Bernstein ('Serenade', 1954), George Rochberg, 1975, Peter Maxwell Davies, 1986, and Dutilleux, 1987. (*See also* ZUKERMAN, PINCHAS.)

Stern, Leo (originally Leopold) [Lawrence] (b. 5 Apr 1862; d. 10 Sept 1904), British cellist (father German). Toured with PATTI, 1888. On a visit to Prague he met Dvořák, and subsequently gave the first performance of Dvořák's Concerto in London, 1896. (Its dedicatee, WIHAN, apparently was not free to accept the London engagement.) Married to ADAMS.

Steuermann, Eduard (b. 18 June 1892; d. 11 Nov 1964), Polish-born American pianist. Emigrated to USA, 1938. Having studied in Berlin with Schoenberg and taken part in the first performance of his *Pierrot lunaire*, 1912, he remained a Schoenberg disciple. Gave the première of the Piano Concerto, 1944, and later became curator of the Schoenberg Institute in Los Angeles. He was a distinguished teacher, latterly at the Juilliard School; also composer.

Stevens (originally Steenberg), **Risë** (b. 11 June 1913), American mezzo-soprano (father Norwegian). In her early career declined an offer from the Metropolitan and went to study in Europe. She performed in Prague and Vienna before making her Metropolitan début, 1938; became one of its cherished stars, especially as Carmen. Sang Cherubino (another favourite role) in *Le nozze di Figaro* at Glyndebourne, 1939. She also acted in films (including *Going My Way* with Bing Crosby, 1944), directed the short-lived Metropolitan Touring Company, 1964–6, and was president of the Mannes College of Music in New York, 1975–8.

Stevenson, Ronald (b. 6 Mar 1928), British pianist, also composer and writer on music. Made Proms début playing his Piano Concerto no. 2, 1972. He has presented radio and television programmes on Busoni (one of his enthusiasms), and recorded his own eighty-minute *Passacaglia on DSCH* (a tribute to Shostakovich, who used these initials).

Stewart, Thomas [James] (b. 29 Aug 1926), American baritone. Sang in Germany and Austria (Berlin City Opera, 1957–64, and Bayreuth, 1960–72) and made his Metropolitan Opera début as Ford in *Falstaff*, 1966. He was notable as Wagner's Wotan as well as in Verdi roles. Married to LEAR.

Stich-Randall, Teresa (b. 24 Dec 1927), American soprano. While still a student took part in the first performance of Virgil Thomson's *The Mother of Us All*, then sang Verdi roles in TOSCANINI's recorded and radio performances. She made her stage début as Violetta in *La traviata* at the Vienna State Opera, 1952, and appeared at the Metropolitan from 1961.

Stiedry, Fritz (b. 11 Oct 1883; d. 8 Aug 1968),

Austrian conductor. His work at the Berlin City Opera (first performance of Weill's *Die Bürgschaft*, 1932) was ended by the Nazis. As a Jewish refugee he went to USSR (conducted in Leningrad and Moscow, 1934–7), then emigrated to USA. In New York he gave the first performance of Schoenberg's Chamber Symphony no. 2, 1940, and worked at the Metropolitan Opera, from 1946. Also conducted at Glyndebourne, 1947, and Covent Garden, 1953–4.

Stignani, Ebe (b. 10 July 1903; d. 5 Oct 1974), Italian mezzo-soprano. Celebrated as Azucena in *Il trovatore* and other Verdi roles, she was associated for many years with La Scala, 1925–56. At Covent Garden, where she first sang in 1937, she was an inappropriately ageing Adalgisa to CALLAS's Norma, 1952 and 1957.

Stilwell, Richard (b. 6 May 1942), American baritone. Made his stage début with the City Opera as Pelléas in Debussy's *Pelléas et Mélisande*, 1970, and repeated the role at Covent Garden, 1974. At Glyndebourne his work has ranged from Monteverdi (title role in *Il ritorno d'Ulisse*) to Verdi (Ford in *Falstaff*).

Stock, Frederick (originally Friedrich) [August] (b. 11 Nov 1872; d 20 Oct 1942), German-born American conductor. Exercised great influence as conductor of the CHICAGO SYMPHONY ORCHESTRA, from 1905 until his death, through his active promotion of modern European works. He conducted the first performances of Prokofiev's Piano Concerto no. 3, 1921 (with the composer as soloist), and Kodály's Concerto for Orchestra and Walton's overture *Scapino*, both 1941.

Stockholm Philharmonic Orchestra, Swedish orchestra founded 1902. Its principal conductors have included Fritz BUSCH, 1937–40, SCHMIDT-ISSERSTEDT, 1955–64, DORÁTI, 1966–74, ROZHDESTVENSKY, 1974–7, and AHRONOVITCH, from 1982.

Stojowski, Sigismund (originally Zygmunt) [Denis Antoni] (b. 14 May 1869; d. 6 Nov 1946), Polish-born pianist, also composer, naturalized American 1938. In Paris studied piano with DIÉMER and composition with Delibes; he played his own Piano Concerto there, 1891, and became a successful performer. Moved to USA, 1906, where he concentrated on teaching.

Stokowski, Leopold (originally Antoni Stanisław Bolesławowicz) (b. 18 Apr 1882; d. 13 Sept 1977), British-born conductor (father Polish), naturalized American 1915. Became London organist, 1902, went to USA, 1905, and in 1912 began his twenty-six-year conductorship of the PHILADELPHIA ORCHESTRA, which decisively influenced American (and world) music. He evolved a highly personal conducting technique (stopped using the baton in 1929), and mastered successive methods of recording; made famous orchestral transcriptions of Bach's organ works. He gave over 2,000 first (or first US) performances, introducing to USA such works as Mahler's Symphony no. 8, 1916, and Berg's *Wozzeck*, 1931; among his premières were Varèse's *Amériques*, 1926, and Rakhmaninov's Symphony no. 3, 1927. Appeared in and conducted the music of Walt Disney's film *Fantasia*, 1941. He was conductor of the HOUSTON SYMPHONY ORCHESTRA, 1955–61, then of the youthful American Symphony Orchestra in New York, 1962–72; with it he gave the first complete performance of Ives's Symphony no. 4, 1965. In London in 1972 he repeated with the LONDON SYMPHONY ORCHESTRA a programme given with them sixty years before. Continued to record till the year of his death (in Hampshire) at the age of ninety-five.

Stoltz, Rosine (originally Victoire Noël) (b. 13 Feb 1815; d. 28 July 1903), French mezzo-soprano. Her mother's maiden name was Stoll. She sang the heroine's roles in important premières of French opera: Halévy's *La Juive* in Brussels, 1836, and, in Paris, Berlioz's *Benvenuto Cellini*, 1838, and Donizetti's *La Favorite*, 1840. As the mistress of the Paris Opera director she caused a scandal that in 1847 forced her (and his) retirement. A new liaison with the Emperor of Brazil led to four lucrative tours there in the period 1850–59.

Stolz, Teresa (originally Terezie Stolzová) (b. 2 June 1834; d. 23 Aug 1902), Czech soprano. After early performances in Russia, established herself in Italy and sang leading roles in Verdi's *Don Carlos* (first performance in Italy, 1867), *La forza del destino* (first performance of revised version, 1869), and *Aida* (first performance in Italy, 1872). She was also soloist in the première of Verdi's Requiem, 1874. The supposition that she was Verdi's mistress is unproven.

Stolze, Gerhard (b. 1 Oct 1926; d. 11 Mar 1979), German tenor. Began his career in East Germany; he became established in Wagner's character parts (for example the dwarf Mime in *The Ring*) at the Bayreuth Festival and won celebrity in such roles on record. Also sang the title role in the first performance of Orff's *Oedipus der Tyrann*, 1959. From 1961 he sang with the Vienna State Opera.

Storace, Nancy (originally Ann Selina; also known as Anna) (b. 27 Oct 1765; d. 24 Aug 1817), British soprano (father Italian). Went to Vienna, 1783, where she married the (much older) British composer John Abraham Fisher. She won much acclaim there, particularly for her part as Susanna in the first performance of *Le nozze di Figaro*, 1786 (though Mozart had originally intended she would sing the Countess). Mozart wrote for her his concert aria 'Ch'io mi scordi di te'. After returning to London, she sang in English operas, including those of her brother Stephen Storace. She later became BRAHAM's musical partner (and lover).

Storchio, Rosina (b. 19 May 1876; d. 24 July 1945), Italian soprano. Prominent in Italian opera from about 1900. Having sung in the first performance of the *La Bohème* composed by Leoncavallo, not Puccini, 1897, she secured her place in Puccini annals as the original heroine of *Madama Butterfly*, 1904. Performed in London and New York, 1920–21.

Strada (also known as Strada del Pò), **Anna Maria** (*fl.* 1720–40), Italian soprano. Celebrated as Handel's leading singer in his London opera seasons from 1729 to 1737, she also sang in the first performances of such English works as the oratorios *Deborah* and *Athaliah*, both 1733, and *Alexander's Feast*, 1736. There is a reference to her in Janáček's opera *The Makropoulos Affair*.

Stratas, Teresa (originally Anastasi Stratakis) (b. 26 May 1938), Canadian soprano of Greek descent. Quickly achieved notice in opera: first appeared at the Metropolitan 1959, Covent Garden 1961 (Mimì in *La Bohème*) and La Scala 1962 (first staged performance of Falla's *La Atlántida*). She sang the title role when Berg's *Lulu* at last achieved its complete staging (Paris, conducted by BOULEZ), 1979. Married to the British poet and opera librettist Tony Harrison.

Stratton Quartet, *see* AEOLIAN QUARTET.

Straumann, Bruno, *see* BUSCH QUARTET.

Straus, Ludwig, *see* JOACHIM QUARTET.

Strehle, Wilfried, *see* BRANDIS QUARTET.

Streich, Rita (b. 18 Dec 1920; d. 20 Mar 1987), German soprano of Russo-German parentage (born in Siberia). Joined Vienna State Opera, 1953, and made her London début with the company in 1954. She was celebrated in high coloratura roles such as Zerbinetta in Strauss's *Ariadne auf Naxos*, which she sang at her Glyndebourne début, 1958. From the 1970s taught in Essen, Salzburg and Nice.

Strepponi, Giuseppina (originally Clelia Maria Josepha) (b. 8 Sept 1815; d. 14 Nov 1897), Italian soprano. Sang in the premières of Verdi's first opera, *Oberto*, 1839, and his *Nabucco* (as Abigaille), 1841. She left the stage in 1846 and from 1847 lived with Verdi, helping him in translations and other professional matters. They were married in 1859; he survived her by three years (d. 27 Jan 1901).

Strongin-Katz, Martha, *see* CLEVELAND QUARTET.

Stucken, Frank van der, *see* VAN DER STUCKEN.

Stuttgart Chamber Orchestra, German orchestra founded 1945 by MÜNCHINGER, who has remained its director.

Sudeten German Quartet, *see* KOECKERT QUARTET.

Südwestfunk Orchestra, German orchestra founded 1946 and based in Baden-Baden. It has been prominent (partly through its contributions to the Donaueschingen Festival) in commissioning and performing new music. Principal conductors have included ROSBAUD, 1948–62, BOUR, 1964–79, KORD, 1980–86, and GIELEN, from 1986.

Suggia, Guilhermina (b. 27 June 1888; d. 31 July 1950). Portuguese cellist. Made her formal début in Leipzig (under NIKISCH) at the age of seventeen. She lived with CASALS, 1906–12 (despite appearances, they seemingly never married). Worked principally in London; she retired to Portugal, but reappeared in 1949 at the Edinburgh Festival. Augustus John made a famous portrait of her, 1923.

Suisse Romande, Orchestre de la, Geneva-based orchestra founded 1918 by ANSERMET, its first conductor. He remained till 1967, and later principal conductors have been SAWALLISCH, 1970–80, STEIN, 1980–85, and then Armin Jordan. As its title indicates, the orchestra belongs to the French-speaking part of Switzerland.

Suitner, Otmar (b. 16 May 1922), Austrian conductor. Active in Dresden, 1960–64, and Berlin (music director of the BERLIN STATE ORCHESTRA and Opera, 1964–71 and again from 1974). He also conducted in Japan and at Bayreuth, from 1965; appeared regularly at San Francisco Opera from 1969. His many recordings include works by Dessau and other East German composers.

Suk, Josef (1), *see* BOHEMIAN QUARTET and SUK, JOSEF (2).

Suk, Josef (2) (b. 8 Aug 1929), Czech violinist. Grandson of Josef SUK (1), violinist and composer, and great-grandson of Dvořák. In 1964 he made his début at the Proms and in USA (with the CLEVELAND ORCHESTRA); performed in a trio with KATCHEN and STARKER, 1967–9. He gave the première of Martinů's Violin Concerto no. 1 (composed in 1932) in 1973, and founded his own string ensemble in Prague the following year.

Suliotis, Elena, *see* SOULIOTIS.

Sumac, Yma (originally Chavarri) (b. 10 Sept 1927), Peruvian soprano. Sang on international concert tours and recordings from 1941, exploiting her freakishly wide five-octave range in arrangements by Moises Vivanco, whom she married. She was still performing in 1984.

Sunderland, Susan [Sykes] (b. 30 Apr 1819; d. 7 May 1905), British soprano. Famous in British oratorio performances in the early Victorian era and known as the 'Yorkshire Queen of Song'. She is commemorated by the Victorian-sounding Mrs Sunderland Competition, still held annually in Huddersfield.

Supervia, Conchita (b. 9 Dec 1895; d. 30 Mar 1936), Spanish mezzo-soprano. Developed her career in Italy. At the age of fifteen she was Octavian in the first Rome performance of Strauss's *Der Rosenkavalier*, 1911. Began to win fame in the mid-1920s for the revival of the (then rarely heard) Rossini coloratura mezzo-soprano roles of *L'Italiana in Algeri* and *La Cenerentola*. She sang at Covent Garden 1934–5 (opposite BORGIOLI), by which time she had married an Englishman, and was highly successful as a concert artist. Died aged forty-one after childbirth, but left recordings that sustained the admiration she had earned from connoisseurs.

Susskind (originally Süsskind), [Jan] **Walter** (b. 1 May 1913; d. 25 Mar 1980), Czech-born conductor, also pianist and composer, naturalized British 1946. Left Prague as a Jew under Nazi threat and worked as music director of the Carl Rosa Opera Company and, 1946–52, the SCOTTISH ORCHESTRA. Thereafter he conducted in Melbourne, Toronto (TORONTO SYMPHONY ORCHESTRA, 1956–65), St Louis, Cincinnati (CINCINNATI SYMPHONY, 1978–80) and elsewhere.

Suthaus, [Heinrich] **Ludwig** (b. 12 Dec 1906; d. 7 Sept 1971), German tenor. Noted in Wagner, appearing at Bayreuth, from 1943, and in London (Albert Hall concert, 1948, later Covent Garden). He sang the title role in Rimsky-Korsakov's *Sadko* at its first German performance, 1947; also appeared at Glyndebourne, 1950.

Sutherland, Joan (b. 7 Nov 1926), Australian soprano. Became one of the reigning operatic celebrities of her day and sustained an active and taxing career until past sixty. Studied in Sydney and London; stylistically she owed most to her fellow-Australian (and from 1954 her husband) BONYNGE. Sang at Covent Garden from 1952, and created the role of Jenifer in Tippett's *The Midsummer Marriage*, 1955. Her international fame came with the title role of *Lucia di Lammermoor*, 1959. She made a speciality of similar Italian coloratura parts, but also revived such rarities as Massenet's *Esclarmonde*

(Covent Garden, 1983, and other locations; also recorded). At the new Sydney Opera House in 1974 she sang all four soprano roles in Offenbach's *Les Contes d'Hoffmann*. Order of Australia, 1975; created Dame, 1979.

Suzuki, Shin'ichi (b. 18 Oct 1898), Japanese violinist, originator of the celebrated method of teaching violin from early childhood. Trained partly in Berlin, and in the 1930s founded the Tokyo String Orchestra. He began to organize classes in 1948 and continued teaching till he was over ninety.

Svanholm, Set [Karl Viktor] (b. 2 Sept 1904; d. 4 Oct 1964), Swedish tenor. His international operatic career, from 1938, embraced the heavier tenor roles such as Verdi's Otello and Wagner's Tristan. He sang at Covent Garden, often opposite FLAGSTAD, between 1948 and 1957. Director of Royal Swedish Opera, 1956–63.

Svetlanov, Yevgeny [Fyodorovich] (b. 6 Sept 1928), Russian conductor, also composer. Principal conductor of the Bolshoi Theatre, 1962–4, and, from 1965, of the USSR STATE SYMPHONY ORCHESTRA. He has also appeared as guest conductor in Britain (with the LONDON SYMPHONY ORCHESTRA, 1970) and elsewhere, and recorded all Tchaikovsky's symphonies. Married to AVDEYEVA.

Swarowsky, Hans (b. 16 Sept 1899; d. 10 Sept 1975), Austrian conductor. Famous as a teacher of conducting in Vienna, where ABBADO and MEHTA studied with him. He was director of the Salzburg Festival, 1940–44, and conductor of the SCOTTISH NATIONAL ORCHESTRA, 1957–9. Conducted at Vienna State Opera, from 1959, and also made many recordings.

Swarthout, Gladys (b. 25 Dec 1900; d. 7 July 1969), American mezzo-soprano. In her long career at the Metropolitan, 1929–45, she was particularly successful as Carmen. Afterwards she devoted herself mainly to concerts and also made films. Retired to Florence after 1954, and died there. Married to the baritone Frank Chapman (1900–66).

Sydney Symphony Orchestra, Australian orchestra. Assumed present name in 1946 (having been preceded by various orchestral foundations); it is the main orchestra of the Australian Broadcasting Corporation. Principal conductors have included Eugene GOOSSENS, 1947–56, MALKO, 1956–61, FRÉMAUX, 1979–82, and MACKERRAS, 1982–5. Zdeněk Mácal was due to take over in 1986, but suddenly withdrew; Stuart Challender was appointed in 1987.

Sýkora , Adolf, *see* JANÁČEK QUARTET.

Szabó, Paul, *see* VÉGH QUARTET.

Székely, Zoltán (b. 8 Dec 1903), Hungarian-born violinist, naturalized Dutch, then American, 1960. In younger years he was a recital partner of Bartók (as pianist); after moving to the Netherlands, gave there the first performance of Bartók's Violin Concerto no. 2, 1939, dedicated to him. Went to USA, 1950. He was leader of the HUNGARIAN QUARTET for most of its life, 1935–70.

Szell, George (originally György Széll) (b. 7 June 1897; d. 30 July 1970), Hungarian-born conductor, naturalized American 1946. Began conducting in Vienna, where he grew up; he made his London début 1933 and conducted the SCOTTISH ORCHESTRA, 1936–9. After moving to USA, 1939, worked at the Metropolitan Opera, 1942–6. He exerted major influence as conductor of the CLEVELAND ORCHESTRA, 1946–70, with which he toured Europe and gave the first performances of Walton's Partita, 1958, and Dutilleux's *Métaboles*, 1965, among other works. Also conducted elsewhere, including the Salzburg Festival (première of Liebermann's opera *Penelope*, 1954).

Szeransky, Péter, *see* HUNGARIAN QUARTET.

Szeryng, Henryk (b. 22 Sept 1918; d. 3 Mar 1988), Polish-born violinist, became Mexican citizen 1946. Made débuts in various countries in 1933; his post-war prominence owed much to the encouragement of Arthur RUBINSTEIN. He discovered and was the first to perform, 1971, a lost concerto by Paganini (no. 3); also gave the première of Benjamin Lees's Concerto, 1963, and of Mexican works. He sometimes performed and recorded as soloist–conductor. Took on a quasi-ambassadorial role for his adopted country. (*See also* WALCHA.)

Szigeti, Joseph (originally József) (b. 5 Sept 1892; d. 19 Feb 1973), Hungarian-born violinist; became American citizen 1951. Made London début 1907 and remained there till 1913. He often played in USSR (first Soviet performance of Prokofiev's Concerto no. 1, 1924), and made his US début 1925. Gave the premières of many works, among them Harty's Concerto (London), 1911, Bloch's Concerto (dedicated to him), 1938, and Bartók's *Contrasts*, 1939, with Bartók (piano) and GOODMAN. Lived in Switzerland from 1960 and died there. (*See also* MAGALOFF.)

T

Tabachnik, Michel (b. 10 Nov 1942), Swiss conductor of Russian extraction, also composer. Settled in France. He studied with BOULEZ and became his assistant conductor; gave the first performance of Xenakis's *Cendrées* (Lisbon), 1974. Artistic director of the Ensemble Intercontemporain, Paris, 1976–7, then appointed conductor of a newly founded orchestra at Metz.

Taddei, Giuseppe (b. 26 June 1916), Italian baritone. Made his London début 1947 and sang extensively at the Vienna State Opera from 1949. He had a repertory of over 135 roles, mainly character rather than lyrical. Took the title role on the first recording of Rossini's *Guillaume Tell*, 1952.

Tadolini [née Savonari], **Eugenia** (b. 1809; d. after 1850), Italian soprano. Worked prominently with Donizetti, for example in the title role of *Linda di Chamonix* at its first performance, Vienna, 1842. She was one of Verdi's earliest prima donnas; sang in *Ernani* shortly after its première, 1844, and in 1845 created the title role of *Alzira*. Her husband was the composer Giovanni Tadolini.

Tagliaferro, Magda (b. 19 Jan 1893; d. 9 Sep 1986), Brazilian pianist. Studied with CORTOT, in Paris. She enjoyed an extraordinarily long career, and gave a solo recital in London in the month of her ninetieth birthday. Dedicatee of Villa-Lobos's *Momoprecoce*, 1927, for piano and orchestra.

Tagliapetra, Giovanni, *see* CARREÑO.

Tagliavini, Ferruccio (b. 14 Aug 1913), Italian tenor. Made début 1939 in Florence and sang at La Scala from 1940; he won distinction in such roles as the Duke (*Rigoletto*) and Nemorino (Donizetti's *L'elisir d'amore*). First appeared at Covent Garden with the visiting La Scala company in 1950. Retired from the stage in 1970.

Tagliavini, Luigi [Ferdinando] (b. 7 Oct 1929), Italian organist and harpsichordist. Noted as soloist and on recordings of two-organ works with Marie-Claire ALAIN. He has toured and taught internationally and is an authority on the conservation of old organs.

Tajo, Italo (b. 25 Apr 1915), Italian-born bass, became American citizen 1979. Noted in opera (Edinburgh Festival, 1947, and the Metropolitan, from 1948), particularly in comic roles. He replaced PINZA in a Broadway production of Rodgers and Hammerstein's *South Pacific*, 1956. Taught singing at the University of Cincinnati from 1966 and in 1980 returned to the Metropolitan, where he was still singing at the age of seventy.

Takács-Nagy, Gábor, *see* TAKÁCS QUARTET.

Takács Quartet, string quartet founded 1975 in Budapest. Members: Gábor Takács-Nagy, Károly Schranz, Gábor Ormai and András Fejér. In 1989 it became based in Boulder, Colorado; tours widely.

Talich, Václav (b. 28 May 1883; d. 16 May 1961), Czech conductor. One of his country's most prominent musicians. For many years he was chief conductor of the CZECH PHILHARMONIC ORCHESTRA, 1919–31 and 1932–41, with which he championed both new and older Czech works; gave the first performance of Janáček's Sinfonietta, 1926. Active also in opera, in 1938 he conducted the première of Martinů's *Julietta* (dedicated to him). The post-1947 communist regime at first penalized, then rehabilitated him.

Talvela, Martti (b. 4 Feb 1935; d. 22 July 1989), Finnish bass. Famous in Wagner and Russian opera (Bayreuth from 1962 and Covent Garden from 1970); his height (over six and a half feet) added to his dramatic effectiveness. Sang the title role of *Boris Godunov* at the Metropolitan, 1974, and also in USSR. Director of the Savonlinna Festival in Finland, 1972–9.

Tamagno, Francesco (b. 28 Dec 1850; d. 31 Aug 1905), Italian tenor. Became the most celebrated singer of his time in the heavier Italian tenor roles. He sang Adorno in the first performance of Verdi's *Simon Boccanegra* in its revised version (Milan, 1881), and Verdi chose him to take the title role of *Otello* at its première (Milan, 1887). He first appeared in London 1889 (*Otello*) and at the Metropolitan 1894 (in Rossini's *Guillaume Tell*). Made early recordings, 1903.

Tamberlik, Enrico (b. 16 Mar 1820; d. 13 Mar 1889), Italian tenor. Won international operatic fame; Verdi wrote for him the role of Alvaro in *La forza del destino*, which he sang at its première in St Petersburg, 1862. By this time he had settled in Paris. Appeared in almost every season at Covent Garden, 1850–70.

Tamburini, Antonio (b. 28 Mar 1800; d. 8 Nov 1876), Italian baritone. One of the brilliant performers (along with Giulia GRISI and LABLACHE) who gave distinction to Italian opera in Paris and London in the 1830s. In Paris he sang in the premières of Bellini's *I puritani* and Donizetti's *Don Pasquale*.

Tamir, Alexander, *see* EDEN.

Tapping, Roger, *see* ALLEGRI QUARTET.

Tarr, Edward [Hankins] (b. 15 June 1936), American trumpeter. Chiefly known as a specialist performer on the Renaissance and baroque instruments (also the cornetto) and a researcher and editor in those fields. Playing modern trumpet, he has recorded Kagel's *Atem* (Breath), 1970, which was written for him.

Tárrega (in full Tárrega y Eixea), **Francisco** (b. 21 Nov 1852; d. 15 Dec 1909), Spanish guitarist. Trained also as a pianist. His performing career (led chiefly in Spain, though he gave concerts in Paris and London in 1880) helped to revalue the guitar in anticipation of its twentieth-century revival. Composed and made many arrangements for guitar, some from works by his friends Albéniz and Granados.

Tate, Jeffrey (b. 28 Apr 1943), British conductor. A qualified physician who turned late to professional music, he worked as an assistant to BOULEZ at Bayreuth, 1976; first conducted at Covent Garden 1982, at the Metropolitan 1980. He was appointed principal conductor of the ENGLISH CHAMBER ORCHESTRA, 1985, and to the new post of principal conductor at Covent Garden, 1986, adding musical directorship of Rotterdam Philharmonic, 1991. Gave the first performance of Saxton's *In the Beginning*, 1988. He suffers from curvature of the spine and conducts seated. CBE, 1990.

Tátrai, Vilmos, *see* TÁTRAI QUARTET.

Tátrai Quartet, Hungarian string quartet founded 1946. Original members were Vilmos Tátrai (who has remained its leader), Albert Rényi, József Iványi and Vera Dénes. It has recorded the complete quartets of Haydn and championed modern Hungarian composers.

Taub, Chaim, *see* TEL AVIV QUARTET.

Tauber (originally Denemy), **Richard** (b. 16 May 1891; d. 8 Jan 1948), Austrian-born tenor, also conductor and composer, naturalized British 1940. Illegitimate, he was given his mother's maiden name and was later adopted by his father, Anton Richard Tauber. Prominent at Vienna State Opera, 1926–38, and was equally acclaimed in concerts and operetta. He played over sixty stage roles, including many of Lehár's (first performance of *The Land of Smiles*, 1929). Under threat as a Jew from Nazi persecution, settled in Britain, 1938. He composed the operetta *Old Chelsea* and starred in its London première, 1943. Sang again with Vienna State Opera when it visited Covent Garden, 1947.

Tausig, Carl (originally Karol) (b. 4 Nov 1841; d. 17 July 1871), Polish pianist. Worked mainly in Germany. He was one of the most famous pupils of LISZT, and had a prodigious memory. Early death from typhoid cut off his brilliant career. Also known as a composer; his many piano transcriptions of other works were once in vogue.

Tausky, Vilem (b. 20 July 1910), Czech-born conductor, also composer, naturalized British 1948. Conducted the première of Williamson's opera *The Violins of Saint-Jacques* (dedicated to him and his wife), 1966, and the first (radio) performance in Britain of Janáček's opera *Destiny* (*Osud*), 1974. He was director of opera at the Guildhall School of Music, 1966–86. CBE, 1981.

Taylor, Franklin (b. 5 Feb 1843; d. 19 Mar 1919), British pianist, also organist. Having studied with MOSCHELES and others in Leipzig and with Clara SCHUMANN in Paris, became one of the most prominent London pianists and teachers. He published editions of piano classics and books of technical instruction.

Tchaikowsky, André (original Polish spelling Andrzej Czajkowski) (b. 1 Nov 1935; d. 26 June 1982), Polish-born British pianist, also composer. A pupil of ASKENASE in Warsaw and of BOULANGER in Paris. He made his British début in 1958. Bequeathed his skull to the Royal Shakespeare Company to use in *Hamlet* (which it has done).

Tchakarov, Emil (b. 29 June 1948), Bulgarian conductor. Secured international engagements while still in his twenties. In 1974 he was appointed to the conductorship of the State Philharmonic at Plovdiv (Bulgaria), and he later worked with the Flanders Philharmonic in Antwerp, 1985–6; also conducted at the Metropolitan Opera, 1979, and elsewhere.

Tear, Robert (b. 8 Mar 1939), British tenor. Equally prominent in concert and opera. He made many performances and recordings of Britten in the composer's English Opera Group. His début at Covent Garden, 1970, was as Dov in the first performance of Tippett's *The Knot Garden*; at Boston he sang in the première of Tippett's *The Mask of Time*, 1984. He has made over 250 records, from Bach to Victorian ballads (with LUXON and PREVIN). From 1985 he has also appeared occasionally as conductor. CBE, 1984.

Tebaldi, Renata (b. 1 Feb 1922), Italian soprano. Became one of the most prominent artists at La Scala from its reopening concert in 1946. She appeared at Covent Garden and San Francisco from 1950 and at the Metropolitan (as Desdemona in *Otello*) in 1955. Her repertory was almost exclusively Italian: recorded *Tosca* three times and the title roles of *Aida* and *Madama Butterfly* twice.

Te Kanawa, Kiri (b. 6 March 1944), New Zealand soprano of partly Maori descent. Brought up by adoptive parents; trained in Auckland and London, she was the first singer of Maori origins to achieve a front-rank career. Her performances as the Countess in *Le nozze di Figaro* at Covent Garden, 1971, and Desdemona in *Otello* at the Metropolitan, 1974, won her immediate acclaim. Appeared as Donna Anna in Joseph Losey's film of *Don Giovanni*, 1979; her lighter recorded repertory includes Bernstein's *West Side Story* with the composer conducting, 1985. She sang at Prince Charles's wedding, 1981; created Dame (New Zealand honours list), 1982.

Tel Aviv Quartet, Israeli string quartet founded 1962. Original members were Chaim Taub, Uri Pianka, Daniel Benyamini and Uzi Wiesel; Pianka was succeeded by Menahem Breuer, then Yefim Boyko. The group gave first performances of works by Tal and other Israeli composers.

Telmányi, Emil (b. 22 June 1892; d. 12 June 1988), Hungarian violinist and conductor. Settled in Denmark, where he made his conducting début in 1919. He was associated with Carl Nielsen, whose younger daughter he married; his second wife was the Danish pianist Annette Schiøler (b. 1904). He was soloist in the first German performance of Elgar's Violin Concerto (Berlin), 1911. In the 1950s he championed a so-called Bach bow with a mechanism for playing multi-string chords.

Temianka, Henri (b. 19 Nov 1906), British-born American violinist and conductor of Polish parentage. He led an international career as soloist and founding leader of the Paganini Quartet, 1946–66. Also conducted and taught, mainly in California.

Temirkanov, Yuri (b. 10 Dec 1938), Russian conductor. Active mainly in Leningrad in concert and opera. Became artistic director of the Kirov Opera there, 1977, and has sometimes also directed the staging of operas. He headed the company's visit to UK, 1987. Appointed principal conductor of the LENINGRAD PHILHARMONIC ORCHESTRA, 1988; also well-known guest conductor with other orchestras.

Tenducci, Giusto Ferdinando (b. *c.* 1735; d. 25 Jan 1790), Italian male soprano (castrato). Nicknamed Triorchis (three-testicled). After settling in London, he sang in opera and was prominent in the Handel commemoration festivals, 1784–90; he also wrote music and a treatise on singing. The boy Mozart, on meeting him in London in 1762, wrote a song for him.

Tennstedt, Klaus (b. 6 June 1926), German conductor. Worked at the Dresden Opera, then moved via Sweden (where he conducted concerts and opera), 1971, to West Germany. He received acclaim after appearing with the TORONTO SYMPHONY ORCHESTRA and the BOSTON SYMPHONY, 1974. Succeeded SOLTI as principal conductor of the LONDON PHILHARMONIC ORCHESTRA, 1983, but cancer compelled him severely to curtail his performances from mid-1987.

Ternina (originally Trnina), **Milka** (b. 19 Dec 1863; d. 18 May 1941), Croatian soprano. Reckoned among the finest operatic performers of her day, particularly in Wagner. She sang more than eighty roles, and was the first Tosca in both London and New York, 1900 and 1901. Forced into retirement by paralysis, 1906.

Tertis, Lionel (b. 29 Dec 1876; d. 22 Feb 1975), British viola player. One of the most distinguished performers of his generation. By his efforts the viola became 'Cinderella no more' (title of his book, 1953): he adapted many works, among them Elgar's Cello Concerto (*see also* GOLANI), and designed a larger viola. Played chamber music with CASALS and others of highest rank. Composers who wrote for him included Bax (Phantasy, with orchestra, 1920). His achievements were finally marked by a CBE, 1950.

Teschemacher, Margarete (b. 3 Mar 1903; d. 19 May 1959), German soprano. Sang at Covent Garden, 1931 and 1936, and also at Salzburg, Chicago, and elsewhere. In 1938 she created the title role in Strauss's *Daphne* (Dresden).

Tessier, Charles (*fl.* 1600), French lutenist. Spent some time in the service of Henri IV of France. Also a composer, he dedicated a volume to the sister of the Earl of Essex, and appears to have sought employment with Essex.

Tetrazzini, Eva, *see* TETRAZZINI, LUISA.

Tetrazzini, Luisa (originally Luigia) (b. 29 June 1871; d. 28 Apr 1940), Italian soprano. Among the first to record extensively and with world-wide success. She made her US début 1904 and her London début 1907 (in *La traviata* at Covent Garden). Became one of the best-known singers of her time, especially for her coloratura agility (and not at all for her acting). Latterly she gave up the stage for the concert hall; toured with AMADIO. Her sister Eva Tetrazzini (1862–1948) was also an operatic soprano and was married to Italo Campanini (1845–96), a tenor.

Teyte, Maggie (originally Margaret Tate) (b. 17 Apr 1888; d. 26 May 1976), British soprano. Adopted the spelling 'Teyte' for French usage. In Paris she appeared in concert with Debussy at the piano and was chosen by him to succeed GARDEN in *Pelléas et Mélisande*; later she sang opera in London, Chicago and elsewhere and created the role of the Princess in Holst's opera *The Perfect Fool* (London), 1923. In 1951 she returned to the stage as Belinda in the Mermaid Theatre's production of *Dido and Aeneas* with FLAGSTAD.

Thalben-Ball, George [Thomas] (b. 18 June 1896; d. 18 Jan 1987), Australian-born British organist. Appointed organist of the Temple Church, London, in 1923 and remained till 1981. He was also a prominent soloist at London concerts and university and city organist in Birmingham, 1949–82. Knighted, 1982. (*See also* LOUGH.)

Thalberg, Sigismond (b. 8 Jan 1812; d. 27 Apr 1871), Swiss-born pianist. It is uncertain whether he was of Austrian or German parentage as the details on his birth certificate have been doubted. Acclaimed for his virtuosity, he toured many countries, including Russia, USA and Brazil. His repertory relied greatly on his own compositions (among them waltzes, caprices, studies and fantasies on tunes from well-known operas), which were published and widely cultivated.

Thaw, David, *see* WATSON.

Thebom, Blanche (b. 19 Sept 1918), American mezzo-soprano of Swedish parentage. Sang at the Metropolitan Opera, 1944–67, and took the role of Dido in London's first complete performance of Berlioz's *Les Troyens* (Covent Garden), 1957.

Thibaud, Jacques (b. 27 Sept 1880; d. 1 Sept 1953), French violinist. While playing in a Paris café, he was discovered by the conductor COLONNE. Became much in demand as a soloist in Paris and then internationally (USA from 1903), and well known in a trio with CORTOT and CASALS, 1905–44. He was also associated with LONG, and a music competition under their names was founded in 1943. Played in London when over seventy and never retired; he was killed in an air crash.

Thill, Georges (b. 14 Dec 1897; d. 16 Oct 1984), French tenor. Enjoyed a long and distinguished operatic career in Paris, 1924–53. He sang about fifty major roles, including Parsifal and Samson in Saint-Saëns's *Samson et Dalila* (Covent Garden, 1928). Appeared in the film of Gustave Charpentier's *Louise* opposite Grace MOORE, 1939.

Thomas, David [Lionel Mercer] (b. 26 Feb 1943) British bass. Celebrated in early-music repertory under the direction of ROOLEY, HOGWOOD and others. He made his US début at the Hollywood Bowl, 1982 (Handel's *Messiah* and Haydn's *Creation*); sang the role of the Devil in the first modern revival of Landi's opera *Sant' Alessio* (Los Angeles), 1988.

Thomas, Jacqueline, *see* BRODSKY QUARTET (2).

Thomas, Jess [Floyd] (b. 4 Aug 1927), American tenor. Prominent in Wagner, sang at Bayreuth from 1961. He performed as Caesar in the première of Barber's *Antony and Cleopatra*, which opened the Metropolitan's new theatre at the Lincoln Center, 1966.

Thomas, John (b. 1 Mar 1826; d. 19 Mar 1913), British harpist. Helped to revive the popularity of the harp in Wales, where he frequently adjudicated at eisteddfod ceremonies. He performed a concerto of his own at the Philharmonic concerts in London, 1852, and became harpist to Queen Victoria, 1871.

Thomas, John Charles (b. 6 Sept 1891; d. 13 Dec 1960), American baritone. Particularly successful in light concert repertory and in Broadway productions of Lehár's and other operettas. He also sang at Covent Garden (Valentin in *Faust*, 1928) and at the Metropolitan, 1934–43.

Thomas, Mary (b. 2 Aug 1932), British soprano. Prominent in modern works, she took part in the first performances of Peter Maxwell Davies's *The Blind Fiddler*, 1971, and *The Medium*, 1981, and Birtwistle's *Entr'actes and Sappho Fragments*, 1964. Also soloist in the première of David Blake's song cycle *In Praise of Krishna*, 1973.

Thomas, Michael, *see* BRODSKY QUARTET (2).

Thomas, Michael Tilson (b. 21 Dec 1944), American conductor and pianist, also television presenter. Became assistant conductor of the BOSTON SYMPHONY ORCHESTRA aged twenty-four (the youngest ever). He conducted the first US production of the complete version of Berg's *Lulu* at Santa Fe, 1979. Appointed principal guest conductor (with RATTLE) of the LOS ANGELES PHILHARMONIC, 1981, and principal conductor of the LONDON SYMPHONY ORCHESTRA, 1988, with which he gave the first British (semi-staged) performance of Rimsky-Korsakov's *Mlada*, 1989. His television presentations have included the Gershwin fiftieth-anniversary programmes on BBC, 1987.

Thomas, Theodore [Christian Friedrich] (b. 11 Oct 1835; d. 4 Jan 1905), German-born

American conductor. Emigrated to USA in boyhood. He was the major creator of orchestral activity in New York from 1862, in Cincinnati (founder and conductor of its biennial festival from 1873 until his death) and especially in Chicago, where he settled permanently in 1891 as conductor of the CHICAGO SYMPHONY ORCHESTRA. Also attempted (unsuccessfully) to promote opera in English. He took his New York and Chicago orchestras on US and Canadian tours, and gave the first US performances of many works, including Dvořák's symphonies nos. 6 and 7, 1883 and 1886, and Saint-Saëns's Symphony no. 3, 1887.

Thompson, Douglas, *see* BLECH QUARTET.

Thomson, Bryden (b. 26 July 1928), British conductor. Held posts with the Royal Ballet, (1962–4), Norwegian Opera, 1964–6, and the RADIO TELEFÍS EIREANN SYMPHONY ORCHESTRA, 1984–5. Held musical directorship of the SCOTTISH NATIONAL ORCHESTRA, 1988–91.

Thomson, César (b. 17 Mar 1857; d. 21 Aug 1931), Belgian violinist. Pupil of VIEUXTEMPS and WIENIAWSKI. His career brought him distinction as solo player and quartet leader; was also noted teacher in Paris, from 1914, and at the Juilliard School, 1924–7.

Thorborg, Kerstin (b. 19 May 1896; d. 12 Apr 1970), Swedish contralto. One of the leading international Wagner singers of her day, she had a long career at the Metropolitan, 1936–50, and also performed at Covent Garden, 1936–9. Sang in the first recording of Mahler's *Das Lied von der Erde* (under WALTER), 1936.

Thurston, Frederick [John] (b. 21 Sept 1901; d. 12 Dec 1953), British clarinettist. Principal clarinet in the newly founded BBC SYMPHONY ORCHESTRA, 1930–46, and a sought-after soloist and chamber-music player. In 1933 (with the GRILLER QUARTET) he gave the first public performance of Bliss's Quintet, one of several British works dedicated to him. Married Thea KING, a former student.

Tibbett (originally Tibbet), **Lawrence** (b. 16 Nov 1896; d. 15 July 1960), American baritone. Adopted what had been a misspelling of his name. He became one of his country's best-known singers and had a long and varied career at the Metropolitan, 1923–60. As well as singing the classic repertory, for example Rigoletto, Falstaff and Wolfram (*Tannhäuser*), he created the title roles of Gruenberg's *The Emperor Jones* (Metropolitan, 1923), Eugene Goossens's *Don Juan de Mañara* (Covent Garden, 1937), and other works. His films include *New Moon* (on Romberg's operetta) with Grace MOORE, 1930.

Tietjens (also spelt Titiens in British usage), **Therese** [Cathline Johanna Alexandra] (b. 17 July 1831; d. 3 Oct 1877), German soprano of Hungarian parentage. Made her home in London, where she was the first to sing the heroine's roles in Verdi's *Un ballo in maschera*, 1861, and *La forza del destino*, 1867, and Gounod's *Faust*, 1863. Also admired as concert singer. Latterly she grew very stout; suffering from cancer, she collapsed after (not, as sometimes said, during) a London performance of Donizetti's *Lucrezia Borgia*, 1877, and died five months later.

Tinsley, Pauline [Cecilia] (b. 27 Mar 1928), British soprano. Made her London opera début in 1961, and was an admired singer with Welsh National Opera from 1962: roles included Strauss's Elektra and Abigaille in Verdi's *Nabucco*. Her US début was in the title role of Donizetti's *Anna Bolena* at Santa Fe, 1969.

Tirimo, Martino (b. 19 Dec 1942), Cyprus-born British pianist. Made London début 1965. He performed and recorded the twenty-one Schubert sonatas with his own completions of unfinished movements, first broadcast 1986–7 on BBC (in twelve programmes). He was the first in London to direct all Beethoven's piano concertos from the keyboard, 1986.

Titiens, Therese, *see* TIETJENS.

Titus, Alan (b. 28 Oct 1945), American baritone. Created the role of the Celebrant in Bernstein's theatre piece *Mass* in Washington, 1971. He has sung various operatic roles in New York, Frankfurt and elsewhere.

Tokyo Philharmonic Orchestra, orchestra founded 1940 as the Central Symphony Orchestra. In 1948 it took its present name and

WATANABE was appointed chief conductor; he remained till 1954. His successors have included OTAKA, from 1974.

Tokyo Quartet, ensemble of Japanese players founded 1969 at the Juilliard School. Original members were Koichiro Harada, Yoshiko Nakura, Kazuhide Isomura and Sadao Harada. Kikuei Ikeda has been second violinist from 1974 and Peter Haig Oundjian (Canadian) first violinist from 1981. The group tours world-wide and has played the complete cycle of Beethoven's quartets several times; it commissioned and performed Takemitsu's Quartet no. 1, 1980.

Tolbecque, Auguste (b. 30 Mar 1830; d. 8 Mar 1919), French cellist. Active in Paris; he was the most celebrated member of a musical family of Belgian descent. Also played the bass viol and established a workshop and collection of early instruments, unusual at that time.

Tomlinson, John [Rowland] (b. 22 Sept 1946), British bass. With English National Opera, from 1974, has sung over forty roles, including Boris Godunov and Rossini's Moses. He has also performed at Covent Garden from 1977 (over twenty roles), and in Continental and US opera houses (Bayreuth from 1988).

Tomowa-Sintow, Anna (b. 22 Sept 1941), Bulgarian soprano. Uses German spelling of her name; normal English transliteration is Tomova-Sintov. She sang with Leipzig Opera, 1967–72, and was chosen by KARAJAN for the 1973 Salzburg Festival première of Orff's *De temporum fine comoedia* (also recorded); often sang with Karajan thereafter. She made her Covent Garden début 1975, Metropolitan 1984, and has pursued an international career in Mozart and Verdi.

Tonhalle Orchestra of Zurich, Swiss orchestra founded 1868. Took its name from its building. Principal conductors have included ANDREAE, 1906–49, ROSBAUD, 1950–62, KEMPE, 1965–72, ALBRECHT, 1975–80, ESCHENBACH, 1982–6, and WAKASUGI, from 1986.

Toronto Symphony Orchestra, Canadian orchestra so named (taking over earlier series) in 1926. Its principal conductors have included MACMILLAN, 1931–56, SUSSKIND, 1956–65, OZAWA, 1965–9, ANČERL, 1969–73, Andrew DAVIS, 1975–89, and HERBIG, from 1990.

Tortelier, Paul (b. 21 Mar 1914; d. 18 Dec 1990), French cellist, also conductor and composer, father of Yan Pascal TORTELIER. Made his Paris concerto début aged seventeen; he was a member of the BOSTON SYMPHONY ORCHESTRA, 1937–9, then returned to Paris. His British début under BEECHAM, 1947, led to top international fame. After spending a year on an Israeli kibbutz, 1955–6, he wrote an *Israel Symphony*. His pupils included DU PRÉ and Maud Martin, whom he married; he recorded in a trio with their son, Yan Pascal, and daughter, Maria de la Pau (b. 1950), a pianist.

Tortelier, Yan Pascal (b. 19 Apr 1947), French violinist and conductor, son of Paul TORTELIER. He has conducted the LONDON PHILHARMONIC (first UK performance of Debussy's *Khamma*, 1986), Scottish Opera and English National Opera, 1988. Appointed principal conductor of the ULSTER ORCHESTRA, 1990–2, thereafter of BBC PHILHARMONIC.

Toscanini, Arturo (b. 25 Mar 1867; d. 16 Jan 1957), Italian conductor. In his early career as a cellist he took the baton in mid-performance of *Aida* in Rio de Janeiro in 1886, and thus launched a conducting career of the highest prestige both in live performances and on record. He had a reputation for absolute fidelity to the score (not quite deserved) and for dictatorial, sometimes furious, behaviour. Conducted the first performances of *Pagliacci* (Milan, 1892), and Puccini's *La Bohème* (Turin, 1896), *La fanciulla del West* (New York, 1910) and *Turandot* (Milan, 1926). He was artistic director of the Metropolitan Opera, 1908–15, and La Scala, 1920–29, and conducted the NEW YORK PHILHARMONIC ORCHESTRA, 1928–36. The first conductor not of German or Austrian origin to appear at the Bayreuth Wagner Festival, he withdrew from it in protest against Nazi victimization of Jews, a political and humanitarian stance that also led him to conduct the inaugural performance of the PALESTINE SYMPHONY ORCHESTRA, 1936. In 1937 in New York the NATIONAL BROADCASTING COMPANY SYMPHONY ORCHESTRA was specially created for him; with it he gave the première of Barber's Adagio for Strings, 1938. His last

British appearance was in 1952. Extremely shortsighted, he committed all scores to his fantastically powerful memory. Although so long active in USA, he never gave up Italian citizenship. His daughter Wanda married HOROWITZ.

Tosi, Pier Francesco (b. *c.* 1653; d. 1732), Italian male alto (castrato). Active in Vienna and London as performer and teacher. His *Observations on the Florid Song*, 1723 (English edition, 1742), remains one of the most celebrated treatises on vocal technique and related matters.

Totenberg, Roman (b. 1 Jan 1911), Polish-born violinist, naturalized American 1943. In the 1930s toured Europe with the composer Szymanowski as his pianist and South America with Arthur RUBINSTEIN. He championed new music and gave the first performance of Hindemith's Violin Sonata in E minor in New York, 1936.

Toth, Aladár, *see* FISCHER, ANNIE.

Tourel (originally Davidovich or Davidson), **Jennie** (b. 26 June 1899; d. 23 Nov 1973), Russian-born mezzo-soprano, naturalized American 1946. Said to have formed her professional name from that of a teacher, Anna El-Tour. She was active in opera in Paris till 1939, then in USA. Won note as a solo recitalist and was chosen by Stravinsky for the first performance of *The Rake's Progress* (Venice), 1951.

Toye, [Edward] Geoffrey (b. 17 Feb 1889; d. 11 June 1942), British conductor, also composer. Conducted the first performance of Vaughan Williams's *A London Symphony*, 1914, and during three seasons as conductor of the D'Oyly Carte Opera Company he gave Sullivan's *Ruddigore* in his own musical revision. Also active in conducting ballet, he wrote his own ballet score *The Haunted Ballroom*, 1935, which includes a famous waltz. He was producer, adapter and conductor of the film version of *The Mikado*, 1939. The music critic Francis Toye was his brother.

Tozzi, Giorgio (originally George) (b. 8 Jan 1923), American bass-baritone of Italian descent. Preferred the Italian form of his given name. He sang Tarquinius in the US première of Britten's *The Rape of Lucretia* (New York, 1948). His roles at the Metropolitan from 1955 included Hans Sachs (*Die Meistersinger*) and Boris Godunov.

Trampler, Walter (b. 25 Aug 1915), German-born viola player, naturalized American 1944. One of the world's leading exponents of his instrument, he gave the first US performance of Henze's concerto *Compases para preguntas ensimismadas*, 1972. Berio's *Sequenza III* and *Chemins II* and *Chemins III* were written for him. Founding member of the New Music Quartet, 1947–56.

Traubel, Helen (b. 20 June 1899; d. 28 July 1972), American soprano. Although she did not attempt a European career, she was one of her country's best-known singers. After FLAGSTAD left the Metropolitan, 1941, Traubel was regarded as its leading Wagner soprano; in 1953, however, she stopped singing there because its director, Rudolf Bing, objected to her performing in night-clubs. She also wrote crime novels.

Trávníček, Jiří, *see* JANÁČEK QUARTET.

Trebelli, Zélia (originally Gloria Caroline Gilbert or Lebert) (b. 1834; d. 18 Aug 1892), French mezzo-soprano. Her adopted surname is supposed to have been a near-anagram of her original one. She was a much appreciated artist in London opera, 1862–87. Continued to sing 'breeches' (young male) roles until she was fifty.

Tree, Michael, *see* GUARNERI QUARTET.

Treigle, Norman (b. 6 Mar 1923; d. 16 Feb 1975), American bass-baritone. A favourite artist of the New York City Opera from 1953, for example in the baritone villain roles of *Les Contes d'Hoffmann*, and in the first professional performance of Carlisle Floyd's *Susannah*, 1956. He also sang at Covent Garden, 1974. Died after taking an overdose of sleeping-pills.

Tretyakov, Viktor (b. 17 Oct 1946), Soviet violinist and conductor. As violinist, won the Moscow Tchaikovsky Competition, 1966. He became known as a soloist and violinist-director of orchestras, and in 1983 was appointed director of the MOSCOW CHAMBER ORCHESTRA, later renamed the USSR State Chamber Orchestra.

Troyanos, Tatiana (b. 12 Sept 1938), American mezzo-soprano. Performed in a wide range of operatic roles: she was Hippolyta in the first New York performance of Britten's *A Midsummer Night's Dream*, 1963, and created the part of Jeanne in Penderecki's *The Devils of Loudun*, 1969, in one of her many appearances with Hamburg State Opera. Also sang Anita in Bernstein's recording of his own *West Side Story*, 1985.

Tsïganov, Dmitry, *see* BEETHOVEN QUARTET.

Ts'ong, Fou, *see* FOU TS'ONG.

Tua, Teresina (originally Maria Felicità) (b. 22 May 1867; d. 29 Oct 1955), Italian violinist. Appeared in Britain from 1883 and USA from 1887 and partnered RAKHMANINOV on tour, 1895. She taught in Milan, 1915–24, then became a nun.

Tubb, Carrie (originally Caroline) [Elizabeth] (b. 17 May 1876; d. 20 Sept 1976), British soprano. Became a favourite in oratorio and Verdi's Requiem; made her Proms début in 1911. She was also, less prominently, an operatic singer (particularly with BEECHAM, from 1910). Sang in the first British performance of Schoenberg's String Quartet no. 2 with the LONDON STRING QUARTET (1), 1912.

Tucker, Richard (originally Reuben Ticker) (b. 28 Aug 1913; d. 8 Jan 1975), American tenor. Began his vocal career as a synagogue cantor. After joining the Metropolitan, 1945, he became one of its most prominent singers; remained up to the time of his sudden death and gave more than 600 performances of some 30 roles in the Italian and French repertory. He sang Cavaradossi in *Tosca* at Covent Garden, 1958. PEERCE, a rival tenor, was his brother-in-law.

Tuckwell, Barry [Emmanuel] (b. 5 Mar 1931), Australian horn player. Moved to UK, 1950, and became one of the world's leading players of his instrument; principal horn with the LONDON SYMPHONY ORCHESTRA, 1955–68. He gave the first performance of Richard Rodney Bennett's *Actaeon* for horn and orchestra, 1977, and many other works dedicated to him. In 1969 formed the Tuckwell Wind Quintet (which toured China, 1984). OBE, 1965.

Tudor, David (b. 20 Jan 1926), American pianist. Celebrated in modern music, he gave the first US performance of Boulez's Sonata no. 2 (New York, 1950), and took part in the premières of Stockhausen's *Refrain* (Berlin, 1959) and *Kontakte* (Cologne, 1960). With the composer John Cage he developed the concept of 'happenings' and gave the first performance of Cage's famous *4′33″* (in which the pianist is silent for the whole of that time), 1952. He also plays the bandoneon (type of accordion), for which he wrote the piece *Bandoneon!* in 1966.

Tunnell, John, *see* LONDON STRING QUARTET (2).

Tureck, Rosalyn (b. 14 Dec 1914), American pianist and harpsichordist, also ensemble director, of Russian and Turkish descent. In early career played much modern American music, but after her European début, 1947, concentrated on Bach. She has taught widely and edited and written about music.

Turner, Eva (b. 10 Mar 1892; d. 16 June 1990), British soprano. Made her British début in 1916 and sang at La Scala from 1924. Admired in Verdi and Wagner, considered outstanding as Puccini's Turandot. Prominent at Covent Garden, 1928–48, Chicago and elsewhere. Taught singing at the University of Oklahoma, 1950–59, and later in London. Created Dame, 1962.

Turnovský, Martin (b. 29 Sept 1928), Czech conductor. Active in Brno and Dresden, 1966–8, then emigrated to Austria. He was music director of Norwegian Opera, 1975–80, and of Bonn Opera, 1979–83.

Tuxen, Erik [Oluf] (b. 4 July 1902; d. 28 Aug 1957), Danish conductor (born in Germany). Conductor of the DANISH RADIO SYMPHONY ORCHESTRA, 1936–57; his performance of Nielsen's symphonies at the Edinburgh Festival, 1950, stimulated a wave of British interest in the composer. He was himself also a composer.

Tyler, James [Henry] (b. 3 Aug 1940), American lutenist. Worked in London and in 1969 founded the Consort of Musicke with ROOLEY; he remained as co-director till 1972. He has also played banjo in a ragtime ensemble. Became university professor in California, 1986.

Tzipine, Georges (b. 22 June 1907), French conductor, formerly violinist. Conductor of the MELBOURNE SYMPHONY ORCHESTRA, 1961–5. Working with French orchestras, he recorded a distinctive French repertory (including Schmitt and Roussel) and accompanied LONG, CHRISTOFF and other celebrated soloists.

Tzveych, Biserka, *see* CVEJIC.

U

Uchida, Mitsuko (b. 20 Dec 1948), Japanese pianist. Studied in Vienna, where she won first prize in a Beethoven piano competition, 1969. Developed an international career (performed in China, 1979). She has recorded Mozart concertos (with TATE) and also the complete Mozart sonatas. Sometimes conducts from the keyboard.

Uhde, Hermann (b. 20 July 1914; d. 10 Oct 1965), German baritone. Sang Creon in the première of Orff's *Antigonae* (Salzburg, 1949). As a member of the Bavarian State Opera visiting Covent Garden, 1953, he was a notable Mandryka in Strauss's *Arabella*. Later performed in Covent Garden's own company and at the Metropolitan Opera, from 1955. He died during a performance of Niels Viggo Bentzon's *Faust III* at Copenhagen.

Ulfung, Ragnar [Sigurd] (b. 28 Feb 1927), Norwegian tenor. His forceful personality contributed to the success of Blomdahl's 'space opera' *Aniara* in 1959 (Stockholm, then Edinburgh Festival). He later became well known at Covent Garden, where he created the title role in Peter Maxwell Davies's *Taverner*, 1972.

Ulster Orchestra, Belfast-based orchestra founded 1966. Principal conductors have included COMISSIONA, 1967–9, Bryden THOMSON, 1977–85, HANDLEY, 1985–9, and Yan Pascal TORTELIER, from 1990.

Umlauf, Ignaz, *see* UMLAUF, MICHAEL.

Umlauf (or Umlauff), **Michael** (b. 9 Aug 1781; d. 20 June 1842), Austrian violinist and conductor, also composer. Conducted the revival of Beethoven's *Fidelio*, 1814, and practically directed from the violin the first performance of the Symphony no. 9, 1824, as the deaf composer's conducting was of little effectiveness. His father, Ignaz Umlauf(f) (1746–96), was also a conductor and composer.

Unger, Georg (b. 6 Mar 1837; d. 2 Feb 1887), German tenor. Recommended to Wagner by Hans RICHTER, created the title role of *Siegfried* at Bayreuth, 1876. He is thus said to have been the first Wagnerian *Heldentenor*, but he did not remain in Wagner's circle.

Unger, Gerhard (b. 26 Nov 1916), German tenor. Began his operatic career in 1947 and became prominent in lighter and character roles. He gave over 300 performances as Pedrillo in *Die Entführung* and sang David in *Die Meistersinger* at Bayreuth under KARAJAN.

Unger, Heinz (b. 14 Dec 1895; d. 25 Feb 1965), German-born conductor; became British citizen 1944. After the Nazis came to power in 1933, worked mainly in London, Leningrad and, from 1948, Toronto. A Mahler specialist, he was prominent as conductor for the Canadian Broadcasting Corporation and toured widely. Made Commander of the Order of Merit (a West German award), 1963.

Unger (or Ungher), **Karoline** (or Caroline) (b. 28 Oct 1803; d. 23 Mar 1877), Austrian contralto. Took part in the first performance of Beethoven's Symphony no. 9 in Vienna, 1824. She then won prominence on the Italian stage as few Austrians did at that time: sang the heroine's roles (written for her) in Bellini's *La straniera* (Milan, 1829) and Donizetti's *Belisario* (Venice, 1836). Other composers also wrote operas for her.

Uninsky, Alexander (b. 2 Feb 1910; d. 19 Dec 1972), Russian-born American pianist. Studied in Warsaw and Paris. Having won first prize at the International Chopin Competition at Warsaw, 1932, he became internationally acclaimed as a Chopin specialist. Went to USA, 1943, and later taught in Toronto and Dallas.

Uppman, Theodor (b. 12 Jan 1920), American baritone. Made a remarkable début in San Francisco, 1947, when he and TEYTE (who was thirty-two years older) sang the title roles in Debussy's *Pelléas et Mélisande* in a concert performance under MONTEUX. Took part in the premières of Britten's *Billy Budd* (title role, London, 1951) and Carlisle Floyd's *The Passion of Jonathan Wade* (New York, 1962); he sang at the Metropolitan Opera from 1953.

Urhan (originally Auerhahn), **Chrétien** (b. 16 Feb 1790; d. 2 Nov 1845), French violinist and viola player. Viola soloist in the first performance of Berlioz's *Harold en Italie* in Paris, 1834. He revived interest in the neglected viola d'amore, and Meyerbeer wrote its part in *Les Huguenots*, 1836, specially for him. A member of the Paris Opera orchestra from 1814, he was also a prominent quartet player, church organist and enthusiast for Bach and Handel.

Ursuleac, Viorica (b. 26 Mar 1894; d. 22 Oct 1985), Romanian soprano. Settled in Austria. She created the title role in Strauss's *Arabella* (Dresden, 1933) and gave over 500 performances of 12 roles in his operas. She was married to KRAUSS, one of Strauss's favourite conductors; they were joint dedicatees of Strauss's opera *Friedenstag*, and she was the dedicatee of some of his songs. She also performed other modern roles as well as Wagner and Puccini. Sang at Covent Garden in 1934 (first British performance of Weinberger's *Švanda the Bagpiper*), but never in USA.

USSR Ministry of Culture Orchestra, Moscow-based orchestra founded 1982. ROZHDESTVENSKY has been principal conductor from its inception.

USSR State Chamber Orchestra, *see* MOSCOW CHAMBER ORCHESTRA.

USSR State Symphony Orchestra, Moscow-based orchestra founded 1936. Erich KLEIBER was conductor for a short time, followed by GAUK, 1936–41, Natan Rakhlin, 1941–6, IVANOV, 1946–65, and then SVETLANOV.

V

Valdengo, Giuseppe (b. 24 May 1914), Italian baritone. Prominent at La Scala and the Metropolitan, 1947–54; also sang at Glyndebourne, 1955. He appeared as SCOTTI in the film *The Great Caruso*, 1951, and recorded the title role of *Falstaff* under TOSCANINI.

Vallin, Ninon (originally Eugénie) (b. 8 Sept 1886; d. 22 Nov 1961), French soprano. Much admired by Debussy, who chose her for the first performance of his *Le Martyre de St Sébastien*, 1911; in 1914 she gave the première of his *Trois poèmes de Mallarmé* at one of their recitals together. She sang the title role in the first recording (abridged, under the composer's supervision) of Gustave Charpentier's *Louise*, and continued a distinguished operatic career in Paris into her sixtieth year.

Valls, Joaquín Cassadó, *see* CASSADÓ.

Van Allan, Richard (originally Alan Philip Jones) (b. 28 May 1935), British bass. Sang at Covent Garden and Glyndebourne (first performance of Maw's *The Rising of the Moon*, 1970). He was particularly prominent at Sadler's Wells Opera (later English National), from 1969, where he took a multiplicity of roles. Became director of the National Opera Studio, 1986, but has continued to perform.

Van Beinum, Eduard [Alexander] (b. 3 Sept 1901; d. 13 Apr 1959), Dutch conductor. Associated with the LONDON PHILHARMONIC ORCHESTRA from 1946 (principal conductor, 1949–51) as well as being principal conductor of the CONCERTGEBOUW ORCHESTRA OF AMSTERDAM, from 1945. He encouraged the young Malcolm Arnold and made the first recording of any of his works (*Beckus the Dandipratt*, 1948). A music education centre in the Netherlands was founded in his memory.

Van Cliburn, *see* CLIBURN.

Van Dam, José (originally Joseph Van Damme) (b. 25 Aug 1940), Belgian bass-baritone. Has become internationally prominent. He sang at Paris Opera from 1961 and later at other major theatres, including Covent Garden (début as Escamillo in *Carmen*, 1973). Took the role of St Francis in the first performance of Messiaen's opera *St François d'Assise*, 1983.

Van der Stucken, Frank [Valentin] (b. 15 Oct 1858; d. 16 Aug 1929), American conductor. Studied in Antwerp and Leipzig, then returned to USA. In Paris, 1889, he conducted the first concert of all-American orchestral music. Settled in Germany, 1907, and died there.

Van der Velde, Jan, *see* GAUDEAMUS QUARTET.

Van der Werff, Ivo-Jan, *see* MEDICI QUARTET.

Van Dyck, Ernest (originally Ernestus) [Maria Hubertus] (b. 2 Apr 1861; d. 31 Aug 1923), Belgian tenor. Performed as Lohengrin in the opera's first French performance, 1887, and remained a prominent Wagner singer; made his Metropolitan début as Tannhäuser, 1898. In 1892 he sang the title role in the première (in Vienna) of Massenet's *Werther*.

Van Egmond, Max (b. 1 Feb 1936), Dutch bass-baritone (born in Java). Won vocal competition at 's Hertogenbosch, 1959. He became noted in Bach, for example as Jesus on a recording of the *St John Passion* under HARNONCOURT. Toured USA and Canada. He took part in the first recording of Lully's opera *Alceste*, 1974.

Vaness, Carol (b. 27 July 1952), American soprano. Made her débuts at Glyndebourne (Donna Anna in *Don Giovanni*, also recorded) and Covent Garden (Mimì in *La Bohème*) in 1982 and at the Metropolitan in 1984 (Armida in Handel's *Rinaldo*). In London she sang the title role in what was claimed as the most complete performance and recording of Monteverdi's *L'incoronazione di Poppea*, 1988.

Van Evera, Emily, *see* PARROTT.

Van Hout, Lucien, *see* YSAŸE QUARTET.

Vanini, Francesca, *see* BOSCHI.

Van Kempen, Paul, *see* KEMPEN.

Vanni-Marcoux, *see* MARCOUX.

Van Otterloo, [Jan] Willem (b. 27 Dec 1907; d. 27 July 1978), Dutch conductor, also composer. As conductor of the RESIDENTIE ORCHESTRA OF THE HAGUE, 1949–73, established its high rank. He continued to work in Europe while he was conductor (later chief guest conductor) of the MELBOURNE SYMPHONY ORCHESTRA, 1967–71. Appointed conductor of the SYDNEY SYMPHONY ORCHESTRA, 1973. He was killed in a car accident in Melbourne.

Van Remoortel, Edouard (b. 30 May 1926; d. 16 May 1977), Belgian conductor, previously cellist. Conducted the Belgian National Orchestra, 1951–8, the ST LOUIS SYMPHONY ORCHESTRA, 1958–62, and the orchestra of Monte Carlo Opera. He made many recordings, including some with SZERYNG.

Van Rooy, Anton (originally Antonius) [Maria Josephus] (b. 1 Jan 1870; d. 28 Nov 1932), Dutch baritone. One of the most distinguished Wagner singers of his day, especially as Wotan in *The Ring*. He sang at Bayreuth from 1897 and the Metropolitan from 1898. His association with Bayreuth came to an end after he participated in the 'pirated' *Parsifal*, which constituted its first US performance, 1903.

Van Zandt, Marie (b. 8 Oct 1861; d. 31 Dec 1919), American soprano. When only seventeen, appeared in Turin as Zerlina in *Don Giovanni* and in London as Amina in Bellini's *La sonnambula*. Delibes wrote the title role of his opera *Lakmé* for her; she performed in its première (Paris), 1883, and in its first London performance, 1885. After her one Metropolitan season, 1891, she sang only occasionally.

Varady, Julia (b. 1 Sept 1941), Romanian soprano. Prominent at Bavarian State Opera in Munich from 1972 in such roles as Donna Anna (*Don Giovanni*) and Strauss's Arabella. She made her British début with Scottish Opera in Gluck's *Alceste*, 1974. Became the fourth wife, 1977, of FISCHER-DIESKAU, with whom she has recorded rare Spohr songs. She was the soloist in the first performance of Reimann's Requiem, 1982.

Varga, Gilbert, *see* VARGA, TIBOR.

Varga, Tibor (b. 4 July 1921), Hungarian-born British violinist. Studied with HUBAY and FLESCH. He founded a chamber orchestra in his name at Detmold (Germany), in 1954, and a festival and summer academy at Sion (Switzerland), 1964. His son Gilbert Varga (b. 1952) is a conductor.

Varnay, Astrid [Ibolyka Maria] (b. 25 Apr 1918), Swedish-born American soprano of Hungarian parentage. Taken to USA as a child. Her distinguished career in Wagner began in 1941 when she deputized without rehearsal for Lotte LEHMANN as Sieglinde in *Die Walküre* at the Metropolitan; performed at Bayreuth from its post-war reopening, 1951. She sang in the first performances of Orff's *Oedipus der Tyrann*, 1959, and Reimann's *Lear*, 1978 (as Cordelia; also recorded).

Varviso, Silvio (b. 26 Feb 1924), Swiss conductor. Active mainly in opera, for example at Basle, San Francisco (first US performance of Britten's *Billy Budd*, 1960), the Metropolitan, from 1961, and Covent Garden, from 1962. He was chief conductor of Royal Swedish Opera, 1965–72; became music director of Paris Opera in 1980, but resigned the following year.

Vásáry, Tamás (b. 11 Aug 1933), Hungarian-born pianist, also from 1970 conductor; became Swiss citizen 1971. Left Hungary on 1956 uprising. He first played in London 1961, New York 1972; has performed and recorded much Chopin and Liszt, and conducted major orchestras. He was music director of the NORTHERN SINFONIA, 1979–82, and became principal conductor of the BOURNEMOUTH SINFONIETTA in 1989.

Vaughan, Denis [Edward] (b. 6 June 1926), Australian conductor and scholar. Worked as assistant to BEECHAM, 1953, and other conductors; later formed his own orchestra in Naples, 1972. In 1959 he exposed discrepancies between the manuscripts and modern scores of Verdi and Puccini.

Vaughan, Elizabeth (b. 12 Mar 1936), British soprano. Made her operatic début with Welsh National Opera and from 1961 sang at Covent Garden, notably as Abigaille in Verdi's *Nabucco*, 1973. She first appeared at the Metropolitan as Donna Elvira in *Don Giovanni*, 1972.

Vaurabourg, Andrée (b. 8 Sept 1894; d. 18 July 1980), Swiss pianist. Married the composer Honegger, 1926, and (as well as composing herself) gave the first performance of many of his works, including the (solo) Toccata and Variations, 1916, and the Concertino (dedicated to her), 1925. She also taught counterpoint at the Paris Conservatory, where her pupils included BOULEZ.

Vázsonyi, Bálint (b. 7 Mar 1936), Hungarian-born American pianist. Left Hungary during the 1956 uprising and settled in USA. A soloist and teacher (Indiana University, 1978), he also wrote a biography of the composer Ernst von Dohnányi, 1971. In 1977 in London (having previously done so in New York) he performed from memory Beethoven's thirty-two sonatas (in chronological order) within two days.

Veasey, Josephine (b. 10 July 1930), British mezzo-soprano. Sang in the chorus of Covent Garden before becoming one of its admired soloists in such roles as Octavian (*Der Rosenkavalier*) and Dido (Berlioz's *Les Troyens*); made her Metropolitan début as Fricka in *Das Rheingold*, 1968. She was the Emperor in the first performance of Henze's *We Come to the River*, 1976. CBE, 1970.

Vecsey, Ferenc (Germanized as Franz von) (b. 23 Mar 1893; d. 6 Apr 1935), Hungarian violinist. Pupil of HUBAY and JOACHIM. A child prodigy, he performed in London in 1904 and New York in 1905; developed a notable career, which was cut off by early death. Sibelius's Violin Concerto was published with a dedication to him, though its first performance was given by HALÍŘ.

Vedernikov, Alexander [Filipyevich] (b. 23 Dec 1927), Russian bass. Studied in USSR and Italy. He sang at the Kirov Theatre, Leningrad, and from 1959 at the Bolshoi. His roles included Dosifey in Musorgsky's *Khovanshchina* and Konchak in Borodin's *Prince Igor* (also recorded). Performed at La Scala, 1961, and elsewhere in the West.

Végh, Sándor (b. 17 May 1905), Hungarian-born violinist, naturalized French 1953. Pupil of HUBAY. He became noted as soloist and quartet player: member of the HUNGARIAN QUARTET and later the VÉGH QUARTET. Performed with many distinguished musicians, including CASALS at the Prades Festival; conducted chamber orchestras and taught in various centres. Founded the Prussia Cove summer course in Cornwall, 1971. Hon. CBE, 1988.

Végh Quartet, Hungarian string quartet founded 1940. Original members were VÉGH, Sándor Zöldy, Georges Janzer and Paul Szabó; in 1978 Philip Nägeli and GIURANNA joined as second violin and viola. The group was based in Switzerland after World War II; disbanded in 1980.

Velde, Jan van der, *see* GAUDEAMUS QUARTET.

Velluti, Giovanni Battista (b. 28 Jan 1781; d. 22 Jan 1861), Italian male soprano (castrato). When he first sang in London in 1825, twenty-five years after the previous castrato, his audience was shocked at the strange phenomenon. Later worked there as a theatre manager, though without success.

Vengerova, Isabella [Afanasyevna] (b. 1 Mar 1877; d. 7 Feb 1956), Russian pianist. Pupil of LESCHETIZKY and YESIPOVA. She taught at the St Petersburg Conservatory, 1913–21. Settled in USA (début in concerto, 1925), where she renewed her distinction as teacher; her students included BERNSTEIN and Samuel Barber.

Verbrugghen, Henri (b. 1 Aug 1873; d. 12 Nov 1934), Belgian violinist and conductor. Studied with HUBAY and YSAŸE. He gave the first British performance of Sibelius's Violin Concerto, 1907. In 1915 went to Australia to work as conductor and conservatory director in Sydney. He conducted the MINNEAPOLIS SYMPHONY ORCHESTRA, 1923–31.

Verhulst, Johannes [Josephus Hermanus] (b. 19 Mar 1816; d. 17 Jan 1891), Dutch conductor, also composer. Became a friend of Mendelssohn and Schumann in Germany. He was an influential conductor in Amsterdam from 1864.

Verkoeyen, Jos, *see* GAUDEAMUS QUARTET.

Verne (originally Wurm), **Adela** (b. 27 Feb 1877; d. 5 Feb 1952), British pianist, sister of Mathilde VERNE and Marie WURM. Studied with her sister Mathilde and with Marie Schumann (daughter of the composer and Clara SCHUMANN); she also had lessons from PADEREWSKI. Made her London début 1891; she partnered ELMAN and YSAŸE, and toured USA. A fourth sister, Alice Verne (1868–1958), was also a pianist.

Verne, Alice, *see* VERNE, ADELA.

Verne (originally Wurm), **Mathilde** (b. 25 May 1865; d. 4 June 1936), British pianist, sister of Adela VERNE and Marie WURM. Having studied with Clara SCHUMANN in Frankfurt, became a popular London performer; she and Adela played Mozart's Concerto for two pianos at the Proms, 1903. Taught Queen Elizabeth the Queen Mother.

Verrett, Shirley (b. 31 May 1931), American mezzo-soprano. Notably successful in a wide repertory ranging from Weill to Meyerbeer (Selika in *L'Africaine*, Paris Opera, 1973); she performed at Covent Garden from 1966. At the first Metropolitan performance of Berlioz's *Les Troyens*, 1973, she sang both Cassandra and Dido.

Vestris (née Bartolozzi), **Lucia Elizabeth** (b. 3 Jan or 2 Mar 1797; d. 8 Aug 1856), British contralto. Deserted after a few years of marriage by the dancer Auguste-Armand Vestris, she established a major presence in London opera. Sang leading roles in the first British performances of *La gazza ladra*, 1821, *La donna del lago*, 1823, and other Rossini operas, and was Fatima in the première of Weber's *Oberon*, 1826. She also acted in spoken drama and from 1831 was a London theatre manager.

Viardot-Garcia (née García), [Michelle Ferdinande] **Pauline** (b. 18 July 1821; d. 18 May 1910), French mezzo-soprano (also sang some soprano roles); also composer. Daughter of Manuel GARCÍA (I), who died when she was eleven. She had piano lessons from LISZT. Visited Russia, 1843, and was the first foreigner to sing Glinka's songs in Russian. Pre-eminent in European opera, she triumphed as Fidès in Meyerbeer's *Le Prophète* (Paris, 1849), written for her; sang the title role of Gluck's *Orpheus* more than 150 times in the edition Berlioz made for her in 1859; helped the young Gounod by singing in his first opera, *Sapho*, 1851, and was the dedicatee of Saint-Saëns's *Samson et Dalila*. She also gave early performances of Brahms's Alto Rhapsody. After retiring from the stage, 1863, she continued to teach and compose. The Russian novelist Turgenev, after falling in love with her in 1843, lived most of his life in her married household.

Vickers, Jon (originally Jonathan) [Stewart] (b. 29 Oct 1926), Canadian tenor. During his first Covent Garden season, 1957, sang Aeneas in the London première of Berlioz's *Les Troyens*. Recorded this role as well as Tristan; his other distinguished roles include Otello. He performed at Bayreuth from 1958 and the Metropolitan from 1960 (Canio in *Pagliacci*).

Victorian Symphony Orchestra, *see* MELBOURNE SYMPHONY ORCHESTRA.

Vienna Philharmonic Orchestra, Austrian orchestra founded 1842. Functions also as the orchestra of Vienna State Opera (formerly Vienna Court Opera). Its principal conductors (though from the late 1920s not necessarily on permanent contracts) have included the composer Otto Nicolai, 1842–8, Hans RICHTER, 1875–98, MAHLER, 1898–1901, WEINGARTNER, 1908–27, FURTWÄNGLER, 1927–30, and KRAUSS, 1930–33. Among its prominent conductors after World War II have been KARAJAN, BÖHM, SOLTI, BERNSTEIN and ABBADO.

Vienna Symphony Orchestra, Austrian orchestra founded 1900. Took present name only in 1919. Principal conductors have included SAWALLISCH, 1958–69, GIULINI, 1973–6, and ROZHDESTVENSKY, 1982–3; at some periods it has depended on guest conductors. It should not be confused with the more illustrious VIENNA PHILHARMONIC.

Vieuxtemps, Henry (b. 17 Feb 1820; d. 6 June 1881), Belgian violinist, also composer. Studied with BÉRIOT. He was highly successful throughout Western Europe (London début 1834) and in Russia and USA (three tours). Encouraged by Paganini, Schumann and Berlioz, he finally accepted a professorship at the Brussels Conservatory, 1871, and continued teaching there till 1879. His students included YSAŸE and HUBAY (who was with him when he died in a sanatorium in Algeria). His compositions include seven violin concertos.

Vignoles, Roger [Hutton] (b. 12 July 1945), British pianist. From 1967 has accompanied leading singers, including STREICH, SÖDERSTRÖM and TE KANAWA, and such instrumentalists as Heinrich SCHIFF (Salzburg, 1984) and PAUK. He has also worked as opera répétiteur.

Vinay, Ramón (b. 31 Aug 1912), Chilean tenor, formerly baritone. Made tenor début in Mexico City, 1943. He sang Otello more than 250 times, at La Scala (début, 1947), Salzburg, the Metropolitan, Covent Garden and elsewhere. At Bayreuth, from 1957, his roles included Tristan. He reverted to baritone towards the end of his career, when he also directed operas.

Viñes, Ricardo (b. 5 Feb 1875; d. 29 Apr 1943), Spanish pianist. Worked mainly in Paris, where he became a friend and advocate of Debussy and Ravel, and taught Poulenc. In a career overwhelmingly devoted to new music, he gave the first performances of Debussy's *Pour le piano*, 1902, and many subsequent works, Ravel's *Gaspard de la nuit*, 1908, and Tailleferre's Ballade for piano and orchestra, 1922.

Viotti, Giovanni Battista (b. 12 May 1755; d. 3 Mar 1824), Italian violinist, also composer. Made London début 1792 after fleeing from the French Revolution. He later worked again in Paris, but returned to London and died there. A pupil of the violinist–composer Pugnani, he was himself a powerful influence on the succeeding generation. Among his compositions are twenty-nine violin concertos.

Visée, Robert de (b. *c.* 1660; d. *c.* 1725), French lutenist and guitarist, also singer. Became a court musician to Louis XIV about 1680, and was succeeded by his son in 1720. He wrote celebrated works for five-string guitar and other music.

Visetti, Alberto [Antonio] (b. 13 May 1846; d. 10 July 1928), Italian pianist and singing teacher. Served the Empress Eugénie (wife of Napoleon III) in Paris, and on the fall of the Empire, 1870, came as she did to Britain. He conducted a concert series at Bath, composed, wrote and taught at the Royal College of Music.

Vishnevskaya, Galina [Pavlovna] (b. 25 Oct 1926), Russian soprano. Vishnevsky was her first husband's name, and in 1955 she married ROSTROPOVICH. She became a major star at the Bolshoi, where she made her début 1953 as Tatyana in Tchaikovsky's *Yevgeny Onegin*. Her first appearances at the Metropolitan, 1961, and Covent Garden, 1962, were both as Aida. Gave the première of Britten's cycle *The Poet's Echo*, 1965, written for her and her husband. The solo soprano part in his *War Requiem* was also intended for her, but she was politically prevented from singing in its first performance, 1962. In 1974 she and Rostropovich were obliged to leave USSR; settled in USA. She was stage director of a student opera at Aldeburgh, 1988. Returned to USSR as visitor, 1990.

Vito, Gioconda de, *see* DE VITO.

Vlach, Josef, *see* VLACH QUARTET.

Vlach Quartet, Prague-based string quartet. Made début 1951. Its original members were Joseph Vlach, Václav Snítil, Soběslav Soukup and Viktor Moučka. Soukup was succeeded by Jaroslav Motlík, 1952, then Josef Kodousek, 1954; Jiři Hanzl became second violinist in 1970.

Vogl, Heinrich (b. 15 Jan 1845; d. 21 Apr 1900), German tenor. Noted in Wagner: he was a distinguished Tristan and created the roles of Loge in *Das Rheingold*, 1869, and Siegmund in *Die Walküre*, 1870. Sang both Loge and Siegmund in London's first production of *The Ring*, 1882, and also performed in Wagner at the Metropolitan. He appeared in the première of his own opera *Der Fremdling* (Munich, 1899). His wife was Therese VOGL.

Vogl, Johann Michael (b. 10 Aug 1768; d. 19 Nov 1840), Austrian baritone. He was a friend and admirer of Schubert and the most distinguished early performer of his songs; sang 'Erlkönig' shortly before its publication in 1821. Also appeared in opera (created Pizarro in Beethoven's final revision of *Fidelio*, 1814) and was a composer.

Vogl (née Thoma), **Therese** (b. 2 Nov 1845; d. 29 Sept 1921), German soprano. Married Heinrich VOGL in 1868 and used his surname professionally. Admired in Wagner, she created the role of Sieglinde in *Die Walküre*, 1870, and sang Brünnhilde in the first Munich and London cycles of *The Ring*, 1878 and 1882.

Voigtschmidt, Joep, *see* GAUDEAMUS QUARTET.

Von Dohnányi, Christoph, *see* DOHNÁNYI.

Vonk, Hans (b. 18 June 1942), Dutch conductor. Held orchestral and operatic posts in the Netherlands, where he became conductor of the RESIDENTIE ORCHESTRA OF THE HAGUE in 1980, and elsewhere. He has worked with London orchestras (début 1974 with the LONDON PHILHARMONIC), and was appointed music director of DRESDEN STATE ORCHESTRA and Opera, 1985.

Von Stade, Frederica (b. 1 June 1945), American mezzo-soprano. Studied piano in Paris. She progressed from a minor part at the Metropolitan Opera (Third Boy in *Die Zauberflöte*, 1970) to a distinctive career; made Covent Garden début as Rosina in *Il barbiere*, 1975. Her recordings range from the title role in Debussy's *Pelléas et Mélisande* (under KARAJAN), 1978, to Magnolia in Kern's *Show Boat*, 1988. She was Tina in the first performance of Argento's opera *The Aspern Papers* at Dallas, 1988. Her unusual concert repertory includes duets with BLEGEN.

Von zur Mühlen, Raimund, *see* ZUR MÜHLEN.

Voss, Gerhard Ernst, *see* MELOS QUARTET.

Voss, Hermann, *see* MELOS QUARTET.

Votto, Antonino (b. 30 Oct 1896; d. 10 Sept 1985), Italian conductor, previously pianist. Worked as assistant to TOSCANINI at La Scala, then conducted *Pagliacci* at Covent Garden, 1924. He was conductor of the rare revival of Spontini's *La vestale* with CALLAS, 1954; recorded this and other works with her, including *Norma*.

Vronsky, Vitya (originally Viktoria) (b. 27 Aug 1909), Russian-born American pianist. Pupil of SCHNABEL and CORTOT in Europe. She went to USA in 1937 with her husband, Victor BABIN. As Vronsky and Babin they were among the leading piano duos; gave the first performance of Milhaud's Concerto for two pianos, 1942.

Vybiral, Břetislav, *see* JANÁČEK QUARTET.

Vyvyan, Jennifer [Brigit] (b. 13 Mar 1925; d. 5 Apr 1974), British soprano. Created the roles of Penelope Rich in Britten's *Gloriana*, 1953, and the Governess in his *The Turn of the Screw*, 1954. She was also well known in Handel and Mozart opera.

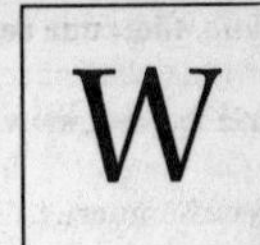

Waart, Edo de, *see* DE WAART.

Wachtel, Theodor (b. 10 Mar 1823; d. 14 Nov 1893), German tenor. Sang in Germany and from 1862 in London; twice toured USA. He was famous for his strong top register and for having displayed it more than 1,000 times in the title role of Adolphe Adam's once popular opera *Le Postillon de Longjumeau.*

Waechter, Eberhard (b. 9 July 1929), Austrian baritone. Performed at Bayreuth from 1958 (Amfortas in *Parsifal* and Wolfram in *Tannhäuser*), Covent Garden from 1956 and the Metropolitan from 1960. He recorded much opera and operetta, including *Die Fledermaus* under KARAJAN. In 1987 he became administrator of the Volksoper in Vienna, and is due also to administer the Vienna State Opera from 1991.

Wagner (or Jachmann-Wagner), **Johanna** (b. 13 Oct 1826; d. 16 Oct 1894), German soprano. Adopted daughter of Richard Wagner's brother Albert. When just nineteen, she sang Elisabeth in the first performance of *Tannhäuser*, 1845; then studied with VIARDOT-GARCIA in Paris. Later she was known both as singer and as actress in spoken tragedy.

Wagner, Roger (b. 16 Jan 1914), French-born American conductor. Taken to USA as a child, but studied in Paris (organ with Marcel DUPRÉ). His professional choir, the Roger Wagner Chorale (founded 1946), became internationally known. In 1973 he conducted some of the opening events of the John F. Kennedy Center, Washington. Conductor of the choir of Radio France, 1977–9.

Wagner, Siegfried [Helferich Richard] (b. 6 June 1869; d. 4 Aug 1930), German conductor, also composer. Son of Richard Wagner. He both conducted and directed productions at his family's Bayreuth Festival, and became festival director after his mother's death in 1908. The stage directors Wieland and Wolfgang Wagner are his sons.

Wakasugi, Hiroshi (b. 31 May 1935), Japanese conductor. Held symphonic and choral posts in Japan, then settled in Germany, where he was conductor of the Cologne Radio Orchestra, 1977–83, and also worked in opera (Deutsche Oper am Rhein). In 1986 he became music director of the TONHALLE ORCHESTRA in Zurich.

Wakefield, [Augusta] **Mary** (b. 19 Aug 1853; d. 16 Sept 1910), British contralto. Her introduction of a competition for vocal quartets at a small-town flower show in Westmorland, 1885, is held to mark the birth of the British competitive festival movement. Its national organization dates from 1905.

Walcha, [Arthur Emil] **Helmut** (b. 27 Oct 1907), German organist. Became blind at the age of sixteen; pupil of RAMIN. He was professor at the Frankfurt Conservatory, 1933–72. Won international fame in recitals (Royal Festival Hall, London, from 1955) and recordings, for example of all Bach's organ music; also (as harpsichordist) recorded Bach sonatas with SZERYNG.

Waldman, Maria (b. 1842; d. 6 Nov 1920), Austrian mezzo-soprano. Prized by Verdi, she sang under his baton in the first performances of his Requiem in Milan, 1874, then in Paris and, in a version specially amended for her (now standard), in London. He also conducted her as Amneris (*Aida*) in Vienna, 1875. She withdrew from the stage on her marriage, 1877.

Walker, Edyth (b. 27 Mar 1867; d. 19 Feb 1950), American mezzo-soprano. Made her début in Berlin, 1894, and became an admired Wagner singer. Having added soprano roles to her repertory, she was the first to sing Strauss's Elektra in London, 1910.

Walker, Sarah (b. 11 Mar 1943), British mezzo-soprano. Took over the doubled role of Diana/Jove in Cavalli's *Calisto* from Janet BAKER at Glyndebourne, 1970. In 1972 she began performing at Sadler's Wells Opera (later English National), where her roles have included Cornelia in Handel's *Giulio Cesare* (also recorded). Sang in the first British performance of Tippett's *The Mask of Time*, 1984 (and on recording); has appeared at Covent Garden and elsewhere.

Wallace, Ian [Bryce] (b. 10 July 1919), British bass. Trained as a lawyer. With Sadler's Wells Opera and at Glyndebourne, 1948–56, he won special success in comic roles such as Don Magnifico in Rossini's *La Cenerentola*. The title of his autobiography, *Promise Me You'll Sing Mud*, 1975, marks his association in light entertainment with Michael Flanders and Donald Swann.

Wallace, John (b. 14 Apr 1949), British trumpeter. Well known as soloist on modern and baroque trumpets. He became principal trumpet of the PHILHARMONIA ORCHESTRA, 1976; leader of the London ensembles Equale Brass and, from 1986, the Wallace Collection.

Wallace, Lucille, *see* CURZON.

Wallenstein, Alfred (b. 7 Oct 1898; d. 8 Feb 1983), American cellist and conductor. As a young man toured with Pavlova (playing the obbligato in Saint-Saëns's 'The Swan'. He was first cellist with the NEW YORK PHILHARMONIC under TOSCANINI, 1926–36. Conducted the LOS ANGELES PHILHARMONIC, 1943–56, the first American-born conductor to hold such a post with a major orchestra.

Wallerstein, Lothar (b. 6 Nov 1882; d. 13 Nov 1949), Austrian conductor and stage director. Worked in Frankfurt, Vienna and Salzburg, collaborated with Strauss in a new version of Mozart's *Idomeneo*, then was forced as a Jew to flee the Nazis. He was a member of the production staff of the Metropolitan Opera, 1941–6.

Wallfisch, Peter, *see* WALLFISCH, RAPHAEL.

Wallfisch, Raphael (b. 15 June 1953), British cellist. Studied with PIATIGORSKY in California. He has toured widely and played many new works; made the first recordings of Bax's Cello Concerto, 1986, and Strauss's Romance, 1988. He sometimes performs in a duo with his father, the pianist Peter Wallfisch (b. 1924).

Walter, Bruno (originally Bruno Walter Schlesinger) (b. 15 Sept 1876; d. 17 Feb 1962), German-born conductor; took French nationality, 1938, then American, 1946. After early work in Hamburg and Berlin, went to Vienna as MAHLER's assistant at the Court Opera; after Mahler's death he conducted the premières of his *Das Lied von der Erde*, 1911, and the Symphony no. 9, 1912. He was conductor of the GEWANDHAUS ORCHESTRA OF LEIPZIG, 1929–33, director of the Vienna State Opera, 1936–8, and a prominent conductor at the Salzburg Festival, 1925–37. Celebrated as symphonic conductor (London from 1909), especially in Mozart, he made important recordings. He was compelled as a Jew to flee Nazi Germany and Austria, but after World War II he again conducted in Vienna, where he engaged the young FERRIER.

Walter, George, *see* GOEHR.

Waltz, Gustavus (d. *c.* 1779), German bass. In London, 1732–51, sang in the first performance of *Athaliah*, 1733, and other works by Handel. He is well known because Handel is supposed to have said disparagingly of Gluck that he knew no more of counterpoint than 'my cook, Waltz', though whether the cook and the bass were the same is not known.

Wand, Günter (b. 7 Jan 1912), German conductor. As city music director in Cologne, conducted the GÜRZENICH ORCHESTRA, 1946–75; made London début 1951. He became chief conductor of the North German Radio Orchestra, 1982. Noted in symphonic repertory, he recorded all Schubert and Bruckner symphonies; also conducted the first performance of Fortner's opera *Bluthochzeit*, 1957.

Wangenheim, Volker (b. 1 July 1928), German conductor, formerly oboist. Worked as principal conductor of the Berlin Mozart Orchestra, 1950–59, later city music director in Bonn. He was principal conductor of the BOURNEMOUTH SINFONIETTA, 1977–80. Also composer.

Ward, David (b. 3 July 1929; d. 16 July 1983), British bass. Began in opera as chorus-singer and became an admired principal at Covent Garden, where he took the key role of Morosus in the first UK performance of Strauss's *Die schweigsame Frau*, 1961. Also sang at Bayreuth from 1960. Died in New Zealand.

Warfield, Sandra, *see* MCCRACKEN.

Warfield, William (b. 22 Jan 1920), American baritone. Became well known in the role of Porgy on a black American company's European tour of *Porgy and Bess*, 1952. He later worked mainly in concert and as a teacher. Married, 1952–72, to Leontyne PRICE.

Warner, H. Waldo, *see* LONDON STRING QUARTET (I).

Warrack, Guy, *see* BBC SCOTTISH SYMPHONY ORCHESTRA.

Warren (originally Warenoff), **Leonard** (b. 21 Apr 1911; d. 4 Mar 1960), American baritone. After making his Metropolitan Opera début in 1939, he became its leading Verdi baritone and also won high esteem elsewhere; sang at La Scala, 1953, and toured USSR, 1958. He died at the peak of his career during a Metropolitan performance of Verdi's *La forza del destino*.

Warsaw Philharmonic Orchestra (also known as the National Philharmonic Orchestra of Warsaw), Polish orchestra founded 1901. Principal conductors have included FITELBERG, 1909–11, PANUFNIK, 1946–7, ROWICKI, 1950–55 and 1958–77, and KORD, from 1977.

Warwick-Evans, C., *see* LONDON STRING QUARTET (I).

Watanabe, Akeo (b. 5 June 1919), Japanese conductor (mother Finnish). Studied in New York, 1950–52, having already begun his career. He was the founding conductor of the Japan Philharmonic Symphony Orchestra, 1958–68, with which he recorded all the Sibelius symphonies and several American works. Also teaches conducting.

Waterman, David, *see* ENDELLION QUARTET and WATERMAN, FANNY.

Waterman, Fanny (b. 22 Mar 1920), British pianist. Founder (with Marion Harewood) and chairman of the Leeds International Piano Competition, 1961. She has adjudicated at other competitions and written educational music. The cellist David Waterman is her nephew. OBE, 1971.

Watkinson, Andrew, *see* ENDELLION QUARTET.

Watson (née McLamore), **Claire** (b. 3 Feb 1927; d. 16 July 1986), American soprano. In opera sang principally at Munich and Covent Garden, both from 1958. She was prized in Mozart roles and others such as Ellen in Britten's *Peter Grimes*. Married to the American tenor David Thaw (b. 1928).

Watts, André (b. 20 June 1946), American pianist (mother Hungarian). Appeared on television with the NEW YORK PHILHARMONIC aged sixteen, then studied with FLEISHER. He made his London début with orchestra and his New York solo début in 1966. Being partly of black parentage he had a special conspicuousness at President Nixon's inaugural concert, 1969. In 1988 a televised concert (with MEHTA conducting) marked his twenty-fifth anniversary.

Watts, Helen [Josephine] (b. 7 Dec 1927), British contralto. Prominent in concert (Proms début 1955 in Bach) and opera. She toured USSR with Britten's English Opera Group, 1964, and sang Erda in *The Ring* at Covent Garden; made her US début in Mahler's *Kindertotenlieder* under SOLTI, 1970. CBE, 1978.

Wayenberg, Daniel [Ernest Joseph Carel] (b. 11

Oct 1929), Dutch pianist (born in Paris). Studied in Paris with LONG. He made his public début in 1949 after winning the Long–Thibaud Competition; US début 1953. His repertory includes Gershwin and Stockhausen. Also composer.

Weathers, Felicia (b. 13 Aug 1937), American soprano. After her marriage used the surname Weathers-Bakony. She sang opera principally in Munich and Hamburg (first performance of Schuller's *The Visitation*, 1967), but also at the Metropolitan, 1965, and elsewhere. Among black singers she was one of the first to win recognition in such standard roles as Violetta (*La traviata*).

Webber, Julian Lloyd, *see* LLOYD WEBBER.

Weber, [Maria] **Aloysia** [Louise Antonia] (b. between 1759 and 1761; d. 8 June 1839), German soprano, sister of Josepha WEBER. Famous for her work with Mozart, who wrote for her various arias and a role in his opera *Der Schauspieldirektor*, 1786. She was distantly related to the composer Carl Maria von Weber.

Weber, [Maria] **Josepha** (b. 1758–9; d. 29 Dec 1819), German soprano, sister of Aloysia WEBER. Mozart wrote for her the exceptionally high role of the Queen of the Night in *Die Zauberflöte*, 1791. Her second husband was the baritone Sebastian Mayer (1773–1835).

Weber, Ludwig (b. 29 July 1899; d. 9 Dec 1974), Austrian bass. Made his Vienna début 1920 and sang at Covent Garden in 1936 and again after World War II, principally in Wagner. He also performed at Bayreuth and on the first recording of Strauss's *Daphne*, 1948. Became professor in Salzburg, 1961.

Weber, Margrit (b. 24 Feb 1924), Swiss pianist, formerly organist. Noted in modern works, she gave the first performance of Martinů's 'Fantasia concertante' (piano concerto no. 5), 1959, and Stravinsky's Movements for piano and orchestra, 1960. Teacher in Zurich.

Weidinger, Anton (b. 9 June 1767; d. 20 Sept 1852), Austrian trumpeter. Member of the court opera orchestra in Vienna; he played the newly evolved keyed trumpet, and for him Haydn wrote his Trumpet Concerto, 1796. Made a concert tour to Germany, France and Britain in 1803.

Weikert, Rolf (b. 10 Nov 1940), Austrian conductor. After winning a Copenhagen competition, 1965, worked in Bonn, Frankfurt and elsewhere. He was director of the MOZARTEUM ORCHESTRA in Salzburg, 1981–4, and in 1983 became music director of Zurich Opera.

Weikl, Bernd (b. 29 July 1942), Austrian baritone. From 1973 sang with Hamburg State Opera and at Bayreuth. A noted Wagner singer, he made his Metropolitan début as Wolfram in *Tannhäuser*, 1977. His varied recordings include the first of Pfitzner's opera *Palestrina*, 1973.

Weilerstein, Donald, *see* CLEVELAND QUARTET.

Weingartner, [Paul] **Felix,** Edler (Count) von Münzberg (b. 2 June 1863; d. 7 May 1942), German conductor, also composer. As a young man won Liszt's commendation as composer. He was conductor (succeeding MAHLER) of Vienna Court Opera, 1908–11, and conducted the VIENNA PHILHARMONIC concerts, 1908–27. His unsurpassed international reputation as a symphonic conductor (London début 1898, New York 1904) was supported by his recordings of Beethoven symphonies in the 1930s. In 1935 gave the first performance of Bizet's Symphony in C (written 1855); he made a famous orchestral arrangement of Weber's *Invitation to the Dance*.

Weir, Gillian [Constance] (b. 17 Jan 1941), New Zealand organist, also harpsichordist. In 1965 made her Proms début in Poulenc's Concerto, and she has led an exceptional career of international tours and teaching, without church posts. Played complete cycles of Messiaen's works in Britain and Australia; her many first performances include concertos by Holloway, 1967, and Mathias, 1984. Resident in UK. CBE, 1989.

Weiss, Amalie, *see* JOACHIM.

Weissenberg, Alexis [Sigismond] (b. 29 July 1929), Bulgarian-born pianist, naturalized French 1956. Studied in Sofia, Jerusalem and New York, where in 1948 he won the Leventritt Competition and made his concerto début under SZELL. His recordings include all Beethoven's concertos under KARAJAN. Also a composer.

Weldon, George (b. 5 June 1906; d. 16 Aug 1963). British conductor. After conducting the CITY OF BIRMINGHAM SYMPHONY ORCHESTRA, 1943–51, became deputy to BARBIROLLI with the HALLÉ ORCHESTRA. Died in South Africa while engaged with the Cape Town Orchestra.

Weldon (née Thomas), **Georgina** (b. 24 May 1837; d. 11 Jan 1914). British soprano. Her association with Gounod, who lived at her London house, 1871–4, was marked by scandal and, afterwards, legal acrimony. She sang in the first performance of Gounod's patriotic cantata *Gallia* (Paris), 1871. Also composed songs and nourished ambitions as an educationist.

Welitsch (originally Velichkova), **Ljuba** (b. 10 July 1913). Bulgarian soprano. Based in Vienna. Her most famous role was Salome, which she first sang under Strauss himself on his eightieth birthday, 1944, and repeated in 1947 at her Metropolitan début and with Vienna State Opera at Covent Garden. Also performed Mozart, Puccini and Janáček.

Weller, Walter (b. 30 Nov 1939). Austrian conductor and violinist. Worked as orchestral and quartet leader in Vienna before making his début as conductor, 1966; he first appeared in London 1973. Principal conductor of the ROYAL LIVERPOOL PHILHARMONIC ORCHESTRA, 1977–80, and the ROYAL PHILHARMONIC ORCHESTRA, 1980–85. He also conducts opera. In 1989 in London conducted a reconstructed 'Beethoven's Tenth Symphony'.

Welser-Möst, Franz, *see* LONDON PHILHARMONIC ORCHESTRA.

Welsh, Moray [Meston] (b. 1 Mar 1947). British cellist. Studied with ROSTROPOVICH in Moscow and made London début 1972. His work as soloist and chamber-music player includes the first performance of Lennox Berkeley's Cello Concerto, 1982.

Wenzinger, August (b. 14 Nov 1905). Swiss cellist, viol player and conductor. Influential in establishing 'authentic' performance, particularly at the Schola Cantorum Basiliensis (an academy in Basle), 1934–70. He made many recordings and gave the first performance of Frank Martin's Ballade for cello, 1949.

Werba, Erik (b. 23 May 1918). Austrian pianist, also composer and writer on music. He is best known as accompanist to GEDDA, LUDWIG and SEEFRIED, among other singers, and as teacher of song-accompaniment courses in Salzburg, Tokyo and elsewhere.

Werff, Ivo-Jan van der, *see* MEDICI QUARTET.

White, John, *see* ALBERNI QUARTET.

White, Robert (b. 27 Oct 1940). American tenor of Irish descent. Studied in Paris and New York. He worked in early music with GREENBERG and appeared in the (televised) première of Menotti's *The Labyrinth*, 1963. Developed a speciality in Irish song, ranging from a homage to MCCORMACK (BBC, 1984) to the classical arrangements by Beethoven and others.

White, Willard (b. 10 Oct 1946). Jamaican bass. One of the very few West Indian singers to become established in opera, his roles have included Colline in *La Bohème* (New York City Opera, 1974, and Glyndebourne, 1978) and Wotan in *Die Walküre* (Scottish Opera, 1989) as well as Porgy in *Porgy and Bess* (Glyndebourne, 1986, and two recordings). Also acted the title role of Shakespeare's *Othello*, 1989.

Whitehill, Clarence [Eugene] (b. 5 Nov 1871; d. 18 Dec 1932). American bass-baritone. Created the title role in Delius's opera *Koanga* (Elberfeld, Germany), 1904, and sang Wotan in *The Ring* under Hans RICHTER at Covent Garden. He went on to lead a distinguished career at the Metropolitan, 1909–32.

Whiteman, Paul (b. 28 Mar 1890; d. 29 Dec 1967). American bandleader. Gave the first performance of Gershwin's *Rhapsody in Blue*, 1924, with the composer at the piano. He toured Europe with his band, 1926; pioneered the concept of 'symphonic jazz'.

Whitney, Robert S[utton] (b. 9 July 1904; d. 22 Nov 1986). American conductor (born in Britain). As founding conductor of the LOUISVILLE ORCHESTRA, 1937–67, he gave the first performances of many newly commissioned works, including Carter's Variations for Orchestra, 1956, and Copland's Orchestral Variations, 1958. He also made the first recordings of these and many others.

Whittaker, W[illiam] **G**[illies] (b. 23 July 1876; d. 5 July 1944), British conductor. Pioneered historically based performance of old choral music, especially with his Newcastle Bach Choir from 1915. It gave the first modern complete performance of Byrd's Great Service, 1924, and toured Germany, 1927. Also composer.

Wich, Günther (b. 23 May 1928), German conductor. Known for performing progressive opera repertory as director at Hanover, 1961–5, and Düsseldorf/Duisburg, 1965–80; he brought the latter company to the Edinburgh Festival, 1972, where it gave the first British performance of Bernd Alois Zimmermann's *Die Soldaten*. Also has appeared as guest conductor (orchestral and operatic) in London and Paris.

Widdop, Walter (b. 19 Apr 1892; d. 6 Sept 1949), British tenor. His operatic career, from 1923, embraced Wagner's heroic parts; in 1924 he sang the title role of *Siegfried* at Covent Garden (where he later created Bagoas in Eugene Goossens's *Judith*, 1929). Performed an excerpt from *Lohengrin* at the Proms the night before he died.

Widor, Charles-Marie [Jean-Albert] (b. 24 Feb 1844; d. 12 Mar 1937), French organist. In 1869 was appointed church organist at St Sulpice, an important Paris post, and he remained there for sixty-four years. Famous as soloist and teacher (succeeded Franck at the Paris Conservatory); he composed orchestral and stage works as well as ten 'symphonies' for organ.

Wieck, Clara, *see* SCHUMANN, CLARA.

Wiener, Otto (b. 13 Feb 1911), Austrian baritone. Performed as concert soloist from 1939. He sang Dr Schön on the first recording of Berg's *Lulu*, 1952, and made his opera stage début 1953; joined Vienna State Opera, 1957. He became noted in Wagner at Bayreuth, Covent Garden (Sachs in *Die Meistersinger*, 1963) and elsewhere.

Wieniawski, Henryk (also known by French form, Henri) (b. 10 July 1835; d. 31 Mar 1880), Polish violinist, also composer. Trained in Paris, where he made his début 1848. He became one of the most celebrated performers of his time. Toured in USA with Anton RUBINSTEIN, 1872, was professor at Brussels, 1875–7, and, despite ill health, began a Russian tour with the singer ARTÔT in 1879. Died in Moscow. His brother Józef Wieniawski (1837–1912) was a pianist; his daughter Irene (1880–1932), who became Lady Dean Paul by marriage, was a composer under the name Poldowski.

Wieniawski, Józef, *see* WIENIAWSKI, HENRYK.

Wiesel, Uzi, *see* TEL AVIV QUARTET.

Wihan, Hanuš (also known by German form, Hans) (b. 5 June 1855; d. 1 May 1920), Bohemian cellist. Celebrated as soloist and quartet player (with the BOHEMIAN QUARTET). He was the dedicatee of the young Strauss's Cello Sonata and gave its première, 1883; Dvořák's Cello Concerto was also written for him, 1894–5, though it was first performed by Leo STERN.

Wild, Earl (b. 26 Nov 1915), American pianist. Had youthful success in New York under TOSCANINI, 1942. He concentrated on performing Liszt's and other works in the romantic style; made London début 1973. He commissioned and gave the first performances of concertos by Creston, 1949, and Marvin David Levy (under SOLTI), 1970.

Wilde, David [Clark] (b. 25 Feb 1935), British pianist. Pupil of SOLOMON, BOULANGER and others. He won a Liszt–Bartók competition in Budapest, 1961, and has performed as soloist (Proms début 1961) and chamber-music player. He is also a college professor in Hanover, a television presenter, composer and occasional conductor.

Wilhelmj, August [Emil Daniel Ferdinand Viktor] (b. 21 Sept 1845; d. 22 Jan 1908), German violinist. Won a far-reaching reputation: he made his London début 1866, led the violins at Wagner's first Bayreuth Festival, 1876, and played before the harem of the Sultan of Turkey, 1885. Taught in London from 1894 and died there. His arrangement of the so-called Air on the G string (his title) popularized this Bach melody.

Wiłkomirska, Maria, *see* WIŁKOMIRSKA, WANDA.

Wiłkomirska, Wanda (b. 11 Jan 1929), Polish violinist. Having won prizes at competitions in Geneva and elsewhere, made London début 1950, New York 1960. Her enterprising repertory has included Britten's Concerto and Penderecki's Capriccio (of which she gave the first performance, 1967). She formed a trio with her stepbrother Kazimierz Wiłkomirski (b. 1900), cellist, and her stepsister Maria Wiłkomirska (b. 1904), pianist. Settled in the West in 1983.

Wiłkomirski, Kazimierz, *see* WIŁKOMIRSKA, WANDA.

Willcocks, David [Valentine] (b. 30 Dec 1919), British organist and conductor. Noted in choral music; organist of Worcester Cathedral, 1950–57, director of music at King's College, Cambridge, 1957–73, conductor of the Bach Choir in London, from 1960, and director of the Royal College of Music, 1974–84. He conducted the first British performance of Duruflé's Requiem, 1952. Knighted, 1977.

Williams, John [Christopher] (b. 24 Apr 1941), Australian guitarist. Based in Britain from 1952. He took courses with Segovia in Siena, and after his formal London début, 1958, developed a distinguished career. Also plays jazz and formed his own semi-pop group, Sky; duo partner of BREAM. He gave the first performance of Previn's Guitar Concerto, 1971, and other new works. OBE, 1980.

Williams, John [Tower] (b. 8 Feb 1932), American conductor, also composer. Best known for his film music, for example *Star Wars*, 1977, which he conducted himself. He has successfully incorporated such works into his concert repertory as conductor of the BOSTON POPS ORCHESTRA, from 1980.

Williams, Louise, *see* CHILINGIRIAN QUARTET and ENDELLION QUARTET.

Windgassen, Fritz, *see* WINDGASSEN, WOLFGANG.

Windgassen, Wolfgang (b. 26 June 1914; d. 8 Sept 1974), German tenor (born in France). Became a leading singer of Wagner's heroic roles at Bayreuth, 1951–70, Covent Garden, from 1955, and the Metropolitan. From 1969 he worked as opera stage director and administrator. His father, Fritz Windgassen (1883–1963), was also a tenor.

Winograd, Arthur, *see* JUILLIARD QUARTET.

Wise, David, *see* BROSA QUARTET.

Wislocki, Stanisław, *see* POLISH RADIO SYMPHONY ORCHESTRA.

Wit, Anton, *see* POLISH RADIO SYMPHONY ORCHESTRA.

Witte, Erich (b. 19 Mar 1911), German tenor. Made début 1930, and from 1941 was active in Berlin (title role in the first German performance of Britten's *Peter Grimes*, 1947); he was noted in Wagner and Strauss. Also worked as stage director and produced *Die Meistersinger* at Covent Garden in 1957.

Wittenberg, Jan, *see* GAUDEAMUS QUARTET.

Wittgenstein, Paul (b. 5 Nov 1887; d. 3 Mar 1961), Austrian-born pianist, naturalized American 1946. Lost the use of his right arm in World War I and developed an extraordinarily skilful one-handed technique. He gave the first performances of specially commissioned concertos by Ravel, 1931, Britten ('Diversions', 1942) and others. The philosopher Ludwig Wittgenstein was his brother.

Wittich, Marie (b. 27 May 1868; d. 4 Aug 1931), German soprano. Made precocious operatic début singing the mezzo-soprano role of Azucena in *Il trovatore* aged fourteen. She was then chosen for the title role in the Dresden première of *Salome*, 1905. Sang also at Bayreuth and Covent Garden.

Wixell, Ingvar (b. 7 May 1931), Swedish baritone. Visited London with Royal Swedish Opera, 1955; he later sang at Glyndebourne, 1972, the Metropolitan, 1973 (début as Rigoletto), and elsewhere. Sang the role of Pentheus in Henze's *The Bassarids*, 1966, but is best known in Italian roles.

Wöldike, Mogens (b. 5 July 1897; d. 20 Oct 1988), Danish conductor and organist. Studied with Carl Nielsen. In the 1950s he was a pioneer conductor of baroque music on record in a conscientiously historical style. Conducted the DANISH RADIO SYMPHONY ORCHESTRA, 1950–67, and was organist of Copenhagen Cathedral, 1959–72.

Wolff, Albert [Louis] (b. 19 Jan 1884; d. 20 Feb 1970), French conductor, also composer. From 1908 prominently (but intermittently) active at the Opéra-Comique, and was also a symphonic conductor; spent the period 1940–45 in South America, then returned to Opéra-Comique. A champion of French composers, he gave the first performances of Roussel's Symphony no. 4, 1935, and of Poulenc's *Les Mamelles de Tirésias*, 1947.

Wölfl (also spelt Woelfl and Wölffl), **Joseph** (b. 24 Dec 1773; d. 21 May 1812), Austrian pianist, also composer. His piano show-pieces such as the sonata *'Non plus ultra'* (Nothing beyond this) were famous in their time. In Vienna in the late 1790s he was held to rival Beethoven in keyboard virtuosity.

Wolstenholme, William (b. 24 Feb 1865; d. 23 July 1931), British organist. Blind from birth; helped by Elgar, who gave him violin lessons. He was a recitalist (also composer), and visited USA, 1908. Held a London church post from 1926.

Wood, Henry J[oseph] (b. 3 Mar 1869; d. 19 Aug 1944), British conductor, also organist and piano accompanist. Among the first Britons to master modern techniques of rehearsal and interpretation, he won fame with the newly established Queen's Hall concerts and particularly the Promenade concerts, 1895–1944, which now bear his name. His Proms programmes contained much new music, including the premières of Schoenberg's Five Orchestral Pieces, 1912, and Vaughan Williams's *Serenade to Music* (composed in his honour), 1938, and the first British performance of Mahler's Symphony no. 1, 1903. In his early career he conducted opera, and gave the first British performance of Tchaikovsky's *Yevgeny Onegin*, 1892, and the première of Stanford's *Shamus O'Brien*, 1896. Among his orchestral arrangements is Bach's Toccata and Fugue in D minor (under the name Paul Klenovsky). (*See also* LAMOUREUX and WOODGATE.)

Woodgate, Leslie [Hubert] (b. 15 Apr 1902; d. 18 May 1961), British conductor, also composer, organist and writer of textbooks. As conductor of the BBC's professional and amateur choruses, from 1934, he became familiar to countless radio listeners. He conducted the first performances of Britten's *A Boy was Born*, 1934, and Walton's *Where Does the Uttered Music Go?* (in memory of WOOD) at the Proms, 1946.

Woodward, Roger [Robert] (b. 20 Dec 1942), Australian pianist. Studied in Sydney, London (with KABOS) and Warsaw; he made his Warsaw and London débuts 1967, and won the Warsaw International Chopin Competition, 1970. To his classical repertory he adds Sculthorpe and other Australian composers as well as Takemitsu's *Far Away*, 1973, and Xenakis's *Mists*, 1981, both dedicated to him. OBE, 1980.

Woodworth, G[eorge] **Wallace** (b. 6 Nov 1902; d. 18 July 1969), American conductor and musicologist. Educated at Harvard and London. He exercised a major influence on US musical education, partly through his conductorship of the Harvard Glee Club (male choir), 1933–58, with which he toured Europe, 1956.

Wöss, Kurt (b. 2 May 1914; d. 4 Dec 1978), Austrian conductor. Held posts in Vienna, 1948–51, Tokyo (NHK SYMPHONY ORCHESTRA, 1951–4) and Melbourne (orchestral and operatic, 1956–60). He then returned to Austria, where he developed a special interest in Bruckner symphonies.

Wührer, Friedrich (b. 29 June 1900; d. 27 Dec 1975), Austrian pianist. Active internationally from 1923. He performed much new music in the 1920s and later; Pfitzner's Six Studies, 1943, were dedicated to him. Recorded all Schubert's sonatas and held professorships in various German and Austrian centres.

Wüllner, Franz (b. 28 Jan 1832; d. 7 Sept 1902), German pianist and conductor, also composer, father of Ludwig WÜLLNER. Worked principally in Munich, where he conducted the first performances of Wagner's *Das Rheingold*, 1869, and *Die Walküre*, 1870, and Cologne (premières of Strauss's *Till Eulenspiegel*, 1895, and *Don Quixote*, 1898).

Wüllner, Ludwig (b. 19 Aug 1858; d. 19 Mar 1938), German baritone, son of Franz WÜLLNER. Won Brahms's commendation and established high standing in recitals in New York, from 1908, as well as in German cities. Also appeared as actor, violinist and conductor.

Wunderlich, Fritz (b. 26 Sept 1930; d. 17 Sept 1966), German tenor. His early death cut off a distinguished career in concert and opera. He made his Covent Garden début as Don Ottavio in *Don Giovanni*, 1965, and in Stuttgart created the role of Tiresias in Orff's *Oedipus der Tyrann*, 1959. His opera recordings range from Handel to Berg.

Wurm, Marie (b. 18 May 1860; d. 21 Jan 1938), British pianist and conductor, sister of Adela VERNE and Mathilde VERNE. Retained her German surname, unlike her sisters. Having studied in Germany with Clara SCHUMANN, she performed there and in England. Founded, 1899, and conducted a women's orchestra in Berlin. She settled in Munich, where she died.

Wylde, Henry (b. 22 May 1822; d. 13 Mar 1890), British conductor, also composer. In opposition to the old, conservative Philharmonic Society he founded the New Philharmonic concerts in London, 1852, some of which were conducted by Berlioz. Wylde gave the British première of Liszt's *St Elisabeth*, 1870, and the first (concert) performance in Britain of *Lohengrin*, 1873.

Wyss, Sophie (b. 5 July 1897; d. 20 Dec 1983), Swiss soprano. Settled in Britain, 1925. She gave the first performance of Britten's song cycles *Our Hunting Fathers*, 1936, and *Les Illuminations*, 1940 (which was dedicated to her).

Y

Yamash'ta, Stomu (originally Tsutomu Yamashita) (b. 10 Mar 1947), Japanese percussionist, also composer. Made solo début in Osaka, 1963, in Milhaud's Concerto; he studied in USA from 1964 and appeared with orchestras and played jazz. In 1970 took part in the première of Henze's *El Cimarrón* (Aldeburgh Festival) and formed his own ensemble.

Yansons, Arvid (b. 24 Oct 1914; d. 21 Nov 1984), Soviet-Latvian conductor, formerly violinist, father of Mariss JANSONS. Worked in Riga (opera and ballet) and Leningrad, then from 1965 till his death was a prominent guest conductor of the HALLÉ ORCHESTRA in Manchester. His revival of Mozart's Requiem, 1969, was the orchestra's first this century.

Yegorov, Yuri (b. 28 May 1954; d. 16 Apr 1988), Russian pianist. Third prizewinner at the Moscow Tchaikovsky Competition, 1974; he left the USSR in 1976 and settled in the Netherlands. Appeared in USA from 1978 and in Britain from 1980, with speciality in romantic music. A victim of AIDS, he died of meningitis.

Yepes, Narciso (b. 14 Nov 1927), Spanish guitarist, also lutenist and composer. From 1964 played a ten-string guitar. He was the first to record the complete works of Bach in two versions, for lute and for guitar, 1973. Among the pieces written for him is Jean Françaix's Guitar Concerto, 1980.

Yershov, Ivan [Vasilyevich] (b. 20 Nov 1867; d. 21 Nov 1943), Russian tenor. Won highest fame on the Russian stage, especially in Wagner. He performed at the Maryinsky (now Kirov) Theatre in St Petersburg from 1895 to 1929, at the end of which time (aged sixty-two) he was still singing Otello. When Leningrad was besieged by the Nazis, he was evacuated with other conservatory teachers to Tashkent, where he died.

Yesipova, Anna [Nikolayevna] (b. 12 Feb 1851; d. 18 Aug 1914), Russian pianist. Said to have given 699 concerts between 1870 and 1885, mainly in Western Europe. She later became a famous teacher at the St Petersburg Conservatory, where Prokofiev was among her students. Married, 1880–92, to her former teacher LESCHETIZKY.

Yomiuri Nippon Symphony Orchestra, Tokyo-based orchestra founded 1962. Its music directors have included FRÜHBECK DE BURGOS, 1980–85, who was followed by Heinz Rögner.

Young (originally Youngs), [Basil] **Alexander** (b. 18 Oct 1920), British tenor. Prominent in concert and opera, especially Handel: complete recording of *Israel in Egypt*, 1985. He sang the hero's roles in the first British (radio) performance of Stravinsky's *The Rake's Progress*, 1953, and in the première of Lennox Berkeley's opera *A Dinner Engagement*, 1954. Also appeared at Covent Garden, 1965–70.

Young, Cecilia (b. *c.* 1710; d. 6 Oct 1789), British soprano. Soloist in the first performances of Handel's *Alexander's Feast*, 1736, and *Saul*, 1737. She married the composer Thomas Arne in 1737; performed her husband's music in Dublin, 1742, and was an admired singer at Vauxhall Gardens, London. Her niece Polly (originally Mary) Young (*c.* 1749–99) was also a soprano.

Young, Polly, *see* YOUNG, CECILIA.

Ysaÿe, Eugène (b. 16 July 1858; d. 12 May 1931), Belgian violinist, also conductor and composer. Active in both Brussels and Paris, where he gave the premières of Franck's Violin Sonata, 1886, and Chausson's *Poème,* 1897; *see also* YSAŸE QUARTET. A greatly esteemed violinist, he first played in USA 1894; he was conductor of the CINCINNATI SYMPHONY ORCHESTRA, 1918–22. After the amputation of his right leg in 1929 he ceased performing as a violinist but continued occasionally to conduct, seated. The Brussels international music competition, now renamed after Queen Elisabeth, originally in 1937 bore his name. His compositions are much valued by violinists. Théophile Ysaÿe (1865–1918), pianist and composer, was his brother.

Ysaÿe, Théophile, *see* YSAŸE, EUGÈNE.

Ysaÿe Quartet, Belgian string quartet founded 1886 by YSAŸE. Other original members were CRICKBOOM, Lucien van Hout and Joseph Jacob. It was active chiefly in Brussels and Paris, where it gave the first performance of Debussy's Quartet, 1893. Although it ceased playing around 1900, it was re-formed in 1906 (with Edouard Dern replacing Crickboom) for the première of Fauré's Piano Quintet no. 1.

Yudina, Maria [Veniaminovna] (b. 9 Sept 1899; d. 19 Nov 1970), Russian pianist. Enjoyed a long concert career, 1921–69; her repertory included works by Schoenberg, Webern and other composers then frowned on in official Soviet musical circles. As a professor at the Moscow Conservatory, 1936–51, she taught singing as well as piano.

Z

Zabaknikov, Nikolay, *see* BEETHOVEN QUARTET.

Zabaleta, Nicanor (b. 7 Jan 1907), Spanish harpist. His reputation in eighteenth- and nineteenth-century classics as well as modern music is unsurpassed; he has toured much. Gave the first performance of Milhaud's Concerto (Venice, 1954), Piston's Capriccio for harp and strings (Madrid, 1964) and other works. He continued to perform into his eighties. His harp has an extra (eighth) pedal to damp the strings.

Zaccaria (originally Zachariou), **Nicola** (b. 9 Mar 1923), Greek bass. Sang at La Scala, 1953–74, where he took part in the first performance of Pizzetti's *Assassinio nella cattedrale*, 1958. He appeared with CALLAS at Covent Garden in *Norma*, 1957, and Cherubini's *Médée*, 1959, and also on recordings of these. Married to HORNE.

Zacher, Gerd (b. 6 July 1929), German organist, also composer. Held church posts in Chile, then Germany. As a recitalist he was a pioneer of the modernist repertory of the 1960s; gave the first performance of Ligeti's *Volumina*, 1962.

Zadek, Hilde (b. 15 Dec 1917), Austrian soprano. Of Jewish origin, she emigrated to Palestine, where she studied with PAULY. Made her European opera début in Vienna as Aida, 1947, and remained with Vienna State Opera. Also sang at Covent Garden, 1950 (in such roles as Aida and Tosca), and at the Metropolitan.

Zagrosek, Lothar (b. 13 Nov 1942), Austrian conductor. Has held various Austrian and German conductorships, including that of the AUSTRIAN RADIO SYMPHONY ORCHESTRA, from 1984; became music director of Paris Opera, 1986–9, and made Glyndebourne début 1987. A specialist in modern works, he conducted the LONDON SINFONIETTA and the BBC SYMPHONY ORCHESTRA, giving with the latter the first performance of Finnissy's *Red Earth*, 1988.

Zamboni, Luigi (b. 1767; d. 28 Feb 1837), Italian bass. His success in comic roles (début 1791) was crowned by his Figaro in the first performance of *Il barbiere*, 1816; he was a friend of Rossini from youth. Retired from the stage in 1825.

Zandt, Marie van, *see* VAN ZANDT.

Zanelli (originally Zanelli Morales), **Renato** (b. 1 Apr 1892; d. 25 Mar 1935), Chilean tenor, previously baritone. Began by taking such roles as Amonasro (*Aida*) at the Metropolitan Opera, 1919–23. He then sang big-scaled tenor roles with distinction (Otello at Covent Garden, 1928–30). Created the principal tenor role in Pizzetti's *Lo straniero*, 1930.

Zavertal, Ladislao (b. 29 Sept 1849; d. 29 Jan 1942), Italian conductor, also composer, of Bohemian descent. Went to Glasgow as a band instructor in 1872. He made a reputation in London as conductor of the Royal Artillery Band, from 1881; using an augmented orchestra, he gave symphony concerts that won high esteem in the 1890s.

Zeani (originally Zehan), **Virginia** (b. 21 Oct 1928), Romanian-born Italian soprano. Made her Italian début as Violetta in *La traviata*, 1948, and repeated the role in London, Moscow and elsewhere. At La Scala she sang Blanche in the first performance of Poulenc's *Dialogues des carmélites*, 1957. Married ROSSI-LEMENI in 1958.

Zecchi, Carlo (b. 8 July 1903; d. 1 Sept 1984), Italian pianist and conductor. Played in a duo with MAINARDI. Having turned to the study of conducting only in 1938, he became well known as conductor of the Vienna Chamber Orchestra, 1974–6; also renowned for his guest performances, recordings and work as a teacher.

Zedda, Alberto (b. 2 Jan 1928), Italian conductor. Taught in Cincinnati, 1957–9, and conducted at West Berlin Opera, 1961–3. He is best known for editing 'cleaned' scores of Rossini operas, which were used on ABBADO's recordings of *Il barbiere* and *La Cenerentola*. He himself conducted the former at Covent Garden, 1975, and San Francisco, 1987.

Zeisler (née Blumenfeld), **Fannie** (b. 16 July 1863; d. 10 Aug 1927), Austrian-born American pianist. Taken to USA in early childhood; she made her Chicago début 1875 and studied in Vienna with LESCHETIZKY. Performed as Fannie Bloomfield until her marriage, 1885. She had an international reputation and a large repertory: in San Francisco gave eight recitals in eighteen days without repeating a piece.

Zeitlin, Zvi (b. 21 Feb 1923), Russian-born American violinist. Taken as an infant to Palestine, where he made his début 1939; gave his first US concert in 1951. He has become known in modern concertos such as Schoenberg's; Ben-Haim's Concerto, 1962, was written for him. Edited a newly discovered concerto by Nardini.

Zelenka, Ladislav, *see* BOHEMIAN QUARTET.

Zenatello, Giovanni (b. 22 Feb 1876; d. 11 Feb 1949), Italian tenor. Performed for a short time as baritone. He sang tenor at La Scala from 1902, and was the first Pinkerton in *Madama Butterfly*, 1904; prominent at Buenos Aires, New York and, from 1905, Covent Garden (Otello, 1926). Settled (and died) in New York, where both he and his wife, GAY, taught.

Zender, Hans (b. 22 Nov 1936), German conductor, also composer. Conductor of the radio orchestra in Saarbrücken, 1972–83, then music director of Hamburg State Opera; he conducted *Parsifal* at Bayreuth, 1975. Prominent in modern music and in 1973 gave the first (posthumous) performance of Bernd Alois Zimmermann's *Ich wandte mich und sah an alles Unrecht, das geschah unter der Sonne*.

Zertsalova, Natalya, *see* OISTRAKH, IGOR.

Zeugheer, Jakob (originally Jakob Zeugheer Herrmann) (b. 20 July 1803; d. 15 June 1865), Swiss violinist and conductor, also composer. Conducted the Gentlemen's Concerts in Manchester, 1831–8. He was an orchestral conductor in Liverpool, from 1843, and thereby a founding father of the ROYAL LIVERPOOL PHILHARMONIC ORCHESTRA.

Zichy, Géza, Count (b. 22 July 1849; d. 14 Jan 1924), Hungarian pianist, also composer. Lost his right arm in a hunting accident at fourteen, but studied piano with LISZT, made his own one-handed arrangements and pursued a concert career. He was also director of the Budapest Conservatory, 1875–1918.

Ziloti (often spelt Siloti in the West), **Alexander** [Ilyich] (b. 9 Oct 1863; d. 8 Dec 1945), Russian pianist and conductor. Studied piano with LISZT. He was a teacher in Moscow (his pupils included his cousin RAKHMANINOV) and conducted the first performance of Rakhmaninov's Piano Concerto no. 2, 1901. He directed his own orchestra in St Petersburg. Settled in USA, 1922, and taught piano at the Juilliard School till 1942.

Zimbalist, Efrem [Alexandrovich] (b. 21 Apr 1889; d. 22 Feb 1985), Russian-born American violinist, also composer. Pupil of AUER. He made his début in USA with the first performance there of Glazunov's Concerto, 1911; won great celebrity. He emerged from retirement in 1952 to give the première of Menotti's Concerto, which was dedicated to him. His first wife was GLUCK; after her death he married Mary Louise

Curtis Bok, 1943, the founder of the Curtis Institute in Philadelphia. He taught there from 1928 and was later its director, 1941–68.

Zimerman, Krystian (b. 5 Dec 1956), Polish pianist. Won the Warsaw International Chopin Competition, 1975; made début in London 1977 and in New York 1979. He specialized in Chopin, but also recorded Brahms's Concerto no. 2, among other works; gave the première of Lutosławski's Piano Concerto, 1988, and its first British performance, 1989.

Zimmermann, Agnes [Maria Jacobina] (b. 5 July 1845; d. 14 Nov 1925), German pianist, also composer. Came to Britain as a child. She was a soloist in London concerts (in partnership with JOACHIM and others) from 1863 for about sixty years. In 1873 she disciplined concertgoers by refusing to let them leave during the last item of a recital.

Zinman, David [Joel] (b. 9 July 1936), American conductor. He was much associated with the NETHERLANDS CHAMBER ORCHESTRA, 1964–77, and then conducted the Rotterdam Philharmonic, 1979–82. In 1985 he became conductor of the Baltimore Symphony Orchestra, which he took to USSR, 1987.

Zisman, Daniel, *see* FITZWILLIAM QUARTET.

Zóldy, Sándor, *see* VÉGH QUARTET.

Zorian, Olive (b. 16 Mar 1916; d. 17 May 1965), British violinist. Founded the Zorian Quartet, which gave the first performances of Tippett's quartets nos. 2 and 3, 1943 and 1946, and other new works. She was also a prominent orchestral leader. Married (1948–55), to the writer and broadcaster John Amis.

Zukerman, Eugenia, *see* ZUKERMAN, PINCHAS.

Zukerman, Pinchas (b. 16 July 1948), Israeli violinist, also viola player and conductor. Studied with GALAMIAN and Isaac STERN in New York. He won the Leventritt Prize there, 1967 (jointly with Kyung-Wha CHUNG), and achieved a brilliant career; made British concert début 1969. He recorded (as viola player) Mozart's Sinfonia concertante with Stern, and has performed chamber music with BARENBOIM and DU PRÉ. Gave the première (with pianist Mark Neikrug) of Lutosławski's Partita. He made his London conducting début 1974 and became director of the St Paul Chamber Orchestra, Minnesota, in 1980. Married Eugenia Rich (b. 1944), a flautist, who performs as Eugenia Zukerman but in 1985 was divorced from him.

Zukofsky, Paul (b. 22 Oct 1943), American violinist. Made his New York recital début 1956 (at Carnegie Hall) and his London début 1969. A specialist in modern works, in 1972 he gave the first performances of Hamilton's 'Amphion' Concerto (Edinburgh Festival) and Wuorinen's Concerto for amplified violin and orchestra.

Zur Mühlen, Raimund von (b. 10 Nov 1854; d. 9 Dec 1931), German-born British tenor. First appeared in Britain 1882, and settled there as soloist and teacher. He reputedly brought the song recital (as distinct from the mixed recital) to Britain, having studied Schumann's and Schubert's songs with Clara SCHUMANN in Germany.

Zylis-Gara, Teresa (b. 23 Jan 1935), Polish soprano. Made her operatic début 1957 in the title role of Moniuszko's *Halka* at Cracow. She later appeared at Vienna, Glyndebourne (Octavian in *Der Rosenkavalier* in 1965), the Metropolitan (début 1968 as Elvira in *Don Giovanni*) and elsewhere. Her concert repertory includes Chopin's songs.

Index of Composers

This alphabetical index gives a cross-reference to composers (with their dates) whose works are specially linked with the performers mentioned. Most commonly, the link will be found to refer to a first performance, a first recording or a first modern revival. In a small number of cases the cross-reference arises because a composer has personally supervised a performance or because of an equally specific connection between a composer's and a performer's work. A merely general mention (that a singer was often heard in Verdi operas, for instance) is not indexed.

An asterisk (*) denotes composers who, as important performers in their own right, also have their appropriate entries in the main body of the book.

Penguin Encyclopedia of Popular Music
Edited by Donald Clarke

'The many entries . . . fairly bristle with information . . . Editor Donald Clarke has in many ways done an admirable job of trying comprehensively to cover . . . country, cabaret, reggae, folk, gospel, blues and pre-eminently, necessarily, the many mutations of jazz and rhythm 'n' blues' – Tim Rostron and Martin Gayford in the *Daily Telegraph*

The Penguin Guide to Compact Discs
Edited by Edward Greenfield, Robert Layton and Ivan March

The Penguin Guide to Compact Discs is the biggest and most comprehensive survey of classical music on CD ever published: an indispensable guide designed to help you make an informed choice from the vast and bewildering range of recordings currently on sale.

'To anyone concerned with serious music it will be absolutely invaluable' – Sir Ian Trethowan

The Heart of Rock and Soul. The 1001 Greatest Singles Ever Made
Dave Marsh

From Marvin Gaye's 'I Heard It Through the Grapevine' downwards, Dave Marsh's list offers a controversial, opinionated catalogue of 1001 greatest pop singles ever pressed into vinyl. Not necessarily chartoppers or Gold Disc winners, they are just the best of their kind, from Prince to the King, from the Righteous Brothers to the Sex Pistols and back again.

PENGUIN REFERENCE BOOKS

The New Penguin English Dictionary

Over 1,000 pages long and with over 68,000 definitions, this cheap, compact and totally up-to-date book is ideal for today's needs. It includes many technical and colloquial terms, guides to pronunciation and common abbreviations.

The Penguin Spelling Dictionary

What are the plurals of *octopus* and *rhinoceros*? What is the difference between *stationary* and *stationery*? And how about *annex* and *annexe*, *agape* and *Agape*? This comprehensive new book, the fullest spelling dictionary now available, provides the answers.

Roget's Thesaurus of English Words and Phrases Betty Kirkpatrick (ed.)

This new edition of Roget's classic work, now brought up to date for the nineties, will increase anyone's command of the English language. Fully cross-referenced, it includes synonyms of every kind (formal or colloquial, idiomatic and figurative) for almost 900 headings. It is a must for writers and utterly fascinating for any English speaker.

The Penguin Dictionary of Quotations

A treasure-trove of over 12,000 new gems and old favourites, from Aesop and Matthew Arnold to Xenophon and Zola.

The Penguin Wordmaster Dictionary
Martin H. Manser and Nigel D. Turton

This dictionary puts the pleasure back into word-seeking. Every time you look at a page you get a bonus – a panel telling you everything about a particular word or expression. It is, therefore, a dictionary to be read as well as used for its concise and up-to-date definitions.

PENGUIN REFERENCE BOOKS

The Penguin Guide to the Law

This acclaimed reference book is designed for everyday use and forms the most comprehensive handbook ever published on the law as it affects the individual.

The Penguin Medical Encyclopedia

Covers the body and mind in sickness and in health, including drugs, surgery, medical history, medical vocabulary and many other aspects. 'Highly commendable' – *Journal of the Institute of Health Education*

The Slang Thesaurus

Do you make the public bar sound like a gentleman's club? Do you need help in understanding *Minder*? The miraculous *Slang Thesaurus* will liven up your language in no time. You won't Adam and Eve it! A mine of funny, witty, acid and vulgar synonyms for the words you use every day.

The Penguin Dictionary of Troublesome Words Bill Bryson

Why should you avoid discussing the *weather conditions*? Can a married woman be *celibate*? Why is it eccentric to talk about the *aroma* of a cowshed? A straightforward guide to the pitfalls and hotly disputed issues in standard written English.

The Penguin Spanish Dictionary James R. Jump

Detailed, comprehensive and, above all, modern, *The Penguin Spanish Dictionary* offers a complete picture of the language of ordinary Spaniards – the words used at home and at work, in bars and discos, at cafés and in the street, including full and unsqueamish coverage of common slang and colloquialisms.

The New Penguin Dictionary of Geography

From *aa* and *ablation* to *zinc* and *zonal soils*, this succinct dictionary is unique in covering in one volume the main terms now in use in the diverse areas – physical and human geography, geology and climatology, ecology and economics – that make up geography today.